CASES AND MATERIALS ON
TORTS

Fourth Edition

■ ■ ■

By

David W. Robertson
W. Page Keeton Chair in Tort Law
University Distinguished Teaching Professor
The University of Texas at Austin

William Powers, Jr.
President
Hines H. Baker & Thelma Kelley Baker Chair in Law
University Distinguished Teaching Professor
The University of Texas at Austin

David A. Anderson
Fred and Emily Marshall Wulff Centennial Chair in Law
The University of Texas at Austin

Olin Guy Wellborn III
William C. Liedtke, Sr. Professor of Law
The University of Texas at Austin

AMERICAN CASEBOOK SERIES®

WEST®
A Thomson Reuters business

Mat #40880835

American Casebook Series is a trademark registered in the U.S. Patent and Trademark Office.

COPYRIGHT © 1989 WEST PUBLISHING
COPYRIGHT © 1998 WEST GROUP
© 2004 West, a Thomson business
© 2011 Thomson Reuters

    610 Opperman Drive
    St. Paul, MN 55123
    1–800–313–9378

Printed in the United States of America

ISBN: 978–0–314–90687–8

PREFACE

There are many intellectual prisms through which tort law can usefully be observed and evaluated. We believe that the best one for the purpose of learning tort law is the litigation perspective. We take note of the most prominent theoretical strands of tort jurisprudence in this book, but our emphasis is on the law as it appears today to the tort lawyer and judge, with all of its controversies, uncertainties, and complex dynamics. For one thing, litigators can access academic theory more readily and proficiently than pure theoreticians can access the realities of litigation. More importantly, we are committed to providing enough of a grounding in procedure, evidence, and litigation practices for the beginning student to make a start on understanding tort law in action. No one can become a good tort lawyer without a deep appreciation of the ways in which the substantive law of torts is influenced by the realities of litigation, such as difficulties of proof and division of responsibility between judge and jury.

The book's organizational scheme reflects our determination to present tort law as it appears to the litigator. The opening chapter is designed to give the beginning law student a primer on the procedural and tactical framework within which tort matters are resolved. After a concise survey of the distinctive world of intentional torts, negligence law is presented in the way lawyers approach it: elements of the prima facie case, defenses, and immunities. We then branch out to other bases of liability, such as strict liability and nuisance.

In every state, tort law today is an amalgam of common law (court-created law) and legislation. In this book we use cases to show the law in action, but we provide a number of representative tort statutes and require students to pay close and rigorous attention to the ways in which they are structured, worded, and (ultimately) applied.

The cases have been tightly edited in recognition of the fact that introductory tort courses, which once were allocated five or six semester hours, now rarely receive more than three or four. Omission of text is indicated by * * *. Footnotes and citations are omitted without indication. We have corrected minor errors of spelling, grammar, and punctuation without indication. Numbered footnotes within the opinions are the courts' and retain their original numbering, although a few may have been relocated to accommodate our editing of the text. Our own footnotes within the opinions generally are indicated with an asterisk and are signed "[Ed.]"

This edition pays significantly more attention to the Torts Restatements than previous ones. The Restatement (Third) of Torts: Products Liability (1998) is sometimes cited as Products Restatement. The Restatement (Third) of Torts: Apportionment of Liability (2000) is sometimes cited as Apportionment Restatement. The Restatement (Third) of Torts: Liability for Physical and Emotional Harm (2010) is sometimes cited as Third Restatement.

We wish to thank other users of the previous editions, especially our good friend Professor William Childs, for very welcome comments and advice. We are also grateful for the assistance of Elizabeth Fitch, Tania Culbertson, Kathryn Hutchinson, and Angel Leffingwell.

Summary of Contents

TABLE OF CONTENTS

TABLE OF CASES

The principal cases are in bold type. Cases cited or discussed in the text
are in roman type. References are to pages. Cases cited in principal
cases and within other quoted materials are not included.

CASES AND MATERIALS ON
TORTS
Fourth Edition

CHAPTER I

TRIAL COURT PROCEDURE IN TORTS CASES

■ ■ ■

Almost all of the cases in this book were decided by appellate courts. It is necessary to study appellate decisions: The opinion of an appeals court is usually the earliest available written record of a tortious occurrence and its treatment by the legal system. But the appellate focus has its drawbacks. Reading the decision of an appellate court to determine what happened at the trial of a torts case—or trying to look even further back in time at what went wrong between the parties to cause them to become adversaries in the first place—is something like looking through the wrong end of a telescope: One can see, but mastering the relevant details demands a certain amount of determination and skill.

The proper starting point in studying an appellate decision is always to ask what the appellate court is telling the trial judge about the handling of this particular case. It is obvious that a torts case comes to an appellate court because at least one of the parties is dissatisfied with the way things turned out in the trial court. What may not be so obvious is that the appellant (the party who initially brings the case to the appellate court) must be complaining of some mistake that the trial *judge* has made. It is not enough to tell the appellate court that the result was unjust or that the jury got the wrong answer. The appellant must pinpoint an error of law committed by the trial judge; otherwise the appeal has no chance.

So when reading an appellate decision, the first thing to look for is, *what does the appellant claim the trial judge did wrong?* You should be able to find the answer to that question for all the lead cases in this book. But you need a rudimentary understanding of trial court procedure to do it. The following material outlines the principal stages at which a trial judge is likely to commit an appealable error while handling a torts case. It is loosely based on the model of a trial judge sitting with a jury and operating under the Federal Rules of Civil Procedure. Most state procedural systems are patterned closely enough after the federal rules that the model is reasonably instructive.

Note that the following discussion proceeds through the torts lawsuit in roughly chronological order, beginning with the filing of the plaintiff's

1

complaint. You should bear in mind that most torts cases are settled (compromised) by agreement of the parties, either before the complaint is filed or at some stage thereafter. Settlements can occur at any stage of the litigation, including the appeal process.

A.

The plaintiff initiates the lawsuit by filing a complaint and causing it to be served on the defendant. The allegations in the complaint set forth the plaintiff's version of the facts. Plaintiff contends that these facts will be proved at trial or conceded by the defendant, and that they provide a basis for an award of damages (or occasionally other relief, such as an injunction) on behalf of the plaintiff.

The defendant's first response can be a motion to dismiss the complaint for failure to state a legally valid claim. What this response says, in effect, is this: Let us assume for purposes of argument that every fact alleged in the plaintiff's complaint is true; even so, it is clear that the law affords no relief, so that the complaint must simply be dismissed, without further ado. For example, suppose that my complaint against you alleges that, as I was painfully and very slowly jogging past your house, you (an ostentatiously fit young stranger) caused me great emotional anguish by calling out, "Look, everyone! It's the Turtleman!" Your motion to dismiss does not admit or deny the accuracy of my complaint, but contends that, even if it is true, it does not describe tortious conduct on your part; ordinary everyday insults are not torts. A trial judge who failed to grant your motion would be making a mistake about tort law.

B.

If the case is not dismissed at a preliminary stage, the defendant must file an answer to the plaintiff's complaint. The answer is a fact pleading in which the defendant typically denies the plaintiff's version of the facts and gives some indication of the defendant's version. (If the case gets that far, eventually a jury will decide which version, if either, is accurate.) The complaint and answer are the only essential pleadings, and once they are on file the case is formally in a posture to be tried. The parties will doubtless spend a great deal of time investigating and negotiating, and this process may well generate disputes about discovery[1] that need sorting out by the trial judge. Moreover, as the discovery process proceeds and the parties' positions begin to crystallize, the trial judge is likely to confront one or more motions for summary judgment.

C.

Either side can move for summary judgment as to a part or all of the dispute. Here we are concerned primarily with defensive summary judgment motions.[2] The defendant's motion for summary judgment (which

---

1. Discovery is the process of investigating a case that follows the initiation of a lawsuit. It includes written interrogatories, depositions, and other formalized evidence-gathering procedures.

2. For a good example of a situation in which a plaintiff's motion for summary judgment should succeed, see Abraham, The Forms and Functions of Tort Law 5 (3d ed. 2007): "[I]f

may precede but more typically follows the filing of the answer) is similar in content and intended effect to the motion to dismiss. The significant difference is that the motion to dismiss is directed solely at what the plaintiff has claimed in the complaint, whereas with the motion for summary judgment the defendant brings additional facts to the court's attention. For example, suppose that my complaint alleges that you deprived me of my liberty by keeping me locked for a period of three months in a room in premises owned and occupied by you. Suppose that your response is a summary judgment motion, accompanied by affidavits attesting that you are a duly accredited psychiatrist and the director of a sanitarium properly licensed by the state, and by a certified copy of the court order whereby I was judicially committed to your institution for three months of psychiatric care and observation. Unless I have further facts, your motion for summary judgment should be granted.

Summary judgment is an important tool, and present-day courts use it much more frequently than in the past. There is a great deal of boilerplate language in reported cases about the standards that should be applied by trial judges in ruling on summary judgment motions and by appellate courts when reviewing such rulings. The following sentence is a recurrent mantra: "Summary judgment is appropriate if the pleadings, depositions, answers to interrogatories, and admissions on file, together with the affidavits, if any, show there is no genuine issue as to any material fact and the moving party is entitled to judgment as a matter of law." Hunley v. Dupont Automotive, 341 F.3d 491, 495 (6th Cir. 2003). When applied to a defensive summary judgment motion, what this means, roughly, is that summary judgment should be granted (a) if a rule of law clearly shields the defendant from liability or (b) if no reasonable person, looking at the evidence presented, could see any legitimate basis for the plaintiff to prevail.

D.

If the plaintiff's case survives the defendant's motion to dismiss and motion for summary judgment, it will need to be tried unless the parties can arrive at a settlement agreement. When the trial date arrives, the lawyers and the judge must first select a jury. If the judge permits it, the lawyers will begin trying to influence the potential jurors at this earliest opportunity, and occasionally an appellant in a torts case will urge that the trial judge erred by permitting improper and prejudicial remarks to be made during the jury selection process.

E.

When the jury selection process is finished, the lawyers for the parties may then make opening statements, each outlining a theory of the case

---

discovery reveals no dispute between the parties that while driving blindfolded down Main Street the defendant struck and injured the plaintiff, * * * [no] jury could legitimately conclude * * * that the defendant was not negligent [and in] all probability the plaintiff would be granted summary judgment * * *."

and alerting the jury to what the evidence will show. A trial judge may commit reversible error at this stage by permitting counsel to make improper remarks (or by forbidding proper remarks) during opening statement. But again, this is relatively rare.

F.

Once the opening statements have been completed, the plaintiff's lawyer puts on the case in chief on behalf of the plaintiff. This involves questioning witnesses under oath and introducing documents and sometimes physical objects into evidence. During this stage of the case the lawyer for the defendant will have the opportunity to cross-examine each witness and to object to the admissibility of documents and other evidence offered by the plaintiff. The trial judge must rule on these objections, and may commit reversible error by allowing the introduction of evidence that should have been kept out or by excluding evidence that should have been let in. For example, the defendant/appellant in South v. National R.R. Passenger Corp., 290 N.W.2d 819 (N.D.1980), urged that the jurors, who found the defendant railroad guilty of negligence in causing a grade crossing accident, had been prejudiced by being allowed to hear irrelevant testimony that the train's engineer refused to put his jacket over an injured man after the wreck because he did not want to soil it. The appellate court reasoned that such testimony would not be irrelevant if the engineer had a tort-law duty to render aid, and concluded that he did.

G.

Eventually the plaintiff's lawyer will complete the presentation of the case in chief on behalf of the plaintiff. At this point the defendant may file a motion for a directed verdict.[3] This motion says, in effect: Now that we've heard all of the evidence the plaintiff has to offer, it is plain that the plaintiff has not shown a sufficient basis for holding defendant responsible under the law. (The plaintiff cannot file a motion for directed verdict at this point, because defendant has not yet put on its factual case.)

For example: My complaint alleges that you ran over me at the corner of 5th and Congress in Austin, Texas, on November 11, 2008. But all I can show at trial is that I was hit by a late-model green Ford sedan and that you own such a car. Your motion for directed verdict should succeed; I have not produced facts from which a reasonable juror could conclude that, more probably than not, you were a cause of my injuries. (In most modern procedural systems, when a judge grants a directed verdict, there is nothing for the jury to do; the judge simply enters judgment for the prevailing party.)

H.

If the trial judge denies the defendant's motion for directed verdict at the conclusion of plaintiff's case in chief, the defendant will then put on

---

3. The Federal Rules of Civil Procedure now call motions for directed verdict and for judgment notwithstanding the verdict "motions for judgment as a matter of law" (JAML). We use the older terminology, which is still in use in many states, because it is the terminology generally used in the opinions in this book.

its case in chief, with plaintiff's lawyer having the opportunity to cross-examine witnesses and object to the introduction of evidence. (Here again the trial judge may commit reversible error by letting in evidence that should be kept out or keeping out evidence that should be let in.)

When defendant's lawyer announces that the case in chief for defendant has been concluded, plaintiff may have the opportunity to present rebuttal evidence. Once that is done, the trial judge (and jury) have heard all the evidence that the parties will present. At this stage either party may move for a directed verdict. If the trial judge believes that there is only one reasonable outcome, she will grant one of these motions.

For example: My complaint alleges that you ran over me at the corner of 5th and Congress in Austin on November 11, 2008. Suppose my trial evidence shows that I was struck and injured on that date by a recklessly driven orange Cadillac convertible bearing longhorn steer horns as a hood ornament, and that you live in Austin and own and regularly drive such a car. Your motion for a directed verdict at the close of my case in chief probably should fail, because the evidence produced at the trial creates a permissible inference that I have correctly identified the tortfeasor. So you put on your case in chief, proving that your Cadillac was stolen from you on November 10, and also proving that you were in New York all day on November 11. Your motion for directed verdict should now succeed; clearly, on all the evidence in the case, I have not met my fundamental burden of proving that you probably caused me an injury.

Defendants' motions for directed verdict are granted with some frequency, and the legal standard for when a directed verdict is appropriate is well established:

> In ruling on the motion, the court must take the strongest legitimate view of the evidence in favor of the non-moving party. In other words, the court must remove any conflict in the evidence by construing it in the light most favorable to the non-movant and discarding all countervailing evidence. The court may grant the motion only if, after assessing the evidence according to the foregoing standards, it determines that reasonable minds could not differ as to the conclusions to be drawn from the evidence.[4]

I.

Even if inclined to believe that there is only one reasonable outcome, the trial judge may well deny a directed verdict motion made at the conclusion of all the evidence. (For one thing, as will be seen in a moment, the judge will have another chance to rule for the party who should prevail.) If the trial judge does not grant a motion for directed verdict at the close of the evidence, the lawyers will then make their closing arguments.[5] The judge may commit reversible error by permitting improp-

---

4. Eaton v. McLain, 891 S.W.2d 587, 590 (Tenn. 1994).

5. In most systems, closing arguments by the lawyers precede the judge's instructions to the jury. Some states do it backward.

er closing argument or, conceivably, by forbidding appropriate closing argument.

J.

After the lawyers' closing arguments, the trial judge instructs (or "charges") the jury on the law they are to apply. Here is perhaps the most fertile source of claims of trial court error. The jury may be told something that is inaccurate or misleading; they may be told too much; they may be told too little. Probably no one fully believes that human beings actually conform their actions and decisions to refined and prolix verbal formulations of the sort often used in jury instructions. Nevertheless, the system's traditions tend to insist on precision and conformity. See, e.g., Bengston v. Estes, 260 Wis. 595, 51 N.W.2d 539 (1952), reversing because the instructions said "clear preponderance of the evidence" instead of "fair preponderance of the evidence."

K.

When closing arguments and instructions are done, the jury retires, deliberates, and returns with a verdict. At this point the winner moves for judgment on the verdict, and the disappointed litigant (there is guaranteed to be at least one) can move for judgment notwithstanding the verdict or for a new trial.[6]

The motion for judgment notwithstanding the verdict (often called judgment non obstante veredicto and abbreviated JNOV) has exactly the same theory and content as the motion for directed verdict at the conclusion of the evidence. So why would a trial judge ever deny a directed verdict motion and then turn around and grant JNOV? It is a purely pragmatic move. If the directed verdict motion is granted and the appellate court eventually disagrees, the case will have to be retried, because the jury never got to rule on it. But if the appellate court disagrees with JNOV, the jury verdict can simply be reinstated.

The motion for JNOV, like the directed verdict motions, asserts that there is only one reasonable and correct outcome and thus seeks a dispositive judgment in the movant's favor. The assertion of a motion for a new trial—whereby the movant seeks not a dispositive judgment in its favor but rather a second chance—is somewhat weaker; it claims in effect that the jury's verdict looks very peculiar and that errors of sufficient importance occurred during the trial to suggest rather strongly that the jurors were prejudiced or misled.

---

6. Other possible post-verdict motions include motions for remittitur or additur. The defendant's remittitur motion asserts that the damages awarded by the jury are unreasonably high. If the trial judge grants the motion, the plaintiff is forced to choose between accepting a specified reduction or submitting to a new trial. The additur motion is just the opposite; the plaintiff claims that the jury's damage award is so low as to defy reason, and seeks to have the defendant forced to choose between agreeing to a specified addition or undergoing a new trial. The federal procedural system does not have the additur device, but quite a few states do.

L.

In summary, here are the major stages at which trial judges make tort-law mistakes:

1. Granting or denying motions to dismiss the complaint.

2. Granting or denying motions for summary judgment.

3. Permitting improper statements by counsel (or squelching proper ones) during jury selection, opening statement, or closing argument.

4. Excluding relevant evidence or admitting improper evidence.

5. Granting or denying motions for directed verdict.

6. Erroneous jury instructions.

7. Granting or denying motions for judgment notwithstanding the verdict.

8. Granting or denying motions for new trial, additurs, or remitturs.

Chapter II

Intentional Harms to Persons and Property

■ ■ ■

A. INTRODUCTION

The cases in this chapter deal with several torts that share a similar analytical structure. They are battery, assault, false imprisonment, intentional infliction of emotional distress, trespass to land, trespass to chattels, and conversion. Each is an intentional tort, meaning that the plaintiff can recover only if the defendant intentionally invaded the specific interest that is protected by the tort. The torts differ from each other in that they protect different interests of the plaintiff.

For each tort, the plaintiff must prove the "elements" of the tort in order to recover. (Some courts call these elements the plaintiff's "prima facie case.") The plaintiff has the burden of introducing evidence tending to prove every element in order to avoid suffering a directed verdict, that is, in order to have the case submitted to the jury. If the plaintiff does produce evidence on every element and the case is submitted to the jury, the plaintiff has the burden of persuading the jury that every element has been met. Even if the plaintiff proves every element of a tort, the defendant can nevertheless escape liability by establishing a defense. The defendant has the burden of producing evidence and persuading the jury on these defenses.

The material is organized to address the elements of each of the several torts and then to address defenses. Although the defenses applicable to each tort are not identical, considerable overlap exists among the available defenses. As you study the elements of each tort, keep in mind that proof of these elements does not guarantee recovery by the plaintiff. A defense, especially consent, may be available to the defendant.

Causation is an element of each of the torts covered in this chapter. Indeed, causation is an element of all tort actions. Issues concerning causation can be difficult. They are addressed in detail in Chapter IV. Causation is not specifically addressed in this chapter, but you should nevertheless be aware that causation is an element of these torts, and the plaintiff must prove it.

8

B. BATTERY

GHASSEMIEH v. SCHAFER

Court of Special Appeals of Maryland, 1982.
52 Md.App. 31, 447 A.2d 84.

MOORE, JUDGE.

In this case, a 13–year–old girl in eighth grade pulled a chair away from her teacher who fell to the floor, hurting her back. Approximately one month less than three years later, the teacher filed a negligence action against her former pupil in the Circuit Court for Baltimore County (Sfekas, J.). From a judgment for the defendant, this appeal is taken. For the reasons stated herein, we shall affirm.

* * *

The appellant, Karen B. Ghassemieh, age 29 on February 24, 1977, was a teacher of art with the Baltimore County Schools, assigned to Old Court Junior High. On that date, she was teaching an 8th grade class of "above average" students, including the appellee, Elaine Schafer, then 13. While the teacher was about to sit down to assist another student, Elaine pulled the chair away. At trial the teacher described what happened:

> I got to Terri's seat and because I am very tall it is my practice either to kneel down next to the children or to sit down. Terri got up very quickly and I went to sit in her seat. As I went to sit down, I tucked the chair underneath me as I usually do. As I relaxed to sit down, the chair was gone. It was pulled out and I fell to the floor hurting my back.

Elaine Schafer testified that she pulled the chair away "as a joke." She further testified on direct examination:

> Q. When you pulled the chair, was there any doubt in your mind that she would miss the chair and fall to the floor?
>
> A. I knew she was going to fall to the floor.
>
> Q. Was that your intent?
>
> A. Yes.

On cross-examination she repeated that, "I did it as a joke." She also said that she did not intend any injury. Thus:

> Q. You mean you did not intend to have any harm done to her, is that right?
>
> A. I intended for her to fall to the floor, not for her to be injured.

The declaration was not filed until January 24, 1980, although in answers to interrogatories, Mrs. Ghassemieh said she was treated for back problems throughout 1977 and 1978.[2]

---

2. This action was brought almost three years after the incident. However, appellant began experiencing back pain in March 1977, a month or so later; she had a myelogram then and again

* * * At the close of the evidence, each side moved for a directed verdict. * * * The appellee's (defendant's) motion was predicated on a claim that the evidence established a battery, an intentional tort, and not negligence, as alleged.

Both motions were denied. With respect to the defendant's motion, the court ruled:

> As to the motion of the defendant, the Court will deny that motion, but I will include in the instructions the definition of a battery and let the jury make the determination whether this in fact was, if it was a negligent act on the part of the defendant or if in fact it was a battery, which would certainly not be encompassed in the action brought by the plaintiff in this case, but I would allow that to go to the jury by way of instruction.

Before the judge instructed the jury, the following exchange occurred:

> MR. CASKEY (counsel for defendant/appellee): I would move that the Court present the question to the jury as a question as to the battery versus negligence issue. I would request that the jury be given the instructions as to what constitutes negligence and as to what constitutes battery and to have them answer the question—do you find that it was negligence, battery, or neither?

> MR. HUESMAN (counsel for plaintiff/appellant): Well, I think, Your Honor, before I respond to that, I guess a lot would depend on exactly the way the questions are phrased.

In the instructions which immediately followed, the court began by saying: "The case before you is an action based on a claim of negligence." * * * The court then instructed on battery, as follows:

> The Court has indicated that this is an action in negligence. *A battery is an intentional touching which is harmful or offensive.* Touching includes the intentional putting into motion of anything which touches another person or the intentional putting into motion of anything which touches something that is connected with or in contact with another person. A touching is harmful if it causes physical pain, injury or illness. A touching is offensive if it offends a person's reasonable sense of personal dignity.

> *If you find that the defendant acted with the intent to cause a harmful or offensive touching of the plaintiff and that that offensive touching directly or indirectly resulted, then this constitutes a battery and your verdict must be for the defendant,* as this suit has been brought in negligence and is not an action in battery. (Emphasis added.)

At the conclusion of the instructions, trial counsel for the plaintiffs (appellants) excepted as follows:

in early 1978. In September 1978, she had a spinal fusion. We observe that appellee did not plead the one-year statute of limitations, Md.Cts. & Jud.Proc.Code Ann., § 5–105 (1980 Repl.Vol.), governing battery, but she had no occasion to do so in light of the allegations in the declaration.

Also, we except to the portion of the charge with regard to the definition of battery. * * * We believe that it is necessary to show that the defendant *actually intended to harm the plaintiff* and we believe on the basis of the defendant's own testimony that she did this as a joke, that she had no intention to commit bodily harm. (Emphasis added.)

The trial court overruled all objections. With respect to the battery objection, the court did not address the definitional point raised, but said:

The battery instruction, the Court felt was appropriate in view of the fact that this is an action in negligence, and if the jury would find from hearing the testimony in the case that in fact there was a battery and not negligence, it may very well have the opportunity to make a determination in favor of the defendant.

Approximately 25 minutes after the jury retired, the court received a request that the definition of battery be given again. Counsel for the teacher objected. The court stated that, in the absence of agreement of counsel, it would decline to repeat the instruction. One-half hour later, the jury returned a verdict for the defendant.

* * *

The gravamen of the plaintiffs' appeal is that the trial court erred in giving the following portion of the instruction on battery quoted above:

If you find that the defendant acted with the intent to cause a harmful or offensive touching of the plaintiff and that that offensive touching directly or indirectly resulted, then this constitutes a battery and your verdict must be for the defendant, as this suit has been brought in negligence and is not an action in battery.

In support of this principal contention, appellants maintain that:

(1) The mere fact that the evidence adduced may have established that the defendant acted intentionally in pulling the chair out from under the appellant, Karen B. Ghassemieh, does not preclude recovery of damages for a cause of action in negligence.

* * *

(3) To permit the defendant to escape liability for her tortious conduct merely because she acted intentionally, rather than negligently, would be fundamentally unjust and contrary to public policy.

We are confronted with a threshold consideration not raised by the appellee and, therefore, neither briefed nor argued but essentially jurisdictional: Was the appellants' objection to the battery instruction, quoted above, a sufficient predicate for their position on appeal? They now argue:

The instruction given by the trial judge was improper because if the jury had found that the defendant acted intentionally in pulling the chair out from under the appellant, Karen B. Ghassemieh, it could nevertheless have awarded damages for negligence.

And further:

> Thus, a finding of gross negligence or of willful and wanton miscon-
> duct may impute a finding of intentional conduct. Consequently, a
> finding that the appellee had acted intentionally would have been
> fully consistent with the allegations of the declaration charging negli-
> gence. The trial court, therefore, erred in instructing the jury to the
> contrary. While it is clear that [appellee] intended to pull the chair
> out from under Mrs. Ghassemieh, it is equally clear that she did not
> intend to injure Mrs. Ghassemieh.

Our problem arises from Maryland Rule 554 (Instructions to the
Jury) (1982 ed.), particularly subsections (d) and (e) concerning, respectively, "objection" and "appeal." Subsection (d) provides in part:

> If a party has an objection to any portion of any instruction given, or
> to any omission therefrom, or the failure to give any instruction, *he
> shall before the jury retires to consider its verdict make such objection
> stating distinctly the portion, or omission, or failure to instruct to
> which he objects and the ground of his objection.* (Emphasis added.)

And subsection (e) provides in its entirety:

> Upon appeal a party in assigning error in the instructions, *shall be
> restricted* to (1) the particular portion of the instructions given or the
> particular omission therefrom or the particular failure to instruct
> *distinctly objected to before the jury retired* and (2) *the grounds of
> objection distinctly stated at the time,* and *no other errors or assign-
> ments of error in the instructions shall be considered by the appellate
> court.* (Emphasis added.)

Trial counsel for the plaintiffs did not object, as appellate counsel now
objects, to *any* instruction on battery, but only to "that portion of the
charge with regard to the *definition* of battery." (Emphasis added.) Trial
counsel was objecting to the court's definition of battery as an "intentional touching which is harmful or offensive" * * *.

Trial counsel never stated as a basis for his objection that no instruction on battery should be given because this was an action in negligence.
The objection at trial was simply that the definition of battery lacked an
essential element, i.e., the defendant actually intended to harm the
plaintiff. However, intent to do harm is not essential to a battery. The gist
of the action is not hostile intent on the part of the defendant, but the
absence of consent to the contact on the plaintiff's part. Thus, horseplay,
pranks, or jokes can be a battery regardless of whether the intent was to
harm. Garratt v. Dailey, 46 Wash.2d 197, 279 P.2d 1091 (1955), aff'd, 49
Wash.2d 499, 304 P.2d 681 (1956).

Trial counsel never argued to the trial court that, as contended at oral
argument before us, negligence and battery are not mutually exclusive, or
that a single intentional act can be the basis for both battery and
negligence, or that the jury could award damages for negligence even if a
battery had also been proved. Only on appeal do appellants make clear

their challenge to the instruction that "this suit has been brought in negligence and is not an action in battery" and if battery were found, "your verdict must be for the defendant." The trial judge was not given to understand that the plaintiff really objected to any instruction on battery. The judge reiterated his negligence versus battery instruction in explaining why he felt the battery instruction was appropriate, and the plaintiff did not object.

Thus, the objection below did not reach the broader issue raised on appeal, and under Rule 554(e) it "may not be considered by the appellate court."

* * *

[T]he presence of an intent to do an act does not preclude negligence. The concepts of negligence and battery are not mutually exclusive.

* * *

We see no reason why an intentional act that produces unintended consequences cannot be a foundation for a negligence action. Here, an intentional act—the pulling away of the chair—had two possible consequences: the intended one of embarrassment and the unintended one of injury. The battery—an indirect offensive touching, a technical invasion of the plaintiff's personal integrity—was proved. However, a specific instruction on negligence—namely, that the defendant had a duty to refrain from conduct exposing the plaintiff to unreasonable risk of injury and breached that duty, resulting in her injury—was not requested. * * * Nor did the plaintiff at trial take the unequivocal position that she was proceeding on a theory of negligence, notwithstanding the co-existence of an intentional act, *i.e.,* a battery. In sum, appellants are asserting now the arguments they should have made at trial. Such hindsight can avail them nothing.

Judgment affirmed; appellants to pay the costs.

NOTE

Generally, a party can raise an issue on appeal only if counsel has "preserved" the issue by a timely and specific objection or request in the trial court. As you read appellate opinions, you should look for the effect trial court procedure has on the posture of the case on appeal.

GARRATT v. DAILEY

Supreme Court of Washington, 1955.
46 Wash.2d 197, 279 P.2d 1091.

HILL, JUSTICE.

The liability of an infant for an alleged battery is presented to this court for the first time. Brian Dailey (age five years, nine months) was visiting with Naomi Garratt, an adult and a sister of the plaintiff, Ruth Garratt, likewise an adult, in the back yard of the plaintiff's home, on July

16, 1951. It is plaintiff's contention that she came out into the back yard
to talk with Naomi and that, as she started to sit down in a wood and
canvas lawn chair, Brian deliberately pulled it out from under her. The
only one of the three persons present so testifying was Naomi Garratt.
(Ruth Garratt, the plaintiff, did not testify as to how or why she fell.) The
trial [judge, sitting without a jury], unwilling to accept this testimony,
adopted instead Brian Dailey's version of what happened, and made the
following findings:

> III. * * * that while Naomi Garratt and Brian Dailey were in the
> back yard the plaintiff, Ruth Garratt, came out of her house into the
> back yard. Some time subsequent thereto defendant, Brian Dailey,
> picked up a lightly built wood and canvas lawn chair which was then
> and there located in the back yard of the above described premises,
> moved it sideways a few feet and seated himself therein, at which
> time he discovered the plaintiff, Ruth Garratt, about to sit down at
> the place where the lawn chair had formerly been, at which time he
> hurriedly got up from the chair and attempted to move it toward Ruth
> Garratt to aid her in sitting down in the chair; that due to the
> defendant's small size and lack of dexterity he was unable to get the
> lawn chair under the plaintiff in time to prevent her from falling to
> the ground. That plaintiff fell to the ground and sustained a fracture
> of her hip, and other injuries and damages as hereinafter set forth.
>
> IV.   That the preponderance of the evidence in this case establishes
> that when the defendant, Brian Dailey, moved the chair in question
> *he did not have any willful or unlawful purpose* in doing so; that *he
> did not have any intent to injure the plaintiff, or any intent to bring
> about any unauthorized or offensive contact with her person* or any
> objects appurtenant thereto; that the circumstances which immediate-
> ly preceded the fall of the plaintiff established that the defendant,
> *Brian Dailey, did not have purpose, intent or design to perform a
> prank or to effect an assault and battery upon the person of the
> plaintiff.*

(Italics ours, for a purpose hereinafter indicated.)

It is conceded that Ruth Garratt's fall resulted in a fractured hip and
other painful and serious injuries. To obviate the necessity of a retrial in
the event this court determines that she was entitled to a judgment
against Brian Dailey, the amount of her damage was found to be $11,000.
Plaintiff appeals from a judgment dismissing the action and asks for the
entry of a judgment in that amount or a new trial.

* * *

It is urged that Brian's action in moving the chair constituted a
battery. A definition (not all-inclusive but sufficient for our purpose) of a
battery is the intentional infliction of a harmful bodily contact upon
another. * * *

* * *

* * * In the comment [to section 13 of the Restatement of Torts] the Restatement says:

> *Character of actor's intention.* In order that an act may be done with the intention of bringing about a harmful or offensive contact * * * to a particular person, * * * the act must be done for the purpose of causing the contact * * * or with knowledge on the part of the actor that such contact * * * is substantially certain to be produced.

We have here the conceded volitional act of Brian, i.e., the moving of a chair. Had the plaintiff proved to the satisfaction of the trial court that Brian moved the chair while she was in the act of sitting down, Brian's action would patently have been for the purpose or with the intent of causing the plaintiff's bodily contact with the ground, and she would be entitled to a judgment against him for the resulting damages.

The plaintiff based her case on that theory, and the trial court held that she failed in her proof and accepted Brian's version of the facts rather than that given by the eyewitness who testified for the plaintiff. After the trial court determined that the plaintiff had not established her theory of a battery (i.e., that Brian had pulled the chair out from under the plaintiff while she was in the act of sitting down), it then became concerned with whether a battery was established under the facts as it found them to be.

In this connection, we quote another portion of the comment [to section 13 of the Restatement of Torts]:

> It is not enough that the act itself is intentionally done and this, even though the actor realizes or should realize that it contains a very grave risk of bringing about the contact * * *. Such realization may make the actor's conduct negligent or even reckless but unless he realizes that to a substantial certainty, the contact * * * will result, the actor has not that intention which is necessary to make him liable under the rule stated in this section.

A battery would be established if, in addition to plaintiff's fall, it was proved that, when Brian moved the chair, he knew with substantial certainty that the plaintiff would attempt to sit down where the chair had been. If Brian had any of the intents which the trial court found, in the italicized portions of the findings of fact quoted above, that he did not have, he would of course have had the knowledge to which we have referred. The mere absence of any intent to injure the plaintiff or to play a prank on her or to embarrass her, or to commit an assault and battery on her would not absolve him from liability if in fact he had such knowledge. Without such knowledge, there would be nothing wrongful about Brian's act in moving the chair and, there being no wrongful act, there would be no liability.

While a finding that Brian had no such knowledge can be inferred from the findings made, we believe that before the plaintiff's action in such a case should be dismissed there should be no question but that the trial court had passed upon that issue; hence, the case should be remanded for clarification of the findings to specifically cover the question of Brian's knowledge, because intent could be inferred therefrom. If the court finds that he had such knowledge the necessary intent will be established and the plaintiff will be entitled to recover, even though there was no purpose to injure or embarrass the plaintiff. If Brian did not have such knowledge, there was no wrongful act by him and the basic premise of liability on the theory of a battery was not established.

It will be noted that the law of battery as we have discussed it is the law applicable to adults, and no significance has been attached to the fact that Brian was a child less than six years of age when the alleged battery occurred. The only circumstance where Brian's age is of any consequence is in determining what he knew, and there his experience, capacity, and understanding are of course material.

* * *

The cause is remanded for clarification, with instructions to make definite findings on the issue of whether Brian Dailey knew with substantial certainty that the plaintiff would attempt to sit down where the chair which he moved had been, and to change the judgment if the findings warrant it.

* * *

Remanded for clarification.

NOTES

1. One of the issues in *Garratt* was whether a battery plaintiff is required to prove that the defendant intended injury. This is a legal issue that was also addressed by the court in *Ghassemieh*. Are the two cases in agreement?

2. You should distinguish the foregoing legal issue from the specific fact issue in *Garratt,* whether the defendant even intended that the plaintiff hit the ground.

On remand, the *Garratt* trial judge re-evaluated the facts in light of the Supreme Court's clarification of the law. He stated that in order to determine Brian's knowledge, "it was necessary for him to consider carefully the time sequence, as he had not done before; and this resulted in his finding that the arthritic woman had begun the slow process of being seated when the defendant quickly removed the chair and seated himself upon it, and that he knew, with substantial certainty, at that time that she would attempt to sit in the place where the chair had been." He accordingly entered judgment in favor of the plaintiff, and on a second appeal the Supreme Court affirmed. 49 Wash.2d 499, 304 P.2d 681 (1956).

3. ***Torts of young children.*** Not all courts would impose battery liability upon a child of Brian Dailey's age on facts like those of *Garratt*. The Supreme Court of Ohio, for example, held that a child under the age of seven cannot be held liable for an intentional tort, reasoning that "[o]ur laws and

our moral concepts assume actors capable of legal and moral choices, of which a young child is incapable." DeLuca v. Bowden, 42 Ohio St.2d 392, 329 N.E.2d 109, 111 (1975). In a case involving defendants who were three and four years of age and who may have caused a fatal injury to a five-week-old baby, the Supreme Court of Colorado rejected *Garratt*'s holding "that infants are liable for their intentional torts irrespective of intent to cause harm." The infant need not intend or foresee the particular harm that resulted, but "must appreciate the fact that the contact may be harmful." Horton v. Reaves, 186 Colo. 149, 526 P.2d 304, 307–08 (1974).

The liability of a young child for negligence is considered in Chapter III.

4. ***Intent to touch vs. intent to injure or offend.*** Cases involving adult defendants can present similar problems and similar judicial disagreements. In White v. University of Idaho, 118 Idaho 400, 797 P.2d 108 (1990), a music professor approached the seated plaintiff, a longtime acquaintance, from behind "and touched her back with both of his hands in a movement later described as one a pianist would make in striking and lifting the fingers from a keyboard. The resulting contact generated unexpectedly harmful injuries * * *." The professor denied any intent to harm or offend. The Idaho Supreme Court affirmed a summary judgment that the act constituted a battery; "under Idaho law the intent required for the commission of a battery is simply the intent to cause an unpermitted contact, not an intent that the contact be harmful or offensive." 118 Idaho at 401, 797 P.2d at 109. In White v. Muniz, 999 P.2d 814 (Colo.2000), an 83–year–old Alzheimer's patient struck the jaw of a caregiver who was attempting to change her diaper. In the ensuing battery action, the trial court, relying upon Horton v. Reaves, note 3, supra, instructed the jury that in order to possess the necessary intent, the patient must have appreciated the offensiveness of her conduct. The jury found against the plaintiff. The Supreme Court of Colorado affirmed, rejecting plaintiff's argument that *Horton* was limited to children and rejecting the reasoning of the Idaho court in White v. University of Idaho.

5. ***The Restatements.*** The *Garratt* court quotes the Restatement of Torts. This was a work published by an organization called the American Law Institute, which was formed in 1923. The ALI is a private organization of lawyers, judges, and legal scholars dedicated to "promot[ing] the clarification and simplification of the law and its better adaptation to social needs," according to its Charter. From its beginning, the ALI has produced "Restatements" of the common law in many areas. The original Restatement of Torts, cited in *Garratt*, was completed in 1939. The Restatement (Second) of Torts, which revised and expanded its predecessor, was produced between 1955 and 1979. The Third Restatement project began in 1991. So far it has produced the Restatement (Third) of Torts: Products Liability (1998), the Restatement (Third) of Torts: Apportionment of Liability (2000), and the Restatement (Third) of Torts: Liability for Physical and Emotional Harm, Volume 1 (2010).* Volume 2 is scheduled for publication in 2011.

The Second Restatement of Torts entirely superseded the First. The Third, however, does not completely supplant the Second. For example,

---

* As we explain in the Preface, throughout this book we will sometimes refer to these as the Products Restatement, Apportionment Restatement, and Third Restatement.

comment *a* to § 5 of the Third Restatement explains that the Second Restatement "remains largely authoritative" concerning detailed doctrines of particular intentional torts such as battery. Accordingly, in the notes in this book we may refer to provisions of the Second as well as the Third Restatement.

The Restatements are not law, but courts often cite them and are influenced by them. See, e.g., Webber v. Sobba, 322 F.3d 1032, 1037 (8th Cir. 2003) (using the Second Restatement to fill a hiatus in Arkansas law, after ascertaining that "[t]he Arkansas Supreme Court frequently looks to the Restatement to answer unsettled questions of tort law"). Sometimes a court will go so far as to expressly adopt a detailed Restatement provision as an expression of its law. See, e.g., Thunder Hawk v. Union Pacific R.R. Co., 844 P.2d 1045, 1048–51 (Wyo.1992) (§ 339 of the Restatement (Second) of Torts).

The Third Restatement § 1 defines intent as follows:

A person acts with the intent to produce a consequence if:

(a) the person acts with the purpose of producing that consequence, or

(b) the person acts knowing that the consequence is substantially certain to result.

6. **Transferred intent.** Intentionally caused harmful or offensive contact is a battery. Intentionally caused apprehension of imminent harmful or offensive contact is an assault. See section C, infra. In a case in which contact occurred but the defendant intended only apprehension, the defendant is still liable for battery, as though the defendant had intended the contact. Similarly, if the defendant intended contact but caused only apprehension, the defendant is liable for assault. Or, if defendant intended contact or apprehension to A, but contact or apprehension resulted to B, the intent element is supplied, by the principle of "transferred intent." See Restatement (Second) of Torts §§ 13, 16, 18, 20, 21, 32 (1965).

FISHER v. CARROUSEL MOTOR HOTEL, INC.

Supreme Court of Texas, 1967.
424 S.W.2d 627.

GREENHILL, JUSTICE.

This is a suit for actual and exemplary damages growing out of an alleged assault and battery. The plaintiff Fisher was a mathematician with the Data Processing Division of the Manned Spacecraft Center, an agency of the National Aeronautics and Space Agency, commonly called NASA, near Houston. The defendants were the Carrousel Motor Hotel, Inc., located in Houston, the Brass Ring Club, which is located in the Carrousel, and Robert W. Flynn, who as an employee of the Carrousel was the manager of the Brass Ring Club. Flynn died before the trial, and the suit proceeded as to the Carrousel and the Brass Ring. Trial was to a jury which found for the plaintiff Fisher. The trial court rendered judgment for the defendants notwithstanding the verdict. The Court of Civil Appeals affirmed. The question before this Court [is] whether there was evidence that an actionable battery was committed * * *.

The plaintiff Fisher had been invited by Ampex Corporation and Defense Electronics to a one day's meeting regarding telemetry equipment at the Carrousel. The invitation included a luncheon. The guests were asked to reply by telephone whether they could attend the luncheon, and Fisher called in his acceptance. After the morning session, the group of 25 or 30 guests adjourned to the Brass Ring Club for lunch. The luncheon was buffet style, and Fisher stood in line with others and just ahead of a graduate student of Rice University who testified at the trial. As Fisher was about to be served, he was approached by Flynn, who snatched the plate from Fisher's hand and shouted that he, a Negro, could not be served in the club. Fisher testified that he was not actually touched, and did not testify that he suffered fear or apprehension of physical injury; but he did testify that he was highly embarrassed and hurt by Flynn's conduct in the presence of his associates.

The jury found that Flynn "forcibly dispossessed plaintiff of his dinner plate" and "shouted in a loud and offensive manner" that Fisher could not be served there, thus subjecting Fisher to humiliation and indignity. It was stipulated that Flynn was an employee of the Carrousel Hotel and, as such, managed the Brass Ring Club. The jury also found that Flynn acted maliciously and awarded Fisher $400 actual damages for his humiliation and indignity and $500 exemplary damages for Flynn's malicious conduct.

The Court of Civil Appeals held that there was no assault because there was no physical contact and no evidence of fear or apprehension of physical contact. However, it has long been settled that there can be a battery without an assault, and that actual physical contact is not necessary to constitute a battery, so long as there is contact with clothing or an object closely identified with the body.

Under the facts of this case, we have no difficulty in holding that the intentional grabbing of plaintiff's plate constituted a battery. The intentional snatching of an object from one's hand is as clearly an offensive invasion of his person as would be an actual contact with the body. "To constitute an assault and battery, it is not necessary to touch the plaintiff's body or even his clothing; knocking or snatching anything from plaintiff's hand or touching anything connected with his person, when done in an offensive manner, is sufficient." Morgan v. Loyacomo, 190 Miss. 656, 1 So.2d 510 (1941).

Such holding is not unique to the jurisprudence of this State. In S.H. Kress & Co. v. Brashier, 50 S.W.2d 922 (Tex.Civ.App.1932, no writ), the defendant was held to have committed "an assault or trespass upon the person" by snatching a book from the plaintiff's hand. The jury findings in that case were that the defendant "dispossessed plaintiff of the book" and caused her to suffer "humiliation and indignity."

* * *

We hold, therefore, that the forceful dispossession of plaintiff Fisher's plate in an offensive manner was sufficient to constitute a battery, and the trial court erred in granting judgment notwithstanding the verdict * * *.

* * * Damages for mental suffering are recoverable without the necessity for showing actual physical injury in a case of willful battery because the basis of that action is the unpermitted and intentional invasion of the plaintiff's person and not the actual harm done to the plaintiff's body. Personal indignity is the essence of an action for battery; and consequently the defendant is liable not only for contacts which do actual physical harm, but also for those which are offensive and insulting. We hold, therefore, that plaintiff was entitled to actual damages for mental suffering due to the willful battery, even in the absence of any physical injury.

* * *

The judgments of the courts below are reversed, and judgment is here rendered for the plaintiff $900 with interest from the date of the trial court's judgment, and for costs of this suit.

NOTES

1. The court at some points describes the plaintiff's suit as one for "assault." Some courts, especially in older opinions, use the term "assault" to describe conduct that today would normally be called "battery."

2. Is it a battery to blow cigar smoke in the face of an anti-smoking activist during a radio talk show? Yes, according to Leichtman v. WLW Jacor Communications, Inc., 92 Ohio App.3d 232, 634 N.E.2d 697 (1994).

3. "A bodily contact is offensive if it offends a reasonable sense of personal dignity." Restatement (Second) of Torts § 19 (1965). The contact "must be one which would offend the ordinary person and as such one not unduly sensitive as to his personal dignity. It must, therefore, be a contact which is unwarranted by the social usages prevalent at the time and place in which it is inflicted." Id. cmt. a.

4. Note that the Carrousel Motor Hotel was liable on the basis of conduct of one of its employees. This is called "vicarious liability." Generally, an employer is liable for torts committed by employees within the scope of employment. Vicarious liability is addressed in Chapter VIII.

C. ASSAULT

VETTER v. MORGAN
Court of Appeals of Kansas, 1996.
22 Kan.App.2d 1, 913 P.2d 1200.

BRISCOE, CHIEF JUDGE.

Laura Vetter appeals the summary judgment dismissal of her * * * assault * * * claim against Chad Morgan for injuries sustained in an automobile accident. * * *

Vetter was injured when her van ran off the road after an encounter with a car owned by Morgan's father and driven by Dana Gaither. Morgan and Jerrod Faulkner were passengers in the car. Vetter was alone at 1:30 or 1:45 a.m. when she stopped her van in the right-hand westbound lane of an intersection at a stoplight. Morgan and Gaither drove up beside Vetter. Morgan began screaming vile and threatening obscenities at Vetter, shaking his fist, and making obscene gestures in a violent manner. According to Vetter, Gaither revved the engine of the car and moved the car back and forth while Morgan was threatening Vetter. Vetter testified that Morgan threatened to remove her from her van and spat on her van door when the traffic light turned green. Vetter stated she was very frightened and thought Morgan was under the influence of drugs or alcohol. She was able to write down the license tag number of the car. Morgan stated he did not intend to scare, upset, or harm Vetter, but "didn't really care" how she felt. He was trying to amuse his friends, who were laughing at his antics.

When the traffic light changed to green, both vehicles drove forward. According to Vetter, after they had driven approximately 10 feet, the car driven by Gaither veered suddenly into her lane, and she reacted by steering her van sharply to the right. Vetter's van struck the curb, causing her head to hit the steering wheel and snap back against the seat, after which she fell to the floor of the van. Morgan and Gaither denied that the car veered into Vetter's lane, stating they drove straight away from the intersection and did not see Vetter's collision with the curb.

* * *

Vetter argues the trial court erred in dismissing her assault claim against Morgan. Assault is defined as "an intentional threat or attempt, coupled with apparent ability, to do bodily harm to another, resulting in immediate apprehension of bodily harm. No bodily contact is necessary." Taiwo [v. Vu], 249 Kan. [585,] 596, 822 P.2d 1024 [(1991)].

The trial court concluded there was no evidence that Morgan threatened or attempted to harm Vetter, that he had no apparent ability to harm her because her van was locked and the windows were rolled up, and there was no claim of immediate apprehension of bodily harm. Vetter contends all of these conclusions involved questions of fact that should have been resolved by a jury.

There was evidence of a threat. Vetter testified in her deposition that Morgan verbally threatened to take her from her van. Ordinarily, words alone cannot be an assault. However, words can constitute assault if "together with other acts or circumstances they put the other in reasonable apprehension of imminent harmful or offensive contact with his person." Restatement (Second) of Torts § 31 (1964).

The record is sufficient to support an inference that Morgan's threat and the acts and circumstances surrounding it could reasonably put someone in Vetter's position in apprehension of imminent or immediate bodily harm. Morgan's behavior was so extreme that Vetter could reasonably have believed he would immediately try to carry out his threat. It is not necessary that the victim be placed in apprehension of instantaneous harm. It is sufficient if it appears there will be no significant delay. See Restatement (Second) of Torts § 29(1), cmt. *b* (1964).

The record also supports an inference that Morgan had the apparent ability to harm Vetter. Although Vetter's van was locked and the windows rolled up, the windows could be broken. The two vehicles were only six feet apart, and Morgan was accompanied by two other males. It was late at night, so witnesses and potential rescuers were unlikely. Although Vetter may have had the ability to flee by turning right, backing up, or running the red light, her ability to prevent the threatened harm by flight or self-defense does not preclude an assault. It is enough that Vetter believed that Morgan was capable of immediately inflicting the contact unless prevented by self-defense, flight, or intervention by others. See Restatement (Second) of Torts § 24, cmt. *b* (1964).

The trial court erred in concluding there was no evidence that Vetter was placed in apprehension of bodily harm. Whether Morgan's actions constituted an assault was a question of fact for the jury.

* * *

NOTES

1. In addition to his own acts, Morgan could have been found liable based upon Gaither's acts (e.g., swerving the car), because the trier could find that they acted in concert. See 913 P.2d at 1205–06.

2. "Finally, we disagree with Geary Huntsberger's claim that the evidence was insufficient to prove that he assaulted Mr. Cleland. An assault occurs when an actor intends to cause an imminent apprehension of a harmful or offensive bodily contact. Restatement (Second) of Torts, § 21. When a person approaches another with two associates wielding chainsaws, screams 'Bring on the chainsaws!,' to which the sawyers respond by dismembering the tree in which the person sits, a factfinder could reasonably conclude that an assault has occurred. Frankly, we are at a loss to understand how a factfinder could arrive at any other conclusion." Sides v. Cleland, 436 Pa.Super. 618, 626, 648 A.2d 793, 796–97 (1994), appeal denied, 540 Pa. 613, 656 A.2d 119 (1995).

3. Like battery, assault is an intentional tort. The plaintiff must prove that the defendant intended to cause apprehension of imminent harmful or offensive bodily contact or intended to cause harmful or offensive bodily contact. See Restatement (Second) of Torts § 32 (1965).

D. FALSE IMPRISONMENT

HERBST v. WUENNENBERG

Supreme Court of Wisconsin, 1978.
83 Wis.2d 768, 266 N.W.2d 391.

ABRAHAMSON, JUSTICE.

Carol Wuennenberg appeals from a judgment entered by the trial court on a jury's special verdict finding that she falsely imprisoned Jason A. Herbst, Ronald B. Nadel, and Robert A. Ritholz ("plaintiffs"). Because there is no credible evidence to sustain a finding of false imprisonment, we reverse the judgment and order the cause remanded so that plaintiffs' complaint can be dismissed and judgment entered in favor of Wuennenberg.

* * *

* * * Plaintiffs' cause of action for false imprisonment arose from an incident which took place on September 19, 1974 in the vestibule of a three-unit apartment building owned and lived in by Wuennenberg and located within the district which Wuennenberg represented as alderperson in the city of Madison. * * *

[T]he plaintiffs were comparing the voter registration list for the city of Madison with names on the mailboxes in multi-unit residential dwellings in Wuennenberg's aldermanic district. Plaintiffs' ultimate purpose was to "purge the voter lists" by challenging the registrations of people whose names were not on mailboxes at the addresses from which they were registered to vote.

The plaintiffs and Wuennenberg gave somewhat differing accounts of the incident which gave rise to the action for false imprisonment, but the dispositive facts are not in dispute.

According to Ritholz, whose version of the incident was corroborated by Herbst and Nadel, when the plaintiffs reached Wuennenberg's house at approximately 4:30 p.m. they entered unannounced through the outer door into a vestibule area which lies between the inner and outer doors to Wuennenberg's building. The plaintiffs stood in the vestibule near the mailboxes, which were on a wall in the vestibule approximately two feet inside the front door to the building. Neither he nor the other plaintiffs touched the mailboxes, stated Ritholz; he simply read the names listed for Wuennenberg's address from a computer printout of the registered voters in Wuennenberg's district, and the others checked to see if those names appeared on the mailboxes.

When they were half way through checking, testified Ritholz, Wuennenberg entered the vestibule from an inner door and asked plaintiffs what they were doing. Ritholz replied that they were working for the Republican party, purging voter lists. According to Ritholz, Wuennenberg became very agitated and told the plaintiffs that she did not want them in her district. "At first she told us to leave," testified Ritholz, "and we agreed to leave, but she very quickly changed her mind and wanted to know who we were. Since we already agreed to leave, we didn't think this was necessary."

After the plaintiffs had refused to identify themselves to her, Wuennenberg asked them whether they would be willing to identify themselves to the police. Ritholz replied that they would be willing to do so. Nonetheless, testified Ritholz, he would have preferred to leave, and several times he offered to leave. Both Nadel and Herbst, who agreed that Ritholz was acting as spokesman for the group, testified to Ritholz's statement to Wuennenberg that the plaintiffs were willing to identify themselves to the police.

Subsequently, Wuennenberg's husband came to the vestibule to see what was going on, and Wuennenberg asked him to call the police. About this time Wuennenberg moved from the inner door to a position in front of the outer door. According to Nadel, Wuennenberg blocked the outer door by "standing there with her arms on the pillars to the door to block our exit." The plaintiffs agreed that Wuennenberg had not threatened or intimidated them and that they neither asked her permission to leave nor made any attempt to get her to move away from the doorway. When asked why he had not attempted to leave the vestibule, each of the plaintiffs answered, in effect, that he assumed he would have had to push Wuennenberg out of the way in order to do so.

The plaintiffs waited in the vestibule, stated Ritholz, until the police came some five minutes later. They gave their names and explained their errand to a police officer who told them that they were not doing anything wrong and that they could continue checking the mailboxes in the district.

* * *

After her husband left to call the police, testified Wuennenberg, she positioned herself in front of the outer doorway because she could watch for the arrival of the police from that vantage and because "I didn't want someone trying to run away at that point." She stated she did not brace her arms against the door frame. She would not have made any effort to stop the plaintiffs had they attempted to leave, stated Wuennenberg, because "I'm not physically capable of stopping anybody."

Plaintiffs' cause of action for false imprisonment [was] tried before a jury. At the close of the evidence, the trial court * * * denied Wuennenberg's motion for a directed verdict * * *.

The jury returned a special verdict finding that Wuennenberg had falsely imprisoned the plaintiffs and awarded Herbst, Nadel and Ritholz a total of $1,500 in actual damages. * * *

* * *

We reiterate the rule which this court must follow in reviewing the record to determine if the jury verdict is supported by the evidence: A jury verdict will not be upset if there is any credible evidence which under any reasonable view fairly admits of an inference supporting the findings. The evidence is to be viewed in the light most favorable to the verdict. A jury cannot base its findings on conjecture and speculation. We hold that the evidence adduced in the case before us does not support a finding that the plaintiffs were falsely imprisoned, and accordingly we reverse the judgment of the trial court.

The action for the tort of false imprisonment protects the personal interest in freedom from restraint of movement. The essence of false imprisonment is the intentional, unlawful, and unconsented restraint by one person of the physical liberty of another. There is no cause of action unless the confinement is contrary to the will of the "prisoner." It is a contradiction to say that the captor imprisoned the "prisoner" with the "prisoner's" consent.

* * *

After review of the record we conclude that the evidence is not sufficient to support the conclusion that Wuennenberg's acts "directly or indirectly result[ed] in * * * a confinement of the [plaintiffs]," a required element of the cause of action.

The Restatement [(Second) of Torts] lists the ways in which an actor may bring about a "confinement": "by actual or apparent physical barriers" [Sec. 38 cmt. *a*]; "by overpowering physical force, or by submission to physical force" [Sec. 39]; "by submission to a threat to apply physical force to the other's person immediately upon the other's going or attempting to go beyond the area in which the actor intends to confine him" [Sec. 40]; "by submission to duress other than threats of physical force, where such duress is sufficient to make the consent given ineffective to bar the action" (as by a threat to inflict harm upon a member of the other's immediate family, or his property) [Sec. 40A]; "by taking a person into custody under an asserted legal authority" [Sec. 41].

The plaintiffs do not contend that confinement was brought about by an actual or apparent physical barrier, or by overpowering physical force, or by submission to duress, or by taking a person into custody under an asserted legal authority. The parties agree that the central issue is whether there was confinement by threat of physical force and thus argue only as to the applicability of section 40 of the Restatement * * *.

* * *

The comments to section 40 provide that a person has not been confined by "threats of physical force" unless by words or other acts the actor "threatens to apply" *and* "has the apparent intention and ability to apply" force to his person. It is not a sufficient basis for an action for false imprisonment that the "prisoner" remained within the limits set by the actor. Remaining within such limits is not a submission to the threat unless the "prisoner" believed that the actor had the ability to carry his threat into effect.

* * *

As plaintiffs state in their brief, the question before this court is whether there is any credible evidence which supports a conclusion that the plaintiffs did not consent to the confinement and that they remained in the vestibule only because Wuennenberg indicated by standing in the doorway that she had "the apparent intention and ability to apply" force to their persons should they attempt to leave. We have reviewed the record, and we find that it does not support this conclusion. Ritholz testified that Wuennenberg had not verbally threatened the plaintiffs, and since none of the plaintiffs asked Wuennenberg to step aside, it could be no more than speculation to conclude that Wuennenberg would not only have refused this request but also would have physically resisted had the plaintiffs attempted to leave. At best, the evidence supports an inference that plaintiffs remained in the vestibule because they *assumed* they would have to push Wuennenberg out of the way in order to leave. This assumption is not sufficient to support a claim for false imprisonment.

We do not intend to suggest that false imprisonment will not lie unless a "prisoner" attempts to assault his captor or unless he fails to make such attempt only because he fears harm. The plaintiffs in the case at bar were not required to obtain their freedom by taking steps dangerous to themselves or offensive to their reasonable sense of decency or personal dignity. At a minimum, however, plaintiffs should have attempted to ascertain whether there was any basis to their assumption that their freedom of movement had been curtailed. False imprisonment may not be predicated upon a person's unfounded belief that he was restrained.

Dupler v. Seubert, [69 Wis.2d 373, 230 N.W.2d 626 (1975)], relied on by plaintiffs, does not support plaintiffs' contention that the trial court properly submitted to the jury the question whether the plaintiffs submitted to "an implied threat of actual physical restraint." We concluded in *Dupler* that the record contained sufficient evidence from which a jury could have concluded that plaintiff had been falsely imprisoned "by an implied threat of actual physical restraint":

> [Plaintiff] testified that defendant Peterson ordered her in a loud voice to remain seated several times, after she expressed the desire to leave. She reported being 'berated, screamed and hollered at,' and said the reason she did not just walk out of the room was that 'Mrs. Seubert had blocked the door, and tempers had been raised with all the shouting and screaming, I was just plain scared to make an effort. There were two against one.'

As Wuennenberg notes in her brief, the only similarity between *Dupler* and the case at bar is that Wuennenberg stood in the doorway. Plaintiffs were not "berated, screamed, and hollered at"; they outnumbered Wuennenberg three-to-one; and they gave no testimony to the effect that they were frightened of Wuennenberg or that they feared she would harm them.

Viewed in the light most favorable to plaintiffs, the evidence shows that the plaintiffs were willing to identify themselves to the police, but that they would have preferred to leave Wuennenberg's premises. It is not a sufficient basis for an action for false imprisonment that the plaintiffs remained on the premises although they would have preferred not to do so. Because plaintiffs did not submit to an apprehension of force, they were not imprisoned.

Judgment reversed, and cause remanded with directions to the trial court to enter judgment in favor of Wuennenberg dismissing plaintiffs' complaint.

NOTES

1. Confinement must be within a boundary. Excluding someone from a place does not constitute a confinement.

2. A reasonable and reasonably discoverable alternative means of escape negates a confinement. In Geddes v. Daughters of Charity of St. Vincent De Paul, Inc., 348 F.2d 144 (5th Cir.1965), the plaintiff alleged that she was falsely imprisoned by a mental hospital. The defendant argued that she had a reasonable means of escape when she was permitted to take escorted trips into town. The court refused to overturn a jury verdict for the plaintiff. Evidence that she was escorted on her trips downtown, that she was old, in ill health and weak, and that she was never given more than ten dollars supported a finding that the alleged means of escape was not reasonable.

3. An often cited case on false imprisonment is Whittaker v. Sandford, 110 Me. 77, 85 A. 399 (1912). The defendant lured the plaintiff onto a yacht for a trip from Jaffa, Syria, to Maine, implicitly agreeing that the plaintiff would be permitted to go ashore in Maine. When the yacht was anchored in a harbor in Maine, the defendant refused to provide a boat to take the plaintiff ashore. The court held that because the defendant had implicitly promised to take the plaintiff ashore, his failure to provide a boat constituted a false imprisonment. This does not mean, however, that, absent an (implicit) agreement, individuals have an affirmative duty to extricate others from a confinement.

Note that it might have been possible for the plaintiff to swim ashore. But this was not considered a "reasonable" means of escape.

4. To recover for false imprisonment, a plaintiff must prove that he or she was aware of the imprisonment at the time *or* that the confinement caused actual harm. In Parvi v. City of Kingston, 41 N.Y.2d 553, 394 N.Y.S.2d 161, 362 N.E.2d 960 (1977), the plaintiff was intoxicated during the imprisonment and could not remember it at the time of trial. The court held that the trial court improperly dismissed the complaint, reasoning that Parvi could have been aware of his confinement at the time and the trial court "failed to distinguish between a later recollection of consciousness and the existence of that consciousness at the time when the imprisonment itself took place."

5. A person may be liable for false imprisonment for wrongfully directing the police to arrest another person. The cases distinguish between "directing" the police to arrest someone and providing the police with information upon which the police exercise judgment. See King v. Crossland Savings Bank, 111 F.3d 251, 256–57 (2d Cir.1997). Knowingly providing the police with incorrect information is the equivalent of "directing" an arrest, but innocently providing incorrect information is not. See Godines v. First Guaranty Savings & Loan Ass'n, 525 So.2d 1321 (Miss.1988).

E. INTENTIONAL INFLICTION OF EMOTIONAL DISTRESS

ECKENRODE v. LIFE OF AMERICA INSURANCE COMPANY

United States Court of Appeals, Seventh Circuit, 1972.
470 F.2d 1.

KILEY, CIRCUIT JUDGE.

Plaintiff, a resident of Pennsylvania, filed this * * * diversity complaint to recover damages for severe emotional injury suffered as a result of the deliberate refusal of Life of America Insurance Company (Insurer), of Chicago, to pay her the proceeds of Insurer's policy covering the life of her husband. The district court dismissed the suit. Plaintiff has appealed. We reverse.

* * *

Taking the allegations, properly pleaded in Counts II and III, as true, the following facts are stated: Defendant's life insurance policy covering plaintiff's husband issued September 22, 1967. Under the policy Insurer agreed to pay plaintiff $5,000 immediately upon due proof of death from "accidental causes." On December 17, 1967, insured was an accidental victim of a homicide. Plaintiff met all conditions of the policy and repeatedly demanded payment, but Insurer refused to pay. Decedent left plaintiff with several children, but no property of value. She had no money, none even for the funeral expenses. Denied payment by Insurer, she was required to borrow money to support her family, while her financial condition worsened. The family was required to live with, and accept charity from, relatives.

Further: Insurer knew or should have known of the death of decedent from accidental causes and of plaintiff's dire need of the policy proceeds. Yet Insurer repeatedly and deliberately refused her demands for payment, and as a proximate result she was caused to suffer "severe distress and disturbance of [her] mental tranquility." Instead of paying her the proceeds of the policy, and being fully aware of the accidental cause of decedent's death and of plaintiff's financial distress, Insurer breached the policy promise to pay immediately upon proof of death. Insurer, knowing full well that plaintiff needed the proceeds of the policy to provide necessaries for her children, applied "economic coercion" in refusing to make payment on the policy, and in "inviting" plaintiff to "compromise" her claim by implying it (Insurer) had a valid defense to the claim.[2]

* * *

The issue before us * * * is whether plaintiff—beneficiary of her husband's life insurance policy—may on the foregoing "facts" recover damages for severe mental distress allegedly suffered as a result of Insurer's conduct. Illinois law controls our decision, and, in anticipation that the Illinois Supreme Court would hold as we do, we decide the issue in favor of plaintiff.

We have no doubt, in view of Knierim v. Izzo, 22 Ill.2d 73, 174 N.E.2d 157 (1961), that the Illinois Supreme Court would sustain plaintiff's complaint against Insurer's motion to dismiss.

In *Knierim,* plaintiff filed a wrongful death action alleging, inter alia, that defendant Izzo threatened her with the murder of her husband, carried out the threat, and thereby proximately caused her severe emotional distress. The trial court dismissed her complaint, but the Illinois Supreme Court reversed and held that plaintiff had stated a cause of action for an intentional causing of severe emotional distress by Izzo's "outrageous conduct."

The court recognized the "new tort" of intentional infliction of severe emotional distress, following similar recognition by an "increasing number of courts," and cited several state decisions. The court rejected reasons given by other courts not recognizing the "new tort." As to the reason that mental disturbance is incapable of financial measurement, the court pointed out that "pain and suffering" and "mental suffering" are elements of damage, respectively, in personal injury and malicious prosecution cases. As to the reason that mental consequences are too evanescent for the law to deal with, the court noted that psychosomatic medicine had learned much in the past "thirty years" about the bodily effects of man's emotions, and that symptoms produced by "stronger emotions" are now visible to the professional eye. As to the reason that recognizing the "new tort" would lead to frivolous claims, the court observed that triers of fact from their own experiences would be able to draw a line between "slight hurts" and "outrageous conduct." And finally, as to the reason that mental consequences vary greatly with the individual so as to pose difficulties too great for the law, the court adopted an objective standard against which emotional distress could be measured. The court thought that the standard of "severe emotional distress to a person of ordinary sensibilities, in the absence of special knowledge or notice" would be a sufficient limit for excluding "mere vulgarities * * * as meaningless abusive expressions." The court noted that the "reasonable man" is well

---

2. Attached to the complaint is a copy of Insurer's letter of January 12, 1968. The letter suggests that in view of a police investigation not likely to be completed until the "very distant future," plaintiff might like to suggest an offer to "settle" rather than wait for the police report.

known to triers of fact who are also well acquainted with "the man of ordinary sensibilities."

The court added a cautionary note, expressing confidence that Illinois trial judges would not permit litigation to introduce "trivialities and mere bad manners" under the cloak of the "new tort." * * *

In *Knierim* the court, inter alia, relied upon State Rubbish Collectors Association v. Siliznoff, 38 Cal.2d 330, 240 P.2d 282 (1952), and Restatement, Torts § 46 (1948 Supp.). In *Siliznoff* the California Supreme Court, in an opinion by Justice Roger Traynor, recognized the "new tort" for the first time and held that Siliznoff could recover from the cross-defendant Rubbish Collectors Association for mental distress caused by the Association's severe threats to beat him up, destroy his truck and put him out of business unless Siliznoff offered to pay over certain proceeds to the Association. Later, the California Supreme Court *en banc* affirmed a trial court judgment against an insurance company, including $25,000 for mental suffering caused by the insurance company's earlier unreasonable refusal to accept a settlement within the limits of the liability policy. Crisci v. Security Ins. Co. of New Haven, 66 Cal.2d 425, 58 Cal.Rptr. 13, 426 P.2d 173 (1967). There Mrs. Crisci's mental distress claim was in addition to her loss of property caused by the insurance company's failure to settle. The court thought that where there were substantial damages apart from the mental distress, the danger of fictitious claims was reduced. Subsequently in Fletcher v. Western National Life Ins. Co., 10 Cal.App.3d 376, 89 Cal.Rptr. 78 (1970), an appellate court, relying upon *Siliznoff* and *Crisci,* held that the defendant insurance company's threatened and actual bad faith refusals to make payments under the disability policy were essentially tortious in nature and could legally be the basis for an action against the company for intentional infliction of emotional distress. The decision rested on the finding that the refusals were maliciously employed by the company in concert with false and threatening communications directed to the badly injured plaintiff-insured for the purpose of causing him to surrender his policy or disadvantageously settle a nonexistent dispute. The court found sufficient evidence showing emotional distress of the "requisite severity" (i.e., outrageousness), and thus affirmed the trial court's denial of judgment N.O.V.

We think that the California court in *Fletcher,* supra, set out correctly the elements of a prima facie case for the tort of "intentional infliction of severe emotional distress":

(1) Outrageous conduct by the defendant;

(2) The defendant's intention of causing, or reckless disregard of the probability of causing emotional distress;

(3) The plaintiff's suffering severe or extreme emotional distress; and

(4) Actual and proximate causation of the emotional distress by the defendant's outrageous conduct.

It is our view that were this case before the Illinois Supreme Court, that court would find the foregoing elements substantially correct; and that plaintiff here has sufficiently pleaded the elements.

It is recognized that the outrageous character of a person's conduct may arise from an abuse by that person of a position which gives him power to affect the interests of another; and that in this sense extreme "bullying tactics" and other "high pressure" methods of insurance adjusters seeking to force compromises or settlements may constitute outrageous conduct. It is also recognized that the extreme character of a persons' conduct may arise from that person's knowledge that the other is peculiarly susceptible to emotional distress by reason of some physical or mental condition or peculiarity.

Here Insurer's alleged bad faith refusal to make payment on the policy, coupled with its deliberate use of "economic coercion" (i.e., by delaying and refusing payment it increased plaintiff's financial distress thereby coercing her to compromise and settle) to force a settlement, clearly rises to the level of "outrageous conduct" to a person of "ordinary sensibilities."

Furthermore, it is common knowledge that one of the most frequent considerations in procuring life insurance is to ensure the continued economic and mental welfare of the beneficiaries upon the death of the insured. The very risks insured against presuppose that upon the death of the insured the beneficiary might be in difficult circumstances and thus particularly susceptible and vulnerable to high pressure tactics by an economically powerful entity. In the case before us Insurer's alleged high pressure methods (economic coercion) were aimed at the very thing insured against, and we think that the insurance company was on notice that plaintiff would be particularly vulnerable to mental distress by reason of her financial plight.

* * *

It is true that settlement tactics may be privileged under circumstances where an insurer has done no more than insist upon his legal rights in a permissible way. But we do not think that a refusal to make payments based on a bad faith insistence on a non-existent defense is privileged conduct against the complaint here.

* * *

For the reasons given, the judgment of the district court dismissing Counts II and III of plaintiff's complaint is hereby reversed.

NOTE

In Vetter v. Morgan, section C, supra p. 20, in addition to assault, the plaintiff claimed intentional infliction of emotional distress. As to the latter claim, the court of appeals affirmed summary judgment for the defendant on the following ground:

There was no evidence that Vetter suffered extreme emotional distress sufficient to support her claim. Her testimony that she was "very, very frightened" during the incident does not establish the kind of extreme emotional distress required for liability. Although Vetter testified that she later became very depressed and was given a prescription for Prozac for a short time, this testimony was given when she was describing her physical injuries and medical treatment for them rather than her emotional reaction to Morgan's actions.

DANA v. OAK PARK MARINA, INC.

Supreme Court of New York, Appellate Division, 1997.
230 A.D.2d 204, 660 N.Y.S.2d 906.

BALIO, JUSTICE.

Defendant Oak Park Marina, Inc. (corporation) owns and operates a marina on the shore of Lake Ontario in North Rose, New York. The individual defendants are officers of the corporation and operators of the marina. One of the buildings on the marina site includes an office area where employees, including lifeguards, are allowed to change. It also includes men's and ladies' rest rooms for use by marina patrons and their guests. The rest rooms include a changing area, shower facilities and toilets. In 1993 the corporation installed a video surveillance camera in each of the rest rooms purportedly for the purpose of detecting and curbing vandalism. The following year the corporation installed two video surveillance cameras in the office area purportedly for the purpose of detecting theft of marina property. Plaintiff, a marina patron who utilized the ladies' rest room, commenced this action * * *, which seeks relief for plaintiff and all others similarly situated, alleg[ing] that defendants video-taped about 150 to 200 female patrons and guests in various stages of undress without their knowledge or consent; that the videotapes were viewed by defendants and others; and that the tapes were displayed to others for purposes of trade. The amended complaint asserts causes of action for * * * reckless infliction of emotional distress * * *.

Defendants brought a preanswer motion to dismiss the causes of action for reckless infliction of emotional distress * * *.

[The trial court] denied the * * * motion. Defendants appeal.

* * *

Defendants contend that New York does not recognize a cause of action for the reckless infliction of emotional distress. We disagree. Although the Court of Appeals has not held that a cause of action exists in a case factually involving reckless, but not intentional, infliction of emotional distress, that Court, in a series of cases, has "adopted" the rule formulated in section 46(1) of the Restatement (Second) of Torts that "[o]ne who by extreme and outrageous conduct intentionally *or recklessly* causes severe emotional distress to another is subject to liability for such emotional distress [emphasis added]." Moreover, the Court has stated that the tort has four elements: "(i) extreme and outrageous conduct; (ii) intent to cause, *or disregard of a substantial probability of causing,* severe emotional distress; (iii) a causal connection between the conduct and injury; and (iv) severe emotional distress [emphasis added]." The italicized phrase comports with general descriptions of recklessness in tort matters and is similar to the Restatement's description of recklessness.*

In our view, reckless conduct is encompassed within the tort denominated intentional infliction of emotional distress. We thus conclude that a complaint alleging that defendants acted "recklessly and with utter disregard that the Plaintiff and others would be harmed, humiliated and suffer extreme mental anguish and distress" alleges that defendants disregarded "a substantial probability of causing" severe emotional distress. Further, the amended complaint alleges that defendants surreptitiously videotaped plaintiff without her consent, viewed videotapes of plaintiff and others in various stages of undress for personal and unjustifiable purposes and displayed those tapes to others for purposes of trade, thereby sufficiently alleging conduct that a jury could find to be extreme and outrageous. Thus, we conclude that the amended complaint states a cause of action for reckless infliction of emotional distress.

NOTE

The Third Restatement § 2 provides:

A person acts recklessly in engaging in conduct if:

(a) the person knows of the risk of harm created by the conduct or knows facts that make the risk obvious to another in the person's situation, and

(b) the precaution that would eliminate or reduce the risk involves burdens that are so slight relative to the magnitude of the risk as to render the person's failure to adopt the precaution a demonstration of the person's indifference to the risk.

F. TRESPASS TO LAND

AMPHITHEATERS, INC. v. PORTLAND MEADOWS

Supreme Court of Oregon, 1948.
184 Or. 336, 198 P.2d 847.

BRAND, JUSTICE.

[Plaintiff owned an outdoor, drive-in movie theater. Defendant owned a horse race track on adjacent property. The race track was equipped with lights for night racing. The plaintiff sued for trespass to land and nui-

---

* Restatement (Second) of Torts § 46 cmt. *i* ("Intention and recklessness") states: "The rule stated in this Section applies where the actor desires to inflict severe emotional distress, and also where he knows that such distress is certain, or substantially certain, to result from his conduct. It applies also where he acts recklessly * * * in deliberate disregard of a high degree of probability that the emotional distress will follow." [Ed.]

sance, claiming that the lights from the race track interfered with the movie screen. The trial court directed a verdict for the defendant.]

In installing outdoor moving picture theaters, it is necessary to protect the premises from outside light interference. For that purpose the plaintiff constructed wing fences for a considerable distance on each side of the screen and along the westerly line of Union Avenue for the purpose of shutting off the light from the cars traveling on that arterial highway. It was also necessary to construct a shadow box extending on both sides and above the screen for the purpose of excluding the light from the moon and stars. The testimony indicates that the construction of the shadow box was necessary if a good picture was to be presented on the screen. The extreme delicacy of plaintiff's operation and the susceptibility of outdoor moving pictures to light in any form was conclusively established by the evidence.

In order to illuminate the defendant's track for night horse racing, approximately 350 1500–watt lights are mounted in clusters on 80–foot poles placed at intervals of approximately 250 feet around the track. The flood lights are in general, directed at the track, but there is substantial evidence to the effect that reflected light "spills" over onto the plaintiff's premises and has a serious effect on the quality of pictures shown on the screen. The nearest cluster of lights on the defendant's track is 832 feet distance from the plaintiff's screen. The light from the defendant's track not only impairs the quality of the pictures exhibited by the plaintiff, but there is also substantial evidence that plaintiffs have suffered financial loss as the result of the illumination of which they complain. On one occasion at least, plaintiffs felt themselves required to refund admission fees to their patrons on account of the poor quality of the picture exhibited. The evidence discloses that the light from the defendant's race track when measured at plaintiff's screen is approximately that of full moonlight.

Upon the opening of the racing season in September, 1946, the plaintiff immediately complained to the defendant concerning the detrimental effect of defendant's lights, and shortly thereafter suit was filed. In the fall of 1946 the defendant, while denying liability, nevertheless made substantial efforts to protect the plaintiff from the effect of defendant's lights. One hundred hoods were installed on the lights, and particular attention was given to those nearest to the plaintiff's property. In 1947, and prior to the spring racing season, which was to last 25 days, thirty louvers were also installed for the purpose of further confining the light to the defendant's property. These efforts materially reduced, but did not eliminate the conditions of which plaintiff complains.

Plaintiff contends that the defendant, by casting light equivalent to that of a full moon upon plaintiff's screen has committed a trespass upon real property and error is assigned by reason of the failure of the court to submit to the jury the question of trespass. While the dividing line between trespass and nuisance is not always a sharp one, we think it clear that the case at bar is governed by the law of nuisance and not by the law of trespass. Under our decisions every unauthorized entry upon land of another, although without damage, constitutes actionable trespass. The mere suggestion that the casting of light upon the premises of a plaintiff would render a defendant liable without proof of any actual damage, carries its own refutation. Actions for damages on account of smoke, noxious odors and the like have been universally classified as falling within the law of nuisance. In fact, cases of this type are described in the Restatement of the Law as "non trespassory" invasions. Restatement of The Law of Torts, Vol. 4, Ch. 40, p. 214, et seq.

Many of the cases on which plaintiff relies in support of its theory of trespass involve the flight of airplanes at low level over plaintiffs' land. The modern law with reference to trespass by airplanes has developed under the influence of ancient rules concerning the nature of property. Ownership of lands, it has been said, "includes, not only the face of the earth, but everything under it or over it, and has in its legal signification an indefinite extent upward and downward * * *." * * *

In support of its theory of trespass, the plaintiff cites Swetland v. Curtiss Airports Corporation, 6 Cir., 55 F.2d 201, 83 A.L.R. 319; United States v. Causby, 328 U.S. 256, 66 S.Ct. 1062, 90 L.Ed. 1206; and Guith v. Consumers Power Co., D.C., 36 F.Supp. 21. They are all cases which involve the flight of airplanes and which reflect the influence of the ancient rules of ownership ad coelum as modified by the rules of privilege set forth in the Restatement. The historical background of these cases distinguishes them from the non trespassory cases which are controlled by the law of nuisance. Portsmouth Harbor Land & Hotel Co. v. United States, 260 U.S. 327, 43 S.Ct. 135, 67 L.Ed. 287, was similar in principle to the *Causby* case, supra. The case involved a taking by the United States by means of the continuous firing of artillery over the petitioners' land. We need not argue the distinction between a cannon ball and a ray of light. Upon this issue plaintiff also cites National Refining Co. v. Batte, 135 Miss. 819, 100 So. 388, 35 A.L.R. 91, and The Shelburne, Inc. v. Crossan Corporation, 95 N.J.Eq. 188, 122 A. 749, both of which cases involve the shedding of light upon defendant's property, but both were decided upon the theory of nuisance and not of trespass. * * *

[The court then held that the defendant's conduct did not constitute a nuisance. See Chapter XVI, infra.]

The trial court did not err in directing a verdict. The judgment is affirmed.

NOTES

1. ***Trespass vs. nuisance.*** To recover for trespass to land (or for battery, assault, or false imprisonment), a plaintiff need not prove that the invasion was unreasonable or that it caused actual damage. Thus, a plaintiff has certain advantages if he can prove an "entry" and fit his case under trespass to land rather than nuisance.

The law of nuisance is addressed in Chapter XV. Basically, the plaintiff must prove that the defendant caused a *substantial, unreasonable* interference with the plaintiff's quiet use and enjoyment of real property. Unlike under trespass to land, a plaintiff need not prove a physical entry. The interference can be caused by a physical, trespassory entry, but it can also be caused by other means, such as odor or noise. On the other hand, under nuisance the plaintiff normally must prove that the interference was unreasonable and that it caused actual damage.

2. ***Title disputes.*** A plaintiff's ability to make out a case for trespass to land without proving damages has at least one important consequence. If two parties dispute ownership, they can resolve their dispute in an action for trespass to land, even though neither party can show actual damage. Moreover, the law of property provides that a trespasser can sometimes acquire legal rights in land if he is in "adverse possession" for a sufficient length of time. An action for trespass to land gives the actual owner the ability to cut off the trespasser's potential rights, even though the owner is not otherwise harmed by the trespass.

3. ***Airplane overflights.*** The court in *Amphitheaters* stated that reasonable overflight by aircraft constitutes a privileged entry. The court cited sections 158 and 159 of the First Restatement of Torts. Under the approach of the First Restatement, an overflight that was not reasonable was not privileged and, therefore, was an actionable trespass.

Section 159 of the Restatement (Second) of Torts provides that overflights into "the immediate reaches" above land constitute an entry. Under the approach of the Second Restatement, higher overflights do not constitute an entry and, therefore, do not require a privilege.

4. ***The intent requirement.*** Trespass to land is an intentional tort in the same sense that battery, assault, and false imprisonment are intentional torts. The plaintiff must prove that the defendant intended (i.e., desired or knew with a substantial certainty) that physical facts constituting an entry would be a result of the defendant's actions. A few older cases suggest that the defendant must merely intend an act that leads to an entry, but the overwhelming modern view is that the defendant must intend facts that constitute an entry. The defendant need not, however, know that the entry is wrongful, or even that it is an "entry." Thus, a defendant who intentionally enters land he mistakenly assumes he owns is liable for trespass to land.

MARTIN v. REYNOLDS METALS COMPANY

Supreme Court of Oregon, 1959.
221 Or. 86, 342 P.2d 790.

O'CONNELL, JUSTICE.

This is an action of trespass. The plaintiffs allege that during the period from August 22, 1951 to January 1, 1956 the defendant, in the operation of its aluminum reduction plant near Troutdale, Oregon caused certain fluoride compounds in the form of gases and particulates to become airborne and settle upon the plaintiffs' land, rendering it unfit for raising livestock during that period. * * *

* * *

Through appropriate pleadings the defendant set up the two-year statute of limitations applicable to nontrespassory injuries to land (ORS 12.110). If the defendant's conduct created a nuisance and not a trespass the defendant would be liable only for such damage as resulted from its conduct during a period of two years immediately preceding the date upon which plaintiffs' action was instituted. On the other hand, if the defendant's conduct resulted in a trespass upon plaintiffs' land the six-year statute of limitations provided for in ORS 12.080 would be applicable and plaintiffs would be entitled to recover damages resulting from the trespasses by defendant during the period from August 22, 1951 to January 1, 1956. [The trial court allowed damages for the full period.]

The gist of the defendant's argument is as follows: a trespass arises only when there has been a "breaking and entering upon real property," constituting a direct, as distinguished from a consequential, invasion of the possessor's interest in land; and the settling upon the land of fluoride compounds consisting of gases, fumes and particulates is not sufficient to satisfy these requirements.

Before appraising the argument we shall first describe more particularly the physical and chemical nature of the substance which was deposited upon plaintiffs' land. In reducing alumina (the oxide of aluminum) to aluminum the alumina is subjected to an electrolytic process which causes the emanation of fluoridic compounds consisting principally of hydrogen fluoride, calcium fluoride, iron fluoride and silicon tetrafluoride. The individual particulates which form these chemical compounds are not visible to the naked eye. A part of them were captured by a fume collection system which was installed in November, 1950; the remainder became airborne and a part of the uncaptured particles eventually were deposited upon plaintiffs' land.

There is evidence to prove that during the period from August, 1951 to January, 1956 the emanation of fluorides from defendant's plant averaged approximately 800 pounds daily. Some of this discharge was deposited upon the plaintiffs' land. There is sufficient evidence to support the trial court's finding that the quantity of fluorides deposited upon the plaintiffs' land was great enough to cause $91,500 damage to the plaintiffs in the use of their land for grazing purposes and in the deterioration of their land as alleged.

* * *

Trespass and private nuisance are separate fields of tort liability relating to actionable interference with the possession of land. They may be distinguished by comparing the interest invaded; an actionable invasion of a possessor's interest in the exclusive possession of land is a trespass; an actionable invasion of a possessor's interest in the use and enjoyment of his land is a nuisance.

The same conduct on the part of a defendant may and often does result in the actionable invasion of both of these interests * * *. * * *

However, there are cases which have held that the defendant's interference with plaintiff's possession resulting from the settling upon his land of effluents emanating from defendant's operations is exclusively nontrespassory. Although in such cases the separate particles which collectively cause the invasion are minute, the deposit of each of the particles constitutes a physical intrusion and, but for the size of the particle, would clearly give rise to an action of trespass. The defendant asks us to take account of the difference in size of the physical agency through which the intrusion occurs and relegate entirely to the field of nuisance law certain invasions which do not meet the dimensional test, whatever that is. In pressing this argument upon us the defendant must admit that there are cases which have held that a trespass results from the movement or deposit of rather small objects over or upon the surface of the possessor's land.

Thus it has been held that causing shot from a gun to fall upon the possessor's land is a trespass.

The dropping of particles of molten lead upon the plaintiff's land has been held to be a trespass. And the defendant was held liable in trespass where spray from a cooling tower on the roof of its theater fell upon the plaintiff's land.

The deposit of soot and carbon from defendant's mill upon plaintiff's land was held to be a trespass * * *.

And liability on the theory of trespass has been recognized where the harm was produced by the vibration of the soil or by the concussion of the air which, of course, is nothing more than the movement of molecules one against the other. * * *

The view recognizing a trespassory invasion where there is no "thing" which can be seen with the naked eye undoubtedly runs counter to the definition of trespass expressed in some quarters. It is quite possible that in an earlier day when science had not yet peered into the molecular and atomic world of small particles, the courts could not fit an invasion through unseen physical instrumentalities into the requirement that a trespass can result only from a *direct* invasion. But in this atomic age even the uneducated know the great and awful force contained in the atom and what it can do to a man's property if it is released. In fact, the now famous equation $E = mc^2$ has taught us that mass and energy are equivalents and that our concept of "things" must be reframed. If these observations on science in relation to the law of trespass should appear theoretical and unreal in the abstract, they become very practical and real to the possessor of land when the unseen force cracks the foundation of his house. The force is just as real if it is chemical in nature and must be awakened by the intervention of another agency before it does harm.

If, then, we must look to the character of the instrumentality which is used in making an intrusion upon another's land we prefer to emphasize the object's energy or force rather than its size. Viewed in this way we may define trespass as any intrusion which invades the possessor's protected interest in exclusive possession, whether that intrusion is by visible or invisible pieces of matter or by energy which can be measured only by the mathematical language of the physicist.

We are of the opinion, therefore, that the intrusion of the fluoride particulates in the present case constituted a trespass.

The defendant argues that our decision in Amphitheaters, Inc. v. Portland Meadows requires a contrary conclusion. In discussing the distinction between trespass and nuisance the court referred to a difference between "a cannon ball and a ray of light" indicating that the former but not the latter could produce a trespassory invasion. The court also said: "The mere suggestion that the casting of light upon the premises of a plaintiff would render a defendant liable without proof of any actual damage, carries its own refutation." We do not regard this statement as a pronouncement that a trespass can *never* be caused by the intrusion of light rays or other intangible forces; more properly the case may be interpreted as stating that the conduct of the defendant in a particular case may not be actionable if it does not violate a legally protected interest of the plaintiff. The court states that the defendant is not liable *without proof of actual damage*. In that case the plaintiff contended that he had suffered damage in the form of a less efficient cinema screen due to the defendant's lights. In denying recovery the court found that there was no damage, apparently because whatever harm the plaintiff suffered was damnum absque injuria.

* * *

The *Amphitheaters* case may also be viewed as a pronouncement that a possessor's interest is not invaded by an intrusion which is so trifling that it cannot be recognized by the law. Inasmuch as it is not necessary to prove actual damage in trespass the magnitude of the intrusion ordinarily would not be of any consequence. But there is a point where the entry is so lacking in substance that the law will refuse to recognize it, applying the maxim *de minimis non curat lex*. Thus it would seem clear that ordinarily the casting of a grain of sand upon another's land would not be a trespass. And so too the casting of diffused light rays upon another's land would not ordinarily constitute a trespass. Conceivably such rays could be so concentrated that their entry upon the possessor's land would result in a trespassory invasion. * * *

* * *

We think that a possessor's interest in land as defined by the considerations recited above may, under the appropriate circumstances, be violated by a ray of light, by an atomic particle, or by a particulate of fluoride and, contrariwise, if such interest circumscribed by these considerations is not violated or endangered, the defendant's conduct, even though it may result in a physical intrusion, will not render him liable in an action of trespass. Amphitheaters, Inc. v. Portland Meadows, supra.

We hold that the defendant's conduct in causing chemical substances to be deposited upon the plaintiffs' land fulfilled all of the requirements under the law of trespass.

The defendant [also] contends that trespass will not lie in this case because the injury was indirect and consequential and that the requirement that the injury must be direct and immediate to constitute a trespass was not met. We have held that the deposit of the particulates upon the plaintiff's land was an intrusion within the definition of trespass. That intrusion was direct. * * * The distinction between direct and indirect invasions where there has been a physical intrusion upon the plaintiff's land has been abandoned by some courts. Since the invasion in the instant case was direct it is not necessary for us to decide whether the distinction is recognized in this state.

* * *

The judgment of the lower court is affirmed.

McALLISTER, CHIEF JUSTICE (specially concurring):

I concur in the result of the above opinion but dissent from that portion thereof that attempts to reconcile the holding in this case with the holding in the case of Amphitheaters, Inc. v. Portland Meadows, 184 Or. 336, 198 P.2d 847.

NOTES

1. ***Direct vs. indirect entry.*** As the court's opinion in *Martin* indicates, some older opinions held that an action for trespass to land could lie only if the defendant directly caused an entry. An indirect entry would not suffice. The prevailing modern view is that the plaintiff need not show a direct entry, as long as the defendant intended the entry.

An example of a case abandoning the directness requirement is Rushing v. Hooper–McDonald, Inc., 293 Ala. 56, 300 So.2d 94 (1974). The defendant dumped asphalt uphill and away from the plaintiff's land, knowing that some of the asphalt would seep downhill and pollute the plaintiff's pond. The court recognized that under the old rule in Alabama, the plaintiff could not recover for trespass to land because the defendant had not directly caused the asphalt to enter the plaintiff's land. The court also recognized, however, that the modern view is to abandon the distinction between direct and indirect entries, as long as the defendant intended the entry. The court held that the trial court erred in directing a verdict for the defendant.

2. ***The writs of trespass quare clausem fregit and trespass on the case.*** The direct-indirect issue arose from the system of writs or forms of action of the early common law. The early writ of trespass *quare clausem fregit* ("wherefore he broke the close") lay for invasions of real property. It originally required neither intent nor negligence nor harm, but it did require that the invasion be "direct." The later writ of trespass on the case covered indirect invasions, but it generally required intent or negligence plus harm.

The modern tort of trespass to land differs from both: it requires an intended entry, which need not be harmful and which may be direct or indirect.

G. TRESPASS TO CHATTELS AND CONVERSION

PEARSON v. DODD

United States Court of Appeals, District of Columbia, 1969.
410 F.2d 701.

WRIGHT, CIRCUIT JUDGE.

This case arises out of the exposure of the alleged misdeeds of Senator Thomas Dodd of Connecticut by newspaper columnists Drew Pearson and Jack Anderson. The District Court has granted partial summary judgment to Senator Dodd, appellee here, finding liability on a theory of conversion. * * *

The undisputed facts in the case were stated by the District Court as follows:

> * * * [O]n several occasions in June and July, 1965, two former employees of the plaintiff, at times with the assistance of two members of the plaintiff's staff, entered the plaintiff's office without authority and unbeknownst to him, removed numerous documents from his files, made copies of them, replaced the originals, and turned over the copies to the defendant Anderson, who was aware of the manner in which the copies had been obtained. The defendants Pearson and Anderson thereafter published articles containing information gleaned from these documents.

* * *

The District Court ruled that appellants' receipt and subsequent use of photocopies of documents which appellants knew had been removed from appellee's files without authorization established appellants' liability for conversion. We conclude that appellants are not guilty of conversion on the facts shown.

* * *

Conversion is the substantive tort theory which underlay [or grew out of] the ancient common law form of action for trover. A plaintiff in trover alleged that he had lost a chattel which he rightfully possessed,[23] and that the defendant had found it and converted it to his own use. With time, the allegations of losing and finding became fictional, leaving the question of

---

23. A threshold question, not briefed by either party and hence not decided by us, is the nature of the property right held by appellee in the contents of the files in his Senate office. Those files, themselves paid for by the United States, are maintained in an office owned by the United States, by employees of the United States. They are meant to contribute to the work of appellee as an officer of the United States. The question thus is not entirely free from doubt whether appellee has title to the contents of the files or has a right of exclusive possession of those contents, or is a bailee, or even a mere custodian of those contents.

whether the defendant had "converted" the property the only operative one.

The most distinctive feature of conversion is its measure of damages, which is the value of the goods converted. The theory is that the "converting" defendant has in some way treated the goods as if they were his own, so that the plaintiff can properly ask the court to decree a forced sale of the property from the rightful possessor to the converter. Because of this stringent measure of damages, it has long been recognized that not every wrongful interference with the personal property of another is a conversion. Where the intermeddling falls short of the complete or very substantial deprivation of possessory rights in the property, the tort committed is not conversion, but the lesser wrong of trespass to chattels.

* * *

The difference is more than a semantic one. The measure of damages in trespass [to chattels] is not the whole value of the property interfered with, but rather the actual diminution in its value caused by the interference. More important for this case, a judgment for conversion can be obtained with only nominal damages, whereas liability for trespass to chattels exists only on a showing of actual damage to the property interfered with.[32] Here the District Court granted partial summary judgment on the issue of liability alone, while conceding that possibly no more than nominal damages might be awarded on subsequent trial. Partial summary judgment for liability could not have been granted on a theory of trespass to chattels without an undisputed showing of actual damages to the property in question.

It is clear that on the agreed facts appellants committed no conversion of the physical documents taken from appellee's files. Those documents were removed from the files at night, photocopied, and returned to the files undamaged before office operations resumed in the morning. Insofar as the documents' value to appellee resided in their usefulness as records of the business of his office, appellee was clearly not substantially deprived of his use of them.

This of course is not an end of the matter. It has long been recognized that documents often have value above and beyond that springing from their physical possession. They may embody information or ideas whose economic value depends in part or in whole upon being kept secret. The question then arises whether the information taken by means of copying appellee's office files is of the type which the law of conversion protects. The general rule has been that ideas or information are not subject to

---

32. "To support an action of trespass to a chattel where the invasion of interests does not result in its destruction or in a dispossession thereof, it was early held there must be some physical harm to the chattel or to its possessor. Unlike the action of trespass quare clausum fregit in the case of land, no action could be maintained for a mere harmless intermeddling with goods. The possessor's proprietary interest in the inviolability of his personal property did not receive that protection which the similar interest in the possession of land or the dignitary interest in the inviolability of the person receives. * * *" 1 F. Harper & F. James, supra Note 25, § 2.3. (Footnotes omitted.)

legal protection, but the law has developed exceptions to this rule. Where information is gathered and arranged at some cost and sold as a commodity on the market, it is properly protected as property. Where ideas are formulated with labor and inventive genius, as in the case of literary works or scientific researches, they are protected. Where they constitute instruments of fair and effective commercial competition, those who develop them may gather their fruits under the protection of the law.

The question here is not whether appellee had a right to keep his files from prying eyes, but whether the information taken from those files falls under the protection of the law of property, enforceable by a suit for conversion. In our view, it does not. The information included the contents of letters to appellee from supplicants, and office records of other kinds, the nature of which is not fully revealed by the record. Insofar as we can tell, none of it amounts to literary property, to scientific invention, or to secret plans formulated by appellee for the conduct of commerce. Nor does it appear to be information held in any way for sale by appellee, analogous to the fresh news copy produced by a wire service.

Appellee complains, not of the misappropriation of property bought or created by him, but of the exposure of information either (1) injurious to his reputation or (2) revelatory of matters which he believes he has a right to keep to himself. Injuries of this type are redressed at law by suit for libel and invasion of privacy respectively, where defendants' liability for those torts can be established under the limitations created by common law and by the Constitution.

Because no conversion of the physical contents of appellee's files took place, and because the information copied from the documents in those files has not been shown to be property subject to protection by suit for conversion, the District Court's ruling that appellants are guilty of conversion must be reversed.

So ordered.

TAMM, CIRCUIT JUDGE, concurring.

Some legal scholars will see in the majority opinion—as distinguished from its actual holding—an ironic aspect. Conduct for which a law enforcement officer would be soundly castigated is, by the phraseology of the majority opinion, found tolerable; conduct which, if engaged in by government agents would lead to the suppression of evidence obtained by these means, is approved when used for the profit of the press. There is an anomaly lurking in this situation: the news media regard themselves as quasi-public institutions yet they demand immunity from the restraints which they vigorously demand be placed on government. That which is regarded as a mortal taint on information secured by any illegal conduct of government would appear from the majority opinion to be permissible as a technique or modus operandi for the journalist. Some will find this confusing, but I am not free to act on my own views under the doctrine of stare decisis which I consider binding upon me.

* * *

Notes

1.   Dodd also sued for invasion of privacy, a tort that is not addressed in this book. His argument had two prongs. First, he argued that the publication of private information invaded his privacy. This theory is usually called "publication of private facts." The court held that the information published "was of obvious public interest," which constitutes a privilege.

Second, Dodd argued that the defendants had physically "intruded" into his private space. The court held that whereas the two former employees might have been liable for intrusion, Pearson and Anderson were not. They merely received the fruits of the intrusion after the fact. Similarly, Dodd might have argued that the defendants were liable for trespass to land. Presumably, the court would have concluded that whereas the two former employees might have been trespassers, Pearson and Anderson were not.

2.   With respect to the conversion claim, the court apparently assumes that had a conversion occurred, Anderson and Pearson could be liable, despite their lack of personal participation in the removal of information from Dodd's files. Section 229 of the Restatement (Second) of Torts states the rule that one who receives converted property from another may also be liable for conversion:

> One who receives possession of a chattel from another with the intent to acquire for himself or a third person a proprietary interest in the chattel which the other has not the power to transfer is subject to liability for conversion to a third person then entitled to immediate possession of the chattel.

According to this well-established doctrine, if A steals a bicycle from B and C innocently buys it at A's garage sale, C is subject to liability to B for conversion. Of course, C may seek indemnity from A on A's implied warranty of title. But if A is insolvent or has vanished, C nevertheless owes B return or full value of the bicycle.

3.   ***Conversion vs. trespass to chattels.*** The difference between trespass to chattels and conversion is one of degree. Trespass to chattels involves a less substantial interference. Conversion involves a more substantial interference, such as outright destruction or long-term interference with use. The remedy for trespass to chattels is damages for repairs, loss of use, and incidental damages. The remedy for conversion is fair market value of the chattel, plus incidental damages. The dividing line between the two torts often depends on the court's evaluation of whether one remedy or the other is more appropriate. For example, if a plaintiff whose car is stolen "covers"—that is, buys a new car—returning the car and paying damages for loss of use is not a very effective remedy.

4.   For both trespass to chattels and conversion, the plaintiff must prove that the defendant intended the interference with the chattel.

H. DEFENSES

If the plaintiff makes out a prima facie case for battery, assault, false imprisonment, trespass to land, trespass to chattels, or conversion, the defendant can still escape liability by establishing one of several defenses. Normally, the defendant has the burden of proof on these defenses.*

Most of the defenses addressed in this section are applicable to each of the six torts listed above, that is, they negate liability for conduct that would otherwise have constituted one of the six torts. (An exception, discussed in more detail below, is the privilege of necessity.) Nevertheless, most of the best treatments of the defenses happen to be battery cases. As you go through the material, you should realize that the defense under consideration would usually also be a defense to the other intentional torts.

1. CONSENT

O'BRIEN v. CUNARD S.S. CO.

Supreme Judicial Court of Massachusetts, 1891.
154 Mass. 272, 28 N.E. 266.

KNOWLTON, JUSTICE.

[The plaintiff sued the defendant for battery and negligence for injuries arising out of a vaccination she received on one of the defendant's ships. The opinion does not reveal the nature of her injuries. The trial court directed a verdict for the defendant. The plaintiff appealed.]

This case presents two questions: First, whether there was any evidence to warrant the jury in finding that the defendant, by any of its servants or agents, committed an assault on the plaintiff; secondly, whether there was evidence on which the jury could have found that the defendant was guilty of negligence towards the plaintiff. To sustain [her action for "assault"], the plaintiff relied on the fact that the surgeon who was employed by the defendant vaccinated her on shipboard, while she was on her passage from Queenstown to Boston. On this branch of the case the question is whether there was any evidence that the surgeon used force upon the plaintiff against her will. In determining whether the act was lawful or unlawful, the surgeon's conduct must be considered in connection with the surrounding circumstances. If the plaintiff's behavior was such as to indicate consent on her part, he was justified in his act, whatever her unexpressed feelings may have been. In determining whether she consented, he could be guided only by her overt acts and the

---

* "Students are sometimes confused on one point. To say that the defendant has the burden of proving an affirmative defense * * * is not to say that the evidence on that topic must originate with the defendant. The plaintiff's own evidence or admissions may suffice * * *. To say that the defendant has the burden is to say that the defendant will be the party to suffer if the evidence is not forthcoming, so that the defendant must be sure that, from whatever source, evidence on the issue does in fact appear." Dobbs, The Law of Torts § 198, p. 493 (2000).

manifestations of her feelings. It is undisputed that at Boston there are strict quarantine regulations in regard to the examination of [immigrants] to see that they are protected from small-pox by vaccination, and that only those persons who hold a certificate from the medical officer of the steamship, stating that they are so protected, are permitted to land without detention in quarantine, or vaccination by the port physician. It appears that the defendant is accustomed to have its surgeons vaccinate all [immigrants] who desire it, and who are not protected by previous vaccination, and give them a certificate which is accepted at quarantine as evidence of their protection. Notices of the regulations at quarantine, and of the willingness of the ship's medical officer to vaccinate such as needed vaccination, were posted about the ship in various languages, and on the day when the operation was performed the surgeon had a right to presume that she and the other women who were vaccinated understood the importance and purpose of vaccination for those who bore no marks to show that they were protected. By the plaintiff's testimony, which, in this particular, is undisputed, it appears that about 200 women passengers were assembled below, and she understood from conversation with them that they were to be vaccinated; that she stood about 15 feet from the surgeon, and saw them form in a line, and pass in turn before him; that he "examined their arms, and, passing some of them by, proceeded to vaccinate those that had no mark;" that she did not hear him say anything to any of them; that upon being passed by they each received a card, and went on deck; that when her turn came she showed him her arm; he looked at it, and said there was no mark, and that she should be vaccinated; that she told him she had been vaccinated before, and it left no mark; "that he then said nothing; that he should vaccinate her again;" that she held up her arm to be vaccinated; that no one touched her; that she did not tell him she did not want to be vaccinated; and that she took the ticket which he gave her, certifying that he had vaccinated her, and used it at quarantine. She was one of a large number of women who were vaccinated on that occasion, without, so far as appears, a word of objection from any of them. They all indicated by their conduct that they desired to avail themselves of the provisions made for their benefit. There was nothing in the conduct of the plaintiff to indicate to the surgeon that she did not wish to obtain a card which would save her from detention at quarantine, and to be vaccinated, if necessary, for that purpose. Viewing his conduct in the light of the surrounding circumstances, it was lawful; and there was no evidence tending to show that it was not. The ruling of the court on this part of the case was correct. * * *

[The court further held that the defendant was not liable for negligence.]

Exceptions overruled.

NOTES

1. In addition to being a defense, consent has a considerable effect on the prima facie case. For example, consent can negate the offensiveness of a touching, and it can negate a confinement.

2. Most courts consider consent to be a defense that the defendant must plead and prove. Some courts, however, define the prima facie case for some intentional torts as an *unconsented* invasion of the particular interest. See, e.g., Ghassemieh v. Schafer, supra at p. 12 ("The gist of [battery] is * * * the absence of consent to the contact on the plaintiff's part"); Fisher v. Carousel Motor Hotel, Inc., supra at p. 20 ("the basis of [battery] is the unpermitted and intentional invasion of the plaintiff's person").

OVERALL v. KADELLA

Court of Appeals of Michigan, 1984.
138 Mich.App. 351, 361 N.W.2d 352.

PER CURIAM.

On April 17, 1975, two amateur hockey teams, the Waterford Lakers and the Clarkston Flyers, played each other in a hockey game. After the game had ended, a fight broke out between defendant, who played for the Flyers, and a member of the opposing team. This fight soon became general, with players leaving the benches to join the melee. During the fight, defendant struck plaintiff, knocking him unconscious and fracturing the bones around plaintiff's right eye.

At trial, defendant stated that he had gone to shake hands with the opposing team after the game when he was struck from behind. Both benches cleared and a scuffle ensued, during which defendant stated he saw a hockey stick coming toward his head. Defendant testified that he was hit several times before he turned around and hit the person swinging the stick. He did not know plaintiff had been injured by the blow and, in fact, did not know whom he had struck until much later. Three witnesses testifying on behalf of defendant stated that plaintiff remained on the bench during the fight, but poked or hit defendant with a hockey stick during the fight. They all saw defendant retaliate by turning and throwing one punch.

Plaintiff's testimony and that of two spectators at the game differed from this testimony in significant respects. According to these witnesses, plaintiff remained on the bench even after all other players had joined the fray. The bench was well removed from the fighting and plaintiff did not poke or hit anyone with a hockey stick. Defendant skated over to the bench and struck plaintiff who had done nothing to provoke the attack. Defendant then skated away.

The hockey referees at the game testified that defendant had engaged in at least three separate fights after the game was over. He was given three game misconducts because fighting is against the rules of the

Michigan Amateur Hockey Association. These rules are designed to stop violence. The bench is considered part of the playing field. One of the referees saw plaintiff poke defendant with a hockey stick to get defendant's attention and then saw defendant attack plaintiff by striking him.

At the conclusion of the bench trial, the district court found that "without provocation the Defendant in the heat of his battles swung his hockey stick at the Plaintiff who was off the field of play and not engaged in the fight and struck him on the right side resulting in the injuries of which he complained." The court also found that plaintiff had suffered damages of $21,000 for out-of-pocket expenses, pain and suffering, and permanent injury, and awarded an additional $25,000 as exemplary damages because defendant's act had been "intentional and malicious."

* * *

Defendant's last objection is to the court's finding that defendant struck plaintiff with a hockey stick. We find, and plaintiff concedes, that this statement is clearly erroneous as there was no evidence that defendant used anything but his fist in striking plaintiff. However, this erroneous finding is harmless as it is clear that the court properly found that a battery was committed.

Defendant's next contention is that plaintiff may not sue for an injury incurred while plaintiff was voluntarily participating in a hockey game. This argument is expressed in the phrase, "*volenti non fit injuria*," or "he who consents cannot receive an injury."

Participation in a game involves a manifestation of consent to those bodily contacts which are permitted by the rules of the game. However, there is general agreement that an intentional act causing injury, which goes beyond what is ordinarily permissible, is an assault and battery for which recovery may be had.

In Nabozny v. Barnhill, 31 Ill.App.3d 212, 334 N.E.2d 258 (1975), a player in an amateur soccer match kicked the opposing goalkeeper in the head while the goalkeeper was in possession of the ball in the penalty area. This act directly violated the safety rules of the game. In deciding whether or not the goalkeeper could bring a tort action against the soccer player, the *Nabozny* Court held that a player is charged with a legal duty to every other player to refrain from conduct proscribed by a safety rule. The Court then rejected the defendant's contention that there should be tort immunity for any injury to another player that occurs during the course of a game:

> This court believes that the law should not place unreasonable burdens on the free and vigorous participation in sports by our youth. However, we also believe that organized, athletic competition does not exist in a vacuum. Rather, some of the restraints of civilization must accompany every athlete onto the playing field. * * *

* * *

It is our opinion that a player is liable for injury in a tort action if his conduct is such that it is either deliberate, wilful or with a reckless disregard for the safety of the other player so as to cause injury to that player, the same being a question of fact to be decided by a jury.

Other cases have also held that the violation of safety rules during a game gives rise to tort liability. In Griggas v. Clauson, 6 Ill.App.2d 412, 128 N.E.2d 363 (1955), a player who intentionally struck an opposing player during a basketball game was found liable, and, in Bourque v. Duplechin, 331 So.2d 40 (La.App.1976), liability was found where a baserunner in a softball game dove into the second baseman five feet from the base and struck him with his forearm in order to break up a double play. We agree with these Courts that liability may be found on such facts. In this case, defendant's own witness testified that the rule against fighting in hockey is designed to stop violence. Defendant's intentional battery certainly violated this rule. In addition, under the facts found by the trial court, it is arguable that the battery did not even occur during the hockey game. It is therefore doubtful whether consent to a battery during a game would constitute consent to a battery after the game.

Defendant also argues that he was merely exercising his right of self-defense by striking back at the person who was hitting him with a hockey stick. The trial court rejected this contention after concluding that plaintiff had not had a hockey stick and that, even if he had had one, the area of the fight was beyond plaintiff's reach. We do not find this conclusion to be clearly erroneous.

Affirmed.

NOTES

1. Many sports involve contacts that may be injurious. By entering the field of play, a player obviously manifests consent to many contacts, but just as obviously does not manifest consent to all imaginable contacts. If the contact in question was accidental, it is governed by the law of negligence, which generally absolves the defendant by holding that a participant in a sport or recreational activity has no duty to avoid the "inherent risks" of the activity. See Chapter IX, section E, infra p. 401. If the contact was intentional, the issue is whether it was outside the boundaries of the implied consent. As the *Overall* opinion indicates, an intentional contact that violates a rule of the game designed to protect the players' safety may be beyond the consent. See, e.g., Kiley v. Patterson, 763 A.2d 583 (R.I.2001) (female second baseman in coed softball game suffered knee injury allegedly from "a so-called forbidden 'take-out slide'" by male base runner; "a boxer may assume the risk of a negligent low blow, but a deliberate punch to his groin would still be actionable.").

2. Analyzing a battery claim arising from a fight requires, first, distinguishing three situations: fighting for sport, e.g., a boxing match; consensual fighting in anger ("Let's settle this outside"); and unconsented attack met with self-defense. The first situation is governed by the usual principles of

sports cases. The third is governed by the self-defense privilege, considered in subsection 2, infra. In the second situation, American courts are divided. Some courts, often said to be the majority, reason rather formalistically that the consent is legally void, since such a fight is a breach of the peace that constitutes a crime (misdemeanor) on the part of each participant. Under this view, therefore, either combatant can recover in battery despite the consent. Other courts uphold the consent defense. The latter view is endorsed by section 60 of the Restatement (Second) of Torts.

McPHERSON v. McPHERSON

Supreme Court of Maine, 1998.
712 A.2d 1043.

DANA, JUSTICE.

Nancy McPherson appeals from the judgment of the Superior Court denying her claims for * * * assault and battery * * *. These claims arise from her claim that her husband, Steven McPherson, infected her with a sexually transmitted disease he acquired through an extramarital affair. * * *

Nancy filed a complaint against Steven, after their divorce, claiming that he had infected her with a sexually transmitted disease, Human Papilloma Virus (HPV). Nancy alleged that Steven acquired HPV through a clandestine extramarital affair with Jane Doe. The complaint further alleges that Steven transmitted the disease to her, prior to their divorce, through sexual intercourse.

Following a jury-waived trial, the court made the following factual findings: that Nancy "has been and may still be infected with HPV"; that it is more likely than not that she was infected with HPV through sexual contact with another individual; that Steven was the only sexual partner that Nancy has ever had; and that it was more likely than not that Steven infected Nancy with HPV. The court also noted that, even though Steven did not then exhibit evidence of the HPV infection, "this is in no way proof that he is not now in a latent stage nor does it demonstrate or have any probative value as to whether or not he was a carrier" at the time he allegedly infected Nancy. The court found further that Steven had a sexual relationship with Doe, that he had sexual intercourse with Nancy after having intercourse with Doe, that he did not disclose his sexual relationship with Doe to Nancy, and that he took no steps to protect Nancy from possible infection with a sexually transmitted disease. Finally, the court found that Steven "did not know or have reason to know" that he might have HPV at the time he infected Nancy because he had no physical symptoms of HPV infection, he had no knowledge of any other partner having symptoms of HPV, and he had no medical diagnosis of any kind of a sexually transmitted disease.

* * *

* * * The [Superior] court found that no assault and battery occurred because the sexual intercourse between Steven and Nancy was consensual. She argues that her consent to have sexual intercourse with Steven was vitiated by the fact that he failed to inform her of his extramarital affair.

"One who effectively consents to conduct of another intended to invade his interests cannot recover in an action of tort for the conduct or for harm resulting from it." Restatement (Second) of Torts § 892A(1) (1977). Consent may be vitiated, however by misrepresentation:

> If the person consenting to the conduct of another is induced to consent by a substantial mistake concerning the nature of the invasion of his interests or the extent of the harm to be expected from it and the mistake is known to the other or is induced by the other's misrepresentation, the consent is not effective for the unexpected invasion or harm.

Id. § 892B(2). By way of illustration, the Restatement provides: "A consents to sexual intercourse with B, who knows that A is ignorant of the fact that B has a venereal disease. B is subject to liability to A for battery." Id. § 892B(2) cmt. *e*, illus. 5.

Nancy argues only that Steven misled her concerning his fidelity. Given the court's finding that Steven neither knew nor should have known of his infection with HPV, however, Nancy cannot argue that Steven misled her "concerning the nature of the invasion of [her] interest or the extent of the harm to be expected" therefrom. If the defendant, ignorant of the fact that he was infected with a sexually transmitted disease, has sexual intercourse with the plaintiff, "the defendant will not be liable, because the plaintiff consented to the kind of touch intended by the defendant, and both were ignorant of the harmful nature of the invasion." Prosser & Keeton, The Law of Torts § 18 at 119 (5th ed.1984). Thus, Steven may not be held liable for assault and battery.

The entry is:

Judgment affirmed.

NOTE

Consent may also be rendered ineffective if it was coerced or if the party was incapacitated on account of infancy, mental incompetency, or intoxication.

2. SELF–DEFENSE AND DEFENSE OF OTHERS

TATMAN v. CORDINGLY

Supreme Court of Wyoming, 1983.
672 P.2d 1286.

BROWN, JUSTICE.

E. Ben Tatman, appellant, sued Gary L. Cordingly, appellee, for assault and battery after the two had an altercation. Judgment was entered pursuant to a jury verdict finding that Cordingly acted out of self-defense. Tatman appeals the judgment on the grounds of faulty jury instructions and lack of sufficient evidence to support the verdict.

* * *

There was a dispute between Tatman and Cordingly. This dispute precipitated a confrontation on June 1, 1982, in Albany County near the Old Fort Fetterman Road, miles from the nearest town. Tatman was 66 years old at the time of the incident, Cordingly in his early 20's. As a result of the fight that occurred Tatman was hospitalized for eight days and incurred substantial medical expenses. There were no witnesses to the scuffle other than the parties themselves, and they disagree as to the details. Both parties contend that the other was the aggressor.

* * *

In this case, judgment was entered on a jury verdict finding that Tatman committed a battery and Cordingly exercised reasonable self-defense. The jury was certainly entitled to believe Cordingly's testimony and find in his favor. There was evidence that Tatman had a bad temper, that he carried a gun and used it often, that he ran over Cordingly's motorcycle with his pickup truck, that Tatman struck Cordingly first, that Tatman was repeatedly trying to get to his rifle and that Cordingly feared for his life. From our review of the record, we find sufficient evidence for the jury to decide as they did.

* * *

The appellant contends that the trial court erred in refusing * * * [the] portion of plaintiff's proposed Instruction 3 [that] reads:

* * * Thus, even acting in self-defense, a person may be liable for injury inflicted upon the aggressor. That is the case when the defender is not justified in his belief that he was in danger, or when the defender uses excessive force, or when the defender continues to exert force after the aggressor is rendered disarmed or helpless.

This instruction is an accurate statement of Wyoming law on self-defense and its limits. The trial judge did, however, properly instruct the jury on these matters. The court gave jury Instructions 7, 8, and 9 which read:

Instruction No. 7

When it is apparent to a person that he is threatened with a battery, he has the right to determine from appearances and the circumstances then existing the necessity of resorting to force to repel any such apparent, threatened battery, and he has the right to do what seems reasonably necessary to protect himself against any such apparent, threatened attack, whether it is real or not, provided he believes it to be real.

Instruction No. 8

The defendant however is not liable to the plaintiff on his claim of battery if the affirmative defense of self-defense of a person is established. This defense is established if you find both of the following:

1. The defendant honestly and reasonably believed (although perhaps mistakenly) that under the circumstances it was necessary for him to use force to protect himself against an actual or apparent threatened harmful contact; and

2. The defendant used no more force than a reasonably prudent person would have used under the same or similar circumstances to protect himself against the actual or apparent threatened contact.

Instruction No. 9

A person who is battered by another has the privilege of self-defense, but that privilege ends when the aggressor is disarmed or helpless, or when all the danger has clearly passed.

Instructions 8 and 9 adequately cover the issue of self-defense and where the privilege of self-defense ends. It was not necessary for the court to duplicate these instructions by giving plaintiff's proposed Instruction 3 in full.

Instruction 7, however, does not fully state the law in regard to the apparent necessity for acting in self-defense. According to Prosser [§ 19, p. 109 (4th Ed. 1971)]:

The privilege to act in self-defense arises, not only where there is real danger, but also where there is a reasonable belief that it exists. * * *

The belief must, however, be one which a reasonable man would have entertained under the circumstances. * * * [I]t is not enough that he really believes that he is about to be attacked, unless he has some reasonable ground for the belief. * * *

* * *

Therefore, the standard to be applied in determining if there is the apparent necessity to act in self-defense is both subjective and objective. Not only must a person believe that a real danger exists, but that belief must also be reasonable. In the court's Instruction 7, a subjective standard is set out but the objective, "reasonable," standard is missing. * * *

This incomplete instruction is not reversible error. When the instructions given by the court are viewed in their entirety, a true and accurate representation of the law is given. Instruction 8 requires that the jury find both a subjective and an objective belief by the defendant that it was necessary for him to protect himself. Appellant has not established any prejudice as a result of this incomplete instruction or that a different result would have occurred had another instruction been given. We find that the error was harmless.

* * *

There was sufficient evidence in the record to support the verdict reached by the jury. The instructions given by the court adequately represented the law of self-defense and its limits. * * *

We affirm.

NOTES

1. *Self-defense vs. retaliation.* Self-defense can be asserted only to prevent or resist an attack, not to retaliate. In Coleman v. Moore, 426 So.2d 652 (La.App.1982), the defendant shot the plaintiff in the buttocks as the plaintiff was leaving the fray. The court held that the defendant could not successfully claim self-defense, even though the plaintiff had been the original aggressor.

2. A person exercising the privilege of self-defense can use only that amount of force that he reasonably believes is necessary to prevent the attack. If he uses excessive force he is liable for the excess but does not lose the privilege altogether.

3. *Deadly force.* A person can use deadly force only if he reasonably believes that doing so is necessary to resist an attack of deadly force. Even if the attack is one of deadly force, however, the person being attacked cannot use more force than he reasonably believes is necessary to prevent the attack.

4. *Retreat, or stand and fight?* Most courts permit a defender to stand and fight, as long as the defender is using non-deadly force. Deadly force may not be used if a completely safe retreat is available, but one defending himself against deadly force may stand and kill if he has any reasonable doubt as to the safety of retreat. Even when a safe retreat is available, a defender threatened with deadly force need not flee from his home or place of business prior to using deadly force.

5. *The breadth of the self-defense privilege.* Self-defense can be asserted as a privilege for conduct that would otherwise be an actionable battery, assault, false imprisonment, intentional infliction of emotional distress, trespass to land, trespass to chattels, or conversion.

6. *What can the self-defender defend against?* The privilege can be used to prevent a battery, assault, false imprisonment, negligently caused bodily injury, or even bodily injury innocently caused or threatened by the person against whom the privilege is asserted.

7. *Defense of others.* At early common law, courts were reluctant to recognize a privilege to use force to defend others, possibly on the ground that people should not meddle in other people's affairs. An early relaxation of this position permitted individuals to use force to defend members of their family. Now, all American jurisdictions recognize a privilege to use force to protect others from attack, without limiting the privilege to family members.

Some courts still suggest that, unlike self-defense, the privilege of defense of others cannot be based on an erroneous but reasonable belief that force is necessary. Under this view, the person exercising the privilege must be correct. Most courts, however, require only that the person exercising the privilege act on a reasonable belief that force is necessary.

3. DEFENSE OF PROPERTY

KATKO v. BRINEY

Supreme Court of Iowa, 1971.
183 N.W.2d 657.

MOORE, CHIEF JUSTICE.

The primary issue presented here is whether an owner may protect personal property in an unoccupied boarded-up farm house against trespassers and thieves by a spring gun capable of inflicting death or serious injury.

We are not here concerned with a man's right to protect his home and members of his family. Defendants' home was several miles from the scene of the incident to which we refer infra.

Plaintiff's action is for damages resulting from serious injury caused by a shot from a 20–gauge spring shotgun set by defendants in a bedroom of an old farm house which had been uninhabited for several years. Plaintiff and his companion, Marvin McDonough, had broken and entered the house to find and steal old bottles and dated fruit jars which they considered antiques.

At defendants' request plaintiff's action was tried to a jury consisting of residents of the community where defendants' property was located. The jury returned a verdict for plaintiff and against defendants for $20,000 actual and $10,000 punitive damages.

After careful consideration of defendants' motions for judgment notwithstanding the verdict and for new trial, the experienced and capable trial judge overruled them and entered judgment on the verdict. Thus we have this appeal by defendants.

* * *

* * * Most of the facts are not disputed. In 1957 defendant Bertha L. Briney inherited her parents' farm land in Mahaska and Monroe Counties. Included was an 80–acre tract in southwest Mahaska County where her grandparents and parents had lived. No one occupied the house thereafter. Her husband, Edward, attempted to care for the land. He kept no farm machinery thereon. The outbuildings became dilapidated.

For about 10 years, 1957 to 1967, there occurred a series of trespassing and housebreaking events with loss of some household items, the breaking of windows and "messing up of the property in general." The latest occurred June 8, 1967, prior to the event on July 16, 1967 herein involved.

Defendants through the years boarded up the windows and doors in an attempt to stop the intrusions. They had posted "no trespass" signs on the land several years before 1967. The nearest one was 35 feet from the house. On June 11, 1967 defendants set "a shotgun trap" in the north bedroom. After Mr. Briney cleaned and oiled his 20–gauge shotgun, the power of which he was well aware, defendants took it to the old house where they secured it to an iron bed with the barrel pointed at the bedroom door. It was rigged with wire from the doorknob to the gun's trigger so it would fire when the door was opened. Briney first pointed the gun so an intruder would be hit in the stomach but at Mrs. Briney's suggestion it was lowered to hit the legs. He admitted he did so "because I was mad and tired of being tormented" but "he did not intend to injure anyone." He gave no explanation of why he used a loaded shell and set it to hit a person already in the house. Tin was nailed over the bedroom window. The spring gun could not be seen from the outside. No warning of its presence was posted.

Plaintiff lived with his wife and worked regularly as a gasoline station attendant in Eddyville, seven miles from the old house. He had observed it for several years while hunting in the area and considered it as being abandoned. He knew it had long been uninhabited. In 1967 the area around the house was covered with high weeds. Prior to July 16, 1967 plaintiff and McDonough had been to the premises and found several old bottles and fruit jars which they took and added to their collection of antiques. On the latter date about 9:30 p.m. they made a second trip to the Briney property. They entered the old house by removing a board from a porch window which was without glass. While McDonough was looking around the kitchen area plaintiff went to another part of the house. As he started to open the north bedroom door the shotgun went off striking him in the right leg above the ankle bone. Much of his leg, including part of the tibia, was blown away. Only by McDonough's assistance was plaintiff able to get out of the house and after crawling some distance was put in his vehicle and rushed to a doctor and then to a hospital. He remained in the hospital 40 days.

* * *

* * * Plaintiff testified he knew he had no right to break and enter the house with intent to steal bottles and fruit jars therefrom. He further testified he had entered a plea of guilty to larceny in the nighttime of property of less than $20 value from a private building. He stated he had been fined $50 and costs and paroled during good behavior from a 60–day jail sentence. * * *

* * * The main thrust of defendants' defense in the trial court and on this appeal is that "the law permits use of a spring gun in a dwelling or warehouse for the purpose of preventing the unlawful entry of a burglar or thief." They repeated this contention in their exceptions to the trial court's instructions 2, 5 and 6. They took no exception to the trial court's statement of the issues or to other instructions.

In the statement of issues the trial court stated plaintiff and his companion committed a felony when they broke and entered defendants' house. In instruction 2 the court referred to the early case history of the use of spring guns and stated under the law their use was prohibited except to prevent the commission of felonies of violence and where human life is in danger. The instruction included a statement [that] breaking and entering is not a felony of violence.

Instruction 5 stated: "You are hereby instructed that one may use reasonable force in the protection of his property, but such right is subject to the qualification that one may not use such means of force as will take human life or inflict great bodily injury. Such is the rule even though the injured party is a trespasser and is in violation of the law himself."

Instruction 6 stated: "An owner of premises is prohibited from willfully or intentionally injuring a trespasser by means of force that either takes life or inflicts great bodily injury; and therefore a person owning a premise is prohibited from setting out 'spring guns' and like dangerous devices which will likely take life or inflict great bodily injury, for the purpose of harming trespassers. The fact that the trespasser may be acting in violation of the law does not change the rule. The only time when such conduct of setting a 'spring gun' or a like dangerous device is justified would be when the trespasser was committing a felony of violence or a felony punishable by death, or where the trespasser was endangering human life by his act."

* * *

The overwhelming weight of authority, both textbook and case law, supports the trial court's statement of the applicable principles of law.

Prosser on Torts, Third Edition [1964], pages 116–118, states:

The law has always placed a higher value upon human safety than upon mere rights in property; it is the accepted rule that there is no privilege to use any force calculated to cause death or serious bodily injury to repel the threat to land or chattels, unless there is also such a threat to the defendant's personal safety as to justify a self-defense. * * * Spring guns and other mankilling devices are not justifiable against a mere trespasser, or even a petty thief. They are privileged only against those upon whom the landowner, if he were present in person would be free to inflict injury of the same kind.

* * *

In Hooker v. Miller, 37 Iowa 613 [1873], we held defendant vineyard owner liable for damages resulting from a spring gun shot although plaintiff was a trespasser and there to steal grapes. * * *

* * *

In United Zinc & Chemical Co. v. Britt, 258 U.S. 268, 275, 42 S.Ct. 299 [1922], the court states: "The liability for spring guns and mantraps arises from the fact that the defendant has * * * expected the trespasser and prepared an injury that is no more justified than if he had held the gun and fired it."

In addition to civil liability many jurisdictions hold a land owner criminally liable for serious injuries or homicide caused by spring guns or other set devices.

In Wisconsin, Oregon and England the use of spring guns and similar devices is specifically made unlawful by statute.

The legal principles stated by the trial court in instructions 2, 5 and 6 are well established and supported by the authorities * * *. There is no merit in defendants' objections and exceptions thereto. Defendants' various motions based on the same reasons stated in exceptions to instructions were properly overruled.

* * *

Affirmed.

NOTE

Most states have statutes dealing specifically with the use of force to protect property. Some of these statutes broaden the common law privilege by giving individuals the right to use deadly force to protect property under certain circumstances. Even those jurisdictions, however, often specifically prohibit the use of lethal devices such as the one employed in *Katko*.

TEEL v. MAY DEPARTMENT STORES CO.

Supreme Court of Missouri, 1941.
348 Mo. 696, 155 S.W.2d 74.

HYDE, COMMISSIONER.

This is an action for $20,000 actual and $20,000 punitive damages for false arrest and imprisonment. The jury returned a verdict for $500 actual and $500 punitive damages, a total of $1,000 for which judgment was entered. Plaintiff appealed and raises only the issue of inadequate damages. Defendant also appealed and assigns error in the refusal of a peremptory instruction [directed verdict] and in Instruction No. 1 on which the case was submitted. * * *

The facts hereinafter stated were shown by plaintiff's evidence (mainly testimony of plaintiff and A.F. Foster) considered most favorably to plaintiff's contentions. (We use the term defendant to refer to the corporate defendant.) Plaintiff's sister-in-law Leona Teel, who was separated from plaintiff's brother and had a divorce suit pending against him, lived with plaintiff in St. Louis during October and November of 1939. She went by the name of Leona Nesslein, the name of her former husband to whom she was married before she married plaintiff's brother. Leona had met Mr. A.F. Foster of Wood River, Illinois, that spring and he frequently came to see her. [Foster told Leona that she could charge on his account and that when she did so, she should say she was Mrs. Foster.] * * *

On November 29th Leona asked plaintiff to accompany her to defendant's store. Leona purchased items there amounting to a total of $93.39.

She told each of defendant's clerks from whom she purchased goods that she was Mrs. A.F. Foster. Plaintiff said that of course she knew Leona was not Mrs. Foster. Leona had left her car in a parking lot nearby and she and plaintiff carried some of the packages there and put them in her automobile, making at least two trips with packages to the car. The largest amount of the purchases were in the bedding department where she bought blankets and linens amounting to $53.26. When they went back to the bedding department to get these purchases defendant's detective Mr. Zytowski came over to plaintiff and asked her if she was charging on the Foster account and she motioned to Leona. Plaintiff testified as to what occurred thereafter as follows:

> He stepped over and asked her if she was charging on the Foster account, and she said that she was, and he said, 'Are you Mrs. Foster?' and she said, 'Yes;' and he said then to the girl at the wrapping desk, 'Well, you can hand each one a package,' and the girl did so, and then Mr. Zytowski said, 'Now, you will have to come along with me.' * * * I was afraid if we didn't go, we would be forced to go, so I didn't want a scene, so I went with him. * * * He took us up to the eighth floor, credit department. * * * Two lady detectives were seated directly behind us, and there were a couple of girls right in front of us at typewriters that looked at us. * * * Mr. Jackson, (the credit manager, who had already called the Foster home, talked to Mrs. Foster, and had been advised by her that no one was authorized to buy on their account) asked Leona then if she was Mrs. Foster, and she said again that she was, and he said, 'You know you are not telling the truth and might as well admit that you are not Mrs. Foster, because I know Mrs. Foster.' * * *

* * *

* * * [T]he owner of property has the right to take action (by force or confinement reasonable under the circumstances) in defense of his property. In such cases, probable cause may be an important element of the defense of justification. Therefore, it has been recognized that an owner of a store or other premises has the right to detain a person therein, for a reasonable time for a reasonable investigation, whom he has reasonable grounds to believe has not paid for what he has received or is attempting to take goods without payment. * * *

* * *

[W]e will separately consider whether the evidence in this case, viewed most favorably to plaintiff, would show any unlawful conduct on the part of defendant, prior to the time of the return of the goods from the automobile in the parking lot to defendant's store, or any conduct so unreasonable that it would be actionable. * * * Plaintiff helped to carry some of the goods to the car, so knew where they were, when, at the credit department, Leona continued to insist that she was Mrs. Foster, and she (plaintiff) was refusing to answer when first asked there who Leona was.

Finally, when Zytowski took her to one side, she did tell him the truth about her identity, and explained about her understanding of Leona's relation with Foster. Even then, in view of the fact that defendant had no notice from Foster of any such authority to buy on his credit, and had found the real Mrs. Foster at the Foster home, defendant's agents were undoubtedly justified in not accepting this explanation as the complete truth, and at least demanding the return of the goods. * * * Under all these circumstances * * *, we cannot say that defendant should have inferred lack of criminal intent. On the contrary, our conclusion is that defendant's agents were within their rights in demanding and thus obtaining the return of the merchandise obtained from defendant by means of such false personation. We would not be willing to hold that the evidence shows unreasonable or unlawful detention of plaintiff and Leona by defendant's agents up to the time of obtaining the return of the goods.

However, we do not think we can say that there could be no jury case of false imprisonment after the goods were returned. Defendant's agents, if they did not believe the explanation made by plaintiff and Leona (and there was evidence of reasonable grounds after investigation for not believing it), might have been within their rights if they had called the authorities to take them into custody and preferred charges against them under the statutes above cited. Instead of doing this (accepting plaintiff's evidence as true) Zytowski undertook to do something that not even the public authorities had any right to do, namely: to compel them to sign confessions under threat of not permitting them to leave his office until they did so. Plaintiff said that after she got back with the merchandise from the car, Zytowski was writing a confession for Leona, and that it was "about twenty-five minutes" after she got back, "before he got it finished," then "he gave it to Leona and wanted her to sign it," but "she said she didn't want to sign it." Plaintiff further testified: "He told us before we would have to sign those statements, or we would not be permitted to leave." * * *

It is well settled that unreasonable delay in releasing a person, who is entitled to be released, or such delay in calling, taking him before or turning him over to proper authorities, or in wrongfully denying opportunity to give bond would thereafter amount to false imprisonment. Although defendant was within its rights in doing what it did to obtain the return of the goods, nevertheless, as said in Restatement, p. 317, Zytowski was "not privileged to use the power, which his custody of another [here held for the purpose of obtaining return of its goods] gives him over the other, to force the other to comply with any demand which has no relation to accomplishing the purpose for which the custody is privileged." Certainly, neither the privilege to restrain plaintiff for the purpose of obtaining return of the goods or in order to turn her over to the proper authorities charged with a felony under the above-cited statutes would give defendant any authority to hold plaintiff to compel her to give a confession * * *. Of course, defendant had evidence to show that this statement and the stay in Zytowski's office for its preparation was wholly voluntary but that issue was for the jury. While it would not be improper to request a written statement, defendant had no right to compel it by coercion. We also approve of the rule adopted by the Restatement that defendant's "misconduct [if found] makes it liable to [plaintiff] only for such harm as is caused thereby and does not make [it] liable for the arrest or for the keeping [of plaintiff] in custody prior to the misconduct." We must, however, hold that the court correctly denied defendant's request for a peremptory instruction.

The court recognized that defendant's conduct was not wholly wrongful, and refused the instructions of plaintiff submitting the case on such theory as well as refusing defendant's theory that defendant had the right to do everything that was shown. The court, of its own motion, gave an instruction which stated that "if you further find and believe from the evidence that such imprisonment, if you find there was such imprisonment, was to a greater extent than was reasonably necessary to enable defendants to recover or retake from plaintiff and her companion Leona Teel the merchandise * * * then such imprisonment, if any, constitutes false imprisonment and plaintiff is entitled to recover."* This was erroneous because it authorized the jury to make imprisonment shown prior to the return of the merchandise (or some part thereof) a basis for recovery, instead of only what occurred thereafter.

The judgment is reversed and the cause remanded.

NOTE

The privilege to protect property against dispossession or destruction, illustrated by *Katko*, does not extend to recapturing property once it has been taken. A different, limited privilege is recognized for recapture after dispossession. It permits necessary nondeadly force to effect recapture in "fresh pursuit," subject to certain limitations. This is the privilege that applied in *Teel* up to the point of recovery of the goods.

After the goods were secured, however, the defendant could no longer invoke any protection-of-property privilege. Its only possibility was some form of arrest privilege. The common law recognized arrest privileges for both law officers and citizens in specific circumstances. Today these common-law doctrines are superseded by statutes in every jurisdiction. Missouri, at the time of *Teel*, typically allowed a shopkeeper a privilege to detain a suspected shoplifter to summon law enforcement. But as the court held, the statutory privilege did not authorize the defendant's conduct in the case.

4. NECESSITY

PLOOF v. PUTNAM
Supreme Court of Vermont, 1908.
81 Vt. 471, 71 A. 188.

MUNSON, JUSTICE.

It is alleged as the ground of recovery that on the 13th of November, 1904, the defendant was the owner of a certain island in Lake Champlain,

---

* This is apparently the instruction that the court, in the first paragraph of its opinion, called "instruction No. 1." [Ed.]

and of a certain dock attached thereto, which island and dock were then in charge of the defendant's servant; that the plaintiff was then possessed of and sailing upon said lake a certain loaded sloop, on which were the plaintiff and his wife and two minor children; that there then arose a sudden and violent tempest, whereby the sloop and the property and persons therein were placed in great danger of destruction; that, to save these from destruction or injury, the plaintiff was compelled to, and did, moor the sloop to defendant's dock; that the defendant, by his servant, unmoored the sloop, whereupon it was driven upon the shore by the tempest, without the plaintiff's fault; and that the sloop and its contents were thereby destroyed, and the plaintiff and his wife and children cast into the lake and upon the shore, receiving injuries. This claim is set forth in two counts—one in trespass, charging that the defendant by his servant with force and arms willfully and designedly unmoored the sloop; the other in case, alleging that it was the duty of the defendant by his servant to permit the plaintiff to moor his sloop to the dock, and to permit it to remain so moored during the continuance of the tempest, but that the defendant by his servant, in disregard of this duty, negligently, carelessly, and wrongfully unmoored the sloop. Both counts are demurred to generally.

There are many cases in the books which hold that necessity, and an inability to control movements inaugurated in the proper exercise of a strict right, will justify entries upon land and interferences with personal property that would otherwise have been trespasses. A reference to a few of these will be sufficient to illustrate the doctrine. In Miller v. Fandrye, Poph. 161, trespass was brought for chasing sheep, and the defendant pleaded that the sheep were trespassing upon his land, and that he with a little dog chased them out, and that, as soon as the sheep were off his land, he called in the dog. It was argued that, although the defendant might lawfully drive the sheep from his own ground with a dog, he had no right to pursue them into the next ground; but the court considered that the defendant might drive the sheep from his land with a dog, and that the nature of a dog is such that he cannot be withdrawn in an instant, and that, as the defendant had done his best to recall the dog, trespass would not lie. * * * If one have a way over the land of another for his beasts to pass, and the beasts, being properly driven, feed the grass by morsels in passing, or run out of the way and are promptly pursued and brought back, trespass will not lie. A traveler on a highway who finds it obstructed from a sudden and temporary cause may pass upon the adjoining land without becoming a trespasser because of the necessity. An entry upon land to save goods which are in danger of being lost or destroyed by water or fire is not a trespass. In Proctor v. Adams, 113 Mass. 376, 18 Am.Rep. 500, the defendant went upon the plaintiff's beach for the purpose of saving and restoring to the lawful owner a boat which had been driven ashore, and was in danger of being carried off by the sea; and it was held no trespass.

This doctrine of necessity applies with special force to the preservation of human life. One assaulted and in peril of his life may run through the close of another to escape from his assailant. One may sacrifice the personal property of another to save his life or the lives of his fellows. In Mouse's Case, 12 Co. 63, the defendant was sued for taking and carrying away the plaintiff's casket and its contents. It appeared that the ferryman of Gravesend took 47 passengers into his barge to pass to London, among whom were the plaintiff and defendant; and the barge being upon the water a great tempest happened, and a strong wind, so that the barge and all the passengers were in danger of being lost if certain ponderous things were not cast out, and the defendant thereupon cast out the plaintiff's casket. It was resolved that in case of necessity, to save the lives of the passengers, it was lawful for the defendant, being a passenger, to cast the plaintiff's casket out of the barge * * *.

It is clear that an entry upon the land of another may be justified by necessity, and that the declaration before us discloses a necessity for mooring the sloop. But the defendant questions the sufficiency of the counts because they do not negative the existence of natural objects to which the plaintiff could have moored with equal safety. The allegations are, in substance, that the stress of a sudden and violent tempest compelled the plaintiff to moor to defendant's dock to save his sloop and the people in it. The averment of necessity is complete, for it covers not only the necessity of mooring, but the necessity of mooring to the dock; and the details of the situation which created this necessity, whatever the legal requirements regarding them, are matters of proof, and need not be alleged. It is certain that the rule suggested cannot be held applicable irrespective of circumstance, and the question must be left for adjudication upon proceedings had with reference to the evidence or the charge.

* * *

Judgment affirmed and cause remanded.

VINCENT v. LAKE ERIE TRANSP. CO.

Supreme Court of Minnesota, 1910.
109 Minn. 456, 124 N.W. 221.

O'BRIEN, JUSTICE.

[Plaintiff sued for damage to his dock caused by defendant's ship, which was tied to the dock during a storm. After the jury rendered a verdict awarding the plaintiff $500, the defendant moved for a new trial. The trial court denied the motion, and the defendant appealed.]

The steamship Reynolds, owned by the defendant, was for the purpose of discharging her cargo on November 27, 1905, moored to plaintiff's dock in Duluth. While the unloading of the boat was taking place a storm from the northeast developed, which at about 10 o'clock p.m., when the unloading was completed, had so grown in violence that the wind was then moving at 50 miles per hour and continued to increase during the night. There is some evidence that one, and perhaps two, boats were able to enter the harbor that night, but it is plain that navigation was practically suspended from the hour mentioned until the morning of the 29th, when the storm abated, and during that time no master would have been justified in attempting to navigate his vessel, if he could avoid doing so. After the discharge of the cargo the Reynolds signaled for a tug to tow her from the dock, but none could be obtained because of the severity of the storm. If the lines holding the ship to the dock had been cast off, she would doubtless have drifted away; but, instead, the lines were kept fast, and as soon as one parted or chafed it was replaced, sometimes with a larger one. The vessel lay upon the outside of the dock, her bow to the east, the wind and waves striking her starboard quarter with such force that she was constantly being lifted and thrown against the dock, resulting in its damage, as found by the jury, to the amount of $500.

We are satisfied that the character of the storm was such that it would have been highly imprudent for the master of the Reynolds to have attempted to leave the dock or to have permitted his vessel to drift away from it. * * * [T]he record in this case fully sustains the contention of the appellant that, in holding the vessel fast to the dock, those in charge of her exercised good judgment and prudent seamanship.

* * *

The appellant contends by ample assignments of error that, because its conduct during the storm was rendered necessary by prudence and good seamanship under conditions over which it had no control, it cannot be held liable for any injury resulting to the property of others, and claims that the jury should have been so instructed. An analysis of the charge given by the trial court is not necessary, as in our opinion the only question for the jury was the amount of damages which the plaintiffs were entitled to recover, and no complaint is made upon that score.

The situation was one in which the ordinary rules regulating property rights were suspended by forces beyond human control, and if, without the direct intervention of some act by the one sought to be held liable, the property of another was injured, such injury must be attributed to the act of God, and not to the wrongful act of the person sought to be charged. If during the storm the Reynolds had entered the harbor, and while there had become disabled and been thrown against the plaintiffs' dock, the plaintiffs could not have recovered. Again, if while attempting to hold fast to the dock the lines had parted, without any negligence, and the vessel carried against some other boat or dock in the harbor, there would be no liability upon her owner. But here those in charge of the vessel deliberately and by their direct efforts held her in such a position that the damage to the dock resulted, and, having thus preserved the ship at the expense of the dock, it seems to us that her owners are responsible to the dock owners to the extent of the injury inflicted.

In Depue v. Flateau, 100 Minn. 299, 111 N.W. 1, 8 L.R.A. (N.S.) 485 [1907], this court held that where the plaintiff, while lawfully in the defendants' house, became so ill that he was incapable of traveling with safety, the defendants were responsible to him in damages for compelling him to leave the premises. If, however, the owner of the premises had furnished the traveler with proper accommodations and medical attendance, would he have been able to defeat an action brought against him for their reasonable worth?

In Ploof v. Putnam, [supra p. 62], the Supreme Court of Vermont held that where, under stress of weather, a vessel was without permission moored to a private dock at an island in Lake Champlain owned by the defendant, the plaintiff was not guilty of trespass, and that the defendant was responsible in damages because his representative upon the island unmoored the vessel, permitting it to drift upon the shore, with resultant injuries to it. If, in that case, the vessel had been permitted to remain, and the dock had suffered an injury, we believe the shipowner would have been held liable for the injury done.

Theologians hold that a starving man may, without moral guilt, take what is necessary to sustain life; but it could hardly be said that the obligation would not be upon such person to pay the value of the property so taken when he became able to do so. And so public necessity, in times of war or peace, may require the taking of private property for public purposes; but under our system of jurisprudence compensation must be made.

Let us imagine in this case that for the better mooring of the vessel those in charge of her had appropriated a valuable cable lying upon the dock. No matter how justifiable such appropriation might have been, it would not be claimed that, because of the overwhelming necessity of the situation, the owner of the cable could not recover its value.

This is not the case where life or property was menaced by any object or thing belonging to the plaintiff, the destruction of which became necessary to prevent the threatened disaster. Nor is it a case where, because of the act of God, or unavoidable accident, the infliction of the injury was beyond the control of the defendant, but is one where the defendant prudently and advisedly availed itself of the plaintiffs' property for the purpose of preserving its own more valuable property, and the plaintiffs are entitled to compensation for the injury done.

Order affirmed.

CHAPTER III

NEGLIGENCE—INTRODUCTION AND STANDARD OF CARE

■ ■ ■

A.   INTRODUCTION

American and English courts developed negligence as a separate cause of action in the early and middle part of the nineteenth century. Prior to that time, these courts used the term "negligence" to refer to any failure to perform a legal obligation; "negligence" did not itself define a legal obligation. The actual standard of liability before the advent of negligence seems to have been very close to strict liability: if an active defendant injured a passive victim, the defendant was liable without much reference to his state of mind or to the reasonableness of his conduct. For example, in The Case of the Thorns, Y.B. 6 Ed. 4, 7a, pl. 18 (1466), the defendant cut a hedge of thorns, some of which fell on the plaintiff's land. The court held for the plaintiff and stated that

> for though a man doth a lawful thing, yet if any damage do thereby befall another, he shall answer for it, if he could have avoided it. As if a man lop a tree, and the boughs fall upon another ipso invito [of their own weight], yet an action lies. If a man shoots at butts [targets] and hurt another unawares, an action lies. If I have land through which a river runs to your mill, and I lop the sallows [willows] growing upon the riverside, which accidentally stop the water, so as your mill is injured, an action lies. If I am building my own house, and a piece of timber falls on my neighbor's house and breaks part of it, an action lies. If a man assault me, and I lift up my staff to defend myself, and in lifting it up hit another, an action lies by that person, and yet I did a lawful thing. And the reason of all these cases is, because he that is damaged ought to be recompensed.

After negligence was established as a separate cause of action in the nineteenth century, a defendant was liable, by and large, only if he was at "fault." This meant that the plaintiff was required to prove that the defendant either injured the plaintiff intentionally or injured the plaintiff negligently by failing to exercise reasonable care.

The exact standard of liability before the nineteenth century has not been free from doubt. One source of uncertainty is that the structure of tort law has changed dramatically during the last two centuries. We now organize tort law according to separate causes of action ("torts") based primarily on the nature of the plaintiff's injury and the defendant's state of mind. As we saw in Chapter 2, battery differs from assault in that battery law compensates a plaintiff who suffers actual harmful or offensive bodily contact, whereas assault law compensates a plaintiff who suffers apprehension of such contact. Battery and assault, in turn, differ from negligence in that the plaintiff in a case of battery or assault must prove that the defendant intended the invasion, whereas a plaintiff in a negligence case need show only that the defendant failed to exercise reasonable care. Before the development of modern tort law in the nineteenth and twentieth centuries, however, the common law principles governing recovery for personal injury and property damage were organized according to the "forms of action" under the English writ system. To bring a case before a royal court, a plaintiff was required to obtain a writ from the chancellor that directed the defendant to appear. The defendant could complain that the case did not fall within the specific writ or form of action, meaning that it was not the type of case over which the royal court had jurisdiction. Much of early English law dealt with the scope of the various writs.

An early writ was the writ of trespass. It covered cases in which the defendant caused *direct* injury to the plaintiff. Direct injuries were more likely to lead to breaches of the peace and were, therefore, within the king's scope of concern. One form of the writ—trespass *vi et armis* (with force of arms)—covered injuries that today would be batteries, assaults, or false imprisonments, though apparently the plaintiff was not required to prove intent. Another form of the writ—trespass *quare clausem fregit* (breaking the "close" or real property)—covered what today we would call trespass to land, though again the plaintiff was not required to prove intent. Later, the chancellor began to issue the writ of trespass on the case. This writ expanded the jurisdiction of the royal courts because it covered indirect injuries (though unlike in cases brought under the writ of trespass, the plaintiff was required to prove actual damages.)

A common question in early English cases was whether the plaintiff had obtained the correct writ. If the injury was direct, the plaintiff had to sue under one of the writs of trespass; if the injury was indirect, the plaintiff had to sue under the writ of trespass on the case. Some people analyzing these early English cases have relied on this feature of the writ system to argue that English tort law has always been based on "fault," that is, that the plaintiff was always required to prove something like intent or negligence. Seemingly contrary statements in early English cases, these people have argued, did not actually address the question of whether a defendant's conduct could, under the correct writ, serve as a basis for liability. Instead, these statements addressed the question of whether the case was brought under the correct writ. For example, in

Brown v. Kendall, 60 Mass. (6 Cush.) 292, 295 (1850), Chief Justice Lemuel Shaw said:

> In these discussions, it is frequently stated by judges, that when one receives injury from the direct act of another, trespass will lie. But we think this is said in reference to the question, whether trespass and not case will lie, assuming that the facts are such, that some action will lie. These dicta are no authority, we think, for holding, that damage received by a direct act of force from another will be sufficient to maintain an action of trespass, whether the act was lawful or unlawful, and neither willful, intentional, or careless.

Oliver Wendell Holmes made a similar argument in his famous book, *The Common Law* (1881).

Notwithstanding these arguments, current scholarship gives substantial support to the conclusion that the law governing personal injury and property damage changed dramatically during the early and middle parts of the nineteenth century. Before that time English and American courts did not require proof of anything like our current notions of intent or negligence. By the middle of the nineteenth century, however, they had begun to do so.

Chief Justice Shaw's opinion in Brown v. Kendall was a landmark event in the development of negligence law in the nineteenth century. Kendall accidentally struck Brown with a stick that Kendall was using to separate two fighting dogs. Brown sued Kendall to recover for his injuries. Writing for the Supreme Judicial Court of Massachusetts, Chief Justice Shaw wrote that no liability existed in the absence of a showing either that Kendall struck Brown intentionally or that Kendall failed to use "ordinary care." Whether or not Shaw misread history in the previously quoted passage, Brown v. Kendall makes clear that, by the middle of the nineteenth century, an injured plaintiff was required to prove that the defendant acted either intentionally or negligently.

Scholars have strenuously debated the reasons negligence law arose as a separate cause of action in the early and middle parts of the nineteenth century. Some scholars have explained the shift from strict liability (that is, liability without proof of fault) to negligence as a "subsidy" to burgeoning industry during the industrial revolution. Others have attributed it to courts' inability to apply strict liability to cases in which both parties were active, such as cases in which two carriages collided. Still others have attributed it to the difference between the old writs of trespass and trespass on the case. Whatever the cause—and it is likely that the development of negligence law had multiple causes—negligence as a separate theory of liability was firmly established by the late nineteenth century. See generally, Morton Horowitz, The Transformation of American Law: 1770–1860, 85–99 (1977).

* * *

Courts today use the term "negligence" in two distinct ways. Sometimes they use the term to refer to a conclusion that the defendant failed to exercise reasonable care, that is, that the defendant acted "negligently." But the defendant's failure to exercise reasonable care is only one element of the liability theory or cause of action known as "negligence." Thus, the term negligence denotes both the overall cause of action and one of its elements.

Under the formal theory of the negligence cause of action, the plaintiff ordinarily has the burden of establishing five elements in order to recover. These five elements are said to constitute the prima facie case in negligence, meaning that the plaintiff will lose if he fails to establish any one of them. (For a similar description with respect to intentional torts, see the Introduction to Chapter II.)

First, the plaintiff must establish that the defendant had a duty to conform its conduct to a specific standard. This matter is addressed in Chapter VI. Usually this standard requires the defendant to exercise "ordinary" or "reasonable" care. In some situations, however, a stricter or more lenient standard is imposed on the defendant.

Second, the plaintiff must prove that the defendant's conduct failed to conform to the appropriate standard. Courts often refer to such failure as a breach of the defendant's duty, or as substandard conduct on the part of the defendant, or (when the standard requires the defendant to exercise reasonable care) as negligence. This element is the subject of this chapter.

Third, the plaintiff must prove that the defendant's substandard conduct was a factual cause or cause in fact of the plaintiff's injuries. This element is treated in Chapter IV.

Fourth, the plaintiff must prove that the defendant's substandard conduct was a "proximate" or "legal" cause of the plaintiff's injuries. This element is addressed in Chapter V.

And fifth, the plaintiff must prove actual damages. Unlike some intentional torts, the cause of action for negligence has actual damage as an element of the plaintiff's prima facie case. This element is addressed in Chapter VII.

The first (duty) issue is normally for the judge to determine, with little or no role for the jury. The other issues are normally for the jury to determine, unless reasonable minds could not differ.

If the plaintiff establishes all five elements, he has made out a prima facie case in negligence. The defendant can still escape liability (or reduce its liability) by establishing one of several affirmative defenses, the most important of which is the plaintiff's own negligence. The affirmative defenses are treated in Chapter IX.

The remainder of this chapter is devoted to the second element of the plaintiff's prima facie case: the determination of whether the defendant exercised reasonable or ordinary care. As you go through the material, you should keep in mind that in order to win, the plaintiff must also satisfy the other four elements of the cause of action in negligence. The defendant may also have one or more affirmative defenses.

B.   SUBSTANDARD CARE

GRACE & CO. v. CITY OF LOS ANGELES

United States District Court, Southern District of California, 1958.
168 F.Supp. 344, affirmed, 278 F.2d 771 (9th Cir. 1960).

WESTOVER, DISTRICT JUDGE.

Defendant, City of Los Angeles, was and now is the owner of Berth 59, Los Angeles Harbor, and together with defendant, Outer Harbor Dock and Wharf Co., operated a certain steel and concrete shed at Berth 59 in that portion of Los Angeles County known as San Pedro.

Plaintiff was the owner of approximately 1,960 bags of coffee, which had been stored in the shed at Berth 59 after having been discharged by various vessels and was awaiting delivery to plaintiff.

Defendants maintained in the public street adjacent to the shed at Berth 59 a certain 8–inch cast-iron water pipe-line. A lateral line leading into the shed from the 8–inch pipe burst, allowing a great quantity of water to escape from the pipe-line under high pressure, which water flooded the floor of the shed at Berth 59 and damaged plaintiff's coffee.

Plaintiff alleges the defendants permitted the pipe to remain beneath the shed, although defendants knew or in the exercise of due care should have known that the pipe was in an ancient, weak, corroded and decaying condition, so that the pipe could not have reasonably been expected to contain water under high pressure.

At the time the pipe was installed it was the best pipe available. Plaintiff makes no contention that the pipe-line or the lateral where the break occurred was negligently installed. At the time of installation defendants did not know of the corrosive nature of the soil, but subsequent to the installation the City, or some of its departments, became cognizant that the soil in the harbor area was highly corrosive. Based upon economic consideration, defendants established a policy of doing nothing about maintaining, repairing or replacing such water pipe-lines until a leak occurred and water was discovered on the surface of the ground.

Plaintiff contends defendants knew or should have known that the pipe was located in highly corrosive soil and, over the period of years involved, defendants should have conducted some sort of inspection to ascertain if the pipe had corroded in order to determine whether there was likelihood of the pipe bursting. Plaintiffs contend that failure to make an inspection for forty years was negligence.

At the trial experts testified the pipe in question failed because of graphitic corrosion. Graphitic corrosion occurs when iron in pipe is leached out and replaced by graphite. The leaching of the iron from the pipe and the replacement thereof by graphite occurs over a long period of time and does not change the pipe shape or contour. The only effect upon the pipe is that it loses strength so that under pressure the pipe in those particular spots where graphitic corrosion occurs gives way.

Plaintiffs contend defendants had knowledge that a break was imminent, for some months prior thereto there appeared to be a leakage in the system of more than 130.00 cubic feet of water per day. However, experts testified at the trial that in a graphitic corrosion break there is no gradual leakage, but that the surface of the pipe gives way all at once and thus allows water to spurt from the pipe.

After defendants received notice of the break in the pipe, the line was repaired by cutting out an eight or ten-foot length of pipe and inserting therein a new piece of cast-iron pipe. Defendants' employees found in the pipe removed an opening, caused by graphitic corrosion, approximately the size of a human hand. They also discovered that within a short distance on either side of the opening the pipe was in sound condition, so that it could be continued in use.

* * *

If, in the case at bar, the court is to find for plaintiff, it will be necessary to find defendants have been negligent either in the installation, maintenance or inspection of the pipe in question. As stated before, there is no contention by plaintiff that the pipe was negligently installed; hence, the negligence, if any, would have to be found in the City's failure to inspect the pipe. Plaintiff's entire case rests upon the theory that defendants were negligent in failing to make inspection of the pipe-line during a period of forty years to determine its condition. * * * Plaintiff admits, however, there was no reasonable manner in which the line could be adequately inspected, other than to excavate the soil along the pipe-line and make physical inspection thereof.

The pipe-line was some ten feet beneath the surface of the ground. The break occurred in a lateral leading into the shed under a cement platform adjacent to Berth 59. To make an inspection, it would have been necessary for the City to excavate the line in its entirety, including the line under the cement platform, which would mean the breaking of the cement platform to get to the pipe below.

According to the testimony of experts, graphitic corrosion occurs sporadically. Graphitic corrosion may occur on the top of the pipe and not on the bottom, or on one side and not the other. Graphitic corrosion may occur in one spot and then may not occur for many feet along the line. It would be necessary to excavate around the entire pipe to locate a corroded area. An examination of the upper half of the pipe would not be sufficient because graphitic corrosion could manifest itself on the lower portion of the pipe and not on the top or sides. To make complete inspection it would be necessary to remove the earth from beneath the line. The removal of earth from beneath the pipe would remove its support, putting a strain upon the pipe itself, and might cause a sinking or bending of the pipe, occasioning damage more extensive than the corrosion itself.

Testimony at the trial indicated the City of Los Angeles has adopted a "do nothing" policy regarding inspection of its water lines. It places water lines in the earth and then neither makes inspection nor replacement until leaks occur. When leaks develop they are repaired. When they become too numerous the pipe-line is replaced.

Defendants contend that when the line was installed it was the best pipe available and that such cast-iron pipe will ordinarily last for many, many years. In fact, evidence indicated that in Pennsylvania similar cast-iron pipe has been in use for more than 150 years in a non-corrosive soil.

If any policy has been adopted by municipalities in California, the policy is the same as that followed by the City of Los Angeles; that is, that after cast-iron water pipe is installed the line is used without inspection or replacement until there are sufficient breaks to indicate the pipe has corroded or has become undependable. Defendants contend there was nothing to indicate the break in question was imminent or the line undependable. In fact, the line was repaired and returned to use, and so far as this court is informed is in use today.

Negligence is a question of fact to be determined from all the surrounding circumstances. Although it might have been desirable to make an inspection of the water lines every two or three years, such inspection would be prohibitively expensive and economically unfeasible. The City, like individuals, is required to take only reasonable precautions.

Although there is some evidence that in other parts of the harbor area there had been pipe failure because of graphitic corrosion, nevertheless, we are of the opinion that considering all the evidence in this case the City was not negligent in failing to inspect the pipe.

Judgment will be for defendants. * * *

NOTES

1. A determination of whether certain conduct constitutes reasonable care is usually a question of fact, to be decided by the jury. *Grace & Co.* was a bench trial, that is, a case tried to the court without the aid of a jury. Thus, the trial judge sat as the fact finder.

2. A determination that a defendant failed to exercise reasonable care has two components. First, the fact finder—usually a jury—must determine what the defendant actually did. For example, in a case involving an automobile accident, a dispute may exist as to whether the defendant actually crossed the center line before the collision. In *Grace & Co.*, a similar issue might have arisen as to whether the city had in fact inspected the pipes. Apparently no such dispute did arise. The parties seemed to agree, by and large, about what actually happened.

Second, the fact finder must evaluate the defendant's behavior to determine whether it was "reasonable" under the circumstances. This evaluation is not about a "fact" in the ordinary sense of the term; it is a judgment about how people ought to behave. Thus, it is sometimes called a "mixed question" of fact and law. Nevertheless, it too is normally a "question of fact" for the jury.

As with any fact issue, a trial or appellate court can take the issue of reasonable care away from the jury only if no evidence supports a finding of substandard care or if reasonable minds could not differ on the issue. A court can do this at various stages of the proceedings: by giving the defendant judgment on the pleadings, by giving the defendant summary judgment, by directing a verdict in favor of the defendant, or by giving the defendant judgment notwithstanding the verdict. (These procedural devices are discussed in Chapter I. They are also part of the subject matter in courses on Civil Procedure.) In such cases, the court may say that the defendant was not negligent as a matter of law. Courts occasionally hold that certain conduct is negligent as a matter of law, but this is rare because the plaintiff has the burden of proof on this issue.

For the purpose of ascertaining the respective roles of the judge and jury, the question of determining what the defendant did is like any other fact. The question of determining whether the defendant's conduct was reasonable is less "factual," and some courts seem to be more willing to substitute their own judgment for that of the jury on such an issue than they would be on a "pure" issue of fact. Most courts, however, *proclaim* that evaluating the defendant's conduct is an issue of fact for the jury, just like any other issue of fact. In *Grace & Co.*, the plaintiff appealed the trial court's decision. The court of appeals affirmed, saying:

> The appellant [plaintiff] had the burden of establishing the negligence of the appellee [defendant]. The District Court found against the claims of the appellant and found that appellee was not negligent. There was ample evidence to support this finding.

278 F.2d 771, 774 (9th Cir.1960).

3. Negligence uses a foresight standard, not a hindsight standard. Thus, reasonable care requires only that a person take reasonable precautions with respect to risks that a reasonable person would foresee. In *Grace & Co.*, both parties seemed to agree that a reasonable party in the City's position could foresee that *some* pipes would break *some* time. The City just argued that digging up all the pipes for inspection would have been too burdensome. What if the City could reasonably have foreseen which pipe would break and when? In this regard, consider the following portion of the court of appeals' decision, which expanded on a point made by the trial court.

> The meters showed that for some months prior to the failure in question there had been a considerable flow of water into the system. The rate of flow was variable, but averaged about 140 cubic feet a day. As this was a "dead-end" system and its sole purpose was to provide water for fighting fires, appellant claims the City should have made a thorough investigation, in the interest of safety, to determine the cause of the flow or loss of water.

However, the meter readings do not indicate that any water was escaping from the pipe at the point where it burst. The evidence of the experts indicates that if there was a failure by reason of graphitic corrosion that there would have been a flood of water, such as occurred, rather than gradual leakage, which does not necessarily indicate a corrosion failure. Further, in the absence of water coming to the surface the source of the leak could not be found without digging up the pipe.

The evidence indicates a number of possible explanations for the flow. The fire line involved was approximately 5,000 to 6,000 feet long, containing a leaded joint every ten feet. Water could be lost through leaks in these joints or through various valves in the line.

278 F.2d at 774–75.

4. ***Learned Hand's famous "formula."*** In United States v. Carroll Towing Co., 159 F.2d 169 (2d Cir.1947), the plaintiff's barge broke loose from its moorings. One issue was whether the custodian of the barge was negligent for leaving the barge unattended. In a famous analysis of the negligence issue, Judge Learned Hand stated:

> Since there are occasions when every vessel will break from her moorings, and since, if she does, she becomes a menace to those about her; the owner's duty, as in other similar situations, to provide against resulting injuries is a function of three variables: (1) The probability that she will break away; (2) the gravity of the resulting injury, if she does; (3) the burden of adequate precautions. Possibly it serves to bring this notion into relief to state it in algebraic terms: if the probability be called P; the injury, L; and the burden, B; liability depends upon whether B is less than L multiplied by P: i.e., whether $B<PL$. Applied to the situation at bar, the likelihood that a barge will break from her fasts and the damage she will do, vary with the place and time; for example, if a storm threatens, the danger is greater; so it is if she is in a crowded harbor where moored barges are constantly being shifted about. On the other hand, the barge must not be the bargee's prison, even though he lives aboard; he must go ashore at times.*

---

* In Brotherhood Shipping Co. v. St. Paul Fire & Marine Ins. Co., 985 F.2d 323 (7th Cir. 1993), Judge Posner offered the following formulation of the *Carroll Towing* standard:

> Under that standard, a defendant is negligent if the burden (cost) of the precautions that he could have taken to avoid the accident (B in Hand's formula) is less than the loss that the accident could reasonably be anticipated to cause (L), discounted (i.e., multiplied) by the probability that the accident would occur unless the precautions were taken. So: $B<PL$. The cost-justified level of precaution (B)—the level that the defendant must come up to on penalty of being found to have violated his duty of due care if he does not—is thus higher, the likelier the accident that the precaution would have prevented was to occur (P) and the greater the loss that the accident was likely to inflict if it did occur (L). Looked at from a different direction, the formula shows that the cheaper it is to prevent the accident (low B), the more likely prevention is to be cost-justified and the failure to prevent therefore negligent. Negligence is especially likely to be found if B is low and both P and L (and therefore PL, the expected accident cost) are high.

The Third Restatement § 3 expresses the same general idea as follows:

> A person acts negligently if the person does not exercise reasonable care under all the circumstances. Primary factors to consider in ascertaining whether the person's conduct lacks reasonable care are the foreseeable likelihood that the person's conduct will result in

5. ***Some cost-benefit exercises.*** In light of *Grace, Carroll Towing,* and the requirement of foreseeability addressed in note 3, consider the following cases:

A.   In Beatty v. Central Iowa Ry., 58 Iowa 242, 12 N.W. 332 (1882), the plaintiff's decedent was killed when the "spirited young" horse he was riding, frightened by the noise of the defendant's train, bolted and collided with it at a crossing. The plaintiff argued that the railroad was negligent for not reconstructing the road near the crossing so that the road and track had more separation and then crossed at right angles, which would have reduced the risk of such events. The court held that the railroad was not negligent.

> If the railway had approached the highway at right angles, and been plainly visible for half a mile before reaching the crossing, it may fairly be assumed that the accident would not have happened. And yet we cannot say, as matter of law, that the railway company was guilty of negligence in not constructing its road in that manner. If deceased had ridden an old, gentle, and well-trained horse, instead of a young, spirited, and not thoroughly trained one it may well be assumed that the accident would not have happened. Yet it would scarcely do to hold that deceased was guilty of contributory negligence because he rode a young and spirited horse. And yet there would be as much propriety in so holding as in declaring, as a matter of law, that the defendant was guilty of negligence because it did not grade the track for the travel on the west line of the highway.

B.   In Kimbar v. Estis, 1 N.Y.2d 399, 153 N.Y.S.2d 197, 135 N.E.2d 708 (1956), the plaintiff broke his nose at a summer camp when he stepped off a path at night and hit a tree. He alleged that the operators of the summer camp were negligent for not illuminating the path. The court held that the summer camp was not negligent for failing to illuminate the path.

C.   In Allien v. Louisiana Power & Light Co., 202 So.2d 704 (La.App. 1967), the plaintiff's decedent was electrocuted when a portable rig was raised by other workers near the place where he was standing, contacting defendant's high-voltage line. The defendant had installed the line in question thinking it went to a working well but later learned that the well was located elsewhere. The defendant installed a new line but did not deactivate the first line, which could have been done for $48. The court held that the defendant was negligent.

> After careful consideration, we think it is unnecessary for us to decide whether a power company is negligent in every case where it installs and maintains an uninsulated high voltage line within 26 feet, and at an elevation of 28 feet, from an oil well which the power company knew or should have known would have to be reworked periodically with portable rigs. In the present case, there is a unique factor which, added to all of the other circumstances, forces us to the conclusion that the power company was negligent. This fact is that

---

harm, the foreseeable severity of any harm that may ensue, and the burden of precautions to eliminate or reduce the risk of harm.

the power line in question had no utility whatever and could have been removed at a nominal cost.

6. *Inadvertence.*

As defined by tort law, negligence does not include any assumption that the actor has failed to advert to the risk. Rather, the balancing approach to negligence tends to assume that the actor is aware of that risk, but has tolerated that risk on account of the burdens involved by risk-prevention measures. In a significant number of cases, however, the actor's alleged negligence consists of an inattentive failure to perceive or appreciate the risk involved in the actor's conduct. When that conduct is allegedly negligent, the relevant burden of precautions is the burden the actor would have borne by paying more attention in the course of his ordinary affairs. In some cases, there may be evidence that bears on the extent of that burden. In many cases, however, the level of the burden, and hence the reasonableness of the person's inattentiveness, are largely matters of common sense. Accordingly, analyzing the factors highlighted in this section may be artificial, and the decisionmaker—typically, the jury—can simply consider whether the reasonably careful person *would* have been aware of the risk. For example, the jury can determine whether a pedestrian should have detected, and hence avoided stumbling over, a banana peel located on a crowded sidewalk.

Third Restatement of Torts § 3 cmt. *k.*

7. *Jury instructions.*
In most jurisdictions the jury is not told very much about how to determine reasonable care. The pattern jury instruction in Texas is typical:

Ordinary Care and Negligence

"Ordinary care" means that degree of care which would be used by a person of ordinary prudence under the same or similar circumstances.

"Negligence" means failure to use ordinary care; that is to say, failure to do that which a person of ordinary prudence would have done under the same or similar circumstances, or doing that which a person of ordinary prudence would not have done under the same or similar circumstances.

State Bar of Texas, Texas Pattern Jury Charges—General Negligence, Intentional Personal Torts 2.1 (2006).

8. *"Sudden emergency."*
One issue that has received much attention is the evaluation of the reasonableness of the behavior of a person who was confronted with an unexpected crisis requiring a quick response. For example, what if a motorist swerves to avoid an object that suddenly falls on the road from a truck, and in hindsight the choice was the wrong one? All courts agree that the court and the jury will take the sudden emergency into account. See, e.g., Third Restatement § 9. Traditionally, a party who acted during a sudden emergency not of his own making has been entitled to a special instruction calling the jury's attention to the circumstance. In recent years, however, a number of courts have moved away from the special instruction. See, e.g., Lyons v. Midnight Sun Transp. Services, Inc., 928 P.2d 1202 (Alaska 1996)

(disapproving of the special instruction, particularly in vehicle cases, and surveying cases from other jurisdictions).

9. **Industry custom.** In *Grace,* the court of appeals relied in part on the fact that "[n]o expert testified that it was the practice in any municipality to dig up underground pipe to ascertain its condition, no matter when it was installed," adding that, "[o]bservance of a custom or practice is evidence of due care, although of course it does not conclusively establish the legal standard." 278 F.2d at 774. The following case is a famous discussion, by a famous jurist, of the role of custom.

T.J. HOOPER

United States Court of Appeals, Second Circuit, 1932.
60 F.2d 737.

L. HAND, CIRCUIT JUDGE.

The barges No. 17 and No. 30, belonging to the Northern Barge Company, had lifted cargoes of coal at Norfolk, Virginia, for New York in March, 1928. They were towed by two tugs of the petitioner, the "Montrose" and the "Hooper," and were lost off the Jersey Coast on March tenth, in an easterly gale. The cargo owners sued the barges under the contracts of carriage; the owner of the barges sued the tugs under the towing contract, both for its own loss and as bailee of the cargoes; the owner of the tug filed a petition to limit its liability. All the suits were joined and heard together, and the judge found that all the vessels were unseaworthy; the tugs, because they did not carry radio receiving sets by which they could have seasonably got warnings of a change in the weather which should have caused them to seek shelter in the Delaware Breakwater en route. He therefore entered an interlocutory decree holding each tug and barge jointly liable to each cargo owner, and each tug for half damages for the loss of its barge. The petitioner appealed, and the barge owner appealed and filed assignments of error.

* * *

A more difficult issue is as to the tugs. We agree with the judge that once conceding the propriety of passing the Breakwater on the night of the eighth, the navigation was good enough. * * * [T]he case as to them turns upon whether they should have put in at the Breakwater.

* * *

[T]he "Montrose" and the "Hooper" would have had the benefit of the evening report from Arlington had they had proper receiving sets. This predicted worse weather; it read: "Increasing east and southeast winds, becoming fresh to strong, Friday night and increasing cloudiness followed by rain Friday." The bare "increase" of the morning had become "fresh to strong." To be sure this scarcely foretold a gale of from forty to fifty miles for five hours or more, rising at one time to fifty-six; but if the four tows thought the first report enough, the second ought to have laid any doubts. The master of the "Montrose" himself, when asked what he would have done had he received a substantially similar report, said that he would certainly have put in. The master of the "Hooper" was also asked for his opinion, and said that he would have turned back also, but this admission is somewhat vitiated by the incorporation in the question of the statement that it was a "storm warning," which the witness seized upon in his answer. All this seems to us to support the conclusion of the judge that prudent masters, who had received the second warning, would have found the risk more than the exigency warranted; they would have been amply vindicated by what followed. To be sure the barges would, as we have said, probably have withstood the gale, had they been well found; but a master is not justified in putting his tow to every test which she will survive, if she be fit. There is a zone in which proper caution will avoid putting her capacity to the proof; a coefficient of prudence that he should not disregard. Taking the situation as a whole, it seems to us that these masters would have taken undue chances, had they got the broadcasts [and not put in].

They did not, because their private radio receiving sets, which were on board, were not in working order. These belonged to them personally, and were partly a toy, partly a part of the equipment, but neither furnished by the owner, nor supervised by it. It is not fair to say that there was a general custom among coastwise carriers so to equip their tugs. One line alone did it; as for the rest, they relied upon their crews, so far as they can be said to have relied at all. An adequate receiving set suitable for a coastwise tug can now be got at small cost and is reasonably reliable if kept up; obviously it is a source of great protection to their tows. Twice every day they can receive these predictions, based upon the widest possible information, available to every vessel within two or three hundred miles and more. Such a set is the ears of the tug to catch the spoken word, just as the master's binoculars are her eyes to see a storm signal ashore. Whatever may be said as to other vessels, tugs towing heavy coal laden barges, strung out for half a mile, have little power to manoeuvre, and do not, as this case proves, expose themselves to weather which would not turn back stauncher craft. They can have at hand protection against dangers of which they can learn in no other way.

Is it then a final answer that the business had not yet generally adopted receiving sets? There are, no doubt, cases where courts seem to make the general practice of the calling the standard of proper diligence; we have indeed given some currency to the notion ourselves. Indeed in most cases reasonable prudence is in fact common prudence; but strictly it is never its measure; a whole calling may have unduly lagged in the adoption of new and available devices. It never may set its own tests, however persuasive be its usages. Courts must in the end say what is required; there are precautions so imperative that even their universal disregard will not excuse their omission. But here there was no custom at all as to receiving sets; some had them, some did not; the most that can be urged is that they had not yet become general. Certainly in such a case we need not pause; when some have thought a device necessary, at least we may say that they were right, and the others too slack. The statute (46 USCA § 484) does not bear on this situation at all. It prescribes not a receiving, but a transmitting set, and for a very different purpose; to call for help, not to get news. We hold the tugs therefore because had they been properly equipped, they would have got the Arlington reports. The injury was a direct consequence of this unseaworthiness.

Decree affirmed.

NOTES

1. The question in *T.J. Hooper* was whether the tugs were "unseaworthy." This is a concept from maritime law; technically, it does not involve negligence. The standard, however, is whether the tugs were "*reasonably* fit," so it is a close cousin of negligence. In any event, courts routinely apply the *T.J. Hooper* rule about industry custom to negligence.

2. *Departure* from industry custom or common usage is evidence of negligence, but it is not conclusive.

C. THE "REASONABLE PERSON"

VAUGHAN v. MENLOVE

Common Pleas, 1837.
3 Bing., N.C., 468.

[The plaintiff owned two cottages near the defendant's land. The defendant had a stack or "rick" of hay on his own land. The hay ignited due to spontaneous combustion caused by heat generated by the hay fermenting. The fire spread and the plaintiff's cottages were burned.]

At the trial it appeared that the rick in question had been made by the defendant near the boundary of his own premises; that the hay was in such a state when put together, as to give rise to discussions on the probability of fire; that though there were conflicting opinions on the subject, yet during a period of five weeks the defendant was repeatedly warned of his peril; that this stock was insured; and that upon one occasion, being advised to take the rick down to avoid all danger, he said "he would chance it." He made an aperture or chimney through the rick; but in spite, or perhaps in consequence of this precaution, the rick at length burst into flames from the spontaneous heating of its materials; the flames communicated to the defendant's barn and stables, and thence to the plaintiff's cottages, which were entirely destroyed.

PATTESON, J., before whom the cause was tried, told the jury that the question for them to consider was, whether the fire had been occasioned by gross negligence on the part of the defendant, adding, that he was bound to proceed with such reasonable caution as a prudent man would have exercised under such circumstances.

A verdict having been found for the plaintiff, a rule nisi for a new trial was obtained, on the ground that the jury should have been directed to consider, not whether the defendant had been guilty of a gross negligence with reference to the standard of ordinary prudence, a standard too uncertain to afford any criterion, but whether he had acted bonâ fide to the best of his judgment; if he had, he ought not to be responsible for the misfortune of not possessing the highest order of intelligence. * * *

TINDAL, C.J. I agree that this is a case primae impressionis; but I feel no difficulty in applying to it the principles of law as laid down in other cases of a similar kind. Undoubtedly this is not a case of contract, such as a bailment or the like, where the bailee is responsible in consequence of the remuneration he is to receive; but there is a rule of law which says you must so enjoy your own property as not to injure that of another; and according to that rule the defendant is liable for the consequence of his own neglect; and though the defendant did not himself light the fire, yet mediately he is as much the cause of it as if he had himself put a candle to the rick; for it is well known that hay will ferment and take fire if it be not carefully stacked. It has been decided that if an occupier burns weeds so near the boundary of his own land that damage ensues to the property of his neighbor, he is liable to an action for the amount of injury done, unless the accident were occasioned by a sudden blast which he could not foresee. Turberville v. Stamp, 1 Salk, 13. But put the case of a chemist making experiments with ingredients, singly innocent, but when combined liable to ignite; if he leaves them together, and injury is thereby occasioned to the property of his neighbor, can any one doubt that an action on the case would lie?

It is contended, however, that the learned judge was wrong in leaving this to the jury as a case of gross negligence, and that the question of negligence was so mixed up with reference to what would be the conduct of a man of ordinary prudence that the jury might have thought the latter the rule by which they were to decide; that such a rule would be too uncertain to act upon; and that the question ought to have been whether the defendant had acted honestly and bonâ fide to the best of his own judgment. That, however, would leave so vague a line as to afford no rule at all, the degree of judgment belonging to each individual being infinitely various; and though it has been urged that the care which a prudent man would take, is not an intelligible proposition as a rule of law, yet such has always been the rule adopted in cases of bailment, as laid down in Coggs v. Bernard, 2 Ld.Raym. 909. * * *

The care taken by a prudent man has always been the rule laid down; and as to the supposed difficulty of applying it, a jury has always been able to say, whether, taking that rule as their guide, there has been negligence on the occasion in question.

Instead, therefore, of saying that the liability for negligence should be coextensive with the judgment of each individual, which would be as variable as the length of the foot of each individual, we ought rather to adhere to the rule, which requires in all cases a regard to caution such as a man of ordinary prudence would observe. That was in substance the criterion presented to the jury in this case, and therefore the present rule must be discharged.

[Concurring opinions were delivered by PARK and VAUGHAN, JJ. GASE-LEE, J., concurred in the result.]

Rule discharged.

NOTES

1. A "rule nisi" is a term used in England to signify an application for an appeal to an appellate court. When the "rule" is "discharged," the appeal fails. When the "rule" is "made absolute," the appeal is successful.

2. *Inferior abilities.* Courts uniformly apply an "objective" standard of negligence—that is, they do not take into account the actor's idiosyncrasies—when the defendant claims mere clumsiness, stupidity, or low mental ability.

3. *Insanity.* Most courts do not take even insanity into account when evaluating a defendant's conduct in a civil, as opposed to a criminal, case. See Jolley v. Powell, 299 So.2d 647 (Fla.App.1974). A few courts take insanity into account when it causes the defendant to have a break with reality or precludes the defendant from conforming his conduct to the appropriate standard. Even in these jurisdictions, however, a defendant who has reason to (and is able to) foresee such episodes might be negligent for putting himself in a position to do harm, such as by driving an automobile. See Breunig v. American Family Insurance Co., 45 Wis.2d 536, 173 N.W.2d 619 (1970).

4. *Superior abilities.* What if the actor possesses knowledge or skill that is not inferior, but superior to that of the average person? Courts have consistently held that the actor's special skills or experience are to be treated as among the circumstances to be considered when the conduct is judged. See, e.g., LaVine v. Clear Creek Skiing Corp., 557 F.2d 730, 734–35 (10th Cir.1977) (expert skier); Cervelli v. Graves, 661 P.2d 1032, 1034–35 (Wyo.1983) (professional truck driver).

5. *Intoxication.* Several courts have said that self-imposed intoxication does not forgive a defendant of conduct that would be negligent if committed by a sober person. See, e.g., Hamilton v. Kinsey, 337 So.2d 344 (Ala.1976).

ROBERTS v. STATE OF LOUISIANA

Louisiana Court of Appeal, 1981.
396 So.2d 566, aff'd on other grounds, 404 So.2d 1221 (La.1981).

LABORDE, JUDGE.

In this tort suit, William C. Roberts sued to recover damages for injuries he sustained in an accident in the lobby of the U.S. Post Office Building in Alexandria, Louisiana. Roberts fell after being bumped into by Mike Burson, the blind operator of the concession stand located in the building.

Plaintiff sued the State of Louisiana, through the Louisiana Health and Human Resources Administration, advancing two theories of liability:

respondeat superior and negligent failure by the State to properly supervise and oversee the safe operation of the concession stand. The stand's blind operator, Mike Burson, is not a party to this suit although he is charged with negligence.

The trial court ordered plaintiff's suit dismissed, holding that there is no respondeat superior liability without an employer-employee relationship and that there is no negligence liability without a cause in fact showing.

We affirm the trial court's decision for the reasons which follow.

On September 1, 1977, at about 12:45 in the afternoon, operator Mike Burson left his concession stand to go to the men's bathroom located in the building. As he was walking down the hall, he bumped into plaintiff who fell to the floor and injured his hip. Plaintiff was 75 years old, stood 5′ 6″ and weighed approximately 100 pounds. Burson, on the other hand, was 25 to 26 years old, stood approximately 6′ and weighed 165 pounds.

At the time of the incident, Burson was not using a cane nor was he utilizing the technique of walking with his arm or hand in front of him.

Even though Burson was not joined as a defendant, his negligence or lack thereof is crucial to a determination of the State's liability. Because of its importance, we begin with it.

Plaintiff contends that operator Mike Burson traversed the area from his concession stand to the men's bathroom in a negligent manner. To be more specific, he focuses on the operator's failure to use his cane even though he had it with him in his concession stand.

In determining an actor's negligence, various courts have imposed differing standards of care to which handicapped persons are expected to perform. Professor William L. Prosser expresses one generally recognized modern standard of care as follows:

> As to his physical characteristics, the reasonable man may be said to be identical with the actor. The man who is blind * * * is entitled to live in the world and to have allowance made by others for his disability, and he cannot be required to do the impossible by conforming to physical standards which he cannot meet * * *. At the same time, the conduct of the handicapped individual must be reasonable in the light of his knowledge of his infirmity, which is treated merely as one of the circumstances under which he acts * * *. It is sometimes said that a blind man must use a greater degree of care than one who can see; but it is now generally agreed that as a fixed rule this is inaccurate, and that the correct statement is merely that he must take the precautions, be they more or less, which the ordinary reasonable man would take if he were blind. (W. Prosser, The Law of Torts § 32, pp.151–52 (4th ed. 1971)).

A careful review of the record in this instance reveals that Burson was acting as a reasonably prudent blind person would under these particular circumstances.

* * *

On the date of the incident in question, Mike Burson testified that he left his concession stand and was on his way to the men's bathroom when he bumped into plaintiff. He, without hesitancy, admitted that at the time he was not using his cane, explaining that he relies on his facial sense which he feels is an adequate technique for short trips inside the familiar building. Burson testified that he does use a cane to get to and from work.

Plaintiff makes much of Burson's failure to use a cane when traversing the halls of the post office building. Yet, our review of the testimony received at trial indicates that it is not uncommon for blind people to rely on other techniques when moving around in a familiar setting. For example George Marzloff, the director of the Division of Blind Services, testified that he can recommend to the blind operators that they should use a cane but he knows that when they are in a setting in which they are comfortable, he would say that nine out of ten will not use a cane and in his personal opinion, if the operator is in a relatively busy area, the cane can be more of a hazard than an asset. Mr. Marzloff further testified that he felt a reasonably functioning blind person would learn his way around his work setting as he does around his home so that he could get around without a cane. Mr. Marzloff added that he has several blind people working in his office, none of whom use a cane inside that facility.

* * *

The only testimony in the record that suggests that Burson traversed the halls in a negligent manner was that elicited from plaintiff's expert witness, William Henry Jacobson. Jacobson is an instructor in peripathology, which he explained as the science of movement within the surroundings by visually impaired individuals. Jacobson, admitting that he conducted no study or examination of Mike Burson's mobility skills and that he was unfamiliar with the State's vending program, nonetheless testified that he would require a blind person to use a cane in traversing the areas outside the concession stand. He added that a totally blind individual probably should use a cane * * * in an unfamiliar environment or where a familiar environment involves a change, whether it be people moving through that environment or strangers moving through that environment or just heavy traffic within that environment.

When cross examined however, Jacobson testified:

Q.   Now, do you, in instructing blind people on their mobility skills, do you tell them to use their own judgment in which type of mobility assistance technique they're to employ?

A.   Yes I do.

Q.   Do you think that three (3) years is a long enough period for a person to become acquainted with an environment that he might be working with?

A.   Yes I do.

Q. So you think that after a period of three (3) years an individual would probably, if he is normal * * * has normal mobility skills for a blind person, would have enough adjustment time to be * * * to call that environment familiar?

A. Yes.

Q. That's not including the fact that there may be people in and out of the building?

A. Right.

Q. Now is it possible that if he's familiar with the sounds of the people inside a building that he may even at some point in time become so familiar with the people in an area, regular customers or what not that you could say that the environment was familiar, including the fact that there are people there, is that possible?

A. Uh * * * I would hesitate to say that, in a public facility where we could not * * * uh * * * control strangers coming in.

Q. Well, let's say that a business has a particular group of clients that are always there, perhaps on a daily or weekly basis. Now you've stated that a blind person sharpens his auditory skills in order to help him articulate in an area?

A. With instruction, yes.

Q. Right. Isn't it possible that if he can rely on a fixed travel of a fixed type and number of persons that it's possible that that is a familiar environment even though there are people there?

A. Only if they were the same people all the time and they know him, yes.

Upon our review of the record, we feel that plaintiff has failed to show that Burson was negligent. Burson testified that he was very familiar with his surroundings, having worked there for three and a half years. He had special mobility training and his reports introduced into evidence indicate good mobility skills. He explained his decision to rely on his facial sense instead of his cane for these short trips in a manner which convinces us that it was a reasoned decision. Not only was Burson's explanation adequate, there was additional testimony from other persons indicating that such a decision is not an unreasonable one. Also important is the total lack of any evidence in the record showing that at the time of the incident, Burson engaged in any acts which may be characterized as negligence on his part. For example, there is nothing showing that Burson was walking too fast, not paying attention, et cetera. Under all of these circumstances, we conclude that Mike Burson was not negligent.

Our determination that Mike Burson was not negligent disposes of our need to discuss liability on the part of the State.

* * *

NOTE

The relevance of Burson's blindness to the question of negligence was clearly a question of law for the court. The subsequent question of the reasonableness of Burson's conduct, taking into account the fact that he was blind, would in most states be one for the jury, unless reasonable minds could not differ. But Louisiana has a practice of appellate review whereby appellate courts review the facts and can actually decide the question of negligence. In a normal jurisdiction that submits the issue of reasonable care to the jury unless reasonable minds could not differ, should the issue have been submitted to the jury on the evidence in *Roberts*?

STRAIT v. CRARY

Court of Appeals of Wisconsin, 1993.
173 Wis.2d 377, 496 N.W.2d 634, review denied, 501 N.W.2d 457 (Wis.1993).

EICH, CHIEF JUDGE.

David Strait, a minor at the time of the events leading up to this action, appeals from a judgment dismissing his personal injury claims against Terry Crary after the jury found him sixty-one percent negligent with respect to the incident upon which the action was based. While Strait raises several issues on the appeal, we consider one to be dispositive: whether the trial court erred in refusing to instruct the jury on the "special" standard of care applicable to children. We agree with Strait that the court's refusal to give the instructions was reversible error. We therefore reverse the judgment and remand for a new trial of the liability issues.

The events leading up to Strait's injury are largely undisputed. In May 1987, when Strait was 16 years old, he and several other teen-agers went riding in Crary's pickup truck. Crary [age 21] purchased beer and other intoxicants for the young people, and they soon became quite intoxicated. Crary, who was not drinking himself and remained sober throughout the evening, continued to drive the group through the countryside as they continued their drinking.

At some point in the evening, while Crary was driving down a country road (within the speed limit), Strait, who was sitting in the front seat, attempted to climb out of the passenger window and join the others in the box of the truck. He fell in the attempt and the truck ran over his leg, breaking it. Crary stopped the truck and, rather than call the police or an ambulance, decided to pick Strait up, place him back in the truck and drive him to the hospital—which he did, causing Strait additional pain and discomfort.

Strait and his parents sued Crary, claiming that he was negligent in the manner in which he operated his truck under the circumstances of the case.

At the trial's conclusion, Strait requested several jury instructions, among them Wis J I–Civil 1010, which sets a separate standard of care for children,[2] and its companion, Wis J I–Civil 1582, which instructs the jury that it must consider that special standard in comparing the parties' negligence.

The trial court denied the requests, concluding that under the rather unusual facts of the case—particularly the drinking and the nature of the acts in which Strait was engaged when he fell from the truck—Strait, although a minor, should be held to the standard of care applicable to adults. The court explained its reasoning at the hearing on Strait's postverdict motions:

> If this had been a year-old child or a six-year-old child and the door was unlocked or the window was open or some such thing as that, then, yes, you have to give that instruction * * * as to children, the driver needs to take special precautions, that's obvious, but when you try to tell me that * * * a 21–year–old driver has got to take extra precautions when there is a 16–year–old passenger * * * crawling out the window to get [into] the back end of the truck, that is preposterous * * *.

As indicated, the jury found both Strait and Crary causally negligent and apportioned the negligence sixty-one percent to Strait and thirty-nine percent to Crary. The trial court denied Strait's postverdict motions and dismissed the action.*

* * *

Here the central issue at trial was the comparative negligence of Strait and Crary. At the time of the accident Strait was a child and Crary was an adult. Thus the proper standard of care to be applied to the litigants was plainly raised by the evidence. Indeed, it was essential to the case. Nonetheless, the trial court declined to give the instructions that would have informed the jury of the law: that "different standards of ordinary care apply to [children and adults]." Brice v. Milwaukee Automobile Ins. Co., 272 Wis. 520, 525, 76 N.W.2d 337, 340 (1956).

Crary argues that we should not find error in the court's refusal. He maintains that the case fits an "exception" to the adult/child rule which holds a child to the adult standard when he or she is "engaged in an activity which is typically engaged in only by adults * * *." See Wis J I–Civil 1010, Comment; Restatement, Law of Torts (Second) cmt c (1965). Prosser explains the rule as follows:

---

2. Wisconsin J I–Civil 1010 provides:

1010 NEGLIGENCE OF CHILDREN

As a child, (_____) was required to use the degree of care which is ordinarily exercised by a child of the same age, intelligence, discretion, knowledge, and experience under the same or similar circumstances.

In determining whether (_____) exercised this degree of care, you should consider the child's instincts and impulses with respect to dangerous acts, since a child may not have the prudence, discretion, or thoughtfulness of an adult.

* Under Wisconsin's system of "modified" comparative negligence, a plaintiff found more negligent than the defendant recovers nothing. [Ed.]

[W]henever a child, whether as plaintiff or as defendant, engages in an activity which is normally one for adults only, such as driving an automobile or flying an airplane, the public interest and the public safety require that any consequences due to his [or her] own incapacity shall fall upon him [or her] rather than the innocent victim, and that he [or she] must be held to the adult standard, without any allowance for * * * age. (Prosser, Law of Torts § 32, at 156–57 (4th ed. 1971).)

Two things are apparent. First, the exception applies only in cases where the child is engaged in an "adults-only" or "licensed" activity, such as driving a car or flying an airplane.[5] Second, the rule is grounded on public policy considerations: that when a child is engaged in such adult activities, public policy requires that the child himself or herself, rather than any "innocent victim[s]" of the child's conduct, should suffer the consequences of that conduct.

Here, while it might be said that drinking to the point of intoxication is—generally, but certainly not exclusively—an adult-type activity, climbing around the outside of a moving vehicle may well not be. Even so, however, the policy underlying the rule—the result it was fashioned to avoid—is not implicated in this case, for there is no "innocent victim" of Strait's conduct. We conclude, therefore, that the exception to the rule holding minors to a different standard of care than adults is inapplicable to the facts of this case. As a result, the trial court erred when it implicitly adopted and applied that exception in rejecting Strait's proffered instructions.

* * *

Here the legal error was plain. The instructions as given told the jury to hold Strait to the same standard of care as Crary, an adult, and to compare that negligence without considering Strait's age. As we have indicated above, the law states otherwise. And we believe the error goes to the heart of the case, which was, as we also have indicated, the assessment and comparison of Strait's and Crary's negligence. We are satisfied that it is probable that the jury was misled by such an instruction and that the result of the jurors' assessment and comparison of the parties' negligence might have been different if they had been properly instructed. We therefore reverse and remand for a new trial on those issues.

Judgment reversed and cause remanded with directions for further proceedings consistent with this opinion.

NOTES

1. *The old "multiples of seven" approach; minimum age for child negligence.* A few courts created presumptions about children in different age groups: children below age seven were conclusively presumed to be

---

5. The comment to Wis J I–Civil 1010 describes the exception as limited to situations where the child is engaged in an adult activity "for which adult qualification or a license is required."

incapable of negligence, children between ages seven and fourteen were presumed to be incapable of negligence, but the presumption could be rebutted by the other party, and children over the age of fourteen were presumed to be capable of negligence, but the presumption could be rebutted by the child. See Dunn v. Teti, 280 Pa.Super. 399, 421 A.2d 782 (1980). Most courts have abolished these presumptions. These courts simply instruct the jury to determine whether the defendant exercised the care of a reasonable child of like age, intelligence and experience. See, e.g., Williamson v. Garland, 402 S.W.2d 80 (Ky.1966) (contributory negligence).

The Third Restatement § 10(b) provides that a child under the age of five is incapable of negligence. Most jurisdictions have agreed that some minimum age is appropriate, and while the cases have varied somewhat as to the specific number, the Restatement reporters found that five appeared to have the most support both in judicial authorities and in contemporary social behavior.

2. ***The "age, intelligence, and experience" standard.*** Note that more than age is taken into account. Unlike adults, children are permitted to excuse their conduct by a showing of low mental ability or lack of experience. In Sherry v. Asing, 56 Haw. 135, 531 P.2d 648 (1975), an issue was whether a seventeen-year-old "mentally slow" plaintiff was contributorily negligent. The plaintiff requested the following jury instruction:

> A minor is not held to the same standard as an adult. A child is only required to use care appropriate to his age and experience and mental capacity.

The trial court gave this instruction, but only after omitting the words "and mental capacity." The defendant requested the following instruction:

> Under the rule of ordinary care which I have just stated, no exception is made for a person who is mentally retarded. A person who is mentally retarded is bound to follow the same standard of care as any person acting under the same circumstances.

The trial court gave this instruction in its entirety. The Hawaii Supreme Court held that because the plaintiff was a child, the trial court erred by deleting the last three words of the plaintiff's proposed instruction and by giving the defendant's proposed instruction.

3. ***The adult activity exception.*** The leading case on the "adult activity" exception to the special standard for children is Dellwo v. Pearson, 259 Minn. 452, 107 N.W.2d 859 (1961). The defendant, a twelve-year-old boy, drove his motorboat across the plaintiff's fishing line. This caused the reel of the plaintiff's fishing rod to fly off, hit her glasses, and injure her eye. The court said:

> A more important point involves the instruction that defendant was to be judged by the standard of care of a child of similar age rather than of a reasonable man. There is no doubt that the instruction given substantially reflects the language of numerous decisions in this and other courts. However, the great majority of these cases involve the issue of contributory negligence and the standard of care that may properly be required of a child in protecting himself against some hazard. The standard of care stated is proper and appropriate for such situations.

However, this court has previously recognized that there may be a difference between the standard of care that is required of a child in protecting himself against hazards and the standard that may be applicable when his activities expose others to hazards. Certainly in the circumstances of modern life, where vehicles moved by powerful motors are readily available and frequently operated by immature individuals, we should be skeptical of a rule that would allow motor vehicles to be operated to the hazard of the public with less than the normal minimum degree of care and competence.

* * * While minors are entitled to be judged by standards commensurate with age, experience, and wisdom when engaged in activities appropriate to their age, experience, and wisdom, it would be unfair to the public to permit a minor in the operation of a motor vehicle to observe any other standards of care and conduct than those expected of all others. A person observing children at play with toys, throwing balls, operating tricycles or velocipedes, or engaged in other childhood activities may anticipate conduct that does not reach an adult standard of care of prudence. However, one cannot know whether the operator of an approaching automobile, airplane, or powerboat is a minor or an adult, and usually cannot protect himself against youthful imprudence even if warned. Accordingly, we hold that in the operation of an automobile, airplane, or powerboat, a minor is to be held to the same standard of care as an adult.

107 N.W.2d at 862–63 (citations and footnotes omitted).

As indicated by the principal case, the adult activity exception has generally been confined to motor vehicle cases. For example, a number of cases involving firearms have applied the child rather than the adult standard. See, e.g., Purtle v. Shelton, 251 Ark. 519, 474 S.W.2d 123 (1971) (17–year–old with deer rifle) ("If we should declare that a minor hunting deer with a high-powered rifle must in all instances be held to an adult standard of care, we must be prepared to explain why the same rule should not apply to a minor hunting deer with a shotgun, to a minor hunting rabbits with a high-powered rifle, to a twelve-year-old shooting crows with a .22, and so on down to the six-year-old shooting at tin cans with an air rifle."). Contra, e.g., Huebner v. Koelfgren, 519 N.W.2d 488 (Minn.App.1994) (14–year–old with BB gun) ("We agree with the trial court that the adult standard of care should be imposed on and expected by a teenager handling a gun; the public generally has a right to expect a single, adult standard of care from individuals who handle guns."). The Third Restatement strongly endorses the latter view. See Third Restatement § 10 cmt. *f.*

D.   VIOLATION OF STATUTE

GORRIS v. SCOTT
Court of Exchequer, 1874.
9 Ex. 125.

KELLY, C.B.

This is an action to recover damages for the loss of a number of sheep which the defendant, a shipowner, had contracted to carry, and which were washed overboard and lost by reason (as we must take it to be truly alleged) of the neglect to comply with a certain order made by the Privy Council, in pursuance of the Contagious Diseases (Animals) Act, 1869. The Act was passed merely for sanitary purposes, in order to prevent animals in a state of infectious disease from communicating it to other animals with which they might come in contact. Under the authority of that Act, certain orders were made; amongst others, an order by which any ship bringing sheep or cattle from any foreign port to ports in Great Britain is to have the place occupied by such animals divided into pens of certain dimensions, and the floor of such pens furnished with battens or footholds. The object of this order is to prevent animals from being overcrowded, and so brought into a condition in which the disease guarded against would be likely to be developed. This regulation has been neglected, and the question is, whether the loss, which we must assume to have been caused by that neglect, entitles the plaintiffs to maintain an action.

The argument of the defendant is, that the Act has imposed penalties to secure the observance of its provisions, and that, according to the general rule, the remedy prescribed by the statute must be pursued; that although, when penalties are imposed for the violation of a statutory duty, a person aggrieved by its violation may sometimes maintain an action for the damage so caused, that must be in cases where the object of the statute is to confer a benefit on individuals, and to protect them against the evil consequences which the statute was designed to prevent, and which have in fact ensued; but that if the object is not to protect individuals against the consequences which have in fact ensued, it is otherwise; that if, therefore, by reason of the precautions in question not having been taken, the plaintiffs had sustained that damage against which it was intended to secure them, an action would lie, but that when the damage is of such a nature as was not contemplated at all by the statute, and as to which it was not intended to confer any benefit on the plaintiffs, they cannot maintain an action founded on the neglect. The principle may be well illustrated by the case put in argument of a breach by a railway company of its duty to erect a gate on a level crossing, and to keep the gate closed except when the crossing is being actually and properly used. The object of the precaution is to prevent injury from being sustained through animals or vehicles being upon the line at unseasonable times; and if by reason of such a breach of duty, either in not erecting the gate, or in not keeping it closed, a person attempts to cross with a carriage at an improper time, and injury ensues to a passenger, no doubt an action would lie against the railway company, because the intention of the legislature was that, by the erection of the gates and by their being kept closed individuals should be protected against accidents of their description. And if we could see that it was the object, or among the objects of this Act, that the owners of sheep and cattle coming from a foreign port should be protected by the means described against the danger of their property being washed overboard, or lost by the perils of the sea, the present action would be within the principle.

But, looking at the Act, it is perfectly clear that its provisions were all enacted with a totally different view: there was no purpose, direct or indirect, to protect against such damage; but, as is recited in the preamble, the Act is directed against the possibility of sheep or cattle being exposed to disease on their way to this country. The preamble recites that "it is expedient to confer on Her Majesty's most honorable Privy Council power to take such measures as may appear from time to time necessary to prevent the introduction into Great Britain of contagious or infectious diseases among cattle, sheep, or other animals, by prohibiting or regulating the importation of foreign animals," and also to provide against the "spreading" of such diseases in Great Britain. * * * That being so, if by reason of the default in question the plaintiffs' sheep had been overcrowded, or had been caused unnecessary suffering, and so had arrived in this country in a state of disease[,] I do not say that they might not have maintained this action. But the damage complained of here is something totally apart from the object of the Act of Parliament, and it is in accordance with all the authorities to say that the action is not maintainable.

POTTS v. FIDELITY FRUIT & PRODUCE CO.

Court of Appeals of Georgia, 1983.
165 Ga.App. 546, 301 S.E.2d 903.

BANKE, JUDGE.

The appellant sued to recover for personal injuries which he allegedly sustained when he was bitten by a spider while unloading bananas from a truck. The incident occurred during the course of his employment with Colonial Stores. The defendants are the local distributor of the bananas, Fidelity Fruit and Produce Co., Inc., and the transporter, Refrigerated Transport Co., Inc. Liability was originally predicated both on ordinary negligence and negligence per se under the Georgia Food Act, OCGA §§ 26–2–20 et seq. However, the appellant has since conceded that the evidence would not sustain a finding of ordinary negligence. This appeal is from a grant of summary judgment in favor of Fidelity Fruit and Produce Co., Inc., as to the negligence per se claim, based on a determination that the appellant is not among the class of persons whom the Georgia Food Act was designed to protect.

In determining whether the violation of a statute or ordinance is negligence per se as to a particular person, it is necessary to examine the purposes of the legislation and decide (1) whether the injured person falls within the class of persons it was intended to protect and (2) whether the harm complained of was the harm it was intended to guard against. Having examined the provisions of the Georgia Food Act, we agree fully with the following analysis made by the trial court: "Clearly, the Act is a consumer protection act, designed not to render the workplace a safe environment, but to prevent the sale and distribution of adulterated or misbranded foods to consumers. While safety in the workplace, and compensation for injuries arising out of work activities, are indeed matters of contemporary concern, they are the subject of other legislative enactments on both the state and federal level." Because the appellant's alleged injuries did not arise incident to his consumption of the bananas, we hold that the trial court was correct in concluding that the Act affords him no basis for recovery.

Judgment affirmed.

NOTE

The test for negligence per se is the following: (1) there must be a statute which prescribes certain actions or defines a standard of conduct, either explicitly or implicitly, (2) the defendant must violate the statute, (3) the plaintiff must be in the class of persons sought to be protected by the statute, and (4) the harm or injury to the plaintiff must generally be of the type the legislature through the statute sought to prevent.

Archibeque v. Homrich, 88 N.M. 527, 543 P.2d 820, 825 (1975).

Generally, violation of a statutory duty is negligence per se. However, in order to establish a violation the statute must have enough specificity to establish a standard of conduct. * * * Section 562A.15(1)(d) does not define what constitutes a good and safe working condition in a furnace, nor does it define adequate maintenance for a furnace. It merely indicates that the landlord shall maintain heating appliances in a safe and working order. The benefit of requiring an absolute and specific standard in a statute before imposing negligence per se is that those who have a duty under the statute can conform their behavior accordingly. This statute does not contain a specific standard of conduct from which a fact finder could find a violation. Therefore we find the trial court did not err when it refused to submit Struve's negligence-per-se theory to the jury.

Struve v. Payvandi, 740 N.W.2d 436, 442–43 (Iowa App. 2007).

MARTIN v. HERZOG
Court of Appeals of New York, 1920.
228 N.Y. 164, 126 N.E. 814.

CARDOZO, JUDGE.

The action is one to recover damages for injuries resulting in death. Plaintiff and her husband, while driving toward Tarrytown in a buggy on the night of August 21, 1915, were struck by the defendant's automobile coming in the opposite direction. They were thrown to the ground, and the man was killed. At the point of the collision the highway makes a curve. The car was rounding the curve, when suddenly it came upon the buggy, emerging, the defendant tells us, from the gloom. Negligence is charged against the defendant, the driver of the car, in that he did not keep to the right of the center of the highway. Highway Law, § 286, subd. 3, and section 332 (Consol.Laws, c. 25). Negligence is charged against the plaintiff's intestate, the driver of the wagon, in that he was traveling without lights. Highway Law, § 329a, as amended by Laws 1915, c. 367. There is no evidence that the defendant was moving at an excessive speed. There is none of any defect in the equipment of his car. The beam of light from his lamps pointed to the right as the wheels of his car turned along the curve toward the left; and, looking in the direction of the plaintiff's approach, he was peering into the shadow. The case against him must stand, therefore, if at all, upon the divergence of his course from the center of the highway. The jury found him delinquent and his victim blameless. The Appellate Division reversed * * *.

We agree with the Appellate Division that the charge to the jury was erroneous and misleading. The case was tried on the assumption that the hour had arrived when lights were due. It was argued on the same assumption in this court. In such circumstances, it is not important whether the hour might have been made a question for the jury. A controversy put out of the case by the parties is not to be put into it by us. We say this by way of preface to our review of the contested rulings. In the body of the charge the trial judge said that the jury could consider the absence of light "in determining whether the plaintiff's intestate was guilty of contributory negligence in failing to have a light upon the buggy as provided by law. I do not mean to say that the absence of light necessarily makes him negligent, but it is a fact for your consideration." The defendant requested a ruling that the absence of a light on the plaintiff's vehicle was "prima facie evidence of contributory negligence." This request was refused, and the jury were again instructed that they might consider the absence of lights as some evidence of negligence, but that it was not conclusive evidence. The plaintiff then requested a charge that "the fact that the plaintiff's intestate was driving without a light is not negligence in itself," and to this the court acceded. The defendant saved his rights by appropriate exceptions.

We think the unexcused omission of the statutory signals is more than some evidence of negligence. It is negligence in itself. Lights are intended for the guidance and protection of other travelers on the highway. By the very terms of the hypothesis, to omit, willfully or heedlessly, the safeguards prescribed by law for the benefit of another that he may be preserved in life or limb, is to fall short of the standard of diligence to which those who live in organized society are under a duty to conform. That, we think, is now the established rule in this state. Whether the omission of an absolute duty, not willfully or heedlessly, but through unavoidable accident, is also to be characterized as negligence, is a question of nomenclature into which we need not enter, for it does not touch the case before us. There may be times, when, if jural niceties are to be preserved, the two wrongs, negligence and breach of statutory duty, must be kept distinct in speech and thought.

In the conditions here present they come together and coalesce. A rule less rigid has been applied where the one who complains of the omission is not a member of the class for whose protection the safeguard is designed. Some relaxation there has also been where the safeguard is prescribed by local ordinance, and not by statute. Courts have been reluctant to hold that the police regulations of boards and councils and other subordinate officials create rights of action beyond the specific penalties imposed. This has led them to say that the violation of a statute is negligence, and the violation of a like ordinance is only evidence of negligence. An ordinance, however, like a statute, is a law within its sphere of operation, and so the distinction has not escaped criticism. Whether it has become too deeply rooted to be abandoned, even if it be thought illogical, is a question not now before us. * * *

In the case at hand, we have an instance of the admitted violation of a statute intended for the protection of travelers on the highway, of whom the defendant at the time was one. Yet the jurors were instructed in effect that they were at liberty in their discretion to treat the omission of lights either as innocent or as culpable. They were allowed to "consider the default as lightly or gravely" as they would (Thomas, J., in the court below). They might as well have been told that they could use a like discretion in holding a master at fault for the omission of a safety appliance prescribed by positive law for the protection of a workman. Jurors have no dispensing power, by which they may relax the duty that one traveler on the highway owes under the statute to another. It is error to tell them that they have. The omission of these lights was a wrong, and, being wholly unexcused, was also a negligent wrong. No license should have been conceded to the triers of the facts to find it anything else.

We must be on our guard, however, against confusing the question of negligence with that of the causal connection between the negligence and the injury. A defendant who travels without lights is not to pay damages for his fault, unless the absence of lights is the cause of the disaster. A plaintiff who travels without them is not to forfeit the right to damages, unless the absence of lights is at least a contributing cause of the disaster. To say that conduct is negligence is not to say that it is always contributory negligence. "Proof of negligence in the air, so to speak, will not do." Pollock Torts (10th Ed.) p. 472.

We think, however, that evidence of a collision occurring more than an hour after sundown between a car and an unseen buggy, proceeding without lights, is evidence from which a causal connection may be inferred between the collision and the lack of signals. If nothing else is shown to break the connection, we have a case, prima facie sufficient, of negligence contributing to the result.

* * *

Here, on the undisputed facts, lack of vision, whether excusable or not, was the cause of the disaster. The defendant may have been negligent in swerving from the center of the road; but he did not run into the buggy purposely, nor was he driving while intoxicated, nor was he going at such a reckless speed that warning would of necessity have been futile. Nothing of the kind is shown. The collision was due to his failure to see at a time when sight should have been aroused and guided by the statutory warnings. Some explanation of the effect to be given to the absence of those warnings, if the plaintiff failed to prove that other lights on the car or the highway took their place as equivalents, should have been put before the jury. The explanation was asked for and refused.

We are persuaded that the tendency of the charge, and of all the rulings, following it, was to minimize unduly, in the minds of the triers of the facts, the gravity of the decedent's fault. Errors may not be ignored as unsubstantial, when they tend to such an outcome. A statute designed for the protection of human life is not to be brushed aside as a form of words, its commands reduced to the level of cautions, and the duty to obey attenuated into an option to conform.

The order of the Appellate Division should be affirmed, and judgment absolute directed * * * in favor of the defendant * * *.

HOGAN, J., dissenting.

* * *

NOTES

1. When giving effect to a statute, courts do not distinguish between cases involving the plaintiff's negligence and cases involving the defendant's negligence.

Several courts have held, contrary to *Martin*, that violation of statute is merely evidence of negligence, which the jury can consider.

2. The statute in *Martin* did not address its effect on tort liability. Like most traffic statutes, it merely imposed a modest fine for violation. It is highly unlikely that the legislature ever thought about the issue of tort liability. Thus, the question for courts is the effect of such statutes in the absence of clear legislative intent. In a few situations, however, the legislature might actually address the effect of the statute on tort liability, or the court might be able to ascertain the legislative intent from the circumstances. In that event, the legislature's decision about the effect of the statute controls.

3. Even in states that follow *Martin* and hold that unexcused violation of statute normally is conclusive on the issue of breach, violation of statute does not conclusively establish liability. The other elements of tort liability are still open for dispute. Thus, in *Martin,* Justice Cardozo still required proof that the plaintiff's failure to have lights was a cause of the accident. Similarly, in a case in which a defendant violates a statute, the defendant can still claim that the plaintiff was contributorily negligent (unless, of course, the statute expressly or impliedly provides a contrary rule).

4. Compliance with a statutory provision is usually just evidence of reasonable care, not conclusive on the issue of reasonable care. See, e.g., Christou v. Arlington Park–Washington Park Race Tracks Corp., 104 Ill. App.3d 257, 60 Ill.Dec. 21, 432 N.E.2d 920 (1982).

TEDLA v. ELLMAN

Court of Appeals of New York, 1939.
280 N.Y. 124, 19 N.E.2d 987.

LEHMAN, JUDGE.

While walking along a highway, Anna Tedla and her brother, John Bachek, were struck by a passing automobile, operated by the defendant Ellman. She was injured and Bachek was killed. Bachek was a deaf-mute. His occupation was collecting and selling junk. His sister, Mrs. Tedla, was engaged in the same occupation. They often picked up junk at the incinerator of the village of Islip. At the time of the accident they were walking along "Sunrise Highway" and wheeling baby carriages containing junk and wood which they had picked up at the incinerator. It was about six o'clock, or a little earlier, on a Sunday evening in December. Darkness had already set in. Bachek was carrying a lighted lantern, or, at least, there is testimony to that effect. The jury found that the accident was due solely to the negligence of the operator of the automobile. The defendants do not, upon this appeal, challenge the finding of negligence on the part of the operator. They maintain, however, that Mrs. Tedla and her brother were guilty of contributory negligence as matter of law.

Sunrise Highway, at the place of the accident, consists of two roadways, separated by a grass plot. There are no footpaths along the highway and the center grass plot was soft. It is not unlawful for a pedestrian, wheeling a baby carriage, to use the roadway under such circumstances, but a pedestrian using the roadway is bound to exercise such care for his safety as a reasonably prudent person would use. The Vehicle and Traffic Law (Consol.Laws, c. 71) provides that "Pedestrians walking or remaining on the paved portion, or traveled part of a roadway shall be subject to, and comply with, the rules governing vehicles, with respect to meeting and turning out, except that such pedestrians shall keep to the left of the center line thereof, and turn to their left instead of right side thereof, so as to permit all vehicles passing them in either direction to pass on their right. Such pedestrians shall not be subject to the rules governing vehicles as to giving signals." Section 85, subd. 6. Mrs. Tedla and her brother did not observe the statutory rule, and at the time of the accident were proceeding in easterly direction on the east bound or right-hand roadway. The defendants moved to dismiss the complaint on the ground, among others, that violation of the statutory rule constitutes contributory negligence as matter of law. They did not, in the courts below, urge that any negligence in other respect of Mrs. Tedla or her brother bars a recovery. The trial judge left to the jury the question whether failure to observe the statutory rule was a proximate cause of the accident; he left to the jury no question of other fault or negligence on the part of Mrs. Tedla or her brother, and the defendants did not request that any other question be submitted. Upon this appeal, the only question presented is whether, as matter of law, disregard of the statutory rule that pedestrians shall keep to the left of the center line of a highway constitutes contributory negligence which bars any recovery by the plaintiff.

Vehicular traffic can proceed safely and without recurrent traffic tangles only if vehicles observe accepted rules of the road. Such rules, and especially the rule that all vehicles proceeding in one direction must keep to a designated part or side of the road—in this country the right-hand side—have been dictated by necessity and formulated by custom. The general use of automobiles has increased in unprecedented degree the number and speed of vehicles. Control of traffic becomes an increasingly difficult problem. Rules of the road, regulating the rights and duties of those who use highways, have, in consequence, become increasingly important. The Legislature no longer leaves to custom the formulation of such rules. Statutes now codify, define, supplement, and, where changing conditions suggest change in rule, even change rules of the road which formerly rested on custom. Custom and common sense have always dictated that vehicles should have the right of way over pedestrians and that pedestrians should walk along the edge of a highway so that they might step aside for passing vehicles with least danger to themselves and least obstruction to vehicular traffic. Otherwise, perhaps, no customary rule of the road was observed by pedestrians with the same uniformity as by vehicles; though, in general, they probably followed, until recently, the same rules as vehicles.

Pedestrians are seldom a source of danger or serious obstruction to vehicles and when horse-drawn vehicles were common they seldom injured pedestrians using a highway with reasonable care, unless the horse became unmanageable or the driver was grossly negligent or guilty of willful wrong. Swift-moving motor vehicles, it was soon recognized, do endanger the safety of pedestrians crossing highways, and it is imperative that there the relative rights and duties of pedestrians and of vehicles should be understood and observed. The Legislature in the first five subdivisions of section 85 of the Vehicle and Traffic Law has provided regulations to govern the conduct of pedestrians and of drivers of vehicles when a pedestrian is crossing a road. Until by chapter 114 of the Laws of 1933, it adopted subdivision 6 of section 85, quoted above, there was no special statutory rule for pedestrians walking along a highway. Then for the first time it reversed, for pedestrians, the rule established for vehicles by immemorial custom, and provided that pedestrians shall keep to the left of the center line of a highway.

The plaintiffs showed by the testimony of a State policeman that "there were very few cars going east" at the time of the accident, but that going west there was "very heavy Sunday night traffic." Until the recent adoption of the new statutory rule for pedestrians, ordinary prudence would have dictated that pedestrians should not expose themselves to the danger of walking along the roadway upon which the "very heavy Sunday night traffic" was proceeding when they could walk in comparative safety along a roadway used by very few cars. It is said that now, by force of the statutory rule, pedestrians are guilty of contributory negligence as matter of law when they use the safer roadway, unless that roadway is left of the center of the road. Disregard of the statutory rule of the road and observance of a rule based on immemorial custom, it is said, is negligence which as matter of law is a proximate cause of the accident, though observance of the statutory rule might, under the circumstances of the particular case, expose a pedestrian to serious danger from which he would be free if he followed the rule that had been established by custom. If that be true, then the Legislature has decreed that pedestrians must observe the general rule of conduct which it has prescribed for their safety even under circumstances where observance would subject them to unusual risk; that pedestrians are to be charged with negligence as matter of law for acting as prudence dictates. It is unreasonable to ascribe to the Legislature an intention that the statute should have so extraordinary a result, and the courts may not give to a statute an effect not intended by the Legislature.

The Legislature, when it enacted the statute, presumably knew that this court and the courts of other jurisdictions had established the general principle that omission by a plaintiff of a safeguard, prescribed by statute, against a recognized danger, constitutes negligence as matter of law which bars recovery for damages caused by incidence of the danger for which the safeguard was prescribed. The principle has been formulated in the Restatement of the Law of Torts: "A plaintiff who has violated a legislative enactment designed to prevent a certain type of dangerous situation is barred from recovery for a harm caused by a violation of the statute if, but only if, the harm was sustained by reason of a situation of that type." § 469. So where a plaintiff failed to place lights upon a vehicle, as required by statute, this court has said: "we think the unexcused omission of the statutory signals is more than some evidence of negligence. It is negligence in itself. Lights are intended for the guidance and protection of other travelers on the highway. Highway Law (Consol.Laws, c. 25) § 329–a. By the very terms of the hypothesis, to omit, willfully or heedlessly, the safeguards prescribed by law for the benefit of another that he may be preserved in life or limb, is to fall short of the standard of diligence to which those who live in organized society are under a duty to conform. That, we think, is now the established rule in this State." Martin v. Herzog, 228 N.Y. 164, 168, 126 N.E. 814, 815, per Cardozo, J. The appellants lean heavily upon that and kindred cases and the principle established by them.

The analogy is, however, incomplete. The "established rule" should not be weakened either by subtle distinctions or by extension beyond its letter or spirit into a field where "by the very terms of the hypothesis" it can have no proper application. At times the indefinite and flexible standard of care of the traditional reasonably prudent man may be, in the opinion of the Legislature, an insufficient measure of the care which should be exercised to guard against a recognized danger; at times, the duty, imposed by custom, that no man shall use what is his to the harm of others provides insufficient safeguard for the preservation of the life or limb or property of others. Then the Legislature may by statute prescribe additional safeguards and may define duty and standard of care in rigid terms; and when the Legislature has spoken, the standard of the care required is no longer what the reasonably prudent man would do under the circumstances but what the Legislature has commanded. That is the rule established by the courts and "by the very terms of the hypothesis" the rule applies where the Legislature has prescribed safeguards "for the benefit of another that he may be preserved in life or limb." In that field debate as to whether the safeguards so prescribed are reasonably necessary is ended by the legislative fiat. Obedience to that fiat cannot add to the danger, even assuming that the prescribed safeguards are not reasonably necessary and where the legislative anticipation of dangers is realized and harm results through heedless or willful omission of the prescribed safeguard, injury flows from wrong and the wrongdoer is properly held responsible for the consequent damages.

The statute upon which the defendants rely is of different character. It does not prescribe additional safeguards which pedestrians must provide for the preservation of the life or limb or property of others, or even of themselves, nor does it impose upon pedestrians a higher standard of care. What the statute does provide is rules of the road to be observed by pedestrians and by vehicles, so that all those who use the road may know how they and others should proceed, at least under usual circumstances. A general rule of conduct—and, specifically, a rule of the road—may accomplish its intended purpose under usual conditions, but, when the unusual occurs, strict observance may defeat the purpose of the rule and produce catastrophic results.

Negligence is failure to exercise the care required by law. Where a statute defines the standard of care and the safeguards required to meet a recognized danger, then, as we have said, no other measure may be applied in determining whether a person has carried out the duty of care imposed by law. Failure to observe the standard imposed by statute is negligence, as matter of law. On the other hand, where a statutory general rule of conduct fixes no definite standard of care which would under all circumstances tend to protect life, limb or property but merely codifies or supplements a common-law rule, which has always been subject to limitations and exceptions; or where the statutory rule of conduct regulates conflicting rights and obligations in [a] manner calculated to promote public convenience and safety, then the statute, in the absence of clear language to the contrary, should not be construed as intended to wipe out the limitations and exceptions which judicial decisions have attached to the common-law duty; nor should it be construed as an inflexible command that the general rule of conduct intended to prevent accidents must be followed even under conditions when observance might cause accidents. We may assume reasonably that the Legislature directed pedestrians to keep to the left of the center of the road because that would cause them to face traffic approaching in that lane and would enable them to care for their own safety better than if the traffic approached them from the rear.

We cannot assume reasonably that the Legislature intended that a statute enacted for the preservation of the life and limb of pedestrians must be observed when observance would subject them to more imminent danger.

* * *

Judgment affirmed.

O'BRIEN and FINCH, JJ., dissent on the authority of Martin v. Herzog * * *.

NOTE

The doctrine of negligence per se applies only to "unexcused" violations. The Third Restatement § 15 recognizes five excuses, including the one illustrated by *Tedla* ("the actor's compliance with the statute would involve a greater risk of physical harm to the actor or to others than noncompliance"). Another is "the actor exercises reasonable care in attempting to comply with the statute," illustrated by Krebs v. Rubsam, 91 N.J.L. 426, 104 A. 83 (1918) (plaintiff's decedent fell in an unlighted stairway in defendant's building; the light, required by a statute, had been "extinguished by the unauthorized act of a third person" very shortly before the fall) and Freund v. DeBuse, 264 Or. 447, 506 P.2d 491 (1973) (brake failure despite reasonable maintenance by vehicle owner). Another is infancy, illustrated by Morby v. Rogers, 122 Utah 540, 252 P.2d 231 (1953) (thirteen-year-old bicyclist who turned without giving a signal was not thereby contributorily negligent as a matter of law; child standard of care applied).

ZERBY v. WARREN

Supreme Court of Minnesota, 1973.
297 Minn. 134, 210 N.W.2d 58.

KELLY, JUSTICE.

* * *

[On August 31, 1969, Steven Zerby, a 14–year–old minor, and Randy Rieken, age 13, went together to the Coast-to-Coast Store in Austin, Minnesota. The store was owned by Chester Warren, who employed Robert Dieke as a clerk in the store.] Rieken purchased two pint containers of Weldwood Contact Cement at the store from Deike, who sold it within the course and scope of his employment as a clerk in the store. The glue contained toluene and was not a part of a packaged kit for construction of a model automobile, airplane, or similar item. At the time of the sale, neither defendant Warren nor Deike were aware that the sale was in violation of Minn. St. 145.38, which had become effective on July 1, 1969.

After Rieken had purchased the glue, he and [Zerby] left the shopping center and within a few hours [intentionally] inhaled the fumes from the glue. [Zerby died as a result of sniffing the glue. The fumes] had an injurious effect on his central nervous system, causing him to fall into a creek and drown. * * *

[Zerby's family brought a wrongful death action against Warren and Deike. Warren and Deike then filed a third-party action against Reiken, seeking contribution. Plaintiffs then amended their complaint to assert a claim against Reiken. All defendants pleaded the affirmative defenses of comparative negligence and assumption of risk by Zerby.

[The trial judge made a pre-trial ruling that Minn. Stat. 145.38 imposed absolute liability on Warren and Deike and that neither comparative negligence nor assumption of risk would be available as defenses. As a result of those rulings, the parties waived a jury trial and submitted the matter on stipulated facts. The trial judge ordered judgment against Warren and Deike and disallowed the third-party claim. Warren and Deike have appeal from the denial of their motion for JNOV or a new trial.]

* * *

In 1969, the Minnesota Legislature recognized the potential harm which could result to minors from the sniffing of glue and enacted provisions to control its sale and use. Minn. St. 145.38 provides:

(1) No person shall sell to a person under 19 years of age any glue or cement containing toluene, benzene, zylene, or other aromatic hydrocarbon solvents, or any similar substance which the state board of health has * * * declared to have potential for abuse and toxic effects on the central nervous system. This section does not apply if the glue or cement is contained in a packaged kit for the construction of a model automobile, airplane, or similar item.

(2) No person shall openly display for sale any item prohibited in subdivision 1.

Minn. St. 145.39 reads:

(1) No person under 19 years of age shall use or possess any glue, cement or any other substance containing toluene, benzene, zylene, or other aromatic hydrocarbon solvents, or any similar substance which the state board of health has * * * declared to have potential for abuse and toxic effects on the central nervous system with the intent of inducing intoxication, excitement or stupefaction of the central nervous system, except under the direction and supervision of a medical doctor.

(2). No person shall intentionally aid another in violation of subdivision 1.

A violation of these statutory provisions is a misdemeanor. Minn. St. 145.40.

I.

The threshold question on this appeal is the nature of tort liability which results from a violation of Minn. St. 145.38. The nature of tort liability created by a statutory violation was considered in the leading case of Dart v. Pure Oil Co., 223 Minn. 526, 27 N.W.2d 555 (1947). That case

involved an action for wrongful death resulting from the explosion of a
mixture of gasoline and kerosene sold in violation of a statute. After
examining many cases, we stated (223 Minn. 534, 27 N.W.2d 559):

> * * * [I]t has been the long-standing rule of this court, *with certain
> exceptions,* that the violation of a statutory standard of conduct does
> not differ from ordinary negligence. (Italics supplied.)

The only difference between a statutorily imposed duty of care and a duty
of care under common law is that the duty imposed by statute is fixed, so
its breach ordinarily constitutes conclusive evidence of negligence, or
negligence per se, while the measure of legal duty in the absence of statute
is determined under common-law principles. After thus establishing the
general rule, the court considered whether the *Dart* case fell within an
exception (223 Minn. 535, 27 N.W.2d 560):

> * * * This brings up the question whether this statute was intended
> for the protection of the public as a whole or for the protection of a
> limited class of persons from their inability to protect themselves.
> There are exceptional statutes which do not permit the defense of
> contributory negligence. * * *
>
>   * * *
>
> The principle of these so-called exceptional statutes is to impose strict
> or *absolute* liability upon the defendant, which is greater than ordi-
> nary negligence liability, by placing upon him the entire responsibility
> for any injury which may result from their violation. (Italics supplied.)

In order to create absolute liability, it must be found that the
legislative purpose of such a statute is to protect a limited class of persons
from their own inexperience, lack of judgment, inability to protect themselves or to resist pressure, or tendency toward negligence. In instances
such as the present case, this legislative intent can be deduced from the
character of the statute and the background of the social problem and the
particular hazard at which the statute is directed.

Types of statutes which would be exceptions to the general rule
include (1) child labor statutes; (2) statutes for the protection of intoxicated persons; and (3) statutes prohibiting sale of dangerous articles to
minors. Obviously, the most direct analogy to the present case is the last-
named type of statute. The obvious legislative purpose of § 145.38 is to
protect minors unable to exercise self-protective care from harm resulting
from sniffing the fumes of glue. This legislative policy inherent in the
statute makes one who violates its provisions entirely responsible for
damages or deaths which are the direct result of the illegal sale. It is one
of the types of statutes referred to by the *Dart* decision as "exceptional
statutes" and therefore violation of its provisions creates absolute liability
for resulting harm.

II.

Having thus concluded that Minn. St. 145.38 is one of these exceptional statutes which impose absolute liability or liability per se upon one

who violates its provisions, we hold that it was proper for the trial court not to allow the defenses of comparative contributory negligence and assumption of risk. If these defenses were permitted, the evident purpose of such statutes would be defeated. Consequently, the legislature must have intended that no defense would displace the responsibility imposed by the statute.

* * *

Defendants [argue] that the enactment of a comparative negligence statute in Minnesota requires the negligence of the parties to be compared in the present case. They argue that the former need to carve exceptions to the general rules of contributory negligence to avoid harsh results is not presently needed under the more equitable comparative negligence statute. However, the adoption of a comparative negligence statute did not create liability where none existed before. Because there can be no contributory negligence as a matter of law when the statute is designed to protect persons from their inability to protect themselves, the adoption of comparative negligence did not alter the exclusion of defenses.

Defendants also argue that decedent's contemporaneous violation of Minn.St. 145.39, which prohibits possession of glue by a minor with the intent to sniff it, should bar his recovery. They cite no cases which support this contention and we must reject it for the same reasons other defenses to the violation of these statutes are barred.

III.

While defendants do not question that the sale of the glue was a direct cause of decedent's death, they argue that the conduct of Randy Rieken in furnishing the glue to him and participating with him in sniffing its fumes in violation of § 145.39, subd. 2, quoted above, was a concurrent cause of the death. For this reason, it is contended that the trial court erred in disallowing defendants' contribution claim against Rieken.

* * *

In the present case, the conduct of Rieken in furnishing the glue to decedent and participating with him in inhaling its fumes was not independent of the original wrongful sale of the glue by defendants. Rather, the sale of the glue set the stage for the subsequent conduct of the minors. While every accident results from a sequence of occurrences or causes, the law disregards all but the substantial. We therefore conclude that the contribution claim against Rieken was properly disallowed because his conduct was merely a reaction to the original wrongful act of defendants and therefore not a proximate cause. * * *

It should not be forgotten that the sale of the glue to Rieken was in violation of Minn. St. 145.38 and that Rieken as a minor was also a member of a limited class of persons that the legislature intended to protect from their inexperience, lack of judgment, and tendency toward negligence. To permit contribution would defeat this legislative purpose.

* * *

Affirmed.

E. RES IPSA LOQUITUR

COLMENARES VIVAS v. SUN ALLIANCE INSURANCE CO.

United States Court of Appeals, First Circuit, 1986.
807 F.2d 1102.

BOWNES, CIRCUIT JUDGE.

Appellants are plaintiffs in a diversity action to recover damages for injuries they suffered in an accident while riding an escalator. After the parties had presented their evidence, the defendants moved for and were granted a directed verdict. The court held that there was no evidence of negligence and that the doctrine of res ipsa loquitur, which would raise a presumption of negligence, did not apply. We reverse the directed verdict and remand the case to the district court because we hold that res ipsa loquitur does apply.

* * *

The relevant facts are not in dispute. On February 12, 1984, Jose Domingo Colmenares Vivas and his wife, Dilia Arreaza de Colmenares, arrived at the Luis Munoz Marin International Airport in Puerto Rico. They took an escalator on their way to the Immigration and Customs checkpoint on the second level. Mrs. Colmenares was riding the escalator on the right-hand side, holding the moving handrail, one step ahead of her husband. When the couple was about halfway up the escalator, the handrail stopped moving, but the steps continued the ascent, causing Mrs. Colmenares to lose her balance. Her husband grabbed her from behind with both hands and prevented her from falling, but in doing so, he lost his balance and tumbled down the stairs. Mr. and Mrs. Colmenares filed a direct action against the Sun Alliance Insurance Company (Sun Alliance), who is the liability insurance carrier for the airport's owner and operator, the Puerto Rico Ports Authority (Ports Authority). Sun Alliance brought a third-party contractual action against Westinghouse Electric Corporation (Westinghouse) based on a maintenance contract that required Westinghouse to inspect, maintain, adjust, repair, and replace parts as needed for the escalator and handrails, and to keep the escalator in a safe operating condition.

* * *

Sun Alliance moved for a directed verdict [at the close of the plaintiff's evidence]. Appellants argued in opposition that the evidence presented was sufficient to show negligence and, in the alternative, that res ipsa loquitur should be applied to raise an inference that the Ports Authority had been negligent. At this point the court decided to allow the trial to continue. Sun Alliance and Westinghouse submitted their case on the basis of the testimony already presented and Sun Alliance renewed its motion for a directed verdict. After hearing the parties' arguments, the court ruled that there was no evidence that the Ports Authority had been negligent, and that the case could not go to the jury based on res ipsa loquitur because at least one of the requirements for its application—that the injury-causing instrumentality was within the exclusive control of the defendant—was not met.

* * *

Under Puerto Rico law, three requirements must be met for res ipsa loquitur ("the thing speaks for itself") to apply: "(1) the accident must be of a kind which ordinarily does not occur in the absence of someone's negligence; (2) it must be caused by an agency or instrumentality within the exclusive control of defendant; [and] (3) it must not be due to any voluntary action on the part of plaintiff." If all three requirements are met, the jury may infer that the defendant was negligent even though there is no direct evidence to that effect.

A. *The First Requirement: Inference of Negligence*

The first requirement that must be met for res ipsa loquitur to apply is that "the accident must be such that in the light of ordinary experience it gives rise to an inference that someone has been negligent." It is not clear to us whether the district court decided that this requirement was met, although the court did suggest that it was giving the benefit of the doubt on this question to the appellants. We hold that this requirement was met because an escalator handrail probably would not stop suddenly while the escalator continues moving unless someone had been negligent.

This requirement would not be met if appellants had shown nothing more than that they had been injured on the escalator, because based on this fact alone it would not be likely that someone other than the appellants had been negligent. Here, it was not disputed that the handrail malfunctioned and stopped suddenly, an event that foreseeably could cause riders to lose their balance and get injured. Thus, the evidence gave rise to an inference that someone probably had been negligent in operating or maintaining the escalator, and the first requirement for the application of res ipsa loquitur was met.

B. *The Second Requirement: Exclusive Control*

The second requirement for res ipsa loquitur to apply is that the injury-causing instrumentality—in this case, the escalator—must have been within the exclusive control of the defendant. The district court found that this requisite was not met, despite the parties' stipulation that "[t]he escalator in question is property of and is under the control of the Puerto Rico Ports Authority." We agree that this stipulation was not by itself enough to satisfy the res ipsa loquitur requirement. It did not exclude the possibility that someone else also had control over the escalator; indeed, the stipulation said that Westinghouse maintained the escalator. We hold, however, that the Ports Authority effectively had exclusive control over the escalator because the authority in control of a public area has a nondelegable duty to maintain its facilities in a safe condition.

Few courts have required that control literally be "exclusive." The Supreme Court, reviewing a case in which this court applied the exclusive control requirement literally, said that the question "really is not whether the application of the rule relied on fits squarely into some judicial definition, rigidly construed," because such an approach unduly restricts "the jury's power to draw inferences from facts." The exclusive control requirement, then, should not be so narrowly construed as to take from the jury the ability to infer that a defendant was negligent when the defendant was responsible for the injury-causing instrumentality, even if someone else might also have been responsible. The purpose of the requirement is not to restrict the application of the res ipsa loquitur inference to cases in which there is only one actor who dealt with the instrumentality, but rather "to eliminate the possibility that the accident was caused by a *third party.*" It is not necessary, therefore, for the defendant to have had actual physical control; it is enough that the defendant, and not a third party, was ultimately responsible for the instrumentality. Thus, res ipsa loquitur applies even if the defendant shares responsibility with another, or if the defendant is responsible for the instrumentality even though someone else had physical control over it. It follows that a defendant charged with a nondelegable duty of care to maintain an instrumentality in a safe condition effectively has exclusive control over it for the purposes of applying res ipsa loquitur. Unless the duty is delegable, the res ipsa loquitur inference is not defeated if the defendant had shifted physical control to an agent or contracted with another to carry out its responsibilities.

We hold that the Ports Authority could not delegate its duty to maintain safe escalators. There are no set criteria for determining whether a duty is nondelegable; the critical question is whether the responsibility is so important to the community that it should not be transferred to another. The Ports Authority was charged with such a responsibility. It was created for a public purpose, which included the operation and management of the airport. A concomitant of this authority is the duty to keep the facilities it operates in a reasonably safe condition. The public is entitled to rely on the Ports Authority—not its agents or contractors—to see that this is done. * * *

* * * We hold, therefore, that the district court erred in ruling that the exclusive control requirement was not met.

C. *The Third Requirement: The Plaintiffs' Actions*

The third requirement that must be met for res ipsa loquitur to apply is that the accident must not have been due to the plaintiff's voluntary actions. The district court found, and we agree, that there was no evidence that Mr. and Mrs. Colmenares caused the accident. Indeed, there is no indication that they did anything other than attempt to ride the escalator in the ordinary manner. Therefore, we hold that all three requirements were met and that the jury should have been allowed to consider whether the Ports Authority was liable based on the permissible inference of negligence raised by the application of res ipsa loquitur.

* * *

Reversed in part, affirmed in part.* Remanded.

TORRUELLA, CIRCUIT JUDGE, dissenting.

* * * Although the majority correctly states the Puerto Rican law as to res ipsa loquitur, it overlooks well-established jurisprudence in applying that law to the circumstances of this case.

The majority concludes that the first requirement of res ipsa loquitur, i.e., inference of negligence arising from the occurrence of the accident, "was met because an escalator handrail probably would not stop suddenly while the escalator continues moving unless someone had been negligent." * * *

In my view, *solely* because the handrail stopped and Mrs. Colmenares fell, without further evidence as to why or how the handrail malfunctioned, does not give rise to an inference of *negligence* by the Ports Authority. * * *

The malfunctioning of an escalator presents [a strong] argument against the raising of an inference of negligence without additional proof as to the cause of the malfunction. Although a court can take notice that an escalator is a complicated piece of machinery, it has no basis of common knowledge for inferring that its malfunction is the result of the operator's negligence. Expert testimony is required to establish the basis for such an inference.

* * *

NOTES

1. Judge Torruella's dissent may find support in Kmart Corp. v. Bassett, 769 So.2d 282 (Ala. 2000), in which a slim (5–4) majority of the Alabama Supreme Court held that the malfunction of an automatic door at a retail store, which injured the 83–year–old disabled plaintiff, did not support an inference of probable negligence on the part of the store in the absence of supporting expert testimony.

2. Note that the Colmenareses sued the tortfeasor's insurer directly. Puerto Rico is not alone in permitting "direct actions" against the insurer. Louisiana and Wisconsin also have "direct action" statutes.

---

* The court affirmed the portion of the lower court's order refusing to allow the plaintiffs leave to amend their complaint six days before trial to add Westinghouse as a defendant. [Ed.]

3. *A res ipsa allegation should not prevent plaintiff from attempting to prove negligence the normal way.* A few courts have held that a plaintiff can rely on res ipsa loquitur only if he "is unable to allege or prove the particular act of negligence which caused the injury." Beatty v. Davis, 224 Neb. 663, 665, 400 N.W.2d 850, 852 (1987). These courts require the plaintiff to choose between proving negligence directly and relying on res ipsa loquitur.

Most courts do not put a plaintiff to such a choice, however. For example, in Newing v. Cheatham, 15 Cal.3d 351, 124 Cal.Rptr. 193, 540 P.2d 33 (1975), the plaintiff's decedent was killed when a small plane in which he was a passenger crashed on a clear day. His estate was able to introduce evidence that the pilot, whose estate was the defendant, had allowed the plane to run out of gas. The court also permitted the plaintiff to rely on res ipsa loquitur.

4. *Defendant's superior access to information is neither necessary nor sufficient for res ipsa.* In addition to the three requirements of res ipsa loquitur addressed in *Colmenares Vivas,* some courts talk about the defendant's better access to information and even the possibility that the defendant is withholding information. This suggests that res ipsa loquitur is a device to force defendants to divulge information. Notwithstanding the language, however, the defendant's having access to information about the accident does not appear to be either a necessary or sufficient predicate for res ipsa loquitur.

5. *The procedural effect of res ipsa.* Some disagreement exists on the procedural effect of res ipsa loquitur. Most courts, including the court in *Colmenares Vivas,* say that res ipsa loquitur raises a "permissive inference" of negligence, which the jury may take or reject, even if the defendant fails to offer evidence. Thus, res ipsa loquitur allows the plaintiff to get the case to the jury by avoiding a directed verdict. A few courts say that res ipsa loquitur raises a "presumption" of negligence, so that the plaintiff is entitled to a directed verdict on the issue of reasonable care if the defendant fails to come forward with evidence. See, e.g., Newing v. Cheatham, note 3, supra.

6. The concept of "nondelegable duty" is explored further in Chapter VIII.

CHAPTER IV

FACTUAL CAUSATION ISSUES

■ ■ ■

The cause-in-fact requirement is typically treated in connection with the negligence cause of action, and we are staying with that tradition. However, it is important to remember that a showing of cause in fact is equally required in intentional tort and strict liability cases. For example, recall that one of the elements of the tort of battery is that defendant must have *caused* physical contact.

As we said in the Introduction to Chapter III, the negligence cause of action has five elements: (1) existence of a duty, usually of reasonable care; (2) breach of that duty (negligence); (3) cause in fact; (4) proximate cause (scope of liability); and (5) damages. Sections A through D of this chapter address the third element—the element that requires the plaintiff to establish a factual causal connection between the defendant's complained-of conduct and the event the plaintiff identifies as harmful. (Section E addresses factual causation issues that are bound up with the assessment and awarding of damages. Further treatment of damages issues is found in Chapter VII.)

In all types of tort cases, normally the plaintiff must prove by a preponderance of the evidence—i.e., that it is more probable than not—that the defendant's substandard conduct was *a* cause of the harmful event complained of. This is typically a jury issue; it will not be decided "as a matter of law" (i.e., second guessed by the trial judge or appellate court) unless reasonable minds could not differ.

Note that the law does not require the plaintiff to prove that defendant's conduct was *the* cause of the harm. This would be an insuperable burden. As was stated in Public Citizen Health Research Group v. Young, 909 F.2d 546, 550 (D.C.Cir.1990), "[e]ver since the first cause brought the world into being, no event has had a single cause." The cause-in-fact requirement is satisfied if defendant's conduct is shown more probably than not to have been among the causes of the result the plaintiff seeks to attribute to the defendant.

Cause in fact is viewed as a bedrock requirement of the law. Some of the broad aims of tort law—compensating injured persons and deterring undesirable behavior—might at times seem to call for dispensing with the requirement in particular cases. But an overarching ideal of *corrective justice*, whereby tort law's central justification is seen in its ability to right wrongs, i.e., to restore the moral balance between injurer and injured, entails the view that the law should hold defendants liable for harms they wrongfully cause and no others.

Cause in fact is the usual name for this issue, but some of the cases refer to it as "proximate cause." In the better usage, "proximate cause" refers to a different issue, which is treated in Chapter V. Properly speaking, "proximate cause" does not refer to factual causation at all, but instead addresses the appropriate scope of responsibility for injuries concededly the factual result of negligent conduct.

A. THE BUT–FOR TEST

EAST TEXAS THEATRES, INC. v. RUTLEDGE

Supreme Court of Texas, 1970.
453 S.W.2d 466.

SMITH, JUSTICE.

This is a damage suit alleging personal injuries were sustained by Sheila Rutledge, on or about September 25, 1966, while attending a midnight movie in a theatre owned and operated by East Texas Theatres, Inc. * * * The jury found the defendant guilty of negligence in failing to remove certain unidentified "rowdy persons" from the theatre and that such negligence was a proximate cause of Sheila's injuries. Damages were assessed by the jury at $31,250.00. Based upon the jury findings, the trial court entered judgment for the plaintiffs. The Court of Civil Appeals has affirmed. We reverse the judgments of both courts and here render judgment that the plaintiffs take nothing.

The defendant presents two major questions for our decision: (1) the error of the Court of Civil Appeals in holding that there was any probative evidence of record to support the jury finding on proximate cause, and (2) the error of the Court of Civil Appeals in holding that the testimony was sufficient to prove a causal connection between the injuries alleged to have been sustained by Sheila and her subsequent complaints of chronic headache, etc. In view of our holding on the first question, it is unnecessary to pass upon the second.

A full and detailed discussion of the evidence bearing on the first question is to be found in the opinion of the Court of Civil Appeals. We briefly summarize the facts. In taking this course, we are mindful of the rule that in deciding whether there is evidence in the record in support of the jury findings, we are required to view the evidence in its most favorable light in support of the verdict.

On September 24 and the early morning of September 25, 1966, Sheila, a paying guest, was attending a special "midnight show" at the Paramount Theatre, one of the several theatres owned by the defendant.

The interior of the theatre was arranged with a lower floor and a balcony for the seating of patrons. Sheila and her friends took seats on the lower floor in the left section close to an aisle which ran parallel with the left wall and out beyond the overhang of the balcony. When the picture came to an end, Sheila started making her exit, after the lights were turned on, using the aisle between the left section and the wall. As she proceeded up the aisle toward the front of the building for the purpose of leaving the theatre and just before she walked under the balcony overhang, some unidentified person in the balcony threw a [whiskey] bottle which struck her on the side of her head just above her left ear.

Conduct of the Theatre Patrons

Since the jury found that the patrons in the balcony were acting in a "rowdy" manner and that the defendant, its agents, servants, and employees negligently failed to remove such rowdy persons from the premises and that such negligence proximately caused the injuries sustained by Sheila, we deem it important to particularly point out the evidence bearing on the conduct of the patrons during the evening. The evidence favorable to the verdict is that during the progress of the show, the patrons in the theatre, both on the lower floor and in the balcony, were engaged in "hollering." Sheila, in describing the "hollering," said that "a few slang words" were used. This "hollering" was intermittent; it occurred "off and on" during "parts of" the movie. One witness testified that " * * * they would holler and maybe slack off a few minutes and then holler again." Buddy Henderson testified that he saw paper or cold drink cups either "drifting down" or being thrown down toward the front of the theatre. Sheila did not see throwing of any type. Henderson testified that he did not recall anything drifting down or being thrown down other than the paper cold drink cups. In regard to the duration of the commotion in the theatre, the evidence shows that there was more commotion on the lower floor than in the balcony. Henderson testified that he thought that the "hollering" seemed to get worse toward the end of the show. Sheila was certain that " * * * [a]bout 30 minutes before the show was over it seemed to be quieter; they didn't seem to be as rowdy then." Sheila, Henderson, and an officer by the name of Burt all agreed in their testimony that before the show was over, and, thus, before the accident, all commotion in the theatre had ceased. The last disturbance of any kind before the show was over was not throwing but "hollering." Henderson further testified that nothing happened, whether "hollering" or the throwing of paper cups, to make him think that something bad was going to happen; he was not worried about the safety of himself or the safety of his friends or anybody that was there.

The Balcony Patrons and Their Conduct

The balcony, which would seat 263 people, was "just about full." The witness, Burt, estimated that about 175 of the balcony seats were occupied. The disturbance in the balcony seemed to come from the balcony generally, "just all over it." The evidence does not identify any particular person as being a "rowdy person." No witness could state which persons in the balcony were rowdy and which were not. No witness could identify the person who threw the bottle. Incidentally, there is no evidence that a hard substance of any character was thrown, other than the bottle which struck Sheila. The witness, Henderson, testified that he could not identify the person who threw the bottle, but that out of the corner of his eye, he saw a "movement, a jerking motion" by someone in the balcony and then saw the bottle hit Sheila. No witness testified that the bottle thrower had been engaged in "hollering" or throwing paper cups. * * *

Assuming without deciding that the finding of negligence is supported by evidence of probative force, we go direct[ly] to the question of whether there is in the record evidence of probative force to support the finding of proximate cause. We hold that there is no evidence to support the finding of the jury that the failure of the defendant to remove "rowdy persons" from its premises was a proximate cause of Sheila's injuries.

"Proximate cause" * * * includes two essential elements: (1) there must be cause in fact—a cause which produces an event and without which the event would not have occurred; and (2) foreseeability. * * * We base our decision here on the ground that the plaintiffs have failed to offer evidence of probative force to establish the cause-in-fact element of proximate cause. In particular, the plaintiffs contend that the act of omission in failing to remove "rowdy persons" from the theatre was a proximate cause of the injuries resulting from the throwing of the bottle by an unknown patron of the theatre. We recognize that cause-in-fact covers the defendant's omissions as well as its acts. However, it cannot be said from this record that had the defendant removed the "rowdy persons" from the premises, the bottle thrower would not have thrown the bottle. The record in this case clearly shows a complete lack of proof that the bottle would not have been thrown "but for" the failure of the defendant to remove "rowdy persons" from the premises. There is no evidence that the bottle thrower was one of the "rowdy persons" engaged in "hollering" and throwing paper cups from the balcony. We cannot say from this evidence what persons would have been removed. We agree with the defendant's contention as made in its Motion for Instructed Verdict; Motion for Judgment non obstante veredicto; Amended Motion for New Trial; points in the Court of Civil Appeals and in this Court that the judgment of the trial court cannot be sustained in that there is no evidence that the alleged injuries were proximately caused by any act of commission or omission of the defendant. * * *

The plaintiffs * * * contend that cause in fact was proved on the theory that "it would be considerably more probable that had even minimum supervision, such as a request by theatre employees to cease such rowdy behavior, or for the policeman to even go to the balcony and stand so that he might be seen by the patrons in the balcony, would have prevented the person who did throw the bottle from doing so because of his fear of being apprehended. That the theatre, by and through its employees, in failing to give this minimum supervision or yet, the more burdensome elements submitted [to the jury] upon the part of the plaintiff, failure to oust persons engaging in rowdy behavior, encouraged the wrongdoer by guaranteeing his anonymity in a crowd to the point that he felt he could and did in fact, get away with throwing the bottle." This theory is related in no way to the single act of throwing the bottle. It is purely speculative as to what would have happened had the defendant attempted to remove the "rowdy persons" from the theatre. The bottle thrower may not have been present at a time when the "rowdy persons" were being ejected. If present at the time of removal of the persons who were "hollering" and throwing paper cups, it would be just a guess as to what subjective effect such action may have had upon the bottle thrower. * * * This cannot be permitted. * * *

We recognize that the theatre was under a duty to exercise reasonable care for the safety of its patrons. Marek v. Southern Enterprises, Inc., 128 Tex. 377, 99 S.W.2d 594 (1936). However, operators of theatres are not insurers of their patrons' safety.

The judgments of the Court of Civil Appeals and the trial court are reversed and judgment is here rendered that plaintiffs take nothing.

MAREK v. SOUTHERN ENTERPRISES, INC.

Commission of Appeals of Texas, 1936.
128 Tex. 377, 99 S.W.2d 594.

HICKMAN, COMMISSIONER.

* * * In the trial court plaintiff recovered judgment against defendant for damages for personal injuries sustained by her while a patron at a theatre conducted by defendant in Dallas, known as Palace Theatre. The Court of Civil Appeals reversed that judgment. * * *

The facts show that plaintiff became a patron of the theatre about midnight on December 31, 1931, for a New Year's Eve performance. Shortly after she and the other members of her party were seated some unidentified persons in the theatre began throwing firecrackers and torpedoes promiscuously over the auditorium. One such torpedo or firecracker exploded near plaintiff's head causing her to suffer, among other injuries, the loss of hearing of one ear. * * *

While the plaintiff's petition is drawn in rather general terms, we think that, as against the general demurrer and special exceptions leveled against it, same is sufficient to charge that the defendant was negligent in not taking the proper precaution to prevent plaintiff's injury after the exploding of firecrackers and torpedoes started in the theatre. That was the theory of liability submitted to the jury in the trial court.

Those who conduct places of public amusement to which an admission fee is charged owe the duty to exercise ordinary care for the safety of their patrons. The relationship of proprietor and patron gives rise to that duty. Although the proprietor may be guilty of no negligence in regard to a danger in its incipiency, still, if after it arises he has time to prevent injuries to his patrons, it is his duty to exercise ordinary care to do so. * * *

We have made an independent investigation of the testimony and, while conceding that, on the question of whether defendant could have prevented plaintiff's injury by the exercise of ordinary care after it knew that the throwing of torpedoes and firecrackers had started in the theatre, it is rather meager, still we are unable to say, as a matter of law, that the record is bare of any evidence on the question. There is evidence that the throwing of fireworks had gone on for several minutes before plaintiff was injured, and that defendant did nothing to stop the practice or to protect its patrons from dangers arising therefrom. There is also evidence tending to show that the theatre was in practical darkness, and that after the throwing of fireworks started no lights were turned on and no remonstrance made.

Let it be presumed that the persons who were throwing the torpedoes and firecrackers knew that they were committing acts in violation of the Penal Statutes of this state and penal ordinances of the city of Dallas. That fact would not relieve the defendant of liability. It owed the same duty to protect its patrons from unlawful acts as it did to protect them from boisterous conduct of others not defined as a penal offense. To our minds the fact that the persons throwing these dangerous fireworks knew that their acts were unlawful constitutes some evidence tending to show that, had defendant turned on the lights and remonstrated with them, such throwing would have stopped. We think the jurors had the right, in the exercise of their best judgment based upon their common knowledge and experience, to conclude that, had the lights been turned on, so that the guilty persons could have been seen and identified, they would have desisted from their unlawful conduct. The question presented is one calling for the exercise of the judgment of the jury and is not a question of law for the determination of this court.

* * *

The judgment of the Court of Civil Appeals will be reversed and that of the trial court affirmed.

Opinion adopted by the [Texas] Supreme Court.

NOTES

1. ***Burden of proof.*** As is implicit in *Rutledge* and *Marek,* the plaintiff generally has the burden of establishing the element of cause in fact by a preponderance of the evidence. ''Preponderance of the evidence means merely the greater weight of the evidence. * * * That is to say that the facts claimed by the plaintiff must be more likely than not to exist.'' Dobbs, The Law of Torts § 150, p. 360 (2000).

2. ***The but-for test.*** The most widely accepted test for cause in fact is the but-for test, which ''may be stated as follows: The defendant's conduct is a

cause of the event if the event would not have occurred but for that conduct; or conversely, the defendant's conduct is not a cause of the event, if the event would have occurred without it." Rudeck v. Wright, 218 Mont. 41, 709 P.2d 621, 628 (1985). Note that the "but for" inquiry addresses a hypothetical situation: what *would have* happened in the absence of the defendant's wrongful conduct. At its core this inquiry is speculative; it asks about a state of affairs that never existed in the world. Because the but-for test calls for inquiry into a hypothetical state of affairs, often there will be room for significant doubt (as was the case in *Rutledge* and *Marek*). In recognition of this reality, courts sometimes caution against raising the proof barrier too high. For example, in Reynolds v. Texas and Pac. Ry., 37 La.Ann. 694, 698 (1885), a passenger fell and was injured while hurrying down inadequately lighted stairs leading from defendant's railroad platform to its tracks. The court answered defendant's contention that the plaintiff might well have fallen even if adequate lighting had been provided by saying:

> [W]here the negligence of the defendant greatly multiplies the chances of accident * * * and is of a character naturally leading to its occurrence, the mere possibility that it might have happened without the negligence is not sufficient to break the chain of cause and effect.

Other cases point in the opposite direction from *Reynolds*. See, e.g., McInturff v. Chicago Title & Trust Co., 102 Ill.App.2d 39, 243 N.E.2d 657, 662 (1968), a broadly similar case to *Reynolds* in which the court showed a completely different attitude, holding that the plaintiff had failed to prove that safer stairs would have avoided a fatal fall and stating that "[d]amages cannot be assessed on mere surmise or conjecture." Cf. Coon v. Ginsberg, 32 Colo.App. 206, 509 P.2d 1293, 1295 (1973) (suggesting that cause in fact needs to be proved "with certainty.") As Professor Dobbs notes, "it is hard to escape the feeling that the but-for rule with its hypothetical alternative case can be applied rigorously in some cases and quite lightly in others." Dobbs, The Law of Torts § 173, p. 422 (2000).

3. ***Expert evidence***. In modern litigation the cause-in-fact issue frequently entails expert testimony, and plaintiffs often lose cases on the basis of complex cause-in-fact questions when their proffered experts cannot be qualified as such or when the experts' opinions are perceived as unconvincing. For further attention to this point, see Note 1 following the *June* case, infra p. 124.

4. ***Common sense***. Amid the flurry of concern about expert testimony and the difficulties of achieving discrimination in its use, it is useful to remember that the ultimate determination of the cause-in-fact issue calls upon the trial judge's and jury's bedrock sense of human reality, their common sense. As Judge Kozinski has noted:

> Not knowing the mechanism whereby a particular agent causes a particular effect is not always fatal to a plaintiff's claim. Causation can be proved even when we don't know precisely *how* the damage occurred, if there is sufficiently compelling proof that the agent must have caused the damage *somehow*. One method of proving causation in these circumstances is to use statistical evidence. If 50 people who eat at a restaurant one evening come down with food poisoning during the night, we can infer that the

restaurant's food probably contained something unwholesome, even if none of the dishes is available for analysis. This inference is based on the fact that, in our health-conscious society, it is highly unlikely that 50 people who have nothing in common except that they ate at the same restaurant would get food poisoning from independent sources.

Daubert v. Merrell Dow Pharmaceuticals, Inc., 43 F.3d 1311, 1314 (9th Cir. 1995) (emphasis in original), *cert. denied*, 516 U.S. 869, 116 S.Ct. 189, 133 L.Ed.2d 126 (1995). Cf. Kramer v. Weedhopper of Utah, Inc., 141 Ill.App.3d 217, 95 Ill.Dec. 631, 490 N.E.2d 104 (1986) (holding that a company that supplied 90% of the bolts distributed in ultralight aircraft kits probably was the source of the defective bolt that caused the crash of an aircraft assembled from one of the kits).

5. ***The five-step approach***. Under the approach to factual causation detailed in Robertson, The Common Sense of Cause In Fact, 75 Tex.L.Rev. 1765, 1768–73 (1997), properly framing and answering the but-for issue in a lawsuit involves five essential steps. *First,* identify the harm for which redress is sought. (Normally this first step will present no difficulty. But see the "lost opportunity" cases treated infra in section D.) *Second,* identify the defendant's wrongful conduct. Care is required here. It is not enough for the plaintiff to show that her injuries would not have occurred if the defendant had never been born; the plaintiff must show that her injuries probably would not have occurred if the defendant had not engaged in the particular conduct alleged (and ultimately proved) in the lawsuit as wrongful.

The *third* step is the trickiest. It involves using the imagination to create a counter-factual hypothesis. One creates a mental picture of a situation identical to the actual facts of the case in all respects save one: the defendant's wrongful conduct is now "corrected" to the minimal extent necessary to make it conform to the standard of conduct the plaintiff claims has been violated. It is important to stress that the mental operation performed at this third step must be careful, conservative, and modest; the hypothesis must be counter-factual only to the extent necessary to ask the but-for question. Only the defendant's wrongful conduct must be "changed," and that only to the extent necessary to make it conform to the standard of conduct the plaintiff claims has been violated.

The *fourth* step asks the key question, whether the harm that plaintiff suffered would probably still have occurred had the defendant behaved correctly in the sense just indicated. The *fifth* and final step is answering the question.

In visualizing the five-step process, a videotape metaphor may be of use. After identifying the injuries in suit and the wrongful conduct, run the tape backward to the period of time immediately preceding the plaintiff's injury. Stop the tape. Change only one thing: change the defendant's behavior to the extent necessary to make it conform to the requisite standard of conduct. In other words, change the accident scene only as necessary to reflect the assumption that the defendant has now been conducting herself properly. *Don't change anything else.* Now, with the defendant behaving properly—with defendant's wrongful conduct out of the picture—run the tape forward. Do you see the plaintiff being harmed? If so, defendant's wrongful conduct was not a cause in fact of the harm; it was irrelevant. Do you see the plaintiff escaping harm? If you see that clearly enough, then the defendant's wrongful conduct was a cause in fact of the harm. Do you see snow on the screen, no picture, just static? If so, the plaintiff may have failed to meet the burden of proof on the issue of factual causation.

6. When struggling with the analytical difficulties occasionally associated with the cause in fact issue, it may be comforting to remember that in most cases the but-for test readily yields an acceptably clear answer. For example, cause in fact was clearly present in most of the cases treated in Chapter III. Cause in fact can be equally clearly absent. For example, in a suit based on an allegedly inadequate warning in an automobile operator's manual, the plaintiff's admission that he had never read any part of the manual was fatal to his case. Bloxom v. Bloxom, 512 So.2d 839, 850–851 (La. 1987).

7. A further useful point of perspective is this: A plaintiff who prevails on cause in fact has not thereby won the case. He has merely prevailed on that one issue, and still must contend with the duty, breach, proximate cause (scope of responsibility), and damages issues, as well as with the affirmative defenses potentially available to the defendant.

B.   LIMITED–PURPOSE SUBSTITUTES FOR THE STANDARD BUT–FOR APPROACH: THE SUBSTANTIAL FACTOR TEST AND THE RESTATEMENT (THIRD) SUBSTITUTE

SANDERS v. AMERICAN BODY ARMOR AND EQUIPMENT, INC.

District Court of Appeal of Florida, 1995.
652 So.2d 883.

LAWRENCE, JUDGE.

* * *

Warren Sanders (Sanders), a law enforcement officer employed by the Jacksonville Sheriff's Office, was killed on July 26, 1990, while participating in an undercover investigation which resulted in heavy gunfire and loss of life. Sanders was shot fifteen times. An expert testified that he died of two bullet wounds—one to the abdomen, and one to the chest—both fatal, and both inflicted "split seconds" apart. One bullet came from the weapon of an assailant, and one, inadvertently, from the weapon of a fellow officer.

Sanders was wearing a vest manufactured and sold by American Body Armor and Equipment, Incorporated (Armor), which met specifications prepared and submitted by the Sheriff's Office. Although several styles of vests were available, including overlapping panels, the Sheriff's Office specifications provided for a "buttfit" style, which Sanders was wearing at the time of his death. The "buttfit" style vest consisted of front and back panels extending to and abutting or joining on each side of his chest. The area of the body at the point of joinder on each side of the chest thus was not protected, because the panels did not overlap. One of the fatal bullets entered his body at this unprotected point. The other fatal bullet entered his abdomen at a point below and outside of the vest area.

* * *

[In a jury trial of the claim by Sanders's estate against Armor, the trial court directed a verdict for the defendant,] reasoning that the bullet to Sanders's chest in the abutment area was not the proximate cause of his death, because he would have died nevertheless from the bullet to his unprotected abdomen. We disapprove of this [reasoning] * * *

* * *

Dean Prosser explains why multiple defendants are liable when the negligence of each one is a substantial factor in bringing about harm, despite that each defendant's negligence is not a cause but for which the harm would not have occurred:

> [T]he "but for" rule serves to explain the greater number of cases; but there is one type of situation in which it fails. *If two causes concur to bring about an event, and either one of them, operating alone, would have been sufficient to cause the identical result, some other test is needed.* * * *. A stabs C with a knife, and B fractures C's skull with a rock; either wound would be fatal, and C dies from the effects of both * * *. *In such cases* it is quite clear that each cause has in fact played so important a part in producing the result that responsibility should be imposed upon it; and it is equally clear that *neither can be absolved from that responsibility upon the ground that the identical harm would have occurred without it, or there would be no liability at all.*

W. Page Keeton et al., Prosser and Keeton on the Law of Torts § 41, at 266–67 (5th ed. 1984) (footnotes omitted; emphasis added) * * *. The instant two fatal bullets, fired split seconds apart, are concurrent causes of a single injury—Sanders' death.

We nevertheless affirm the trial court's directed verdict for Armor [on other grounds]. * * *

NOTE

Restatement (Second) of Torts § 432(2) (1965) phrases the substantial factor test differently than *Prosser & Keeton*, but the thought is the same:

> If two forces are actively operating, one because of the actor's negligence, the other not because of any misconduct on his part, and each of itself is sufficient to bring about harm to another, the actor's negligence may be found to be a substantial factor in bringing it about.

The Third Restatement takes a significantly different approach. See supra p. 122.

MAVROUDIS v. PITTSBURGH–CORNING CORP.

Court of Appeals of Washington, 1997.
86 Wash.App. 22, 935 P.2d 684.

KENNEDY, ACTING CHIEF JUDGE.

* * *

Michael M. Mavroudis, Jr., had a long and successful career in the United States Navy before retiring in 1993. Twice he worked on ship conversions, once in Philadelphia in the early 1950s and again at the Puget Sound Naval Shipyard in the late 1950s and early 1960s. The work at the Puget Sound Naval Shipyard involved the conversion of the *U.S.S. Wright.* That assignment lasted nearly four years * * *. An asbestos-based product known as Kaylo [produced by defendant Owens–Corning Fiberglass Corporation (OCF)] was one of only three types of insulation used on the *U.S.S. Wright* conversion project * * *. An industrial hygienist testified that Kaylo gave off very substantial amounts of asbestos when it was cut.

Within a few months after his retirement, Mr. Mavroudis discovered that he had mesothelioma.* He was 59 years old at that time. Mr. Mavroudis is now deceased. Denise J. Mavroudis, his personal representative, has been substituted as a party plaintiff.

Dr. Samuel Hammar, a pathologist specializing in asbestos-related disease, testified that the asbestos included in the Kaylo product and the asbestos contained in other asbestos-based products handled by Mr. Mavroudis can cause mesothelioma. He also testified that scientific information indicated that all of Mr. Mavroudis's exposure to asbestos at Puget Sound Naval Station from 1957 to 1963 probably played a role in causing the mesothelioma, and that he could not say which exposures were, in fact, the cause of the condition. He also testified that as little as 10 percent of Mr. Mavroudis's asbestos exposure would have been sufficient to cause mesothelioma.

* * *

Mr. Mavroudis and his wife brought this suit against OCF and others. The case was submitted to the jury with claims against OCF for (1) strict liability for selling a product not reasonably safe as designed, (2) strict liability for selling a product not reasonably safe in that adequate warnings were not given with respect to the dangers presented by the product, and (3) negligence in failing to warn of the danger of exposure to Kaylo. The jury rendered a verdict in favor of the Mavroudises on the warning and negligence theories, and against the Mavroudises on the not-reasonably-safe-as-designed theory. The jury entered a single damages award in

---

* In the asbestos case law and literature, mesothelioma is referred to as a "signature disease," meaning that it virtually never results from anything but asbestos exposure. [Ed.]

a sum in excess of one million dollars. [The trial judge entered judgment on the jury verdict.]

* * *

The trial court gave one proximate cause instruction for all theories of liability. This instruction is commonly known as a "substantial factor" instruction. It relieved the plaintiff of proving that, but for the exposure to Kaylo, Mr. Mavroudis would not have contracted mesothelioma and instead allowed the plaintiff to establish causation by showing that the defendant's negligence or product was a substantial factor in bringing about the injury, even though the injury would have occurred without it. [The heart of the instruction was this:]

> If you find that two or more causes have combined to bring about an injury and any one of them operating alone would have been sufficient to cause the injury, each cause is considered to be a proximate cause of the injury if it is a substantial factor in bringing it about, even though the result would have occurred without it. A substantial factor is an important or material factor and not one that is insignificant.

* * *

Although we are aware that substantial factor causation instructions are commonly given in asbestos-injury cases tried in Washington, no published Washington case cited by the parties or found by this court through independent research directly addresses the propriety of substantial factor instructions in asbestos-injury cases.

* * *

As noted by Dean Prosser, the substantial factor test * * * is used where either one of two causes would have produced the identical harm, thus making it impossible for plaintiff to prove the "but for" test. In such cases, it is quite clear that each cause has "played so important a part in producing the result that responsibility should be imposed on it." * * * W. Keeton, D. Dobbs, R. Keeton & D. Owen, Prosser and Keeton on Torts § 41, p. 267 (5th ed.1984).

OCF argues that this is not an appropriate case for application of the substantial factor test because Mr. Mavroudis failed to show that he could not prove that one event alone was the cause of the injury. We disagree with that view of the evidence in the record. Dr. Hammar testified that although all of Mr. Mavroudis's exposures to asbestos while working at the Puget Sound Naval Station from 1957 to 1963 probably played a role in causing the mesothelioma, and that as little as 10 percent of the total exposure would have been sufficient to cause the injury, he could not say which exposures were, in fact, the cause of the mesothelioma. This is exactly the kind of situation that calls for application of the substantial factor test, in order that no supplier enjoy a causation defense solely on the ground that the plaintiff probably would have suffered the same disease from inhaling fibers originating from the products of other suppliers. In sum, we conclude that multi-supplier asbestos-injury cases call for the substantial-factor test of causation rather than the but-for test, in cases such as this one, wherein the expert witness testifies, as did Dr. Hammar, that all of the plaintiff's exposure probably played a role in causing the injury and that it is not possible to determine which exposures were, in fact, the cause of the condition.

* * *

AFFIRMED.

JUNE v. UNION CARBIDE CORPORATION

United States Court of Appeals, Tenth Circuit, 2009.
577 F.3d 1234.

HARTZ, CIRCUIT JUDGE.

The lawsuit before us arises out of alleged radiation injuries to residents of Uravan, Colorado, a former uranium and vanadium milling town owned and operated by Defendants Union Carbide Corporation and Umetco Minerals Corporation. * * * Mining and milling have been conducted in the Uravan area for many years. The Standard Chemical Company was producing radium in the region as early as 1914. In 1928 Defendants purchased Standard Chemical's holdings, and in 1936 began milling vanadium and uranium. To accommodate workers, Defendants founded the community of Uravan, constructing homes and a number of facilities, including a medical clinic, elementary school, community center, tennis courts, and a swimming pool.

Defendants ceased operations in Uravan in 1984, having produced 42 million pounds of uranium oxide. This production did not come without environmental costs. In 1986 the Environmental Protection Agency placed Uravan on the National Priorities List, which ranks the nation's most environmentally hazardous sites to prioritize remedial action. About this time, Uravan's remaining residents were evacuated and remedial activities began. The last structures standing in Uravan were razed after this lawsuit was filed.

* * *

Twenty-seven Plaintiffs are pursuing personal-injury claims * * *. [Eleven] have been diagnosed with nonthyroid cancer and 16 have been diagnosed with thyroid disease (including one case of thyroid cancer).

[In the district court, Defendants moved for summary judgment, arguing that the Plaintiffs] had failed to show the but-for causation required by Colorado tort law. * * * [Plaintiffs responded] that causation in Colorado is determined not by a but-for test but by a "substantial factor" test requiring only that the defendant's tortious conduct be "a substantial contributing cause of the injury." Plaintiffs contended that their experts' opinions created a triable issue of fact "as to whether the

Defendants' emission of radiation over the course of decades substantially contributed" to the personal-injury Plaintiffs' illnesses. * * *The district court rejected the [Plaintiffs'] substantial-contributing-cause argument * * *. Because Plaintiffs had submitted no evidence of but-for causation, the court granted summary judgment.

* * *

In Colorado, as elsewhere, * * * [t]he general rule for causation is that the plaintiff must prove that the alleged "injury would not have occurred but for the defendant's negligent conduct." Plaintiffs do not dispute that proposition but argue that when there are "potential multiple or concurring causes" for an injury, Colorado applies a "substantial factor test" for causation, not the more stringent but-for test. Under the substantial-factor test, Plaintiffs contend, an actor's conduct can be deemed causal "where it is of sufficient significance in producing the harm as to lead reasonable persons to regard it as a cause and to attach responsibility." Because the illnesses at issue in this case (cancer and thyroid disease) can have multiple causes, Plaintiffs conclude that this more permissive substantial-factor test applies.

* * * Plaintiffs' statement of the substantial-factor test * * * misstates the law * * *.

* * *

The term *substantial factor* appears in the treatment of causation in the Restatement (Second) of Torts (as well as its predecessor, the original Restatement of Torts). It has been abandoned, however, in the [Restatement (Third) of Torts: Liability for Physical and Emotional Harm § 26 cmt. *j* (2010)] because of the misunderstanding that it has engendered. [Under the Restatement (Third)], [o]rdinarily a cause is a "factual cause" only if it is a but-for cause, see id. § 26, although there is a potential exception * * * when there are multiple causes, see id. § 27. * * * Section 27 * * * recognizes that it is sometimes appropriate to impose liability even when the harm would have occurred without the defendant's act. This exceptional circumstance is narrowly defined to impose liability only "when a tortfeasor's conduct, while not necessary for the outcome, would have been a factual cause if the other competing cause had not been operating." Id. § 27 cmt. *a*. [The black letter of § 27 states: "If multiple acts occur, each of which under § 26 alone would have been a factual cause of the physical harm at the same time in the absence of the other act(s), each act is regarded as a factual cause of the harm."] An illustration clarifies the concept:

> Rosaria and Vincenzo were independently camping in a heavily forested campground. Each one had a campfire, and each negligently failed to ensure that the fire was extinguished upon retiring for the night. Due to unusually dry forest conditions and a stiff wind, both campfires escaped their sites and began a forest fire. The two fires, burning out of control, joined together and engulfed Centurion Company's

hunting lodge, destroying it. Either fire alone would have destroyed the lodge. Each of Rosaria's and Vincenzo's negligence is a factual cause of the destruction of Centurion's hunting lodge.

* * *

[The caption of § 27] speaks of "multiple sufficient causes," but it could more precisely speak of "multiple sufficient causal *sets*." See id. § 27 cmt. *f*. For example, the evidence at trial may show (1) that conditions A, B, C, D, E, and F were present; (2) that if only A, B, and C had been present, the injury would probably have occurred; and (3) that if only D, E, and F had been present, the injury would probably have occurred. If F is the defendant's misconduct, then F was not a but-for cause of the injury; even without F, the injury would have occurred (all it took was A, B, and C). But since D, E, and F would also have caused the injury, F is a component of a second causal set. F must, of course, be a *necessary* component of the second causal set to be a factual cause of the injury. That is, F would not be a factual cause if D and E alone would have been enough to cause the injury; F must be a "but for" component of at least one causal set for liability to attach.

Moreover, multiple causal sets may share some components. If A, B, and C would probably have caused the injury (with each of A, B, and C being necessary) and so would have A, B, and D, the tortfeasor who committed D would be liable. The Restatement (Third) [at § 27 cmt. *f*, illus. 3] provides the following example:

> Able, Baker, and Charlie, acting independently but simultaneously, each negligently lean on Paul's car, which is parked at a scenic overlook at the edge of a mountain. Their combined force results in the car rolling over the edge of a diminutive curbstone and plummeting down the mountain to its destruction. The force exerted by each of Able, Baker, and Charlie would have been insufficient to propel Paul's car past the curbstone, but the combined force of any two of them is sufficient. Able, Baker, and Charlie are each a factual cause of the destruction of Paul's car.

A real-world example would be a typical asbestosis lawsuit. A person suffering from asbestosis may have been exposed to asbestos from a number of sources (say, four), and the total exposure may have been more than enough to cause asbestosis. It may well be (1) that asbestosis would probably have arisen even without exposure of the victim to Source A, so Source A is not a but-for cause; and (2) that Source A by itself would not have caused asbestosis. But Source A may be a factual cause if it was a necessary component of a causal set that included, say, two of the other sources and the three together would probably have caused asbestosis.

* * *

To sum up, as we understand the * * * Restatement (Third), a defendant cannot be liable to the plaintiff unless its conduct is either (a) a but-for cause of the plaintiff's injury or (b) a necessary component of a causal set that (probably) would have caused the injury in the absence of other causes. * * *

To be sure, it is Colorado law that governs here, not the Restatement[]. The Colorado Supreme Court may * * * decide[] to disagree with the Restatement[] and adopt a different standard for causation. But we see no evidence of this. * * * We therefore hold that Defendants would be liable only upon proof of one of the following: (1) that exposure of a Plaintiff to Uravan radiation was a but-for cause of the Plaintiff's medical condition or (2) that such exposure to Uravan radiation was a necessary component of a causal set that would have caused the medical condition.

We now examine whether Plaintiffs supplied such evidence.[This was a close call, because, even if the Uravan operations had never occurred, the Plaintiff's diseases could have resulted from background radiation; more significantly, many of the plaintiffs had been exposed to radiation from the detonation of atomic weapons at a testing site in Nevada conducted between 1959 and 1970. The court ultimately concluded that] Plaintiffs failed to raise in district court a genuine issue of fact regarding factual causation. That is, they failed to present to the court evidence * * * that Uravan radiation was either a but-for cause of any medical condition suffered by one of the Plaintiffs or that Uravan radiation was a necessary component of a causal set that would probably have caused one of those conditions.

* * *

The judgment of the district court is affirmed.

[Judge Holloway dissented in part, taking the position that one of the Plaintiff's experts had come close enough to opining that radiation from the Uravan operations was a but-for cause of the thyroid diseases to enable the thyroid-disease Plaintiffs to survive summary judgment.]

NOTES

1. **Expert evidence.** The problem of presenting qualified expert cause-in-fact testimony can be particularly acute in cases asserting that toxic substances caused disease.[1] See, e.g., Ranes v. Adams Laboratories, Inc., 778 N.W.2d 677, 687–88 (Iowa 2010), where (in the course of rejecting plaintiff's expert's testimony and upholding summary judgment for the defendant in a prescription-drug injury case), the court provided a useful perspective on the toxic-tort area (citations omitted):

> Courts have commonly bifurcated toxic-tort-causation analysis into two separate but related parts: general causation and specific causation. General causation is a showing that the drug or chemical is capable of causing the type of harm from which the plaintiff suffers. Specific

---

1. See generally Gerald W. Boston, A Mass–Exposure Model of Toxic Causation: The Content of Scientific Proof and the Regulatory Experience, 18 Colum. J. Envtl. L. 181, 279–326 (1993) (surveying the scientific evidence of causation in most of the major toxic-substances cases of the late 20th century).

causation is evidence that the drug or chemical in fact caused the harm from which the plaintiff suffers. * * * The Restatement (Third) of Torts: Liability for Physical and Emotional Harm [§ 28 cmt. *c*, p. 405 (2010)] has recognized this relatively recent common practice as a "device[] to organize a court's analysis" and not as an additional element of the tort. The Restatement authors supplement their explanation by asserting factual causation is a necessary element in every tort case; the "general and specific" language has simply become more prevalent in toxic-tort cases. * * * The primary difference between toxic-tort cases and other types of tort cases is that, in nontoxic-tort cases, both general and specific causation are often easily proven with the same evidence. Id. (noting [that] when a plaintiff is injured in an automobile accident, for example, "potential causal explanations other than the collision are easily ruled out [i.e., specific causation]; common experience reveals that the forces generated in a serious automobile collision are capable of causing a fracture [i.e., general causation]").

The bifurcated analysis has not been explicitly used as the standard in Iowa. However, due to its general acceptance among scholars and courts of other jurisdictions, as well as the relative ease of application the analysis offers to courts examining complex issues of causation, we believe it is appropriate for courts to use the bifurcated causation analysis in toxic-tort cases. In the toxic-tort case before us, both types of causation must be proven, and expert medical and toxicological testimony is unquestionably required to assist the jury.

The Third Restatement gives detailed treatment to the evidentiary issues that arise in toxic substances cases in § 28 cmt. *c* (pp. 402–413) and in the Reporters' Note on cmt. *c* (pp. 433–63).

On one reading of *June*, plaintiffs' counsel need to worry not only about finding scientifically qualified expert witnesses but also about teaching the scientists enough law to enable them to testify in language that is currently acceptable to the legal community. Part of the *June* plaintiffs' problem seemed to be that their experts packaged their conclusions in "substantial factor" language, and this was a language that the court strongly disliked.

2. ***Uses and misuses of the substantial factor test.*** Robertson, The Common Sense of Cause in Fact, 75 Tex. L. Rev. 1765, 1776 (1997), discussed the "uses and misuses of the substantial factor test" as follows:

The term "substantial factor" has come to have a number of different meanings in the jurisprudence. * * * In the narrowest and only fully legitimate usage, the term describes a cause-in-fact test that is useful as a substitute for the but-for test in a limited category of cases in which two causes concur to bring about an event, and either cause, operating alone, would have brought about the event absent the other cause * * *. [Malone, Ruminations on Cause in Fact, 9 Stan. L.Rev. 60, 88–90 (1956), calls these "combined force" cases. Another frequently-used term is "duplicative causation" cases. A third term is "overdetermined causation."] In a looser and potentially confusing usage, the substantial factor test is treated as more or less interchangeable with the but-for test; in this usage courts seem to feel that it is appropriate to shift to the substantial factor vocabulary whenever the but-for test is proving difficult to work with for whatever reason. In a third usage, "substantial factor" describes an approach to the issue of legal [proximate] causation or ambit of duty, a matter that should be kept entirely distinct from the cause-in-fact issue.

Sanders is a classic example of what Robertson calls the "narrowest" use of the substantial factor test. *Mavroudis* stretches the traditional substantial factor approach to some extent, using it in a three-causal-candidates situation, rather than the normal two, and in a situation in which it was not as clear as in the classic cases that defendant's candidate would have been a but-for cause of the harm in the absence of the other(s). *June* describes a "causal set" substitute for the traditional substantial factor approach that is potentially quite a bit more expansive than substantial factor. See generally Robertson, Causation in the Restatement (Third) of Torts: Three Arguable Mistakes, 44 Wake Forest L. Rev. 1007 (2009).

3. ***The justification for a "duplicative causation" or "overdetermined causation" exception to the normal but-for requirement***. Some analysts believe the but-for test captures the essential meaning of factual causation. From this point of view, substituting a more lenient test in the "combined force" cases is difficult or impossible to justify. See, e.g., Callahan v. Cardinal Glennon Hospital, 863 S.W.2d 852, 861–862 (Mo. 1993):

> Some lawyers and judges have come to look upon the "but for" test as a particularly onerous and difficult test for causation. Nothing could be further from the truth. "But for" is an absolute minimum for causation because it *is* merely causation in fact. Any attempt to find liability absent actual causation is an attempt to connect the defendant with an injury or event that the defendant had nothing to do with.

See also Price Waterhouse v. Hopkins, 490 U.S. 228, 282, 109 S.Ct. 1775, 1807, 104 L.Ed.2d 268 (1989) (Kennedy, J., dissenting, stating that using "[a]ny standard less than but-for * * * represents a decision to impose liability without causation.")

The opposing viewpoint, which is the traditional one, sees the substantial factor test as an alternative way of establishing the existence of factual causation. This view was elaborated in Boeing Co. v. Cascade Corp., 207 F.3d 1177, 1184–85 (9th Cir. 2000):

> In the special circumstance of causal overdetermination, conduct can be a cause of a result even though it is not a *sine qua non*. [Imagine a kitchen with a light switch at each end. When one person flips up the front switch at precisely the same time another person flips up the rear switch], the light goes on. Neither person's conduct is a *sine qua non* because the light would have gone on anyway. Neither individual's conduct made a difference to the outcome. [Under the but-for test], neither person caused the light to go on. * * * But the light went on. And it did so by human agency, not spontaneously. So the conclusion that [the but-for test] compels, that *no one* caused the light to go on, is false. Because the correct answer has to be the same for the two individuals, by eliminating the false answer we have left only one possible answer which must be true: Each of the two persons caused the light to go on.

See also Judge Posner's opinion in United States v. Feliciano, 45 F.3d 1070, 1075 (7th Cir. 1995):

> A barrel of gasoline is sitting on the street. Through negligence two people toss lighted matches into the barrel at the same time and it explodes. It would have exploded if only one lighted match had been thrown into it; so neither person was a "but for" cause of the explosion; yet both would be held liable in tort (or criminally, if they had acted recklessly or deliberately), both having "caused" the explosion in a perfectly reasonable sense.

C. LIMITED–PURPOSE SUBSTITUTES FOR THE STANDARD BUT–FOR APPROACH: THE ALTERNATIVE LIABILITY, CONCERTED ACTION, AND MARKET SHARE THEORIES

PENNFIELD CORP. v. MEADOW VALLEY ELECTRIC, INC.

Superior Court of Pennsylvania, 1992.
413 Pa.Super. 187, 604 A.2d 1082.

CAVANAUGH, JUDGE.

* * *

This action has its origin in the untimely demise of 1,537 swine, who suffocated when an electrically operated ventilation system in their abode failed. The swine were housed at Mountain View Farms, Berks County, Pennsylvania, and were owned by Pennfield Corporation. Pennfield brought an action against Meadow Valley Electric, Inc. [MVE] the corporation which allegedly performed repair and maintenance services on the electrical equipment at Mountain View Farms. The Pennfield complaint alleged that a defective electrical system installed by MVE caused the ventilation system to fail, thus resulting in the suffocation of the swine.

MVE in turn filed a complaint to join numerous additional defendants including York Electrical Supply Co. MVE's joinder complaint alleged that the ventilation system failed and that the cause of the failure was defective electrical cable purchased either from York or from another distributor, Tri–State Electrical Supply Company. MVE claimed that York was liable * * * on theories of strict liability, negligence, and breach of warranties.[3]

York responded to MVE's joinder complaint with preliminary objections in the nature of a demurrer. The gravamen of York's objections is that to make out a cause of action in strict liability, negligence, or breach of warranties MVE has to specifically identify which defendant supplied the defective cable. York notes specifically that [MVE pleaded that the] "electrical cable installed at Mountain View was bought either from York

---

3. MVE alleged the same theories of liability against Tri–State as against York. Tri–State answered the complaint but did not file preliminary objections to MVE's complaint as did York.

or Tri–State" and that "[t]he electrical cable bought by MVE from York and Tri–State cannot be identified or distinguished."

* * * [T]he trial court sustained York's preliminary objections [and] dismissed with prejudice [MVE's complaint against York]. This appeal followed.

* * *

MVE's first argument is based on what MVE deems the "alternative liability" theory of Restatement (Second) of Torts, § 433(B)(3) (1965) and Summers v. Tice, [33 Cal.2d 80, 199 P.2d 1 (1948)]. Section 433(B)(3) states * * *:

> Where the conduct of two or more actors is tortious, and it is proved that harm has been caused to the plaintiff by only one of them, but there is uncertainty as to which one has caused it, the burden is upon each actor to prove that he has not caused the harm.

* * * [MVE argues that under the quoted subsection (3)], because it cannot prove that either York or Tri–State harmed it, the burden is on York or Tri–State to prove that they were not the tortfeasor. This is a mischaracterization of the law. The predicate for applying subsection (3) is that "the conduct of two or more actors is tortious." Subsection (3) is based on the rationale that "injustice [lies in] permitting proved wrong-doers, who among them have inflicted an injury upon the entirely inno-cent plaintiff, to escape liability merely because the nature of their conduct and the resulting harm has made it difficult or impossible to prove which of them has caused the harm." § 433B(3) cmt. *f*. Here, MVE has not alleged that the conduct of two or more actors is tortious. Rather, MVE asserts one actor may be tortious while admitting the other actor may not be tortious. It is quite obvious from the rule and the rationale that the burden of proof remains on MVE, and subsection (3) does not apply.

* * *

This case is * * * a far cry from the seminal case in this area, the well-known hunting case of Summers v. Tice [supra]. In Summers v. Tice, three persons were hunting fowl when suddenly a bird flew from the brush. Notwithstanding that one of the hunters was in close proximity to the brush, the other two hunters simultaneously fired their weapons, accidentally wounding the hunter. In such circumstances, it was impossi-ble for the injured hunter to determine which party caused the injury. The California Supreme Court felt it was appropriate to shift the burden to the two careless hunters to prove which hunter fired the shot. The court emphasized that both parties were wrongdoers who had brought about a situation where the negligence of one of them had injured their compan-ion. Either of the two was in a better position to know which of them caused the injury, while the nature of their conduct made it difficult or impossible for the injured party to determine who was liable.

MVE implicitly admits in its [complaint] that either York or Tri–State bears no culpability whatsoever in bringing about the suffocation. * * * Thus, unlike in Summers v. Tice or the usual alternative liability theory case, MVE cannot with certainty state that York and Tri–State are * * * tortfeasors.

* * *

* * * [It is essential to refuse to] extend Summers v. Tice * * * to the present fact scenario. Our system of jurisprudence rightly balks at assigning liability to an innocent party. Our reluctance has been overcome only when compelling circumstances demand that we deviate from the rule that a cause of action must fail unless defendant's conduct is shown to have been [a but-for cause] of plaintiff's injury.

* * *

We affirm the trial court's order as to the preliminary objections, but instruct the trial court to allow MVE the opportunity to amend its complaint.*

NOTES

1. ***Dobbs wants to call it "alternative causation."*** Professor Dobbs thinks "alternative liability" is a misleading name, because the "liability [that results when the theory is applied] is joint and several,[1] not in the alternative. It is rather causation that is in the alternative, because one or the other but not both tortfeasors are causes of the harm." Dobbs, The Law of Torts § 175, p. 427 (2000).

2. ***A remedy-impairment rationale for the alternative liability theory.*** Dobbs does not think the "dubious suggestion that defendants might know more than plaintiffs" can explain many of the alternative liability cases. He suggests that a better justification for the theory was set forth in Justice Rand's opinion in Lewis v. Cook, [1951] S.C.R. 830 (Supreme Court of Canada 1951):

> What * * * the culpable actor [in cases like Summers v. Tice] has done by his * * * negligent act is, first, to have set in motion a dangerous force which embraces the injured person within the scope of its probable mischief; and next, * * * to have made more difficult if not impossible the means of proving the possible damaging results of his own act or the similar results of the act of another. He has violated not only the victim's

---

* The court thought that MVE should be allowed to replead, omit the allegation that the supplier of the defective cable couldn't be identified, and thus "have the opportunity to utilize discovery to pin-point which company distributed the allegedly defective cable. However, if after an opportunity to submit all the relevant evidence, the probabilities are * * * still evenly divided between York and Tri–State as to causation, it would [then] be the duty of the trial court to dismiss the complaint." [Ed.]

1. In this usage, "joint and several liability" means that the judgment is for a single sum, representing the total value of the plaintiff's injury, and that the plaintiff is entitled to collect his money from either or both of the defendants, up to but not exceeding the amount of the judgment.

substantive right to security, but he has also culpably impaired the latter's remedial right of establishing liability.

3. ***Alternative liability sometimes applies against product suppliers.*** Presumably the alternative liability theory would have been available to MVE if it had been able to show that, while only one of the two suppliers was the source of the particular cable that killed the pigs, both suppliers' cables were identically defective. See Minnich v. Ashland Oil Co., 15 Ohio St.3d 396, 473 N.E.2d 1199 (1984) (holding that each of two suppliers of cleaning fluid— neither of whom provided a proper warning of the product's explosive qualities—had the burden of negating cause in fact in a lawsuit by a worker who had no way of telling which supplier's fluid he was using when hurt in an explosion); Wysocki v. Reed, 222 Ill.App.3d 268, 164 Ill.Dec. 817, 583 N.E.2d 1139 (1991) (similar result against two providers of an allegedly defective drug).

4. ***Why should the alternative liability theory require plaintiff to join both tortfeasors as defendants?*** Most courts will refuse to apply alternative liability in cases like *Summers* unless both tortfeasors are joined as defendants. We have not found an explanation of this requirement, but it is relatively easy to understand. The ultimate result in *Summers* was a judgment that the two shooters were jointly and severally liable for the plaintiff's injury. From the corrective justice viewpoint, such a result is guaranteed to be unjust as to one of the shooters, whose bullet did not strike the victim. Courts insist that both shooters be in court because they want to be sure they are at least doing something right (holding the true shooter liable) while they are also obviously—at least from the corrective justice standpoint—doing something wrong (imposing liability on the other shooter for a harm that he did not cause).

5. ***How many tortfeasors?*** Alternative liability gets more difficult to justify as the number of defendants increases. Yet courts have used the theory against relatively large groups. See, e.g., Huston v. Konieczny, 52 Ohio St.3d 214, 556 N.E.2d 505 (1990) (five possible furnishers of the beer that made a teenage driver drunk); Snoparsky v. Baer, 439 Pa. 140, 266 A.2d 707 (1970) (twelve boys, any one of whom might have thrown the rock that struck the plaintiff).

The perceived difficulty of justifying using the alternative liability theory against more than two defendants—i.e., of moving from accepting a 50/50 chance of cause in fact (*Summers*) to a 1/12 chance (*Snoparsky*) or even smaller—was a major reason for the Oregon Supreme Court's total rejection of the alternative liability theory in Senn v. Merrell–Dow Pharmaceuticals, Inc., 305 Or. 256, 751 P.2d 215, 222 (1988).

6. ***The Third Restatement.*** Section 28(b) of the Third Restatement embraces the alternative liability theory and indicates that there is no particular problem with using the theory against groups of defendants larger than two.

POOLE v. ALPHA THERAPEUTIC CORPORATION

United States District Court, Northern District of Illinois, 1988.
696 F.Supp. 351.

MORAN, DISTRICT JUDGE.

[Plaintiffs have sued three defendants, seeking to hold defendants liable for manufacturing, processing, marketing, and distributing a blood product that caused the death of Stephen Poole. Plaintiffs now move to add counts IX and X to their third amended complaint in order to assert additional theories of liability]. For the reasons stated herein we reject plaintiffs' proposed market share and concerted action theories but grant them leave to amend to include allegations setting forth a theory of alternative liability modeled after Summers v. Tice, 199 P.2d 1, 4 (Cal. 1948).

* * *

Accepting the truth of all of plaintiffs' well-pleaded allegations, from 1975 until 1987, Stephen Poole, a hemophiliac, purchased and internally injected an antihemophilic factor known as factor VIII. The named defendants comprise the complete market of manufacturers, processors, marketers, and distributors from which Poole purchased factor VIII over his lifetime. According to the complaint, as the result of defendants' solicitation of blood donors from a high-risk segment of the population, their failure to perform screening and heat-treating tests, and their failure to warn decedent of factor VIII risks, Poole contracted Acquired Immune Deficiency Syndrome (AIDS) and died on July 10, 1987.

Plaintiffs specifically labeled counts IX and X "Market Share Liability" claims. In these counts plaintiffs assert that from 1982 to 1985 defendants solicited donors known to have a high risk of contracting AIDS without informing Poole of this risk, and that they marketed improperly-treated factor VIII products, despite the fact that they knew that these products could lead to the contraction of AIDS. Plaintiffs further assert that * * * they have identified all those defendants from whom decedent purchased factor VIII * * *. The proposed counts seek damages based on the respective market share of each defendant and assert theories of liability that would allocate the burden of proof in such a way that each defendant would be required to show that its product did not cause Poole's death.

* * *

While plaintiffs have labeled their proposed counts "Market Share Liability" claims, we look to the substance of the allegations themselves to determine whether they support valid theories of liability.

A. *Market Share*

The concept of market share liability was first developed by the California Supreme Court in Sindell v. Abbott Laboratories, 26 Cal.3d 588,

607 P.2d 924 (1980), to address the unique causation problems raised by diethylstilbestrol (DES) litigation. In *Sindell*, the plaintiff alleged that she was injured by DES which her mother ingested while she was pregnant with the plaintiff. The plaintiff brought an action naming several drug manufacturers and alleging that they had produced DES pursuant to an agreed-upon formula. Her claims sounded in negligence, strict liability, violation of express and implied warranties, and false and fraudulent representations. The court acknowledged the general rule that a plaintiff bears the burden of establishing that the damages suffered were caused by the defendant. It modified the rule because the plaintiff was unable to identify the manufacturer responsible for making the DES taken by her mother while she was *in utero*. Specifically, the *Sindell* court determined that if the plaintiff joined in the litigation the manufacturers of a substantial share of the DES that her mother might have taken, the burden of proof would shift to the defendants to demonstrate that they could not have supplied the DES which caused her injuries. The court ruled further that each defendant failing to make such a showing would be held liable for the proportion of the judgment represented by its share of the drug market.

In Illinois, the market share theory of liability has met with limited success. * * * [O]nly one Illinois court has applied the theory, [and that court (an intermediate appellate court)] explained that its holding was limited to the DES action before it and recounted factors making DES litigation unique. As plaintiffs' action involves factor VIII and AIDS, not DES, we find [the Illinois DES case] of limited relevance here. Further, [the fact that] plaintiffs have identified all those defendants responsible for Poole's injury [makes the market share theory inapplicable here]. * * * As a federal court, we refuse to expand Illinois tort law in new ways where there is no indication that the state courts would do the same. * * * We thus decline to adopt the market share theory of liability here.

B. *Concerted Action*

Under their concerted action theory plaintiffs must show that a tacit agreement existed among defendants to perform a tortious act. Illinois has adopted the approach set forth in the Restatement of Torts for determining whether defendants have engaged in concerted action. [Restatement (Second) of Torts § 876 (1979)] provides:

> For harm resulting to a third person from the tortious conduct of another, one is subject to liability if he
>
> (a) does a tortious act in concert with the other or pursuant to a common design with him, or
>
> (b) knows that the other's conduct constitutes a breach of duty and gives substantial assistance or encouragement to the other to so conduct himself, or

(c) gives substantial assistance to the other in accomplishing a tortious result and his own conduct, separately considered, constitutes a breach of duty to the third person.

Plaintiffs here have failed to allege that the named defendants pursued a common plan or tacitly agreed to commit the tortious acts about which they complain. Instead, plaintiffs assert that defendants committed parallel tortious acts, which they specifically describe as "identical negligent conduct." Not only is the complaint wholly devoid of the assertions necessary to sustain a concerted action claim, but the type of allegations that plaintiffs do include have generally been rejected as inadequate to support such a theory. We therefore find the proposed amendments insufficient to support a concert-of-action theory.

C. *Alternate Liability*

Unlike the newly developed concept of market share liability, the theory of alternate liability was introduced in 1948 in Summers v. Tice and has been adopted by the Restatement. Under [Restatement (Second) § 433B],

> [w]here the conduct of two or more actors is tortious, and it is proved that the harm has been caused to the plaintiff by only one of them, but there is uncertainty as to which one has caused it, the burden is upon each such actor to prove that he has not caused the harm.

As traditionally applied, the theory requires that each negligent actor prove that his actions did not cause the plaintiff's injury, and in failing such proof all defendants are liable.

The Illinois Supreme Court has yet to address the precise issue before us—whether the theory embodied in *Summers* applies to shift the burden in a case where an AIDS victim is able to identify the universe of negligent defendants responsible for transmitting the disease to him. Despite the dearth of case law and the uniqueness of the facts before us, we do not now reject plaintiffs' theory. Although the Illinois Supreme Court has not yet ruled on its applicability in AIDS cases, we attempt a prediction of Illinois law based on lower state court decisions, the general rule on the issue before us, and legal sources such as treatises. * * *

[Courts around the country that have rejected] the alternative liability theory have done so primarily because not all of the defendants were named in the suits. Since plaintiffs have identified all of the defendants that could have possibly caused Poole to contract AIDS, this case presents the classic situation contemplated by the alternative liability doctrine. When all defendants are present, courts have adopted the theory. * * *

AIDS is a relatively recently discovered and newly publicized disease without a cure, responsible for taking the lives of increasing numbers of Americans and people worldwide. The case before us presents a set of circumstances not yet confronted by the Illinois Supreme Court and indeed few courts, federal or state, have had the opportunity to consider the legal implications of AIDS-related injuries and deaths—and we anticipate the advent of many more such actions in the future. At this early stage of the litigation, in light of the fact that plaintiffs are able to identify all possible defendants responsible for Poole's death, we are unprepared to reject the theory of alternative liability here. We recognize, however, that factual development in this case, and legal development in the AIDS field, may mandate later rejection of the theory. We simply hold, for now, that the Illinois Supreme Court would follow the vast majority of courts in allowing plaintiffs to proceed on a theory of alternate liability. * * *

BUCHANAN v. VOWELL

Court of Appeals of Indiana, 2010.
926 N.E.2d 515.

BARTEAU, SENIOR JUDGE.

* * *

[Jerry Buchanan's complaint for damages against defendants Candice Vowell, Shannon Vowell, and Brad's Gold Club pleaded the following facts.] During the early morning hours of July 29, 2007, Jerry was a pedestrian walking westbound near the edge of the eastbound lane of Kessler Boulevard close to its intersection with Ditch Road in Marion County. At that same time, Defendant Candice Vowell ("Candice") was driving her vehicle eastbound on Kessler Boulevard and struck Jerry, throwing him on the hood of her car and into the windshield. Jerry suffered permanent brain damage and fractures to various bones.

Prior to the accident, Candice had, during her hours of employment or immediately thereafter, consumed sufficient alcohol to become intoxicated. The alcohol was provided by Candice and Shannon's employer, Brad's Gold Club. Candice and Shannon, who is Candice's mother, determined that rather than call a cab or leave Candice's car at Brad's Gold Club, they would traverse the Marion County streets with Candice leading and Shannon following. At the time of the accident, Shannon was following Candice in a separate vehicle, and was engaging Candice in conversation on a cellular telephone.

[Jerry alleged] that at the time of the accident Shannon knew that Candice was operating her vehicle while intoxicated and knew or should have known that talking on her cell phone would further impair or distract Candice, making her even more dangerous to other persons using the streets. Jerry further alleged that Shannon "negligently made the affirmative, conscious effort to call Candice, distracting her from maintaining a proper lookout." Jerry noted that Candice and Shannon elected to leave the scene of the accident, "leaving Jerry in his wounded and unconscious states to fend for himself."

Jerry [alleged] that the negligence of Candice, Shannon, and Brad's Gold Club resulted in physical and emotional injuries, as well as significantly impairing or eliminating his ability to earn income to support himself and his daughter. * * * Shannon filed a motion for dismissal pursuant to Indiana Trial Rule 12(B)(6) for failure to state a claim upon which relief could be granted, which the trial court granted. [The case is before this court on interlocutory appeal.]

* * *

[T]the crux of Jerry's [case] is that Shannon engaged in a negligent activity with Candice that was the proximate result of Jerry's injuries. * * * [Jerry] alleges that Shannon acted in concert with Candice * * *. [He also claims] that Shannon's cellular communication with Candice negligently distracted an intoxicated driver.

* * *

* * * Jerry may show that Shannon is liable for Candice's negligent acts if Shannon is found to be acting in concert with Candice. Restatement (Second) of Torts § 876 is relevant here, and it provides that a person is liable for tortious conduct of another if she:

(a) does a tortious act in concert with the other or pursuant to a common design with [her], or

(b) knows that the other's conduct constitutes a breach of duty and gives substantial assistance or encouragement to the other so to conduct [herself], or

(c) gives substantial assistance to the other in accomplishing a tortious result and [her] own conduct, separately considered, constitutes a breach of duty to the third person.

Pursuant to this language, a person will be held liable for the injuries that flow from her participation in a joint concerted tortious activity, if that activity was the proximate cause of the plaintiff's injuries. Although Indiana cases have not addressed the issue before us under Restatement § 876, Illinois cases have addressed the use of the Restatement provision in similar circumstances. In Clausen v. Carroll, 684 N.E.2d 167, 171 (Ill.App. 1997), the court held that all participants in a drag race may be held jointly liable when a third party is injured by one race participant. More importantly, in Sanke v. Bechina, 576 N.E.2d 1212 (Ill.App.1991), the court held that a passenger in the driver's vehicle may be held jointly liable to a third party when the passenger verbally encourages the driver to exceed the posted speed limit and disregard a stop sign, and the driver thereafter fatally injures a third person. Liability is found where a person is engaged in a joint concerted tortious activity and any alleged injuries were the result of such activity.

The allegations made by Jerry * * * show that Shannon agreed to enter into a concerted activity whereby Shannon would follow the drunken Candice and would direct and/or distract her by calling her on her cell phone. The allegations also show that Candice and Shannon conspired to leave the scene of an accident where serious injury to Jerry had occurred. Thus, like the passenger in *Sanke,* Shannon encouraged Candice's tortious activity. It is possible that Shannon, like the passenger in *Sanke,* could be held jointly liable for Jerry's injuries.

Furthermore, we note that Shannon owed a duty of reasonable care to those that shared the road with her, both motorists and pedestrians. Shannon, as an individual, may have breached this duty by calling and distracting a person she knew was operating a vehicle while under the influence of alcohol. Thus, Shannon may be found liable for Jerry's injuries even if she did not * * * act in concert with Candice.

* * *

Reversed and remanded.

NOTES

1. ***The concerted action theory is different from vicarious liability.*** Dobbs, The Law of Torts § 175, p. 428 (2000), says that when "two defendants are acting in concert, as part of a common plan or design, they are true joint tortfeasors and each is vicariously liable for the other's negligence." But that does not seem quite right, because courts seem to insist that the defendant must himself have engaged in tortious behavior. See, e.g., Orser v. Vierra, 252 Cal.App.2d 660, 60 Cal.Rptr. 708, 713–714 (1967), a two-shooters, single-wound case in which the court quoted approvingly from an early version of the Prosser torts treatise as follows:

> All those who, in pursuance of a common plan or design to commit a tortious act, actively take part in it, or further it by cooperation or request, or who lend aid or encouragement to the wrongdoer, or ratify and adopt his acts done for their benefit, are equally liable with him. * * * [M]ere knowledge by each party of what the other is doing is [not] sufficient "concert" to make each liable for the acts of the other since one man ordinarily owes no duty to take affirmative steps to interfere with another's activities absent some special relationship. * * * It is * * * essential that each particular defendant who is to be charged with responsibility shall be proceeding tortiously, that is to say with intent to commit a tort, or with negligence.

On this view, the concerted action theory is not full-blown vicarious liability (see Chapter VIII) but might instead be termed a theory of "vicarious causal responsibility."

2. ***The concerted action theory seldom works in multiple-source products cases.*** Many courts have agreed with the view taken in *Poole* that drug companies' cooperation with each other—for example, in securing FDA approval of a product that they have reason to suspect may be dangerous—is mere "parallel" conduct that is not alone sufficient to show (in the words of the *Poole* court) "a tacit agreement to perform a tortious act." See, e.g., Hymowitz v. Eli Lilly and Co., 73 N.Y.2d 487, 541 N.Y.S.2d 941, 539 N.E.2d 1069, 1074 (1989):

> [T]he theory of concerted action, in its pure form, [does not] supply a basis for recovery [in a DES case]. This doctrine, seen in drag racing

cases, provides for joint and several liability on the part of all defendants having an understanding, express or tacit, to participate in "a common plan or design to commit a tortious act." * * * [D]rug companies were engaged in extensive parallel conduct in developing and marketing DES. There is nothing in the record, however, beyond this similar conduct to show any agreement, tacit or otherwise, to market DES for pregnancy use without taking proper steps to ensure the drug's safety. Parallel activity, without more, is insufficient to establish the agreement element necessary to maintain a concerted action claim.

3. *The position of the Third Restatements on concerted action.* Section 15 of the Apportionment Restatement addresses how courts should handle concerted-action cases in comparative-fault regimes (see infra Chapter IX) but "does not address the rules regarding when concerted activity exists." Id. cmt. *a*. Restatement (Third) of Torts: Liability for Physical and Emotional Harm (2010) does not appear to treat the concerted action theory.

4. *The market share theory.* In creating the market-share response to the DES problem, the California Supreme Court in *Sindell* (see the discussion in *Poole*), relied heavily on a law review article authored by a law student (Naomi Sheiner), Comment, DES and a Proposed Theory of Enterprise Liability, 46 Fordham L. Rev. 963 (1978). In the wake of *Sindell*, many other courts (including the New York high court in *Hymowitz*) developed their own versions of a DES-specific market-share theory. Only a very few courts have taken the theory beyond the DES context. See, e.g., Smith v. Cutter Biological, Inc., 72 Haw. 416, 823 P.2d 717 (1991) (antihemophilic factor infected with AIDS virus).

The Restatement (Third) of Torts: Liability for Physical and Emotional Harm(2010) takes no position on the validity of the market share theory but (in § 28 cmt. *o*) offers a helpful explanation:

> [T]he drug diethylstilbestrol (DES) [was] prescribed in the middle part of the 20th century to prevent miscarriages. DES, because it was not patented, was manufactured by hundreds of pharmaceutical companies. DES caused disease in the [daughters] of the mothers who took the drug, typically 20 years after exposure, and at a time when evidence of which manufacturer produced the DES the mother had consumed was, quite often, unavailable. * * * A number of courts * * * adopted a new "market share" theory that permitted apportionment of liability among defendant-manufacturers based on each one's share of the relevant market for DES. Many of the details of the specific market-share theory adopted vary from court to court, but common to all is that liability is several, rather than joint and several, and is limited to the market share of each defendant, so that in theory each will pay roughly the amount that represents the overall harm caused by that defendant's DES. A roughly equal number of courts have declined to craft a new theory for DES patients, expressing concern that to do so would rend too great a chasm in the tort-law requirement of factual causation. Despite several decades of development, the number of jurisdictions that have addressed and resolved this question for DES victims is quite small; the vast majority of states has not yet been confronted with or decided this issue.

However, with DES having been withdrawn from the market in 1971, a latency period of approximately 20 years, and very little judicial activity over the past decade, it appears unlikely that there will be any significant further development of market-share liability in the DES context. Virtually all courts that have considered the question have declined to apply a market-share liability theory to products that are not fungible and therefore do not pose equivalent risks to all of those exposed to the products.

D. LIMITED–PURPOSE SUBSTITUTES FOR THE STANDARD BUT–FOR APPROACH: THE LOST OPPORTUNITY DOCTRINE

GRANT v. AMERICAN NATIONAL RED CROSS

District of Columbia Court of Appeals, 2000.
745 A.2d 316.

FARRELL, ASSOCIATE JUDGE.

* * *

In July 1982 Calvin Grant * * *, then age twelve, underwent surgery at Children's Hospital in Washington, D.C. to repair a congenital heart defect. During the surgery he received five units of whole blood, which had been provided to Children's Hospital by * * * the American National Red Cross * * *.

All of the five donors whose blood was used on Grant satisfied the blood screening requirements then utilized by the Red Cross. However, in compliance with the Red Cross's procedures at the time, none of the blood had been tested for alanine aminotransferase ("ALT") levels. In September 1993, after a liver biopsy, Grant was found to have the hepatitis C virus. He filed a complaint in the Superior Court charging the Red Cross with negligence in not having screened the blood administered to him during the 1982 surgery for ALT. During the litigation, it was determined that one of the five donors of the donated blood had been positive for hepatitis C. At the Red Cross's request, blood samples from the positive donor and [Grant] were tested by means of DNA, and it was confirmed that [Grant] had been infected with the virus during the 1982 transfusion.

In 1982, when Grant underwent surgery, scientists and doctors were aware that besides hepatitis A and hepatitis B there was a form referred to as "non-A, non-B" (or "NANB") hepatitis. Although today scientists know that most NANB hepatitis is caused by the hepatitis C virus ("HCV"), that virus was not isolated until 1989, and the first test to screen blood for HCV antibodies was not available until 1990. In his suit Grant asserted, nonetheless, that the Red Cross should have tested all donor blood for ALT levels as a "surrogate test" for NANB hepatitis,[2]

---

2. A surrogate test, while not testing directly for the causative agent of a disease or its antibodies, may reveal a statistical association between a disease and a particular agent.

because blood containing elevated levels of ALT has an increased chance of carrying the NANB hepatitis virus. According to [Grant], at the time of his surgery ALT testing could identify a significant portion (up to 40%) of the blood supply infected with the NANB hepatitis, and—he asserted—the Red Cross itself believed that ALT testing might prevent as many as a third of the expected serious cases of NANB hepatitis cases annually, yet made a "business" (or cost-benefit) decision to forgo the testing.

The Red Cross defended by asserting that in 1982, all of the available data and the practice of national blood suppliers counseled against routine screening by ALT donor testing. It proffered evidence that, according to the consensus of leading experts nationwide, ALT testing would not have detected approximately 70 percent of donors infected with the then-unknown viral agent HCV; that [30 percent] of the donors excluded on the basis of ALT testing would have been healthy and not affected by that agent; and that as a result routine ALT testing would have annually excluded many thousands of units of healthy blood from donors not carrying hepatitis, while failing to detect the vast majority of donors carrying NANB hepatitis.

Grant responded by conceding that he could not prove by greater than 50% (more likely than not) that he would not have been infected even if ALT testing had been performed. Specifically, he admitted that his expert testimony would be able to establish no more than a 40 percent correlation between ALT levels and infection with the NANB hepatitis * * *.[3] Grant argued nonetheless—as he does on appeal—that a jury should be allowed to decide whether the Red Cross's negligence in not screening for elevated ALT levels "depriv[ed] him of an opportunity to avoid" the infection he incurred even if that "opportunity" were measured at less than fifty-percent likelihood. Citing decisions of other courts that have applied the so-called "loss of chance" doctrine, he argued that it was "a jury question whether the Red Cross's negligent failure to test proximately caused Calvin Grant's injury by increasing his chances of getting NANB infected blood by at least 30%." The trial court, on the strength of decisions of this court cited by the Red Cross, concluded as a matter of law that Grant had failed to present triable issues of fact on both negligence and proximate causation. It therefore granted summary judgment to the Red Cross.

* * *

Grant concedes, as he did in the trial court, his inability to prove that the Red Cross's assumed negligence more likely than not caused his

---

3. * * * In her deposition Grant's expert witness, Dr. Johanna Pindyck, acknowledged that Grant's chance of not being infected would have improved by "at least 30 percent" had ALT testing been used, but that she could not "say for certain whether it would have been greater than that." This approximated the affidavit of Dr. Thomas Zuck, past president of the Council of Community Blood Centers, that in 1982 there was "only a 30% chance that the implicated donor would have had an elevated ALT level and his blood discarded" as a result of ALT testing. Similarly, a study performed by the National Institutes of Health at about the same time confirmed that ALT testing "would fail to detect about 70% of the blood that would infect recipients with non-A, non-B hepatitis" (Affidavit of Dr. Paul V. Holland).

hepatitis infection, i.e., that blood testing for ALT levels would—as a matter of probability—have detected the donor carrying the hepatitis C virus, leading to rejection of that blood donation. Instead Grant urges us to depart from that standard and accept the view of some courts in cases such as this that a plaintiff makes out a triable issue on causation by showing that the defendant's conduct deprived him of a substantial, though less than fifty percent, chance of a better outcome had due care been exercised. * * *

Grant argues * * * that this court has already applied the "loss of chance" doctrine in Ferrell v. Rosenbaum, [691 A.2d 641 (D.C. 1997)] * * *. Upon analysis, we do not read *Ferrell* as deviating from the basic standard of proof of causation by probability. In that case, the plaintiff sued her physician and hospital for misdiagnosing her infant child's potentially fatal blood disorder of Fanconi anemia. She proffered evidence that the child's best hope of survival into adulthood had been through a bone marrow transplant from a compatible donor sibling. Indeed, her expert witness would have testified that, according to recent scientific reports, "*70 to 90 percent* of Fanconi anemia patients can be cured of their hematological disease if transplanted with a matched sibling at an early age." The plaintiff's theory was that the defendants' negligence in misdiagnosing the child's condition deprived her of the opportunity she would have seized—but which she later lost through circumstances—to bear a child or children who could have donated the necessary bone marrow. In reversing summary judgment to the defendants, we acknowledged that "[t]he bare possibility that the Ferrells could have had another child, or children, that could have been a suitable bone marrow donor" would not suffice * * *. But we held that, given the proffered testimony that the mother "would have done anything to help [the affected child], including having another child or children," the "significant" chances that this "would have yielded a suitable donor" for the child, and the even stronger evidence (cited above) of correlation between a transplant and likely cure, the plaintiff had presented a triable issue on whether the alleged negligence "substantial[ly]" contributed to the child's reduced chances for survival. * * * Id. at 651–52 (citing and relying on conclusion of the court in Daniels v. Hadley Mem'l Hosp., 185 U.S.App.D.C. 84, 93, 566 F.2d 749, 758 (1977), "that there was an 'appreciable chance' that [the] patient's life would have been saved, after [a] bench trial includ[ed] testimony that 75–80% of patients survived if given proper treatment").

The "lost chance" recognized in *Ferrell* was thus the opportunity for the plaintiff to avail herself of a medical procedure with a high likelihood (a 70–90 percent chance) of success if carried out. No similar claim is made in the present case, given Grant's inability to offer proof that screening blood for ALT levels would have offered a more than thirty-percent-plus chance of detecting a donor's hepatitis. *Ferrell* thus synchronizes with the standard of probability required by our decisions, whereas Grant's proof does not.

* * *

Grant's conceded inability to prove that the Red Cross's assumed negligence more likely than not caused his injury required the entry of summary judgment for the Red Cross. Accordingly, the judgment of the Superior Court is affirmed.

NOTES

1. ***The genesis of the lost opportunity doctrine.*** The lost opportunity doctrine came out of cases grappling with the normal requirement of expert testimony to establish factual causation in medical malpractice cases. The law's burden-of-proof standard on factual causation is "by a preponderance of the evidence," meaning "more probably than not." But medical experts are often loath to give an opinion that "X probably caused Y." They seem more comfortable with expressing their opinions in the form of estimates of the mathematical chances that avoiding X would have avoided Y. At one time courts were inclined to regard such estimates as too conjectural to serve as evidence of factual causation in medical cases, sometimes suggesting that "even a conjecture that a better than fifty percent chance of [medical] recovery would have been in prospect but for the defendant's negligence will not justify a submission [of the cause-in-fact] issue to the jury." Malone, Ruminations on Cause-in-Fact, 9 Stan.L.Rev. 60, 88 (1956).

In Hamil v. Bashline, 481 Pa. 256, 392 A.2d 1280 (1978), expert testimony established that an emergency room physician's failure to diagnose and treat a patient's heart attack—which proved fatal—deprived the patient of a 75% chance of surviving. Reversing a jury verdict for the defendant, the Pennsylvania Supreme Court held, in effect, that such testimony is readily translatable into terms with which the law is comfortable: When a medical witness gives an expert opinion that "X deprived the patient of a 75% chance of avoiding Y," courts can take that to mean "X probably caused Y."

That's all there was to *Hamil.* Nevertheless, courts in cases like Herskovits v. Group Health Co-op., 99 Wash.2d 609, 664 P.2d 474 (1983), picked up on *Hamil* and used it as authority for allowing damages when the medical testimony put the chance of survival that the defendant's negligent conduct cost the patient at less than 50%. The experts in *Herskovits* testified that the defendant's negligent failure to timely diagnose and begin treating a patient's lung cancer lowered the patient's chances of surviving the cancer from 39% to 25%. In a divided opinion, the court held that damages should be awarded (presumably calculated at 14% of whatever the damages would have been if plaintiff had been able to prove the defendant's negligent conduct caused the death). *Herskovits* became the leading case for the "lost opportunity" doctrine.

2. ***The lost opportunity doctrine in medical malpractice cases.*** The arguments for using the lost opportunity doctrine in the medical malpractice context are very strong. In Murrey v. United States, 73 F.3d 1448 (7th Cir. 1996), the plaintiffs could not show that a V.A. Hospital's delay in administering surgical treatment caused their decedent's death, but they did have evidence that prompt treatment would have given decedent a 5 to 10

percent chance of surviving. Judge Posner's opinion for the court explained why the hospital's negligent destruction of this small chance was actionable:

> It does not matter, as far as liability is concerned, how good or bad [the patient's] prospects were (obviously it matters greatly to the amount of damages). * * * A loss is a loss even if it is only probable, as are most things in life. No doubt Murrey would have paid a lot (if he had a lot to pay) for a 5 percent chance of survival if the alternative was a certainty of immediate death. This shows that he lost something by being deprived of that chance. If 200 people were in Murrey's situation and received improper care, we would expect 10 to have survived if all 200 had received proper care, so that if none of the 200 was entitled to any damages the hospital would have escaped liability for malpractice that had caused a number of deaths in a realistic sense of "cause." Damages for loss of a chance are necessary to prevent the underdeterrence of medical negligence.

Despite the strength of these arguments—which seem convincing on economic efficiency *and* corrective justice grounds—the lost opportunity doctrine is controversial. In Smith v. State Dep't of Health & Hosp., 676 So.2d 543, 547 (La.1996) (adopting the doctrine), the court said "it has been recognized by a majority of the states." But in an omitted footnote the *Grant* court said the majority of jurisdictions have rejected the doctrine. Third Restatement § 26 cmt. *n* "takes no position" on the validity of the lost opportunity doctrine.

3. ***The lost opportunity doctrine outside the medical malpractice context?*** Third Restatement § 26 cmt. *n* indicates that the lost opportunity doctrine has "almost universally" been confined to medical malpractice cases, explaining:

> Three features of that context are significant: (1) a contractual relationship exists between patient and physician (or physician's employer), in which the *raison d'etre* of the contract is that the physician will take every reasonable measure to obtain an optimal outcome for the patient; (2) reasonably good empirical evidence is available about the general statistical probability of the lost opportunity; and (3) frequently the consequences of the physician's negligence will deprive the patient of a less-than–50–percent chance for recovery.

4. ***The lost opportunity theory does not address emotional suffering***. The fear, anxiety, grief, anger, etc. resulting from medical negligence that deprives a patient of an opportunity of a medical cure must be carefully distinguished from the lost opportunity itself. The principles governing recovery for the emotional consequences in lost opportunity cases are treated in section E of Chapter VI, infra at pp. 233–51.

E. APPORTIONING DAMAGES ACCORDING TO CAUSATION

"Causation in fact is an all-or-nothing proposition. * * * [S]pecific conduct is either a cause in fact, or it is not."[1] A single indivisible injury—

---

1. Waste Management, Inc. v. South Central Bell Tel. Co., 15 S.W.3d 425, 433 (Tenn.App. 1997).

no matter how many causes in fact it has—cannot be apportioned by causation. Thus, for example, in Summers v. Tice, supra p. 128, the wound to the plaintiff's eye was a single indivisible injury, and each of the tortious shooters was treated as a cause in fact of the entirety.[2]

But obviously damages should be apportioned by causation whenever there is a reasonable basis for doing so, because otherwise, a bedrock cause-in-fact tenet—that no one should be held responsible for consequences that she had nothing to do with—will be offended. Thus, if the evidence in *Summers* had shown that one shooter wounded the plaintiff's eye and the other simultaneously wounded his knee, each shooter's liability would have been limited to the consequences that could be traced to his conduct, i.e., to the wound that he produced.[3]

We have just discussed a clear case of a single indivisible injury and a clear case of separate injuries that can and should be apportioned. The subject of this section is a large middle ground between these two poles. Quite often the injuries of which the plaintiff complains will be theoretically separate and divisible, but as a practical matter it will be impossible to sort out which injuries stemmed from which causes. Broadly speaking, the question addressed in this section is this: When the plaintiff can show that the defendant's tortious conduct was a cause in fact of some significant part (but probably not all) of an inextricable tangle of injuries, how do and should the courts respond?

1. APPORTIONING HARM CAUSED BY MULTIPLE TORTFEASORS

HOLTZ v. HOLDER

Supreme Court of Arizona, 1966.
101 Ariz. 247, 418 P.2d 584.

UDALL, JUSTICE.

* * *

On February 6, 1960, [plaintiff] Cynthia A. Holtz was driving north on 24th Street in the city of Phoenix. She stopped for a red light, in the lane nearest the center line, at the intersection of 24th Street and Thomas Road. Defendant James E. Holder also stopped for the light in the lane immediately to the right of the plaintiff. At a short distance across the intersection, the right lane of 24th Street was partially blocked by piles of dirt, which had been placed there by a construction crew that was installing a water line along the east edge of 24th Street, thus causing the street to narrow to a single lane of traffic on the left, nearest the center line. When the light changed to green, Cynthia Holtz and James Holder

---

2. Only one of them actually caused it, but the alternative liability doctrine legitimated treating each as though he had done so.

3. This would be true unless the concerted action theory applied to make each shooter responsible not only for his own shot but also for the other's.

both started north on 24th, but as a result of the narrowing of the street at the point of construction, there was not enough room for both cars to travel abreast, and a collision occurred between the two vehicles.

As a result of the collision the automobile driven by the plaintiff was forced in a westerly direction across the center line of 24th Street and into a pickup truck, which was facing south on 24th and was stopped in a line of cars which had been waiting for the light to change. Following the impact with the truck, plaintiff's vehicle came to rest in a crosswise direction across the lane in which she had been driving.

Plaintiff remained in her automobile after it came to a stop, and some five or ten minutes later a milk truck owned by defendant Carnation Company and being driven by one of its employees, turned north onto 24th Street from Thomas Road. As the driver of the truck approached the vehicle occupied by plaintiff, he became aware that there was little room for his truck to pass. He slowed down and proceeded to pass on the right, driving over a mound of dirt. In some manner, not clearly established by the evidence, the truck struck the car of the plaintiff before the passing maneuver was completed.

In the lower court plaintiff sought recovery for injuries allegedly received due to the negligent operation of their vehicles by defendants Holder and Carnation. * * * In the subsequent trial before a jury, an issue arose concerning the extent of injuries received in the separate collisions. Plaintiff offered testimony of her doctor to the effect it was medically impossible to determine which impact caused which injuries, or whether one or the other of the collisions caused all the injuries, and that the only way to tell would have been by an examination of the plaintiff immediately after the first collision with the vehicle driven by Holder. * * *

On this appeal from a general verdict in favor of both defendants, plaintiff assigns as error the giving of two instructions and the failure to give two others. The first instruction complained of was given on behalf of defendant Holder and reads as follows:

> You are instructed that as a matter of law defendant Carnation Company is not responsible for the injuries, if any, sustained by the plaintiff as a result of the impact between the Holder Ford and plaintiff's Buick, or the plaintiff's Buick and the Chevrolet pickup. You are further instructed that as a matter of law defendant Holder is not responsible for the injuries, if any, sustained by the plaintiff as a result of the impact between plaintiff's Buick and the Carnation milk truck. You are instructed where the evidence shows an injury may have resulted from one of two causes, but only one can be attributed to a defendant's negligence, the plaintiff cannot recover from that defendant.

The second allegedly erroneous instruction was given on behalf of defendant Carnation Company as follows:

You are further instructed the law of this state is when the plaintiff's injuries and damages have been a proximate result of one of several causes, but only one of such causes can be attributed to the negligence, it any, of the defendant Carnation Company, the plaintiff cannot recover. You are further instructed that if you find from the evidence that the personal injuries if any, suffered by the plaintiff Cynthia Holtz may have been the proximate result of the prior accident in which the defendant Carnation Company was not involved, or if you cannot determine from the evidence whether any injuries [that] may have been received by the plaintiff Cynthia Holtz existed prior to the accident with the Carnation Company truck, then in either of such events, the plaintiff cannot recover and your verdict must be for the defendant Carnation Company.

Plaintiff claims that the above instructions incorrectly state the law in a case where a plaintiff is unable to prove which defendant caused which injuries or whether all were caused by one defendant or the other. Plaintiff argues that her requested instructions No. 6 and No. 9, which were refused, contain a correct statement of the law applicable to such cases. Since we think that instruction No. 6 merely repeats the legal principles stated in No. 9, we will consider only the latter instruction. It reads as follows:

You are instructed * * * that if you find from the evidence that the defendant Holder was negligent, and that the defendant Carnation Milk Company was also negligent, and if you further find that the plaintiff's injuries were the proximate result of the negligence of both of the defendants, then it is your duty to apportion the total amount of damages suffered by the plaintiff between these defendants, rendering your verdict against each defendant in the amount of damages that you feel each defendant caused the plaintiff; however, if from the facts of this case you feel that there is no reasonable basis upon which to apportion the damage among the defendants, then it is your duty to award plaintiff a verdict for the full amount of [her] damages against the defendants and each of them.

In view of the errors alleged with regard to the above instructions, the precise question raised on this appeal is whether two or more independent tortfeasors may be held to a joint and several liability for the entire damages or injuries suffered by the plaintiff, because of the indivisibility of the harm caused by the separate acts of negligence; or whether the negligent actors will escape liability altogether, on an application of the general rule that an independent tortfeasor is liable only for the harm caused by his act, and that a plaintiff must carry the burden of proving the extent of damage or injury caused by each tortfeasor.

The majority of courts which have been confronted with this question have found that the two or more tortfeasors involved could be held to a joint and several liability, under a theory which has come to be known as the "single injury" or "single, indivisible injury" rule * * *.

* * *

On this appeal, plaintiff urges this Court to adopt the "single injury" rule, with its resulting imposition of joint and several liability upon independent tortfeasors. The weight of well-reasoned authority supports the rule. The "single injury" rule is based on the proposition that it is more desirable, as a matter of policy, for an injured and innocent plaintiff to recover his entire damages jointly and severally from independent tortfeasors, one of whom may have to pay more than his just share, than it is to let two or more wrongdoers escape liability altogether, simply because the plaintiff cannot carry the impossible burden of proving the respective shares of causation * * *. We are in agreement with this proposition, and consequently, we adopt the "single injury" rule as the correct one to be applied in multiple collision, indivisible injury cases.

* * *

For the reasons indicated, the judgment of the trial court is reversed and a new trial is ordered.

NOTES

1. ***Joint and several liability (and the "one satisfaction" rule).*** The term "joint and several liability" describes the feature of a judgment against multiple defendants—as to each of whom cause in fact has been established under the normal but-for test or one of the established limited-purpose alternatives—that enables the plaintiff to collect the entire amount from any one or any combination of them. A judgment imposing joint and several liability "means that each defendant is liable to the plaintiff for the whole of the plaintiff's damages, except that the plaintiff may not collect, from all of the defendants together, more than those damages." McKinnon v. City of Berwyn, 750 F.2d 1383, 1387 (7th Cir.1984). The principal function of the joint and several liability doctrine is to protect the plaintiff against the risk of "uncollectability," i.e., the risk that one or more of the tortfeasors may be insolvent or otherwise unable to satisfy its liability.

Ordinarily each defendant held subject to joint and several liability has a right of *contribution* from the other(s). The right of contribution means "that a defendant forced to pay a disproportionate amount of the plaintiff's damages [can ordinarily] insist that other defendants (or even nondefendant tortfeasors) reimburse him for some of the cost. [T]he whole point of contribution is to mitigate the effect of joint and several liability, which allows liability to fall disproportionately on one or some of a group of joint tortfeasors." *McKinnon,* 750 F.2d at 1387. Judgments imposing joint and several liability and recognizing contribution rights shift the risk of uncollectability from the plaintiff to the group of tortfeasors.

2. ***The single indivisible injury rule.*** The appropriateness of shifting the apportionment burden to defendants in what the *Holtz* court variously

calls "single injury" and "single indivisible injury" cases is widely accepted. It is endorsed by Apportionment Restatement § 26 cmt. *h* and by Third Restatement § 28 cmt. *d(1)*. The leading case for the approach is probably Maddux v. Donaldson, 362 Mich. 425, 108 N.W.2d 33 (1961), in which the plaintiff's tangle of injuries resulted from two collisions separated by about 30 seconds. The court allowed recovery in full from the second motorist. (The first, impecunious and uninsured, was not pursued.)

3. ***How far apart is too far?*** There is no agreement on how far apart in time the two accidents can be before the "single indivisible injury" burden-shifting rule loses its plausibility and gives way to the normal allocation of the burden of proof. The *Maddux* 30–second interval and the *Holtz* 5–10 minute interval were not particularly problematic. Pang v. Minch, 53 Ohio St.3d 186, 559 N.E.2d 1313 (1990), applied the burden-shifting rule against traffic tortfeasors responsible for three separate wrecks spread over a five-month period. But the court in Potts v. Litt, 171 Ariz. 98, 828 P.2d 1239 (App. 1991), thought two wrecks 13 days apart were outside the legitimate applicability of the rule, stating that "[w]e have been unable to find a case that was submitted to a jury under the indivisible injury rule in which the successive accidents were as distant in time as the accidents involved here."

2. APPORTIONING HARM CAUSED BY A COMBINATION OF TORTIOUS CONDUCT AND OTHER CAUSES

FOLLETT v. JONES

Supreme Court of Arkansas, 1972.
252 Ark. 950, 481 S.W.2d 713.

HOLT, JUSTICE.

* * * Chauncy G. Jones was driving a pick-up truck when a collision occurred between it and a car driven by [Frank Follett]. Jones sustained three nondisplaced broken ribs, contusions, abrasions, and a blow to his head as a result of the accident. He was taken to a hospital where he died 17 days later. Prior to the date of the accident, Jones had regularly worked at his job and, also, on his farm. However, it is undisputed that on the date of the accident, unbeknownst to the deceased, he had terminal cancer of the lung. The cancerous condition was discovered from the x-rays taken to determine the extent of the injuries to his chest. An autopsy report listed the cancer as the cause of his death. A jury found * * * that [Follett] was negligent in causing the accident and that [Follett's] negligence was the proximate cause of Jones' death. The jury awarded $3,867.89 damages to [Jones's estate in compensation for Jones's 17 days of suffering from the broken ribs, etc.] and $8,000.00 to [Jones's widow in wrongful death damages. Follett has appealed the award of wrongful death damages.] * * *

We first consider [Follett's] assertion * * * that the trial court erred in not directing a verdict in his favor as to the wrongful death because the evidence failed to establish that the "accident was the proximate cause of the decedent's death." Medical testimony from two physicians was presented to establish that the death was proximately caused by the accident. One of the doctors testified that "the injuries received in the automobile accident hastened his death" and, further, the death was a result of "a combination" of the injuries and the cancer. However, decedent would have eventually died of the cancer had the accident never occurred. The other medical expert testified: "I believe that his injuries hastened his death." This evidence when viewed most favorably to the appellees, as we must do on appeal, is sufficient to present a question of fact for a jury's determination as to whether the accident proximately caused Jones's death.

We next consider [Follett's] contention that the jury's award for wrongful death is based upon speculation in that the record is void of any evidence relating to the "period of time that the accident shortened the life span of the decedent." Although the evidence as adduced is sufficient to present a jury question as to proximate causation, there is no evidence * * * from which the jury could determine the relative time span that this accident "shortened" Jones's life. In the absence of such evidence the jury's award is without a reasonable basis and is, therefore, speculative. * * *. However, * * * upon a retrial it is not impossible that the deficiency of proof as to decedent's "shortened" life span could be supplied. In such a situation a remand [for a new trial] is proper.* * * [T]he judgment is reversed and the cause remanded.

LANCASTER v. NORFOLK AND WESTERN RAILWAY CO.

United States Court of Appeals, Seventh Circuit, 1985.
773 F.2d 807.

POSNER, CIRCUIT JUDGE.

This [is an] appeal by the Norfolk and Western from a judgment for $850,000 in a suit under the Federal Employers' Liability Act (45 U.S.C. §§ 51–60)* by a former employee of the railroad, Gary Lancaster * * *.

The jury could have found the following facts in favor of Lancaster. In 1975 he was a 30–year–old mechanic working in the railroad's locomotive shop in Decatur, Illinois. Lachrone, a short-tempered foreman in the shop who had once been disciplined for roughing up a worker, became angry at Lancaster and several other workers who Lachrone thought were soldiering on the job. After flipping over a table on which one of the workers (not Lancaster) was sleeping, and smashing a bench, Lachrone grabbed a

---

* Most workplace injury claims by employees against employers are taken out of the tort system by workers' compensation statutes, which impose a limited responsibility upon the employer regardless of fault and immunize the employer against tort liability. The Federal Employers' Liability Act (FELA) is an unusual (and important) alternative approach; it enables injured railway employees to sue their employers in tort. The Jones Act, 46 U.S.C. § 30104, does the same thing for seamen. [Ed.].

broom handle, approached Lancaster in a menacing fashion, screamed at him for about 15 seconds, and shook the broomstick in his face. * * *

The incident upset Lancaster abnormally. He thought people were following him, thought his phone was tapped, felt that the pressures of working for the railroad were too much, and went to Georgia to look for a new job. But after a couple of months his distress subsided and he went back to the old one. He was assigned to another foreman, Funderburk, who liked to "goose" workers, pull their hair, and hit them on the arms. He did these things to Lancaster, over the latter's protest. This behavior culminated in an incident in 1976 when Funderburk twice stuck his hand down the back of Lancaster's pants—once squeezing a buttock, the other time sticking his finger into Lancaster's anus. Lancaster became very upset, had trouble working, consulted a doctor, and on the doctor's advice took a leave of absence. [Lancaster was exhibiting definite symptoms of mental illness—most notably in the form of a hallucination in which he thought he saw a bug-like creature, almost a foot long, that had humanoid hands, feet, and face.] The doctor diagnosed Lancaster as suffering from anxiety * * *.

Lancaster returned to work early in 1977 and worked uneventfully until an incident in 1979 involving another supervisor, Boyd. Lancaster and another worker were repairing a locomotive under Boyd's supervision when Boyd picked up a sledgehammer—though as a supervisor he was not supposed to wield a sledgehammer—and swung it at a pin that was stuck. The sledgehammer flew out of Boyd's hands when he completed his swing, and struck Lancaster. Although only bruised, Lancaster became very upset because he thought Boyd had thrown the sledgehammer at him ("I swear before God the man throwed that sledgehammer, because when he throwed it, it went right where my head was back, and when I moved back is the only thing that saved my life").

Two months later Lancaster found himself working under another hot-tempered supervisor, like Lachrone—Tynan, a burly six-footer, who while fondling a pickax handle told Lancaster that if he didn't "keep on the job and do it right, I'll put your name on it." About a week later Lancaster happened to deliver some papers to Tynan that were folded. Tynan said, "I told you not to fold the papers," to which Lancaster replied that he had not folded them, they had been folded when he had received them to give to Tynan. Tynan, enraged, charged Lancaster with pickax handle in hand ("I turned around, and here's Jack [Tynan] coming at me, and I says, don't Jack, don't") and struck the door frame over Lancaster's head with the handle ("I heard his pickax handle hit the door frame, and I turned around, and there's Jack, and he wasn't smiling"). Lancaster became even more upset than after the previous incidents. Indeed his mental condition deteriorated rapidly. His doctor referred him to a psychiatrist who, two weeks after the incident with Tynan, diagnosed Lancaster as schizophrenic. Lancaster quit work, tried unsuccessfully to return, and is expected never to be well enough to work again.

A psychologist who testified for the railroad opined that Lancaster's latent schizophrenia would surely have been triggered by some other traumatic event if no supervisor misconduct had occurred. The two psychiatrists who testified for Lancaster thought this unlikely, among other reasons because Lancaster had got through two divorces before 1970 without incident. They thought that Lancaster's sense of self-worth was bound up with his work for the railroad and that his supervisors' hostile acts had exerted unbearable psychological pressure on him. All three expert witnesses agreed that the incident with Tynan, coming on top of the earlier incidents, had precipitated a descent into madness from which Lancaster will never recover.

Surprisingly, the railroad does not dispute the reasonableness of the damage award (which is made up of $40,000 in medical expenses, $200,000 in past and future pain and suffering, and $610,000 in lost earnings), although it does challenge one of the instructions on damages.

* * *

[The railroad also argues that most of the incidents that allegedly precipitated Lancaster's psychosis—the assault by Lachrone, the batteries by Funderburk, the battery or negligent infliction of personal injury by Boyd—are time-barred under the FELA's three-year statute of limitations. However, it is clear that the assault by Tynan—the pickax-handle episode—is not time-barred.] It was [Tynan] (the jury could have found) who pushed Lancaster over the edge. That Lancaster may have been made especially susceptible to such misconduct by earlier acts for which the railroad might or might not be liable would be no defense. Under the "thin skull," or more colorfully the "eggshell skull," rule, the railroad would be fully liable for the consequences of Tynan's assault.

* * *

Suppose the jury had been instructed that the only tortious conduct that it could consider was Tynan's assault in 1979, which clearly was not time-barred. The expert witnesses seem agreed that it was that assault which triggered the schizophrenia on which Lancaster's entire claim of damages rests. The fact that the railroad had weakened Lancaster by earlier misconduct for which it could not be held liable would be irrelevant to its liability for Tynan's assault and to the amount of damages it would have to pay. The tortfeasor takes his victim as he finds him (emphatically so if the victim's weakened condition is due to earlier, albeit time-barred, torts of the same tortfeasor); that is the eggshell-skull rule. The single act of Tynan made the railroad fully liable for all the damages that Lancaster sought and the jury awarded.

* * *

The last issue relates to the judge's refusal to instruct the jury to reduce Lancaster's damages by the probability that he would have become schizophrenic even if the railroad's supervisors had not misbehaved.

Lancaster points out that since the tortfeasor takes his victim as he finds him, if the victim is highly vulnerable that is the tortfeasor's bad luck; there is no discount to average damages. This is a thoroughly sensible principle, by the way. If a tortfeasor never had to pay more than the average victim's damages, victims as a class would be systematically undercompensated and tortfeasors as a class therefore systematically underdeterred, because victims with above-average injuries would get their damages cut down while victims with below-average injuries would not get an offsetting increase.

But a corollary to this principle is that the damages of the "eggshell skull" victim must be reduced to reflect the likelihood that he would have been injured anyway, from a nonliable cause, even if the defendant had not injured him. The purpose of this corollary is transparent in a case like Dillon v. Twin State Gas & Elec. Co., 85 N.H. 449, 163 A. 111 (1932). The estate of Dillon, who was electrocuted by the defendant's negligence on his way down from the bridge he had just jumped off, was allowed to get damages only for the short time Dillon would have lived had it not been for the defendant's negligence. But the principle also applies to cases such as this where the tort victim is highly vulnerable to injury and the damages he suffered must therefore be discounted (multiplied) by the probability, distinctly less than one, that but for the tort he would have lived a normal life.

It is desirable in such cases to direct the jury's attention to the issue by a specific instruction. But the failure to give such an instruction in this case was not reversible error. The judge's instruction on damages was sufficiently general to allow (though it did not compel, as it should have done) the jury to adjust damages downward for the probability that something other than tortious misconduct would have triggered Lancaster's latent schizophrenia; for he told the jury simply that they should award Lancaster the damages proximately caused by the alleged wrongdoing if they found the railroad liable. In its closing argument the railroad reminded the jurors of the psychologist's testimony that, had it not been for the alleged wrongdoing, something else in Lancaster's life would have set him off. Lancaster's counsel argued the contrary evidence of his expert witnesses but did not suggest that it would be improper for the jury to apportion damages according to the probability that Lancaster would have gone through the rest of his life without incident if he had not been victimized by the railroad. The jury was thus at least apprised of the issue.

More important, the railroad failed to offer a specific instruction. In a civil case it is not enough for a party, especially a sophisticated litigant like the Norfolk and Western Railway, merely to point out a subtle omission in the instructions and leave it to the plaintiff and the district judge to figure out as best they can how to repair it. A failure to offer a correct instruction normally will excuse the trial judge's giving an incorrect alternative, and the same principle should apply to the failure to offer any instruction. Furthermore, the defendant put in no evidence that would have enabled the jury to make a sensible apportionment of damages between the defendant's conduct and the normal vicissitudes of life that would have confronted Lancaster, and might have precipitated his madness, even if his supervisors had behaved. The instruction that the defendant requested, even if given, would thus have left the jury up in the air. It is the defendant's own fault that the jury was allowed to bring in a verdict that, given Lancaster's pre-existing vulnerability to psychosis, may seem high.

Affirmed.

NOTES

1. *The eggshell skull rule and its flip side*. The eggshell skull rule means that the victim's pre-accident vulnerability, however extreme, affords the tortfeasor no excuse. Thus, if the victim has unusually fragile bones, the injuries may be far more extensive than would have been those of an average person, but the tortfeasor is nevertheless responsible for the full extent of the injuries she culpably brought about. See, e.g., McNabb v. Green Real Estate Co., 62 Mich.App. 500, 233 N.W.2d 811 (1975) (contemplating full recovery for the extensive consequences of a "brittle diabetic's" fall on defendant's defective stairway).

By the same token, the victim may have unusually strong bones, so that his or her injuries are less extensive than would have been those of an average person. Here, too, the tortfeasor's responsibility is measured by the actual consequences. This is the flip side of the eggshell skull rule. Both sides flow from the premise that our tort law is a system of corrective justice. The maxim repeatedly recited by Judge Posner "the tortfeasor takes his victim as he finds him" succinctly captures that premise.

2. *The causation principle applied in Follett and Lancaster.* The eggshell rule does not address factual causation; it deals with the scope of a defendant's responsibility for consequences that concededly resulted from defendant's tortious conduct. But the rule that Judge Posner termed a "corollary" of the eggshell rule does address factual causation. In holding that the railroad's liability should have been limited to the value of the difference between the schizophrenia Tynan induced and the schizophrenia that Lancaster's pre-existing mental illness would eventually have brought about regardless of Tynan's attack, the court was applying the basic rule that a tortfeasor should not be held accountable for consequences that would have befallen the victim regardless of the tortfeasor's wrongful conduct. This same rule was applied in *Follett* to protect the tortfeasor from liability for the death that the victim's pre-existing cancer would have brought about regardless of the traffic accident.

3. *The problem presented by Dillon v. Twin State*. Dillon v. Twin State, supra p. 151, is arguably different from *Follett* and *Lancaster* in that Dillon (who did not jump, by the way; it was an accidental fall) was not suffering from a pre-existing illness at the time of the tort. But the difference seems slight, because Dillon was at least as certain to die from the fall that was already in progress when the tort occurred as Follett was from the cancer

(and probably more certain to die than Lancaster was to become schizophrenic).

But once the principle of the pre-existing condition cases is extended to a case like *Dillon*—in which the problem is not a pre-existing condition but a looming threat—the question arises, why shouldn't a defendant who kills a person in a car accident get a big discount if the decedent was on her way to catch an airplane that crashed on takeoff? Dobbs, The Law of Torts § 177, p. 433 (2000), suggests courts are adamantly resistant to such arguments because "it is both impractical and logically improper to devalue the plaintiff's life, limb, or property in the light of subsequent losses from extraneous forces that no one present at the time would have taken into account." King, Causation, Valuation, and Chance in Personal Injury Torts Involving Pre-existing Conditions and Future Consequences, 90 Yale L.J. 1353, 1356–57 (1981), gets at the difference between *Dillon* and the plane-crash hypothetical as follows:

> [A] tortfeasor should be charged only with the value of the interest he destroyed. In determining what that value is, the preinjury condition of the victim should be taken into account. Valuation therefore requires that there be a workable definition of pre-existing conditions—those conditions that should be considered in assessing the value of the interest destroyed. * * * Generally, a pre-existing condition may be defined as a disease, condition, or force that has become sufficiently associated with the victim to be factored into the value of the interest destroyed, and that has become so before the defendant's conduct has reached a similar stage. A threatening force or condition should qualify when it has "attached"— that is, its association with the value of the interest in question could not be avoided even if the victim were aware of its existence * * *.

See also Robertson, The Common Sense of Cause In Fact, 75 Tex.L.Rev. 1765, 1797–98 (1997).

4. *Note that Lancaster was an intentional tort case.* *Lancaster* is an important reminder that the cause-in-fact requirement is fully applicable in intentional tort cases.

5. *Assigning the burden of proof.* In noting that the railroad "put in no evidence that would have enabled the jury to make a sensible apportionment of damages," Judge Posner may suggest that the apportionment burden should be on the defendant in the present context, just as it is in the multiple-tortfeasor context. The next case indicates that the suggestion is somewhat controversial.

BLATZ v. ALLINA HEALTH SYSTEM

Court of Appeals of Minnesota, 2001.
622 N.W.2d 376.

LANSING, JUDGE.

Allina Health System, doing business as HealthSpan Transportation Services, contracts [with Scott County] to provide paramedic and ambulance services to Jordan, Minnesota, and surrounding communities.

* * *

In the summer of 1995, Mary Blatz lived at 18555 Halifax Lane in Jordan with her husband, Patrick Sherman, and their two children. On the morning of June 18, 1995, shortly after awakening, Blatz told Sherman she was having trouble breathing. * * * Sherman dialed 911.

The Scott County 911 tape indicates that Sherman's call was received at approximately 8:50 a.m. Sherman told the dispatcher that his wife was "having severe chest pains in a bad way right now." The dispatcher confirmed the family's address and telephone number, notified the Scott County Sheriff's Office, and notified the HealthSpan dispatcher. The HealthSpan dispatcher, in turn, notified HealthSpan paramedics, and the ambulance was en route at 8:53 a.m.

* * *

[Scott County Deputy Brian Wondra was not familiar with the immediate area but had no trouble finding the Blatz–Sherman residence. He arrived between 9:03 and 9:04 a.m. and began administering CPR to Blatz. The paramedics—who did have trouble finding the house—did not arrive until five or six minutes later. By then, Blatz had no heartbeat and was not breathing.] The paramedics inserted an oropharyngeal airway and gave Blatz 100% oxygen; they also established an IV line. One paramedic testified that within three minutes of their arrival, the monitor showed perfusion—that the heart was pumping and the blood was flowing. The other paramedic testified that Blatz's color improved within 30 to 60 seconds and her pulse returned within one to two minutes.

Blatz remained in a coma for approximately four weeks. No one has been able to determine what caused her initial cardiopulmonary arrest. But the arrest caused an anoxic brain injury that resulted in a severe loss of mental and physical capacity. Blatz is permanently disabled, is incapable of caring for herself, and lives in a nursing home. The medical evidence uniformly indicated that her condition will not improve. By January 2000, Blatz had incurred medical expenses of about $469,000.

Blatz's theory of [liability was that the paramedics were negligent] because "a reasonably prudent driver" would have [avoided the navigational mistakes made by the paramedics and therefore reached the Sherman residence significantly sooner. Blatz presented evidence that if the paramedics had not been delayed by their mistakes, they would have arrived at the Blatz–Sherman household approximately two to five minutes earlier. Blatz's theory of causation was based on the testimony of a physician who works as assistant director of a hospital's emergency department. He testified that the two-to-five minute] time period was within the window of opportunity in which Blatz could have been revived and irreversible brain damage could have been prevented.

Allina's defense theory rested on the testimony of two expert witnesses, a physician specializing in neurology and a physician specializing in pulmonary and respiratory disorders. Both expressed the opinion that the irreversible brain damage was complete before the deputy's arrival, and thus the paramedics' initial inability to locate the house had no effect on the brain injury Blatz suffered. * * *

The jury found that Allina was negligent in responding to the 911 call and that this negligence was a direct cause of Blatz's injuries. [It awarded $11 million in damages.] Allina brought post-trial motions for JNOV and a new trial. * * * The district court denied the motions, and Allina [has appealed, contending that the evidence does not support a finding of negligence or causation. Allina also challenges a jury instruction relating to damages.]

* * *

[We believe the evidence supports the jury's finding of negligence and causation and thus turn to Allina's challenge to the jury instruction.] Allina alleges that the district court's instruction on a pre-existing condition, based on CIVJIG 91.40, misstates the law. See 4A Minnesota Practice, CIVJIG 91.40 (1999). Allina argues that the last sentence [of the instruction] impermissibly shifts the burden of proving causal damages from the plaintiffs to the defendants. The instruction given at trial reads:

> Now, there is evidence that Mary Blatz had a pre-existing medical condition prior to the arrival of the Allina ambulance. Allina Health Systems is liable only for the damages that you find to be directly caused by the negligence, if any. *If you cannot separate damages caused by the pre-existing medical condition from those caused by Allina's negligence, if any, then Allina is to be held liable for all of the damages.*

4A Minnesota Practice, CIVJIG 91.40 (1999) (emphasis added). * * *

CIVJIG 91.40 is intended to take the place of CIVJIG 163 from the 1986 edition of the Jury Instruction Guides, which read:

> A person who has a defect or disability at the time of an accident is nevertheless entitled to damages for any aggravation of such pre-existing condition, even though the particular results would not have followed if the injured person had not been subject to such pre-existing condition. Damages are limited, however, to those results which are over and above those which normally followed from the pre-existing condition, had there been no accident.

[It is argued that CIVJIG 91.40's last sentence is consistent with the treatment of liability apportionment among at-fault defendants in] Mathews v. Mills, 288 Minn. 16, 22, 178 N.W.2d 841, 845 (1970). Analyzing liability for a passenger's injuries in a multiple-impact collision, the court held that "unless the damage caused by each [tortfeasor] is clearly separable, permitting the distinct assignment of responsibility to each, each is responsible for the entire damage." The burden of proving that the harm is capable of being divided lies with each defendant who contends it can be divided. If the court determines the harm is divisible, the actual apportionment is a fact question for the jury. The court, relying on principles of joint and several liability, reasoned that placing the burden of proof on the defendant "is a result of a choice made as to where a loss * * * shall fall—on an innocent plaintiff or on defendants who are clearly proved to have been at fault."

CIVJIG 91.40 extends beyond *Mathews* * * *. [I]t embraces the [appropriateness of] apportioning harm not just among at-fault defendants, but between a pre-existing condition and an at-fault defendant. [And] it places the burden of proof for the apportionment of aggravation on the at-fault defendant. Because the apportionment of aggravation of an injury is not between two at-fault defendants, as in *Mathews*, but rather between a pre-existing condition and an at-fault defendant, the principles underlying joint and several liability have thus been extended to circumstances in which they do not apply.

There is precedent in other states for placing the burden of proof on the at-fault defendant when apportioning damages between an at-fault defendant and an innocent or pre-existing cause. [The most frequently cited case in this line may be] Newbury v. Vogel, 151 Colo. 520, 379 P.2d 811, 813 (1963) (holding that defendant was responsible for the entire damage when court found it impossible to apportion between damages from accident and damages from pre-existing arthritic condition). * * * See generally Dan B. Dobbs, The Law of Torts § 174, at 425 (2000).

* * *

* * * With some rewording, [CIVJIG 91.40] may be a correct statement of the law in a case apportioning damage among two or more defendants whose combined conduct causes a plaintiff harm. But applying the instruction to aggravation of a pre-existing medical condition to apportion damage between that pre-existing condition and an at-fault defendant not only extends Minnesota law but also conflicts with existing caselaw.*

In this case, however, the instruction neither destroyed the substantial correctness of the charge nor created substantial prejudice on a vital issue. First, the district court crafted the instruction to state that Allina was liable only for damages directly caused by "its negligence, if any," rather than "any damages" caused by "the accident." The instruction is narrowed to the pre-existing medical condition and Allina's negligence, not incorporating any theoretical injuries "caused by the accident" that might not result from Allina's negligence or a pre-existing condition. Second, the effect of the instruction is limited by the facts of the case. Blatz's expert testified that Blatz sustained irreversible brain injury in the time period between arrival of the deputy at 9:03 to 9:04 a.m. and the paramedics' arrival at 9:08 to 9:09 a.m. Allina's causation experts both testified that Blatz sustained brain damage before the deputy arrived; thus, under Allina's theory of the case, an earlier arrival of the paramedics would not have made a difference because the irreversible injury was

---

* Rowe v. Munye, 702 N.W.2d 729, 738 (Minn. 2005), has confirmed that "CIVJIG 91.40 misstates Minnesota law because it erroneously combines joint and several liability rules with aggravation of pre-existing injury rules." [Ed.]

completed before 9:03–9:04 when the deputy arrived. The jury was thus presented two alternative theories of causation; those theories were separate, and the evidence did not overlap in a way that resulted in a shifting of the burden of proof. Furthermore, Allina did not argue for apportionment. The jury instruction, while not helpful to the jury, was not prejudicial. Allina is not entitled to a new trial because of the jury instruction on a pre-existing condition.

* * *

Affirmed.

NOTES

1. ***Restatements.*** Third Restatement § 28 cmt. *d(2)* puts cases like *Blatz* in a category it labels "apportioning harm between tortious conduct and innocent causes or nonparty actors," describes a split in the jurisprudence on the placement of the burden of proving up a basis for apportionment in these cases (Reporters' Note), and "takes no position on who should bear the burden of proof." The Apportionment Restatement § 26 cmt. *h* endorses placing the burden on the defendant. The Apportionment Restatement Reporters' Note acknowledges that the burden-placement question here is more difficult than in the multiple-tortfeasors context.

2. ***Why is burden-shifting more controversial here than in multiple-tortfeasor cases?*** We have found no clear explanation of the widely shared view that placing the burden on the defendant in cases like *Follett*, *Lancaster*, and *Blatz* is less readily justified than in cases like *Holtz*, supra p. 143. But it may be as simple as this: Our tort law is a system of corrective justice, which means that tortfeasors can routinely take advantage of their victims' extraneous bad luck—e.g., in being old, sick, poor, and/or unable to prove up a case. But allowing tortfeasors to benefit from one another's bad conduct just seems too powerfully unfair to countenance.

3. ***The apportionment burden should never be very heavy.*** Third Restatement § 28 cmt. *d* states: "However the burden of proof is allocated * * *, the preferred approach is to employ a modest threshold for the party with the burden of proof to satisfy the burden of production on the magnitude of harm." Cf. DePass v. United States, 721 F.2d 203, 209 (7th Cir.1983) (Posner, J., dissenting): "[A] tort plaintiff's burden of proving the extent of his injury is not a heavy one. Doubts are resolved against the tortfeasor."

CHAPTER V

PROXIMATE CAUSE (SCOPE OF LIABILITY)

■ ■ ■

A. INTRODUCTION TO CLASSIFICATION AND TERMINOLOGY PROBLEMS

Again we begin with a reminder that the plaintiff's prima facie case in negligence law comprises five issues or elements: duty, breach, cause in fact, proximate cause (scope of liability), and damages. In traditional thinking, the duty element is regarded as an issue of law for the trial judge to decide. The other four elements are loosely classified as issues of "fact," for the jury to decide unless reasonable minds could not differ.

The five-element formulation is a good tool (or tool kit) for resolving and understanding negligence cases provided the elements are kept separate and the boundaries among them maintained. Boundary-maintenance is an ongoing problem, principally because judges are often tempted to avoid subjecting cases to jury determination by classifying breach or proximate cause issues as duty issues.[1] We discuss this technique more fully in Chapter VI. For now, it will suffice to point out that some of the cases in this chapter use the terminology of duty or no-duty in treating issues that we believe should have been classified as proximate cause issues.

The proximate cause area of the law is famously rococo. Dobbs, The Law of Torts § 193, p. 484 (2000) notes that "a good deal of [the] terminology in proximate cause cases is superfluous." Having fun with this idea, Leon Green once spun out a list of what he deemed utterly useless "ruffles and decorations" that have been attached in front of the word *cause*, including "remote, proximate, direct, immediate, adequate, efficient, operative, inducing, moving, active, real, effective, decisive, supervening, primary, original, contributory, ultimate, concurrent, causa causans, legal, responsible, dominating, natural, probable, and others."[2]

---

1. See generally Powers, Judge and Jury in the Texas Supreme Court, 75 Tex.L.Rev. 1699 (1997); Robertson, The Vocabulary of Negligence Law: Continuing Causation Confusion, 58 La.L.Rev. 1 (1997).

2. Leon Green, Rationale of Proximate Cause 135–36 (1927).

The First and Second Restatements tried to encourage courts to use the term "legal cause" rather than "proximate cause," but the effort failed. Restatement (Third) of Torts: Liability for Physical and Emotional Harm (2010) includes (at p. 492) a "Special Note on Proximate Cause" announcing that the effort to shift to "legal cause" usage is being abandoned, deploring the term "proximate cause," and explaining why "proximate cause" must nevertheless be used. The Restatement (Third) calls this issue "Scope of Liability (Proximate Cause)."

B. THE RESTATEMENT (THIRD) APPROACH

ROYAL INDEMNITY CO. v. FACTORY MUTUAL INSURANCE CO.

Supreme Court of Iowa, 2010.
786 N.W.2d 839.

BAKER, JUSTICE.

[Factory Mutual Insurance Co. (FM) entered into an agreement with Deere & Company whereby FM undertook to conduct a fire-safety inspection of a warehouse that Deere was contemplating leasing as a place to store equipment. After the inspection was conducted, Deere leased the warehouse and moved the equipment into it. About two months later, the warehouse and all of Deere's equipment were destroyed by a fire. The evidence did not show what caused the fire, but the fire chief gave uncontradicted testimony that it would have been fairly quickly extinguished if there had been sufficient water pressure. Nothing in the FM–Deere contract contemplated any responsibility of FM to look into the warehouse's water-supply sources.

[Deere's equipment was insured against fire loss. The insurer, Royal Indemnity Company, paid the claim, thereby acquiring the right to step into Deere's shoes in order to pursue Deere's claims against FM.* At the close of the evidence in Royal's negligence action against FM,** the trial court directed a verdict for FM, concluding that the evidence was insufficient to establish a jury question on proximate cause. Royal appealed.]

The trial court's grant of a motion for directed verdict is reviewed for correction of errors at law. In reviewing the grant of a motion for a directed verdict, the court must determine whether reasonable minds could differ on the issue presented; if so, the grant was inappropriate. We view the facts in a light most favorable to the nonmoving party.

* * *

Viewing the evidence in a light most favorable to Royal, a jury could find that FM did not test the sprinkler system * * *. [This was probably

---

* The legal doctrine that entitled Royal to sue FM in Deere's stead is called *subrogation*. See infra p. 306 n.4. [Ed.]

** Royal also made breach of contract claims, which ultimately failed for reasons broadly similar to those that sank the negligence action. [Ed.]

negligent on FM's part. But a proper inspection of the sprinkler system would not have prevented the fire damage, because even if the sprinkler system had worked perfectly, the lack of water pressure would still have led to the destruction of Deere's equipment. Royal does not contend that an adequate inspection would have prevented the fire or that an adequate inspection would have revealed the source of the water-pressure failure. Royal's causation theory is that if the inspection had been adequate, the resulting information would have dissuaded Deere from leasing the warehouse.]

* * *

* * * "No serious question exists that some limit on the scope of liability for tortious conduct that causes harm is required." [Restatement (Third) of Torts: Liability for Physical and Emotional Harm § 29 cmt. *a*]. The Restatement (Third) expresses this limitation by providing that "[a]n actor's liability is limited to those harms that result from the risks that made the actor's conduct tortious." Id. § 29. "Central to the limitation on liability of this section is the idea that an actor should be held liable only for harm that was among the potential harms—the risks—that made the actor's conduct tortious." Id. cmt. *d*. [Section 30 adds: "An actor is not liable for harm when the tortious aspect of the actor's conduct was of a type that does not generally increase the risk of that harm."] * * *

The Restatement (Third) [at § 30 cmt. *a*, illus. 1] cites the following example for determining scope of liability:

> Gordie is driving 35 miles per hour on a city street with a speed limit of 25 miles per hour with Nathan as his passenger. Without warning, a tree crashes on Gordie's car, injuring Nathan. Gordie's speeding is a factual cause of Nathan's harm because, if Gordie had not been traveling at 35 miles per hour, he would not have arrived at the location where the tree fell at the precise time that it fell. Gordie is not liable to Nathan because Gordie's speeding did not increase the risk of the type of harm suffered by Nathan. The speeding merely put Gordie at the place and time at which the tree fell. * * *.

* * * This limitation on the scope of liability is important for creating appropriate incentives to deter tortious behavior and to address corrective-justice concerns. Restatement (Third) § 30 cmt. *b* [sets forth the rationale for the scope of liability (proximate cause) limitation as follows:

> This limitation on scope of liability contributes both to appropriate incentives for deterrence and to affirming corrective-justice concerns. Limiting liability to instances in which the tortious conduct increased the risk of harm is essential for appropriate incentives in a tort system that retains a factual-cause requirement. Deterrence, it is true, can be obtained by criminal and regulatory systems, but those devices remain outside the tort system. From a corrective-justice perspective, a merely serendipitous causal connection between the tortious aspect of the actor's conduct and the other's harm provides

little reason for requiring the defendant to correct for that which has been wrongfully taken from the plaintiff.]

With these principles in mind, we must examine the facts to determine whether the loss suffered is within the scope of liability, i.e., whether the loss was more likely to occur because of the deficiencies in the inspection or whether the loss was merely a case of the inventory being in the wrong place at the wrong time.

Under the Restatement (Third) analysis, to impose liability, something FM did or did not do must have increased the risk to Deere's product. There is no evidence that a proper or competent inspection would have either identified the source of the fire and prevented it, or discovered the problem with the water pressure and corrected it. [Royal] does not so claim. [Royal] asserts that [Deere] would not have leased the facility had it known of the problems. Thus, [Royal] may have established factual causation, i.e., but for the bad inspection, [Deere] would not have leased the facility [thereby placing its equipment in harm's way].

* * *

[It is helpful to consider] Gorris v. Scott, 9 L.R. Exch. 125 (1874) as an example of when but-for causation is not enough to establish civil liability for wrongdoing. In that case,

> [t]he plaintiff's sheep were being transported on a ship owned by the defendant. A storm arose and the sheep were swept overboard to a watery death. The defendant had failed to equip the ship with pens for the sheep, as he was required to do in order to prevent the spread of disease among the animals. Had he complied with his duty the sheep would have been saved. And so the violation of the duty was a "but for" cause of their loss. Yet the plaintiff was not allowed to recover any damages. The loss of the sheep was a consequence, but not a foreseeable consequence, of the violation of a legal duty, because the duty was to take precautions against a different kind of loss from the one that materialized.

[Movitz v. First National Bank of Chicago, 148 F.3d 760, 762–63 (7th Cir. 1998), (citing Gorris v. Scott, 9 L.R. Exch. 125).] * * * We agree with this analysis. * * * Royal failed to prove that a condition or deficiency overlooked by FM in its inspection increased the risk of the loss that actually occurred. We hold that the loss to Deere's inventory was outside the scope of liability. [The trial court's entry of judgment for FM is affirmed.]

NOTES

1. ***An additional insight from the Third Restatement***. In § 29 cmts. *b* and *d*, the Restatement (Third) explains that jury instructions on proximate cause should convey the idea that "the harm that occurred must be one that results from the hazards that made the defendant's conduct tortious in the first place." "Thus, the jury should be told that, in deciding whether the plaintiff's harm is within the scope of liability, it should *go back to the*

reasons for finding the defendant engaged in negligent or other tortious conduct.'' (Emphasis supplied.)

2. ***The Gorris v. Scott analogy.*** The *Royal* opinion presented *Gorris* via a quotation from Judge Posner's opinion in *Movitz.* Arguably the Posner version of *Gorris* took liberties with the case; as we saw in Chapter III at p. 89, *Gorris* was a negligence per se case, not an ordinary negligence case, and it was not couched in unforeseeability terms but rather in terms of the scope of intended protection of the statute the defendant had violated. But Judge Posner's somewhat blithe reconstruction of *Gorris* can be seen as an economical way to make an important point. The proximate cause element can indeed usefully be seen as the ordinary negligence law's analog to the threshold criteria for imposing liability (under the rubric of "negligence per se") on the basis of defendant's violation of a penal or regulatory (non-tort) statute. The ultimate question addressed by both the negligence per se criteria and the proximate cause issue is this: Was the rule of law violated by the defendant designed to protect people like the plaintiff against harm of the sort the plaintiff suffered?

In an ordinary negligence case, identifying the "rule of law" violated by the defendant is not as easy as in a negligence per se case (where the plaintiff is pointing to the language of a particular statute). But—to sharpen the analogy—here is a way of looking at the "rule of law" problem: In an ordinary negligence case, the plaintiff establishes that the defendant violated the law by satisfying the breach element, i.e., by proving that the defendant engaged in conduct that was less than reasonable care under the circumstances. In order to establish that the defendant's conduct fell below reasonable care, the plaintiff must show that the defendant's conduct created or exacerbated one or more foreseeable risks of harm to others. That array of risks—the array of foreseeable risks of harm that the defendant should have guarded against—identifies and defines the rule of law the defendant violated. The proximate cause issue then becomes: was the injury that befell the plaintiff among the array of foreseeable risks the existence of which called upon the defendant to alter his or her conduct?

3. ***The Third Restatement analysis is a good synthesis of typical proximate cause outcomes.*** Courts have long bemoaned the lack of any clear test for proximate cause. See, e.g., Derosier v. New England Tel. & Tel. Co., 81 N.H. 451, 130 A. 145, 152 (1925):

> No legal question has been more discussed in the cases than this one of legal cause, or, as it has commonly been termed, proximate cause. Very many attempts have been made to frame a definition or state a test which will determine whether there is or is not liability in all cases. None of these attempts have been successful.

But when one looks at the outcomes (rather than the language) of proximate cause cases, the sense of chaos is much diminished. As Judge Friendly put it, "what courts do in [proximate cause] cases makes better sense than what they, or others, say." In re Kinsman Transit Co., 338 F.2d 708, 725 (2d Cir. 1965). See also Johnson v. Greer, 477 F.2d 101, 106 (5th Cir. 1973): "[W]e will not attempt to reconcile all of the varying judicial pronouncements on the subject [of proximate cause], which differ more in semantics than in substance." Regardless (more or less) of what courts may have been *saying* in their proximate cause rulings, the Third Restatement articulates what we believe courts have most often *done* with the proximate cause issue: they have *allowed the trier of fact to find proximate cause whenever the plaintiff's injury was among the array of risks the creation or exacerbation of which led to the conclusion that the defendant's conduct was negligent.*

4. ***Why do we need a proximate cause limit?*** *Royal* and the Third Restatement say we need it for both economic efficiency and corrective justice reasons. Not everyone agrees. See Robertson, Metaphysical Truth vs. Workable Tort Law: Adverse Ambitions? (Book Review), 88 Tex. L. Rev. 1053, 1063–65 (2010) (sketching an argument that the corrective justice and economic efficiency justifications for the proximate cause limit are unconvincing and that proximate cause is best viewed as "a justice-rationing device—meant largely for the courts' own protection—that is closely analogous to the standing-to-sue requirement"). Cf. Zipursky, Rights, Wrongs, and Recourse in the Law of Torts, 51 Vand. L. Rev. 1 (1998) (discussing a concept of "substantive standing").

C. SOME FAMOUS OLD CASES

The *Wagon Mound* case just below was seen as a sea change in British tort jurisprudence. In overruling In Re Polemis, (1921) L.R. 3 K.B. 560, the Privy Council seemed to shift from a time-honored (and relatively lenient) approach to the proximate cause issue to a much more restrictive (defendant-friendly) one.

Polemis was an action for extensive fire damage that resulted when defendant's employees, working aboard plaintiff's ship, dropped a heavy plank into the hold. Defendants' employees' conduct was negligent because of the risk of impact damage to the ship, but no one could have foreseen the spark and fire that occurred. The English Court of Appeal held that foreseeability of the fire was irrelevant to the question presented, stating:

> The presence or absence of reasonable anticipation of damage determines the legal quality of the conduct as negligent or innocent. If it be thus determined to be negligent, then the question whether particular damages are recoverable depends only on the answer to the question whether they are the direct consequences of the act.

OVERSEAS TANKSHIP LTD. v. MORTS DOCK & ENGINEERING CO. LTD. (WAGON MOUND)

Privy Council 1961.
[1961] A.C. 388, [1961] 2 W.L.R. 126, [1961] 1 All E.R. 40.

VISCOUNT SIMONDS.

[Plaintiffs were Sydney shipbuilders who owned and operated Sheerlegs Wharf. While plaintiffs were engaged in welding operations there, defendant's negligence caused a large quantity of furnace oil to escape from defendant's ship *Wagon Mound*, moored 600 feet from Sheerlegs Wharf. The oil spilled into the bay and spread beneath the wharf. Plaintiffs stopped welding for a time, but resumed after investigating and forming the belief that furnace oil would not ignite on the surface of the water. Welding operations continued for the rest of that day and until 2 p.m. the following day (November 1, 1951), when a fire started in the oil beneath plaintiffs' wharf. The wharf was destroyed.

[In a bench trial, the trial judge found that the fire occurred because sparks from the welding operations set fire to cotton waste or rags floating in the water; this in turn ignited the furnace oil. The trial judge also specifically found that the defendants "did not know and could not reasonably be expected to know that [the oil] was capable of being set afire when spread on water." Nevertheless, the trial judge held that plaintiffs were entitled to recover, reasoning that the release of the furnace oil was negligence because of the pollution damage it could be expected to cause, and that the rule of *Polemis* [supra p. 163] mandated recovery on concluding that the fire was a direct consequence of the release of the oil.

[Defendants appealed to the Supreme Court of New South Wales, which affirmed the trial judge's judgment in favor of plaintiff. Defendants then appealed to the Privy Council in England.]

[The trial judge] made the all-important finding, which must be set out in his own words: "The *raison d'etre* of furnace oil is, of course, that it shall burn, but I find the defendant did not know and could not reasonably be expected to have known that it was capable of being set afire when spread on water." This finding was reached after a wealth of evidence which included that of a distinguished scientist, Professor Hunter. * * *

One other finding must be mentioned. The learned judge held that apart from damage by fire the [plaintiffs] had suffered some damage from the spillage of oil in that it had got upon their slipways and congealed upon them and interfered with their use of the slips. He said: "The evidence of this damage is slight and no claim for compensation is made in respect of it. Nevertheless it does establish some damage which may be insignificant in comparison with the magnitude of the damage by fire, but which nevertheless is damage which beyond question was a direct result of the escape of the oil." It is upon this footing that their Lordships will consider the question whether the [defendants] are liable for the fire damage. * * *

It is inevitable that first consideration should be given to the [*Polemis* case]. For it was avowedly in deference to that decision and to decisions of the Court of Appeal that followed it that the [court below] was constrained to decide the present case in favor of the [plaintiffs]. * * *

* * *

[T]he decision of the Court of Appeal in *Polemis* plainly asserts that, if the defendant is guilty of negligence, he is responsible for all the consequences whether reasonably foreseeable or not. The generality of the proposition is perhaps qualified by the fact that each of the Lords Justices refers to the outbreak of fire as the direct result of the negligent act. There is thus introduced the conception that the negligent actor is not responsible for consequences which are not "direct," whatever that may mean. * * *

* * *

If the line of relevant authority had stopped with *Polemis,* [we] might, whatever [our] own views as to its unreason, have felt some hesitation about overruling it. But it is far otherwise. * * *

* * *

[T]he authority of *Polemis* has been severely shaken though lip-service has from time to time been paid to it. In [our] opinion it should no longer be regarded as good law. It is not probable that many cases will for that reason have a different result, though it is hoped that the law will be thereby simplified, and that in some cases at least palpable injustice will be avoided. For it does not seem consonant with current ideas of justice or morality that for an act of negligence, however slight or venial, which results in some trivial foreseeable damage the actor should be liable for all consequences however unforeseeable and however grave, so long as they can be said to be "direct." It is a principle of civil liability, subject only to qualifications which have no present relevance, that a man must be considered to be responsible for the probable consequences of his act. To demand more of him is too harsh a rule, to demand less is to ignore that civilised order requires the observance of a minimum standard of behaviour.

* * * [I]f some limitation must be imposed upon the consequences for which the negligent actor is to be held responsible—and all are agreed that some limitation there must be—why should that test (reasonable foreseeability) be rejected which, since he is judged by what the reasonable man ought to foresee, corresponds with the common conscience of mankind, and a test (the "direct" consequence) be substituted which leads to nowhere but the never ending and insoluble problems of causation. * * *

* * *

In the same connexion may be mentioned the conclusion to which the [court below] finally came in the present case. Applying the rule in *Polemis* and holding, therefore, that the unforeseeability of the damage by fire afforded no defence, [the court below] went on to consider the remaining question. Was it a "direct" consequence? Upon this Manning, J., said: "Notwithstanding that, if regard is had separately to each individual occurrence in the chain of events that led to this fire, each occurrence was improbable and, in one sense, improbability was heaped upon improbability, I cannot escape from the conclusion that if the ordinary man in the street had been asked, as a matter of common sense, without any detailed analysis of the circumstances, to state the cause of the fire at Mort's Dock, he would unhesitatingly have assigned such cause to spillage of oil by the appellants' employees." Perhaps he would, and probably he would have added: "I never should have thought it possible." But with great respect to the [court below] this is surely irrelevant, or, if it is relevant, only serves to show that the *Polemis* rule works in a very strange way. After the event even a fool is wise. But it is not the hindsight of a fool; it is the foresight of the reasonable man which alone can determine responsibility. The *Polemis* rule by substituting "direct" for "reasonably foreseeable" consequence leads to a conclusion equally illogical and unjust.

* * *

* * * Suppose an action brought by *A* for damage caused by the carelessness (a neutral word) of *B,* for example a fire caused by the careless spillage of oil. It may, of course, become relevant to know what duty *B* owed to *A,* but the only liability that is in question is the liability for damage by fire. It is vain to isolate the liability from its context and to say that *B* is or is not liable and then to ask for what damage he is liable. For his liability is in respect of that damage and no other. If, as admittedly it is, *B*'s liability (culpability) depends on the reasonable foreseeability of the consequent damage, how is that to be determined except by the foreseeability of the damage which in fact happened—the damage in suit? And, if that damage is unforeseeable so as to displace liability at large, how can the liability be restored so as to make compensation payable?

* * *

[We] will humbly advise Her Majesty that this appeal should be allowed and the respondents' action so far as it related to damage caused by the negligence of the appellants be dismissed with costs * * *.

NOTES

1. ***A refocused breach analysis?*** As we saw in note 4 following *Grace,* supra p. 74, the PL side of the B<PL? inquiry for determining breach will often include not only the risk of the harm that actually befell the plaintiff but also other relevant foreseeable risks that the evidence shows the defendant created or exacerbated. Thus, Judge Hand discussed not only the risk of harm to the breakaway barge—which is what actually happened in *Carroll Towing*—but also the risk of harms the breakaway barge might have done to other vessels in the vicinity. Similarly, in applying the B<PL? formula in *Brotherhood* (supra p. 74)—a case of tortious damage to a ship whose crew members fortunately escaped injury—Judge Posner said the "L" in that case included "endanger[ed] human life." 985 F.2d at 329.

In *Wagon Mound*, the Privy Council summarized its new formula for determining proximate cause in the paragraph beginning "Suppose an action brought by A for damages." That paragraph seems to call for determining proximate cause by refocusing the breach inquiry, narrowing it so that, for proximate cause purposes, the B<PL inquiry addresses solely the particular

injury that befell the plaintiff. The court in The Glendola, 47 F.2d 206, 207 (2d Cir. 1931), expressed the same idea in suggesting that the best proximate cause analysis might be to "treat remote consequences as though the [defendant's] wrong consisted in causing these alone, and [to] hold the [defendant liable] only for such as he should have foretold." The Oregon Supreme Court seemed to reject that approach in Fazzolari v. Portland School Dist., 303 Or. 1, 734 P.2d 1326, 1331 n. 9 (1987), stating that "aggregate risks may make conduct negligent even though the specific risk to the particular plaintiff might in isolation be neither sufficiently unreasonable nor foreseeable [to call for precautions]."

A crisp statement of the question asked by the refocused breach approach is found in Calabresi, Concurrent Cause and the Law of Torts: An Essay for Harry Kalven, Jr., 43 U.Chi. L. Rev. 69 (1975): Would the plaintiff's accident "*by itself*" have justified calling defendant's conduct wrongful?" Id. at 92 n. 31; emphasis in original.

2. *A matter of critical importance*. It is essential to understand the difference between the refocused breach approach and the Restatement (Third) approach set forth in section B, supra.

3. *Judge Friendly's view*. In Petition of Kinsman Transit Co., 338 F.2d 708 (2d Cir.1965), the defendants relied heavily on *Wagon Mound*. A dissenting judge was convinced by the argument, but not Judge Friendly. Kinsman was an Ohio company that owned five ships. During the winter of 1958–59, four of its ships were tied up in the Buffalo River for the winter awaiting the thaw of Lake Erie and the resumption of navigation on the lake. Because it was not securely enough fastened to its winter mooring in the river, one of Kinsman's ships broke away under the pressure of an especially heavy current in the river, drifted downstream, struck other moored ships and broke them loose, and ended up causing the collapse of the City of Buffalo's drawbridge. The ships and the collapsed bridge combined to dam up the river, causing extensive flooding and property damage for many miles upstream. The dissenting judge characterized the accident as "an extraordinary concatenation of * * * extraordinary events, not unlike the humorous and almost-beyond-all-imagination sequences depicted by the famous cartoonist Rube Goldberg." Unpersuaded, the majority held that Kinsman should be liable for the damages shown. Judge Friendly's opinion for the court evaluated *Wagon Mound* as follows:

> We have no difficulty with the result of *The Wagon Mound,* in view of the finding that the appellant had no reason to believe that the floating furnace oil would burn. * * * On that view the decision simply applies the principle which excludes liability where the injury sprang from a hazard different from that which was improperly risked. [But] some language in the [*Wagon Mound I* opinion] goes beyond this * * *.

The *Wagon Mound* language that Judge Friendly disagreed with was the paragraph discussed in Note 1 above. Friendly flatly rejected the *Wagon Mound* court's suggestion that the refocused breach limitation on negligence liability is morally compelled:

> We see no reason why an actor engaging in conduct which entails a large risk of small damage and a small risk of other and greater damage, of the

same general sort, from the same forces, and to the same class of persons, should be relieved of responsibility for the latter simply because the chance of its occurrence, *if viewed alone*, may not have been large enough to require the exercise of care. By hypothesis, the risk of the lesser harm was sufficient to render his disregard of it actionable; the existence of a less likely additional risk that the very forces against whose action he was required to guard would produce other and greater damage than could have been reasonably anticipated should inculpate him further rather than limit his liability. (338 F.2d at 725; emphasis supplied.)

4. ***Four rough categories of proximate cause cases.*** As we saw in section B, the Third Restatement adopts a "harm within risks" vocabulary that does not use the term "foreseeability." This seems to us a healthy development, because the concept of foreseeability has been greatly overworked. But at this point, we find it necessary to observe that the Third Restatement approach is unavoidably foreseeability-driven, because the array of "risks" that the plaintiff's harm needs to be within (in order to avoid proximate-cause defeat) are those that comprise the PL part of the PL<B? inquiry, and P in that inquiry *is* foreseeable probability.

So, it is hard to talk about the following categories of proximate cause problems without getting into questions like "what was it about the plaintiff's accident that was arguably unforeseeable?" In thinking about the progression from least-to-most difficult in the categories below, keep in mind that we've put "rule" in quotation marks because these are rules of thumb, not rules of law. The judicial tendencies signaled by this loose use of the term "rule" are reliable enough to justify the term, but the take-away message is that these categories are useful analytical tools but they are neither precise nor invariably trustworthy.

(a) ***Unforeseeable extent of harm: the eggshell skull "rule."*** If the only unforeseeable feature of the plaintiff's accident was that the damages incurred were much greater than could have been anticipated, the plaintiff will typically have no trouble reaching the jury on proximate cause, and may even get a pre-trial ruling, directed verdict, or instruction that on that issue plaintiff should prevail. See, e.g., Smith v. Leech Brain & Co. Ltd., [1962] 2. Q.B. 405 (Q.B.), in which a worker suffered a burned lower lip while handling molten metal in defendant's factory. The defendant was negligent for not having an adequate shield between the worker and the metal. The burn developed into a cancerous condition from which the worker died. Answering the defendant's argument that *Wagon Mound* defeated liability because the cancer and death were highly unforeseeable consequences, the court said: " * * * I am quite satisfied that the [Privy Council] in the *Wagon Mound* case did not have what I may call, loosely, the thin skull cases in mind. It has always been the law of this country that a tortfeasor takes his victim as he finds him. * * * The [Privy Council] were [holding] that a man is no longer liable for the *type* of damage which he could not reasonably anticipate. [They] were not * * * saying that a man is only liable for the *extent* of damage which he could anticipate * * *." (Emphasis supplied.)

We encountered the foregoing idea—that defendant will be liable if some injury of the general type plaintiff sustained was a foreseeable consequence of defendant's negligent conduct, although the extent of the injuries may be quite unexpected—in Chapter IV (the *Lancaster* case, supra p. 148). The concept has various names, including the "eggshell skull rule" and "the extent rule." It has wide currency. See, e.g., Hammerstein v. Jean Development West, 111 Nev. 1471, 907 P.2d 975 (1995), where the court imposed liability on a hotel whose fire alarm kept going off needlessly. The twelfth or so false alarm in a three-month period caused a 70–year–old diabetic guest to hurry down the stairs; he twisted his ankle, which eventually led to a very serious gangrenous infection. The court said the plaintiff did not have to establish the foreseeability of either "the extent of [his] harm or the manner in which the harm occurred."

(b) *Unforeseeable manner of occurrence: the mechanism "rule."* The preceding quotation from *Hammerstein* combines the extent rule with a concept sometimes called "the mechanism rule," which was put by Justice Holmes in Munsey v. Webb, 231 U.S. 150, 156, 34 S.Ct. 44, 58 L.Ed. 162 (1913) as follows: "It was not necessary that the defendant should have had notice of the particular method in which an accident would occur, if the possibility of an accident was clear to the ordinarily prudent eye." What Justice Holmes meant was this: If the plaintiff and the general type of harm sustained by the plaintiff were foreseeable, recovery is usually permitted, even though the particular way in which the harm came about—the *manner of occurrence* of the harm—may be fairly bizarre without defeating plaintiff's proximate cause case. E.g., in Hughes v. Lord Advocate, [1963] A.C. 837, [1963] 1 All E.R. 705 (H.L.), defendants were workmen who went to tea and left a manhole in an Edinburgh street surrounded by paraffin lamps and unattended. An eight-year-old boy entered the tent around the manhole and knocked or lowered one of the lamps into the hole. There was an explosion, and the boy was badly hurt. The lower courts held for defendants, reasoning that while it was foreseeable that a child might enter the unattended tent and suffer burns from the lamps, the explosion and consequent injuries were not foreseeable. Reversing, the House of Lords held that the *Wagon Mound* principle exonerates a defendant only "if the damage [that occurred] can be regarded as *differing in kind* from what was foreseeable. * * * [The] mere fact that the *way in which the accident happened* could not be anticipated is [not] enough to exclude liability * * *." (Lord Reid) (emphasis added.)

(c) *Unforeseeable type of harm.* The perception that plaintiff's accident consisted of harm of a wholly different type from those comprising the array of risks that made the defendant's conduct negligent spells defeat for the plaintiff. This is the *holding* of *Wagon Mound*, and it remains good law. So the boundary between the *unforeseeable mechanism* and *unforeseeable type* categories is an important one. But it's murky, because when a court perceives that the mechanism is just too weird, it is free to characterize the situation as one involving a different type of harm than was put at risk by the defendant's negligent conduct. See, e.g., Doughty v. Turner, [1964] 1 Q.B. 518 (Court of Appeal 1963), an action by a worker who was burned when the defendant negligently dropped the heavy cover of a large vat of molten liquid (800 degrees centigrade) into the vat, bringing about a chemical eruption that flung the liquid onto the worker. The court held that the worker could not recover, because, while dropping the cover into the vat had caused a foreseeable risk of causing injuries through simple splashing, the chemical eruption—a violent one—was not foreseeable.

Unforeseeable extent cases can be turned into *unforeseeable type* cases, too, if the court perceives the need as great enough. If you negligently drive your car into the rear end of mine, I doubt I'll get away with characterizing the mutilation of the multi-million-dollar Rembrandt in my car's trunk as just some more property damage to go along with my spare tire.

(d) *Unforeseeable plaintiffs*. This is the most dangerous territory for plaintiff. See *Palsgraf* and the notes infra at p. 172.

5. *More rules of thumb*. The courts have developed some consensus on the proper treatment of "foreseeability" problems of certain recurrent types. Here, as with the categories treated in note 4, we are not talking about true rules of law, but about generally reliable judicial tendencies. Sometimes these "rules" lead to plaintiff-favorable rulings from the bench; sometimes all they do is get to the plaintiff to the jury.

(a) *Subsequent medical injuries*. A defendant who is liable for negligently causing a personal injury will generally be held liable for subsequent injuries done by rescue and medical personnel in responding to and treating the injury. Unless there is something fairly extraordinary about the subsequent injury, it is generally deemed foreseeable. This is true although the medical personnel may be negligent and liable in their own right. The "rule" has a fairly broad sweep. See, e.g., Younger v. Marshall Industries, Inc., 618 So.2d 866 (La. 1993) (holding the original injurer liable when a defective seat in a hospital shower bath collapsed, causing further injury to the victim); Smith v. Hardy, 144 Ga.App. 168, 240 S.E.2d 714 (1978) (contemplating liability of a negligent motorist when the traffic accident caused plaintiff's pre-existing ulcer to flare up 27 days later, necessitating a blood transfusion—negligently administered—that caused the victim to lose her eyesight); Pridham v. Cash & Carry Bldg. Ctr., 116 N.H. 292, 359 A.2d 193 (1976) (holding original injurer liable for victim's death in ambulance wreck).

In sharp contrast, courts have been reluctant to hold the original wrongdoer liable for the results of subsequent negligence of mechanics and repairers. In Exner Sand & Gravel Corp. v. Petterson Lighterage & Towing Corp., 258 F.2d 1 (2d Cir.1958), the defendant negligently caused $500 worth of bow damage to the plaintiff's barge. While that was being fixed, the repairer negligently caused $11,000 worth of bottom damage. Denying recovery against the original negligent party for the bottom damage, the court distinguished the "subsequent medical negligence" cases by saying that "the risks which in view of 'human fallibility' are 'normally recognized as inherent in the necessity of submitting to medical, surgical or hospital treatment' [are not] 'normally recognized as inherent' in the services of the repairman." (Another justification for this distinction might be that it is much easier to successfully sue a negligent repairer than a negligent physician. See infra Chapter XII.)

(b) *Rescuers*. Within broad limits, they are deemed foreseeable. The most famous rescuer case is Wagner v. International Ry. Co., 232 N.Y. 176, 133 N.E. 437 (1921), in which negligence in the operation of defendant's railroad caused plaintiff's cousin to be jostled out of the train. Plaintiff's injury occurred when he walked back along the trestle to look for his cousin's body and fell off. Judge Cardozo's opinion reversed the trial judge for having told the jury to find for defendant unless they concluded that there was separate negligent conduct directed toward the plaintiff himself, stating:

> Danger invites rescue. The cry of distress is the summons to relief. The law does not ignore these reactions of the mind in tracing conduct to its consequences. It recognizes them as normal. It places their effects within the range of the natural and probable. The wrong that imperils life is a wrong to the imperiled victim; it is a wrong also to his rescuer. * * * The risk of rescue, if only it be not wanton, is born of the occasion. The emergency begets the man. The wrongdoer may not have foreseen the coming of a deliverer. He is accountable as if he had.

This is another "rule" that sweeps pretty broadly. It applies in actions against tortfeasors who put innocent victims at risk as well as against those who negligently or intentionally put themselves at risk. See, e.g., Thomas v. Garner, 284 Ill.App.3d 90, 219 Ill.Dec. 737, 672 N.E.2d 52 (1996) (nine-year-old girl, trying to cross the street to fetch her little brother from where defendant school bus driver had let him off on the wrong side of the street from the house, treated as rescuer); Thompson v. Summers, 567 N.W.2d 387 (S.D. 1997) (hot air balloon pilot was subject to liability under the rescue doctrine when he brought the balloon too close to a high-voltage power line, causing a bystander who was trying to help to sustain serious electrical burns); Talbert v. Talbert, 22 Misc.2d 782, 199 N.Y.S.2d 212 (Sup.Ct. 1960) (man trying to commit suicide in his garage held liable to his son for the injuries the son sustained in breaking into the garage).

In many states, a so-called "firefighters' rule" prevents firefighters, police officers, and other professional risk takers from invoking the rescue doctrine. See, e.g., Maltman v. Sauer, 84 Wash. 2d 975, 530 P.2d 254 (1975), where the court denied the benefits of the rescue doctrine to the crew of an army helicopter that crashed while en route to the scene of a traffic accident. The firefighters' rule has applications beyond the context of the rescue doctrine, and there is tremendous state-to-state variety on the breadth and strength of the rule. See Dobbs, The Law of Torts §§ 285–87 (2000).

6. ***Scope of liability for intentional tortfeasors.*** A traditional viewpoint was expressed by Justice Marshall, dissenting in Associated Gen. Contractors v. California State Council of Carpenters, 459 U.S. 519, 547–48, 103 S.Ct. 897, 74 L.Ed.2d 723 (1983) (emphasis in original):

> Although many legal battles have been fought over the extent of tort liability for remote consequences of *negligent* conduct, it has always been assumed that the victim of an *intentional* tort can recover from the tortfeasor if he proves that the tortious conduct was a cause-in-fact of his injuries. An inquiry into proximate cause has traditionally been deemed unnecessary in suits against intentional tortfeasors.

The Third Restatement proposes a considerably more restrictive approach than Justice Marshall's. Section 33 provides:

> (a) An actor who intentionally causes harm is subject to liability for that harm even if it was unlikely to occur.

(b) An actor who intentionally or recklessly causes harm is subject to liability for a broader range of harms than the harms for which that actor would be liable if only acting negligently. In general, the important factors in determining the scope of liability are the moral culpability of the actor, as reflected in the reasons for and intent in committing the tortious acts, the seriousness of harm intended and threatened by those acts, and the degree to which the actor's conduct deviated from appropriate care.

(c) Notwithstanding Subsections (a) and (b), an actor who intentionally or recklessly causes harm is not subject to liability for harm the risk of which was not increased by the actor's intentional or reckless conduct.

Section 33 ct. *f*, illus. 3 states:

> After leaving a shopping mall one night, Joe was confronted by Alex and Rob, two young hoodlums who approached Joe with threatening gestures and words, and who were carrying martial-arts weapons. Joe began to run from Alex and Rob, but was struck by lightning, causing Joe serious burns. Alex and Rob, despite their assault on Joe, are not liable for his harm because their assault, while a factual cause of Joe's burns, did not increase the risk of being struck by lightning and suffering burns.

The Restatement's authors do not say why they think it is a good idea to let such bad actors as Alex and Rob off the hook on no-increased-risk grounds, and it may be that the case they cite in support of the illustration is limited to intentional torts committed "without malice or bad intent." Johnson v. Greer, 477 F.2d 101, 107 (5th Cir. 1973).

PALSGRAF v. LONG ISLAND R. CO.

Court of Appeals of New York, 1928.
248 N.Y. 339, 162 N.E. 99.

CARDOZO, C.J.

Plaintiff was standing on a platform of defendant's railroad after buying a ticket to go to Rockaway Beach. A train stopped at the station, bound for another place. Two men ran forward to catch it. One of the men reached the platform of the car without mishap, though the train was already moving. The other man, carrying a package, jumped aboard the car, but seemed unsteady as if about to fall. A guard on the car, who had held the door open, reached forward to help him in, and another guard on the platform pushed him from behind. In this act, the package was dislodged, and fell upon the rails. It was a package of small size, about fifteen inches long, and was covered by a newspaper. In fact it contained fireworks, but there was nothing in its appearance to give notice of its contents. The fireworks when they fell exploded. The shock of the explosion threw down some scales at the other end of the platform many feet away. The scales struck the plaintiff, causing injuries for which she sues.

The conduct of the defendant's guard, if a wrong in its relation to the holder of the package, was not a wrong in its relation to the plaintiff, standing far away. Relatively to her it was not negligence at all. Nothing in the situation gave notice that the falling package had in it the potency of peril to persons thus removed. Negligence is not actionable unless it involves the invasion of a legally protected interest, the violation of a right. The plaintiff, as she stood upon the platform of the station, might claim to be protected against intentional invasion of her bodily security. Such invasion is not charged. She might claim to be protected against unintentional invasion by conduct involving in the thought of reasonable men an unreasonable hazard that such invasion would ensue. These, from the point of view of the law, were the bounds of her immunity * * *. If no hazard was apparent to the eye of ordinary vigilance, an act innocent and harmless, at least to outward seeming, with reference to her, did not take to itself the quality of a tort because it happened to be a wrong, though apparently not one involving the risk of bodily insecurity, with reference to some one else. * * * The plaintiff sues in her own right for a wrong personal to her, and not as the vicarious beneficiary of a breach of duty to another.

A different conclusion will involve us, and swiftly too, in a maze of contradictions. A guard stumbles over a package which has been left upon a platform. It seems to be a bundle of newspapers. It turns out to be a can of dynamite. To the eye of ordinary vigilance, the bundle is abandoned waste, which may be kicked or trod on with impunity. Is a passenger at the other end of the platform protected by the law against the unsuspected hazard concealed beneath the waste? If not, is the result to be any different, so far as the distant passenger is concerned, when the guard stumbles over a valise which a truckman or a porter has left upon the walk? The passenger far away, if the victim of a wrong at all, has a cause of action, not derivative, but original and primary. His claim to be protected against invasion of his bodily security is neither greater nor less because the act resulting in the invasion is a wrong to another far removed. In this case, the rights that are said to have been violated, the interests said to have been invaded, are not even of the same order. The man was not injured in his person nor even put in danger. The purpose of the act, as well as its effect, was to make his person safe. If there was a wrong to him at all, which may very well be doubted, it was a wrong to a property interest only, the safety of his package. Out of this wrong to property, which threatened injury to nothing else, there has passed, we are told, to the plaintiff by derivation or succession a right of action for the invasion of an interest of another order, the right to bodily security. The diversity of interests emphasizes the futility of the effort to build the plaintiff's right upon the basis of a wrong to some one else. The gain is one of emphasis, for a like result would follow if the interests were the same. Even then, the orbit of the danger as disclosed to the eye of reasonable vigilance would be the orbit of the duty. One who jostles one's neighbor in a crowd does not invade the rights of others standing at the outer fringe when the unintended contact casts a bomb upon the ground. The wrongdoer as to them is the man who carries the bomb, not the one who explodes it without suspicion of the danger. Life will have to be made over, and human nature transformed, before prevision so extravagant can be accepted as the norm of conduct, the customary standard to which behavior must conform.

The argument for the plaintiff is built upon the shifting meanings of such words as "wrong" and "wrongful," and shares their instability. What the plaintiff must show is "a wrong" to herself; i.e., a violation of her own right, and not merely a wrong to some one else, nor conduct "wrongful" because unsocial, but not "a wrong" to any one. We are told that one who drives at reckless speed through a crowded city street is guilty of a negligent act and therefore of a wrongful one, irrespective of the consequences. Negligent the act is, and wrongful in the sense that it is unsocial, but wrongful and unsocial in relation to other travelers, only because the eye of vigilance perceives the risk of damage. If the same act were to be committed on a speedway or a race course, it would lose its wrongful quality. The risk reasonably to be perceived defines the duty to be obeyed, and risk imports relation; it is risk to another or to others within the range of apprehension. This does not mean, of course, that one who launches a destructive force is always relieved of liability, if the force, though known to be destructive, pursues an unexpected path. "It was not necessary that the defendant should have had notice of the particular method in which an accident would occur, if the possibility of an accident was clear to the ordinarily prudent eye." * * *. The range of reasonable apprehension is at times a question for the court, and at times, if varying inferences are possible, a question for the jury. Here, by concession, there was nothing in the situation to suggest to the most cautious mind that the parcel wrapped in newspaper would spread wreckage through the station. If the guard had thrown it down knowingly and willfully, he would not have threatened the plaintiff's safety, so far as appearances could warn him. His conduct would not have involved, even then, an unreasonable probability of invasion of her bodily security. Liability can be no greater where the act is inadvertent.

Negligence, like risk, is thus a term of relation. Negligence in the abstract, apart from things related, is surely not a tort, if indeed it is understandable at all. Negligence is not a tort unless it results in the commission of a wrong, and the commission of a wrong imports the violation of a right, in this case, we are told, the right to be protected against interference with one's bodily security. But bodily security is protected, not against all forms of interference or aggression, but only against some. One who seeks redress at law does not make out a cause of action by showing without more that there has been damage to his person. If the harm was not willful, he must show that the act as to him had possibilities of danger so many and apparent as to entitle him to be protected against the doing of it though the harm was unintended. * * * The victim does not sue derivatively, or by right of subrogation, to vindicate an interest invaded in the person of another. Thus to view his cause of action is to ignore the fundamental difference between tort and crime. He sues for breach of a duty owing to himself.

The law of causation, remote or proximate, is thus foreign to the case before us. The question of liability is always anterior to the question of the measure of the consequences that go with liability. If there is no tort to be redressed, there is no occasion to consider what damage might be recovered if there were a finding of a tort. We may assume, without deciding, that negligence, not at large or in the abstract, but in relation to the plaintiff, would entail liability for any and all consequences, however novel or extraordinary. There is room for argument that a distinction is to be drawn according to the diversity of interests invaded by the act, as where conduct negligent in that it threatens an insignificant invasion of an interest in property results in an unforeseeable invasion of an interest of another order, as, e.g., one of bodily security. Perhaps other distinctions may be necessary. We do not go into the question now. The consequences to be followed must first be rooted in a wrong.

The judgment of the Appellate Division and that of the Trial Term should be reversed, and the complaint dismissed, with costs in all courts.

ANDREWS, J., dissenting.

* * *

* * * The result we shall reach depends upon our theory as to the nature of negligence. Is it a relative concept—the breach of some duty owing to a particular person or to particular persons? Or, where there is an act which unreasonably threatens the safety of others, is the doer liable for all its proximate consequences, even where they result in injury to one who would generally be thought to be outside the radius of danger? This is not a mere dispute as to words. We might not believe that to the average mind the dropping of the bundle would seem to involve the probability of harm to the plaintiff standing many feet away, whatever might be the case as to the owner or to one so near as to be likely to be struck by its fall. If, however, we adopt the second hypothesis, we have to inquire only as to the relation between cause and effect. We deal in terms of proximate cause, not of negligence.

Negligence may be defined roughly as an act or omission which unreasonably does or may affect the rights of others * * *.

* * *

But we are told that "there is no negligence unless there is in the particular case a legal duty to take care, and this duty must be one which is owed to the plaintiff himself and not merely to others." This I think too narrow a conception. Where there is the unreasonable act, and some right that may be affected there is negligence whether damage does or does not result. That is immaterial. Should we drive down Broadway at a reckless speed, we are negligent whether we strike an approaching car or miss it by an inch. The act itself is wrongful. It is a wrong not only to those who happen to be within the radius of danger, but to all who might have been there—a wrong to the public at large. Such is the language of the street. * * *

* * *

The proposition is this: Every one owes to the world at large the duty of refraining from those acts that may unreasonably threaten the safety of others. Such an act occurs. Not only is he wronged to whom harm might reasonably be expected to result, but he also who is in fact injured, even if he be outside what would generally be thought the danger zone. There needs be duty due the one complaining, but this is not a duty to a particular individual because as to him harm might be expected. Harm to some one being the natural result of the act, not only that one alone, but all those in fact injured may complain. * * * Unreasonable risk being taken, its consequences are not confined to those who might probably be hurt.

* * *

* * * [W]hen injuries * * * result from our unlawful act, we are liable for the consequences. It does not matter that they are unusual, unexpected, unforeseen, and unforeseeable. But there is one limitation. The damages must be so connected with the negligence that the latter may be said to be the proximate cause of the former.

* * *

* * * What we * * * mean by the word "proximate" is that, because of convenience, of public policy, of a rough sense of justice, the law arbitrarily declines to trace a series of events beyond a certain point. This is not logic. It is practical politics. * * *

Take the illustration given in an unpublished manuscript by a distinguished and helpful writer on the law of torts. A chauffeur negligently collides with another car which is filled with dynamite, although he could not know it. An explosion follows. *A*, walking on the sidewalk nearby, is killed. *B*, sitting in a window of a building opposite, is cut by flying glass. *C*, likewise sitting in a window a block away, is similarly injured. And a further illustration: A nursemaid, ten blocks away, startled by the noise, involuntarily drops a baby from her arms to the walk. We are told that *C* may not recover while *A* may. As to *B* it is a question for court or jury. We will all agree that the baby might not. Because, we are again told, the chauffeur had no reason to believe his conduct involved any risk of injuring either *C* or the baby. As to them he was not negligent.

But the chauffeur, being negligent in risking the collision, his belief that the scope of the harm he might do would be limited is immaterial. His act unreasonably jeopardized the safety of any one who might be affected by it. *C*'s injury and that of the baby were directly traceable to the collision. Without that, the injury would not have happened. *C* had the right to sit in his office, secure from such dangers. The baby was entitled to use the sidewalk with reasonable safety.

The true theory is, it seems to me, that the injury to *C,* if in truth he is to be denied recovery, and the injury to the baby, is that their several injuries were not the proximate result of the negligence. And here not what the chauffeur had reason to believe would be the result of his conduct, but what the prudent would foresee, may have a bearing—may have some bearing, for the problem of proximate cause is not to be solved by any one consideration. It is all a question of expediency. There are no fixed rules to govern our judgment. There are simply matters of which we may take account. * * * There is in truth little to guide us other than common sense.

* * * We draw an uncertain and wavering line, but draw it we must as best we can.

[I]t is all a question of fair judgment, always keeping in mind the fact that we endeavor to make a rule in each case that will be practical and in keeping with the general understanding of mankind.

* * *

* * * The act upon which defendant's liability rests is knocking an apparently harmless package onto the platform. The act was negligent. For its proximate consequences the defendant is liable. If its contents were broken, to the owner; if it fell upon and crushed a passenger's foot, then to him; if it exploded and injured one in the immediate vicinity, to him also as to *A* in the illustration. Mrs. Palsgraf was standing some distance away. How far cannot be told from the record—apparently 25 or 30 feet, perhaps less. Except for the explosion, she would not have been injured. We are told by the [railroad in its] brief, "It cannot be denied that the explosion was the direct cause of the plaintiff's injuries." So it was a substantial factor in producing the result—there was here a natural and continuous sequence—direct connection. The only intervening cause was that, instead of blowing her to the ground, the concussion smashed the weighing machine which in turn fell upon her. There was no remoteness in time, little in space. * * *

Under these circumstances I cannot say as a matter of law that the plaintiff's injuries were not the proximate result of the negligence. That is all we have before us. * * *

The judgment appealed from should be affirmed, with costs.

POUND, LEHMAN, and KELLOGG, JJ., concur with CARDOZO, C.J.

ANDREWS, J., dissents in opinion in which CRANE and O'BRIEN, JJ., concur.

NOTES

1. ***The railroad's negligent conduct.*** Judge Cardozo's statement that it "may very well be doubted" whether defendant's employees were guilty of any negligent conduct is puzzling. In the intermediate appellate court (the "Appellate Division"), the decision (by a 3–2 vote) was to affirm the plaintiff's

judgment. Palsgraf v. Long Island R. Co., 222 App.Div. 166, 225 N.Y.S. 412 (1927). The majority opinion in that court justified the jury finding of negligent conduct as follows:

> Two of the defendant's employees undertook to help [the man with the bundle to board] the train while it was in motion, one of them the trainman and the other the man on the platform. During their efforts to assist the man onto the moving train, these men knocked the bundle out from under the passenger's arm, and it fell under the train. * * * The sole question of defendant's negligence submitted to the jury was whether the defendant's employees were "careless and negligent in the way they handled this particular passenger after he came upon the platform and while he was boarding the train." This question of negligence was submitted to the jury by a fair and impartial charge, and the verdict was supported by the evidence. The jury might well find that the act of the passenger in undertaking to board a moving train was negligent, and that the acts of the defendant's employees in assisting him while engaged in that negligent act were also negligent. Instead of aiding or assisting the passenger engaged in such an act, they might better have discouraged and warned him not to board the moving train. It is quite probable that without their assistance the passenger might have succeeded in boarding the train, and no accident would have happened, or without the assistance of these employees the passenger might have desisted in his efforts to board the train. (225 N.Y.S. at 413).

The dissenting judges in the Appellate Division did not dispute the existence of negligent conduct: "[The] door of the train should have been closed before the train started, which would have prevented the passenger making the attempt." Id. at 414.

2. *Mrs. Palsgraf's lawyer's theory of the case.* Aside from res ipsa loquitur cases, a plaintiff's lawyer proves the breach element by identifying questionable conduct of the defendant and using the evidence to convey a picture of an array of risks created or exacerbated by that conduct. It has always been a mystery why Helen Palsgraf's lawyer chose to paint such a picture that didn't have his client in it. Perhaps counsel overestimated the health and strength of the directness test for proximate causation.

3. *Is Palsgraf a duty case or a proximate cause case?* Judge Cardozo could easily have reached the result he thought appropriate by saying that no reasonable juror could think that Mrs. Palsgraf's accident was among the array of foreseeable risks that made defendant's conduct negligent. This was roughly the view of the Appellate Division dissenters, who said:

> [T]he negligence of defendant was not a proximate cause of the injuries to plaintiff. Between the negligence of defendant and the injuries there intervened the negligence of the passenger carrying the package containing an explosive. This was an independent, and not a concurring, act of negligence. The explosion was not reasonably probable as a result of defendant's act of negligence. The negligence of defendant was not a likely or natural cause of the explosion, since the latter was such an unusual occurrence. Defendant's negligence was a [factual] cause of plaintiff's injury, but too remote. (225 N.Y.S. at 414–15).

In choosing a no-duty articulation, Judge Cardozo put forward a new mode of analysis. And we do not think Cardozo's analysis has stood the test of time.

When Judge Andrews said that "[n]egligence may be defined roughly as an act or omission which unreasonably does or may affect the rights of others," he was echoing the principle of a seminal case, Heaven v. Pender, [1883] 11 Q.B.D. 503, 509:

> [W]henever one person is by circumstances placed in such a position with regard to another that every one of ordinary sense who did think would at once recognize that if he did not use ordinary care and skill in his own conduct with regard to those circumstances, he would cause danger of injury to the person or property of the other, a duty arises to use ordinary care and skill to avoid such danger.

As we will see in Chapter VI, this is also the viewpoint of the Third Restatement. From this perspective, a defendant whose activities have brought about physical injury to another will presumptively have owed a duty of reasonable care unless the case falls into a category as to which there is a rule of law providing otherwise. Chapter VI treats some of these categorical no-duty rules, including, for example, rules restricting recovery for negligently-inflicted emotional harm or purely economic harm.

What Judge Cardozo laid down in *Palsgraf* was not a no-duty rule in that same sense. "Unforeseeable plaintiff" does not describe a legal category; instead it is a summary characterization of the facts of the particular case. Remember always that the duty issue is assigned to the judge, not the jury; this assignment is what gives no-duty rules their power. A correlative proposition is that a no-duty rule should have enough breadth and clarity to permit the trial judge in most cases raising the problem to dismiss the complaint or award summary judgment for the defendant on the basis of the rule. If the case is of a sort that typically the judge will need to know the details of the occurrence before ruling for the defendant (as was certainly true of *Palsgraf*), then the appropriate formulation is in terms of plaintiff's failure to establish breach or legal cause rather than "no duty." It is pertinent here that Cardozo acknowledged that his new candidate for a no-duty rule—no duty to the unforeseeable plaintiff—will "at times [be] a question for the jury." The court in Moning v. Alfono, 400 Mich. 425, 254 N.W.2d 759, 762 (1977), had Cardozo's *Palsgraf* opinion in mind when it said: "It obscures the separate issues in a negligence case (duty, proximate cause, and * * * standard of care) to combine and state them together in terms of whether there is a duty to refrain from particular conduct."

4. ***The concept of superseding cause.*** Recall that in the view of the Appellate Division dissenters in *Palsgraf*, the conduct of the passenger with the package "intervened" as an "independent" negligent cause of the harm. That serious misconduct by someone other than the defendant—or any other causal force that might be similarly deemed dramatic and highly unexpected— might "intervene" between the defendant's negligent conduct and the injury in such a way as to become a "superseding" or a "supervening" cause, insulating the defendant from liability, is a plausible concept of long standing. See, e.g., Watson v. Kentucky & Indiana Bridge & R. Co., 137 Ky. 619, 126 S.W. 146 (1910) (holding that a rail carrier that negligently spilled gasoline

that was then ignited by a man trying to light a cigar, causing an explosion that harmed the innocent plaintiff, could be liable if the cigar man was merely negligent but not if his act was "wanton or malicious"). Section 34 of the Third Restatement tucks the superseding cause concept neatly into its general scope of liability (proximate cause) test, stating:

> When a force of nature or an independent act is also a factual cause of harm, an actor's liability is limited to those harms that result from the risks that made the actor's conduct tortious.

5. ***The core risk qualification of the superseding cause concept.*** "An intervening act may not serve as a superseding cause, and relieve an actor of responsibility, where the risk of the intervening act occurring is the very same risk which renders the actor negligent." Derdiarian v. Felix Contracting Corp., 51 N.Y.2d 308, 434 N.Y.S.2d 166, 414 N.E.2d 666, 671 (1980). See also Commonwealth v. Babbitt, 172 S.W.3d 786, 793 (Ky. 2005) (citing Third Restatement § 34 cmt. *d* in the course of concluding that a motorist's negligently leaving the roadway is "precisely the risk that renders tortious" the defendant's failure to erect guardrails). In Jutzi–Johnson v. United States, 263 F.3d 753 (7th Cir. 2001), Judge Posner expanded on the idea:

> [T]he doctrine of supervening cause is not applicable when the duty of care claimed to have been violated is precisely a duty to protect against ordinarily unforeseeable conduct. * * * And so a hospital that fails to maintain a careful watch over patients known to be suicidal is not excused by the doctrine of supervening cause from liability for a suicide, any more than a zoo can escape liability for allowing a tiger to escape and maul people on the ground that the tiger is the supervening cause of the mauling. (Id. at 756; citations omitted.)

D. CONTROVERSIAL MODERN CASES

EDWARDS v. HONEYWELL, INC.

United States Court of Appeals, Seventh Circuit, 1995.
50 F.3d 484.

Posner, Chief Judge.

A fireman's widow has sued Honeywell, the provider of an alarm system intended to protect the house where her husband was killed in the line of duty. The suit, filed in an Indiana state court, charges that David John Edwards died because of Honeywell's negligence in failing to call the fire department promptly upon receiving a signal from the alarm. As a result of the delay, the floor of the burning house was in a severely weakened condition by the time the firemen entered, and it collapsed beneath Edwards, plunging him to his death. The district court, to which the suit had been removed under the diversity jurisdiction, granted summary judgment for Honeywell. The court held that Honeywell owed no duty of care to fireman Edwards under the common law of Indiana. * * *

In 1982 Honeywell had made a contract with a couple named Baker to install (for $1,875) and monitor (for $21 a month) an alarm system in the Bakers' house [located in a suburb of Indianapolis]. * * * The contract limited Honeywell's liability to the Bakers for the consequences of any failure of the system to $250. The validity of this limitation is not questioned.

The alarm system was of a type that has become common. If the house was entered while the alarm was turned on, and the alarm was not promptly disarmed, or if someone in the house pushed either a "panic button" or a button on the alarm console labeled fire, police, or emergency medical service, a signal was automatically transmitted over the telephone lines to a central station maintained by Honeywell. The person manning the station (called the "alarm monitor") would call the fire department if the fire or medical-emergency button had been pressed, and otherwise would call the police department. * * *

[In the winter of 1988, Mrs. Baker discovered a fire in the furnace room in the basement. She ran upstairs and pushed the two buttons on the control panel of the alarm system.] * * * Then she grabbed her dog and ran out the front door. * * *

The signals from the Bakers' house [came] into [Honeywell's] central station at 2:54 p.m., triggering an audible alarm. The alarm monitor, hearing it, * * * pressed a function key, causing the relevant information about the Bakers to flash on the screen of her computer. The display told her to call the Indianapolis Fire Department * * *. So she pushed the "direct fire button" to the Indianapolis Fire Department, connecting her immediately with the department's dispatcher. She gave the dispatcher the Bakers' address. The dispatcher told her that it was within the jurisdiction of a different fire department, that of the City of Lawrence, to which the dispatcher transferred the call. That was wrong too. It was the fire department of Lawrence Township that had jurisdiction over the Bakers' house. So the dispatcher for the City of Lawrence transferred the call [to the Lawrence Township] fire department.

Had Honeywell's operator called the township's fire department first, rather than reaching that department as it were on the third try, it would have taken no more than 45 seconds for the department to learn of the fire at the Bakers' house. Because of the jurisdictional error, it was not until 2:58 that the department received the call. The 45 seconds had been stretched to four minutes because of the misinformation in Honeywell's computer. The plaintiff claims, and for purposes of this appeal we accept, that Honeywell was careless in not having a procedure for verifying and updating such essential information as which fire department to call in the event of a fire in a subscriber's premises, since the boundaries between fire districts are shifted from time to time.

A Lawrence Township fire chief arrived at the scene at 3:00 p.m. (This was remarkably prompt, the call having come in only two minutes earlier. But the Bakers' residence was only a mile or a mile and a half from the firehouse. This shows by the way the importance of notifying the right fire department.) He saw dark smoke but no flames. Mrs. Baker was there and told him that she thought her furnace had exploded. The chief did not ask her when the fire had started but assumed that, because Mrs. Baker had been at home, she had notified the fire department immediately. This implied that the fire was less than three minutes old. Five minutes later, at 3:05 p.m., two parties of firemen began leading hoses into the house, entering through the front door and the garage (which was on the side of the house) respectively. The floor was hot to the touch (firemen customarily enter a burning building on all fours because smoke and heat rise), and the group that had entered through the front door quickly withdrew, fearing that the floor would collapse. The smoke thickened. Fire was seen darting from the roof. Edwards, an experienced fireman, was one of two men who had entered the house from the garage. Sometime between 3:10 and 3:15, before he could withdraw from the house, the floor collapsed and he fell into the basement and was asphyxiated.

The house was severely damaged by the fire, and the Bakers have since moved to another house. They no longer subscribe to Honeywell's alarm service.

We may assume that the firemen would have arrived a little more than three minutes earlier (to be exact, four minutes minus 45 seconds earlier) had Honeywell's call gone to the right fire department directly rather than having to be relayed. Whether fireman Edwards' life would have been saved is obviously a highly speculative question. It depends on what the firemen would have done with the extra three minutes and 15 seconds. If they would have brought the fire under control in that time, then the floor might not have collapsed. But if at the end of that period they would still have been laying their hoses (no water had yet been applied to the fire when the firemen withdrew and the floor collapsed), the floor would have collapsed just as it did and Edwards would have been killed just as he was. Absence of evidence that the delay of which the plaintiff complains made any difference to Edwards' fate was not, however, the ground on which the district judge dismissed the suit. Nor does Honeywell urge it as an alternative ground for affirming the judgment.

* * *

As the premise of our further discussion, we may assume without having to decide not only that Honeywell breached its duty of care to the Bakers by not updating the information in its computer on which fire department to call if the Bakers' house caught on fire, but also that as a consequence of this breach fireman Edwards died. We are speaking of a tort duty of care * * *, not a contractual duty; there is no suggestion that Edwards was a third-party beneficiary of the contract between Honeywell and the [Bakers].

The question we must decide, therefore, is whether Honeywell's duty of care extended to firemen who might be summoned to fight the blaze, for, if not, the plaintiff's suit was properly dismissed. Why duty should be an issue in a negligence case is not altogether clear, however, and the quest for an answer may guide us to a decision.

* * * [O]riginally negligence signified carelessness only in the performance of * * * a duty arising from an undertaking (for example that of a surgeon) or a [specific] duty imposed by law, such as an innkeeper's duty to look after his guests' goods. It was not until the nineteenth century that a general principle of liability for the careless infliction of harm was securely established. But as liability for negligence expanded, the judges felt a need to place limitations on its scope and to rein in juries, and the concept of duty was revived to name some of these limitations and to exert some control over juries. Negligence was redefined as the breach of a duty running from the injurer to the injurer's victim to exercise due care, and the question whether there was such a duty in the particular case or class of cases was, and remains, a matter for the judge to decide, not the jury. * * *

* * *

Of particular relevance to the present case are two lines of precedent. Indeed the present case could be said to lie at their intersection. One concerns the duty of care to an unforeseeable victim. The classic case is *Palsgraf* * * * The Indiana courts accept *Palsgraf's* exclusion of liability to unforeseeable victims. So if fireman Evans [sic] was an unforeseeable victim of Honeywell's negligence, this suit must fail.

The other line of cases concerns the duty of care of water companies, telephone companies, and other providers of services of the public utility type—today including alarm services—to the general public as opposed to customers. Again the most famous cases are Judge Cardozo's. H.R. Moch Co. v. Rensselaer Water Co., 247 N.Y. 160, 159 N.E. 896 (1928), held that a company which had contracted to supply water to a city and its residents was not liable for the consequences of a fire that the fire department was unable to bring under control (with resulting damage to the plaintiff's property) because the water company failed through carelessness to maintain adequate pressure in the water mains. Kerr S.S. Co. v. Radio Corp. of America, 245 N.Y. 284, 157 N.E. 140 (1927), held that careless failure to transmit the plaintiff's telegram, a failure that caused the plaintiff to lose a valuable contract, was not a tortious wrong to the plaintiff. Telegraph companies have gone by the board. But there have been cases which hold that telephone companies can be liable for fire damage resulting from an operator's failure to transmit a distress call, and an equal number of cases rejecting such liability.

We do not know the standing of the public utility cases in Indiana law. * * * Even so, if the rest of the states were in agreement on the scope of the limitation with respect either to a case such as the present one or to the class of cases illustrated by *Moch* and *Kerr*, we could assume that Indiana would fall into line. They are not. The principle of these cases is accepted in some jurisdictions, rejected in others. The split is mirrored in the cases closest to the present one—cases involving the liability of alarm services to noncustomers (none of them, however, firemen, policemen, or other rescue workers) for the consequences of the service's negligence. There are no Indiana cases concerning the liability of alarm services to noncustomers.

The basic criticism of both the *Palsgraf* and *Moch–Kerr* lines of decisions, articulated with characteristic force by Judge Friendly in Petition of Kinsman Transit Co., [supra p. 167], is that since by assumption the defendant was careless (for the concept of duty would have no liability-limiting function otherwise), why should its carelessness be excused merely because either the particular harm that occurred as a consequence, or the person harmed as a consequence, was unforeseeable? If the Long Island Railroad's employees had avoided jostling the passenger carrying the bundle of fireworks, as due care required them to do, Mrs. Palsgraf would not have been injured. If the water company had kept up the pressure, as it was contractually obligated to do, the fire would not have raged out of control. And if Honeywell had used due care in identifying the fire department with jurisdiction over a fire in the Bakers' house, Edwards (we are assuming for purposes of this appeal) would not have been killed. In none of these cases would the defendant, in order to prevent the injury of which the plaintiff was complaining, have had to exercise more care than it was required by law to exercise anyway.

The arguments on the other side, the arguments in favor of the duty limitation in these cases, are twofold. The first arises from the fact that a corporation or other enterprise does not have complete control over its employees, yet it is strictly liable under the principle of respondeat superior for the consequences of their negligent acts committed in the scope of their employment. [See Chapter VIII.] It is not enough to say to the enterprise be careful and you have nothing to fear. The carelessness of its employees may result in the imposition of a crushing liability upon it. In order to know how many resources (in screening new hires and in supervising and disciplining workers after they are hired) to invest in preventing its employees from being careless, the employer must have some idea, some foresight, of the harms the employees are likely to inflict. Imposing liability for unforeseeable types of harm is unlikely, therefore, to evoke greater efforts at preventing accidents; it is likely merely to constitute the employer an insurer. The railroad in *Palsgraf* did not know that conductors who jostle boarding passengers pose a threat of injury by explosion to people standing elsewhere on the platform, and the water company in *Moch* did not know the likelihood of fires or the value of the property that might be damaged by them.

The second argument in favor of using the concept of duty to limit the scope of liability for careless acts, an argument relevant to *Moch* and *Kerr* though not to *Palsgraf*, is that the defendant may not be in the best position to prevent a particular class of accidents, and placing liability on it may merely dilute the incentives of other potential defendants. In most cases the best way to avert fire damage is to prevent the fire from starting rather than to douse it with water after it has started. The water company represents a second line of defense, and it has no control over the first. It cannot insist that people not leave oil-soaked rags lying about or that they equip their houses and offices with smoke detectors and fire extinguishers.

How far in general these arguments outweigh the consideration emphasized by Judge Friendly [in *Kinsman*] is a matter of fair debate; but they are especially powerful in this case, and remember that Indiana is a jurisdiction that follows *Palsgraf*. The provider of an alarm service not only has no knowledge of the risk of a fire in its subscribers' premises, and no practical ability to reduce that risk (though we suppose an alarm service like a fire insurer could offer a discount to people who installed smoke detectors in their premises); it also lacks knowledge of the risk of a fire to firemen summoned to extinguish it. That risk depends not only on the characteristics of the particular premises but also on the particular techniques used by each fire department, the training and qualifications of the firemen, and the quality of the department's leadership. The alarm company knows nothing about these things and has no power to influence them.

The death of a fireman in fighting a residential fire appears to be a rare occurrence. And we have not been referred to a single case in which such a death was blamed on a malfunction, human or mechanical, in an alarm system. The problem of proving causation in such a case is, as we saw, a formidable one, and the plethora of potential defendants makes it difficult (we should think) for an alarm company to estimate its likely liability even if it does foresee the kind of accident that occurred here. If "unforeseeable" is given the practical meaning of too unusual, too uncertain, too unreckonable to make it feasible or worthwhile to take precautions against, then this accident was unforeseeable. Honeywell would have difficulty figuring out how careful it must be in order to satisfy its legal obligations or how much more it ought to charge its subscribers in order to cover its contingent liability to firemen and to any others who might be injured in a fire of which the alarm company failed to give prompt notice. Similar problems of debilitating legal uncertainty would arise if the person injured were a police officer or a paramedic rather than a firefighter.

The alarm service constitutes, moreover, not a first or second line of defense against fire but a third line of defense—and in this case possibly a fourth, fifth, or *n*th. The first is the homeowner. We do not know why the Bakers' furnace exploded—whether it was because of a defect in the furnace or a failure by the Bakers or others to inspect or maintain it properly. The second line of defense is the fire department. Potential defendants in this case included not only the alarm service and the fire department (though presumably the plaintiff's only remedy against the department would be under Indiana's public employees' compensation law), but [also] the Bakers, the manufacturer of the furnace, any service company that inspected or maintained the furnace, possibly even the supplier of the wood for the floor that collapsed or the architect or builder of the house. The plaintiff has chosen to sue only the alarm service. Of course none of the others may be negligent. And if any of the others are, conceivably the alarm service might implead them so that liability could come to rest on the most culpable. Yet it is also possible that the principal attraction of the alarm service as a defendant is that it is a large out-of-state firm with deep and well-lined pockets. We can only speculate. All things considered, however, the creation of a duty of care running from the alarm service to Edwards is likely to make at best a marginal contribution to fire safety and one outweighed by the cost of administering such a duty. That at least is our best guess as to how the Supreme Court of Indiana would evaluate this case were it before that court.

Pointing to the $250 limitation of the alarm service's liability to the Bakers, the plaintiff argues that if Honeywell prevails in this suit, alarm services will have no incentive to take care. But they will. Honeywell lost the Bakers' business. Our society relies more heavily on competition than on liability to optimize the quality of the goods and services supplied by the private sector of the economy. A case such as this does Honeywell's customer relations no good even if it wins the case—as we think it must.

* * *

AFFIRMED.

NOTES

1. *Edwards is a proximate cause (scope of liability) case.* Judge Posner cast his opinion in no-duty terms, but we consider *Edwards* to be a proximate cause case for the same reason that we put *Palsgraf* in that category: the decision does not set forth or invoke criteria for defining a legally cognizable category of "unforeseeable" plaintiffs but only determines that the particular plaintiff was not (in some sense or another) foreseeable enough.

2. *Further on the economic efficiency justification for the proximate cause limitation.* For another phrasing of Judge Posner's first argument "in favor of [what he called] the duty limitation in these cases," see his opinion in Jutzi–Johnson v. United States, 263 F.3d 753, 756 (7th Cir. 2001):

A person is not liable for such improbable consequences of negligent activity as could hardly figure in his deciding how careful he should be. Liability in such circumstances would serve no deterrent, no regulatory purpose; it would not alter behavior and increase safety. Nothing would be gained by imposing liability in such a case but compensation, and compensation can be obtained more cheaply by insurance.

Do you think the Third Restatement's approach to proximate cause restricts liability enough to accommodate Judge Posner's view of economic policy? Or would it take something more restrictive, such as the refocused breach test? Did Judge Posner apply the refocused breach test?

3. *"No duty" versus "no legal cause as a matter of law."* Courts often indicate that it makes little or no difference whether a scope-of-responsibility issue is framed in duty language or proximate cause language.

(See, e.g., fn. 1 in *Meyering*, infra at 189.) But of course it matters tremendously. If Judge Posner had not determined that "[t]he Indiana courts accept *Palsgraf*[]"* he probably would have been led to discuss Honeywell's responsibility to fireman Edwards under the rubric of proximate cause and to explain why Edwards's case failed as a matter of law to establish proximate causation. The normal meaning of the phrase "no proximate cause as a matter of law" is that no reasonable juror could find that the harm to the plaintiff was among the array of risks the creation or exacerbation of which led to the conclusion that the defendant's conduct was negligent. This might have been difficult to say with a straight face under the facts of *Edwards*. (Does Judge Posner's undocumented and seemingly casual remark that "[t]he death of a fireman in fighting a residential fire appears to be a rare occurrence" seem plausible?)

Our point is that the choice between the duty and proximate cause approaches to particular scope-of-liability issues has potentially determinative rhetorical consequences. A defendant who succeeds in characterizing a scope-of-liability issue as one of duty benefits from the tradition that duty issues are for the judge, not the jury, and the court's concomitant freedom to soar far above the facts of the case into a high realm of legal theory. A plaintiff's successful characterization of such an issue as one of legal cause invokes the presumption that juries get such issues unless reasonable minds could not differ and the concomitant implication that the answer ought to be sensitive to the particular facts of the case.

4. ***The shift-of-responsibility cases***. It is questionable whether a policy of steering plaintiffs toward the most obviously and immediately responsible tortfeasors and away from others (expressed by Judge Posner as a caution against "dilut[ing] the incentives of other potential defendants") can justify the result in *Edwards*. But it does seem to justify some cases in which defendants escape liability because the plaintiff's harm occurs after responsibility for the danger has shifted in a meaningful sense from the defendant to another responsible actor. See, e.g., Kent v. Commonwealth, 437 Mass. 312, 771 N.E.2d 770 (2002) (state parole board's negligent release of dangerous murderer to the federal INS was not a proximate cause of a violent crime by the murderer eight years later); Braun v. New Hope Township, 646 N.W.2d 737 (S.D. 2002) (farmer who broke a road-hazard sign was not responsible for an accident that occurred after township had negligently repaired the sign); Sisco v. Broce Mf'g, Inc., 1 Fed. Appx. 420 (6th Cir. 2001) (Tenn. law) (unpublished) (plaintiff's employer's negligent failure to repair brakes of highway sweeper was a supervening act between the manufacturer's defective design or manufacture of the brakes and the brake-failure accident).

MEYERING v. GENERAL MOTORS CORP.

Court of Appeal, Fourth District, Division 1, California, 1990.
232 Cal.App.3d 1103, 275 Cal.Rptr. 346.

WIENER, ACTING PRESIDING JUSTICE.

Plaintiff Kurt Meyering was severely injured when he was struck on the head by a chunk of concrete thrown from a freeway overpass by two

---

* Under the influence of *Palsgraf*, many courts treat the unforeseeable plaintiff problem as a duty issue and the remaining categories (type of harm, manner of occurrence, extent of harm) under the rubric of proximate cause.

juveniles. At the time of his injury, Meyering was driving a 1984 Chevrolet Corvette recently purchased by his girlfriend, Jane Casey. The concrete chunk struck him after penetrating the car's sunroof. The Corvette was designed and manufactured by defendant General Motors Corporation (GM) * * *.

Meyering's complaint alleges * * * that [GM was] negligent in the design, manufacture and distribution of the automobile. * * * Meyering's theory is that the sunroof was made from a type of plexiglass which was too thin and too weak. He contends there is a relatively inexpensive alternative—lexan polycarbonate sheeting—which is shatterproof and would have prevented the injury he suffered in this case.

In sustaining [GM's demurrer], the trial court accepted [GM's] argument that the criminal conduct of the two juveniles constituted an unforeseeable intervening act which the manufacturer * * * of the vehicle had no duty to guard against.

* * *

The role played by "foreseeability" in a negligence cause of action has proven to be a confusing one for courts grappling with questions of duty, negligence and proximate cause. * * * [I]n Ballard v. Uribe (1986) 41 Cal.3d 564, 715 P.2d 624, the California Supreme Court * * * caution[ed] lower courts against deciding fact-specific issues of foreseeability in the guise of determining whether the plaintiff has pleaded a valid cause of action. "[A] court's task—in determining 'duty'—is not to decide whether a *particular* plaintiff's injury was reasonably foreseeable in light of a *particular* defendant's conduct, but rather to evaluate more generally whether the category of negligent conduct at issue is sufficiently likely to result in the kind of harm experienced that liability may appropriately be imposed on the negligent party." [*Ballard* court's emphasis.]

The trial court's comments here in sustaining defendant's demurrer do not make clear whether it understood the limited nature of the foreseeability question before it. To the extent the court was focusing on the particular facts of this incident, *Ballard* makes clear it is an inappropriate basis for denying a plaintiff the opportunity to plead a cause of action. Moreover, it must be remembered that a defendant "may be liable if his conduct was a 'substantial factor' in bringing about the harm, though he neither foresaw nor should have foreseen the extent of the harm or the manner in which it occurred." Thus here, even if one could consider fact-specific foreseeability issues at the pleading stage, it is not necessary that GM anticipate that someone might throw a rock off a freeway overpass. Rather, in designing the Corvette's sunroof, it is only necessary that GM foresee the possibility that objects could fall from above a car and thus pose a danger to its occupants. (See Green v. Denney (1987) 87 Or.App. 298, 742 P.2d 639 (affirming judgment against auto manufacturer relating to freak accident where horse fell on top of car, collapsing roof).)

Meyering points out that objects can fall from trucks onto cars below; roadside signs frequently warn of the danger of falling rocks; indeed, the rock in question here could have been accidentally or negligently kicked off the overpass and onto a passing car. In addition, it may well be that the sunroof in question would provide inadequate protection to the car's occupants during rollover accidents. It is certainly a question of fact as to the extent of the risk posed by the sunroof's design and whether GM was negligent in failing to use stronger materials.

It may be, however, the trial court truly understood that fact-specific foreseeability was not an issue at the demurrer stage. The court may have reasoned—and GM certainly argues—that regardless of how foreseeable the risk of falling objects may be and how negligent GM may have been in failing to take account of that risk, policy considerations dictate a limitation on GM's liability for its negligence. In more familiar but perhaps less useful terms, GM claims it had no "duty" to guard against the criminal acts of third persons.[1]

* * * GM's argument anachronistically recalls a view long rejected by California courts as well as most other jurisdictions. "The view * * * that an intervening criminal act is by its very nature a superseding cause * * * is rejected by many courts and writers as an illogical and undesirable formula. They point out that in a large number of situations the very reason why the defendant's conduct is negligent is that it creates the risk of the particular intervening criminal act, and that it is absurd to invoke the very fact which establishes negligence to absolve the negligent person from liability * * *. The later California cases have fully accepted this theory as to both negligent and intentional intervening acts." See, e.g., Richardson v. Ham (1955) 44 Cal.2d 772, 285 P.2d 269 (lack of an ignition lock permits intoxicated persons to joyride in a 26–ton bulldozer); Bigbee v. Pacific Tel. & Tel. Co. (1983) 34 Cal.3d 49, 665 P.2d 947 (improper siting of a phone booth causes injury to caller when booth is struck by a drunk driver); Peterson v. San Francisco Community College Dist. (1984) 36 Cal.3d 799, 685 P.2d 1193 (untrimmed foliage provides hiding place for potential rapist); Isaacs v. Huntington Memorial Hospital (1985) 38 Cal.3d 112, 695 P.2d 653 (inadequate lighting and security contributes to shooting of doctor in hospital parking lot).

It is well established that manufacturers must design their products to perform in a reasonably safe manner. This obligation includes taking into account the possibility that foreseeable negligence or misconduct of the user or third persons may contribute to causing the injury. Illustrative of this principle and particularly relevant to the facts of this case is the Ninth Circuit Court of Appeals decision in d'Hedouville v. Pioneer Hotel Co. (9th Cir.1977) 552 F.2d 886. Plaintiff's decedent in *d'Hedouville* was

---

1. As the opinions of Judges Cardozo and Andrews in [*Palsgraf*] illustrate, the concepts of "duty" and "proximate cause" are effectively interchangeable ideas addressing the identical issue: At what point do external policy considerations require that a concededly negligent defendant's liability be restricted? Having previously expressed our concerns with the "duty" rubric, we nonetheless employ that formulation as the lesser of two evils. * * *

killed in a hotel fire started by an arsonist. Plaintiff sued Monsanto Company, the manufacturer of the hotel carpet, for wrongful death alleging that the fiber in the carpet ignited readily, did not self-extinguish and contributed to the outbreak and rapid spread of the fire. Applying Arizona law, the Ninth Circuit affirmed a jury verdict in plaintiff's favor. Monsanto had argued, as does GM here, that the arsonist's criminal act constituted a superseding cause of the victim's death which cut off any liability on its part. Rejecting this argument, the Ninth Circuit observed that "[w]hile this appears to have been the rule stated in early Arizona cases, more recent decisions apply the general principle of foreseeability to intervening criminal acts." The court went on to explain that Monsanto could foresee the possibility of fires in buildings in which its carpeting was installed and had the obligation to design its product with these hazards in mind. * * *

The obligations of automobile manufacturers have been particularly well defined by case law. In what is perhaps the seminal case nationally on the issue, the Eighth Circuit Court of Appeals rejected GM's argument that it had no duty to design a car to withstand collisions because the intended purpose of an automobile is not to crash into other vehicles or objects. "This duty of reasonable care in design rests on common law negligence [law] that a manufacturer of an article should use reasonable care in the design and manufacture of his product to eliminate any unreasonable risk of foreseeable injury. The duty of reasonable care in design should be viewed in light of the risk. While all risks cannot be eliminated nor can a crash-proof vehicle be designed under the present state of the art, there are many common-sense factors in design, which are or should be well known to the manufacturer that will minimize or lessen the injurious effects of a collision. The standard of reasonable care is applied in many other negligence situations and should be applied here." Larsen v. General Motors Corporation (8th Cir.1968) 391 F.2d 495, 503.

It is perhaps unnecessary to add that these principles apply regardless of whether the car is colliding with some other object or, as in this case, some other object is colliding with the car. * * *

* * *

Our conclusion does not suggest that an intentional criminal act can never be a superseding cause of injury. [GM refers] us to Restatement Second of Torts section 442B which [indicates that an intervening force will relieve a negligent actor of liability for resulting harm when] "the harm is intentionally caused by a third person and is not within the scope of the risk created by the actor's conduct." * * * The facts here do not present a similar issue. There is no suggestion that Meyering's juvenile assailants were intent on harming him, knew of the defective sunroof and deliberately took advantage of his vulnerability. It appears, rather, that the boys were engaged in reckless behavior * * * likely with no intent to cause personal injury. There is certainly no superseding cause on these facts which can be resolved as a matter of law.[4]

* * *

The judgment of dismissal is reversed. The trial court is directed to overrule GM's demurrer * * *.

FROEHLICH, ASSOCIATE JUSTICE, dissenting.

The majority here determines that a willfully tortious, criminal act which concurs with the antecedent negligence of another party is not a superseding cause of the resulting damage when the occurrence and the injury are foreseeable by the first actor in terms of noncriminal conduct. The majority * * * elects to expand the scope of tort liability in California * * *.

* * *

The majority cites and relies upon cases and authority which, I respectfully suggest, are inapposite. * * * Where one's conduct can specifically be anticipated to induce criminal conduct, he will be held to foresee it. * * * [This explains] Richardson v. Ham (lack of an ignition lock permits intoxicated persons to joyride in a 26–ton bulldozer). * * * Our case does not fit this category. Nothing General Motors did can be deemed to have induced or made more likely the subsequent tortious act of the rock thrower. Our record discloses no evidence suggesting the tortfeasor selected Meyering's car because it had a sunroof, or that he had some knowledge that it was a defective sunroof.

* * *

[Another] line of cases which is distinguishable is that which deals with superseding *negligence*, as opposed to superseding intentional or criminal acts. Typical of these is *Bigbee*, in which liability of the telephone company was found possible when the plaintiff, using its telephone booth, was injured by a drunk driver who ran into it. Although drunk driving may be a crime, its civil nature is essentially that of negligence. * * *

The authority asserted by the majority to be definitively in point consists [principally] of *d'Hedouville*, * * * which involved the liability of Monsanto Company for furnishing a hotel with flammable carpet. One of Monsanto's defenses was that the fire which damaged the plaintiffs was the result of arson, contending the arson was a superseding cause. The only portion of the lengthy opinion directed to the issue before us is the brief paragraph as follows:

---

4. We wholeheartedly agree with the dissent that the facts of this case and our status as an intermediate appellate court do not call for the creation of expansive new theories of tort liability. Our point of disagreement is that we believe the result we reach is compelled by existing—indeed well-established—precedent. As a result, we eschew reliance on "enlightened" legal thought (see, e.g., Huber, Liability, The Legal Revolution And Its Consequences (1988) which fervently exhorts a substantial change in the legal status quo because of perceived disastrous consequences caused by existing legal rules.) * * *

Monsanto argues that under Arizona decisions the criminal act of a third person constitutes a superseding cause as a matter of law. While this appears to have been the rule stated in early Arizona cases, more recent decisions apply the general principle of foreseeability to intervening criminal acts.

It is to be noted that this brief passage makes no reference to Restatement principles, nor does it cite any California cases. * * * [This was a federal court's interpretation of Arizona law, and it] should not be deemed controlling in that little or no consideration or discussion is devoted to the question, and the [Arizona] authority it cites does not support the broad proposition espoused.

* * *

If one is to go out of state, he will find considerable authority which supports the concept that criminality (absent the special circumstances set forth above) constitutes a superseding cause of damage. This authority is relatively current and certainly not an anachronism. * * *

* * *

* * * [T]he ruling of the majority is a departure from current law. * * * Saying this, the logical next question is "Why shouldn't we depart from current law?" Admittedly, there is no binding Supreme Court authority on the subject. Since the majority avers that it is simply applying existing law, it provides little by way of argument for its position. * * * [However the majority has effectively reached] a policy decision favoring recovery by plaintiffs from remote actors, increasing the potential scope of liability for manufacturers, and fostering claims and litigation. Is this the direction in which we are presently headed in the California judiciary? I think not, and therefore dissent from the policy decision implicit in the majority's opinion.

Whether plaintiffs' litigation potential vis-a-vis manufacturers of products should be increased or decreased is no doubt a matter of politics and philosophy, presumably best determined by the legislature. The function of an intermediate appellate court is, I contend, not to determine such philosophy but simply to reflect it. We have known periods of great expansion in the rights of plaintiffs. We are not now in one of those periods. * * * We should not now in the Court of Appeal be expanding grounds for liability in negligence * * *. The Supreme Court has [repeatedly] recognized * * * that litigation is not and cannot be the ultimate answer to all grievances. We are in a trend of restriction, not expansion, of litigation rights. This, I suggest, is in harmony with enlightened legal thought.[5]

* * *

---

5. See, for instance, Huber, Liability, The Legal Revolution and Its Consequences (1988) where it is persuasively argued that our system of determination of compensation for injuries through tort litigation is haphazard, poorly directed, excessively expensive, and generally detrimental to our competitive world position. Huber states at page 221:

NOTE

1. The California Supreme Court granted a writ of review. It did not reverse the Court of Appeal's decision, but it designated the Court of Appeal's opinion as "unpublished" and thus—under California practice—not citable as authority.

2. ***Intervening crimes and intentional torts.*** The *Meyering* case was inherently difficult because of the perception that a criminal and intentionally tortious act (the juveniles' throwing the chunk of concrete) had intervened between the defendant's negligent conduct (marketing a car with a weak roof) and the plaintiff's injury. As we will see in Chapter VI, this area of the law gives the courts a great deal of trouble. The jurisprudence is chaotic. Compare Kitchen v. K–Mart Corp., 697 So.2d 1200 (Fla. 1997), holding that K–Mart could be liable for selling a .22 rifle to a visibly drunk man who then used the weapon to intentionally shoot the plaintiff, with Buczkowski v. McKay, 441 Mich. 96, 490 N.W.2d 330 (1992), holding that K–Mart had "no duty" to avoid selling .410 ammunition to a visibly drunk man who then used the shells to intentionally shoot the plaintiff.

For further treatment of this troubled area of the law, see the *Doe* and *Galanti* cases in the nonfeasance section of Chapter VI (pp. 208 and 211) and the section in Chapter VI dealing with the creation of no-duty rules (pp. 217–32).

3. ***Dutification.*** In the notes following *Palsgraf*, supra p. 172, and *Edwards*, supra p. 180, we argue that these courts translated proximate cause issues into duty issues—*viz.*, that the courts "dutified" proximate cause issues. From this viewpoint, GM's argument to the *Meyering* court that it had no duty to guard against the risk that someone would throw concrete from an overpass onto the roof of a Corvette was an effort at dutification. When it succeeds, dutification is a powerful defensive move, because it presents the dispositive issue as a question for the judge rather than a jury.

In this chapter, we have been looking at dutification of proximate cause issues. In Chapter VI, we will see that courts are also often inclined to dutify breach issues.

Applied as it has been in recent years, open-ended tort law serves only as an engine of social destruction. Sometimes the effect is to alienate individuals from each other. The freedom of contract is undermined, private bilateral deals are curtailed. Sometimes the effect is to alienate the individual from community and state. Each individual is issued his own quiver of claims against the state and the publicly risky activities it has sanctioned; the state strikes back with more and more paternalistic legislation to protect citizens willy-nilly from injury. The unchecked inflation of the nonnegotiable right to sue eventually undercuts a panoply of other freedoms.

CHAPTER VI

THE DUTY ISSUE

■ ■ ■

A. INTRODUCTION: THE PRINCIPLE OF HEAVEN v. PENDER

Here again, we begin with a reminder that duty is traditionally listed as the first of five elements of the cause of action in negligence. Duty is an issue of law, for the judge; the other four are "issues of fact,"[1] for the jury unless reasonable minds could not differ.

The twelfth paragraph of Judge Posner's opinion in Edwards v. Honeywell, supra p. 183 (first full paragraph), is a useful quick overview of the history of Anglo–American tort law's use of the concept of duty. In what we will (somewhat arbitrarily) call the first stage, some forms of overt misconduct were actionable, but in general duties to guard against negligent conduct arose only from specific undertakings, such as a bailee's agreeing for a price to look after a bailor's goods; entailed in such an undertaking was an obligation to use due care. In the second stage, the courts began synthesizing the duties attached to specific undertakings into a general duty of reasonable care. (In Vaughan v. Menlove (1837), supra p. 79, we saw this process of synthesis in action; the court cobbled together a neighbor-to-neighbor duty of reasonable care on the basis of principles found in bailment cases.[2]) In the third stage, courts began selectively using the concept of duty to "rein in juries."

The second-stage synthesis can be seen at its zenith in the broad proclamation of Heaven v. Pender (1883), supra p. 179, that anyone engaged in an activity that potentially places others at risk of harm

---

1. *Issues of fact* needs to be in quotation marks here, because in the negligence-law context the term routinely includes inquiry into not only what actually happened but also what should have or might have happened.

2. The "neighbor" concept proved expansive. In Donoghue v. Stevenson, 1932 S.L.T. 317 (House of Lords 1932), the court held that the manufacturer of a bottle of ginger beer containing a decomposed snail should be liable to a sickened consumer whose friend had bought the beverage for her. The main opinion in the case (Lord Atkin, id. at 323) explained: "In English law, * * * [t]he rule that you are to love your neighbour becomes * * *, you must not injure your neighbour. * * * Who, then, in law is my neighbour? The answer seems to be—persons who are so closely and directly affected by my act that I ought reasonably to have them in contemplation as being so affected when I am directing my mind to the acts or omissions which are called into question. This appears to be the doctrine of Heaven v. Pender * * *."

presumptively has a duty to use reasonable care to minimize the risk.[3] Speaking very generally, the Heaven v. Pender principle has the useful practical meaning that "[i]n the usual run of cases, a general duty to avoid negligence is assumed, and there is no need for the court to undertake detailed analysis of precedent and policy" in order to conclude that a duty exists.[4]

Restatement (Third) of Torts: Liability for Physical and Emotional Harm § 7 (2010) embraces the Heaven v. Pender principle, stating: "An actor ordinarily has a duty to exercise reasonable care when the actor's conduct poses a risk of physical harm." Section 6 cmt. *d* provides two compelling justifications for the principle:

> One justification for imposing liability for negligent conduct that causes physical harm is corrective justice; imposing liability remedies an injustice done by the defendant to the plaintiff. An actor who permits [his] conduct to impose a risk of physical harm on others that exceeds the burden the actor would bear in avoiding that risk impermissibly ranks personal interests ahead of the interests of others. This, in turn, violates an ethical norm of equal consideration when imposing risks on others. Imposing liability remedies this violation.
>
> Another justification for imposing liability for negligence is to give actors appropriate incentives to engage in safe conduct. The actor's adoption of appropriate precautions improves overall social welfare and thereby advances broad economic goals.

Judge Posner's third—"reining in juries"—stage is ongoing. In present-day law it takes two major forms: the group of general-category no-duty rules that are treated in sections B, C, and E through G of this chapter, and the process of creating new no-duty rules that is treated in section D. These limitations on the Heaven v. Pender principle are not static. The privity limitation treated in section B has been shrinking but continues to show intermittent vigor. Limitations of the sort discussed in section D are very much in dispute and in flux. Those treated in the other sections are fairly stable, although they can be narrowed or broadened from time to time and place to place.

When a duty is found to exist, it is usually a duty to use reasonable care, but it can be a lesser or greater duty. In section G we will see that occupiers of land are often held to something less than the full duty of reasonable care. Conversely, common carriers are sometimes said to owe their passengers a duty of utmost care. See, e.g., Markwell v. Whinery's Real Estate, Inc., 869 P.2d 840 (Okla. 1994).

---

3. The law of most—perhaps all—states includes some version of the Heaven v. Pender principle. The versions range from the facially overbroad pronouncement in Miller v. Wal–Mart Stores, 219 Wis.2d 250, 580 N.W.2d 233, 238 (1998) that "[i]n Wisconsin, everyone has a duty to the whole world" to the considerably more informative formulation in Doe v. Johnson, 817 F.Supp. 1382, 1386 (W.D. Mich. 1993), that Michigan's law of negligence "imposes on every person engaged in the prosecution of any undertaking an obligation to use due care, [i.e.,] to so govern his actions as not to unreasonably endanger the person or property of others."

4. Dobbs, The Law of Torts § 227, p. 578 n. 1 (2000) (quoting from Hamilton v. Accu–Tek, 62 F.Supp.2d 802 (E.D.N.Y. 1999)).

B. PRIVITY OF CONTRACT

At one stage of its development, English tort law pulled against the Heaven v. Pender principle in some contexts by requiring that the plaintiff have a contractual relationship of some kind with the defendant tortfeasor. This "privity of contract" requirement can be seen at work in Langridge v. Levy, 2 M. & W. 510, 50 E.R. 863 (1836), in which a young man was hurt by a defective gun that his father had bought for him. (Thus the father had a privity-of-contract relationship with the seller, but the injured son did not.) The court held the seller of the gun liable to the son for fraud—he had lied about the identity of the gun's maker—but stated that negligence liability could not be imposed because the injured son could not show "a breach of a public duty [flowing from a recognized public calling such as that of surgeon or blacksmith] or a violation of a private right existing between himself and the defendant."

In Winterbottom v. Wright, 10 M. & W. 109, 152 E.R. 402 (1842)—the seminal privity-of-contract case—the court held that the defendant's negligence in the performance of his contract with the owner of a mail coach to keep the coach in safe running condition could not serve as the basis for liability to a driver of the coach who was "lamed for life" when the coach collapsed. The *Winterbottom* court explained its ruling:

> There is no privity of contract between [defendant and plaintiff]; and if the plaintiff can sue, every passenger, or even any person passing along the road, who was injured by the upsetting of the coach, might bring a similar action. Unless we confine the operation of such contracts as this to the parties who entered into them, the most absurd and outrageous consequences, to which I can see no limit, would ensue. * * * By permitting this action, we should be working this injustice, that after the defendant had done everything to the satisfaction of [the coach's owner], and after all matters between them had been adjusted, and all accounts settled on the footing of their contract, we should subject them to be ripped open by this action of tort being brought against him.

As we will spell out in a bit more detail in section A of Chapter XIV, in its heyday the privity-of-contract doctrine insulated manufacturers of defective products from responsibility to consumers who did not buy the product directly from the manufacturer. In MacPherson v. Buick Motor Co., 217 N.Y. 382, 111 N.E. 1050 (1916), Judge Cardozo effectively abolished the privity rule in the products-liability context. However, vestiges of *Winterbottom's* "privity" idea can still be found in other areas of negligence law. Consider the following case.

BUSH v. SECO ELECTRIC CO.

United States Court of Appeals, Seventh Circuit, 1997.
118 F.3d 519.

CUDAHY, CIRCUIT JUDGE.

The law of Indiana has long held that once an owner accepts a piece of construction work from an independent contractor, the owner takes full responsibility for it. The contractor's duty of care to a third party for personal injury thereby ceases, for the contractor and the third party are not in privity. And with the contractor's duty goes its liability as well. In embracing this "acceptance rule," Indiana has not been alone. In the related area of warranties in sales of personal property, American courts many years ago shed a requirement of privity between injured parties and manufacturers. MacPherson v. Buick Motor Co. [supra p. 196]. But, in the world of construction contracts, courts have been much slower to relax the privity strictures of the nineteenth-century common law.

Defendants SECO Electric Company and Jack Satkamp (collectively SECO) argue that the acceptance rule remains potent in Indiana and that it blocks any liability to plaintiff Jerri Bush. Bush was a temporary employee at an Indianapolis recycling plant owned by Rumpke Recycling, Inc. (Rumpke). The plant recycled aluminum cans; Bush's main job was "densifying" the cans inside the plant building. Delivery trucks would drop cans into a deep pit, and a giant conveyor contraption would pick them up and deposit them in a hopper. (Rumpke had hired SECO to install the wiring of the conveyor.) The conveyor sometimes failed to gather all the aluminum cans, which then needed to be cleaned up. The proper way to do this was to go down into the pit, pick the cans up, dump them in big garbage bins and haul the bins out. The safety protocol called for shutting off the conveyor with controls located outside the pit. A yellow safety guard was supposed to be fitted on the conveyor's mouth, making it impossible to feed cans into the conveyor. There was no emergency shut-off button actually in the pit.

Bush was picked to go clean the pit. Bush says she knew nothing of the safety protocol, and it was her first day on pit duty. She began shoveling cans onto the conveyor while it was still running. The safety guard was not on, apparently taken off to be cleaned or repaired. The conveyor snagged her clothes and Bush lost her arm.

* * *

SECO moved for summary judgment, raising the acceptance rule as its defense. That Rumpke had accepted the wiring job was not in dispute: the conveyor had been operating for four weeks when Bush was injured, and Rumpke's control over the conveyor was beyond doubt. Bush argued that the acceptance rule did not defeat her action, because she fitted into a narrow "humanitarian" exception. Under this exception, lack of privity could be overlooked if a contractor produced "a product or work in a condition that was dangerously defective, inherently dangerous or imminently dangerous such that it created a risk of imminent personal injury"—but mere negligence would not suffice. The absence of an emergency stop-button in the pit itself constituted such a condition, Bush argued.

The district court thought not. Because SECO therefore owed no duty of care to Bush, the district court granted summary judgment to SECO. Bush appeals. * * *

While this appeal was awaiting oral argument, the Indiana Supreme Court in Blake v. Calumet Construction Corp., 674 N.E.2d 167 (Ind.1996), recast the acceptance rule. In her briefs before this court, Bush forecast that the Indiana Supreme Court would overrule the privity-based acceptance rule for personal injuries in favor of a negligence standard rooted in foreseeability. In this, Bush was disappointed: the acceptance rule survives in Indiana.

Yet in its explication of the "imminent personal injury" exception upon which Bush relied in the district court, *Blake* may have delivered what Bush seeks. *Blake* is peppered with words like "expectable," "reasonable," and "foreseeable," words alien to the privity analysis of the acceptance rule. In spirit, it seems, *Blake* looks to the granddaddy of negligence cases, *Palsgraf* [supra p. 172]. *Blake* goes so far as to remark upon the advantages of junking the acceptance rule in favor of a "*Palsgraf*-like foreseeability standard." Such a standard, *Blake* notes, would "obviate[] possible confusion caused by terms like 'acceptance' or 'imminently dangerous.'" Yet rather than trace this logic to its implicit conclusion, *Blake* in the end declines to set aside the acceptance rule.

So the acceptance rule survives; but in what form? For the humanitarian exception widens enough in *Blake* to re-shape the acceptance rule itself. Where a contractor hands over work "in a defective or dangerous state," "important considerations of deterrence and prevention militate in favor of imposing an ongoing duty of care." And *Blake* grounds this view on a foundation that is positively Palsgrafian: "The possibility of harm from the condition is foreseeable by the contractor." The spirit of *Palsgraf* is evident as well in *Blake's* elaboration of the humanitarian exception. The exception applies to contractors' work that is (1) dangerously defective, (2) inherently dangerous, or (3) imminently dangerous. *Blake* supplies definitions for each. Because the "inherently dangerous" sub-exception best applies to "dangerous activities such as blasting, rather than conditions or instrumentalities" (like SECO's wiring), we quote only the first and third definitions. SECO's wiring would be "'dangerously defective' if the work is turned over in a condition that has a propensity for causing physical harm to foreseeable third parties using it in reasonably expectable ways." Or its work might be "'imminently dangerous' if it 'is reasonably certain to place life or limb in peril.'"

In *Blake*, the defendant contractor had built a loading dock attached to a maintenance building. The contractor had not put up a guardrail. Wrapping up some work in the building, plaintiff Blake took a break mid-evening and exited onto the darkened loading dock. Stepping off the edge, Blake fell four feet to the concrete below and broke his hip. The trial court invoked the acceptance rule and granted summary judgment to the defendant contractor. The Court of Appeals affirmed. Equipped with the re-visited humanitarian exception, the Indiana Supreme Court decided that Blake should have survived summary judgment. "[T]he lack of a safety device on a darkened construction site," the *Blake* court held, "is enough to present a jury question on the loading dock's status as an imminently dangerous condition."

The district court decided against Bush under pre-*Blake* law. Whether Bush can surmount summary judgment under current Indiana law is puzzling. Maybe a reasonable jury could conclude that the absence of an emergency stop-button down in the pit was "reasonably certain to place life or limb in peril." We do not know. The acceptance rule has shifted enough to make extrapolating from the district court's decision little more than divination. We believe the district court must take a second look in light of *Blake*. Additional submissions might lead to summary judgment. And, if not, a trial would seem appropriate.

The opinion of the district court is vacated and this case remanded for further proceedings.

NOTES

1. ***The acceptance rule is dying.*** Having fatally wounded the acceptance rule in its decision in *Blake*, the Indiana Supreme Court abolished it in Peters v. Forster, 804 N.E.2d 736 (Ind. 2004). This came too late for Jerri Bush, who presumably settled her case under the shadow of whatever was left of the acceptance rule after *Blake*. For other recent abolitions, see Davis v. Baugh Industrial Contractors, Inc., 159 Wash.2d 413, 150 P.3d 545 (2007); Dorell v. South Carolina Dept. of Transp., 361 S.C. 312, 605 S.E.2d 12 (2004). For a more elderly abolition, see Strakos v. Gehring, 360 S.W.2d 787 (Tex. 1962).

2. ***The acceptance rule has at least one healthy cousin***. Restatement (Second) of Torts §§ 352 and 353 treat a rule protecting real-property sellers in most situations from liability for injuries (caused by conditions of the property existing at the time of sale) that occur after the transfer of possession and control. For a recent application of this "ordinary vendor" rule, see Tindle v. Pulte Home Corp., 607 F.3d 494 (7th Cir. 2010) (Illinois law) (concealed sinkhole in back yard).

3. Even when the lack of privity is not the direct basis for a no-duty ruling, it can be an influential factor. For example, in Strauss v. Belle Realty Co., 65 N.Y.2d 399, 492 N.Y.S.2d 555, 482 N.E.2d 34 (1985), the court held that even though the ConEd Power Company was guilty of gross negligence in bringing about a massive 25–hour power failure in New York City (the blackout of 1977), the company's liability for injuries caused by the blackout was limited to persons with whom the company had a contractual relationship. Thus, the complaint of a tenant of a ConEd customer, who lost running water because of the blackout and then fell on darkened basement stairs while seeking an alternative water source, was properly dismissed by the lower court. The *Strauss* court stated that "while the absence of privity does not foreclose recognition of a duty, * * * [c]onsiderations of privity are not entirely irrelevant in implementing policy." 482 N.E.2d at 36. The court

defined its policy goal as "extend[ing] defendant's duty to cover specifically foreseeable parties but at the same time [containing] liability to manageable levels." Id. at 37.

4. ***Physician-nonpatient cases.*** The privity concept may help to account for the significant number of cases insulating physicians from liability for negligence in facilitating or failing to prevent their patients' infecting or otherwise harming others. See, e.g., Brown v. United States, 583 F.3d 916 (6th Cir. 2009) (under Michigan law, Department of Veterans Affairs doctors owed no duty to veteran's family members to whom veteran spread a parasitic infection that he contracted while serving in the Persian Gulf War); McNulty v. City of New York, 100 N.Y.2d 227, 762 N.Y.S.2d 12, 792 N.E.2d 162 (2003) (doctors who treated a patient with infectious meningitis owed no duty of care to the patient's friend, who stuck close to the patient after the doctors led her to believe she was not at great risk of infection); Schmidt v. Mahoney, 659 N.W.2d 552 (Iowa 2003) (physician who negligently told his epileptic patient that it was safe to drive a car had no duty to a person the patient injured in a car wreck during a seizure).

There are cases going both ways on this point. For a lively debate, see the four opinions in Coombes v. Florio, 450 Mass. 182, 877 N.E.2d 567 (2007).

5. In reading *Bush,* were you surprised to see "the spirit of *Palsgraf*" working for a plaintiff?

C. DUTY TO ACT? NONFEASANCE vs. MISFEASANCE

Leon Green called the misfeasance/nonfeasance line "the most definite boundary of negligence law" and offered an explanation in The Duty Problem in Negligence Cases, 28 Colum.L.Rev. 1014, 1026–27 (1928):

> Broadly speaking no person is under a duty to another unless he has entered upon some course of conduct towards such other. As long as a person does nothing he comes under no duty imposed by law. This is one of the most dependable limitations upon duties * * *. [I]n the tort field at least, this power we call law is merely designed to *control* conduct and not to *compel* it. We have enough to do to keep our activities within control, without attempting to regulate the directions the latent energies of individuals should take.

The Third Restatement's treatment of the nonfeasance area is set out in Chapter 7, §§ 37–44, of *Proposed Final Draft No. 1 (April 6, 2005).* The chapter is complete and has been approved by the American Law Institute. (It will be published along with a chapter on liability of hirers of independent contractors when the latter is completed.) Section 37 states the basic nonfeasance rule. Section 39 describes an exception based on defendant's *prior conduct.* Section 40 sets forth certain "special relationships" between defendant and plaintiff that may generate an affirmative duty of care; we will call this the *relationship with victim* exception. Section 41 deals with the situation in which the plaintiff is injured by the affirmative conduct of a third person and sets forth certain relationships between the defendant and the third person that may generate an affirmative duty of care; we will call this the *relationship with perpetrator* exception. Sections 42–44 treat what we will call the *volunteer* exception. Another name for the volunteer exception is the Good Samaritan doctrine. (Some analysts see this doctrine as a way of taking a case out of the nonfeasance category rather than as an exception to the nonfeasance rule.)

In the cases and notes below we will see the nonfeasance rule applied, challenged, and tested, and we will observe the courts struggling toward designing appropriate limits and exceptions to it. Broadly speaking, there are two battlefronts. The first is how to draw the misfeasance/nonfeasance line; is the case at hand a misfeasance care, or is it a nonfeasance case? The second is, assuming that the case at hand falls into the nonfeasance category, does it fall into one (or more) of the four loosely delineated exceptions to the nonfeasance rule?

SATTERFIELD v. BREEDING INSULATION CO.

Supreme Court of Tennessee, 2008.
266 S.W.3d 347.

WILLIAM C. KOCH, JR., J.

* * *

[The facts recited below are taken from the plaintiff's complaint.] Alcoa, Inc. is an international manufacturer of aluminum and aluminum products. It owns and operates facilities in various locations throughout the United States, including a facility in Alcoa, Tennessee. Alcoa uses materials containing asbestos in many of its manufacturing operations. Since the 1930s, Alcoa has been aware that asbestos is a highly dangerous substance, and it has closely monitored the research into the dangers posed by asbestos.

* * *

Alcoa became aware in the 1960s that the dangers posed by asbestos fibers extended beyond its employees who were in constant direct contact with the materials containing asbestos or the asbestos fibers in the air. It learned * * * that persons living near facilities that made extensive use of materials containing asbestos were experiencing higher disease rates, as were the family members of its employees who were being exposed regularly and repeatedly to the asbestos fibers on the employees' work clothes.

In 1972, the Occupational Safety and Health Administration ("OSHA") promulgated regulations prohibiting employees who had been exposed to asbestos from taking their work clothes home to be laundered. Tests that Alcoa conducted at a number of its facilities, including those in Tennessee, revealed that the levels of asbestos fibers on the workers' clothes were extremely high.

In 1973, Doug Satterfield began working at Alcoa's facility in Alcoa, Tennessee. He worked there for two years until he entered the United States Army in 1975. After three years of military service, Mr. Satterfield resumed working at the Alcoa plant in 1978. He continued to work for Alcoa until at least 1984. His job assignments resulted in his exposure to high levels of asbestos dust and fibers on a daily basis.

Contrary to the OSHA regulations, Alcoa failed to educate Mr. Satterfield and its other employees regarding the risk of asbestos or how to handle materials containing asbestos. * * * Despite the fact that Alcoa was aware of the dangers posed by asbestos before Mr. Satterfield became an employee, it failed to apprise him or its other employees of the dangers of asbestos or specifically of the danger associated with wearing home their asbestos-contaminated work clothes. In addition, Alcoa failed to provide protective coveralls for its employees, discouraged the use of its on-site bathhouse facilities, and did not offer to launder its employees' work clothes at its facility. Accordingly, Alcoa's employees, including Mr. Satterfield, left the plant each day unaware of the dangers posed by the asbestos fibers on their contaminated work clothes and without Alcoa making an effort to prevent others from being exposed to the asbestos fibers on its employees' clothes.

* * *

[This action was brought by Doug Satterfield's daughter, Amanda, who alleged that she contracted mesothelioma from being exposed throughout her life to the asbestos fibers on her father's work clothes. Not long after initiating the litigation, Amanda died from mesothelioma at the age of 25. Her father (as personal representative of his daughter's estate) was substituted as plaintiff. Alcoa moved to dismiss the complaint on no-duty grounds. The trial court granted the motion. The intermediate appellate court reversed and remanded the case for further proceedings. The supreme court then granted Alcoa's application for permission to take an interlocutory appeal.]

* * * Alcoa asserts that it did not owe a duty to Ms. Satterfield. It contends that imposing such a duty on it would improperly create an affirmative obligation to act despite the absence of any special relationship between Alcoa and either Ms. Satterfield or her father. On the other hand, Mr. Satterfield insists that his daughter's complaint is premised on the assumption that Alcoa owed Ms. Satterfield a duty of reasonable care because it created an unreasonable and foreseeable risk of harm to her.

The underlying dispute in this case is fundamentally one of characterization and classification. Has Alcoa engaged in an affirmative act that created an unreasonable and foreseeable risk of harm to Ms. Satterfield? * * * Or, alternatively, does this case involve an omission by Alcoa in failing to control the actions of Mr. Satterfield, its employee? If so, then does Alcoa have the sort of special relationship with either Mr. Satterfield or Ms. Satterfield that gives rise to a duty to restrain Mr. Satterfield or to protect Ms. Satterfield? * * *

* * *

[M]ore than a century ago, Professor Francis H. Bohlen asserted that "[t]here is no distinction more deeply rooted in the common law and more fundamental than that between misfeasance and nonfeasance, between active misconduct working positive injury to others and passive inaction, a failure to take positive steps to benefit others, or to protect them from harm not created by any wrongful act of the defendant."

* * *

The distinction between misfeasance and nonfeasance can be easily misunderstood. One can be led astray by thinking that a defendant's negligent act must be characterized "as an affirmative act for a duty to exist, rather than appreciating that it is the defendant's entire course of conduct that must constitute an affirmative act creating a risk of harm and that negligence may consist of an act or omission creating an unreasonable risk." A classic illustration of this point is the example of a driver who fails to apply his or her brakes to avoid hitting a pedestrian walking in a crosswalk. Even though the driver's negligent act—failing to apply the brakes—is an omission, the "driver's careless failure to apply the brakes is negligent driving, not negligent failure to rescue." Accordingly, distinguishing between misfeasance and nonfeasance can best be accomplished, not by focusing on whether an individual's "specific failure to exercise reasonable care is an error of commission or omission," but rather by focusing on whether the individual's entire course of conduct created a risk of harm. Thus, even though the specific negligent act may constitute an omission, the entirety of the conduct may still be misfeasance that created a risk of harm.

* * *

The distinction between misfeasance and nonfeasance is far from academic. It has practical significance, and Tennessee's courts regularly employ it when called upon to decide whether a duty exists. With regard to misfeasance, this Court has held that "all persons have a duty to use reasonable care to refrain from conduct that will foreseeably cause injury to others." As for nonfeasance, Tennessee's courts generally have declined to impose a duty to act or to rescue. Simply stated, persons do not ordinarily have a duty to act to protect others from dangers or risks except for those that they themselves have created.

* * *

A compelling argument in opposition to the no duty to act or to rescue rule rests comfortably "on the perception that, as a matter of inarticulate common sense, it is wrong for one person to stand by as another suffers an injury that could easily be prevented." An expert swimmer who stands on the shore watching a child drown or a passerby on the bridge who cannot be bothered to throw a rope to a person in distress in the waters below stand as illustrations that demonstrate the unreasonableness that can be exemplified by a failure to rescue. Even staunch defenders of the no duty to act or to rescue rule must concede that failure to do so may, in certain circumstances, not only be unreasonable, a normal measure for negligent conduct, but actually "outrageous."

Nevertheless, common-law courts * * * have preserved * * * the no duty to act or to rescue rule. The reason is not intransigency or lack of consideration. Quite to the contrary, the rule survives because its limitations continue to be of considerable importance and value. Imposing a duty to act or to rescue strays dangerously into interference with individual liberty. By adhering to a no duty to act or to rescue rule, the courts are not rendering the common law amoral but instead are prioritizing liberty over altruism in circumstances where the defendant did not create the risk of harm. * * *

* * *

Searching for reasonable ground between the competing viewpoints * * *, Tennessee's courts have maintained the general rule but have carved out exceptions to mitigate against some of its harshest applications. These exceptions arise when certain special relationships exist between the defendant and either the person who is the source of the danger or the person who is foreseeably at risk from the danger. These relationships create an affirmative duty either to control the person who is the source of the danger or to protect the person who is endangered.

* * *

Courts across the country have disagreed as to how these broad principles of tort law should be used to determine whether an employer owes a duty to persons who develop asbestos-related illnesses after exposure to asbestos fibers on its employees' clothing. * * * The opinions of many state courts contain well-reasoned and insightful analyses of the legal principles implicated in these so-called "take-home" asbestos exposure cases. * * *

* * *

While [some courts have held that employers have no duty in take-home asbestos exposure cases because of the absence of a special relationship between the employer and the employee's family], this argument is misplaced under Tennessee tort law * * *. Whether a case involves a simple automobile accident or a complicated toxic tort, Tennessee law currently provides that one owes a duty to refrain from engaging in conduct that creates an unreasonable and foreseeable risk of harm to others.

Our decision in [West v. East Tennessee Pioneer Oil Co., 172 S.W. 3d 545 (Tenn. 2005)] illustrates this principle. That case required us to determine whether a convenience store had a duty to the occupants of a vehicle who were injured when an intoxicated motorist struck their vehicle after the store's employees had helped the obviously intoxicated motorist fuel his vehicle shortly before the accident. The store asserted that the intoxicated motorist was only a customer and, therefore, that no special relationship existed between the store and the intoxicated driver that would be sufficient to require the store employees to control the intoxicated driver's conduct. We did not hold that the convenience store's liability was predicated on the existence of a special relationship between the store and the intoxicated driver. Instead, we held that

> the defendant misconstrues the plaintiffs' claims as being based upon a "special relationship" arising from the sale of gasoline to Mr. Tarver (the intoxicated driver). The plaintiffs' allegations do not revolve around any duty of the defendant to control the conduct of a customer. Instead, the claims are predicated on the defendant's employees' affirmative acts in contributing to the creation of a foreseeable and unreasonable risk of harm, i.e., providing mobility to a drunk driver which he otherwise would not have had, thus creating a risk to persons on the roadways. (Id. at 551.)

* * * Under the facts alleged in Ms. Satterfield's complaint, Alcoa's alleged misfeasance created a significant risk of harm to Ms. Satterfield. Despite Alcoa's protestations to the contrary, this is not a [nonfeasance case]. * * * Instead, this case involves a risk created through misfeasance. * * * [L]liability for misfeasance is not cabined within the confines of boxes created by particular relationships. To the contrary, "[l]iability for 'misfeasance' * * * may extend to any person to whom harm may reasonably be anticipated as a result of the defendant's conduct * * *; while for 'nonfeasance' it is necessary to find some definite relation between the parties, of such a character that social policy justifies the imposition of a duty to act." Alcoa engaged in misfeasance that set in motion a risk of harm to Ms. Satterfield. Because Ms. Satterfield's complaint rests on the basic tort claim of misfeasance, it is not necessary to analyze in detail whether Alcoa also had duties arising from special relationships * * *.

We affirm the Court of Appeals and remand the case to the trial court for further proceedings consistent with this opinion.

LACEY v. UNITED STATES

United States District Court, District of Massachusetts, 1951.
98 F.Supp. 219.

SWEENEY, CHIEF JUDGE.

* * * [T]he administrator of the estate of a pilot who lost his life in Massachusetts Bay after his plane had fallen into the water seeks to recover against the United States * * * by reason of the allegedly negligent failure of the Coast Guard to rescue his decedent. * * *

It is well settled common law that a mere bystander incurs no liability where he fails to take any action, however negligently or even intentionally, to rescue another in distress. [Plaintiff urges] here that the Coast Guard is charged by statute with the responsibility of saving lives at sea, and a civil tort liability for negligence is thereby created which would be otherwise non-existent. With this I cannot agree. The statute, 14 U.S.C.A. § 1 et seq., invokes a military discipline of rewards and punishments to promote the proper performance of their duties by Coast Guard personnel, but nowhere in the statute is there created a right to be rescued in the sense of an award of civil damages for the negligent failure of the Coast Guard to attempt to rescue a person in distress. It is not for the Court to create this right where such a novel tort liability is neither contemplated by the basic statute nor recognized by prior law. It is true that, while the common law imposes no duty to rescue, it does impose on the Good Samaritan the duty to act with due care once he has undertaken rescue operations. The rationale is that other would-be rescuers will rest on their oars in the expectation that effective aid is being rendered. Under this theory it is argued here that the Coast Guard is liable because it did undertake to rescue the deceased but negligently failed to reach [him] while [he was] still alive. That the Government does not come within the Good Samaritan rule is demonstrated by the fact that the complaint does not show that the Coast Guard's rescue attempt reached the stage where other would-be rescuers were induced to cease their efforts in the belief that the Coast Guard had the situation in hand. Since the deceased [was] in no way deprived of other available help by the Coast Guard operations, there is no tort liability on the Coast Guard for its allegedly negligent failure to save the deceased. * * *

[T]he Government's * * * motion to dismiss is allowed.

NOTES

1. In United States v. Gavagan, 280 F.2d 319 (5th Cir. 1960), the volunteer exception led to liability for a failed Coast Guard rescue mission, on the finding that reliance on the Coast Guard's effort had induced the friends and families of the imperiled fishermen to forgo private efforts "which, in all probability, would have been successful."

2. When the volunteer exception applies, it gives rise to a duty not to worsen the victim's situation. Some courts add that it also generates a duty to avoid "reckless and wanton conduct in performing the rescue." Berg v. Chevron U.S.A., Inc., 759 F.2d 1425, 1430 (9th Cir. 1985). Note that this is less than a full-blown duty of reasonable care.

3. *An exercise in statutory interpretation.* The cases holding that the common law imposes no duty to rescue constitute the most controversial application of the nonfeasance rule. Statutes in many European countries make it a misdemeanor to refuse assistance to a person in serious or mortal danger. See also Vt.Stat.Ann. tit. 12 § 519, which provides as follows:

(a) A person who knows that another is exposed to grave physical harm shall, to the extent that the same can be rendered without danger or peril to himself or without interference with important duties owed to others, give reasonable assistance to the exposed person unless that assistance or care is being provided by others.

(b) A person who provides reasonable assistance in compliance with subsection (a) of this section shall not be liable in civil damages unless his acts constitute gross negligence or unless he will receive or expects to receive remuneration. Nothing contained in this subsection shall alter existing law with respect to tort liability of a practitioner of the healing arts for acts committed in the ordinary course of his practice.

(c) A person who willfully violates subsection (a) of this section shall be fined not more than $100.00.

Does this statute impose a tort-law duty to rescue? There are good arguments both ways. In thinking about them, pay close attention to the *Lacey* court's treatment of the Coast Guard statute.

4. ***Does the law need a nonfeasance rule?*** The nonfeasance rule is controversial in applications like *Lacey*, but courts seem to regard it as fundamental. Wisconsin is unusual in not having such a rule. In Rockweit v. Senecal, 197 Wis.2d 409, 541 N.W.2d 742 (1995), the Rockweit family—father, mother, and 18–month–old Anthony—were camping at a proprietary campground. One night they were joined around their campfire by a number of acquaintances, including Ann Tynan, a friend who was camping several sites away. Everyone eventually went to bed—Tynan was one of the last—and nobody put out the fire. The next morning, Anthony Rockweit slipped away from his mother and slid into the fire pit, sustaining severe burns. One of the defendants was Tynan—allegedly negligent for going to bed without dousing the fire—and the lower court determined that she should share in the responsibility for the child's injuries. In reviewing that decision, the Wisconsin Supreme Court said that a jury could find that Tynan's conduct was negligent and that it was a proximate cause of Anthony's injuries. It also said that Tynan's argument—that because her conduct was pure nonfeasance, she owed no duty of care—was "incorrect" and "without merit." The court— which has frequently stated that Wisconsin has no nonfeasance rule—explicitly held that Tynan owed a duty of care and breached it. But it then turned to a "public policy" analysis that led it to stress a number of factual considerations—Tynan's conduct was an "omission," she did not select the fire site nor start the fire, she never had any custody or control over Anthony, she "did not create the hazard," she did not "assume any responsibility to maintain the fire pit"—in support of the conclusion that Anthony's injury was "too remote from any alleged negligence on [Tynan's] part to impose liability."

5. ***Should the common law impose a duty to rescue?*** Hyman, Rescue Without Law: An Empirical Perspective on the Duty to Rescue, 84 Tex. L. Rev. 653 (2006) says no, we don't need one. Professor Hyman concludes (id. at 716) that "Americans, motivated by the imperfect obligations of beneficence, have proven themselves more than up to the task of rescuing those in need, irrespective of whatever the law might happen to say on the subject."

DOE v. CORPORATION OF THE PRESIDENT OF THE CHURCH OF JESUS CHRIST OF LATTER–DAY SAINTS

Court of Appeals of Utah, 2004.
98 P.3d 429, *cert. denied*, 106 P.3d 743 (Utah 2004).

GREENWOOD, J.

* * *

[The facts recited below are taken from the plaintiffs' complaint.]

For many years, Jane [Doe] and her son John were members of the Church and regularly attended a ward in the Salt Lake Holladay Stake.[2] George Tilson was also a member of the Church, and held the positions of "High Priest"[3] and scout leader within the Church.

Beginning in 1966 and continuing through 2002, COP [Corporation of the President] received several complaints from its members that Tilson was sexually abusing children within his ward.[4] However, COP not only failed to do anything in response to these complaints, it actively concealed Tilson's sexual abuse from its members and secular authorities. Moreover, COP allowed Tilson to continue to hold the positions of High Priest and scout leader.

Two of Tilson's victims during the time period that he was alleged to have engaged in child sexual abuse were Jane and John. In the summer of 1976, Tilson enticed Jane, who was then thirteen years old, into his home where he fondled her under her clothing. Tilson sexually abused John, Jane's son, some time between 1993 and 1996 when John was approximately five years old. John's abuse also occurred in Tilson's home after Tilson lured him away from a neighbor's yard where he was playing.

In the fall of 2001, Jane learned of news reports that led her to believe that COP had prior knowledge of Tilson's propensities to sexually abuse children. Jane's subsequent investigation of these reports ultimately prompted her to file a complaint in June of 2002 against Tilson, alleging that he had sexually abused Jane and John, and against COP, alleging negligence, breach of fiduciary duty, and intentional infliction of emotional distress arising out of Tilson's alleged sexual abuse. [The trial court granted COP's motion to dismiss the complaint.]

[In the court of appeals, the dispositive issue was] whether COP had a common law duty to warn Plaintiffs about Tilson's prior acts of child sexual abuse. "Traditionally, the common law has not required a defen-

---

2. COP administers the Church through a multi-level structure. At the local level are wards which are administered by bishops. Wards are grouped into stakes which are administered by stake presidents.

3. According to Plaintiffs, "[a] High Priest is held out by the church as someone who is 'morally worthy' and deserving of the trust of its members."

4. None of the alleged sexual abuse occurred on COP property or in connection with a COP sponsored activity.

dant to prevent harm when doing so requires that the defendant control the conduct of another person or warn others about such conduct." However, an exception to this rule exists when

(a) a special relation exists between the actor and the third person which imposes a duty upon the actor to control the third person's conduct, or

(b) a special relation exists between the actor and the other which gives the other a right to protection.

Higgins v. Salt Lake County, 855 P.2d 231, 236 (Utah 1993). Moreover, "in determining the existence of a duty, we examine such factors as the identity and character of the actor, the victim, and the victimizer, the relationship of the actor to the victim and the victimizer, and the practical impact that finding a special relationship would have." With this background in mind, we examine whether COP had a special relationship with either Tilson or Plaintiffs.

In support of their argument that COP had a special relationship with Tilson, Plaintiffs rely primarily on language from *Higgins,* stating that a special relationship exists if

the one causing the harm has shown him-or herself to be uniquely dangerous so that the actor upon whom the alleged duty would fall can be reasonably expected, consistent with the practical realities of that actor's relationship to the one in custody or under control, to distinguish that person from others similarly situated, to appreciate the unique threat this person presents, and to act to minimize or protect against that threat.

What Plaintiffs have failed to mention, however, is that this analysis applies "[i]n the context of a claim that an actor having *custody and control* of another owed a duty to prevent harm to or by that other." Id. (emphasis added). Here, Plaintiffs have not alleged any facts demonstrating that COP had custody and control over Tilson at the time he sexually abused Plaintiffs. For example, Plaintiffs do not allege that Tilson was a COP agent or employee, or that he was a member of COP's clergy. Nor do they allege that the abuse occurred on COP property, during a COP sponsored activity, or in connection with Tilson's position as a High Priest or scout leader. Although Plaintiffs do allege that "COP had the power to remove Tilson as a High Priest, and even had the power to excommunicate him from the church," these facts alone are insufficient to establish that COP had custody and control over Tilson. Therefore, we conclude that no special relationship existed between COP and Tilson at the time Plaintiffs were sexually abused that would give rise to a duty on COP's part to warn Plaintiffs about Tilson.

We next turn to Plaintiffs' argument that COP had a special relationship with them at the time they were sexually abused because they were child church members at risk of harm by Tilson. According to Plaintiffs, COP "had a system of disciplinary action in place which was meant to, among other things, identify sexual predators and other dangerous individuals within the membership in order to protect innocent members from harm." However, a special relationship that would have created a duty on COP's part to protect Plaintiffs from Tilson would have existed only if they had been in COP's custody at the time Tilson sexually abused them. * * *

In Meyer v. Lindala, 675 N.W.2d 635 (Minn.App.2004), the court specifically considered whether a defendant church had a special relationship with its plaintiff child members, who were sexually abused by another church member, while outside the defendant's custody. [As in] the instant case, the *Meyer* plaintiffs alleged that the defendant had concealed its knowledge that the perpetrator had previously engaged in child sexual abuse. Although the abuse did not occur on the defendant's property and was unconnected to the defendant, the plaintiffs argued that the defendant had a special relationship with them because it provided them with faith-based advice. The court rejected this argument, noting that "[p]roviding faith-based advice or instruction, without more, does not create a special relationship." Id.; see also Bryan R. v. Watchtower Bible & Tract Soc'y, Inc., 738 A.2d 839, 847 (Me.1999) ("The allegation[s] that [the plaintiff church member] placed 'substantial trust and confidence' in the elders of the church and trusted them 'to protect him and guide him' * * * are wholly insufficient to make out a claim of a special relationship between the organization and its members.").

As in *Meyer,* the sexual abuse in this case was unconnected to COP and did not occur while Plaintiffs were in COP's custody. Accordingly, we also reject Plaintiffs' argument that COP membership alone was sufficient to establish a special relationship between COP and Plaintiffs that created a duty on COP's part to warn Plaintiffs about Tilson. Moreover, because we conclude that COP did not have a duty to warn Plaintiffs about Tilson's history of child sexual abuse, based on a lack of a special relationship with either Tilson or Plaintiffs, it is unnecessary to consider Plaintiffs' other claims. * * * [T]he decision of the trial court is affirmed.

NOTES

1. *The "relationship with victim" exception.* In connection with the Does' argument that the Church owed them a duty of care by virtue of their relationship with the Church, note that § 40 of the Third Restatement provides:

(a) An actor in a special relationship with another owes the other a duty of reasonable care with regard to risks that arise within the scope of the relationship.

(b) Special relationships giving rise to the duty provided in Subsection (a) include:

(1) a common carrier with its passengers,

(2) an innkeeper with its guests,

(3) a business or other possessor of land that holds its premises open to the public with those who are lawfully on the premises,

(4) an employer with its employees who are:

    (a) in imminent danger; or

    (b) injured and thereby helpless,

(5) a school with its students,

(6) a landlord with its tenants, and

(7) a custodian with those in its custody if: (a) the custodian is required by law to take custody or voluntarily takes custody of the other; and (b) the custodian has a superior ability to protect the other.

The items enumerated in subsection (b) of § 40 are not presented as an exhaustive listing, but (as the *Doe* case illustrates), courts are not much inclined to go beyond the list. For a notable exception, see Farwell v. Keaton, 396 Mich. 281, 240 N.W.2d 217 (1976) (holding that Keaton, a 16–year–old companion of the 18–year–old Farwell, "had an affirmative duty to come to Farwell's aid" when Farwell was left injured and semi-conscious after a fight with a gang the two boys had encountered).

    2. ***The "relationship with perpetrator" exception.*** Do you understand why the Church's relationship with Tilson was insufficient to require the Church to do something about him? We will return to this matter in the notes following *Galanti*, just below.

GALANTI v. UNITED STATES

United States Court of Appeals, Eleventh Circuit, 1983.
709 F.2d 706, cert. denied, 465 U.S. 1024, 104 S.Ct. 1279, 79 L.Ed.2d 683 (1984).

MORGAN, SENIOR CIRCUIT JUDGE.

Vivian W. Galanti, plaintiff-appellant, brought this action against the government in the District Court for the Northern District of Georgia under the Federal Tort Claims Act (FTCA), 28 U.S.C. § 1346(b), claiming that her husband, Isaac N. Galanti, died as a result of negligence committed by an agent of the Federal Bureau of Investigation (FBI). The district court concluded that no actionable negligence exists under the pertinent facts and granted the government's motion to dismiss for failure to state a claim. We affirm the district court's order for the following reasons.

The facts giving rise to appellant's claim are undisputed.[1] In October of 1978, Isaac N. Galanti and Roger Dean Underhill were shot to death on a secluded tract of undeveloped property in Fulton County, Georgia. Galanti was interested in purchasing the property from Underhill, and the two men were inspecting it at the time of their deaths. Unknown to Galanti, Underhill was a key witness in the government's investigation into the criminal activity of Michael G. Thevis. Thevis, a convicted felon,

---

    1. Our statement of the facts is taken from a detailed stipulation which the parties prepared and submitted to the district court.

had escaped from federal custody six months earlier and was still a fugitive at the time of the murders. He was apprehended a month later and eventually convicted in federal court of violating Underhill's civil rights by having him murdered, along with the innocent bystander Galanti, in order to prevent Underhill's testimony in the government's case.

For several months before his death, Underhill traveled a great deal and kept a low profile, although he frequently contacted F.B.I. Agent Paul V. King, Jr. King was in charge of the Thevis investigation and knew that Thevis had made earlier attempts to kill Underhill. King considered Underhill to be in extreme danger at all times. For this reason, the government arranged for Underhill to enter a witness protection program in which Underhill would be given a permanent, new identity with government assistance, but Underhill refused to enter the program until he sold the undeveloped property in Fulton County. He ignored advice to retain a real estate agent and insisted on personally handling the sale of his property. In the week preceding his death, Underhill repeatedly visited the property even though King advised him of the needless danger involved. On the night before the murders, Underhill called and informed King that he would be showing the property the next day to Galanti who had answered a newspaper advertisement. King made no attempt to contact and warn Galanti of the potential danger, nor did he arrange for surveillance of the property. This is the conduct which formed the basis of appellant's suit in the district court. She claimed that King's failure to warn or protect Nicholas Galanti against a specific, foreseeable danger was a negligent act and the proximate cause of her husband's death.[2]

This action was necessarily filed in federal court under the provisions of the FTCA since appellant seeks to hold the government liable for the negligence of its employee, but both parties agree that Georgia law controls the negligence issue. In Georgia there are four essential elements of a negligence action: (1) A legal duty to conform to a standard of conduct raised by the law for the protection of others against unreasonable risks of harm; (2) a breach of this standard; (3) a legally attributable causal connection between the conduct and the resulting injury; and (4) some loss or damage flowing to the plaintiff's legally protected interest as a result of the alleged breach of the legal duty. It is the first element with which we are concerned in this appeal. The court below concluded that under no circumstances could appellant establish a legal duty owed by King to Nicholas Galanti, and accordingly granted the government's motion to dismiss for failure to state a claim. Appellant vigorously challenges this conclusion and relies on a large number of state and federal cases, some very recent, in order to support her argument. After a careful review of the various claims and the relevant law, we find that the district court's order must be affirmed.

---

2. Mrs. Galanti also argued below that the government was negligent in allowing Thevis to escape from custody, but the district court concluded that this theory of relief was not properly included in the pleadings and refused to consider it. Appellant does not challenge that decision in this appeal.

The general rule in Georgia is that one has no duty to warn or protect another person from a foreseeable risk of harm simply because of one's knowledge of the danger. In other words, the mere foreseeability of injury to another person does not of itself create a duty to act. This rule is not applicable in three distinct factual situations, however, and appellant contends that each of the three exceptions is present here. First, the duty to protect or warn against danger will arise if the defendant has in any way taken an affirmative step to create the danger. In the recent case of United States v. Aretz, 248 Ga. 19, 26, 280 S.E.2d 345, 350 (1981), the Georgia Supreme Court held that "where one by his own act, although without negligence on his part, creates a dangerous situation, he is under a duty to remove the hazard or give warning of the danger so as to prevent others from being injured where it is reasonably foreseeable that this will occur." In that case, the United States Army provided one of its contractors with mistaken information concerning the appropriate storage classification of explosive materials. The Army later realized the mistake, but failed to communicate it to the contractor, and the materials exploded causing injury and death to several of the contractor's employees. The Georgia court, upon certification from the Fifth Circuit Court of Appeals, held that the Army's failure to inform the contractor of the change in classification was a breach of duty which arose when the Army mistakenly classified the materials in the first place. The *Aretz* decision relied heavily on an earlier Georgia case, Hardy v. Brooks, 103 Ga.App. 124, 118 S.E.2d 492 (1961), where the defendant hit and killed a cow without negligence while driving his car on a public road. The Georgia Court of Appeals held that the defendant's act of killing the cow created the duty to act in the face of foreseeable danger to other drivers on the road. Therefore, *Aretz* and *Hardy* stand for the proposition that a duty to warn or protect a third person from danger will arise if the defendant affirmatively contributes to the creation of the danger. In the present case, FBI Agent King did nothing to create the foreseeable danger. He was merely aware of the risk to Galanti and for whatever reason chose not to act. Georgia law does not hold him legally responsible for knowledge alone.

A second exception to the general rule concerns the defendant's failure to properly exercise his ability to control the foreseeably dangerous instrument. The most recent Georgia decision involving this principle is Bradley Center, Inc. v. Wessner, 250 Ga. 199, 296 S.E.2d 693 (1982). In that case, a private mental hospital released one of its patients despite its ability to keep the patient confined, and despite its knowledge that the patient might cause harm to a specific third party. Under these facts the Georgia court held that the hospital owed a legal duty to the third party even in the absence of the usual doctor-patient privity. Appellant argues that *Bradley* stands for the proposition that one must always warn or protect a third person from a foreseeable criminal act, but this argument is incorrect. *Bradley*, and other cases like it, hold that the legal duty arises only if the defendant failed to exercise his ability to control the potential criminal. This is not the situation we are faced with here. Appellant has not alleged, and the relevant facts do not support the theory, that FBI Agent King or his associates had the ability and failed to control Michael Thevis.[5] Thevis was a wanted fugitive beyond King's control during the relevant time period, and thus King had no duty to warn or protect Galanti merely because of the danger posed by Thevis' known criminal intent.

Finally, law enforcement officials may have the legal duty to warn or protect against danger if they have voluntarily assumed or incurred that duty to a specific individual. However, this duty, if at all applicable here, would extend only to Roger Dean Underhill, and he repeatedly ignored warnings and refused protection. Appellant cannot cite to any Georgia statute or case which charges law enforcement officials with the duty to warn or protect members of the general public simply upon learning of a possible danger.

We recognize that the result in this case may appear harsh because Galanti's death very likely would have been avoided if King had chosen to act rather than to remain silent. Nonetheless, Georgia law did not impose any legal duty on King to act on behalf of Galanti, and therefore appellant's complaint did not establish a viable claim. For this reason, the order of the district court is affirmed.

NOTES

1. The Federal Tort Claims Act is the principal waiver of the federal government's "sovereign immunity" from tort liability. It is set forth in Chapter XI, infra pp. 449–51.

2. ***Identifying the arguments in Galanti.*** The court's sentence at footnote signal 2 might be read to indicate that Mrs. Galanti was arguing that King's negligent conduct was misfeasance rather than nonfeasance. The second-to-last paragraph of the opinion indicates that she was also urging the relationship-with-victim exception to the nonfeasance rule. But it is reasonably clear that her main hopes were (a) the exception illustrated by *Aretz* and *Hardy* and (b) the exception illustrated by *Bradley Center*.

3. ***The prior conduct exception.*** *Aretz* and *Hardy* applied the "prior conduct" exception to the nonfeasance rule. Section 39 of the Third Restatement phrases the exception as follows: "When an actor's prior conduct, even though not tortious, creates a continuing risk of physical harm of a type characteristic of the conduct, the actor has a duty to exercise reasonable care to prevent or minimize the harm." The phrasing in Restatement (Second) of Torts § 321(1) may be slightly clearer: "If the actor does an act, and subsequently realizes or should realize that it has created an unreasonable risk of causing physical harm to another, he is under a duty to exercise reasonable care to prevent the risk from taking effect."

It is useful to see this exception as containing two ingredients: the defendant's prior conduct, which is not itself being asserted as a basis for

---

5. See note 2, supra.

liability; and the defendant's subsequent failure to take steps to deal with a danger that has arisen out of the prior conduct, which failure *is* being asserted as the basis for liability. (Another way to say this: the plaintiff in a prior conduct case is not claiming that the original conduct was actionable misfeasance, but that its existence makes the later nonfeasance actionable.)

The government's prior conduct in *Galanti* included allowing Thevis to escape from custody, but let's assume that the court's footnote 2 takes that conduct completely out of the case. The other prior conduct candidate was King's use of Underhill as an informant. Why didn't that conduct suffice to bring the plaintiff under the prior conduct exception? In pondering this question, consider notes 4 and 6 below.

4. ***Informative applications and rejections of the prior conduct exception.*** The prototypical application of the prior conduct exception holds the motorist who non-negligently creates a highway obstruction to a duty of reasonable care to try to alleviate the problem. Cases like *Hardy,* supra p. 213, holding such motorists liable for negligently failing to remove the obstruction or take other reasonable steps to protect highway users, are numerous. However, even in this situation, some courts have seemed inclined to keep the exception narrow by refusing to apply it when the defendant's contribution to the creation of the highway obstruction was in some fashion indirect or attenuated. For example, in Dubus v. Dresser Industries, 649 P.2d 198 (Wyo.1982), two W.S. Hatch Company trucks became disabled on a windswept highway during a blizzard. A short time later a Dresser Industries pickup had to swerve to avoid colliding with the Hatch trucks and spilled boxes of drill bits from the bed of the pickup onto the highway. All three drivers left the scene without clearing away the drill bits. Plaintiff came along shortly thereafter, stopped to investigate the tangle of vehicles, and tripped and fell on one of the drill bits. The court held that the Dresser driver had a duty of reasonable care to clear away the drill bits, but upheld summary judgment on behalf of the Hatch drivers, stating that "the record [does not] reflect that Hatch is responsible for the dropping and scattering of the boxes from the Dresser vehicle." See also Buchanan v. Rose, 138 Tex. 390, 159 S.W.2d 109 (1942), holding that a trucker was free to drive away and do nothing about a bridge that broke down under the weight of his vehicle because the bridge was in such bad shape that "it is hardly fair to say that the [trucker] created the dangerous situation."

5. ***The relationship-with-perpetrator exception.*** The principle applied in *Bradley Center*, supra p. 213, exposes the defendant to liability on the basis of the relationship between the defendant and the person who was the active and immediate cause of the harm. Restatement (Third) § 41 provides:

(a) An actor in a special relationship with another owes a duty of reasonable care to third persons with regard to risks posed by the other that arise within the scope of the relationship.

(b) Special relationships giving rise to the duty provided in Subsection (a) include:

(1) a parent with dependent children,

(2) a custodian with those in its custody,

(3) an employer with employees when the employment facilitates the employee's causing harm to third parties, and

(4) a mental-health professional with patients.

This exception to the nonfeasance rule enabled the plaintiffs to survive defendant's motion for summary judgment in Texas Home Management, Inc. v. Peavy, 89 S.W.3d 30 (Tex. 2002), in which a dangerous 17–year–old committed a murder while on authorized home leave from defendant's facility that was supposed to be maintaining court-mandated control over the mentally retarded youngster. But the courts are grudging with this exception and seem disinclined to move beyond the Restatement list of relationships that are subject to the principle. See, e.g., Daniel v. Webb, 110 S.W.3d 708 (Tex.App. 2003) (woman had no duty to keep her obviously dangerous 92–year–old grandfather from driving his car); Remsburg v. Montgomery, 376 Md. 568, 831 A.2d 18 (2003) (man who accompanied his 27–year–old son during a deer hunt had no duty to supervise even though he had told his son to "shoot the first thing that moves"). See also *Doe,* supra p. 208.

6. ***Responsibility for others' crimes and intentional torts.*** *Galanti* was an inherently difficult case for the same reason that *Meyering,* supra p. 187, was: courts do not feel confident in their handling of lawsuits (increasingly prevalent) in which crime victims seek to pin responsibility for the results of a crime on someone other than the criminal. In such cases the arguments for liability can often be strong. But in any case asserting that the defendant should be held liable for his negligence in failing to prevent or guard against another's crime or intentional tort, if the issue is at all close the judge will be inclined to characterize the defendant's conduct as nonfeasance rather than misfeasance and to construe any potentially applicable exceptions to the nonfeasance rule pretty narrowly.

We take up the issue of liability for negligently facilitating or failing to prevent a crime again in section D, infra p. 217.

7. ***An advocacy perspective.*** Plaintiffs seem fairly often to mischaracterize their cases. For example, in Ventura v. Picicci, 227 Ill.App.3d 865, 169 Ill.Dec. 881, 592 N.E.2d 368 (1992), a mother whose adult son habitually engaged in violent and crazy behavior let him live with her, bought him cocaine and a gun, and let him keep ammunition in the house. When the man eventually shot his girlfriend, the girlfriend sued the mother, evidently treating the case as a nonfeasance case and relying principally or solely on the relationship-with-perpetrator exception. The complaint was dismissed.

In Lauer v. City of New York, 95 N.Y.2d 95, 711 N.Y.S.2d 112, 733 N.E.2d 184 (2000), the City Medical Examiner (ME) wrongly diagnosed the death of a three-year-old as a homicide and so noted on the autopsy report and death certificate. The police suspected the child's father and immediately began investigating and harassing him. A month or two later the ME discovered his mistake—the child had died of a ruptured brain aneurysm, not a beating—but the ME notified no one, and the police investigation of the father continued for another couple of years before a newspaper expose finally brought the truth to light. The father, whose life was completely ruined, sued the City (as vicariously liable for the ME's negligent conduct). Because of a doctrine of governmental immunity, the ME's original mistake was not actionable, so the lawsuit necessarily focused on the ME's subsequent failure to let the police know as soon as the mistake was discovered. A divided court exonerated the city, holding that the complaint should be dismissed. From reading the several opinions in the case, it appears that the plaintiff relied principally on the relationship-with-victim exception (perhaps on the view that the nature of the ME's office generated that kind of relationship with the family of the murdered child). The prior conduct exception does not seem to have been emphasized.

The introductory note to this section warned that the exceptions to the nonfeasance rule are loosely delineated, and by now you are probably convinced. But trying to keep them separated is usually worth the effort. Consider Zylka v. Leikvoll, 274 Minn. 435, 144 N.W.2d 358 (1966). In winter darkness at 30 degrees below zero, Leikvoll, who owned and operated a wrecker service, was using his wrecker to push Traphagan's disabled car. A vehicle driven by Bounds came along and collided with Traphagan's right front fender. Other traffic piled up, and eventually plaintiff, a pedestrian, was struck by a car. The jury found that Leikvoll was not negligent respecting the Traphagan–Bounds collision but that he was negligent thereafter in not doing a better job of lighting and flagging the scene. Leikvoll argued that he was entitled to a directed verdict because "his position was that of a volunteer and * * * [t]hus * * * unless his conduct increased the danger to plaintiff, he is not liable." Wrong, said the court; "Leikvoll was a participant in the creation of the first accident * * *, not * * * a volunteer but * * * one called upon to exercise reasonable care, either to remove the hazard or give adequate warning to others." Translation: The court saw through Leikvoll's attempt to characterize the case against him as confined to the volunteer exception. In the court's view, the proper characterization was the prior conduct exception.

D. CREATING NO–DUTY RULES

When a court rules "no duty" in a particular case, it is saying that there are legal reasons—reasons of law—for concluding that proof of breach, cause in fact, proximate cause, and damages do not suffice to support liability. In the cases treated in the other sections of this chapter, these legal reasons are found in established no-duty rules covering categories of cases—*viz., categorical no-duty rules*[1]—and in the jurisprudence that, over time, established, developed, and set forth the conditions justifying and setting the boundaries of the categorical rules. For example, the nonfeasance rule rests on the considerations outlined in the introduction to section C, supra p. 200, and in *Satterfield*, supra p. 201. The dispositive question in *Satterfield* was not whether a no-duty rule existed, but rather whether the case fell into the no-duty *category*.

The cases in this section are different. Here the defendants were not protected by pre-existing categorical no-duty rules. Letting such a defen-

---

1. See note 3 following *Palsgraf*, supra p. 178.

dant escape liability on a no-duty basis requires the creation of a new no-duty rule. As we saw in Chapter V[2] and in section A of this chapter, judges who are eager to control results—in Posnerian terms, to "rein in juries"—have fairly frequently been hospitable to defense arguments calling for new no-duty rules.

As we pointed out in section A, the Third Restatement embraces the principle of Heaven v. Pender. At the same time, the Third Restatement acknowledges that judges will sometimes believe that new exceptions to it—new no-duty rules—are needed. Striving for balance, § 7 provides:

> (a) An actor ordinarily has a duty to exercise reasonable care when the actor's conduct creates a risk of physical harm.

> (b) In exceptional cases, when an articulated countervailing principle or policy warrants denying or limiting liability in a particular class of cases, a court may decide that the defendant has no duty or that the ordinary duty of reasonable care requires modification.

Section 7 has three important implications. The first is that the existence of a duty is not something that has to be fought out in every case. In most cases it will be clear that subsection (a) applies and there is no need for any further consideration of the duty issue. Although duty has traditionally been considered an element of the prima facie case, the Third Restatement takes the position that a defendant has the procedural obligation to raise the issue; until the defendant has done so, the plaintiff has no obligation to show that a duty existed.

The second implication from § 7—a fairly obvious one—is that creating new no-duty rules on a case-by-case basis would be improper. The fundamental common-law maxim that "like cases must be treated alike" begs many questions but still has tremendous potency.

Section 7's third implication follows in a somewhat subtle way from the second. If the court's reasons for denying liability depend on the facts of the particular case, creating a new no-duty rule is not the way to proceed; such a case should be resolved on the basis of no proximate cause or no breach, and the court may do so as a matter of law only if reasonable minds could not differ. "No-duty rules are appropriate only when a court can promulgate relatively clear, categorical, bright-line rules of law applicable to a general class of cases." Third Restatement § 7 cmt. *a.* Expressing a proximate cause or breach ruling in no-duty terms can usefully be called *dutification,* a term of respectful disparagement.

Like the framers of the Third Restatement, we deplore dutification because it entails a shift of decisional authority from jury to trial judge and from trial court to appellate court.[3] We also deplore it because it

---

2. See notes 1 and 3 following *Edwards, supra* p. 186; note 3 following *Meyering, supra* p. 193.

3. A trial judge's duty determination addresses an issue of law and is therefore reviewed on appeal under a *de novo* standard that affords the determination no deference, whereas—at least

obscures the true grounds of decision. In a case falling naturally into the breach or proximate cause category, a disappointed plaintiff should not be told that there are reasons of law for her loss when the law really doesn't have any pre-established reasons.Instead the losing plaintiff should be told either that "a reasonable jury has concluded (or no reasonable juror could avoid concluding) that under the particular circumstances of your case, the defendant was not negligent," or in similar fashion that under the circumstances of the particular case, the element of proximate cause was lacking.

Does foreseeability have a legitimate role in duty determinations? Going all the way back to *Palsgraf* (or even earlier), the concept of foreseeability has played a major role in deciding duty issues. Whether the Third Restatement's effort to confine foreseeability inquiries to the breach and proximate cause realms will succeed (as it does in the following case) remains to be seen.

THOMPSON v. KACZINSKI

Supreme Court of Iowa, 2009.
774 N.W.2d 829.

HECHT, JUSTICE.

* * *

[Defendants] James Kaczinski and Michelle Lockwood resided in rural Madison County, near Earlham, on property abutting a gravel road. During the late summer of 2006, they disassembled a trampoline and placed its component parts on their yard approximately thirty-eight feet from the road. Intending to dispose of them at a later time, Kaczinski and Lockwood did not secure the parts in place. A few weeks later, on the night of September 16 and morning of September 17, 2006, a severe thunderstorm moved through the Earlham area. Wind gusts from the storm displaced the top of the trampoline from the yard to the surface of the road.

Later that morning, while driving from one church to another where he served as a pastor, plaintiff Charles Thompson approached the defendants' property. When he swerved to avoid the obstruction on the road, Thompson lost control of his vehicle. His car entered the ditch and rolled several times. Kaczinski and Lockwood were awakened by Thompson's screams at about 9:40 a.m., shortly after the accident. When they went outside to investigate, they discovered the top of their trampoline lying on the roadway. Lockwood dragged the object back into the yard while Kaczinski assisted Thompson.

Thompson and his wife filed suit, alleging [that] Kaczinski and Lockwood breached * * * common law duties by negligently allowing the

---

as a matter of theory—trial-court determinations on any of the other four issues go up on appeal cloaked with some measure of presumed correctness. The shift of authority to the appellate level moves the matter from the trial-level courthouse, where decisions are based on live testimony, up to an appellate chamber where all decisions are based on a cold paper or electronic record.

trampoline to obstruct the roadway. Kaczinski and Lockwood moved for summary judgment, contending they owed no duty under the circumstances because the risk of the trampoline's displacement from their yard to the surface of the road was not foreseeable. The district court granted the motion, concluding Kaczinski and Lockwood breached no duty and the damages claimed by the plaintiffs were not proximately caused by the defendants' negligence. * * *

* * *

Plaintiffs contend Kaczinski and Lockwood owed a common law duty to exercise reasonable care to prevent their personal property from obstructing the roadway and to remove their property from the roadway within a reasonable time after it became an obstruction. Whether a duty arises out of a given relationship is a matter of law for the court's determination.

Our cases have suggested [that] three factors should be considered in determining whether a duty to exercise reasonable care exists: "(1) the relationship between the parties, (2) reasonable foreseeability of harm to the person who is injured, and (3) public policy considerations." * * *

The role of foreseeability of risk in the assessment of duty in negligence actions has recently been revisited by drafters of the Restatement (Third) of Torts. "An actor ordinarily has a duty to exercise reasonable care when the actor's conduct creates a risk of physical harm." [Restatement (Third) of Torts: Liability for Physical and Emotional Harm § 7(a).] Thus, in most cases involving physical harm, courts "need not concern themselves with the existence or content of this ordinary duty," but instead may proceed directly to the [negligence, cause in fact, and scope of responsibility (proximate cause)] elements of liability. Id. § 6 cmt. *f*. The general duty of reasonable care will apply in most cases, and thus courts "* * * need not refer to duty on a case-by-case basis." Id. § 7 cmt. *a*.

However, in exceptional cases, the general duty to exercise reasonable care can be displaced or modified. Id. § 6 cmt. *f*. An exceptional case is one in which "an articulated countervailing principle or policy warrants denying or limiting liability in a particular class of cases." Id. § 7(b). In such an exceptional case, when the court rules as a matter of law that no duty is owed by actors in a category of cases, the ruling "should be explained and justified based on articulated policies or principles that justify exempting [such] actors from liability or modifying the ordinary duty of reasonable care." Id. § 7 cmt. *j*. Reasons of policy and principle justifying a departure from the general duty to exercise reasonable care do not depend on the foreseeability of harm based on the specific facts of a case. "A lack of foreseeable risk in a specific case may be a basis for a no-breach determination, but such a ruling is not a no-duty determination."

The assessment of the foreseeability of a risk is allocated by the Restatement (Third) to the fact finder, to be considered when the jury decides if the defendant failed to exercise reasonable care.

Foreseeable risk is an element in the determination of negligence. In order to determine whether appropriate care was exercised, the fact-finder must assess the foreseeable risk at the time of the defendant's alleged negligence. The extent of foreseeable risk depends on the specific facts of the case and cannot be usefully assessed for a category of cases; small changes in the facts may make a dramatic change in how much risk is foreseeable * * *. [C]ourts should leave such determinations to juries unless no reasonable person could differ on the matter.

Id. The drafters acknowledge that courts have frequently used foreseeability in no-duty determinations, but have now explicitly disapproved the practice in the Restatement (Third) and limited no-duty rulings to "articulated policy or principle in order to facilitate more transparent explanations of the reasons for a no-duty ruling and to protect the traditional function of the jury as factfinder." We find the drafters' clarification of the duty analysis in the Restatement (Third) compelling, and we now, therefore, adopt it.

The district court clearly considered foreseeability in concluding the defendants owed no duty in this case. When the consideration of foreseeability is removed from the determination of duty, as we now hold it should be, there remains the question of whether a principle or strong policy consideration justifies the exemption of Kaczinski and Lockwood—as part of a class of defendants—from the duty to exercise reasonable care. We conclude no such principle or policy consideration exempts property owners from a duty to exercise reasonable care to avoid the placement of obstructions on a roadway. * * * Accordingly, we conclude the district court erred in determining Kaczinski and Lockwood owed no common law duty under the circumstances presented here.

* * *

[W]e reverse the district court's dismissal of this claim and remand this case for trial.

NOTES

1. For other decisions adopting or endorsing the Third Restatement's analysis of the duty issue, see A.W. v. Lancaster County School District, 280 Neb. 205, 784 N.W.2d 907, 913–18 (2010); Gipson v. Kasey, 214 Ariz. 141, 150 P.3d 228, 231 (2007).

2. *Competing approaches and philosophies in take-home toxins cases.* In general terms, the Third Restatement's shift away from the foreseeability-oriented approach to duty is a plaintiff-friendly move, but it will not always work that way. In *Satterfield*, supra p. 201, the court rejected the Third Restatement's approach to duty and used a foreseeability-based approach to hold that asbestos-using employers owe employees' family members a duty of care. And in Van Fossen v. MidAmerican Energy Co., 777 N.W.2d 689, 696 (Iowa 2009), the court used the Third Restatement approach to

support its no-duty holding in a take-home asbestos case, stating: "We conclude this case presents an instance in which the general duty to exercise reasonable care is appropriately modified."

The "take-home" injury problem is not limited to asbestos injuries. See Doe v. Pharmacia & Upjohn Co., 388 Md. 407, 879 A.2d 1088 (2005) (holding that the employer of a technician who contracted HIV–2 at work owed no duty to the worker's spouse).

3. In *Satterfield*, one justice wrote separately to urge adoption of the Third Restatement approach to duty, stating:

> I fully concur in the majority's conclusion that Alcoa owed a duty to Ms. Satterfield to take reasonable steps to prevent her from suffering harm as a result of the risks created by the operation of Alcoa's facility. I write separately to express my belief that any discussion of foreseeability in the context of duty encroaches upon the role of the finder of fact. * * * [T]he foreseeability of an injury or risk is more properly considered an element of breach of duty or proximate cause. This observation is important primarily because the existence of duty is determined by courts as a matter of law while breach of duty and proximate cause are fact-based inquiries to be determined by juries. By incorporating foreseeability into an analysis of duty, the majority transforms a factual question into a legal issue and expands the authority of judges at the expense of juries. It is with good reason that determinations of breach of duty and proximate cause, and therefore foreseeability, have traditionally been entrusted to juries. A collection of twelve people representing a cross-section of the public is better suited than any judge to make the common-sense and experience-based judgment of foreseeability. * * *

> To be candid, I must acknowledge that my understanding of duty remains a minority position. I firmly believe, however, that analyzing foreseeability in the context of duty is inherently problematic and that the Restatement (Third) of Torts presents a wiser approach. * * *

4. ***Two hills to climb?*** According to one commentator, 47 states "plainly do give foreseeability a significant role in duty analysis," See Zipursky, Foreseeability in Breach, Duty, and Proximate Cause, 44 Wake Forest L. Rev. 1247, 1260 (2009). Obviously, the Third Restatement's effort to expunge foreseeability inquiries from duty analysis confronts a sizeable challenge.

The challenge is not confined to the foreseeability front, either. Sometimes judges claim virtually plenary authority to declare no-duty rules whenever they feel the need. For example, in Fisher v. Miami–Dade County, 883 So.2d 335 (Fla.App. 2004), *rev. denied*, 901 So.2d 873 (Fla. 2005), the court used policy reasoning to determine that police owe no duty to innocent passengers who die as the result of high-speed police pursuits. A concurring justice applauded the policy analysis and added: "The dispositive issue of whether a passenger in a fleeing vehicle is owed a 'duty' of care by the pursuer is determined * * * simply by a consideration of whether we believe that one should." The concurrer went on to quote from another case: "[A] common law duty exists when a court says it does because it thinks it should." 883 So.2d at 337–38.

Liability for Facilitating or Failing to Prevent Crimes

As we noted in note 3 following *Meyering*, supra p. 193, and again in connection with the *Doe* and *Galanti* cases in the nonfeasance section of this chapter (supra pp. 208 and 211) courts have visible trouble figuring out how to handle cases against defendants who are alleged to have done something (or failed to do something) that caused the plaintiff to be harmed by the crime or intentional tort of a third person. No one should be surprised to learn that this has been a particularly fertile field for the creation of new no-duty rules.

The third person's conduct in the next case was probably neither a crime nor an intentional tort, but the case lays a good foundation for analyzing the third-party-crimes cases.

STAGL v. DELTA AIRLINES

United States Court of Appeals, Second Circuit, 1995.
52 F.3d 463.

CALABRESI, CIRCUIT JUDGE.

* * *

Plaintiff, Eleanor M. Stagl, appeals from a judgment granting summary judgment to defendant, Delta Air Lines, Inc., and dismissing her personal injury action against Delta which was based upon the airline's alleged negligent supervision and management of its baggage retrieval system. * * *

On May 1, 1993, Mrs. Stagl, then 77 years old, was a passenger on a Delta flight from Orlando, Florida to LaGuardia Airport in New York City. The plane was delayed for approximately one-half hour, and Mrs. Stagl noted that upon its arrival in New York the passengers were visibly upset. After disembarking from the aircraft, Mrs. Stagl proceeded to a designated baggage carousel located in Delta's terminal in order to retrieve her luggage.

In her affidavit in opposition to Delta's motion for summary judgment, Mrs. Stagl describes the Delta terminal as "bedlam." According to her, "[p]eople were crowded around the baggage carousel and everyone seemed in a hurry to get out of the airport." Moreover, they were "rowdy and unruly, pushing and shoving each other, grabbing their luggage from the moving carousel by whatever means possible." She further claims that Delta did not provide any personnel, or make any cautionary announcement to quell the turmoil; nor did the airline cordon off a separate area in which elderly and disabled passengers could safely obtain their luggage.

In an attempt to reclaim her own belongings, Mrs. Stagl made her way to the "front rank" of the throng surrounding the baggage carousel. Apparently, an unidentified man to one side of her reached across the conveyor belt, grabbed his satchel with great force, and unwittingly triggered a domino effect. His bag collided with another's suitcase, which, in turn, fell off the carousel, toppling Mrs. Stagl. As a result, she suffered a broken hip.

Mrs. Stagl brought this diversity action in the district court, claiming that Delta did not exercise reasonable care to ensure her safety. She complained that the airline negligently failed to take any crowd-control measures or to provide a safe method by which elderly and disabled people could retrieve their luggage. Mrs. Stagl alleged that her physical injuries were the proximate result of Delta's inaction.

* * *

[T]he district court granted Delta summary judgment [concluding] that, under New York law, Mrs. Stagl had "failed to establish that Delta's duty as an air carrier encompasses a duty to control the crowd at the baggage retrieval area or designate a separate area for elderly passengers." * * *

* * *

The district court ruled that "Delta owed no duty to protect [Mrs. Stagl] from the particular injury involved here." * * * [T]he district court concluded that Delta had no obligation "to protect against or warn of potential negligent conduct by third persons within the terminal building." This was error.

There is no question that Delta, as an owner or occupier of the premises, owed a duty to take reasonable steps in maintaining the safety of its baggage retrieval area.

This duty is a broad one, and it includes the obligation "to take reasonable precautions to protect [patrons] from dangers which are foreseeable from the arrangement or use of the property," as well as to exercise reasonable care in protecting visitors from the foreseeable, injurious actions of third parties.

* * *

In the present case, the district judge refused to impose an obligation upon Delta to safeguard passengers against the foreseeable risks created by its concentration of allegedly unruly travelers around a congested baggage carousel. In the district court's opinion, such a duty would "offer little if any real public benefit, and yet would impose upon the airline burdensome and costly obligations." Although we appreciate that, under New York law, the "existence and scope of an alleged tortfeasor's duty is usually a policy-laden declaration reserved for Judges" that, in part, weighs competing socioeconomic factors in an attempt to distribute "burdens of loss and reparation on a fair, prudent basis," we also note that New York courts do not exercise this authority on an ad hoc basis.

[W]here, as here, the applicable duty relationship is well established, we do not believe New York law condones the limitation of a familiar liability rule simply to avoid placing a disproportionate burden on a defendant in a particular case. The law deals with that problem not by redefining the defendant's duties in each case, but by asking whether—

considering all the circumstances of the particular case—the defendant breached its duty of care.

* * *

[We reverse the summary judgment and remand the case for further proceedings.]

NOTES

1. As we saw in the introductory note to this section, the Restatement (Third) shares Judge Calabresi's view that courts should not announce no-duty rules "on an ad hoc basis." See also Sugarman, Assumption of Risk, 31 Val.U.L.Rev. 833, 872 (1997) (deploring "ad hoc, free-standing [duty] doctrines"); Dobbs, The Law of Torts § 227, p.580 (2000) ("Courts often find it useful or necessary to eliminate the defendant's duty of care by a rule of law. But in many cases, courts may be using the language of duty with all its breadth for what is or should be essentially a negligence question to be decided case by case rather than by a rule of law.")

2. ***Narrow-category no-duty rules, case-specific no-duty rules, and dutification.*** In Kentucky Fried Chicken v. Superior Court, 14 Cal.4th 814, 59 Cal.Rptr.2d 756, 927 P.2d 1260 (1997), a KFC customer taken hostage during an armed robbery was injured when the robber turned violent after the store clerk failed to promptly comply with the robber's demand to turn over the store's cash. After an extended policy discussion, the majority ruled that KFC was entitled to summary judgment, holding: "[T]here is no duty to comply with a robber's unlawful demand for the surrender of property. Simple refusal to obey does not breach any duty to third persons present on the premises." As far as the process of its creation goes, this no-duty rule seems to comply with the Third Restatement's proposed strictures. The court was reasonably candid about what it was doing, it "articulated [a] policy" basis for the new rule, and (in the terms of Third Restatement § 7(b)), it effectively labeled the case as "exceptional." (This is not to say that the rule was wise, or even to concede that any narrow-category no-duty rule can be wise; we mean only to concede that the new rule was arrived at by a principled process.)

In contrast, the no-duty rule the district judge announced in *Stagl* seemed to be case-specific: "Delta owed no duty to protect [Mrs. Stagl] from the particular injury involved here." In Judge Calabresi's terms, it was "ad hoc" in a quite narrow sense. The process of its creation would not pass muster under the Third Restatement. And it was objectionable in a fundamental way: While the rule may have been contrived only for Delta and only for that day, announcing it in no-duty terms presented it as a rule of law suitable for extrapolation and expansion in other cases.

Dissenting in *Kentucky Fried Chicken*, Justice Kennard evidently did not think the majority had used a principled process. After taking the majority to task for "usurp[ing] the jury's historic function in a negligence case to determine the reasonableness of defendant's conduct under the surrounding circumstances," Justice Kennard launched into a discussion of misuse of duty analysis:

> It is always possible to recast any question of whether the standard of care has been breached as a question of "duty" * * *. Thus, instead of asking whether an automobile driver who failed to stop in time used the care of a reasonable driver under like circumstances, we could ask whether the driver had a "duty" to begin braking sooner; instead of asking whether a doctor treated a feverish patient with the care of a reasonable physician we could ask whether the doctor had a "duty" to administer penicillin. If a court does so, however, it abandons the flexibility inherent in the application of the reasonable person standard and instead dictates a rigid, inflexible rule of conduct * * *.

Justice Kennard went on to say that her objection stemmed mainly from the fear that such "rigid, inflexible rule[s] of conduct" will spread from the cases in which they originate to "all defendants in future cases who are confronted by a risk of the same type of harm to another, regardless of differences in the surrounding circumstances."

  3. *Arguments for maintaining the jury's authority over the breach issue.* Justice Kennard's *Kentucky Fried Chicken* dissent presented three arguments:

> There are at least three good reasons why negligence law has allocated the judgment of the reasonableness of a defendant's conduct to the jury as a matter for case-by-case determination, rather than having courts, under the rubric of "duty," establish as a matter of law fixed and unvarying rules of conduct for various categories of human activity. The first reason arises from the irreducible variety of circumstances which may surround an event that causes harm to someone. Because of this variety, an individualized rather than categorical determination of what constitutes reasonable care to avoid a particular type of harm usually will provide a more precise measure of what conduct is reasonable under the circumstances.

  Justice Kennard's second reason was that leaving the question to the jury "allows successive juries to reassess what precautions are reasonable as social, economic, and technological conditions change over time." The third was that the jury brings a wider array of practical experience and knowledge to that task than does a judge. "The jury is a repository of collective wisdom and understanding concerning the conditions and circumstances of everyday life that it can bring to bear on the determination of what conduct is reasonable."

  Compare Justice Kennard's view with that expressed in Moning v. Alfono, 400 Mich. 425, 254 N.W.2d 759, 763 (1977): "The preference for jury resolution of the issue of negligence is not * * * simply an expedient reflecting the difficulty of stating a rule that will readily resolve all cases; rather, it is rooted in the belief that the jury's judgment of what is reasonable under the circumstances of a particular case is more likely than the judicial judgment to represent the community's judgment of how reasonable persons would conduct themselves." Cf. Leon Green, The Duty Problem in Negligence Cases, 28 Colum.L.Rev. 1014, 1029 (1928): "[T]he very purpose of jury trial is to give a new deal in each case."

McCARTHY v. OLIN CORPORATION

United States Court of Appeals, Second Circuit, 1997.
119 F.3d 148.

MESKILL, CIRCUIT JUDGE.

Plaintiffs include two surviving victims and the estate of one deceased victim of the December 7, 1993 assault on the 5:33 p.m. Long Island Railroad commuter train. * * *

* * *

On December 7, 1993, Colin Ferguson boarded the Long Island Railroad's 5:33 p.m. commuter train departing from New York City and opened fire on the passengers. Six people, including Dennis McCarthy, were killed and nineteen others, including Kevin McCarthy and Maryanne Phillips, were wounded in the vicious attack. Ferguson was armed with a 9mm semiautomatic handgun, which was loaded with Winchester "Black Talon" bullets (Black Talons). The injuries to Dennis and Kevin McCarthy and Maryanne Phillips were enhanced by the ripping and tearing action of the Black Talons because, unfortunately, the bullets performed as designed.

The Black Talon is a hollowpoint bullet designed to bend upon impact into six ninety-degree angle razor-sharp petals or "talons" that increase the wounding power of the bullet by stretching, cutting and tearing tissue and bone as it travels through the victim. The Black Talon bullet was designed and manufactured by Olin Corporation (Olin) through its Winchester division and went on the market in 1992. Although the bullet was originally developed for law enforcement agencies, it was marketed and available to the general public. In November 1993, following public outcry, Olin pulled the Black Talon from the public market and restricted its sales to law enforcement personnel. Colin Ferguson allegedly purchased the ammunition in 1993, before it was withdrawn from the market.

Plaintiffs brought this action against Olin. * * *

Olin moved to dismiss the complaint pursuant to Fed.R.Civ.P. 12(b)(6) for failure to state a claim upon which relief can be granted. The district court granted the motion. First addressing the issue of negligence, the court held that plaintiffs' negligence theories must fail because Olin owed no duty to plaintiffs to protect them from criminal misuse of the Black Talon ammunition. * * *

Plaintiffs appeal the dismissal of their complaint, claiming that the issue of whether they will ultimately prevail is a matter to be determined on a factual basis and not merely on the pleadings. In the alternative, plaintiffs request that because the complaint is based on novel theories of liability under New York law, we certify the questions raised in this case to the New York Court of Appeals.

* * *

Recently, the New York courts have had the opportunity to address issues almost identical to those raised in this case. See Pekarski v. Donovan, Nos. 95–11161, 95–1175, 95–1187, slip op. (N.Y.Sup.Ct. Oneida County Sept. 27, 1995); Forni v. Ferguson, 232 A.D.2d 176, 648 N.Y.S.2d 73 (1st Dep't 1996). Basing their decisions on well-settled principles of New York tort law, the New York courts held that the plaintiffs could not state a cause of action upon which relief could be granted against Olin for the manufacture and marketing of the Black Talon bullet. [Many federal courts have stated that "while a federal court is not bound by lower state court decisions, they do have great weight in informing the court's prediction on how the highest court of the state would resolve the question."] Although the New York Court of Appeals has not addressed the issue of ammunition manufacturer liability, the *Forni* and *Pekarski* decisions, as well as existing precedents in New York law, provide us with sufficient guidance to analyze the district court's dismissal of this case. Therefore, we decline to certify any questions of law to New York's highest court. We will now address the merits of plaintiffs' appeal.

* * *

[The court held that the trial judge had properly dismissed plaintiffs' claims based on strict products liability.]

* * *

In their complaint, appellants also asserted causes of action for the negligent marketing and manufacture of Black Talon bullets. On appeal, appellants do not appear to pursue their negligent manufacturing claim but rather focus their argument on Olin's negligent marketing of the ammunition. For the reasons discussed below, appellants cannot assert a cause of action under either theory of negligence.

The crux of appellants' negligence theory is that Olin negligently marketed and placed the Black Talon ammunition for sale to the general public. Appellants argue that because of the severe wounding power of the bullets, Olin should have restricted sales to law enforcement agencies, for whom the bullet was originally designed. They also argue that Olin should have known that their advertising, which highlighted the ripping and tearing characteristics of the bullet, would attract "many types of sadistic, unstable and criminal personalities," such as Ferguson.

To state a cause of action for negligence, the plaintiffs must show: (1) that Olin owed them a "duty, or obligation, recognized by law", (2) a breach of the duty, (3) a "reasonably close causal connection between [defendant's] conduct and the resulting injury" and (4) loss or damage resulting from the breach.

* * *

The existence of a duty is a question of law to be decided by the court. New York courts are reluctant to impose a duty of care where there is little expectation that the defendant could prevent the actions of a third party.

* * *

While there are of course many exceptions to this rule, we find that none of them is applicable here.

New York courts do not impose a legal duty on manufacturers to control the distribution of potentially dangerous products such as ammunition. Accordingly, although it may have been foreseeable by Olin that criminal misuse of the Black Talon bullets could occur, Olin is not legally liable for such misuse. As the district court pointed out, appellants have not alleged that any special relationship existed between Olin and Ferguson. Here, Olin could not control the actions of Ferguson.

* * *

To impose a duty on ammunition manufacturers to protect against criminal misuse of its product would likely force ammunition products— which legislatures have not proscribed, and which concededly are not defectively designed or manufactured and have some socially valuable uses—off the market due to the threat of limitless liability. Because Olin did not owe a legal duty to plaintiffs to protect against Colin Ferguson's horrible action, appellants' complaint does not state a cause of action for negligence and the claim was properly dismissed.

* * *

CALABRESI, CIRCUIT JUDGE, dissenting.

* * *

In cases that are dramatic and involve "hot" issues, there is a tendency for the parties to describe themselves as raising new issues that are remarkable in their legal context.[9] But in fact, such cases are usually best looked at in the most traditional of ways. Courts must see how these cases fit into old categories before considering whether it is either necessary or proper to expand those old categories or to create new ones. And so it is with the case before us. For this reason, I begin with the most traditional of the causes of action that the plaintiffs have raised—negligence—and address it in its most "black letter" terms.

* * *

In doing this I do not, of course, seek to determine whether liability for negligence lies in a case like this one in New York. I examine the issue only to discern whether the question is sufficiently open to warrant certification.

* * *

---

9. The plaintiffs in the instant case are guilty of this mistake. See McCarthy v. Sturm, Ruger and Co., 916 F.Supp. 366, 372 (S.D.N.Y.1996) ("Plaintiffs candidly argue that I should expand existing tort doctrines to cover this case * * *.").

To hold a defendant liable in negligence in New York, a plaintiff must show: 1) a duty on the part of the defendant; 2) a breach of that duty by conduct involving an "unreasonable risk of harm"; 3) damages suffered by the plaintiff; and 4) causation, both in fact and proximate, between the breach and the plaintiff's harm. So viewed, three of the four elements of a cause of action for negligence—damages, causation, and conduct involving an unreasonable risk of harm—are either readily present or sufficiently cognizable under New York law on the facts of this case that a federal court would err mightily to hold on its own to the contrary. * * *

* * *

The only aspect of this case—viewed as a negligence action—that is problematic is the existence of a duty.

* * *

[Under New York law as set forth in Waters v. New York City Housing Authority, 69 N.Y.2d 225, 513 N.Y.S.2d 356, 505 N.E.2d 922, 923–24 (1987)]:

> The question of the scope of an alleged tortfeasor's duty is, in the first instance, a legal issue for the court to resolve. In this analysis, not only logic and science, but policy play an important role. The common law of torts is, at its foundation, a means of apportioning risks and allocating the burden of loss. While moral and logical judgments are significant components of the analysis, we are also bound to consider the larger social consequences of our decisions and to tailor our notion of duty so that the legal consequences of wrongs are limited to a controllable degree.

* * *

This does not mean that the court is required—or even permitted—to weigh such policy considerations to determine the existence of a duty in each individual New York negligence case. Once the New York Court of Appeals has established that the relationship between plaintiffs and defendants in certain circumstances or categories of cases suffices to establish a duty of due care, all cases of like kind are covered by that finding, and there is no warrant to take a case from the jury for a separate judicial examination of duty.

It follows that, before we can be confident that there is a jury question as to negligence in this case, we must find precedents that establish a duty between the parties in cases akin to this one. I am not prepared to make such a finding. Nor, however, am I prepared to say that the New York Court of Appeals would not find that such a precedent exists or create one in this case. I am not, in other words, satisfied that the New York Court of Appeals has made a policy determination, one way or the other, in circumstances akin to those here.

* * *

New York law is quite clear that the defendant in many circumstances can be under a duty to the plaintiff that makes him liable for the harm caused by the intervening negligent acts of a third party.

* * *

In fact, under appropriate conditions, a defendant can even be held liable for the intervening criminal acts of a third party. See, e.g., Nallan v. Helmsley–Spear, Inc., 50 N.Y.2d 507, 429 N.Y.S.2d 606, 612–13, 407 N.E.2d 451, 457–58 (1980) (holding that a commercial landlord has a duty to take reasonable precautionary measures to minimize the risk of foreseeable criminal activity and to make the premises safe for the visiting public); Stevens v. Kirby, 86 A.D.2d 391, 450 N.Y.S.2d 607, 610 (1982) ("A tavern owner owes a duty to his patrons to protect them from personal attack when he has reasonable cause to anticipate conduct on the part of third persons which is likely to endanger their safety.").

* * *

What of this case? On the one hand, it seems that the defendant could have substantially reduced the harm caused by these unusually destructive bullets by not marketing them to the general public. And the danger of exposing the defendant to liability beyond sound public policy might not be present here, especially if the New York courts were to conclude that marketing Black Talons to the general public causes more harm than benefit. On the other hand, this case may well involve "the expansion * * * of new channels of liability" since it involves a criminal intervenor in a case where no direct relationship exists between the injured plaintiff and the defendant.

* * *

Under the circumstances, it is hard to know whether the New York Court of Appeals would find a duty. The fact that the foreseeable intervenor behaved in a criminal, rather than a negligent, manner does not change matters for the purposes of proximate cause.*

* * *

Does it do so for purposes of duty? That is a question to which the New York Court of Appeals has given us no answer.

* * *

Since the Court of Appeals has neither countenanced nor foreclosed liability in cases involving a criminal intervenor and the absence of a direct relationship, I believe that we are bound to allow that Court to make a policy determination of duty in the instant case.

---

* In an edited-out portion of the opinion, Judge Calabresi explained this statement by quoting from Derdiarian v. Felix Contracting Corp., 51 N.Y.2d 308, 414 N.E.2d 666, 671 (1980): "An intervening act may not serve as a superseding cause * * * where the risk of the intervening act occurring is the very same risk which renders the actor negligent." [Ed.]

In this respect, the argument that, because it is legal to sell and advertise Black Talons, there can be no liability, is misplaced.

* * *

There is all of the difference in the world between making something illegal and making it tortious. Making an activity tortious forces the people who derive benefit from it to internalize the costs associated with it, thereby making sure that the activity will only be undertaken if it is desired by enough people to cover its costs.[22] It does not proscribe it altogether. As a result, very different policy considerations go into the decision of whether to forbid something and the decision of whether to find a duty that permits liability for the harm it causes. The fact that the New York legislature has failed to prohibit Black Talons is certainly one factor that the New York Court of Appeals is likely to consider in deciding the "policy-laden declaration reserved for Judges" that it must make in resolving whether a duty exists. But the weight to be given to this factor is just the sort of thing that only the New York Court of Appeals itself can determine.

* * *

NOTES

1. ***Certified questions.*** When a federal court encounters a question of state law the answer to which is not clear, it has two choices: it can make an educated guess as to how the state courts would rule, or it can seek an answer from a state court. Most states have established procedures permitting the state court of last resort to answer certified questions submitted by federal courts (and sometimes lower state courts). In the principal case, the Second Circuit could have asked the New York Court of Appeals whether New York law imposed a duty on the manufacturer of Black Talons, but the majority thought it unnecessary to do so.

2. Does the process the Second Circuit used to create the no-duty rule in *McCarthy* comply with the recommendations in Third Restatement § 7(b)?

3. In response to this case and others like it, Congress passed the "Protection of Lawful Commerce in Arms Act," 15 U.S.C. § 7901 et seq., which gives manufacturers of guns and ammunition immunity from tort suits arising from use of their products for criminal purposes.

---

22. Cf. Note, Absolute Liability for Ammunition Manufacturers, 108 Harv.L.Rev. 1679, 1691 (1995) ("The primary advantage of [imposing tort liability on ammunition manufacturers] is that it will force consumers of ammunition to internalize costs that have heretofore been borne by third parties and society in general. Such internalization will provide manufacturers and consumers with the proper incentives to choose care and activity levels that more closely equate costs and benefits.") (footnote omitted); id. at 1690 (noting that, unlike banning ammunition, imposing liability "does not reflect any moral or ethical condemnation of ammunition manufacturers").

E. MENTAL AND EMOTIONAL HARM

A defendant held liable for an intentional tort will usually be required to compensate for attendant emotional suffering, even in the absence of physical injury. Furthermore, when the defendant has caused a bodily injury compensable under negligence law, emotional pain is a recognized element of damages. In the latter case, the emotional suffering damages are often said to be "parasitic" to the physical injury.

The present section addresses the courts' treatment of negligently-inflicted emotional suffering that is not parasitic to a compensable physical harm. The movement of the law has been from a rule prohibiting recovery toward cautious recognition of some kinds of emotional suffering claims. The law on emotional injuries varies from state to state, but the Pennsylvania cases in this section illustrate a typical pattern.

Note that abolition of the broad no-duty rule for emotional injuries does not mean that such injuries will be treated identically with physical harms. Virtually all courts recognize a need for some special restrictions for non-physical injuries.

BOSLEY v. ANDREWS

Supreme Court of Pennsylvania, 1958.
393 Pa. 161, 142 A.2d 263.

BELL, JUSTICE.

Defendant's cattle strayed onto plaintiffs' farm and injured their crops, for which the jury gave plaintiffs a verdict of $179.99. Mrs. Mary Louise Bosley, the wife-plaintiff, sought to recover damages for a heart disability which resulted from her fright and shock upon being chased by a Hereford bull owned by defendant. The bull did not strike or touch plaintiff, and plaintiff suffered no physical injury. The Superior Court sustained the entry of a nonsuit. * * *

* * *

[T]he evidence does not show that [the bull] got any nearer to Mrs. Bosley than approximately 25 feet. Plaintiff collapsed on the ground and had an attack of coronary insufficiency—shortness of breath, pain in her chest and an insufficiency of blood flowing into the artery into the heart. * * *

* * *

The rule is long and well established in Pennsylvania that there can be no recovery of damages for injuries resulting from fright or nervous shock or mental or emotional disturbances or distress, unless they are accompanied by physical injury or physical impact.

In the leading case of Koplin v. Louis K. Liggett Co., 322 Pa. 333, 185 A. 744 [1936], plaintiff claimed damages because she became nauseated by the presence of a centipede in the spoon with which she was eating her

soup, and was made sick for several weeks. This Court denied recovery
* * *.

In Morris v. Lackawanna & Wyoming Valley Railroad Co., 228 Pa. 198, 77 A. 445 [1910], plaintiff claimed damages for a miscarriage resulting from a nervous shock occasioned by the electric car in which she was riding *bumping* over the track at an open switch. This Court denied recovery * * *.

In Ewing v. Pittsburgh, C. & St. L. Ry. Co., 147 Pa. 40, 23 A. 340, 14 L.R.A. 666 [1892], plaintiff's statement of claim averred that by a collision on defendant's railroad which occurred through the negligence of defendant's employees, defendant's cars were derailed and thrown against plaintiff's dwelling and she was thereby subjected to great fright, fear and nervous distress, became sick and disabled and was unable to attend to her usual work and duties. A demurrer to the statement of claim was sustained * * *.

In Fox v. Borkey, 126 Pa. 164, 17 A. 604 [1889], plaintiff was husking [corn] with her husband. An explosion occurred which was caused by defendant's blasting; the earth trembled and dirt blew over them as if it were hail. Plaintiff fell to the ground, trembling all over with shock; she became very nervous and had heart trouble * * *. The Court denied recovery.

In Potere v. City of Philadelphia, 380 Pa. 581, 112 A.2d 100 [1955], a contractor and the city were held jointly liable for a cave-in of a city street as the result of which plaintiff suffered physical injuries and a severe shock to his nervous system which was diagnosed as an anxiety neurosis. The Court said:

> It has been well established that in the absence of physical injury or physical impact, mental or emotional distress is not the subject of legal redress. However, where, as here, a plaintiff sustains *bodily injuries,* even though trivial or minor in character, *which are accompanied by fright or mental suffering directly traceable* to the peril in which the defendant's negligence placed the plaintiff, then mental suffering is a legitimate element of damages.

* * *

Plaintiff cites a number of decisions of this Court to support her claim but fails to realize that in those cases where recovery was allowed for nervous shock, *the nervous shock was accompanied by physical injuries,* and that all of her cases recognized and reiterate the above mentioned well settled rule. What plaintiff is really asking us to do is to review and change the rule which has been so long and clearly established by our cases * * *.

To allow recovery for fright, fear, nervous shock, humiliation, mental or emotional distress—with all the disturbances and illnesses which accompany or result therefrom—where there has been no physical injury or impact, would open a Pandora's box. * * * [A]ny one of a dozen * * * every-day events can cause or aggravate fright or nervous shock or emotional distress or nervous tension or mental disturbance. Such an event, if compensable, may cause normal people, as well as nervous persons and persons who are mentally disturbed or mentally ill, to honestly believe that the sudden and unexpected event caused them fright or nervous shock or nervous tension with subsequent emotional distress or suffering or pain or miscarriage or heart attack, or some kind of disease. * * * For every wholly genuine and deserving claim, there would likely be a tremendous number of illusory or imaginative or "faked" ones. Medical science * * * could not prove that these could not have been caused or precipitated or aggravated by defendant's alleged negligent act.

We have considered all of the contentions of the plaintiffs but find no merit in them.

The judgment of the Superior Court is affirmed * * *.

MUSMANNO, JUSTICE, dissenting.

* * *

The great fear of the Majority seems to be that if we should allow the plaintiff in this case to submit her case to a jury, and, incidentally, *that is all she is seeking,* the courts would be besieged with "faked" cases. * * *

But are our courts so naive, are they so gullible, are they so devoid of worldly knowledge, are they so childlike in their approach to realities that they can be deceived and hoodwinked by claims that have no factual, medical, or legalistic basis? If they are, then all our proud boasts of the worthiness of our judicial system are empty and vapid indeed.

The Majority's apprehension that if we should allow the instant case to go to a jury for factual determination, the Courts would be engulfed in a tidal wave of lawsuits, is to look upon a raindrop and visualize an inundation. Many jurisdictions now permit recovery where physical disablement tortiously caused is not made manifest through visible trauma, and I have seen no report that in those States the Courts are awash in trumped-up cases. * * *

* * *

NOTES

1. The rule permitting recovery for emotional suffering only if it was "accompanied by physical injury or physical impact" does not insist that the physical injury or impact cause the emotional harm. For example, in the *Potere* case discussed by the *Bosley* majority, the plaintiff suffered a sprained ankle and a bruised elbow when his truck fell into a 19–foot–deep hole in the street. These were indisputably physical injuries. He also suffered a much more serious "anxiety neurosis," which clearly resulted from the fall and not from the physical injuries. Recovery for the anxiety neurosis was allowed.

2. At the same time it was clear that physical injuries *caused by* the emotional stress did not qualify. Mrs. Bosley had a heart ailment, and the

plaintiffs in *Koplin, Morris, Ewing,* and *Fox* got physically sick. None was permitted recovery.

3. What exactly was required to constitute an *impact* under the "physical injuries or impact" rule? Mrs. Bosley fell to the ground; the plaintiff in *Fox* was showered with dirt falling "as if it were hail"; neither was good enough. What if Mrs. Bosley had run into a tree while fleeing the bull, and then fallen to the ground with an emotionally induced heart ailment? What if she had run into a tree, breaking her nose, and then had the emotionally induced heart ailment?

NIEDERMAN v. BRODSKY

Supreme Court of Pennsylvania, 1970.
436 Pa. 401, 261 A.2d 84.

ROBERTS, JUSTICE.

Appellant, Harry Niederman, alleges that on November 4, 1962 he was walking with his son at the corner of 15th and Market Streets in Philadelphia. At that time * * * appellee was driving a motor vehicle in a reckless and negligent manner as a result of which the automobile skidded onto the sidewalk and destroyed or struck down a fire hydrant, a litter pole and basket, a newsstand and appellant's son, who at that time was standing next to appellant. Almost immediately after this destructive path was cut by appellee's car, appellant claims that he suffered severe chest pain and that upon examination in the hospital, where he was confined for five weeks, appellant was diagnosed to have sustained acute coronary insufficiency, coronary failure, angina pectoris, and possible myocardial infarction. Consequently, appellant sought recovery from appellee for both these severe disabilities and the accompanying shock and mental pain.

Appellant's complaint was reluctantly dismissed on preliminary objections for failing to state a cause of action under the "impact rule" which provides that there can be no recovery for the consequences of fright and shock negligently inflicted in the absence of contemporaneous impact. * * *

Today we decide that on the record before us, appellant may go to trial and if he proves his allegations, recovery may be had from a negligent defendant, despite the fact that appellant's injuries arose in the absence of actual impact. * * * By our holding today Pennsylvania proceeds along the path recently followed by our neighboring jurisdictions and removes this ancient roadblock to appellant's recovery.

* * *

An analysis of the prior case law indicates that there have been three basic arguments which in the past would have defeated appellant. The first deals with medical science's difficulty in proving causation between the claimed damages and the alleged fright. The second involves the fear of fraudulent or exaggerated claims. Finally, there is the concern that such a rule will precipitate a veritable flood of litigation.

* * * While we agree that [the first argument might once] have been an appropriate conclusion because of the lack of sophistication in the medical field * * *, it would presently be inappropriate for us to ignore all of the phenomenal advances medical science has achieved in the last eighty years. * * *

* * *

The logical invalidity of this objection to medical proof can be demonstrated further by noting that the rule has *only* been applied where there is absolutely no impact whatsoever. Once there is even the slightest impact, it has been held that the plaintiff can recover for any damages which resulted from the accompanying fright, even though the impact *had no causal connection* with the fright-induced injuries. [The court here quoted *Potere*. See note 1 after *Bosley*, supra p. 235.]

It appears completely inconsistent to argue that the medical profession is absolutely unable to establish a causal connection in the case where there is no impact at all, but that the slightest impact (e.g., a bruised elbow and sprained ankle in *Potere*) suddenly bestows upon our medical colleagues the knowledge and facility to diagnose the causal connection between emotional states and physical injuries. * * *

Finally, even if we assume *arguendo* that a great deal of difficulty still remains in establishing the causal connection, this still does not represent sufficient reason to deny appellant an *opportunity* to prove his case to a jury. There is no reason to believe that the causal connection involved here is any more difficult for lawyers to prove or for judges and jurors to comprehend than many others which occur elsewhere in the law. * * *

The second major objection includes the fear of fictitious injuries and fraudulent claims. * * *

The charge that fraudulent claims will arise is not unique to this Commonwealth. Every court that has been confronted with a challenge to its impact rule has been threatened with the ominous spectre that an avalanche of unwarranted, trumped-up, false and otherwise unmeritorious claims would suddenly cascade upon the courts of the jurisdiction. The virtually unanimous response has been that (1) the danger of illusory claims in this area is no greater than in cases where impact occurs and that (2) our courts have proven that any protection against such fraudulent claims is contained within the system itself—in the integrity of our judicial process, the knowledge of expert witnesses, the concern of juries and the safeguards of our evidentiary standards.

* * *

The last argument urged by the proponents of the impact rule is that: "If we permitted recovery in a case such as this, our Courts would be swamped by a virtual avalanche of cases for damages for many situations and cases hitherto unrecoverable in Pennsylvania." However, it is our view that this argument is currently refuted on two grounds. First, it is not at all clear that the flood of litigation has occurred in states without the impact rule. * * *

Secondly, and more compelling * * * is the fundamental concept of our judicial system that any such increase should not be determinative or relevant to the availability of a judicial forum for the adjudication of impartial individual rights. "It is the business of the law to remedy wrongs that deserve it, even at the expense of a 'flood of litigation'; and it is a pitiful confession of incompetence on the part of any court of justice to deny relief upon the ground that it will give the courts too much work to do." Prosser, Intentional Infliction of Mental Suffering: A New Tort, 37 Mich.L.Rev. 874 (1939). * * *

* * *

We today choose to abandon the requirement of a physical impact as a precondition to recovery for damages proximately caused by the tort in only those cases like the one before us where the plaintiff was in personal danger of physical impact because of the direction of a negligent force against him and where plaintiff actually did fear the physical impact. Since appellant's complaint alleges facts which if proven will establish that the negligent force was aimed at him and put him in personal danger of physical impact, and that he actually did fear the force, this case must proceed to trial.

The order of the Court of Common Pleas of Philadelphia County is reversed and appellee's preliminary objections are dismissed.

BELL, CHIEF JUSTICE, dissenting.

The Majority too often forget that an emotionally appealing or heart-rending claim often produces bad law and sets a dangerous precedent.

* * *

The majority Opinion commits three tremendous and grievous errors in overruling Pennsylvania's "impact rule." The first regrettable and disastrous error is that they open Pandora's famous Box, out of which will flow a multiplicity of trespass suits for personal injuries and/or diseases. These will include the most fictitious or false or exaggerated claims that the imagination can conceive * * *.

The second major error of the Majority is that they not only substitute a "medical guessing game" for Pennsylvania's clear and definite and well-established "impact rule," but add a "Judicial guessing game." Few writers and few States can agree on a clear and definite formula for recovery, and the Majority itself cannot formulate a clear, specific, definite and boundarized rule or standards for recovery in this so-called "impact" field, which the Majority now abolish. * * *

The third major error of the Majority is that they deal another fatal or near-fatal blow to stare decisis. Once again a majority of the present Supreme Court has cavalierly buried or ignored the basic principle and the fundamental precept upon which the House of Law was built and maintained. Upon this Rock of Gibraltar, all Judges and all public officials, as well as all the people of Pennsylvania, can see and know and rely on their respective rights, their powers, their duties, their obligations and limitations. It is regrettable to be compelled to say that a decision of the present Court of Pennsylvania is good "for this day and this train only." What a catastrophe, and what a mockery of Law and of Justice!

* * *

NOTES

1. When judges change the law by moving from no-duty rules toward legal cause treatment of particular issues, the stated justifications are usually much like those of the *Niederman* majority. And the objections to such movement are likewise similar from area to area.

2. What if Mr. Niederman had pleaded that his emotional suffering resulted from fear and anguish over the injuries to his son, standing right beside him, rather than fear for his own safety? See the following case.

SINN v. BURD

Supreme Court of Pennsylvania, 1979.
486 Pa. 146, 404 A.2d 672.

NIX, JUSTICE.

At issue in this appeal is the vexing and complex question of when a plaintiff should be allowed to recover damages for negligently caused mental trauma. The specific question presented for our review is whether the trial court properly sustained appellee's demurrer to the fourth count of appellant's complaint in which she sought to recover damages for physical and mental injuries incurred when she saw her minor daughter struck and killed by an automobile, although the plaintiff herself was not within any zone of personal physical danger and had no reason to fear for her own safety. * * *

* * *

The averred facts are as follows. Appellant JoAnne Marie Sinn lived with her husband and two minor children in Elizabeth Township, Allegheny County. On June 12, 1975, at approximately 5:53 p.m., the deceased, Lisa Sinn, and her sister, Deborah, were standing by the Sinn's mail box located alongside the Greenock–Buena Vista Road, approximately 36 feet from the nearest intersection. An automobile operated by the appellee struck Lisa and hurled her through the air, causing injuries which resulted in her death. Deborah was not struck by the vehicle, although it narrowly missed her. Appellant witnessed the accident from a position near the front door of her home. * * * The fourth count was brought by appellant for damages she sustained from the emotional stress of witnessing her daughter's death. * * *

* * *

Since the *Niederman* decision, experience has taught us that the zone of danger requirement can be unnecessarily restrictive and prevent recovery in instances where there is no sound policy basis supporting such a result. It has unquestionably not been effective in every instance of assuring that one may "seek redress for every substantial wrong." The restrictiveness of the zone of danger test is glaringly apparent where it is allowed to deny recovery to a parent who has suffered emotional harm from witnessing a tortious assault upon the person of his or her minor child. A majority of the commentators and a growing number of jurisdictions have considered this problem in recent years and have concluded that it is unreasonable for the zone of danger requirement to exclude recovery in such cases.

This new awareness of the unfairness of the zone of danger requirement in these cases is based upon the implicit acceptance that the emotional impact upon a parent witnessing the killing of a minor child is at least as great and as legitimate as the apprehension that is inspired by a plaintiff being personally within the zone of danger. * * *

* * *

In an attempt to still the concerns of those troubled by "the fear of unlimited liability" the Supreme Court of Hawaii [in Leong v. Takasaki, 55 Haw. 398, 520 P.2d 758 (1974), which allowed recovery by a 10–year–old boy who saw his step-grandmother struck and killed by an automobile] suggested the limiting of recovery "to claims of serious mental distress." We believe this is a reasonable response to the concern. * * *

The *Leong* court attempted to achieve an objective standard by defining serious mental distress as being properly found where a reasonable person "normally constituted, would be unable to adequately cope with the mental stress engendered by the circumstances" of the event. Such a test focuses upon the situation producing the emotional stress and requires it to be [of] a nature that would be likely to produce a response in a person of average sensitivities. In this determination factors such as the context in which the trauma occurred, the development of physical ramifications, and the duration and severity of the emotional distress are available to make the judgment an objective—as opposed to a subjective—one.

* * *

[One of the policy arguments against bystander recovery has been the difficulty of reasonably circumscribing the area of liability.] This issue raises the question of the extent to which bystander recovery will be permitted. We are confident that the application of the traditional tort concept of foreseeability will reasonably circumscribe the tortfeasor's liability in such cases. Foreseeability enters into the determination of liability in determining whether the emotional injuries sustained by the plaintiff were reasonably foreseeable to the defendant.

[Dillon v. Legg, 68 Cal.2d 728, 441 P.2d 912 (1968), is the seminal case in this area. In determining that a mother who saw her daughter struck and killed by an automobile should be allowed to recover], the California Supreme Court identified three factors determinative of whether the injury to the plaintiff [in such a case] was reasonably foreseeable: (1) whether plaintiff was located near the scene of the accident as contrasted with one who was a distance away from it; (2) whether the shock resulted from a direct emotional impact upon plaintiff from the sensory and contemporaneous observance of the accident, as contrasted with learning of the accident from others after its occurrence; [and] (3) whether plaintiff and the victim were closely related, as contrasted with an absence of any relationship or the presence of only a distant relationship. In elaborating upon these factors, the court stated:

> The evaluation of these factors will indicate the *degree* of the defendant's foreseeability: obviously defendant is more likely to foresee that a mother who observes an accident affecting her child will suffer harm than to foretell that a stranger witness will do so. Similarly, the degree of foreseeability of the third person's injury is far greater in the case of his contemporaneous observance of the accident than that in which he subsequently learns of it. The defendant is more likely to foresee that shock to the nearby, witnessing mother will cause physical harm than to anticipate that someone distant from the accident will suffer more than a temporary emotional reaction. All these elements, of course, shade into each other; the fixing of obligation, intimately tied into the facts, depends upon each case.

> In light of these factors the court will determine whether the accident and harm was *reasonably* foreseeable. Such reasonable foreseeability does not turn on whether the particular defendant as an individual would have in actuality foreseen the exact accident and loss; it contemplates that courts, on a case-to-case basis, analyzing all the circumstances, will decide what the ordinary man under such circumstances should reasonably have foreseen. The courts thus mark out the areas of liability, excluding the remote and unexpected.

* * *

* * * Since we have determined that a tortfeasor's liability for mental distress is not to be denied solely because the plaintiff was beyond the zone of physical danger, we must examine whether the injuries sustained by appellant were reasonably foreseeable. It is clear that appellant's injuries were of a nature reasonably foreseeable under the circumstances alleged. Where the bystander is a mother who witnessed the violent death of her small child and the emotional shock emanated directly from personal observation of the event, we hold as a matter of law that the mental distress and its effects is a foreseeable injury.[21]

* * *

---

21. * * * We need not here consider the case where the mother is notified of the accident by another. Nor do we consider the situation where the relationship between the plaintiff-bystander

ROBERTS, JUSTICE, dissenting.

* * * The depth and inconsolable nature of a parent's loss at the death of a child is unique in human experience. And where that death is caused by another's irresponsible act, it is not unexpected that parents turn to the law to seek redress for the harm done to them. * * * Yet * * * the law must recognize that not every human loss arising out of another's conduct constitutes a legal injury for which compensation shall be available.* * *

* * *

The central problem this kind of action brings before the courts is not that of the genuineness of the emotional distress, but that of rationally limiting defendant's liability. The opinion of Mr. Justice Nix disingenuously would have us believe that today we need not consider whether it is possible to limit recovery solely to plaintiff's class. If, however, there is no principled means of distinguishing this plaintiff from any other, then to decide her case is to decide the question the majority claims is not before us. One can say that question is not before us only by assuming its answer.

Mr. Justice Nix asserts that he sufficiently limits liability by narrowing recovery to "foreseeable injuries." But what constitutes a foreseeable injury is the conclusion of legal analysis, not its principal tool. Indeed there is remarkable disagreement about how to distinguish the "foreseeable" from the "unexpected." In Massachusetts one who does not witness an accident to a third party may still suffer foreseeable emotional distress from learning of the death. In Hawaii, such injuries are not foreseeable. In Connecticut, seeing an accident will foreseeably cause emotional distress, while hearing one will not. In California, witnessing a negligent stillbirth does not create a foreseeable injury, while coming upon an already injured victim may.

In Rhode Island a mother may recover, but not a close personal friend. In Arizona, anyone who was a close friend of the victim may suffer a foreseeable injury. In Hawaii, not every one who is close will suffer a foreseeable injury, but a step-grandson's emotional distress is foreseeable. This variety of rules "limiting" recovery is eloquent testimony that there is no natural non-arbitrary way to limit liability for this injury.

* * *

Mr. Justice Nix's foreseeable injury "test," adopted from *Dillon*, predicates recovery upon plaintiff's (1) witnessing an accident, (2) close-up (3) in which a "close" relative is injured. This test, ostensibly simple, will produce monumental problems both of application and fair limitation. If recovery is extended in the present case, can the law close its eyes to the emotional distress of bystanders who recently witnessed the traumatic

and the accident victim is more remote. These are questions which may properly be left to another day. Jurisprudentially, the remote and unexpected can best be excluded by reaching these issues on a more appropriate record.

amputation of a young woman's hand by a subway car? Does the majority's "rule" give us any principle at all in the following situation? Three siblings get off a bus. Two attempt to cross the street. The third begins to walk away from them down the block. A moment later he hears screeching car brakes, screams and one of his siblings yelling, "My God, Jim is dead." Does the brother have a foreseeable injury? Is there any way to judge whether his emotional distress "resulted from a direct emotional impact upon the plaintiff from the sensory and contemporaneous observance of the accident" or from "learning of the accident from others after its occurrence?" How many steps down the street distinguish immediate observation from indirect learning? * * *

* * *

NOTES

1. The California Supreme Court's *Dillon* decision has been so influential that the uninjured bystander problem is also often called the Dillon v. Legg problem.

2. Some of the Pennsylvania bystander cases after Sinn v. Burd are described in the following case.

ARMSTRONG v. PAOLI MEMORIAL HOSPITAL

Superior Court of Pennsylvania, 1993.
430 Pa.Super. 36, 633 A.2d 605, appeal denied, 538 Pa. 663, 649 A.2d 666 (1994).

CIRILLO, JUDGE.

In this appeal we are asked to consider whether the trial court erred when it ruled that a jury award of $1,000 on a claim of negligent infliction of emotional distress warranted a new trial on the damages question alone and whether the trial court erred when it refused to enter a judgment *non obstante veredicto* (j.n.o.v.). On both questions, we reverse.

As she was dressing her young son for a birthday party one morning, Dawn Armstrong received a telephone call from Paoli Memorial Hospital, informing her that her husband had been in an accident and asking her to come to the hospital.

The hospital had summoned Mrs. Armstrong because a critically injured accident victim named Thomas Armstrong had been brought in unconscious by ambulance. Following a hospital policy to notify the next-of-kin as quickly as possible, an emergency room employee asked information for a telephone number of Thomas Armstrong in Chester. Based on that information, she called Dawn Armstrong.

Once at the hospital, Dawn Armstrong met with a neurosurgeon and examined X-rays of a man with a crushed cranium. She was not allowed to see the patient. Only after she had been at the hospital for more than an hour did her sister see the accident victim's driver's license. Then, it was clear the accident victim was not Dawn Armstrong's husband, Thomas *J.*

Armstrong, but Thomas *H.* Armstrong, also of Chester. Dawn Armstrong testified that when she heard the injured man was not her husband, "I just lost it. I urinated, defecated, and I just lost it completely."

As a result of the misidentification, Dawn Armstrong testified she suffers from depression, nightmares, insomnia and unreasonable fears about the safety and whereabouts of her husband and son for which she has undergone psychological counseling.

The Armstrongs filed suit against Paoli Memorial Hospital, alleging negligent infliction of emotional distress, intentional infliction of emotional distress and asking for compensatory and punitive damages. The count of intentional infliction of emotional distress and the request for punitive damages were dismissed by the trial judge at the close of testimony. Only the question of negligent infliction of emotional distress went to the jury. The claims for intentional infliction of emotional distress and punitive damages were not revived in post-trial motions. In response to post-trial motions the trial court entered a single order granting a new trial as to damages, calling a verdict of $1,000 "inadequate, indeed supremely embarrassing," and denying the hospital a j.n.o.v.

* * *

Not every wrong constitutes a legally cognizable cause of action. Lubowitz v. Albert Einstein Med. Center, 424 Pa.Super. 468, 472, 623 A.2d 3, 5, (1993) (false report of exposure to AIDS is not a legally cognizable injury). The law cannot be expected to compensate for every minor psychic shock incurred in the course of everyday living. Not every loss constitutes a legal injury for which compensation is available.

The fundamental question underlying this appeal is whether Pennsylvania recognizes an independent tort of negligent infliction of emotional distress.

* * *

The tort of negligent infliction of emotional distress has evolved almost exclusively in the context of those who observe injury to close family members and are as a consequence of the shock emotionally distressed. To state a cause of action for negligent infliction of emotional distress the plaintiff must demonstrate that she is a foreseeable plaintiff and that she suffered a physical injury as a result of the defendant's negligence.

Physical injury must be averred to sustain a cause of action for negligent infliction of emotional distress. See Covello v. Weis Markets, Inc., 415 Pa.Super. 610, 610 A.2d 50 (1992), appeal denied, 533 Pa. 644, 622 A.2d 1376 (1993), (policeman who was unable to extricate a child from a trash compactor failed to allege physical harm to himself); Abadie v. Riddle Memorial Hospital, 404 Pa.Super. 8, 589 A.2d 1143 (1991) (demurrer sustained for failure to state a cause of action when plaintiff failed to allege physical harm from a raucous hospital staff birthday celebration while she was being treated); Wall by Lalli v. Fisher, 388 Pa.Super. 305, 565 A.2d 498, allocatur denied, 526 Pa. 636, 584 A.2d 319 (1990) (mother who witnessed a dog bite her child failed to aver physical injury to herself); Banyas v. Lower Bucks Hospital, 293 Pa.Super. 122, 437 A.2d 1236 (1981) (plaintiff who was charged with murder after hospital records were altered to blame him for a death and to conceal malpractice failed to aver physical harm and, thus, stated no cause of action for negligent infliction of emotional distress).

The requirement that physical harm must accompany emotional distress to state a cause of action is based on the Restatement (Second) of Torts § 436A. Temporary fright, nervous shock, nausea, grief, rage, and humiliation if transitory are not compensable harm; but, long continued nausea or headaches, repeated hysterical attacks or mental aberration are compensable injuries. This court applied the Restatement standards to a case in which the plaintiff averred "headaches, shaking, hyperventilation, nightmares, shortness of breath, lack of control over the bowels, and tightening of the muscles in the neck, back and chest" and found that she had stated a cause of action for negligent infliction for emotional distress when her employer wrongfully coerced her to enter an abusive substance abuse program. Crivellaro v. Pennsylvania Power and Light, 341 Pa.Super. 173, 491 A.2d 207 (1985). Relying on cmt. *c* to § 436A, a panel of this court held that "symptoms of severe depression, nightmares, stress and anxiety, requiring psychological treatment, and * * * ongoing mental, physical and emotional harm" sufficiently stated physical manifestations of emotional suffering to sustain a cause of action. Love v. Cramer, 414 Pa.Super. 231, 606 A.2d 1175 (1992). Cases which the *Crivellaro* court collected from other jurisdictions cite depression, nightmares, nervousness, insomnia and hysteria as physical symptoms warranting recovery.

In this case, Armstrong's allegation of loss of continence when she learned the accident victim coupled with her claim of depression, nightmares and insomnia meet the requirement of allegation of physical injury.

While physical injury is necessary to recovery, it is not sufficient. Armstrong must still demonstrate that she was a foreseeable plaintiff towards whom the hospital acted negligently.

The requirement that a plaintiff allege physical injury is intrinsic to the question of who is a foreseeable plaintiff. The original test for whether a tortfeasor was liable for the emotional distress of another was the "impact rule." There was no recovery for emotional disturbance unless it was accompanied by physical injury or physical impact. The impact rule yielded to a zone of danger test in *Niederman* [supra p. 236]. When *Niederman*'s "zone of danger" rule became unworkable, Pennsylvania adopted the foreseeability test of Sinn v. Burd [supra p. 239.]

* * *

* * * Since Sinn v. Burd, the debate has centered on the meaning of "sensory and contemporaneous observance." In Yandrich v. Radic, 495 Pa.

243, 433 A.2d 459 (1981), the state supreme court held that a father who arrived on the accident scene after his son had been taken to the hospital had not stated a cause of action. Five years later the court reached the same conclusion in Mazzagatti [v. Everingham, 512 Pa. 266, 516 A.2d 672 (1986)] regarding a mother who arrived on the scene minutes after the accident and saw her child's body in the street. *Mazzagatti,* 512 Pa. at 280, 516 A.2d at 679. The court reasoned that where the close relative is not present at the scene of the accident, but instead learns of the accident from a third party, the close relative's prior knowledge of the injury to the victim serves as a buffer against the full impact of observing the accident scene. By contrast the relative who contemporaneously observes the tortious conduct has no time in which to brace his or her emotional system. The negligent tortfeasor inflicts upon this bystander an injury separate and apart from the injury to the victim.

In Brooks v. Decker, 512 Pa. 365, 516 A.2d 1380 (1986), our Supreme Court held that a father who followed an ambulance to the scene of an accident and saw his injured son in the street failed to state a cause of action. And, in Bloom v. Dubois Regional Medical Center, 409 Pa.Super. 83, 597 A.2d 671 (1991), this court denied recovery to a husband who found his wife hanging by her neck in a hospital room, allegedly due to the failure of the hospital and her doctor to treat her suicidal tendencies. The panel held that the husband had not witnessed the tortious conduct, only its aftermath.

The next year, a panel of this court allowed recovery by a woman whose mother died in her arms after a doctor failed to diagnose or treat a serious heart ailment. The daughter had taken her mother for treatment and was present when the doctor was dismissive of the woman's symptoms. Love v. Cramer, supra (Cirillo, J., dissenting). This court has also allowed a wife to recover when she saw a speeding vehicle heading for her husband's car, heard the collision, and immediately realized her husband had been struck. Neff v. Lasso, 382 Pa.Super. 487, 555 A.2d 1304 (1989). Most recently, this court *en banc* allowed recovery for negligently inflicted emotional distress to a mother who was standing at the head of a supermarket checkout line near a plate glass window when her children were terribly injured by a drunken driver just outside the window. Krysmalski v. Tarasovich, 424 Pa.Super. 121, 622 A.2d 298 (1993) (Cirillo, J., dissenting).

Thus, the impact rule became the zone of danger test, *Niederman,* supra, and finally the three-part test of Sinn v. Burd, supra. In the evolution, the change was not in the need to allege physical harm but in the expansion of the proximate cause of the harm. Originally the law required that the harm be caused by the impact; today we recognize that the shock of apprehending an injury to a loved one can cause physical manifestation of emotional disturbance.

In the case at hand, Dawn Armstrong fails to meet the bystander test of Sinn v. Burd because she was not related to the accident victim and she did not have a contemporaneous perception of the accident. She posits her theory of recovery on a separate and independent tort, that which was allegedly committed when she was mistakenly summoned to the hospital.

Only two appellate cases in Pennsylvania have held that the question of negligent infliction of emotional distress in a context other than bystander recovery should go to the jury. In Stoddard v. Davidson, 355 Pa.Super. 262, 513 A.2d 419 (1986), the question was whether there was sufficient "impact" to allow recovery when the plaintiff was emotionally distressed after he ran over the body of a woman whom the defendant killed and left lying in the road. The plaintiff alleged that his distress arose when he had to hold a cover over the corpse for three hours during the police investigation of the victim's death. The panel, with one concurrence and one dissent, found sufficient impact alleged to allow a jury to decide if there was negligent infliction of emotional distress.

In the second case, *Crivellaro,* supra, the question was whether an employee who was coerced by her employer into entering an controversial drug and alcohol rehabilitation program has alleged sufficient physical manifestation of her injury to recover. A panel of this court found that she had.

This case asks us to expand the tort of negligent infliction of emotional distress beyond the fact situations of liability to close family members who actually witness an accident, something which, with the exception of *Stoddard,* supra, and *Crivellaro,* supra, Pennsylvania has consistently refused to do.

Among the cases in which this court has refused to recognize an independent tort of negligent infliction of emotional distress is *Lubowitz,* supra, in which a false report of exposure to AIDS was insufficient to support a cause of action for negligent infliction of emotional distress. *Lubowitz* followed the reasoning of the asbestos cases in Pennsylvania in which this court has found that fear of disease is not a compensable wrong. * * *

* * *

Few if any jurisdictions recognize an independent cause of action for negligent infliction of emotional distress. More often the tort of negligent infliction of emotional distress is premised on the violation of a pre-existent duty based on a contractual or implied contractual relationship. Cf. *Crivellaro,* supra, (pre-existent employer-employee relationship).

California experimented with allowing recovery on an independent tort of negligent infliction of emotional distress. The Armstrongs argue that Molien v. Kaiser Foundation Hospitals, 27 Cal.3d 916, 167 Cal.Rptr. 831, 616 P.2d 813 (1980), is persuasive. In *Molien,* the California Supreme Court held that a general duty to refrain from inflicting serious mental distress was based on the foreseeability of the plaintiff. The *Molien* case allowed a husband to recover for his mental distress after his wife was wrongly diagnosed as having syphilis. Only a few years later, the same court expressed reservations about the "limitless exposure to liability." *Thing v. LaChusa*, 48 Cal.3d 644, 771 P.2d 814, 821 (Cal.1989). A second California appellate court decision found that *Molien* created a "quagmire of novel claims." *Andalon v. Superior Court*, 162 Cal.App.3d 600, 208 Cal.Rptr. 899, 903 (1984). By 1992, California had abolished negligent infliction of emotional distress as an independent tort and had narrowed its scope to include only those cases in which a contractual relationship existed, *Burgess v. Superior Court*, 2 Cal.4th 1064, 831 P.2d 1197 (1992), or those in which a bystander witnessed an injury to a loved one.

* * *

The law is not the guarantor of an emotionally peaceful life. Tort law cannot protect any of us from the emotional slings and arrows of daily living. Not every mistake that happens will be legally cognizable. Were we to allow Dawn Armstrong to collect, we would risk opening the floodgates of litigation in Pennsylvania, something we decline to do.

Factually, Dawn Armstrong is in a particularly perilous position. Had the telephone call from Paoli Memorial Hospital been accurate, she could not have stated a cause of action for any emotional distress she suffered learning of her husband's injuries. Consequently, Dawn Armstrong is forced to argue that she was injured when she learned it was not her husband who was injured, information which foreseeably would cause relief, not distress. Indeed, Armstrong testified that it was when she learned it was not her husband in the hospital that she "lost it."

Our review of the law of Pennsylvania and our sister states makes it clear that to state a cause of action for negligent infliction of emotional distress, Dawn Armstrong must demonstrate that she is a bystander who meets the criteria of *Sinn v. Burd*, supra, or that the defendant, Paoli Memorial Hospital, owes her a pre-existing duty of care, either through contract or fiduciary duty. *Crivellaro*, supra. This she cannot do. Dawn Armstrong was not a bystander who witnessed an injury to a close family member, nor did Paoli Memorial Hospital owe her a pre-existing duty of care.

Since we find that the Armstrongs have not stated a cause of action, we reverse the trial court's denial of a j.n.o.v. and order judgment in favor of the defendant. The trial court's order of a new trial on damages alone is also reversed.

NOTES

1. Did subsequent developments vindicate Justice Roberts's dissent in *Sinn v. Burd*?

2. ***The "physical manifestation" requirement.*** *Armstrong* states that in addition to other requirements, "physical injury" is necessary to recover for negligently caused emotional distress, but the requirement is satisfied by depression, nightmares and insomnia. A more common and

precise term in this context is "physical manifestation," meaning a physical ailment consequent to the emotional distress, and thereby corroborative of its severity (to be distinguished from physical trauma resulting directly from an impact). Most jurisdictions likewise require physical manifestation but are lenient in interpreting the condition. A number of jurisdictions have abandoned the requirement. The Texas Supreme Court gave five reasons for doing this: (a) "The requirement is overinclusive because it permits recovery for mental anguish when the suffering * * * results in any physical impairment, regardless of how trivial the injury." (b) "[T]he requirement is underinclusive because it arbitrarily denies court access to persons with valid claims they could prove if permitted to do so." (c) "[T]he requirement is defective because it 'encourages extravagant pleading and distorted testimony.' '[I]n most instances of severe mental disturbance some deleterious physical consequence can, with a little ingenuity, be found * * * ' and characterization of an injury as physical or mental may depend on the ingenuity of counsel in framing the pleadings." (d) "[T]he concept of 'physical manifestation' has been expanded to the point where the term has lost much of its former significance." (e) "[M]edical research has provided modern mankind with a much more detailed and useful understanding of the interaction between mind and body. It is well recognized that certain psychological injuries can be just as severe and debilitating as physical injuries." St. Elizabeth Hospital v. Garrard, 730 S.W.2d 649, 652–53 (Tex.1987).

3. *The* Dillon *factors.* As illustrated by the Pennsylvania bystander cases surveyed in *Armstrong,* many cases have encountered problems with the first two *Dillon* factors, whether plaintiff was located near the scene of the accident and whether the plaintiff experienced direct sensory perception of it. The third factor, whether plaintiff and the victim were closely related, has less often been at issue but has presented its own difficulties. See, e.g., Elden v. Sheldon, 46 Cal.3d 267, 250 Cal.Rptr. 254, 758 P.2d 582 (1988) (unmarried cohabitant lacked sufficiently close relationship); Dunphy v. Gregor, 136 N.J. 99, 642 A.2d 372 (1994) (unmarried cohabitant had sufficiently close relationship); Blanyar v. Pagnotti Enterprises, Inc., 451 Pa.Super. 269, 679 A.2d 790 (1996), aff'd, 551 Pa. 313, 710 A.2d 608 (1998) (plaintiff who witnessed drowning of cousin lacked sufficiently close relationship). See also Roman v. Carroll, 127 Ariz. 398, 621 P.2d 307 (App.1980) (no bystander recovery for plaintiff who witnessed dismemberment of her poodle by defendant's St. Bernard).

4. *Thing v. La Chusa.* In Thing v. La Chusa [cited in *Armstrong* at p. 248], the California Supreme Court slightly modified the *Dillon* factors and turned them into formal requirements for bystander recovery. Citing the need to limit liability and provide predictability, the court expressly abandoned any case-by-case determination of foreseeability as the test.

5. Stoddard v. Davidson, described in *Armstrong* at p. 247, indicates that at least in Pennsylvania "impact" survives as an alternative theory available to a plaintiff who fails to make out the elements of bystander recovery or zone of danger. More recent Pennsylvania cases agree. See Doe v. Philadelphia Community Health Alternatives AIDS Task Force, 745 A.2d 25, 28–29 (Pa.Super.2000); Brown v. Philadelphia College of Osteopathic Medicine, 449 Pa.Su-

per. 667, 674 A.2d 1130 (1996); Tomikel v. Commonwealth Dept. of Transp., 658 A.2d 861 (Pa.Cmwlth.1995).

6. ***Fear of disease.*** The cases cited in *Armstrong* denying recovery for fear of a disease are in accord with most decisions elsewhere with similar facts. See, e.g., Metro–North Commuter R.R. Co. v. Buckley, 521 U.S. 424, 117 S.Ct. 2113, 138 L.Ed.2d 560 (1997) (railroad worker negligently exposed to carcinogen but without symptoms of disease cannot recover under Federal Employers' Liability Act for negligently inflicted emotional distress because facts fail to make out zone of danger or physical impact); Potter v. Firestone Tire & Rubber Co., 6 Cal.4th 965, 25 Cal.Rptr.2d 550, 863 P.2d 795 (1993) (no recovery for fear of cancer in a negligence action for exposing plaintiffs to carcinogens unless plaintiff is "more likely than not" to develop cancer). With *Metro–North*, compare Norfolk & Western Railway Co. v. Ayers, 538 U.S. 135, 123 S.Ct. 1210, 155 L.Ed.2d 261 (2003), permitting (5–4) recovery for fear of cancer as part of pain and suffering by plaintiffs who had actually contracted asbestosis, which increases the risk of cancer.

A number of cases involve "fear of AIDS." The cases present a great variety of facts and outcomes. A number of courts have required that the plaintiff show "actual exposure" to the virus. See, e.g., K.A.C. v. Benson, 527 N.W.2d 553 (Minn.1995). Some courts further require that plaintiff prove a medically possible "channel of transmission" of the virus. See, e.g., Brown v. New York City Health & Hosp. Corp., 225 A.D.2d 36, 648 N.Y.S.2d 880 (1996). California requires, in addition to actual exposure, that plaintiff show that he is more likely than not to contract AIDS. See Kerins v. Hartley, 27 Cal. App.4th 1062, 33 Cal.Rptr.2d 172 (1994). On the other hand, a few courts require only that plaintiff show a reasonable fear of AIDS. See, e.g., Williamson v. Waldman, 150 N.J. 232, 696 A.2d 14 (1997) (fear must be reasonable based upon accurate generally available public knowledge about AIDS transmission); Faya v. Almaraz, 329 Md. 435, 620 A.2d 327 (1993).

In many of the fear-of-disease cases denying recovery, a toxic substance has come into actual contact with the plaintiff's body, or plaintiff has been touched with possibly contaminated medical equipment. What do these outcomes indicate about the current content of the zone of danger and impact doctrines? Can you formulate those doctrines so as to incorporate these cases?

Suppose that as a result of defendant's negligence, plaintiff is pricked by a needle that might be contaminated. Plaintiff suffers fear of AIDS and other diseases (and perhaps physical manifestations resulting from the mental distress) but develops no infectious disease and repeatedly tests negative for HIV. On these facts, some courts have denied any recovery. See, e.g., Carroll v. Sisters of St. Francis Health Services, 868 S.W.2d 585 (Tenn.1994); Babich v. Waukesha Memorial Hospital, Inc., 205 Wis.2d 698, 556 N.W.2d 144 (App.1996). Others have allowed recovery based upon "impact." See, e.g., Marchica v. Long Island R.R. Co., 31 F.3d 1197 (2d Cir.1994), cert. denied, 513 U.S. 1079, 115 S.Ct. 727, 130 L.Ed.2d 631 (1995).

7. ***"Pre-existing duty of care."*** In addition to impact, zone of danger, and bystander, *Armstrong* recognizes a fourth possible basis for emotional-harm recovery, "a pre-existing duty of care, either through contract or fiduciary duty." This category is further recognized in Toney v. Chester

County Hospital, 961 A.2d 192 (Pa.Super.2008) (hospital providing medical care to plaintiff), and in Third Restatement § 46 ("An actor whose negligent conduct causes serious emotional disturbance to another is subject to liability to the other if the conduct * * * (b) occurs in the course of specified categories of activities, undertakings, or relationships in which negligent conduct is especially likely to cause serious emotional disturbance.").

F. "PURE ECONOMIC LOSS"

Tort law has no general problem with awarding recovery for economic loss. Economic loss is recoverable in the torts of intentional misrepresentation and intentional interference with contract. It is recoverable in wrongful death actions, see Chapter VII, infra. It is sometimes recoverable, though severely limited, in negligent misrepresentation. Even in ordinary negligence-based personal injury cases, all of the traditional elements of damages, aside from the pain and suffering portions, are designed to compensate for economic loss. This includes damages for medical expenses and lost earnings. See generally Chapter VII.

But a special problem arises when a defendant's negligent conduct causes financial detriment not resulting from an injury to the plaintiff's person or tangible property. Such an injury is called *pure economic loss.* Traditional Anglo–American tort law denied recovery in negligence for such losses, and there is still a pronounced reluctance to redress them. Perlman, Interference With Contract and Other Economic Expectancies: A Clash of Tort and Contract Doctrine, 49 U.Chi.L.Rev. 61, 70–72 (1982),offers useful speculation about one of the principal reasons for that reluctance:

> The consequences of any act can be traced indefinitely, but tort law has never made a defendant pay for all harm caused by his tortious act.

* * *

> At some point, it is generally agreed that the defendant's act cannot fairly be singled out from the multitude of other events that combine to cause loss. A number of doctrinal devices—proximate cause, intervening cause, and duty—have served to limit liability.

* * *

> There is little agreement on where to draw the line.

* * *

> Moreover, courts faced with the problem of limiting liability in individual cases have concerns beyond locating the limit at precisely the right point. They can be expected to search for a rule that can be applied consistently and articulated sensibly to guide future cases and to avoid the appearance of arbitrariness.

In cases of physical injury to persons or property, the task of defining liability limits is eased, but not eliminated, by the operation of the laws of physics. Friction and gravity dictate that physical objects eventually come to rest. The amount of physical damage that can be inflicted by a speeding automobile or a thrown fist has a self-defining limit. Even in chain reaction cases, intervening forces generally are necessary to restore the velocity of the harm-creating object. These intervening forces offer a natural limit to liability.

The laws of physics do not provide the same restraints for economic loss. Economic relationships are intertwined so intimately that disruption of one may have far-reaching consequences. Furthermore, the chain reaction of economic harm flows from one person to another without the intervention of other forces. Courts facing a case of pure economic loss thus confront the potential for liability of enormous scope, with no easily marked intermediate points and no ready recourse to traditional liability-limiting devices such as intervening cause.

In another large group of cases, the principal reason for denying recovery for pure economic losses seems to be a reluctance to allow a tort remedy when the plaintiff could have secured (or perhaps did secure) a remedy contractually.

The next two cases assay the considerations for and against the no-duty rule in the contexts mentioned above.

CORPUS CHRISTI OIL & GAS CO. v. ZAPATA GULF MARINE CORP..

United States Court of Appeals, Fifth Circuit, 1995.
71 F.3d 198.

E. GRADY JOLLY, CIRCUIT JUDGE.

[During a storm in the Gulf of Mexico, a tugboat and barge owned by Zapata broke loose from their moorings and drifted into an offshore platform owned by Corpus Christi Oil and Gas. Attached to a leg of the platform was a gas riser (a vertical pipe) owned by Houston Pipeline Co. The riser was connected to a pipeline carrying natural gas to the shore eight miles away.]

Workers on the Corpus Christi platform foresaw the allision* and promptly shutdown operations to prevent a fire or explosion. The force of the allision crushed the concrete riser coating and damaged the riser. Houston ordered Corpus Christi to shut in its wells [disconnect them from the riser] so that it could inspect the riser and replace the damaged section. The repair took two weeks, during which time Corpus Christi could not use the riser to convey its gas. During the repairs, Corpus Christi flared gas to prevent the loss of the wells. [Corpus Christi sued

---

* In maritime law, an allision is a collision between a moving vessel and a fixed object. [Ed.]

Zapata and Houston for its losses resulting from its inability to use the riser.]

The district court conducted a bench trial. At its close, the district court allocated fault** for damage to the riser two-thirds to Zapata, and the remaining one-third, collectively, to Corpus Christi and Houston.[2] Zapata argued at trial—and now argues on appeal—that Corpus Christi did not sustain physical damage to any proprietary interest; [and] thus, under the "bright line" rule of this circuit announced in Louisiana ex rel. Guste v. M/V Testbank, 752 F.2d 1019 (5th Cir.1985) (en banc), cert. denied, 477 U.S. 903, 106 S.Ct. 3271, 91 L.Ed.2d 562 (1986), may not recover its losses incurred due to Zapata's negligence. In support of its argument, Zapata notes that Corpus Christi did not own the damaged riser, and that it voluntarily flared the gas, the cost of which it now seeks to recover. Zapata does not dispute, however, that Corpus Christi would have incurred great harm to its wells if it had not flared the gas during Houston's repair of its riser.

The district court held that the flaring of the gas constituted physical damage to a proprietary interest of Corpus Christi, thus permitting Corpus Christi to avoid the *Testbank* bar.

* * *

The district court thus awarded to Corpus Christi the value of the gas and condensate that was flared. In addition, the district court awarded Corpus Christi the revenue lost while its wells were shut in for the repair of the riser. The proportionate share of these items amounted to $232,628.64. * * *

* * *

II.

A.

In Pennzoil Producing Co. v. Offshore Express, Inc., 943 F.2d 1465, 1473 (5th Cir.1991), we reviewed a district court's application of the rule of law announced in Robins Dry Dock & Repair Co. v. Flint, 275 U.S. 303, 309, 48 S.Ct. 134, 135, 72 L.Ed. 290 (1927), and reaffirmed by this court in *Testbank*. Noting the applicable standard of review, we wrote:

> It is well settled law that, as in most federal actions, in maritime actions the "clearly erroneous" rule applies to the review of the factual findings of the trial court. Thus we must accept the district court's findings of fact unless, upon reading the record and examining the exhibits, we are convinced that they are demonstrably incorrect.

** This was done in accordance with principles of proportionate liability that we will consider in Chapter XI, infra.[Ed.]

2. The district court found Houston negligent for failing to protect the riser from accidental vessel damage, and Corpus Christi negligent either for failing to review plans for the riser before allowing Houston to attach the riser, or failing to require Houston adequately to protect its riser before allowing Houston to attach the riser.

B.

The damages award in this case had three components—the cost of gas flared by Corpus Christi to preserve the wells, the revenue lost by Corpus Christi during the period of the riser's repair, and the cost incurred by Houston of repairing the damage to the riser. We address each award in turn.

(1)

Zapata argues that Corpus Christi suffered no physical damage from the allision, and is therefore entitled to no damages award. In the alternative, it argues that, if the flaring of the gas (in order to save the wells) suffices as physical damage, then Corpus Christi is entitled only to the costs incurred by the voluntary flaring of gas, and not the purely economic loss in gas production for the two weeks while Houston repaired its riser.

In this circuit, an admiralty plaintiff cannot recover negligently inflicted economic losses where there is no physical damage to the plaintiff's property. *Testbank.* In *Testbank,* we reviewed a summary judgment entered against numerous plaintiffs, each claiming purely economic losses arising from a spill of a toxic chemical in the Mississippi River Gulf outlet. Later, in Consolidated Aluminum Corp. v. C.F. Bean Corp., 772 F.2d 1217 (5th Cir.1985), cert. denied, 486 U.S. 1055, 108 S.Ct. 2821, 100 L.Ed.2d 922 (1988), a panel of this court reviewed *Testbank,* noting:

> The "character of the interest harmed" for which the plaintiffs sought relief in *Testbank* was solely economic. Given this character of the interest harmed, the Court reaffirmed the holding of [a panel of] this Court that physical damage to a proprietary interest [is] a prerequisite to recovery for economic loss in cases of unintentional tort. The Court emphasized that to abandon the physical injury requirement would impose a "limitless type of liability," and the result would be wave upon wave of successive consequences. The Court also noted the corresponding difficulty to courts in managing such economic claims on a discrete basis under traditional tort principles. Thus, where the character of the interest harmed was solely economic, the Court held that no recovery could be allowed under *Robins* as a "pragmatic limitation upon the tort doctrine of foreseeability."

Corpus Christi points out that in *Consolidated,* we held that physical damage that was a *consequence* of an accident was sufficient to satisfy *Testbank*'s requirement. In that case, Consolidated Aluminum Corporation's plant machinery was damaged by the slowing of the flow of gas that was caused by Bean's negligent puncture to a pipeline some six miles from Consolidated's facility. We held that Consolidated had stated a claim for physical damages to its machinery as a result of Bean's negligence and that, therefore, *Testbank* did not preclude Consolidated's recovery of associated economic losses.

Corpus Christi also points to *Pennzoil,* a case factually similar to the one at bar. There we held that damage to a well resulting from the *failure* to flare gas after a well was shut in following an allision constituted the kind of physical damage that made the *Testbank* bar inapplicable. Corpus Christi argues that here, it did "what this Circuit told Pennzoil it should have done"—flared the gas and prevented the loss of its wells.

We think that it does no violence to *Testbank* or its underlying principles to find recovery appropriate in the case before us. Except for its acts in mitigation, Corpus Christi would have suffered great physical damages to its wells as a result of Zapata's negligence. *Testbank* must not be construed as mandating the narrow and impractical result urged by Zapata: finding a defendant free of liability when the plaintiff incurs losses, although "voluntarily" so, that nevertheless are directly attributable to its efforts to avoid the physical damages that would have rendered that defendant liable for much larger sums. We therefore agree with the district court that Corpus Christi's costs incurred in flaring the gas to save its wells constitutes the physical damage to a proprietary interest, i.e., its gas, sufficient to satisfy the *Testbank* requirements. Corpus Christi is thus entitled to $58,613, representing the economic loss it suffered because of the flaring of the gas, to be reduced by one-third (reflecting the amount of Corpus Christi's own negligence), for a total award of $39,075.33.

(2)

We disagree, however, that Corpus Christi is further entitled to damages resulting from its inability to produce and sell its gas in the two weeks during which Houston repaired its riser. *Testbank* denies recovery for pure economic losses not associated with physical injuries. Although we hold that the recovery Corpus Christi seeks for its flared gas is based upon injury to its property—that is, its gas—no such argument can be made with respect to the purely economic losses resulting from failure to sell its gas during the two-week repair. That gas remains in the ground, unaffected by the property damage suffered by Corpus Christi, that is, the gas that was flared. The additional economic losses that Corpus Christi seeks to recover occurred solely and only because of the physical damage *that was done to Houston's property,* i.e., the riser, which shut down Houston's pipeline. Corpus Christi lost its gas sale profits because it could not use the pipeline, not because it was flaring its own gas.

We recognize that, although *Testbank* suggests an association between recovery sought and damage to the plaintiff's property, it left undecided the degree of association required. Neither did *Consolidated* clearly resolve this question. It simply made clear that economic losses that flowed directly from the physical damage to Consolidated's property were recoverable. In the present case, however, we are squarely presented with the question of whether the principle of *Testbank*—that is, a limitation on the doctrine of foreseeability[3]—requires that recoverable economic damages

---

3. In *Testbank* we wrote, "Denying recovery for pure economic losses is a pragmatic limitation on the doctrine of foreseeability, a limitation we find to be both workable and useful."

have some direct tie to the plaintiff's specific physical loss or damage, or whether the *Testbank* principle simply requires a showing of damage to some proprietary interest of the plaintiff, in order to open the door to recovery for *all* purely economic damages that were foreseeable from the initial tort. For help in answering this question, we turn first to the principles underlying *Testbank*.

In *Testbank,* when considering the basis of the subject rule, we explained as follows:

> *Robins* broke no new ground but instead applied a principle * * * which refused recovery for negligent interference with "contractual rights." Stated more broadly, the prevailing rule denied a plaintiff recovery for economic loss *if that loss* resulted from physical damage to property in which he had no proprietary interest.

We concluded that "*Robins Dry Dock* is both a widely used and necessary limitation on recovery for economic losses." Thus, *Testbank* strongly suggests that recoverable losses somehow be tied to the damage to the *plaintiff's* property, here the flared gas. Clearly, *Testbank* sought to preclude wave upon wave of damages. For example, assuming Corpus Christi were a vertically integrated operation, *Testbank*'s bright line rule serves to preclude not only recovery for lost gas sales from the well, but also any damages related to refineries that could not process the gas, or damages related to trucking operations that could not transport the gas or to retail outlets that could not sell the final product.

Although one might try to extrapolate an argument from *Consolidated* that, once physical damage to any proprietary interest is proven, all pure economic losses are recoverable, such a reading, we think, is inconsistent with *Consolidated*'s holding. In *Consolidated,* all the awarded damages flowed directly from the destruction of Consolidated's production facilities. Consolidated sued not solely for any lost income or other *economic* loss from the interruption of its supply of natural gas (e.g., due to being forced to pay higher prices for an alternative supply) but instead for *physical* losses, as well as *attendant* economic damages, to its own property which occurred as a result of the interruption of Consolidated's supply of gas "within minutes" of the pipeline's rupture.

As we have emphasized, Corpus Christi's claimed economic loss was not "attendant" to the physical damage to Corpus Christi's proprietary interest; the loss was instead occasioned only by the physical injury to Houston's riser, property in which Corpus Christi had no proprietary interest. To allow recovery for those losses plainly would abrogate the bright line rule of *Testbank*. To insure that the principles underlying *Testbank* are preserved, we hold that simply meeting the requirement of showing physical damage to a proprietary interest does not automatically open the door to all foreseeable economic consequences. We therefore reverse the district court on this point, and deny Corpus Christi's recovery of revenue lost while its wells were shut in for the repair of Houston's riser.

* * *

Affirmed in part and reversed in part.

BENAVIDES, CIRCUIT JUDGE, concurring in part and dissenting in part:

I join the majority in affirming the award of damages to Corpus Christi for the flared gas and to Houston for the riser.

* * *

However, the majority's denial of Corpus Christi's delay damages resulting from the shut-in under the guise of *Testbank* ignores controlling authority in this Circuit and forges a new rule of law unintended by *Testbank* and its progeny. I must dissent.

Testbank stands for a single proposition: physical damage to a proprietary interest is a prerequisite to recovery for economic loss. We adopted the "bright-line" *Testbank* rule to exclude entire categories of potential plaintiffs who had suffered only economic harm. These would-be plaintiffs, whose claims were potentially indeterminate and indefinite, created the specter of wave upon wave of successive economic consequences. We drew our bright line with full recognition that some plaintiffs with foreseeable economic injury would be denied recovery. Nonetheless, our rule of law is not only consistent with established precedent, but also with the appropriate adjudicative role of our courts.

Thus *Testbank* operates as a threshold to recovery. Those plaintiffs with physical injury to a proprietary interest may enter; those without may not. This gateway to recovery makes sense. Having satisfied the prerequisite, the rationale for foreclosing relief for economic harm does not apply because the plaintiff no longer belongs to the putative class of indeterminate and indefinite claimants; the plaintiff now belongs to the finite fold of those suffering some physical damage. Simply put, once a plaintiff demonstrates physical damage to a proprietary interest, *Testbank* is simply inapplicable.

Clearing the *Testbank* threshold, however, is not the end of the matter. A plaintiff's right to recovery still hinges on application of traditional tort principles including legal duty and foreseeable injury. These principles, of course, include recovery for foreseeable economic loss caused by a defendant's negligence. These well-settled principles of negligence, not *Testbank,* control the ultimate outcome.

In this case, we correctly hold that Corpus Christi's sensible action in flaring gas to save its wells "constitutes the physical damage to a proprietary interest, i.e., its gas, sufficient to satisfy the *Testbank* requirements." At this point, Corpus Christi meets the prerequisite; our *Testbank* inquiry is over. General principles of negligence now govern whether Corpus Christi can recover damages. The majority, however, resurrects *Testbank* and fashions a new requirement that each element of recoverable loss must satisfy *Testbank.* I cannot condone this new rule because it ignores the lessons of our previous authority in this area of law.

[Judge Benevides went on to argue that the majority's reliance on *Consolidated Aluminum* was inappropriate; he said Consolidated was denied recovery because its loss was not sufficiently foreseeable, not because of the economic loss rule—*Testbank* having been found inapplicable because Consolidated suffered physical harm to its own equipment.]

* * *

In the case before us today, Corpus Christi suffered two types of economic damages: flared gas and delay damages from the shut-in. Having satisfied the *Testbank* prerequisite, fundamental negligence principles determine Corpus Christi's recovery. Applying traditional tort principles, these economic damages are recoverable unless they are unforeseeable or causally unrelated to the allision. When Zapata's barge collided with the Corpus Christi platform it damaged the gas riser. This necessitated Corpus Christi's prudent action in flaring gas to avoid permanent damage to the well. Is it unforeseeable that Corpus Christi would also suffer economic damages from a shut-in caused by a need to repair the gas riser? Certainly not. The damages from both the flared gas and the subsequent shut-in directly flow from the allision. This is not a situation, as presented in *Consolidated Aluminum,* where the damages occur in some remote location unknown and unseen by the tortfeasor. The Zapata barge ran into the Corpus Christi platform and the attached riser directly leading to both the flared gas and necessary shut-in.

* * *

I would affirm the award of the foreseeable delay damages to Corpus Christi.

NOTES

1. Corpus Christi had physical harm (destruction of the natural gas it was forced to flare off) as well as economic loss (its inability to produce gas while the riser was repaired). The dissenting judge thought that was enough to avoid the economic loss rule. The majority demanded more; it denied recovery because the economic loss did not have "a direct tie to" or was not "attendant to" the harm to Corpus Christi's property. When the specific economic loss is clearly *caused by* the physical damage to the plaintiff's property, courts are agreed that the economic loss rule has no application; the claim is treated as one for damage to property rather than economic loss. As the principal case suggests, courts are in disagreement as to whether proof of *some* physical harm opens the door to recovery for economic loss not caused by (or only indirectly caused by) the physical damage. If it does, it appears to function as an exception to the economic loss rule, much as proof of "impact" triggers an exception to the general rule barring recovery for negligently inflicted emotional harm. See Section D, supra. Cases can be found embracing either interpretation. Which is the better view may depend on the work the

economic loss rule is intended to do. If its purpose is to restrict the universe of potential claimants to a manageable number, the door-opening role may be sufficient. If its purpose is broader—to limit the damages recoverable even by claimants who can show some physical harm—the interpretation favored by the majority is obviously better.

Under either interpretation, a holding that the economic loss rule does not bar recovery leaves open the possibility that the claim may still be denied on foreseeability grounds, as it was in the *Consolidated Aluminum* case discussed in both opinions above.

2. Even when the claimant has suffered no physical harm at all, the economic loss rule is not always a bar to recovery. In *Testbank*, discussed in the principal case, commercial fishermen who were unable to fish during the time the waterway was closed due to the spill were allowed to recover, apparently for reasons peculiar to maritime law. When the Exxon Valdez spilled more than 275,000 barrels of oil into Prince William Sound in 1989, Exxon paid $20 million to settle claims by Native Americans who lost the use of the sound for fishing and ceremonial purposes. Because the case was settled, there was no definitive judicial determination that the economic loss rule was inapplicable. After that spill, Congress passed the Oil Pollution Act of 1990, which made companies liable for some economic losses, such as loss of profits and impairment of earning capacity resulting from damage to natural resources.

In the aftermath of the worst spill in history, the Deepwater Horizon (or Macondo) spill in the Gulf of Mexico in 2010, British Petroleum announced it would pay "all legitimate claims" and expressed no intention to deny claims on the basis of the economic loss rule. Its early payments included some claims for lost wages and rents, but those payments may have been mandatory under the 1990 Act. Whether BP contemplated paying economic loss claims beyond those it was required to pay by the statute was not clear.

3. In some other countries courts are not as hostile to economic loss claims as the U.S. courts are. The Supreme Court of Canada allowed a railroad to recover for losses incurred when it had to reroute its trains because defendant's tugboat negligently damaged a bridge owned by a third party. The court emphasized that the railroad owned the track on either end of the bridge and accounted for 86 per cent of the traffic across the bridge, and the defendant knew that the bridge was essential to the railroad's operations. See Canadian National Railway v. Norsk Pacific Steamship Co., (1992) 91 DLR (4th) 289.

In a case very similar to *Corpus Christi*, the High Court of Australia permitted an oil company to recover for losses incurred when the defendant's dredge negligently severed a pipeline owned by a third party but used to deliver the plaintiff's petroleum. The judges emphasized that the defendant knew that the pipeline served the plaintiff's refinery and that damage to it would require the plaintiff to pay for alternative means of getting its oil to the refinery. See Caltex Oil (Australia) Pty Ltd v. The Dredge "Willemstad", (1976) 136 CLR 529. In their separate judgments, one or more of the High Court justices embraced each of the following requisites for recovery of economic losses:

—Defendant knew or should have known that the negligent act would cause economic loss to the plaintiff.

—The loss occurred through loss of use of the (third party's) damaged property.

—The loss was not merely loss of profits, but the out-of-pocket expense of providing an alternative to the damaged method of transport.

—Economic harm to a specific claimant, as opposed to a class of claimants, was foreseeable.

—The harm was caused by physical effects on property located in such proximity to the site of the negligent conduct that the effects were foreseeable.

Do these cases indicate that there are workable ways to limit recovery for economic loss short of the "bright line" prohibition adhered to in *Corpus Christi*?

———

Another reason for the economic loss rule, in addition to those mentioned in the *Testbank* and *Corpus Christi* cases, is to preserve a boundary between tort and contract. In cases seeking damages for economic loss resulting from defective products, courts generally deny recovery in tort. The rationale is that the seller and buyer were in a contractual relationship and tort law should leave the adjustment of losses arising from that relationship to contract law unless the defect results in personal injury or damage to property other than the product itself. The most famous cases denying tort recovery for this reason are East River Steamship Corp. v. Transamerica Delaval, Inc., 476 U.S. 858, 106 S.Ct. 2295, 90 L.Ed.2d 865 (1986), and Seely v. White Motor Co., 63 Cal.2d 9, 45 Cal.Rptr. 17, 403 P.2d 145 (1965).

The deference to contract principles goes only so far, however. In suits for legal malpractice, for example, the same argument could be made: the plaintiff and defendant were parties to a contract and the resolution of their dispute therefore ought to be left to contract law. But it is well established that legal malpractice is a tort, even though the harm usually is purely economic.

In the following case, the court must decide which of these lines of authority to follow when the loss arises neither from a defective product nor from legal malpractice.

2314 LINCOLN PARK WEST CONDOMINIUM ASS'N v. MANN, GIN, EBEL & FRAZIER, LTD.

Supreme Court of Illinois, 1990.
136 Ill.2d 302, 555 N.E.2d 346, 144 Ill.Dec. 227.

JUSTICE MILLER.

[The Condominium Association (Lincoln) consisted of the owners of the 39 condominium units located at 2314 Lincoln Park West in Chicago.

Mann, Gin, Ebel & Frazier, Ltd. (Mann), was the architectural firm that designed the project. Lincoln sued Mann and the owners and developers of the project, alleging that windows and glass doors were loose, the roof leaked, the heating and cooling systems and other utilities were inadequate and did not function property, and the garage was settling. Basing its action on both contract and tort theories, the plaintiff requested compensatory damages for the cost of repairing those problems. The trial court dismissed all the claims except the negligence claim against Mann. As to that claim, the judge submitted a certified question asking the Supreme Court whether Illinois law "would permit Plaintiffs seeking to recover purely economic losses due to defeated expectations of a commercial bargain to recover from an architect or engineer in tort."]

In Moorman Manufacturing Co. v. National Tank Co. (1982), 91 Ill.2d 69, 61 Ill.Dec. 746, 435 N.E.2d 443, this court held that recovery generally cannot be had in tort for what is termed purely economic loss. The plaintiff in that case had purchased a grain storage tank from the defendant manufacturer. A crack developed in the tank some years later, and the plaintiff then sued the manufacturer, seeking damages for the cost of repairing the tank and for the loss of its use. * * *

Central to the court's discussion in *Moorman* are the appropriate characterization of economic loss and the recognition of the distinct functions served by the regimes of tort and contract. Regarding the term "economic loss," the court stated:

> "Economic loss" has been defined as "damages for inadequate value, costs of repair and replacement of the defective product, or consequent loss of profits—without any claim of personal injury or damage to other property" as well as "the diminution in the value of the product because it is inferior in quality and does not work for the general purposes for which it was manufactured and sold." These definitions are consistent with the policy of warranty law to protect expectations of suitability and quality.

In *Moorman,* the court concluded that the plaintiff in that case was seeking compensation for economic loss. The court held that such damages are not recoverable under the tort theories of strict liability, negligence, or innocent misrepresentation.

The court cited several considerations as militating against allowing recovery of damages for economic loss in strict liability. The court believed that the relationships between suppliers and consumers of goods are more appropriately governed by contract law than by tort law, and referred to the large statutory apparatus, such as the Uniform Commercial Code, applicable to the field of sales. The court also observed that the rules of warranty serve to limit the potentially far-reaching consequences that might otherwise result from imposing tort liability for disappointed commercial or consumer expectations; the court noted, moreover, that contracting parties are free to bargain over the terms of their warranties.

In addition, the court rejected the notion that there is something arbitrary in allowing recovery in strict liability only when physical harm or personal injury results. Quoting Justice Traynor's opinion for the court in Seely v. White Motor Co. (1965), 63 Cal.2d 9, 18, 45 Cal.Rptr. 17, 23, 403 P.2d 145, 151, the court in *Moorman* stated:

> "The distinction that the law has drawn between tort recovery for physical injuries and warranty recovery for economic loss is not arbitrary and does not rest on the 'luck' of one plaintiff in having an accident causing physical injury. The distinction rests, rather, on an understanding of the nature of the responsibility a manufacturer must undertake in distributing his products. He can appropriately be held liable for physical injuries caused by defects by requiring his goods to match a standard of safety defined in terms of conditions that create unreasonable risks of harm. He cannot be held for the level of performance of his products in the consumer's business unless he agrees that the product was designed to meet the consumer's demands. A consumer should not be charged at the will of the manufacturer with bearing the risk of physical injury when he buys a product on the market. He can, however, be fairly charged with the risk that the product will not match his economic expectations unless the manufacturer agrees that it will. Even in actions for negligence, a manufacturer's liability is limited to damages for physical injuries and there is no recovery for economic loss alone."

Thus, the rule appropriately reflects the distinction between tort and contract.

For those reasons, the court in *Moorman* declined to allow a cause of action in strict liability for the recovery of solely economic loss. With respect to the plaintiff's claim for negligence, the court believed that "[t]he policy considerations against allowing recovery for solely economic loss in strict liability cases apply to negligence actions as well" and accordingly held that the plaintiff did not have a cause of action under that theory.

* * *

The question certified in the present case is whether an exception to the *Moorman* rule should be recognized for actions alleging architectural malpractice. A similar issue was raised, but not decided, in two prior cases before this court. [The court noted that courts of other states and intermediate appellate courts of Illinois were divided on the question.]

* * *

Consistent with *Moorman* and its progeny, we answer the certified question in the negative and hold today that a tort action will not lie in the circumstances described.

* * *

The plaintiff argues that recovery of economic losses is permitted in malpractice actions against other professionals and contends that no different result should obtain here. At oral argument, plaintiff's counsel warned that application of *Moorman* to the present claim for architectural malpractice would upset settled principles of malpractice liability in other professions. Apparently the plaintiff's theory is that denial of recovery in tort for economic loss in the present case will mean that economic loss is never recoverable in an action for malpractice. In this regard, the plaintiff contends that the licensing requirements applicable to architects under the Illinois Architecture Act confirm the professional nature of the services they render.

* * *

In a variety of circumstances this court has distinguished *Moorman* and has allowed tort actions to proceed. See Board of Education of City of Chicago v. A, C & S, Inc. (1989), 131 Ill.2d 428, 439–51, 137 Ill.Dec. 635, 546 N.E.2d 580 (installation of asbestos-containing material in buildings tantamount to contamination of other property, making available tort recovery); Scott & Fetzer Co. v. Montgomery Ward & Co. (1986), 112 Ill.2d 378, 387–88, 98 Ill.Dec. 1, 493 N.E.2d 1022 (tort action allowed where alleged defects in alarm system failed to detect warehouse fire; damage to property other than product itself was caused by sudden and dangerous conflagration, so tort action not barred by *Moorman*); Vaughn v. General Motors Corp. (1984), 102 Ill.2d 431, 436, 80 Ill.Dec. 743, 466 N.E.2d 195 (tort action allowed where defective brakes on truck caused truck to roll over and lose load; "The allegations of the complaint * * * allege a sudden and calamitous occurrence caused by a defect in the product and state a cause of action based on strict liability".) * * *

* * *

The gravamen of the plaintiff's claim for negligence against Mann is dissatisfaction with the way in which the building was designed and constructed, and the failure of the building to meet the unit owners' expectations. It may be noted that the unit owners received express warranties from the developer at the time they purchased their units, and the plaintiffs are currently seeking recovery from their seller on that basis. The present claim, however, is limited to the plaintiff's theory that the defendant architectural firm was negligent in its design of the structure. As our prior decisions concerning the construction industry fully illustrate, such a claim concerns the quality, rather than the safety, of the building and thus is a matter more appropriately resolved under contract law. We decline to impose on Mann a duty in tort to protect the unit owners from the sort of loss asserted. The architect's responsibility originated in its contract with the original owner, and in these circumstances its duties should be measured accordingly. Recovery of the nature requested here essentially seeks damages for a difference in quality. "There is room in the market for goods of varying quality, and if the purchaser buys goods which turn out to be below its expectations, its remedy should be against the person from whom it bought the goods, based upon the contract with that person."

While we do not intend in the present case to determine the future application of *Moorman* in all areas of professional malpractice, we must reject the plaintiff's theory that denial of the negligence claim against the present architect would signal in general the end of malpractice recovery in tort. It may be noted that in suits involving malpractice claims against health care professionals, personal injury will generally be the alleged result, and therefore *Moorman* would not bar recovery in any event. Moreover, we believe that other professional relationships are readily distinguishable from the present case. For example, since *Moorman*, malpractice actions against attorneys have gone forward, without any suggestion that the form of recovery traditionally recognized in such actions would no longer be allowed. Moreover, those cases recognize an extracontractual duty not only to the client but also to the group of persons the client intended to benefit. Such a duty arises from a consideration of the nature of the undertaking and the lawyer's traditional responsibilities. The same cannot be said with respect to the defendant architect in the present case.

For the reasons stated, the question certified by the circuit court is answered in the negative. The cause is remanded to the circuit court of Cook County for further proceedings not inconsistent with this opinion.

NOTES

1. Does the court provide a persuasive reason for treating architectural malpractice differently than legal malpractice?

2. The condominium owners were not parties to the contract with Mann. For an argument that "An agreement to which the plaintiff is not a party provides no basis for limiting whatever rights the plaintiff may have under tort law," see Vincent R. Johnson, The Boundary–Line Function of the Economic Loss Rule, 66 Wash. & Lee L. Rev. 523 (2009).

3. The tort of negligent misrepresentation, which originated as an offshoot of the ancient common law action of deceit and its modern counterpart, intentional misrepresentation, operates as a rather large exception to the economic loss rule. That tort recognizes a cause of action against those who, in the course of their business, negligently supply false information intended to be used by a limited group of recipients in their business transactions. See Restatement (Second) of Torts § 552. Claims by third parties against negligent architects are sometimes actionable as negligent misrepresentation. See, e.g., Bilt–Rite Contractors, Inc. v. The Architectural Studio, 581 Pa. 454, 866 A.2d 270 (2005) (holding architects potentially liable for errors in specifications that caused construction to be more difficult than anticipated). In other cases courts deny negligent misrepresentation claims in the interest of encouraging parties to protect themselves contractually. See, e.g., Berschauer/Phillips Const. Co. v. Seattle School Dist. No. 1, 124 Wash.2d 816, 881 P.2d 986 (1994) ("contract principles override the tort principles in

§ 552 and, thus, purely economic damages are not recoverable" by contractor that was not in privity with architect but that could have protected itself from architect negligence in its contract with owner).

In the principal case, the plaintiffs did not plead negligent misrepresentation. In an omitted portion of the opinion, the court said it doubted that this tort would be applicable in any event, because the business of architects is designing buildings, not merely furnishing information.

4. In negligent misrepresentation cases, the danger of indeterminate liabilities is addressed by limitations on damages: the tortfeasor is liable only to parties for whose benefit and guidance he intends to supply the information or knows that the recipient intends to supply it, and only for losses arising from transactions of the sort the tortfeasor intended to influence. See Restatement (Second) of Torts § 552(2). Under the Oil Pollution Act, liability is capped at a fixed dollar amount. Are these better liability-limiting devices than the economic loss rule?

G. OWNERS AND OCCUPIERS OF LAND

The duty questions we have seen up to this point arose because the defendant argued that it owed no duty to exercise reasonable care. Now we encounter an area in which the contention is not that the defendant owed no duty, but that its duty was something less than the full duty of reasonable care.

Historically, landowners* were not held to the full duty of reasonable care when conditions on their premises caused injury to persons or property of others. They received the benefit of a reduced standard of care. How much the standard was reduced depended upon the circumstances of the claimant's presence on the premises.

1. INVITEES AND LICENSEES

NELSON v. FREELAND

Supreme Court of North Carolina, 1998.
349 N.C. 615, 507 S.E.2d 882.

WYNN, JUSTICE.

[T]his case presents us with the simplest of factual scenarios— [defendant Dean] Freeland requested that plaintiff John Harvey Nelson ("Nelson") pick him up at his house for a business meeting the two were attending, and Nelson, while doing so, tripped over a stick that Freeland had inadvertently left lying on his porch. Nelson brought this action against Freeland and his wife seeking damages for the injuries he sus-

---

* Like most courts, we use the term "landowner" as shorthand for the universe of defendants who may be eligible for these special limited-duty rules. A more precise term would be "occupier," which includes a person occupying the land with intent to control it, a former occupier if no one has subsequently occupied it, or a person who is entitled to immediately occupy it. A lessee, for example, is an occupier and thus a member of the favored category even if not a landowner.

tained in the fall. The trial court granted summary judgment for the defendants, and the Court of Appeals affirmed.

Although the most basic principles of tort law should provide an easy answer to this case, our current premises-liability trichotomy—that is, the invitee, licensee, and trespasser classifications—provides no clear solution and has created dissension and confusion amongst the attorneys and judges involved. Thus, once again, this Court confronts the problem of clarifying our enigmatic premises-liability scheme—a problem that we have addressed over fourteen times. * * *

* * *

I. ANALYSIS

A. Current North Carolina Premises Liability Law

Under current North Carolina law, the standard of care a landowner owes to persons entering upon his land depends upon the entrant's status, that is, whether the entrant is a licensee, invitee, or trespasser. An invitee is one who goes onto another's premises in response to an express or implied invitation and does so for the mutual benefit of both the owner and himself. The classic example of an invitee is a store customer. A licensee, on the other hand, "is one who enters onto another's premises with the possessor's permission, express or implied, solely for his own purposes rather than the possessor's benefit." The classic example of a licensee is a social guest. Lastly, a trespasser is one who enters another's premises without permission or other right.

In a traditional common-law premises-liability action, the threshold issue of determining the plaintiff's status at the time of the injury is of substantial import. The gravity of this determination stems from the fact that there is a descending degree of duty owed by a landowner based upon the plaintiff's status.

The highest degree of care a landowner owes is the duty of reasonable care toward those entrants classified as invitees. Specifically, a landowner owes an invitee a duty to use ordinary care to keep his property reasonably safe and to warn of hidden perils or unsafe conditions that could be discovered by reasonable inspection and supervision.

A landowner's duty toward a licensee, on the other hand, is significantly less stringent. The duty of care owed to a licensee by an owner or possessor of land ordinarily is to refrain from doing the licensee willful injury and from wantonly and recklessly exposing him to danger. Thus, a licensee enters another's premises at his own risk and enjoys the license subject to its concomitant perils.

Finally, with respect to trespassers, a landowner need only refrain from the willful or wanton infliction of injury. Wilful injury constitutes actual knowledge of the danger combined with a design, purpose, or intent to do wrong and inflict injury. Similarly, a wanton act is performed intentionally with a reckless indifference to the injuries likely to result.

B. *Premises–Liability Nationwide—The Modern Trend*
    of Abolishing The Common–Law Trichotomy in
    Favor of a Reasonable–Person Standard

Although the common-law trichotomy has been entrenched in this country's tort-liability jurisprudence since our nation's inception, over the past fifty years, many states have questioned, modified, and even abolished it after analyzing its utility in modern times. At first, states believed that although the policies underlying the trichotomy—specifically those involving the supremacy of land ownership rights—were no longer viable, they nonetheless could find means to salvage it. In particular, states attempted to salvage the trichotomy by engrafting into it certain exceptions and subclassifications which would allow it to better congeal with our present-day policy of balancing land-ownership rights with the right of entrants to receive adequate protection from harm. Accordingly, North Carolina, along with the rest of the country, witnessed the burgeoning of novel jurisprudence involving entrant-protection theories such as the active-negligence and attractive-nuisance doctrines. Unfortunately, these exceptions and subclassifications ultimately forced courts to maneuver their way through a dizzying array of factual nuances and delineations.

Additionally, courts were often confronted with situations where none of the exceptions or subclassifications applied, yet if they utilized the basic trichotomy, unjust and unfair results would emerge. Therefore, these courts were forced to define terms such as "invitee" and "active conduct" in a broad or strained manner to avoid leaving an injured plaintiff deserving of compensation without redress. Although these broad or strained definitions may have led to just and fair results, they often involved rationales teetering on the edge of absurdity. For example, in Hansen v. Richey, 237 Cal.App.2d 475, 480–81, 46 Cal.Rptr. 909, 913 (1965), under the trichotomy the court would not have been able to compensate the plaintiffs for their licensee son's drowning because the defendant did not maintain his pool in a manner which wantonly or recklessly exposed the decedent to danger. Therefore, to reach a just result, the court in *Hansen* read the phrase "active conduct" broadly to include the general "active" act of having a party. Under this strained reading, however, "active conduct" could plausibly exist whenever a landowner "actively" invites someone to his home.

* * *

The first significant move toward abolishing the common-law trichotomy occurred in 1957 when England—the jurisdiction giving rise to the trichotomy—passed the Occupier's Liability Act which abolished the distinction between invitees, licensees and so-called contractual visitors. Shortly thereafter, the United States Supreme Court decided not to apply the trichotomy to admiralty law after concluding that it would be inappropriate to hold that a visitor is entitled to a different or lower standard of care simply because he is classified as a "licensee." See Kermarec [v. Compagnie Generale Transatlantique, 358 U.S. 625 (1959)]. In so ruling, the Court noted that "[t]he distinctions which the common law draws between licensee and invitee were inherited from a culture deeply rooted to the land, a culture which traced many of its standards to a heritage of feudalism."

* * *

Nine years later, the Supreme Court of California decided the seminal case of Rowland v. Christian, 69 Cal.2d 108, 443 P.2d 561, 70 Cal.Rptr. 97 [(1968)], which abolished the common-law trichotomy in California in favor of modern negligence principles. Specifically, the court in *Rowland* held that the proper question to be asked in premises-liability actions is whether "in the management of his property [the landowner] has acted as a reasonable man in view of the probability of injury to others."

* * *

The *Rowland* decision ultimately served as a catalyst for similar judicial decisions across the country. Indeed, since *Rowland,* twenty-five jurisdictions have either modified or abolished their common-law trichotomy scheme—seven within the last five years.

Specifically, eleven jurisdictions have completely eliminated the common-law distinctions between licensee, invitee, and trespasser.

Further, fourteen jurisdictions have repudiated the licensee-invitee distinction while maintaining the limited-duty rule for trespassers.

In summation, nearly half of all jurisdictions in this country have judicially abandoned or modified the common-law trichotomy in favor of the modern "reasonable-person" approach that is the norm in all areas of tort law.

C. *The Advantages and Disadvantages of Abolishing the Common–Law Trichotomy*

* * *

2. Reasons For and Against Abolishing the Trichotomy

Although the modern trend of premises-liability law in this country has been toward abolishing the trichotomy in favor of a reasonable-person standard, there are some jurisdictions that have refused to modify or abolish it. One of the primary reasons that some jurisdictions have retained the trichotomy is fear of jury abuse—a fear similar to the reason it was created in the first place. Specifically, jurisdictions retaining the trichotomy fear that plaintiff-oriented juries—like feudal juries composed mostly of land entrants—will impose unreasonable burdens upon defendant-landowners. This argument, however, fails to take into account that juries have properly applied negligence principles in all other areas of tort law, and there has been no indication that defendants in other areas have had unreasonable burdens placed upon them. Moreover, given that modern jurors are more likely than feudal jurors to be landowners themselves, it is unlikely that they would be willing to place a burden upon a defendant that they would be unwilling to accept upon themselves.

Another fear held by jurisdictions retaining the trichotomy is that by substituting the negligence standard of care for the common-law categories, landowners will be forced to bear the burden of taking precautions such as the expensive cost associated with maintaining adequate insurance policies. This argument, however, ignores the fact that every court which has abolished the trichotomy has explicitly stated that its holding was not intended to make the landowner an absolute insurer against all injuries suffered on his property. Rather, they require landowners only to exercise reasonable care in the maintenance of their premises.

Lastly, opponents of abolishing the trichotomy argue that retention of the scheme is necessary to ensure predictability in the law [but the court asserted that it in fact produced little predictability.]

* * *

The complexity and confusion associated with the trichotomy is twofold. First, the trichotomy itself often leads to irrational results not only because the entrant's status can change on a whim, but also because the nuances which alter an entrant's status are undefinable. Consider, for example, the following scenario: A real-estate agent trespasses onto another's land to determine the value of property adjoining that which he is trying to sell; the real-estate agent is discovered by the landowner, and the two men engage in a business conversation with respect to the landowner's willingness to sell his property; after completing the business conversation, the two men realize that they went to the same college and have a nostalgic conversation about school while the landowner walks with the man for one acre until they get to the edge of the property; lastly, the two men stand on the property's edge and speak for another ten minutes about school. If the real-estate agent was injured while they were walking off the property, what is his classification? Surely, he is no longer a trespasser, but did his status change from invitee to licensee once the business conversation ended? What if he was hurt while the two men were talking at the property's edge? Does it matter how long they were talking?

The Supreme Court of Wisconsin asked whether there is any reason why one who invites a guest to a party should have less concern for that individual's well-being than he has for the safety of an insurance salesman delivering a policy to his home.

* * *

[Second,] the trichotomy often forces the trier of fact to focus upon irrelevant factual gradations instead of the pertinent question of whether the landowner acted reasonably toward the injured entrant. For instance, in the real-estate agent hypothetical posed above, the trier of fact would be focused on determining the agent's purpose for being on the land at the time of injury instead of addressing the pertinent question of whether the landowner acted as a reasonable person would under the circumstances.

Corresponding to this argument is the fact that "[i]n many instances, recovery by an entrant has become largely a matter of chance, dependent upon the pigeonhole in which the law has put him, e.g., 'trespasser,' 'licensee,' or 'invitee'—each of which has radically different consequences in law." Significantly, this pigeonholing is essentially an attempt to transmute propositions of fact into propositions of law—a transmutation that has only distracted the jury's vision away from the proper consideration of whether the defendant acted reasonably. For instance, the three experienced Court of Appeals judges who initially decided this case—Judge Smith, Chief Judge Arnold, and Judge Walker—disagreed not only with respect to whether plaintiff was an invitee or a licensee, but also as to whether this case involved a question of law or fact.

Lastly, we note that the trichotomy has been criticized because its underlying landowner-immunity principles force many courts to reach unfair and unjust results disjunctive to the modern fault-based tenets of tort law. For example, the Kansas Supreme Court noted that "modern times demand a recognition that requiring all to exercise reasonable care for the safety of others is the more humane approach." Likewise, the California Supreme Court noted that using the trichotomy to determine whether a landowner owed the injured plaintiff a duty of care "is contrary to our modern social mores and humanitarian values." Indeed, modern thought dictates that "[a] man's life or limb does not become less worthy of protection by the law nor a loss less worthy of compensation * * * because he has come upon the land of another without permission or with permission but without a business purpose." Simply put, "the traditional rule confers on an occupier of land a special privilege to be careless which is quite out of keeping with the development of accident law generally and is no more justifiable here than it would be in the case of any other useful enterprise or activity."

* * *

[O]ur cases show that the trichotomy is no longer viable because of the complexity and confusion surrounding the numerous exceptions and subclassifications engrafted into it. [The court cited cases in which the outcome depended on whether the negligence was active or passive, whether a landlord had control over a common way; whether the plaintiff was a police officer, whether a defect was known to the occupier, whether the hazard was created by an independent contractor; whether the dangerous condition was obvious, whether an invitee had exceeded the scope of his invitation, whether there were conditions diverting the injured party's attention, whether criminal activity was known or knowable, and whether the hazard was an attractive nuisance.] These exceptions and subclassifications have created a labyrinth of jurisprudence through which the trier of fact must make its way with difficulty to determine liability. Instead of clarifying premises-liability law, these exceptions and subclassifications have created such subtle nuances that a typical landowner can never be sure what constitutes actionable conduct.

* * *

In sum, there are numerous advantages associated with abolishing the trichotomy. First, it is based upon principles which no longer apply to today's modern industrial society. Further, the preceding cases demonstrate that the trichotomy has failed to elucidate the duty a landowner owes to entrants upon his property. Rather, it has caused confusion amongst our citizens and the judiciary—a confusion exaggerated by the numerous exceptions and subclassifications engrafted into it. Lastly, the trichotomy is unjust and unfair because it usurps the jury's function either by allowing the judge to dismiss or decide the case or by forcing the jury to apply mechanical rules instead of focusing upon the pertinent issue of whether the landowner acted reasonably under the circumstances. Thus, we conclude that North Carolina should join the twenty-four other jurisdictions which have modified or abolished the trichotomy in favor of modern negligence principles.

II. THE NEW APPROACH TO PREMISES LIABILITY IN NORTH CAROLINA

Given the numerous advantages associated with abolishing the trichotomy, this Court concludes that we should eliminate the distinction between licensees and invitees by requiring a standard of reasonable care toward all lawful visitors. Adoption of a true negligence standard eliminates the complex, confusing, and unpredictable state of premises-liability law and replaces it with a rule which focuses the jury's attention upon the pertinent issue of whether the landowner acted as a reasonable person would under the circumstances.

In so holding, we note that we do not hold that owners and occupiers of land are now insurers of their premises. Moreover, we do not intend for owners and occupiers of land to undergo unwarranted burdens in maintaining their premises. Rather, we impose upon them only the duty to exercise reasonable care in the maintenance of their premises for the protection of lawful visitors.

Further, we emphasize that we will retain a separate classification for trespassers. We believe that the status of trespasser still maintains viability in modern society, and more importantly, we believe that abandoning the status of trespasser may place an unfair burden on a landowner who has no reason to expect a trespasser's presence. Indeed, whereas both invitees and licensees enter another's land under color of right, a trespasser has no basis for claiming protection beyond refraining from willful injury.

* * *

[P]laintiff Nelson is entitled to a trial at which the jury shall be instructed under the new rule adopted by this opinion. Specifically, the jury must determine whether defendant Freeland fulfilled his duty of reasonable care under the circumstances. This case is therefore remanded to the Court of Appeals for further remand to the Superior Court, Guilford County, for proceedings consistent with this opinion.

Reversed and remanded.

[The vote to reverse was unanimous, but only four justices endorsed the new approach to premises liability cases. The three concurring justices believed plaintiff was an invitee and the defendant violated the duty of care owed an invitee; they voted to reverse on that ground and thought it unnecessary to decide whether to abandon North Carolina's previous method of analyzing premises liability claims.]

NOTES

1. Under the traditional scheme Nelson would have lost had he been classified as a licensee, because North Carolina, together with a handful of other states, allowed licensees to recover only for wilful or wanton conduct and there was no indication Freeland was guilty of that. Most other states do not treat licensees that harshly. They usually permit licensees to recover for occupier negligence if they were injured by a hazard the landowner (1) had reason to know about and (2) could not expect the visitor to discover. These states also might well have denied Nelson recovery on a finding that he could have been expected to discover the stick on his own.

2. As to invitees, the court says landowners under the old regime were held to the full duty of reasonable care. That too may be atypical. Usually it is said landowners owe a duty of reasonable care as to hazards that they should know about and should realize pose an unreasonable risk of harm, if they should expect that invitees will not appreciate the danger or will fail to protect themselves against it. This formula appears to give the landowner a couple of chances to avoid liability in addition to the possibility that he or she will be found to have used reasonable care.

3. Under the usual standards, the difference in duties owed to licensees and invitees is not as great as in the principal case, but is still significant: invitees may recover by showing that the landowner *should* have discovered the risk (e.g., that reasonable care required the occupier to inspect for risks), while licensees win only if they can show that the occupier had *reason to know* of the risk (e.g., was aware of the facts giving rise to the risk).

4. The plaintiff's status is not the only variable in the traditional scheme. In some cases courts have imposed a duty of reasonable care with respect to injuries caused by *activities* on the land but not by passive *conditions*, *artificial* conditions on the land but not *natural* conditions, or injuries occurring on the land but not injuries to passersby. These are among the "subclassifications" that the court in the principal case determined to get rid of, along with the invitee-licensee division.

2. TRESPASSERS

In the preceding case, the court noted that its new "unitary" approach to premises liability would not include trespassers. Most of the states that have abolished limited-duty rules for invitees and licensees have kept them for trespassers. The Third Restatement, however, proposes to extend the full duty of care to all trespassers except those it calls "flagrant trespassers," which it describes as persons whose presence "is so antithetical to the rights of the land possessor to exclusive use and possession of the land that the land possessor should not be subject to liability for failing to exercise the ordinary duty of reasonable care"— burglars, for example. Third Restatement of Torts § 52 cmt. *a.*

The traditional rule is that occupiers are liable to trespassers only for wilful and wanton conduct—not mere negligence. Almost from the beginning, however, the courts made an exception for some trespassing children. In the late 19th and early 20th centuries, railroads maintained spur lines to hundreds of small towns, and at the end of the line they often installed a turntable for the purpose of reversing the direction of a locomotive. These were usually in out-of-the-way places and unguarded. Children were attracted to them because by climbing onto the turntable and tripping a lever, they could take a ride as the device rotated. Unfortunately, the mechanism often severed limbs and mangled bodies. Because the children were trespassers, the railroads could not be held liable for negligently failing to guard against such injuries. But in 1873 the United States Supreme Court held that a railroad could be held liable to a six-year-old boy whose foot was crushed by its turntable. Sioux City & Pacific R. Co. v. Stout, 84 U.S. (17 Wall.) 657, 21 L.Ed. 745 (1873). This precedent eventually came to be explained on the theory that the turntable was an "attractive nuisance"—a dangerous condition that naturally tended to attract children who would not appreciate the danger—and that exempted the child from the usual trespasser rule. Since then, the exception has expanded and is now applied to many hazards that result in injury to trespassing children.

BENNETT v. STANLEY
Supreme Court of Ohio, 2001.
92 Ohio St.3d 35, 748 N.E.2d 41.

PFEIFER, J.

In this case we are called upon to determine what level of duty a property owner owes to a child trespasser. We resolve the question by adopting the attractive nuisance doctrine set forth in Restatement of the Law 2d, Torts (1965), Section 339. We also hold that an adult who attempts to rescue a child from an attractive nuisance assumes the status of the child, and is owed a duty of ordinary care by the property owner.

Factual and Procedural Background

When Rickey G. Bennett, plaintiff-appellant, arrived home in the late afternoon of March 20, 1997, he found his two young daughters crying.

The three-year-old, Kyleigh, told him that "Mommy" and Chance, her five-year-old half-brother, were "drowning in the water." Bennett ran next door to his neighbors' house to find mother and son unconscious in the swimming pool. Both died.

* * *

The Bennetts rented the house next to the Stanleys. The houses were about one hundred feet apart. There was some fencing with an eight-foot gap between the two properties.

The Stanleys were aware that the Bennetts had moved next door and that they had young children. They had seen the children outside unsupervised. Stacey Stanley had once called Chance onto her property to retrieve a dog. The Stanleys testified, however, that they never had any concern about the children getting into the pool. They did not post any warning or "no trespassing" signs on their property.

Rickey Bennett testified that he had told his children to stay away from the pool on the Stanleys' property. He also stated that he had never seen the children playing near the pool.

Kyleigh told her father that she and Chance had been playing at the pool on the afternoon of the tragedy. The sheriff's department concluded that Chance had gone to the pool to look at the frogs and somehow fell into the pool. His mother apparently drowned trying to save him.

Bennett * * * filed a wrongful death and personal injury suit against the Stanleys. The complaint alleged that appellees had negligently maintained an abandoned swimming pool on their property and that appellees' negligence proximately caused the March 20, 1997 drowning of Chance and Cher.

* * *

[The trial court entered a summary judgment in favor of the Stanleys on the ground that Chance and Cher were trespassers on the Stanleys' property and that the Stanleys therefore owed them only a duty to refrain from wanton and willful misconduct. The intermediate appellate court affirmed.]

Law and Analysis

Ohio has long recognized a range of duties for property owners vis-à-vis persons entering their property. Currently, to an invitee the landowner owes a duty "to exercise ordinary care and to protect the invitee by maintaining the premises in a safe condition." To licensees and trespassers, on the other hand, "a landowner owes no duty except to refrain from willful, wanton or reckless conduct which is likely to injure [the licensee or trespasser]." Today, we face the issue of whether child trespassers should become another class of users who are owed a different duty of care.

* * *

[T]his court has never adopted the attractive nuisance doctrine. The doctrine as adopted by numerous states is set forth in Restatement of the Law 2d, Torts (1965), Section 339:

A possessor of land is subject to liability for physical harm to children trespassing thereon caused by an artificial condition upon land if:

(a) the place where the condition exists is one upon which the possessor knows or has reason to know that children are likely to trespass, and

(b) the condition is one of which the possessor knows or has reason to know and which he realizes or should realize will involve an unreasonable risk of death or serious bodily harm to such children, and

(c) the children because of their youth do not discover the condition or realize the risk involved in intermeddling with it or in coming within the area made dangerous by it, and

(d) the utility to the possessor of maintaining the condition and the burden of eliminating the danger are slight as compared with the risk to children involved, and

(e) the possessor fails to exercise reasonable care to eliminate the danger or otherwise to protect the children.

* * *

Ohio is one of only three states that have not either created a special duty for trespassing children or done away with distinctions of duty based upon a person's status as an invitee, licensee, or trespasser.

In more recent years, this court has failed to address the issue of attractive nuisance head-on. In Elliott v. Nagy (1986), 22 Ohio St.3d 58, 22 OBR 77, 488 N.E.2d 853, this court avoided the opportunity to adopt the attractive nuisance doctrine, stating that the case at hand "present[ed] no compelling reasons meriting the adoption of the attractive nuisance doctrine." *Elliott* was a swimming pool case. However, in that case, the child who perished in the pool was visiting her grandparents, who lived one hundred to three hundred feet from the neighbor who owned the pool. Rather than rejecting the doctrine of attractive nuisance, this court simply declined to apply it in *Elliott,* finding that the neighbors could not have foreseen that a nineteen-month-old child would be visiting her grandparents and wander into their yard. The court held in its syllabus:

The attractive nuisance doctrine will not extend tort liability to the owner of a residential swimming pool where the presence of a child who was injured or drowned therein was not foreseeable by the property owner.

That ruling is not contradictory to the attractive nuisance doctrine as set forth in the Restatement of Torts. One of the key elements of the doctrine as defined in the Restatement is that "the place where the condition exists is one upon which the possessor knows or has reason to know that children are likely to trespass." Section 339(a). * * *

* * *

In this case, there is at least a genuine issue of fact regarding the foreseeability of one of the Bennett children entering onto the Stanley property. In *Elliott,* the injured child was a visitor; here, the child resided next door. Reasonable minds could conclude that it was foreseeable that one of the Bennett children would explore around the pool.

Thus, in this case we cannot decline to adopt the attractive nuisance doctrine because of a lack of foreseeability. Any failure to adopt attractive nuisance would be to reject its philosophical underpinnings and would keep Ohio in the small minority of states that do not recognize some form of the doctrine.

Adopting the attractive nuisance doctrine would be merely an incremental change in Ohio law, not out of line with the law that has developed over time. It is an appropriate evolution of the common law. While the present case is by no means a guaranteed winner for the plaintiff, it does present a factual scenario that would allow a jury to consider whether the elements of the cause of action have been fulfilled.

We therefore use this case to adopt the attractive nuisance doctrine contained in Restatement of the Law 2d, Torts (1965), Section 339. In doing so, we do not abandon the differences in duty a landowner owes to the different classes of users. In this case we simply further recognize that children are entitled to a greater level of protection than adults are. We remove the "distinctions without differences" between the dangerous instrumentality doctrine and the attractive nuisance doctrine. Whether an apparatus or a condition of property is involved, the key element should be whether there is a foreseeable, "unreasonable risk of death or serious bodily harm to children." Restatement, Section 339(b).

The Restatement's version of the attractive nuisance doctrine balances society's interest in protecting children with the rights of landowners to enjoy their property. Even when a landowner is found to have an attractive nuisance on his or her land, the landowner is left merely with the burden of acting with ordinary care. A landowner does not automatically become liable for any injury a child trespasser may suffer on that land.

The requirement of foreseeability is built into the doctrine. The landowner must know or have reason to know that children are likely to trespass upon the part of the property that contains the dangerous condition. See Section 339(a). Moreover, the landowner's duty "does not extend to those conditions the existence of which is obvious even to children and the risk of which should be fully realized by them." Also, if the condition of the property that poses the risk is essential to the landowner, the doctrine would not apply:

"The public interest in the possessor's free use of his land for his own purposes is of great significance. A particular condition is, therefore, regarded as not involving unreasonable risk to trespassing children unless it involves a grave risk to them which could be obviated without any serious interference with the possessor's legitimate use of his land." *Id.* at cmt. *n.*

We are satisfied that the Restatement view effectively harmonizes the competing societal interests of protecting children and preserving property rights. * * * We are not a rural society any longer, our neighbors live closer, and our use of our own property affects others more than it once did.

Despite our societal changes, children are still children. They still learn through their curiosity. They still have developing senses of judgment. They still do not always appreciate danger. They still need protection by adults. Protecting children in a changing world requires the common law to adapt. Today, we make that change.

[The court held that although the attractive nuisance doctrine is not ordinarily applicable to adults, it may be invoked by an adult injured while trying to rescue a child from an attractive nuisance, and the Stanleys therefore could be found to have owed a duty of ordinary care to Cher Bennett.]

Accordingly, we reverse the judgment of the court of appeals and remand the cause to the trial court.

DOUGLAS, RESNICK and FRANCIS E. SWEENEY, SR. JJ., concur.

[MOYER, C.J., concurred with respect to the Stanleys's potential liability for Chance's death but dissented with respect to the claim arising from his mother's death.]

COOK, J., dissenting.

* * *

The procedural history of this case shows that the Bennetts, at every stage of the litigation, have deliberately declined to raise the attractive nuisance doctrine as a theory of the Stanleys' liability. The Bennetts have accordingly waived any argument for adopting the attractive nuisance doctrine.

* * *

Admittedly, the briefs submitted to this court are not entirely devoid of arguments concerning the attractive nuisance doctrine and, in particular, Section 339 of the Restatement of Torts. But these arguments appear only in the brief of *amicus curiae,* Ohio Academy of Trial Lawyers, and in the Bennetts' reply brief. Neither brief properly brings the issue before us. An *amicus curiae* is not a party to the case and may not interject issues and claims not raised by the parties. And a reply brief cannot raise a new issue that the appellants failed to raise in their merit brief.

Although the majority offers compelling reasons for adopting the attractive nuisance doctrine, it is not appropriate to establish this groundbreaking rule in the case at bar. The Bennetts chose to litigate avenues other than the attractive nuisance doctrine and successfully petitioned this court for review on those issues. The majority ignores the Bennetts' legal claims in favor of reaching an issue that the Bennetts waived in the lower courts. I would address only the propositions of law actually raised by the Bennetts and affirm the judgment of the court of appeals for the reasons stated in its opinion.

* * *

LUNDBERG STRATTON, J., concurs in the foregoing dissenting opinion.

NOTES

1. Note that the plaintiffs in the preceding case did not invoke the attractive nuisance doctrine, at least until the Ohio Academy of Trial Lawyers urged it in an amicus brief. That is probably not surprising, in view of nearly 100 years of consistent nonrecognition of the doctrine by the Ohio courts; a litigant may be reluctant to try the judge's patience by challenging a well-settled proposition. And, as the dissent points out, courts normally will not consider a theory not pursued by the litigants. So courts may not get an opportunity to change a deeply entrenched rule unless they are willing to bend their usual rules a bit. The majority in the principal case resolved to "use this case to adopt the attractive nuisance doctrine" without addressing the dissent's point.

2. In some states there are other exceptions for "discovered trespassers," "tolerated trespassers," and "habitual trespassers." The drafters of the Third Restatement cited the proliferation of exceptions as evidence that imposing a general duty of care toward trespassers comes closer to reflecting current reality than the conventional "categorical" treatment of them. See Restatement (Third) of Torts § 51 cmt. c(2).

————

3. STATUTORY PROTECTION OF LANDOWNERS

Currents sometimes flow in opposite directions in tort law, and landowner liability is a case in point. While the Third Restatement and many of the state courts have been expanding potential liabilities by abandoning the categorical limited-duty rules or creating exceptions to them, many legislatures have been curtailing landowner liability. Among the most common of these statutory limitations are "Recreational Use Statutes," one of which is applied in the following case.

MacVANE v. S.D. WARREN CO., LLC

United States District Court, Maine, 2009.
641 F.Supp.2d 54.

D. BROCK HORNBY, DISTRICT JUDGE.

* * *

On August 18, 2006, thirteen-year-old Mackenzie MacVane and two friends went swimming in the Presumpscot River near the Eel Weir Dam [owned by the S.D. Warren Co.]. Mackenzie decided that he wanted to jump from the Eel Weir Dam building into the river below. He had successfully completed such a jump from the building's roof the day before while swimming with his older brother and his brother's friend. Mackenzie gained access to the premises through [a] hole in the perimeter fence. He then climbed stairs to the topmost part of the main dam building. At the top of a flight of stairs, Mackenzie encountered and scaled another chain-link fence that was blocking his access to the main building's rooftop. In contrast with the perimeter fence, this roof fence was not topped with barbed wire, but the fence gate was chained and padlocked. To access the roof of a tower-like building adjoining the main building, Mackenzie then climbed an antenna pole using horizontal brackets extending off of the pole as footholds. Unlike the preceding day, Mackenzie did not jump from the roof of this tower, but instead chose to leap from a catwalk platform extending off of the side of the tower building, roughly forty feet above the Presumpscot River. To reach the catwalk, Mackenzie had to drop down a short distance from the tower's rooftop onto the platform. Three 11,000 volt electrical transmission lines were connected to the tower building, attaching above the metal catwalk platform. When Mackenzie stood to jump into the river, he backed into one of the power lines. The shock knocked him off of the catwalk into the water below, resulting in his death.

Before Mackenzie's accident, S.D. Warren was on notice that swimmers, including children, frequented the area near the Eel Weir Dam facility. The hole through which Mackenzie gained access to the premises had been present for at least a few months, and S.D. Warren had knowledge of repeated holes in the perimeter fence in the past. Furthermore, three years prior to Mackenzie's accident, S.D. Warren commissioned a private risk consulting company to conduct a security assessment of the Eel Weir station in Standish and another facility in a different town, Gorham, Maine. This report stated that:

> [T]he highest occurrence of crime at the site * * * is trespassing. This is a major issue * * * as the site is very tempting for trespassers. The site can also be very dangerous for these people, therefore this simple misdemeanor must be taken very seriously. Damaged fence and graffiti indicates that the traffic in and around the dams is a common occurrence. Reports from the Line Crew indicate that the

fences are continuously being mended due to unauthorized entry attempts.

The report pointed out that numerous holes in the perimeter fence at the Eel Weir facility "indicate[d] a problem with unauthorized access," and that these holes might "indicate to potential trespassers that [S.D. Warren] is not actively trying to keep people out." Moreover, with respect to the other facility being assessed (in Gorham, Maine), the report expressly noted the potential for the type of accident that claimed Mackenzie's life:

> The roof of the building has been a regular issue as youths access the roof to jump into the water below. The biggest problem with this access is the presence of the electric lines on the roof of the building. If a person makes contact with these lines serious injury is possible. This has occurred in the past and is a major concern.

For the Eel Weir Dam facility, the risk assessment company recommended that S.D. Warren "install more substantial outriggers on the side of the building and fencing on the roof above the stairway to ensure a person could not climb to the roof from this stairway."

Private security officers patrolled the Eel Weir Dam property multiple times daily. Signs were posted throughout the Eel Weir Dam premises, including warnings of "No Trespassing" and "Danger High Voltage." However, Mackenzie may not have seen these signs on his path to the catwalk, because warning signs were not posted on the side of the building on which Mackenzie was swimming. Although a sign reading "Danger High Voltage Keep Out" was posted on a door directly across from where Mackenzie emerged through the hole in the fence, and an additional sign reading "Danger High Voltage Keep Out" was posted on a door leading into the tower building near the antenna that Mackenzie climbed to get onto the tower roof, Mackenzie or other children may have understood the signs to refer to danger only *inside* the building through the doors on which the signs were posted. There were no warning signs expressly indicating that the cables attached to the tower above the catwalk were active electrical power lines.

ANALYSIS

Maine's Recreational Use statute provides:

> An owner * * * of premises does not have a duty of care to keep the premises safe for entry or use by others for recreational * * * activities or to give warning of any hazardous condition, use, structure or activity on these premises to persons entering for those purposes. This subsection applies regardless of whether the owner * * * has given permission to another to pursue recreational * * * activities on the premises.

14 M.R.S.A. § 159–A(2). The statute defines "premises" as "improved and unimproved lands, private ways, roads, any buildings or structures on those lands and waters standing on, flowing through or adjacent to those

lands." The statute expressly includes "swimming" in the definition of recreational activities, and states that the statute's coverage "includes entry of, * * * use of and passage over premises in order to pursue these activities." The Maine Law Court has held that the statute protects owners of commercial property and bars the claims even of children based on the common law doctrine of attractive nuisance.

Here, Mackenzie's swimming in the Presumpscot River, adjacent to S.D. Warren's land and the Eel Weir Dam, was a recreational activity as expressly defined in the statute. Furthermore, the S.D. Warren facility and land were "premises" under the statute. Mackenzie entered and passed over S.D. Warren's premises in order to pursue his swimming activities in the river, and thus the events as described fell within the parameters of the statute.

The MacVanes attempt to bypass the statute on two grounds: "Either * * * the statute does not apply to any property that poses an unreasonable risk of death or serious bodily injury to children, or * * * ownership of such property inadequately protected against a child's trespass is by definition wilful." I deal with both arguments.

As to the first, the statute does not exempt categorically "property that poses an unreasonable risk of death or serious bodily injury to children," and I decline to read such a limitation into the text. See *Stanley,* 541 A.2d at 952 (explaining that "[w]hen the language of the [Recreational Use] statute is clear and unambiguous, [courts] will give the statute its plain meaning," and refusing to read in a limitation that was not specifically listed in "[t]he exceptions expressed in the statute to the rule of limited liability"). The Maine Law Court has expressly advised that the immunity provision of the Recreational Use statute should be broadly construed. Dickinson v. Clark, 767 A.2d 303, 305 (Me.2001).

[The judge reviewed numerous Maine cases rejecting claims that defendants had been guilty of wilful and wanton conduct.]

Under Maine law, then, failing to mend a hole in a barbed-wire-topped perimeter fence is insufficient to rise to willful or malicious conduct. I cannot accept the MacVanes' argument that, under the Recreational Use statute, where property "poses an unreasonable risk of death or serious bodily injury to children, ownership of such property inadequately protected against a child's trespass is by definition willful." * * * Here, although S.D. Warren failed to place warning signs on the river side of the Eel Weir Dam facility or to follow all the recommendations of the risk consultants' report, it did post multiple signs, including signs describing high voltage danger on doorways visible to Mackenzie in his ascent to the tower rooftop. Furthermore, S.D. Warren installed a second padlocked fence blocking access to the roof of the main building, and hired a private security patrol to monitor the premises. Such precautions, although they were insufficient to prevent Mackenzie's tragic death, belie any argument that S.D. Warren's conduct was willful or malicious. It had taken steps to prevent access to the roof and to warn of dangerous high voltage. That

S.D. Warren knew or had reason to know that children were trespassing into the Eel Weir Dam property is alone insufficient to find that S.D. Warren acted willfully or maliciously under Maine law.

Because of Maine's Recreational Use statute, I grant summary judgment to the defendant.

SO ORDERED.

NOTE

Recreational use statutes were initially proposed as a means of encouraging owners to open their land to the public for such uses as hunting and fishing. They generally do not apply to commercial recreational facilities or to users who have paid for the right to use the premises. But as the principal case indicates, they are often used to cut off liability in contexts that have little to do with encouraging recreation. The Maine statute, for example, is not limited to *authorized* recreational uses. It applies to "recreational activities conducted out-of-doors, including, but not limited to, hunting, fishing, trapping, camping, environmental education and research, hiking, recreational caving, sight-seeing, operating snow-traveling and all-terrain vehicles, skiing, hang-gliding, noncommercial aviation activities, dog sledding, equine activities, boating, sailing, canoeing, rafting, biking, picnicking, swimming or activities involving the harvesting or gathering of forest, field or marine products." M.R.S.A. § 195–A(1)(B).

CHAPTER VII

DAMAGES

■ ■ ■

A. INTRODUCTION

The law of damages is complex and demanding. It is addressed in depth in upper-level law school courses on remedies. This chapter does no more than introduce the general principles and examine selected problems that are particularly important in modern torts litigation.

The three broad categories of damages that may be awarded in torts cases are nominal damages, compensatory damages, and punitive damages.

The cause of action for some intentional torts—e.g., battery, assault, false imprisonment, and trespass to land—is complete without proof of actual damages. When a plaintiff wins such a case without proving any damages, the court awards *nominal damages,* which may be defined as "a trivial sum of money awarded to a litigant who has established a cause of action but has not established that he is entitled to compensatory damages." Restatement (Second) of Torts § 907.

Compensatory damages "are the damages awarded to a person as compensation, indemnity, or restitution for harm sustained by him." Restatement (Second) of Torts § 903. The basic theory of compensatory damages in tort cases is restoration of the plaintiff to his or her pre-injury condition, to the extent that an award of money can do that. (By way of rough contrast, a basic theory of damages for breach of contract is said to be giving the plaintiff the reasonably expectable benefits of the bargain.)

In causes of action based on negligence and strict liability, the plaintiff must prove compensatory damages as part of the prima facie case. This is true of some intentional torts, as well. Even when the plaintiff can establish a cause of action without proving damages, it is rarely worthwhile to do so. In practice, the amount of damages is often the most important and intensely contested part of the case.

Punitive damages "are damages, other than compensatory or nominal damages, awarded against a person to punish him for his outrageous conduct and to deter him and others like him from similar conduct in the future." Restatement (Second) of Torts § 908(1).

We do not treat damages for harms to property in this chapter because that subject is too intricate to be covered briefly and our primary focus in this book is on torts resulting in personal injury or death.

B. COMPENSATORY DAMAGES IN PERSONAL INJURY CASES

There are three main types of compensatory damages in personal injury cases:

medical (and related) expenses (past and future);

loss of earning capacity (past and future); and

physical and mental pain and suffering (past and future).

The first two categories are sometimes called "special damages" and the third category is sometimes called "general damages." The common law meaning of these terms has become debased, but in some jurisdictions they still have specific statutory meanings and consequences. Today one is more likely to encounter the terms "pecuniary" or "economic" damages, referring to the first two categories, and "nonpecuniary" or "noneconomic" damages referring to pain and suffering and other losses that cannot be easily measured in dollars.

Damages issues may come up on appeal in any of the procedural contexts discussed in Chapter I. One highly visible impact of the law of damages on torts cases is the judge's instructions to the jury. A fairly typical jury instruction is set forth below. Like all such pattern jury charges, the following—which is a modification of those promulgated by the California Bar Association—will be tailored and streamlined by the trial judge to fit the circumstances of the particular case.

If you find that plaintiff is entitled to a verdict against defendant, you must then award plaintiff damages in an amount that will reasonably compensate her for each of the following elements of claimed injury:

(a) The reasonable value of medical, hospital, and nursing care, services, and supplies reasonably required and actually given in the treatment of the plaintiff to the present time, and the present cash value of the reasonable value of similar items reasonably certain to be required and given in the future.

(b) The reasonable value of working time lost to date. In determining this amount, you should consider evidence of plaintiff's earning capacity, her earnings, how she ordinarily occupied herself, and what she was reasonably certain to have earned in the time lost if she had not been injured. A person's ability to work may have a monetary value even though she is not employed by another. In determining this amount, you should also consider evidence of the reasonable value of services performed by others in doing things for the plaintiff which, except for her injury, plaintiff would ordinarily do for herself.

(c) The present cash value of earning capacity reasonably certain to be lost in the future as a result of the injury in question.

(d) Reasonable compensation for any pain, discomfort, fears, anxiety, and other mental and emotional distress suffered by the plaintiff and of which her injury was a proximate cause, and for similar physical, mental, and emotional suffering reasonably certain to be experienced in the future from the same cause. No definite standard or method of calculation is prescribed by law by which to fix reasonable compensation for pain and suffering. Nor is the opinion of any witness required as to the amount of such reasonable compensation. Furthermore, the argument of counsel as to the amount of damages is not evidence of reasonable compensation. In making an award for pain and suffering you shall exercise your authority with calm and reasonable judgment and the damages you fix shall be just and reasonable in the light of the evidence.

RODRIGUEZ v. McDONNELL DOUGLAS CORP.

California Court of Appeal, 1978.
87 Cal.App.3d 626, 151 Cal.Rptr. 399.

JEFFERSON, JUSTICE.

[Plaintiff Richard Rodriguez was a sprinkler fitter's apprentice for a fire protection company engaged as a subcontractor on a major construction project to modify a McDonnell Douglas hangar. Through the negligence of another subcontractor and the general contractor, a 630–pound pipe fell on Rodriguez, striking the back of his helmet, his back, and his legs. The accident happened in 1970. At the conclusion of the trial in 1975, the jury exonerated McDonnell Douglas but found the negligent contractors liable to Rodriguez for $4,235,996.* Because the verdict was general, it did not specify how much of the award was for each element of damage. On appeal the defendants argued that the trial judge should have granted their motion for a new trial on the ground (among others) that the size of the award suggested that the jury acted on passion and prejudice.]

* * *

VI.

THE ISSUE OF WHETHER THE DAMAGES AWARDED WERE EXCESSIVE

A.   The Nature of the Injuries

As the contention is made on appeal that the award of damages was excessive, we summarize here the relevant medical testimony presented on behalf of plaintiff Richard Rodriguez. Eight doctors described to the jury various aspects of the massive injuries sustained by the plaintiff Richard and problems encountered as a result thereof.

---

* $183,874 of this was set aside to repay the State Workers' Compensation Fund for benefits it provided Rodriguez.—Ed.

Prior to the accident, Richard Rodriguez had been a happy and healthy young man 22 years of age. He was approximately six feet tall, and engaged in an active life with family and friends. He had been married to Mary Anne, aged 20 years, for sixteen months.

Dr. Christos Papatheodorou, a neurosurgeon, treated Rodriguez from the date of the accident until March 1971. The plaintiff's brain had been severely injured by the falling pipe; his spine was fractured and there was substantial, irreparable damage to the spinal cord. Richard's mind gradually became clear, although he does not remember the events surrounding the accident. It was Dr. Papatheodorou's task to advise Richard and his wife Mary Anne, that Richard would never walk again nor would he ever regain any function in the lower part of his body. Plaintiff Richard is triplegic as a result of this accident, paralyzed from the middle of the chest down. He has lost all bladder, bowel and sexual function. In addition, there are complications associated with the left side of his entire body, ranging from his left eye to a left arm which is practically useless.

The consequences of the spinal cord injury and the resultant paralysis have been tremendously heavy. Shortly after his admission to the hospital after the accident, Richard developed bleeding ulcers which were life-threatening. Dr. John Sweeney, a surgeon, performed a partial gastectomy, removing part of his patient's stomach.

Surgery was later performed on plaintiff's left hand by an orthopedic surgeon, Dr. Eric Widell, in an effort to restore some function. The "tendon transplant surgery" resulted in limited improvement in the left hand, but the arm is still significantly impaired.

Dr. Alan Shanberg, a urologist, was called upon in December 1970, to take charge of bladder, kidney and bowel problems. Richard was experiencing serious infection in these areas. The first surgery performed to provide an alternative method of disposing of urine was a suprapubic cystotomy which involved placing a tube in the stomach, to which a bag could be attached. The operation was unsuccessful. It was then necessary to form an urethroileo conduit, and an ileostomy was performed. This is a method of urinary diversion effected by opening a hole in the stomach, a stoma, to which a bag-type "artificial bladder" is attached. At some point in time, it may be necessary to repeat this surgical procedure, if the stoma should close. Richard requires enemas and laxatives relative to bowel care; there have been problems with impaction from time to time. Kidney stones and other kidney complications regularly occur in patients with spinal cord injuries; prevention requires a carefully prescribed diet.

In addition, a major area of concern to a triplegic are ulcerated pressure sores, decubitis. Simple weightbearing produces these sores; while the triplegic cannot feel them, such sores may extend from the surface of the skin down to the bone, and osteomyelitis may develop, requiring amputation of the legs. The triplegic must shift position constantly and must avoid such small pressures as those resulting from wrinkled clothing. Dr. Billy De Shazo, a plastic surgeon, testified that he had operated on three extensive pressure sores developed by Richard, plugging the holes with skin taken from other parts of the body.

Since 1973, Dr. Frederick Amerongen has been the neurosurgeon who has cared for plaintiff Richard. Certain procedures were undertaken to block the constant pain in plaintiff's left arm. Surgery was performed to remove ganglia, but the operation was not successful. Pain remains, particularly when the arm is cold. Dr. Amerongen testified that Richard has clonics (spasms) beyond his control on occasion. Richard must wear a support corset in order to sit up; he cannot bathe himself, nor can he dress and undress himself.

Thomas Gucker III, M.D., an orthopedic specialist, has been the coordinator of Richard's medical care. He operated on Richard to remove a bone deposit which had formed near the right hip; he has also treated Richard with a brine pool immersion technique to heal recurring pressure sores. Dr. Gucker enumerated the various medical specialists who must see Richard several times a year for the rest of his life.

Psychiatrist James McGinnis testified at trial concerning two in-depth interviews he had conducted with plaintiff and his wife, Mary Anne, in 1973 and just prior to trial in 1975. Richard expressed his desire to live. While he and his wife have remained devoted to one another, the details of their daily lives involve matters physically and psychologically overwhelming. By 1975, the burden had become evident.

Several of the treating physicians expressed the opinion that plaintiff Richard has a normal life expectancy, despite his injuries. However, from the date of the accident to time of trial, Richard had been hospitalized fourteen times.

B. The Amount of the Award

Defendants assert that the size of the award suggests that the jury acted on the basis of passion and prejudice. Upon appeal, we apply the familiar rule that "[a] reviewing court must uphold an award of damages whenever possible and all presumptions are in favor of the judgment." The fact that an award may set a precedent by its size does not in and of itself render it suspect. The determination of the jury can only be assessed by examination of the particular circumstances involved. It was cogently stated in Niles v. City of San Rafael, (1974) 42 Cal.App.3d 230, 241, 116 Cal.Rptr. 733, 739: "The determination of damages is primarily a factual matter on which the inevitable wide differences of opinion do not call for the intervention of appellate courts. An appellate court, in reviewing the amount of damages, must determine every conflict in the evidence in respondent's favor and give him the benefit of every reasonable inference. An appellate court may not interfere with an award unless 'the verdict is so large that, at first blush, it shocks the conscience and suggests passion, prejudice or corruption on the part of the jury.'"

In *Niles*, an eleven-year old boy had been rendered mute and quadriplegic due to the negligence of the defendants. The award of damages was

$4,025,000. As is true in the case at bench, such items as lost earnings and the need for attendant care were properly considered by the jury in the *Niles* case. It is argued here that since plaintiff Richard Rodriguez is not as limited in movement as was Kelly Niles, the plaintiff in Niles, an award larger than the *Niles* award is subject to criticism. On the other side, seeking to justify the award in the case before us, plaintiffs point to other large personal injury judgments obtained in specific cases in California and in other jurisdictions. This species of argument is not helpful to a reviewing court. For us to measure the validity of an award of damages by making a comparison with other cases would constitute a "serious invasion into the realm of factfinding" specifically disapproved of by the California Supreme Court. There is no merit in a principle that would countenance measuring a monetary distinction to be applied to triplegia, as opposed to quadriplegia.

The injuries sustained herein can only logically be described as catastrophic. Plaintiff Richard was a young person just beginning a happy and productive life. The power to enjoy sexual relations and to father children has been taken from him. The ability to take care of personal needs is not his to enjoy. Without dispute, the record establishes the unalterable tragic consequences of the injuries the intense pain and suffering and the recurrent need for hospitalization as well as the permanent limitations all of this places on the task of just existing and living. As difficult as it may appear to place a monetary value on such a loss, the trier of fact, under our judicial system, must do so. We conclude that the award in this case was within the jury's discretion.

C.   The Economic Evidence

Defendants challenge the amount of the award of damages on the ground that the evidence offered by the plaintiffs with respect to wages lost by Richard Rodriguez from the date of the accident to time of trial, and with respect to the loss of future earning capacity, militates against the sufficiency of the evidence to support the judgment.

Plaintiffs did not introduce evidence of the actual amount plaintiff Richard had earned as an apprentice sprinkler fitter prior to the accident. We know of no rule of law that requires that a plaintiff establish the amount of his actual earnings at the time of the injury in order to obtain recovery for loss of wages although, obviously, the amount of such earnings would be helpful to the jury in particular situations.

In the instant case, Richard was an apprentice, without an economic track record of any consequence; information concerning actual earnings at the time of the accident could well have been misleading. The plaintiffs did introduce into evidence the union contract applicable to Richard's employment, which showed, along with other information, the annual increase in wages earned by sprinkler fitters from 1970 forward. This financial data was offered on the assumption that plaintiff would have continued to work at his chosen trade had he not been injured, a reasonable assumption to make.

With respect to loss of future earnings, the decisional law and other authorities carefully point out that "[l]oss of earning power is an element of general damages which can be inferred from the nature of the injury, without proof of actual earnings or income either before or after the injury, and damages in this respect are awarded for the loss of ability thereafter to earn money."

"[O]ne's earning capacity is not a matter of actual earnings. The impairment of the power to work is an injury wholly apart from any pecuniary benefit the exercise of such power may bring and if the injury has lessened this power, the plaintiff is entitled to recover. In short, the test is not what the plaintiff would have earned, but what he could have earned." The important distinction just discussed is particularly applicable when the plaintiff is a student or an apprentice.

* * *

In *Niles v. City of San Rafael, supra,* the award was based upon statistics of the United States Department of Labor showing the average lifetime earnings of an American male.

In the case before us, in addition to the evidence of the union contract (past and present), the plaintiffs offered the testimony of an expert economist, Robert Edward Schultz, a professor at the graduate school of business at the University of Southern California. He possessed solid educational qualifications and had taught at the University of Southern California since 1952. Schultz's expert qualifications included varied experience as an economic consultant and having been involved as an expert witness in considerable litigation, making projections of future economic trends.

Schultz was asked to make certain economic projections concerning Richard's lost earnings, both past and future, based upon certain assumptions. He had been provided with the union data; it showed that in 1969, a journeyman sprinkler fitter was earning $8.69 per hour, excluding fringe benefits, while in 1976, the same individual would earn $14.66 per hour, exclusive of fringe benefits. Schultz determined that the wages of such a worker had increased during the 1969–1976 period at a rate of 9 percent per year. Schultz also took into account the fact that an apprentice sprinkler fitter's wages constituted a percentage of the journeyman's wages, a percentage which would increase as the apprentice progressed from one apprentice period to the next.

Schultz assumed that Richard would have continued as an apprentice during the period of past lost wages (from 1970 until time of trial) and also assumed that he would have been fully employed; Schultz arrived at a figure for wages lost to time of trial of $111,646. No objection to this testimony was made by the defendants.

With respect to future loss of wages—loss of earning capacity— Schultz arrived at an annual base wage for 1975 of $16.62 per hour, including fringe benefits, totaling $34,569 per year. He then projected this figure into the future on the basis that (1) Richard would have become a journeyman in 1976; (2) he would have worked at his trade for 35 years until he was 62 years of age; (3) he would have received wages increasing annually at a rate of 7 percent; and (4) the [future wage estimates should be] discounted at a rate of 6 percent. Schultz also assumed that, had he not been injured, Richard would have worked full time, 40 hours per week, 52 weeks of the year (including a paid vacation period), with the exception of the year 1975, as the evidence had established that during that particular year, a 32–hour week was the norm.

By projecting the union wages at a strict hourly rate, without allowance for overtime or "moonlighting" (secondary employment capacity), Schultz calculated that by the year 2010, Richard would have had annual earnings of over $300,000. Schultz arrived at a lost earnings figure, or a loss of earning capacity, of $1,440,144. No objection was made by the defendants to this testimony given on direct examination by Schultz.

On cross-examination, the defendants explored with Schultz the assumptions upon which he had made his calculations. It developed that Schultz had not been informed of what Richard's actual earnings had been prior to the accident, nor did he know what were the average annual earnings of a sprinkler fitter, past or present. Defendants elicited from Schultz the estimate that, in the construction industry generally, the average worker was only employed in Southern California 80 percent of the year at the union rate. Schultz testified that he had not taken this circumstance into account when making his calculations; he did not know if sprinkler fitters followed the construction industry average, commenting that the nature of the work (often inside buildings) was not as subject to weather limitations as some construction work would be. Defendants also cross-examined Schultz with respect to the potential impact on future earnings of strikes, use of nonunion labor and business recession.

* * *

[D]efendants moved to strike the testimony of Schultz, on the ground that his assumptions in making his calculations had no evidentiary support.

* * *

[W]e find no error in the trial court's ruling refusing to strike the testimony of Schultz; the cross-examination of Schultz exposed the full-employment fallacy upon which his calculations were based, and there was no timely objection to his testimony given on direct or cross-examination; in addition, the jury verdict was not returned in a form from which it can be determined what actual sum the jury allocated for Richard's earnings loss. Unlike *Niles,* supra, the jury was not required to specify particular sums for the various items of damage sought by plaintiffs. But the jury may well have rejected the amounts claimed by the plaintiffs as lost earnings; the verdict was considerably less than the total requested.

Furthermore, the gravity of the injuries and the pain and suffering of the plaintiff are of such magnitude that the award is easily justified.

D. Attendant Care

Defendants assert that the jury should not have been provided, as it was, with information concerning the past and future cost of attendant care, because the evidence was insufficient to establish the need for such care on the part of plaintiff Richard. This assertion lacks merit.

Dr. Gucker testified that Richard should presently have one and one-half shifts of attendant care, and that, when he reached 45 years of age, two shifts of attendant care were indicated. Dr. McGinnis, a psychiatrist, expressed an opinion that, in years to come, the mental health of Richard and his wife, Mary Anne, would be protected, as would be their interpersonal relationship, if an attendant could provide certain personal care for plaintiff, particularly with respect to problems of bladder and bowel.

From the date of the accident to the time of trial, with the exception of periods of hospitalization, 24–hour–a–day attendant care has been provided to Richard by his wife, Mary Anne. For this care, Richard has received an allowance of $280 per month from the State [Workers' Compensation] Fund. It is not too clear from the record why Mary Anne has provided such care without outside assistance; she testified that she had, on occasion, attempted, without success, to find an adequate attendant for her husband. While all of the doctors who testified expressed their admiration for this wife's devotion in caring for her husband, there was evidence that the burden placed upon her has become overwhelming. Dr. Amerongen testified that just prior to trial he had hospitalized Mary Anne for a few days of sleep.

We reject the premise that the cost of attendant care, past or future, should not have been an item for consideration by the jury because of the presence of Mary Anne. It is not part of her duties as a wife to render 24–hour–a–day attendant care. As to past care, the jury was entitled to determine that the sum of $280 per month was not anywhere near enough for the services rendered, in light of the evidence presented by plaintiffs on this issue.

No attack has been made here on the estimate testified to by Schultz concerning the cost of attendant care from the time of the accident to the time of trial, based upon the wage history of such attendants during that period of time, $124,586.

Projecting present wages into the future ($4.50 per hour) and assuming a 5 percent annual increase in those wages, reduced to present value, the economist expressed an opinion that a fund of $693,733 would be required to provide one and one-half shifts of attendant care per day for plaintiff Richard's life (43.8 years from time of trial); a total of $924,978 would be required if another half-shift were added.

* * *

[T]he necessity for attendant care and the reasonable value thereof are questions for jury determination.

* * *

E. *Admissibility of Evidence of Inflation*

It is claimed that, in making its award, it was improper for the jury to take into account inflationary trends. California law has long approved consideration of the factor of inflation as a matter of economic reality. No claim has been made here that the percentages employed by plaintiffs' economist in varying contexts had no basis in fact. We therefore reject this claim of error asserted by defendants.

F. *The Claim that the Awards Were Excessive as a Result of Inflammatory Evidence*

Defendants contend that the jury was prejudicially affected by the introduction into evidence of certain photographs of plaintiff Richard and by the receipt into evidence of certain testimony concerning Richard's physical condition.

We have examined the photographs which were introduced into evidence. The claim is made that they were "gory," "gruesome" depictions, unnecessarily cumulative of other evidence concerning plaintiff Richard's injuries. While they are not pleasant photographs, they served a relevant function in the fact-finding process. These photographs were relevant on the issue of the nature and extent of plaintiff Richard's injuries to guide the jury in making a fair assessment of adequate compensation for such injuries. The photographs show different portions of the body of plaintiff Richard—the scars, the pressure sores, the opening in his stomach, and the useless legs.

* * *

It is also asserted that the testimony of eight doctors was unnecessarily cumulative. The assertion is without merit. Each doctor called by the plaintiffs testified in substantial part to different aspects of the medical care that had been provided from the time of the accident to time of trial. That testimony, too, was highly relevant on the issue of damages.

Finally, it is asserted that undue emphasis was placed on plaintiff Rodriguez' impotence, pressure sores, and the problems resulting from disfunction of bladder and bowel. We know of no delicate way of approaching these subjects, with which plaintiffs must concern themselves on a daily basis.

[The court concluded that the amount of the award was reasonable in light of the grievousness of Richard's injuries, and that the defendants had made no showing that it was the product of passion and prejudice.]

NOTES

1. As the principal case indicates, a general verdict reveals nothing about the components of the jury's award. Often the jury is asked to return a special verdict that shows the jury's allocation. Here is a fairly typical example of a special verdict on damages:

GENERAL DAMAGES

Pain & suffering, both physical and mental	$ _____
Physical impairment	$ _____
Permanent disability	$ _____
Loss of enjoyment of life	$ _____

SPECIAL DAMAGES

Past lost wages	$ _____
Future lost wages/loss of earning capacity	$ _____
Past medical expenses	$ _____
Future medical expenses	$ _____

Whatever the verdict form, the trial judge must also give the jury instructions of the sort quoted at the beginning of this section. If the judge gives the jury a form of this type, he or she can tie each instruction to the appropriate blank on the form.

2. Note that the form above contains a blank for "loss of enjoyment of life." That category of damages is considered in Banks v. Sunshine Hospital, infra p. 295.

3. *Reducing awards.* If the trial or appellate court believes that the award is excessive, it usually has three options: grant a new trial on all issues, grant a new trial on the damage issues only, or order a remittitur, whereby a (partial or complete) new trial is ordered unless the plaintiff agrees to remit a specified amount of the award. If a court grants a remittitur, the plaintiff is under considerable pressure to accept, even if the plaintiff thinks the amount left after remittitur is too low, because if the plaintiff declines he or she faces new trial (or appeal) before a court that has already expressed a view as to what the maximum award should be. Moreover, plaintiffs' lawyers generally dislike new trials on damage issues only, because in those the focus of attention is on the plaintiff and his or her claimed losses rather than on the defendant's misconduct. Some jurisdictions require a complete new trial on all issues even if the error in the first trial related only to the amount of damages.

Present Value

Note that the economic expert's projection of Rodriguez's loss of future earning capacity was "discounted at a rate of 6 per cent" and also that the projected cost of future attendant care was "reduced to present value." These are both references to a standard accounting adjustment reflecting the time value of money. When he collects the judgment, Rodriguez will receive a lump sum, part of it representing compensation for future lost earning capacity and future costs of attendant care. As the court observes, in arriving at the estimates for such future losses, it is appropriate to take expectations about inflation into account. But they also need to be adjusted downward, to take into account the fact that Rodriguez will receive all the money immediately.

Suppose, for example, his award includes $10,000 for attendant care for the year 1998; if the judgment is paid in 1978, he has the use of the money for 20 years before he has to spend it on attendants. If he invests it prudently, the $10,000 will have increased substantially when the time comes to pay the attendants. For example, if he invests the $10,000 in U.S. Treasury bonds at 6 per cent interest and invests each year's dividends similarly, he will have $32,071 in 20 years (ignoring the tax payable on the dividends). This is simply the effect of compounding interest; each year he earns interest not only on the $10,000 but also on the previous years' earnings.

Discounting to present value is the reverse of compounding interest. The question it addresses is, "what sum of money, awarded today, will equal $10,000 in 20 years?" The answer depends, of course, on the rate of interest that the money can be expected to return over the 20–year period. This rate is called the discount rate. The higher that rate, the less the money that needs to be awarded today to reach the $10,000 goal in 20 years.

Once a discount rate is chosen, reduction to present value is a purely mathematical task. For most lawyers, the easiest way to make this calculation is to use a present value table, which can be found in most standard financial reference books, or a financial calculator that has a present value function. (In our example, if we use a discount rate of 6 per cent, the present value of $10,000 due in 20 years is $3,118.) Following is a portion of a typical present value table, showing what $1, to be paid in the future, is worth today, assuming annual compounding:

YEAR	4%	5%	6%	7%	8%	9%	10%
1%	.9615	.9524	.9434	.9346	.9259	.9174	.9091
2	.9246	.9070	.8900	.8734	.8573	.8417	.8264
3	.8890	.8638	.8396	.8163	.7938	.7722	.7513
4	.8548	.8227	.7921	.7629	.7350	.7084	.6830
5	.8219	.7835	.7473	.7130	.6806	.6499	.6209
6	.7903	.7462	.7050	.6663	.6302	.5963	.5645
7	.7599	.7107	.6651	.6227	.5835	.5470	.5132
8	.7307	.6768	.6274	.5820	.5403	.5019	.4665
9	.7026	.6446	.5919	.5439	.5002	.4604	.4241
10	.6756	.6139	.5584	.5083	.4632	.4224	.3855
11	.6496	.5847	.5268	.4751	.4289	.3875	.3505

YEAR	4%	5%	6%	7%	8%	9%	10%
12	.6246	.5568	.4970	.4440	.3971	.3555	.3186
13	.6006	.5303	.4688	.4150	.3677	.3262	.2897
14	.5775	.5051	.4423	.3878	.3405	.2992	.2633
15	.5553	.4810	.4173	.3624	.3152	.2745	.2394
16	.5339	.4581	.3936	.3387	.2919	.2519	.2176
17	.5134	.4363	.3714	.3166	.2703	.2311	.1978
18	.4936	.4155	.3503	.2959	.2502	.2120	.1799
19	.4746	.3957	.3305	.2765	.2317	.1945	.1635
20	.4564	.3769	.3118	.2584	.2145	.1784	.1486

In jury trials, reduction to present value usually is handled as it was in *Rodriguez*: the expert witnesses incorporate the present value calculation into their estimates of the plaintiff's losses, and are free to challenge each other's assumptions as to the appropriate discount rate. It is for the jury to decide which expert's assumptions to accept. In bench trials judges sometimes do the reduction themselves.

There is general agreement that awards for future pecuniary losses, such as medical expenses and loss of earning capacity, should be reduced to present value. Awards for future nonpecuniary losses, such as pain and suffering and loss of enjoyment, often are not reduced, probably in the belief that these calculations are so imprecise to begin with that reduction to present value would add only an illusion of accuracy. The California pattern jury charges quoted at the beginning of this section reflect this view.

BANKS v. SUNRISE HOSPITAL

Supreme Court of Nevada, 2004.
120 Nev. 822, 102 P.3d 52.

AGOSTI, J.

[While undergoing rotator cuff surgery at Sunrise Hospital, James Banks, Jr. suffered cardiac arrest and did not regain consciousness. He remained in a permanent vegetative state. Through a guardian, Banks sued Sunrise Hospital, the surgeon and the anesthesiologist alleging that all were negligent in connection with the administration of anesthesia. The surgeon and anesthesiologist settled with Banks for $1.9 million shortly before trial. A jury found Sunrise liable for Banks's injury and awarded damages of $5,412,030. The jury apparently awarded separate sums for (a) loss of enjoyment of life, and (b) pain and suffering; the opinion does not state the amounts, or reveal whether there were other components of the damage award as well. The district court subsequently reduced the award by the amount paid in settlement by the two physicians, added prejudgment interest, and entered judgment in the amount of $4,825,450. Sunrise appealed, alleging that various reversible errors occurred at trial.]

* * *

Hedonic damages

Sunrise contends that the district court erred in permitting expert testimony concerning the monetary range of hedonic damages, *i.e.,* loss of enjoyment of life damages.

We turn first to whether hedonic damages are a compensable element of damages. The term "hedonic" is derived from the Greek language and refers to the pleasures of life. Hedonic damages are therefore monetary remedies awarded to compensate injured persons for their noneconomic loss of life's pleasures or the loss of enjoyment of life. The Supreme Court of South Carolina has succinctly explained hedonic loss, as distinguished from pain and suffering:

> An award for pain and suffering compensates the injured person for the physical discomfort and the emotional response to the sensation of pain caused by the injury itself. Separate damages are given for mental anguish where the evidence shows, for example, that the injured person suffered shock, fright, emotional upset, and/or humiliation as the result of the defendant's negligence.

> On the other hand, damages for "loss of enjoyment of life" compensate for the limitations, resulting from the defendant's negligence, on the injured person's ability to participate in and derive pleasure from the normal activities of daily life, or for the individual's inability to pursue his talents, recreational interests, hobbies, or avocations.

Boan v. Blackwell, 343 S.C. 498, 541 S.E.2d 242, 244 (2001) (citation omitted).

Awarding damages for hedonic losses appears to be a recent concept. The long-standing objection to such an award was the "fear of speculativeness and duplication." While the majority of jurisdictions recognize hedonic loss as a recoverable element of damages, the jurisdictions differ as to how hedonic loss should be presented and awarded. In particular, jurisdictions disagree as to whether an expert should be permitted to testify concerning the value of hedonic loss. Some jurisdictions will not permit an expert to testify concerning the value of a person's life on the grounds that the loss is subjective, that the damages are incapable of being accurately measured, or that the methods used by experts to measure hedonic losses are unreliable. Other courts permit experts, such as economists, to testify concerning the value of hedonic loss, recognizing that the jury is ultimately responsible for computing damages and that expert testimony will often assist the jury in making its determination.

We agree with these latter jurisdictions. In Nevada, the district court has discretion to qualify a witness as an expert. * * *

Here, Banks offered Robert Johnson, a forensic economist, as an expert on hedonic damages to assist the jury in determining the monetary value of the pleasure of living that James will be denied as a result of his injury. In cases permitting experts to testify as to the value of hedonic loss, economists have used various methods to arrive at their conclusions. Johnson's methodology for the valuation of hedonic damages is called the "willingness to pay" theory. Johnson testified that he relied on particular studies written about and evaluated by other authors concerning two methods under the "willingness to pay theory." The first method, the "survey" method, asks people how much they are willing to spend to reduce the probability of death from 3 deaths per 20,000 to 1 death per 20,000. The second method, the "wage risk" method, examines the salary people in high fatality risk jobs receive and the amount of money people are willing to forego to work a lower fatality risk job. [Using a combination of these two methods, Johnson estimated that Banks' loss of enjoyment was worth at least $2.5 million.]

Johnson's methodology for the valuation of hedonic damages assisted the jury to understand the amount of damages that would compensate James for the loss of his enjoyment of life. Johnson's valuation theories were matters within the scope of his specialized knowledge concerning the monetary value of intangibles. Moreover, the probative value of Johnson's testimony was not substantially outweighed by the danger of unfair prejudice. Therefore, the district court properly exercised its discretion in qualifying Johnson as an expert and permitting him to testify concerning hedonic damages. We observe that Sunrise had the ability to use traditional methods of disputing Johnson's testimony, such as presenting witnesses on its behalf to persuade the jury that Johnson's methods were inaccurate or unreliable. The jury was then free to determine whether Johnson's valuation theories were credible and to weigh his testimony accordingly.

* * *

[S]ome jurisdictions permit an award of hedonic damages as a separate and distinct compensatory award, in addition to the three common compensatory damages of lost earnings, medical expenses and pain and suffering. These jurisdictions believe that compensating a victim for hedonic loss in a separate award prevents inadequate awards to the victim and facilitates judicial review. Other jurisdictions permit the trier of fact to treat hedonic loss as a factor in determining general damage awards or pain and suffering awards. These courts reason that, because of the intangible nature of hedonic loss, separating hedonic loss into a distinct category will produce duplicative damage awards or overcompensate the victim.

For example, in Huff v. Tracy, [57 Cal.App.3d 939, 129 Cal.Rptr. 551, 553 (1976)] a California court determined that the injured plaintiff, who suffered severe lacerations to his tongue during an automobile accident that permanently impaired his sense of taste, was entitled to argue, as one factor for a pain and suffering award, that he should receive compensation of his loss of enjoyment of life. The court noted that California did not have a "rule restrict[ing] a plaintiff's attorney from arguing this element [of damages] to a jury." The court analogized the treatment of hedonic loss to the treatment of mental damages, another element of a pain and suffering award of damages.

We agree with California and those jurisdictions permitting plaintiffs to seek compensation for hedonic loss as an element of the general award for pain and suffering. Like California, Nevada does not restrict a plaintiff's attorney from arguing hedonic damages. Moreover, by including hedonic losses as a component of pain and suffering, we perceive no problem of confusion or duplication of awards by the jury. Accordingly, we hold that hedonic damages may be included as an element of a pain and suffering award of damages.

Here, however, the district court permitted the jury to award hedonic damages as a separate and distinct damage award, rather than including hedonic loss as a component of the pain and suffering damages award. Although the district court erroneously permitted the jury to give Banks a separate award for hedonic damages, the error was not prejudicial because the jury could have easily added the value of the hedonic loss to the pain and suffering award. Therefore, the record does not reveal that the hedonic damages award was duplicative or excessive. Accordingly, the error was harmless.

[Judgment affirmed.]

SHEARING C.J., ROSE, GIBBONS AND DOUGLAS, J.J., concur.

[MAUPIN, J., with whom BECKER, J., agrees, dissented on other issues but concurred in the portion of the opinion reprinted above.]

NOTES

1. One issue is whether tort victims should be compensated at all for loss of enjoyment of life. Most courts agree that they should, one way or another. The case for doing so is easiest to see in cases involving amateur athletes and artists, whose inability to perform will not be compensated by the award for lost earning capacity and may be unrelated to pain. A second issue is whether loss of enjoyment should be treated as a separate category of damages. Some courts, like the court in *Banks*, say the jury should simply be instructed to consider it in making the award for pain and suffering. Others say it is a distinct type of harm and should be submitted separately. See, e.g., Fantozzi v. Sandusky Cement Products Co., 64 Ohio St.3d 601, 597 N.E.2d 474 (1992). A third issue is whether the court should admit expert testimony on the amount of damages for loss of enjoyment.

In the principal case, the court appears to have collapsed all three issues into one. The defendant's contention was that the expert's testimony should not have been admitted; in the course of deciding that the testimony was admissible, the court also decided that loss of enjoyment was properly compensable, that it should be treated as a component of pain and suffering, and that submitting it separately was not reversible error.

2. Courts are usually skeptical of economists' attempts to establish a "market price" for noneconomic losses. Judges usually exclude testimony based on surveys asking people how much money would induce them to endure a certain type of pain or disability, on the ground that answers to such hypothetical questions are unreliable and tell jurors little that their own intuitions can't tell them. Courts are not much more receptive to methods like the attempt by Banks' expert to ascertain how much money actually does induce people to take specified risks or how much they actually do pay to avoid dangers. See, e.g., Mercado v. Ahmed, 974 F.2d 863 (7th Cir. 1992), holding that the trial court properly excluded testimony similar to that given by Banks' expert. Courts usually prefer to leave the estimating to the intuitions of jurors, with guidance no more precise than the admonition to be "just and reasonable" in subsection (d) of the pattern jury charge quoted at p. 285 supra.

3. Damages for loss of enjoyment are sometimes denied to comatose plaintiffs like Banks, on the ground that a plaintiff who is unaware of his or her situation suffers no loss of enjoyment, or on the ground that the money can have no value to such a person. See, e.g., McDougald v. Garber, 73 N.Y.2d 246, 538 N.Y.S.2d 937, 536 N.E.2d 372 (1989).

4. Legislatures in many states have imposed caps on noneconomic damages, such as pain and suffering and loss of enjoyment, in medical malpractice cases. Nineteen such statutes, with caps ranging from $250,000 to $1.05 million, are cited in Lebron v. Gottlieb Memorial Hosp., 237 Ill.2d 217, 341 Ill.Dec. 381, 930 N.E.2d 895 (2010). Most of these statutes have survived constitutional challenges, but the Illinois Supreme Court in the Lebron case held that a statute capping physicians' liability at $500,000 and hospitals' at $1 million violated the separation of powers clause of the state constitution because it encroached upon "the fundamentally judicial prerogative of determining whether a jury's assessment of damages is excessive within the meaning of the law." As for the existence of similar statutes in other states, "That 'everybody is doing it' is hardly a litmus test for the constitutionality of the statute." The court was also unimpressed by citations indicating that separation of powers challenges had been rejected in nine states. "That the courts of other states would hold differently based on their constitutional jurisprudence applied to their statutes is of no moment."

In a few states legislatures have imposed caps not just in malpractice cases, but in broader categories of tort cases. See, e.g., Md. Ann. Code, Ct. & Jud. Proc. § 11–108 (all tort cases); Me. Rev. Stat. Ann. tit. 14 § 8105 (suits against public entities).

Collateral Benefits

Suppose a tort victim incurs $10,000 in medical bills as a result of her injuries and sues the tortfeasor for that amount. In the course of discovery the defendant learns that the victim's medical insurance policy paid $7,500 of the bill and her grandfather paid the remaining $2,500. What should the defendant have to pay?

Until recently the answer in most jurisdictions would have been, the full $10,000. The collateral source rule said that these payments (considered "collateral" because they were made by third parties not on behalf of the defendant or his insurance company) were none of the defendant's business. The grandfather meant his gift to benefit his granddaughter, not the tortfeasor. As for the insurance payment, the plaintiff (or someone acting for her benefit) bought and paid for that benefit and the defendant should not be able to appropriate it. Moreover, the medical insurance company may be entitled under the terms of the policy to subrogation, i.e, to be reimbursed from the proceeds of the plaintiff's tort suit. If so, giving the defendant a deduction for the insured amount would either deny the plaintiff the benefits of her insurance policy or defeat the insurance company's right of subrogation. On the other hand, allowing the plaintiff to recover the full $10,000 from the tortfeasor, even though her medical bills have been paid by others, means she ends up better off (financially, at least) than she was before the tort.

In the past two or three decades, the collateral source rule has been under attack.

BOZEMAN v. STATE

Supreme Court of Louisiana, 2004.
879 So.2d 692.

JOHNSON, JUSTICE.

[Tommy Bozeman suffered brain damage and numerous fractures, bruises, and abrasions in an auto accident. He was hospitalized for a month, then transferred to a long term care facility where he remained in a semi-conscious state until his death more than three years later. Bozeman's wife filed suit on her husband's behalf against the Louisiana Department of Transportation and Development (DOTD), alleging that the accident was caused an unreasonably dangerous highway. After two appeals and two remands to the trial court, the Court of Appeals eventually determined that Bozeman's medical expenses were $622,086, that the Louisiana Department of Health and Hospitals (DHH) had paid $319,838 of that under the Medicaid program and had denied $35,368 in claims, and that Bozeman's various health care providers had written off the remaining $266,879 as they were required to do by state and federal Medicaid regulations. After a bench trial, the judge initially awarded the plaintiff the full amount of his medical expenses, but the Court of Appeals subtracted the amounts that were written off, permitting recovery of $355,206, the sum of the claims paid and denied by Medicaid. The DHH applied to the court for reimbursement of the $319,838 it had paid in Medicaid benefits but that claim was denied. The plaintiff appealed the deduction of the write-off amount. DHH did not appeal. Bozeman's death did not affect the outcome of this case for reasons that will become clear in section C, infra.]

* * *

Under the collateral source rule, a tortfeasor may not benefit, and an injured plaintiff's tort recovery may not be reduced, because of monies received by the plaintiff from sources independent of the tortfeasor's procuration or contribution. Hence, the payments received from the independent source are not deducted from the award the aggrieved party would otherwise receive from the wrongdoer, and, a tortfeasor's liability to an injured plaintiff should be the same, regardless of whether or not the plaintiff had the foresight to obtain insurance. As a result of the collateral source rule, the tortfeasor is not able to benefit from the victim's foresight in purchasing insurance and other benefits.

The collateral source rule has been applied to a variety of factual circumstances, although it typically applies to tort cases involving insurance payments or other benefits. * * *

> The collateral source rule has been held to apply not only where plaintiff directly purchased insurance against which the plaintiff recovered, but also where there have been Medicare payments, sick leave and annual leave payments, retirement pension payments, free medical services rendered as a professional courtesy, Federal Social Security Benefits, free medical care rendered by the Veteran's Administration, insurance paid for by the employer for the employee as a result of a collective bargaining agreement in a F.E.L.A. case, and suits brought under the Jones Act and Longshoremen's and Harbor Worker's Compensation Act. [Citing cases from Lousisiana and other jurisdictions].

[Bryant v. New Orleans Public Serv. Inc., 406 So.2d 767, 768 (La.App. 4th Cir.1981)].

In *Bryant*, supra, the court also provided a lucid discussion of the policy reasons supporting the collateral source rule. The court stated the following:

> There are several reasons for the existence of the collateral source rule. The reason most often stated is that the defendant should not recover from outside benefits provided to the plaintiff or procured by the plaintiff. For years the Louisiana courts struggled with the so-called "windfall" or "double-dip" aspect of the collateral source rule only to discover that no "windfall" or "double dip" in fact occurred. No "windfall" or "double dip" occurred because the injured party's patrimony was diminished to the extent that he was forced to recover against outside sources and the diminution of patrimony was *additional* damage suffered by him.

> For example, if the payment received by plaintiff was from annual leave or sick leave time, then those resources which would have been available to him but for the accident or injury, are no longer available and he has suffered the loss of annual or sick leave time for which he should be recompensed. This same logic applies to pension payments, government benefits, and gratuitous services.

In the case of insurance purchased by the plaintiff or deductions made from the plaintiff's paycheck, the plaintiff has paid premiums which are a diminution of his patrimony as that cash would have otherwise been available to him. By going against his own insurance policy, he is diminishing the benefits of that policy which would otherwise be available, he has suffered a diminution of the patrimony by premium payments and his rates will rise providing a third area of loss.

Where insurance is provided by the employer, then that fringe benefit is in the nature of deferred compensation. The deferred compensation would have been available to him as cash per paycheck, but for the existence of the deferred compensation plan. Likewise, the benefits of the deferred compensation would have been available but for the injury.

Lastly, if the collateral source rule were not applied, then there would be no reason for an individual to purchase insurance. For example, if in a wrongful death case the tortfeasor was allowed a set-off for proceeds from the deceased's life insurance policy, then the deceased's estate suffered the loss not only of the amounts paid as premiums but also for the *use* of the money over the years, so that the deceased's estate could, theoretically, bring an action against the defendant to recover back the set-off amount.

As stated earlier, the collateral source rule is a rule of evidence and damages. From an evidentiary perspective, the rule bars the introduction of evidence that a plaintiff has received benefits or payments from a collateral source * * *.

From an evidentiary perspective, there is no dispute here, since the evidence of the collateral source payments was jointly introduced at trial. Thus, we are called upon to make a determination regarding the damages aspect of the collateral source rule.

The major policy reason for applying the collateral source rule to damages has been, and continues to be, tort deterrence. The underlying concept is that tort damages can help to deter unreasonably dangerous conduct. Tort deterrence has been an inherent, inseparable, aspect of the collateral source rule since its inception over one hundred years ago.

* * *

[The court described three approaches to the issue presented by this case. One was advanced by the plaintiff, who argued that the collateral source rule required that he be awarded the entire amount of the medical expenses that were reasonably billed to him, including those amounts that were written off by healthcare providers. For this position, he relied on Restatement (Second) of Torts § 920A cmt. *b*:

If the plaintiff was himself responsible for the benefit, as by maintaining his own insurance or by making advantageous employment arrangements, the law allows him to keep it for himself. If the benefit was a gift to the plaintiff from a third party *or established for him by law,* he should not be deprived of the advantage that it confers. The law does not differentiate between the nature of the benefits, so long as they did not come from the defendant or a person acting for him.

(Emphasis added).The court conceded that this was the position of the majority of states, but rejected it.]

Defendant, DOTD, * * * argues that the Medicaid "write-off" amount is an illusory amount that is simply used by healthcare providers to set their fee payments with Medicaid. DOTD argues that the plaintiff never incurred this bill, and by operation of state and federal law, the Medicaid provider is required to accept as full payment the amount paid by Medicaid, and no more. Thus, to allow the plaintiff to recover this additional amount would violate the law of compensatory damages, which is to make the plaintiff whole. According to defendant, allowing plaintiff to recover an amount that neither he nor anyone was ever obligated to repay, an amount over and above what was actually paid for his medical expenses, would be to grant the plaintiff a windfall because plaintiff would recover damages in excess of what it took to make the plaintiff whole, thus, violating the goal of tort recovery. We disagree.

* * *

The third approach used by courts is to award plaintiffs the full value of their medical expenses, including the "write-off" amount, where the plaintiff has paid some consideration for the benefit of the "write-off" amounts. Louisiana's First Circuit Court of Appeal adopted this rationale in [Griffin v. Louisiana Sheriff's Auto Risk Association, 802 So.2d 691 (La.App. 2001)] when it concluded that the plaintiff's patrimony was continually diminished to the extent that she had to pay premiums in order to secure the benefits of her insurance. According to the First Circuit, to the extent that the write-offs were procured through the payment of the premiums, they cannot properly be considered a windfall. Rather, the write-off amount was viewed as a benefit to plaintiff's contractual bargain with her insurance provider.

Similarly, the Virginia Supreme Court, in Acuar v. Letourneau, 260 Va. 180, 531 S.E.2d 316, 322–323 (2000), concluded the following:

we conclude that Acuar (the tortfeasor) cannot deduct from that full compensation any part of the benefits Letourneau (the victim) received from his contractual arrangement with his health insurance carrier, whether those benefits took the form of medical expense payments or amounts written off because of agreements between his health insurance carrier and his health care providers. Those amounts written off are as much of a benefit for which Letourneau paid consideration as are the actual cash payments made by his health insurance carrier to the health care providers. The portions of medical expenses that health care providers write off constitute 'compensation or indemnity received by a tort victim from a source collateral to the tortfeasor.

Additionally, the Virginia Supreme Court stated that this conclusion is consistent with the purpose of compensatory damages, which is to make the victim whole. The court noted that "the injured party should be made whole by the tortfeasor, not by a combination of compensation from the tortfeasor and collateral sources. The wrongdoer cannot reap the benefit of a contract for which the wrongdoer paid no compensation." Further, the California Supreme Court, in Helfend v. S. California Rapid Transit District, 2 Cal.3d 1, 84 Cal.Rptr. 173, 465 P.2d 61, 66–67 (1970) made specific reference to insurance and other benefits being an investment made by the plaintiff, for which the plaintiff should get the benefit. The California Supreme Court stated the following:

> The collateral source rule expresses a policy judgment in favor of encouraging citizens to purchase and maintain insurance for personal injuries and for other eventualities. Courts consider insurance a form of investment, the benefits of which become payable without respect to any other possible source of funds. If we were to permit tortfeasor to mitigate damages with payments from plaintiff's insurance, plaintiff would be in a position inferior to that of having bought no insurance, because his payment of premiums would have earned no benefit. Defendant should not be able to avoid payment of full compensation for the injury inflicted merely because the victim has had the foresight to provide himself with insurance.

We embrace this reasoning for plaintiffs who have paid some consideration for the collateral source benefits, including the "write-off." * * * Several courts have distinguished Medicaid benefits from Medicare and private insurance.

The Supreme Court of Kansas, in Rose v. Via Christi, 276 Kan. 539, 552, 78 P.3d 798 (2003), concluded that based upon the payment of premiums by Medicare participants, "we find that Medicare is akin to private insurance and can be distinguished from Medicaid in that regard." * * * A clear discussion of this distinction is provided by the Ohio Supreme Court in Hodge v. Middletown Hospital Assoc., 91–3232 (1991), 62 Ohio St.3d 236, 240, 581 N.E.2d 529. * * *

> Medicaid payments, however, are significantly different from benefits paid as Medicare Part A. Medicaid is a system for providing payment of medical costs for the poor. Neither the beneficiary nor his employer pays premiums or underwrites the cost of the program * * * Payment into the (Medicare) trust fund, though involuntary, is in exchange for health care coverage, and gives rise to a duty on the part of the government to pay benefits when required. In addition, the language of the statute specifically refers to "policy or contract" of insurance. In short, Medicare Part A is funded by payments made by beneficiaries and their employers, is actuarily determined, and is described by its enabling statute as insurance.

Care of the nation's poor is an admirable social policy. However, where the plaintiff pays no enrollment fee, has no wages deducted, and otherwise provides no consideration for the collateral source benefits he receives, we hold that the plaintiff is unable to recover the "write-off" amount. This position is consistent with the often-cited statement in Gordon v. Forsyth County Hospital Authority, Inc., 409 F.Supp. 708 (M.D.N.C.1975), affirmed in part and vacated in part, 544 F.2d 748 (4th Cir.1976), that "(i)t would be unconscionable to permit the taxpayers to bear the expense of providing free medical care to a person and then allow that person to recover damages for medical expenses from a tort-feasor and pocket the windfall." After careful review, we conclude that Medicaid is a free medical service, and that no consideration is given by a patient to obtain Medicaid benefits. His patrimony is not diminished, and therefore, a plaintiff who is a Medicaid recipient is unable to recover the "write off" amounts. The operative words here are "free medical care," which, again, we hold is applicable to plaintiffs who receive Medicaid, not plaintiffs who receive Medicare or private insurance benefits.

* * *

KNOLL, JUSTICE, concurring.

I additionally concur with the majority opinion to emphasize the narrowness of our holding.

* * * There are many and varied origins of collateral sources which may provide compensation for the tort victim's injuries. In addition to Medicare, Medicaid and insurance benefits, collateral sources can also comprise payment of wages unless for services performed, worker's compensation, unemployment compensation, sick pay and related employee benefit programs, Social Security, pension and retirement funds, and benefits provided gratuitously by private parties or government agencies under compulsion of neither contract nor statute. Often an injured person receives gratuitous medical, economic or other assistance from governmental agencies or private benefactors.

Write-offs, as in this case before us however, are technically not payments from a collateral source. Therefore, we correctly find the plaintiff is not entitled to recover these amounts from the defendant, where the write-offs are mandated by the Medicaid program.

The majority opinion is strictly limited to the amounts written off by the health care providers in accordance with the Medicaid program. Our holding today does not include a tort victim who is the beneficiary of largesse from a private benefactor, where there is no consideration provided for that benefit and the plaintiff's patrimony was not diminished; under these circumstances the collateral source rule is applicable and the tort victim is still entitled to recover damages otherwise recoverable from the wrongdoer. Simply stated, gratuitous collateral sources are not excluded from the collateral source rule under our holding. Our holding here is limited to the amounts written off by the health care provider, where no consideration was provided for that benefit, as contrasted with Medicare and private insurance, where consideration is provided for the benefit.

NOTES

1. Some courts disagree with the *Bozeman* result. See, e.g., Wills v. Foster, 229 Ill.2d 393, 892 N.E.2d 1018, 323 Ill.Dec. 26 (2008), permitting recovery of amounts written off under Medicaid, describing that as the majority position, and citing numerous cases. *Bozeman* is typical, however, of a tendency by courts to construe the collateral source rule narrowly. See, e.g., Haynes v. Yale–New Haven Hospital, 243 Conn. 17, 699 A.2d 964 (1997) (refusing to apply the rule to proceeds from an underinsured motorist insurance policy).

2. Apparently DOTD conceded that amounts *paid* by Medicaid were collateral payments. If the agency had not made that concession, would the court's logic as to write-offs also preclude recovery for the amounts paid?

3. A number of states have statutes that would preclude recovery of the paid amounts and the write-off amounts alike. See, e.g., Mont. Code Ann. § 21–1–308. The collateral source rule has been a major target of the tort reform movement, and it is said that about half of the states have abolished or limited the rule at least for some types of claims, such as medical malpractice. See D. Dobbs, The Law of Torts 1059 (2000).

4. *Subrogation.* By the terms of the Medicaid regulations, DHH had a right of subrogation against Bozeman's tort recovery—that is, DHH was entitled to be reimbursed for the amounts it had paid, to the extent that Bozeman recovered for those expenses. The court of appeals refused to let DHH pursue its subrogation claim because it had failed to timely intervene, even though it had notice of the litigation.

Most insurance policies contain subrogation clauses providing that if the policy holder recovers a judgment or settlement from a tortfeasor (or a tortfeasor's insurance company), the plaintiff's insurance company has a subrogation right in that recovery. As a practical matter, that often means that the first-party insurer (e.g., the victim's own health insurance carrier) pays the victim's bills and then brings suit against the tortfeasor to enforce its subrogation rights. This has an important bearing on collateral source questions. If benefits such as health insurance payments are deducted from the recovery, allowing subrogation against what remains of the plaintiff's recovery defeats the purpose of carrying health insurance, while disallowing subrogation defeats the objective of transferring the loss from the victim's insurance company to wrongdoer's.

To avoid this, the statutes requiring deduction of collateral payments often contain an exception for payments that are subject to a right of subrogation. For example, Idaho Code § 6–1606 provides that "judgment may be entered for the claimant only for damages which exceed amounts received by the claimant from collateral sources as compensation for the personal injury or property damage, whether from private, group or governmental sources, and whether contributory or noncontributory," but adds that this does not apply to amounts "paid under federal programs which by law must seek subrogation, death benefits paid under life insurance contracts, * * * and benefits paid which are recoverable under subrogation rights created under Idaho law or by contract."

C. WRONGFUL DEATH AND SURVIVAL ACTIONS

The common law permitted no recovery for a tort that caused death. The explanation generally given is the "felony-merger rule," an early English doctrine premised on the notion that any intentional or negligent killing was a felony. The primary offense was the breach of the King's peace rather than the wrong to the victim, so the tort was considered "merged" into the crime. Moreover, as in all felonies, the punishment was death for the felon and forfeiture of his estate to the Crown; thus there was no defendant left to sue and no assets from which a recovery might be had. See Moragne v. States Marine Lines, 398 U.S. 375, 381–82, 90 S.Ct. 1772, 26 L.Ed.2d 339 (1970). Another explanation may be that the law generally does not give one person a cause of action for a tort committed against another. Another may be that such claims generally are barred by the rule precluding recovery for purely economic losses.

Whatever the explanation, the rule created the untenable result that a tortfeasor whose victim died was better off than one whose victim was merely injured. Beginning in the mid-nineteenth century, England and every American jurisdiction adopted statutes permitting actions for "wrongful death." These specified who could recover—usually the spouse and children, sometimes also parents and siblings, sometimes all the decedent's legal heirs. At first the statutes permitted recovery only for pecuniary losses, such as loss of support, and often they had fixed dollar ceilings, e.g., $5,000, but gradually most states dropped these limitations, and now nonpecuniary losses such as loss of the decedent's guidance and companionship are an important part of wrongful death recovery.

It is difficult to generalize about wrongful death because the cause of action remains almost entirely statutory and courts generally adhere to the specific dictates of the statute even when those seem inconsistent with the general principles that the statute is supposed to embody. For example, it is often said that the purpose of wrongful death recovery is to provide for the decedent's dependents, and the statutes usually name classes of survivors that the legislature probably assumed would be dependents (e.g. spouses and children). Nevertheless, courts routinely deny recovery to dependents who do not fit the statutory description (e.g. unadopted stepchildren). See, e.g., Klossner v. San Juan County, 21 Wash.App. 689, 586 P.2d 899 (1978), aff'd 93 Wash.2d 42, 605 P.2d 330 (1980). (In California a similar decision led the legislature to amend the statute to allow recovery by stepchildren and other dependent minors who lived in decedent's household. See Cal.Civ.Proc. Code § 377.60.) On the other hand, persons who fit the statutory classification but are not dependent (e.g. adult children) routinely recover.

Survival statutes do something different. They provide that the cause of action the decedent would have had survives his or her death and can be maintained by and for the benefit of the decedent's estate. In theory, wrongful death and survival actions are clearly distinct. The wrongful death action seeks recovery for the losses suffered by the decedent's surviving family members, e.g., their loss of support; the survival action seeks recovery for the decedent's (or his estate's) losses, e.g., the pain he suffered before death and the medical expenses chargeable to his estate. In practice, the courts (and sometimes the statutes themselves) often blur the lines. For example, some allow recovery in a wrongful death action for the decedent's pain and suffering, see, e.g., McDavid v. United States, 213 W.Va. 592, 584 S.E.2d 226 (2003), and some measure wrongful death recovery by the amount that the decedent would have accumulated had his or her life not been cut short, e.g., Iowa–Des Moines Nat. Bank v. Schwerman Trucking Co. 288 N.W.2d 198 (Iowa 1980). Sometimes this blurring is a result of "hybrid" statutes that combine the two actions into one, but often it appears to be the result of confusion.

In non-fatal cases, immediate family members are sometimes allowed to sue for "loss of consortium," which is conceptually similar to the recovery for loss of society in wrongful death actions. The following case required the court to sort out the three types of claims: loss of consortium, wrongful death, and survival.

WEIGEL v. LEE

Supreme Court of North Dakota, 2008.
752 N.W.2d 618.

* * *

I.

On May 6, 2004, Darlyne Rogers arrived at the emergency room of St. Luke's Hospital in Crosby, North Dakota, complaining of abdominal pain, nausea and vomiting. X-rays revealed Rogers suffered from pneumonia and a bowel obstruction. A doctor at St. Luke's Hospital contacted Dr. Lane Lee who agreed to treat Rogers. Rogers was transferred as Lee's patient to Trinity Hospital in Minot. Rogers, despite being critically ill, was admitted to a room on the "regular" floor of the hospital. Three and one-half hours later, Rogers began vomiting bodily waste and aspirating it into her lungs. Rogers ultimately died.

Rogers' [four] adult children, the Weigels, brought a suit on their own behalf against Lee and Trinity Hospital, alleging negligence. The complaint stated,

> This is an action to recover damages for the wrongful death of Darlyne Rogers * * * pursuant to N.D.C.C. Chapter 32–21. * * * [T]he Plaintiffs have sustained injuries and damages, both economic and non-economic. * * * The Plaintiffs have sustained mental and emotional anguish as a result of the Defendants' negligence and their

mother's death. Furthermore, the Plaintiffs have been denied the society, comfort, counsel and companionship of Darlyne Rogers.

[The Weigels' case was tried to a jury, but the judge dismissed the case before verdict on the ground the children were seeking recovery for loss of parental consortium, which the state did not allow. After several motions for reconsideration, the judge decided the case should have gone to the jury on the children's mental and emotional anguish claim. Later the judge modified that order, stating "Rather than allowing the jury to consider awarding damages for mental anguish/emotional distress allegedly sustained by the *surviving children* of the decedent * * * the jury should instead be allowed to consider awarding compensation for non-economic damages-such as, pain, suffering, mental anguish, emotional distress or humiliation-allegedly sustained by the *decedent herself,* prior to her death. * * * Otherwise stated, Darlyne Rogers' surviving heirs * * * 'step into her shoes' in terms of the cause of action available against the Defendants in this matter." The Weigels then made clear that they were suing for their own losses, not those of their mother, and the judge dismissed their suit. The Weigels appeal the judgment of dismissal, contending the district court's interpretation of the wrongful death act was erroneous.]

II.

The district court erred by blending three distinct claims for tortious conduct. At various points in its orders, the district court discussed (1) loss of consortium claims arising out of personal injury actions, (2) survival actions and (3) wrongful death actions. This Court and North Dakota's statutes distinguish between these three claims, as we explain below.

First, English common law recognized an action for loss of consortium arising out of tortious conduct that resulted in *personal injury.* Historically, "a husband's right to recover for the loss of his wife's consortium was considered a property right" with a loss of consortium being defined as "love, companionship, affection, society, comfort, solace, support, sexual relations, and services." Under this original approach, "only a husband could recover for the loss of [his wife's] consortium." The contemporary interpretation of this common law concept includes recovery for wives as well as for husbands. [In Hastings v. James River Aerie No. 2337, 246 N.W.2d 747, 749 (N.D.1976)], this Court acknowledged both spouses' right to recover for loss of consortium, but refused to extend this type of recovery to children who suffer the loss of a parent's consortium. Nonetheless, this is not the basis of the Weigels' action, and as this Court importantly clarified in *Hastings,* the inability of children to recover for loss of consortium arising out of personal injury to a parent "should not be construed to prohibit recovery where a parent dies and recovery is allowed under the Wrongful Death Act."

The distinction between loss of consortium in personal injury and in wrongful death actions is important here because Lee argues this Court's decision in [Butz v. World Wide, Inc., 492 N.W.2d 88 (N.D. 1992)] indicates a decedent's children are not entitled to damages in a wrongful death action. Lee misapplies *Butz. Butz* was not a claim under the wrongful death act because the tortious conduct resulted in severe injury, not in death. This Court acknowledged the loss of consortium claim made in *Butz* was like that made in *Hastings,* arising out of the common law. Because *Butz* does not address claims made under the wrongful death statutes, it is not applicable to the Weigels' claim.

Second, N.D.C.C. § 28–01–26.1 provides for survival actions: "No action or claim for relief, except for breach of promise, alienation of affections, libel, and slander, abates by the death of a party or of a person who might have been a party had such death not occurred." For example, in, 647 N.W.2d 133 (N.D. 2002), an individual was seriously injured in an automobile accident. He underwent hospital treatment, but died approximately two weeks later. This Court stated, "Clearly a personal injury action existed on behalf of [the injured party] against [the tortfeasor] for various damages, including the medical expenses occasioned by the accident, and that action survived [the injured party's] death." Survival statutes "are remedial in nature, and are intended to permit recovery by the representatives of the deceased for damages the deceased could have recovered had he lived. * * * A survival action merely continues in existence an injured person's claim after death as an asset of his estate." Sheets v. Graco, Inc., 292 N.W.2d 63, 66–67 (N.D.1980). Although they could have, the Weigels' complaint indicates they are not seeking damages on Rogers' behalf as part of a survival action. Instead, the Weigels brought a wrongful death action for their own injuries: "The Plaintiffs have sustained mental and emotional anguish as a result of the Defendants' negligence and their mother's death. Furthermore, the Plaintiffs have been denied the society, comfort, counsel and companionship of Darlyne Rogers, all to their injury and damage."

Third, N.D.C.C. ch. 32–21 provides for wrongful death actions. The Weigels offer the wrongful death act as the legal basis for their claim. We conclude the Weigels are entitled to seek compensation for Rogers' wrongful death for the reasons stated below.

There was no wrongful death claim at common law. Early wrongful death statutes severely limited compensable damages. Generally, only pecuniary losses were awarded, with no compensation available for mental anguish or loss of companionship. Contemporary wrongful death statutes tend to address a broader scope of injuries, including those considered non-pecuniary.

> Wrongful death actions are intended to compensate the survivors of the deceased for the losses they have sustained as a result of a wrongful killing. Dependent upon the specific statutory language, losses recoverable by survivors in wrongful death actions often include the prospective loss of earnings and contribution; prospective expenses; loss of services; *loss of companionship, comfort, and consortium; and mental anguish and grief.*

Sheets, 292 N.W.2d at 66 (emphasis added).

North Dakota's wrongful death act, N.D.C.C. ch. 32–21, provides:

> Whenever the death of a person shall be caused by a wrongful act, neglect, or default, and the act, neglect, or default is such as would have entitled the party injured, if death had not ensued, to maintain an action and recover damages in respect thereof, then and in every such case the person who, or the corporation, limited liability company, or company which would have been liable if death had not ensued, shall be liable to an action for damages, notwithstanding the death of the person injured or of the tort-feasor, and although the death shall have been caused under such circumstances as amount in law to felony.

N.D.C.C. § 32–21–01. This statute "is not a survival statute intended to increase the estate of the deceased, but its purpose is to give a measure of protection to those persons within a fixed degree of relationship to and dependency on the deceased because of actual injury sustained by them by reason of the wrongful killing of the deceased." Damages under the wrongful death act are "based on the loss suffered by the beneficiaries, and not on the loss sustained by the decedent's estate." A jury determines the quantity of damages and "shall give such damages as it finds proportionate to the injury resulting from the death to the persons entitled to the recovery." N.D.C.C. § 32–21–02.

Compensable damages available in wrongful death actions are enumerated in N.D.C.C. § 32–03.2–04:

> In any civil action for damages for wrongful death or injury to a person and whether arising out of breach of contract or tort, damages may be awarded by the trier of fact as follows:
>
> 1. Compensation for economic damages, which are damages arising from medical expenses and medical care, rehabilitation services, custodial care, loss of earnings and earning capacity, loss of income or support, burial costs, cost of substitute domestic services, loss of employment or business or employment opportunities and other monetary losses.
>
> 2. Compensation for noneconomic damages, which are damages arising from pain, suffering, inconvenience, physical impairment, disfigurement, *mental anguish,* emotional distress, fear of injury, loss or illness, *loss of society and companionship, loss of consortium,* injury to reputation, humiliation, and other nonpecuniary damage.

(Emphasis added.)

Section 32–21–04, N.D.C.C., clarifies that intended recipients of damages under the wrongful death act are "the decedent's heirs at law." This Court has determined "heirs at law" for purposes of this statute are "those persons who by the laws of descent would succeed to the property of the decedent in case of intestacy, but in addition, that if members of a preferred class are precluded from recovery for reasons other than death those next entitled to inherit may be considered beneficiaries." Broderson v. Boehm, 253 N.W.2d 864, 869 (N.D.1977) (holding collateral heirs may recover only when no recovery is possible by a closer relative). * * *

Persons entitled to recover damages under the wrongful death act should not be confused with persons statutorily authorized to bring an action. Section 32–21–03, N.D.C.C., states: [The statute names, in order: surviving spouse, surviving children, surviving parent, surviving grandparent, personal representative, and "A person who has had primary physical custody of the decedent before the wrongful act."]

The distinction between persons eligible to seek damages from wrongful death actions and those entitled to bring such actions is important because the trial judge is charged with splitting the recovery among eligible heirs. Section 32–21–04, N.D.C.C., states:

> The amount recovered shall not be liable for the debts of the decedent, but shall inure to the *exclusive benefit of the decedent's heirs at law in such shares as the judge before whom the case is tried shall fix in the order for judgment, and for the purpose of determining such shares, the judge after the trial may make any investigation which the judge deems necessary.*

(Emphasis added.) In specific wrongful death actions, overlap will likely exist between plaintiffs bringing the action under N.D.C.C. § 32–21–03 and those entitled to any damages. However, those with authority to bring the action do "not have an absolute right to the damages recovered, and, instead, bring the action in a representative capacity for the exclusive benefit of the persons entitled to recover." Goodleft v. Gullickson, 556 N.W.2d 303, 306 (N.D.1996). The wrongful death act "thus differentiate[s] between the capacity to bring an action and the right to share in the damages recovered." Surviving children are eligible to bring a wrongful death action under N.D.C.C. § 32–21–03(2) if the decedent had no eligible spouse or if the spouse fails to bring an action for thirty days after the children made a demand. But this issue is separate from the children's ability to recover damages in a wrongful death action.

Because the wrongful death act does not exclude the decedent's children from parties entitled to damages and because the damages requested are permitted under N.D.C.C. § 32–03.2–04, the Weigels' claim should not have been dismissed.

* * *

NOTES

1. The statutes quoted in the principal case are typical. They keep the wrongful death and survival actions separate, with one large exception: by using the general compensatory damage statute, N.D.C.C. § 32–03.2–04, to specify the damages recoverable in wrongful death, the legislature muddied the water. Pain and suffering and loss of earning capacity are the decedent's

losses, not those of the survivors, so they should not be recoverable in the wrongful death action. Medical and burial expenses and the costs of rehabilitation and custodial care might properly be included in the wrongful death recovery if the family members paid them, but if they were paid for by the decedent's estate they should be recoverable only in the survival action.

2. There is a necessary relationship, of course, between the survivors' recovery and what the decedent has lost: the survivors' loss of support cannot exceed the decedent's prospective earnings less what he would have spent on himself. Likewise, amounts the decedent would have spent in support of the family are sums that would not have benefitted the decedent's estate.

3. Often the wrongful death beneficiaries will be the same persons who will inherit from the decedent's estate. In those instances, if actions are brought under both the wrongful death and survival statutes, it makes little difference which claims are assigned to which cause of action. But it can make a great deal of difference if the decedent's will leaves his or her estate to someone other than the beneficiaries named in the wrongful death statute. The following case, for example, probably would not have arisen if the decedent had left a will.

ASPINALL v. McDONNELL DOUGLAS CORP.

United States Court of Appeal, Ninth Circuit, 1980.
625 F.2d 325.

CHAMBERS, CIRCUIT JUDGE.

Appellant Aspinall, individually and as personal representative of the estate of Anthony Price, appeals from the district court's order for summary judgment holding that she and her children are not his "heirs" for the purposes of the California wrongful death act (Section 377, California Code of Civil Procedure).

Price was killed in March 1974, with 345 other passengers and crew members, when a DC–10 crashed at Paris. The plane had been manufactured by appellee McDonnell Douglas Corporation and it had been designed in part by appellee General Dynamics Corporation. At the time of his death Price, a resident of England, was unmarried and had no issue. His parents were deceased and he had no collateral heirs. But he and appellant had lived together in the roles of husband and wife for over four years and Price left his entire estate to appellant by will. He had been the sole support (except for a small pension) of appellant and her children during the four years, but he had never married appellant and he had never adopted her children.

* * *

[On defendants' motion for summary judgment, the district court] held that appellant and her children were not eligible for relief under

California's wrongful death statute as they did not qualify as "heirs" for the purpose of that statute.[2]

Under California law the right of a survivor to recover under the wrongful death theory is purely statutory; the Legislature's intent in adopting the statute was to create an entirely new cause of action where none existed theretofore. At the time that the cause of action arose in this case, the courts of California defined "heirs," as used in Section 377, as those "who would have been eligible to inherit from the decedent's estate had he died intestate," i.e. under the intestacy provisions of the California Probate Code. Nowhere in those Probate Code provisions, as worded at the time this cause of action arose, would appellant come within the definition of an "heir," entitled to succeed to decedent's estate. And nowhere in those Probate Code provisions would her children be considered his "heirs."

Appellant contends that she would be entitled to succeed to some of decedent's estate because she was his "putative spouse." Even if we were to accept, for purposes of argument, her interpretation of the rights of putative spouses under California case law, it is clear that she was not a "putative spouse" according to the California definition, i.e. a surviving spouse of a marriage that was "solemnized in due form and celebrated in good faith by at least one of the parties but which, by reason of some legal infirmity, is either void or voidable." In this case there is no claim of any marriage, whether legal, void or voidable.

* * *

Appellant also urges this Court to extend the California wrongful death statute to her and her children on some equitable basis. While we might like to do so, our hands are tied. We cannot legislate this change in California's statute law. Finally, we cannot accept appellant's argument that the California statute denies her and her children equal protection.

Affirmed.

<h3 style="text-align:center">N<small>OTES</small></h3>

1. A survey of caselaw showed that all reported decisions reached the same result as *Aspinall,* including one case in which the cohabitants had been engaged to be married a few days after the death and another in which they had cohabited for 24 years. See Note, The Right of a Cohabitant to Recover in Tort: Wrongful Death, Negligent Infliction of Emotional Distress and Loss of Consortium, 32 U.Louisville J.Fam.L. 531 (1994) (observing that the 1990 census found almost three million unmarried couples cohabiting in the United States and concluding that wrongful death statutes embody an obsolete vision of family relationships).

2. Logic has its limits in understanding wrongful death law. The theory is that surviving family members have a cause of action for their own losses arising from the death, distinct from the decedent's losses. But the family

---

2. Section 377, as worded at the time that this cause of action arose, stated:

When the death of a person is caused by the wrongful act or neglect of another, his heirs, and his dependent parents, if any, who are not heirs, or personal representatives on their behalf may maintain an action for damages against the person causing the death.

members' wrongful death recovery is not fully independent of the decedent's claim. For example, as we shall see in Chapter IX, section D, infra, the decedent's negligence reduces (or bars) the family members' recovery, even if they have been guilty of no negligence themselves. If the decedent's personal injury action is resolved before death, the settlement or judgment precludes a survival action, because that statute only preserves the cause of action the decedent would have had. That logic would not apply to a wrongful death action if the family members are considered to be suing for their own losses rather than the decedent's, but some courts hold that a release of the decedent's personal injury claim precludes a wrongful death action as well as a survival suit. See, e.g., Varelis v. Northwestern Memorial Hospital, 167 Ill.2d 449, 657 N.E.2d 997, 212 Ill.Dec. 652 (1995).

Evidentiary considerations

Because major elements of wrongful death recovery require predictions about the support and services the decedent would have given the survivors, some delicate evidentiary questions arise. The jury is entitled to know how much money the decedent was likely to make and how generous and attentive the decedent was to the needs of the survivors. To that extent, evidence of decedent's frugality or profligacy and sobriety or intemperance is admissible, as is evidence (positive and negative) about the decedent's relationships with the survivors. On the other hand, courts often exclude evidence about the decedent's moral transgressions, such as marital infidelities, apparently in the belief that they are likely to be more prejudicial than probative. See, e.g., Gamble v. Hill, 208 Va. 171, 156 S.E.2d 888 (1967) (excluding evidence of decedent's two extramarital pregnancies on the ground that such immoralities would not diminish survivors' losses). With similar reservations, it can be said that the character and habits of the survivors may be admissible to show how long or how much the decedent was likely to support and nurture them.

A recurring issue is remarriage of the surviving spouse; is the defendant entitled to show that the spouse is better off with his or her new mate? Many states do not allow the jury even to be told of the remarriage, apparently on the theory that what the survivor does after the death should not benefit the tortfeasor. See, e.g., Gilmer v. Carney, 608 N.E.2d 709 (Ind.App.1993).

Proving pain and suffering in death cases

Damages for the decedent's pain and suffering from the time of injury to death are recoverable in a survival action. In a few states, survivors are permitted to recover for the decedent's pain and suffering under the wrongful death statute. See, e.g, McDavid v. United States, 213 W.Va. 592, 584 S.E.2d 226 (2003). Under either theory, most courts hold that there must be evidence that the decedent was conscious. See, e.g., Morrissey v. Welsh Co., 821 F.2d 1294, 1301 (8th Cir.1987) (decedent was aware that she had been buried alive under a collapsed wall but died before being removed from the rubble; recovery allowed for pain and suffering); Higgins v. State, 192 A.D.2d 821, 596 N.Y.S.2d 479 (1993) (award for conscious pain and suffering allowed when decedent received electrical shock after entering a lake; decedent contemplated death for several minutes because electrical shock rendered him unable to escape the water, then caused him to come into contact with a more intense source of electricity). When death is instantaneous, or when there is no evidence that the decedent consciously perceived pain and suffering before death, damages for pain and suffering are generally disallowed. See, e.g., Baker v. Slack, 319 Mich. 703, 30 N.W.2d 403 (1948) (evidence failed to show that decedent-pedestrian struck by automobile was conscious at any time during a thirty-minute interval before death, though she did make an outcry at the moment she was struck).

Losses to the Decedent's Estate

Most survival statutes limit recovery to losses sustained before death, but that puts the tortfeasor whose victim dies in better position than one whose victim is permanently disabled. The victim who is permanently disabled is entitled to recover for lost earning capacity for the remainder of his or her expected life. When the victim is killed, in most states the tortfeasor has to pay (as support damages under the wrongful death statute) only the portion of the earnings that the decedent would have contributed to survivors plus (under the survival statute) the decedent's lost earnings from the tort until death. The tortfeasor escapes liability for (a) earnings the decedent would have spent on himself or herself and (b) earnings the decedent would have saved and thus passed on to his or her estate.

Suppose the decedent is a professional with rising earnings, two grown children who are eligible to recover under the wrongful death statute, and a long-term companion who is ineligible under the wrongful death statute but is the beneficiary of decedent's will. Since the decedent's years of supporting the children are over, their wrongful death recovery is likely to be modest. The loss to the companion is likely to be substantial because the decedent had reached a point where he or she was able to accumulate wealth. The damages-before-death limitation assures that in this situation the tortfeasor will pay considerably less than the true cost of the death.

A few states avoid this situation by construing their survival statutes to permit the estate to recover for the wealth the decedent would have likely accumulated during his or her natural lifetime. See, e.g., Weil v. Seltzer, 873 F.2d 1453 (D.C.Cir.1989) (allowing recovery under survival action for decedent's probable future earnings less decedent's projected personal expenses and amounts decedent would have contributed to those entitled to recover under the wrongful death statute).

Loss of Consortium in Non–Fatal Cases

From early times the common law recognized a husband's cause of action for "loss of consortium" produced by non-fatal injury to the wife. The traditional rule denied a similar cause of action to the wife for loss of the husband's consortium. See, e.g., Best v. Samuel Fox & Co., Ltd., [1952] A.C. 716 (H.L.). Most of the modern American cases confronting the issue have eliminated the discrimination by recognizing a wife's cause of action for lost consortium, as North Dakota did in the *Hastings* case cited in *Weigel*, supra.

The recovery for loss of consortium is similar to the survivors' recovery for loss of society in wrongful death actions, and in those parents and children usually are allowed to recover for their loss of the decedent's society. Influenced by the trend to allow recovery for loss of society in wrongful death cases, some recent decisions have allowed children's claims for loss of an injured parent's consortium and parents' claims for loss of an injured child's consortium. In some states, statutes grant parents a right to recover for the loss of an injured child's society. But the majority of jurisdictions confine the cause of action in non-fatal cases to spouses, and at least as many recent decisions have rejected the children's or parents' claims for loss of consortium as have accepted them. Compare Gallimore v. Children's Hospital Medical Center, 67 Ohio St.3d 244, 617 N.E.2d 1052 (1993) (recognizing both parents' and childrens' consortium claims) with Dearborn Fabricating & Engineering Corp. v. Wickham, 551 N.E.2d 1135 (Ind.1990) (denying child's claim) and Roberts v. Williamson, 111 S.W.3d 113 (Tex. 2003) (denying parent's claim).

In Rodriguez v. McDonnell Douglas Corp., supra p. 285, the victim's wife was awarded $500,000 for loss of consortium. In a portion of the opinion not reproduced, the California Supreme Court rejected the defendant's claim that the amount was excessive. The court said consortium "embraces such elements as love, companionship, affection, society, sexual relations, solace and more.' Considering the youth of plaintiffs, the deprivation to be suffered by Mary Anne will extend over an inordinately long period of time."

D. OTHER COMPENSATORY DAMAGE ISSUES

Interest

Once a judgment is entered, the amount normally is treated as a debt owed by the defendant and interest begins to accrue at a rate that is usually set by statute.

As to prejudgment interest, there is less uniformity of treatment. The traditional view was that since the amount of the debt in a personal injury or death case is "unliquidated," i.e., not known until judgment, no interest should accrue until that time. Increasingly, however, courts have been inclined (or directed by legislatures) to award prejudgment interest on the theory that the tortfeasor's obligation to make the victim whole arises when the injury occurs, or at least when suit is filed. See, e.g., McCrann v. United States Lines, Inc., 803 F.2d 771 (2d Cir.1986).

Taxation

Punitive damages are subject to federal income tax, but compensatory damages for physical injuries or sickness (or death) are not. See 26 U.S.C. § 104(a). In O'Gilvie v. United States, 519 U.S. 79, 117 S.Ct. 452, 136 L.Ed.2d 454 (1996), the Supreme Court said Congress intended plaintiffs to receive the benefit of the exclusion. The best way to achieve that result would be to tell jurors to ignore the effects of taxation in fixing the compensatory award. If they are told nothing, they may assume the award is taxable. Suppose the jury believes the plaintiff has suffered a $100,000 loss of earning capacity and mistakenly believes the award will be taxed at 33 per cent; the jury might award $150,000 to make sure the plaintiff gets $100,000 after taxes. In that event, the plaintiff would get not only the tax break that Congress presumably intended, but an additional $50,000 that overcompensates the plaintiff at the defendant's expense. To prevent that, the Supreme Court has held that defendants in Federal Employers Liability Act (FELA) cases are entitled to have the jury told that compensatory damages will not be taxed. Norfolk & W. Ry. Co. v. Liepelt, 444 U.S. 490, 100 S.Ct. 755, 62 L.Ed.2d 689 (1980).

There is little agreement as to what, if anything, jurors should be told about taxation. In *Rodriguez*, supra p. 285, the trial court forbade the parties from introducing evidence relating to taxation. In a portion of the opinion not reproduced in the casebook, the court of appeals approved that procedure and said most jurisdictions agree that jurors should be told nothing about taxation.

A related problem is whether the jury should be given pre-tax or after-tax estimates of the plaintiff's earnings losses. The *Liepelt* majority held that it was error, under the FELA, to exclude evidence of the tax that would have been payable on the earnings, but that seems inconsistent with *O'Gilvie*'s theory as to the purpose of Sec. 104(a)(2). The plaintiff will get the windfall that *O'Gilvie* says Congress intended only if both the earnings estimate and the award ignore the effects of taxation. Reducing both the earnings estimate and the award on account of taxation would subject the plaintiff to double taxation; reducing either denies the plaintiff the windfall.

Periodic Payments

As we saw above, supra p. 293, awards for pecuniary losses usually are reduced to present value on the theory that the plaintiff can use the award to make more money by investing it. Of course, the successful plaintiff need not invest the award, prudently or otherwise. If the plaintiff chooses to fritter away the money, the tort system's objective of helping the injured plaintiff achieve self-sufficiency is frustrated. This is only one of the weaknesses of the traditional lump sum judgment. Another is that it requires all future losses to be calculated at one moment in time, precluding future adjustments for changes in earnings, medical costs, treatment methods, inflation, and most importantly, the plaintiff's condition. But courts have shown little interest in retaining jurisdiction to permit such ongoing adjustments and seem firmly committed to the finality of a one-time determination of all these variables. That does not preclude paying the one-time sum out periodically, however, and there has been some movement in that direction. A number of states permit or even require the court to arrange for periodic payment of certain types of judgments, for example, judgments for medical malpractice or against governmental entities. See, e.g., American Bank & Trust Co. v. Community Hospital, 36 Cal.3d 359, 204 Cal.Rptr. 671, 683 P.2d 670 (1984); Bernier v. Burris, 113 Ill.2d 219, 100 Ill.Dec. 585, 497 N.E.2d 763 (1986); Smith v. Myers, 181 Ariz. 11, 887 P.2d 541 (1994).

Structured Settlements

Far more common are settlement agreements to pay part of the agreed amount as a lump sum and the remainder as periodic payments. Parties often negotiate "structured settlements" in which the defendant typically agrees to buy the plaintiff an annuity that guarantees the plaintiff a specified monthly or annual payment for a specified period such as the rest of the plaintiff's life, a fixed number of years, or until the plaintiff's children reach a certain age. Because of the time value of money, this arrangement costs the defendant less than the total the plaintiff ultimately receives. The annuity provider (usually a life insurance company) in effect manages the money until it is time to pay it to the plaintiff. These arrangements are so popular—and sometimes so intricate—that they have spawned a new profession, the structured settlement broker. Lawyers employ these brokers to advise them on the many annuity options available.

Caps on Damages

In more than half the states, legislatures have imposed caps on compensatory damages. In some states the cap applies only to certain types of cases or certain types of damages. In California, for example, damages in medical malpractice cases for noneconomic losses (including pain and suffering, disfigurement, physical impairment, and inconvenience) are capped at $250,000, Cal. Civ. Code § 3333.2. In Utah total damages against liquor providers are capped at $500,000. Utah Code. Ann. 32A–14a–102. The cap in Maryland applicable to all personal injury cases, limits noneconomic damages to $500,000 plus an annual upward adjustment. Md. Ann. Code, Ct. & Jud. Proc. § 11–108. Colorado limits damages against health care providers to $300,000 for noneconomic damages and $1 million total for all categories of damages. Colo. Rev. Stat. § 13–64–302.l.

Opponents of caps argue that they make the most seriously injured plaintiffs bear the costs of tortious conduct and do nothing, in the vast majority of cases where damages do not reach the cap, to cure whatever imperfections were thought to produce excessive damage awards. Proponents say caps are a simple way of reducing the cost of tort liability, and therefore of insurance premiums. Both sides agree that caps affect far more cases than those in which recovery is actually reduced to conform to the cap, because the existence of the cap reduces settlement value of cases by giving defendants a ceiling on their potential losses if they refuse to settle.

Alternative Compensation Schemes

The best-known alternative to tort liability as a means of compensating personal injuries or wrongful death is workers' compensation. All states and the federal government have statutes giving employers immunity from most tort liability for on-the-job injuries or occupational diseases in exchange for their contributions to a fund or insurance plan which pays injured workers benefits in amounts that are administratively determined. Benefits are payable without regard to the fault of either the employer or the employee, usually do not cover the full amount of employee's lost earnings, and do not include anything for pain and suffering. There are numerous exclusions (intentional torts are often excluded, for example). Attempts by employees to get out of the workers' compensation scheme and into the tort scheme, and by employers to get out of the tort scheme and into workers' compensation, generate considerable litigation. See, e.g., Karen A. Lerner, Workers' Compensation Law and Practice (1989).

Another alternative is no-fault insurance. The idea is that certain classes of injuries, e.g., from auto accidents, are compensated by the victim's own insurance, at least up to a specified threshold amount. The theory is that this is less costly than a system in which the defendant's insurance pays only after the victim establishes the defendant's liability under tort law. A no-fault auto accident plan was advanced in Robert E. Keeton and Jeffrey O'Connell, Basic Protection for the Traffic Victim (1965), and is often called the Keeton–O'Connell plan. A few states (most notably New York) have employed such plans with apparent success for a number of years, but the idea has not caught on nationally. See Roger C. Henderson, No–Fault Insurance for Automobile Accidents: Status and Effect in the United States, 56 Or. L. Rev. 287 (1977).

Occasionally Congress creates ad hoc compensation plans to bypass tort liability in specific situations. For example, to encourage manufacturers to quickly produce enough vaccine for mass immunization campaigns, Congress created a federal compensation fund to pay those who suffer injurious side effects from the vaccinations. Benefits are limited and procedures for establishing entitlement are standardized. See, e.g., National Childhood Vaccine Injury Act, 42 U.S.C. § 300aa–1 et seq. For a description of the statutory scheme, see Schafer v. American Cyanamid Co., 20 F.3d 1 (1st Cir. 1994).

Another example is the Victim Compensation Fund created for survivors and relatives of those killed in the September 11, 2001, attacks on the World Trade Center and the Pentagon. Congress hastily created the Fund in the aftermath of the attacks to protect airlines, insurance companies, and building owners from tort claims that they claimed would bankrupt them. Ninety-seven per cent of the families of deceased victims chose to waive their tort claims in exchange for compensation from the Fund. The Fund distributed over $7 billion to survivors of 2,880 persons killed in the attacks and 2,680 individuals who were injured in the attacks or in the rescue efforts that followed. Average awards were in excess of $2 million for families of victims killed and nearly $400,000 for injured victims. See Final Report of the Special Master for the September 11th Victim Compensation Fund of 2001, available at http://www.justice.gov/final _ report.

A similar fund was set up with $20 billion in funds from BP Exploration & Production, Inc. to compensate victims of the 2010 Deepwater Horizon oil spill in the Gulf of Mexico. It was to be administered by

Kenneth Feinberg, the lawyer who was the special master for the 9/11 fund.

E. PUNITIVE DAMAGES

The availability and amount of punitive damages is governed in the first instance by tort law—that is, by state law (or, as in the following case, federal maritime law). Generally, states permit punitive damages only on a showing of an elevated level of fault such as "conscious disregard of a high degree of risk"—never on a showing of mere negligence. Some states do not permit them at all, and most provide for heightened appellate scrutiny of punitive damage awards.

In addition to these limitations, the Supreme Court has decided that some punitive damage awards violate defendants' due process rights. As a result of a series of cases beginning in the 1990s, the law of punitive damages has become increasingly constitutionalized. The most important of those decisions are discussed in the following case. It is important to remember, however, that punitive damages are a creation of tort law, and as this case shows, there is no constitutional question to be considered until the tort law analysis is completed.

EXXON SHIPPING CO. v. BAKER

Supreme Court of the United States, 2008.
554 U.S. 471, 128 S.Ct. 2605, 171 L.Ed.2d 570.

JUSTICE SOUTER.

There are three questions of maritime law before us: whether a shipowner may be liable for punitive damages without acquiescence in the actions causing harm, whether punitive damages have been barred implicitly by federal statutory law making no provision for them, and whether the award of $2.5 billion in this case is greater than maritime law should allow in the circumstances. We are equally divided on the owner's derivative liability,* and hold that the federal statutory law does not bar a punitive award on top of damages for economic loss, but that the award here should be limited to an amount equal to compensatory damages.

I.

On March 24, 1989, the supertanker *Exxon Valdez* grounded on Bligh Reef off the Alaskan coast, fracturing its hull and spilling millions of gallons of crude oil into Prince William Sound. The owner, petitioner Exxon Shipping Co. (now SeaRiver Maritime, Inc.), and its owner, petitioner Exxon Mobil Corp. (collectively, Exxon), have settled state and federal claims for environmental damage, with payments exceeding $1 billion, and this action by respondent Baker and others, including com-

---

* The want of a majority on this point left in place the Ninth Circuit's determination that acts of its managers could be charged to Exxon for purposes of imposing punitive damages.—Ed.

mercial fishermen and native Alaskans, was brought for economic losses to individuals dependent on Prince William Sound for their livelihoods.

A.

The tanker was over 900 feet long and was used by Exxon to carry crude oil from the end of the Trans–Alaska Pipeline in Valdez, Alaska, to the lower 48 States. On the night of the spill it was carrying 53 million gallons of crude oil, or over a million barrels. Its captain was one Joseph Hazelwood, who had completed a 28–day alcohol treatment program while employed by Exxon, as his superiors knew, but dropped out of a prescribed follow-up program and stopped going to Alcoholics Anonymous meetings. According to the District Court, "[t]here was evidence presented to the jury that after Hazelwood was released from [residential treatment], he drank in bars, parking lots, apartments, airports, airplanes, restaurants, hotels, at various ports, and aboard Exxon tankers." The jury also heard contested testimony that Hazelwood drank with Exxon officials and that members of the Exxon management knew of his relapse. Although Exxon had a clear policy prohibiting employees from serving onboard within four hours of consuming alcohol, Exxon presented no evidence that it monitored Hazelwood after his return to duty or considered giving him a shoreside assignment. Witnesses testified that before the *Valdez* left port on the night of the disaster, Hazelwood downed at least five double vodkas in the waterfront bars of Valdez, an intake of about 15 ounces of 80–proof alcohol, enough "that a non-alcoholic would have passed out."

[Hazelwood left the bridge and went to his cabin two minutes before the ship was to make a difficult maneuver, leaving only an unlicensed officer and a nonofficer to navigate. The tanker failed to make a turn and ran aground on Bligh Reef, tearing the hull open and spilling 11 million gallons of crude oil into Prince William Sound. Hazelwood returned to the bridge and tried to rock the *Valdez* off the reef, "a maneuver which could have spilled more oil and caused the ship to founder." His blood-alcohol level was .061 eleven hours after the spill, which expert witnesses said indicated that he must have had a blood-alcohol level of around .241 at the time of the spill. The jury found Hazelwood guilty of recklessness. The instructions allowed the jury to impose punitive damages on Exxon if it believed either that Exxon was itself reckless in knowingly allowing a relapsed alcoholic to pilot a vessel filled with millions of gallons of oil, or that Hazelwood was a managerial employee whose recklessness would be imputed to Exxon as a matter of law.]

* * *

In the aftermath of the disaster, Exxon spent around $2.1 billion in cleanup efforts.

Exxon pleaded guilty to violations of the Clean Water Act, the Refuse Act, and the Migratory Bird Treaty Act and agreed to pay a $150 million fine, later reduced to $25 million plus restitution of $100 million. A civil action by the United States and the State of Alaska for environmental harms ended with a consent decree for Exxon to pay at least $900 million toward restoring natural resources, and it paid another $303 million in voluntary settlements with fishermen, property owners, and other private parties.

B.

The remaining civil cases were consolidated into this one against Exxon, Hazelwood, and others. The District Court for the District of Alaska divided the plaintiffs seeking compensatory damages into three classes: commercial fishermen, Native Alaskans, and landowners. At Exxon's behest, the court also certified a mandatory class of all plaintiffs seeking punitive damages, whose number topped 32,000. Respondents here, to whom we will refer as Baker for convenience, are members of that class.

For the purposes of the case, Exxon stipulated to its negligence in the *Valdez* disaster and its ensuing liability for compensatory damages.

* * *

[T]he jury heard about Exxon's management's acts and omissions arguably relevant to the spill. At the close of evidence, the court instructed the jurors on the purposes of punitive damages, emphasizing that they were designed not to provide compensatory relief but to punish and deter the defendants. The court charged the jury to consider the reprehensibility of the defendants' conduct, their financial condition, the magnitude of the harm, and any mitigating facts. The jury awarded $5,000 in punitive damages against Hazelwood and $5 billion against Exxon.

[On appeal, the Court of Appeals for the Ninth Circuit reduced the award against Exxon to $2.5 billion.]

* * *

IV.

Finally, Exxon raises an issue of first impression about punitive damages in maritime law, which falls within a federal court's jurisdiction to decide in the manner of a common law court, subject to the authority of Congress to legislate otherwise if it disagrees with the judicial result.

* * *

[The Court reviewed the history of punitive damages, the limitations that many state legislatures have imposed on them in recent years, and the laws of other countries, which it said show that "punitive damages overall are higher and more frequent in the United States than they are anywhere else."]

D.

American punitive damages have been the target of audible criticism in recent decades, see, e.g., Note, Developments, The Paths of Civil

Litigation, 113 Harv. L.Rev. 1783, 1784–1788 (2000) (surveying criticism), but the most recent studies tend to undercut much of it, see id., at 1787–1788. A survey of the literature reveals that discretion to award punitive damages has not mass-produced runaway awards, and although some studies show the dollar amounts of punitive-damages awards growing over time, even in real terms, by most accounts the median ratio of punitive to compensatory awards has remained less than 1:1.[14] Nor do the data substantiate a marked increase in the percentage of cases with punitive awards over the past several decades. The figures thus show an overall restraint and suggest that in many instances a high ratio of punitive to compensatory damages is substantially greater than necessary to punish or deter.

The real problem, it seems, is the stark unpredictability of punitive awards. Courts of law are concerned with fairness as consistency, and evidence that the median ratio of punitive to compensatory awards falls within a reasonable zone, or that punitive awards are infrequent, fails to tell us whether the spread between high and low individual awards is acceptable. The available data suggest it is not. A recent comprehensive study of punitive damages awarded by juries in state civil trials found a median ratio of punitive to compensatory awards of just 0.62:1, but a mean ratio of 2.90:1 and a standard deviation of 13.81. [T. Eisenberg, Juries, Judges, and Punitive Damages, 3 J. of Empirical Legal Studies 263, 269 (2006)]. Even to those of us unsophisticated in statistics, the thrust of these figures is clear: the spread is great, and the outlier cases subject defendants to punitive damages that dwarf the corresponding compensatories. The distribution of awards is narrower, but still remarkable, among punitive damages assessed by judges: the median ratio is 0.66:1, the mean ratio is 1.60:1, and the standard deviation is 4.54.

* * *

Starting with the premise of a punitive-damages regime, these ranges of variation might be acceptable or even desirable if they resulted from judges' and juries' refining their judgments to reach a generally accepted optimal level of penalty and deterrence in cases involving a wide range of circumstances, while producing fairly consistent results in cases with similar facts. But anecdotal evidence suggests that nothing of that sort is going on. One of our own leading cases on punitive damages, with a $4 million verdict by an Alabama jury, noted that a second Alabama case with strikingly similar facts produced "a comparable amount of compensatory damages" but "no punitive damages at all." See *Gore*, 517 U.S., at 565, n. 8, 116 S.Ct. 1589. As the Supreme Court of Alabama candidly explained, "the disparity between the two jury verdicts * * * [w]as a

---

14. See, *e.g.,* Juries, Judges, and Punitive Damages 269 (reporting median ratios of 0.62:1 in jury trials and 0.66:1 in bench trials using the Bureau of Justice Statistics data from 1992, 1996, and 2001); Vidmar & Rose, Punitive Damages by Juries in Florida, 38 Harv. J. Legis. 487, 492 (2001) (studying civil cases in Florida state courts between 1989 and 1998 and finding a median ratio of 0.67:1). But see Financial Injury Jury Verdicts 307 (finding a median ratio of 1.4:1 in "financial injury" cases in the late 1980s and early 1990s).

reflection of the inherent uncertainty of the trial process." BMW of North America, Inc. v. Gore, 646 So.2d 619, 626 (1994) (per curiam). We are aware of no scholarly work pointing to consistency across punitive awards in cases involving similar claims and circumstances.[17]

E.

The Court's response to outlier punitive damages awards has thus far been confined by claims at the constitutional level, and our cases have announced due process standards that every award must pass. See, *e.g.,* State Farm Mut. Automobile Ins. Co. v. Campbell, 538 U.S. 408, 425, 123 S.Ct. 1513, 155 L.Ed.2d 585 (2003); *Gore,* 517 U.S., at 574–575, 116 S.Ct. 1589. Although "we have consistently rejected the notion that the constitutional line is marked by a simple mathematical formula," *id.,* at 582, 116 S.Ct. 1589, we have determined that "few awards exceeding a single-digit ratio between punitive and compensatory damages, to a significant degree, will satisfy due process," *State Farm,* 538 U.S., at 425, 123 S.Ct. 1513; "[w]hen compensatory damages are substantial, then a lesser ratio, perhaps only equal to compensatory damages, can reach the outermost limit of the due process guarantee," ibid.

Today's enquiry differs from due process review because the case arises under federal maritime jurisdiction, and we are reviewing a jury award for conformity with maritime law, rather than the outer limit allowed by due process; we are examining the verdict in the exercise of federal maritime common law authority, which precedes and should obviate any application of the constitutional standard. Our due process cases, on the contrary, have all involved awards subject in the first instance to state law. These, as state-law cases, could provide no occasion to consider a "common-law standard of excessiveness," and the only matter of federal law within our appellate authority was the constitutional due process issue.

Our review of punitive damages today, then, considers not their intersection with the Constitution, but the desirability of regulating them as a common law remedy for which responsibility lies with this Court as a source of judge-made law in the absence of statute. Whatever may be the constitutional significance of the unpredictability of high punitive awards, this feature of happenstance is in tension with the function of the awards as punitive, just because of the implication of unfairness that an eccentrically high punitive verdict carries in a system whose commonly held notion of law rests on a sense of fairness in dealing with one another.

---

17. The Court is aware of a body of literature running parallel to anecdotal reports, examining the predictability of punitive awards by conducting numerous "mock juries," where different "jurors" are confronted with the same hypothetical case. See, *e.g.,* C. Sunstein, R. Hastie, J. Payne, D. Schkade, W. Viscusi, Punitive Damages: How Juries Decide (2002); Schkade, Sunstein, & Kahneman, Deliberating About Dollars: The Severity Shift, 100 Colum. L.Rev. 1139 (2000); Hastie, Schkade, & Payne, Juror Judgments in Civil Cases: Effects of Plaintiff's Requests and Plaintiff's Identity on Punitive Damage Awards, 23 Law & Hum. Behav. 445 (1999); Sunstein, Kahneman, & Schkade, Assessing Punitive Damages (with Notes on Cognition and Valuation in Law), 107 Yale L.J. 2071 (1998). Because this research was funded in part by Exxon, we decline to rely on it.

Thus, a penalty should be reasonably predictable in its severity, so that even Justice Holmes's "bad man" can look ahead with some ability to know what the stakes are in choosing one course of action or another. See The Path of the Law, 10 Harv. L.Rev. 457, 459 (1897). And when the bad man's counterparts turn up from time to time, the penalty scheme they face ought to threaten them with a fair probability of suffering in like degree when they wreak like damage. The common sense of justice would surely bar penalties that reasonable people would think excessive for the harm caused in the circumstances.

F.

1.

[The Court said experience with criminal sentencing guidelines convinced it that nothing less than a firm quantitative limitation would provide sufficient predictability. The Court said a "slim majority" of the states that have imposed such a quantitative limit have selected a ratio of 3:1 punitive to compensatory damages, but "a legislative judgment that 3:1 is a reasonable limit overall is not a judgment that 3:1 is a reasonable limit in this particular type of case," where the tortious action was worse than negligent but less than malicious and exposed Exxon to regulatory sanctions and inevitable damage actions in addition to punitive damages. It rejected the 2:1 ratio reflected in federal statutes authorizing treble damages in actions such as antitrust on the ground that those were designed to encourage enforcement through private litigation, an objective that "has no traction here, in this case of staggering damage inevitably provoking governmental enforcers to indict and any number of private parties to sue."]

There is better evidence of an accepted limit of reasonable civil penalty, however, in several studies mentioned before, showing the median ratio of punitive to compensatory verdicts, reflecting what juries and judges have considered reasonable across many hundreds of punitive awards. We think it is fair to assume that the greater share of the verdicts studied in these comprehensive collections reflect reasonable judgments about the economic penalties appropriate in their particular cases.

These studies cover cases of the most as well as the least blameworthy conduct triggering punitive liability, from malice and avarice, down to recklessness, and even gross negligence in some jurisdictions. The data put the median ratio for the entire gamut of circumstances at less than 1:1, meaning that the compensatory award exceeds the punitive award in most cases. In a well-functioning system, we would expect that awards at the median or lower would roughly express jurors' sense of reasonable penalties in cases with no earmarks of exceptional blameworthiness within the punishable spectrum (cases like this one, without intentional or malicious conduct, and without behavior driven primarily by desire for gain, for example) and cases (again like this one) without the modest economic harm or odds of detection that have opened the door to higher awards. It also seems fair to suppose that most of the unpredictable outlier cases that call the fairness of the system into question are above the median; in theory a factfinder's deliberation could go awry to produce a very low ratio, but we have no basis to assume that such a case would be more than a sport, and the cases with serious constitutional issues coming to us have naturally been on the high side, see, *e.g., State Farm,* 538 U.S., at 425, 123 S.Ct. 1513 (ratio of 145:1); *Gore,* 517 U.S., at 582, 116 S.Ct. 1589 (ratio of 500:1). On these assumptions, a median ratio of punitive to compensatory damages of about 0.65:1 probably marks the line near which cases like this one largely should be grouped. Accordingly, given the need to protect against the possibility (and the disruptive cost to the legal system) of awards that are unpredictable and unnecessary, either for deterrence or for measured retribution, we consider that a 1:1 ratio, which is above the median award, is a fair upper limit in such maritime cases.[27]

The provision of the [Clean Water Act] respecting daily fines confirms our judgment that anything greater would be excessive here and in cases of this type. Congress set criminal penalties of up to $25,000 per day for negligent violations of pollution restrictions, and up to $50,000 per day for knowing ones. 33 U.S.C. §§ 1319(c)(1), (2). Discretion [given by the statute] to double the penalty for knowing action compares to discretion to double the civil liability on conduct going beyond negligence and meriting punitive treatment. And our explanation of the constitutional upper limit confirms that the 1:1 ratio is not too low. In *State Farm,* we said that a single-digit maximum is appropriate in all but the most exceptional of cases, and "[w]hen compensatory damages are substantial, then a lesser ratio, perhaps only equal to compensatory damages, can reach the outermost limit of the due process guarantee." 538 U.S., at 425, 123 S.Ct. 1513.[28]

V.

Applying this standard to the present case, we take for granted the District Court's calculation of the total relevant compensatory damages at $507.5 million. A punitive-to-compensatory ratio of 1:1 thus yields maximum punitive damages in that amount.

We therefore vacate the judgment and remand the case for the Court of Appeals to remit the punitive damages award accordingly.

---

27. The reasons for this conclusion answer Justice Stevens's suggestion that there is an adequate restraint in appellate abuse-of-discretion review of a trial judge's own review of a punitive jury award (or of a judge's own award in nonjury cases). We cannot see much promise of a practical solution to the outlier problem in this possibility. Justice Stevens would find no abuse of discretion in allowing the $2.5 billion balance of the jury's punitive verdict here, and yet that is about five times the size of the award that jury practice and our judgment would signal as reasonable in a case of this sort.

* * *

28. The criterion of "substantial" takes into account the role of punitive damages to induce legal action when pure compensation may not be enough to encourage suit, a concern addressed by the opportunity for a class action when large numbers of potential plaintiffs are involved: in such cases, individual awards are not the touchstone, for it is the class option that facilitates suit, and a class recovery of $500 million is substantial. In this case, then, the constitutional outer limit may well be 1:1.

It is so ordered.

[Justice Alito took no part in the consideration or decision of the case. Justices Scalia and Thomas concurred but reiterated their belief that the Court's earlier decisions imposing constitutional limits on punitive damages were wrong. Justices Stevens and Ginsburg dissented from Parts IV and V of the opinion, arguing that the any limitation on punitive damages in maritime suits should be left to Congress. Justice Breyer agreed with the majority's view that a limit was appropriate, but dissented from the decision to apply the limit in this case because he believed Exxon's conduct was exceptionally egregious.]

NOTES

1. After this decision, Exxon agreed to pay $507.5 million in punitive damages, an amount equal to the compensatory damages awarded in this branch of the litigation, plus $470 million in interest on that amount. See 568 F.3d 1077 (9th Cir. 2009).

2. At an earlier stage in its appeal, Exxon argued that the disparity between the $5,000 awarded against the man who directly caused the oil spill and the $5 billion awarded against Exxon impugned the rationality of the jury's evaluation of reprehensibility. The district court said: "What is sufficient to effect just but not excessive deterrence of Captain Hazelwood, and what is sufficient to effect just and not excessive deterrence of the Exxon defendants are vastly different." Hazelwood's career was destroyed, he would not again be piloting a tanker, and his conduct was brought on by alcoholism, a disease. On the other hand, Exxon was an economic powerhouse and would remain so despite the cost of the *Valdez* disaster, and it would continue to transport crude oil across Prince William Sound for many years. "Its callous inattention to Captain Hazelwood's relapse and its reckless failure to remove him from command of the *Exxon Valdez,* knowing that he had relapsed into drinking, calls for major deterrence." 236 F. Supp.2d 1043, 1065 (D. Alaska 2002). The disparity was not discussed by the Supreme Court.

3. This case established only that a 1:1 ratio of punitive to compensatory damages is the maximum allowable in federal maritime cases. It ostensibly left the states free to establish their own maximums in other tort cases, within the federal due process limit of "a single digit ratio." But note that in footnote 28, the Court said "the *constitutional* outer limit may well be 1:1" in cases like Exxon. (Emphasis added.) That led Justice Ginsburg to wonder whether the Court was signalling that at the next opportunity it would rule "that 1:1 is the ceiling due process requires in all of the States, and for all federal claims." 128 S.Ct. at 2639.

4. The Supreme Court's imposition of federal constitutional limitations on punitive damages, which traditionally have been exclusively within the domain of state law, has led to some tests of wills between the Court and state supreme courts. For example, see Williams v. Philip Morris Inc., 344 Or. 45, 176 P.3d 1255 (2008) (refusing, after two remands from the U.S. Supreme

Court, to reduce a punitive damage award of $79.5 million). The Supreme Court dismissed Philip Morris's third challenge. 129 S.Ct. 1436 (2009).

5. In some states a portion of a punitive damage award is payable to the state. See, e.g., Mo. Rev. Stat. Sec. 537.567, authorizing the state to assert a lien on 50% of any final judgment for punitive damages on behalf of the state's tort victim compensation fund.

Chapter VIII

Vicarious Liability

■ ■ ■

When the defendant's employee, contractor, or child hurts someone, the defendant may be liable on the basis of defendant's own negligence. Thus, the company that hires an obviously incompetent driver to operate a heavy truck is subject to liability when the driver runs over someone. The developer who engages a contractor with a terrible job-safety record may be liable when the contractor hurts a construction worker. The parent who entrusts a reckless teenager with a powerful vehicle may be liable for harm the child does with the machine. Indeed, anyone whose substandard conduct enables another person to hurt the plaintiff may be liable for the resulting injuries, on familiar principles of negligence law.

Vicarious liability is something different. When A is held *vicariously* liable for damages done by B, the liability is not based on any view that A has been at fault; it is imposed solely on the basis that B was at fault and that the relationship between A and B justifies holding A responsible.

The most important instance of vicarious liability, often called "respondeat superior," is the liability of an employer ("master") for the tort of an employee ("servant") who was acting in the scope of the employment. As a general rule, one who employs an independent contractor, rather than an employee, is not subject to vicarious liability for the contractor's torts. There are exceptions to this general rule, however, which are introduced in this chapter.

Whether the employed party is characterized as an employee or an independent contractor depends upon the nature of the relationship. If the employer exercises or has the right to exercise control over the physical conduct ("manner and means") of the work, the one employed is an employee or servant. If the relationship is such that the employer directs only the result, and the party employed is free to determine the manner and means, then the relationship is one of independent contractor. See Restatement (Second) of Agency § 220 (1958). Many factors may be considered in determining whether the relationship is one of employee or independent contractor, including the length of time of the employment; who provides the tools, instrumentalities, and place of work; the method of payment (by time or by the job); and the degree of skill and judgment required. See id. (listing ten nonexclusive factors).

Under the common law, parents are not vicariously liable for the torts of their children. Many jurisdictions have imposed limited vicarious liability upon parents by statute. These "parental liability" statutes vary widely, but typically they cap liability at a fairly low amount, apply only to children in a specified age range, and often apply only to acts in the nature of malicious mischief (vandalism).

Other relationships that have supported vicarious liability under certain circumstances include partnerships and joint enterprises. Vicarious liability has also sometimes been imposed on the basis of statutes making the owner of a car liable for the fault of anyone driving it with the owner's permission.

IRA S. BUSHEY & SONS, INC. v. UNITED STATES

United States Court of Appeals, Second Circuit, 1968.
398 F.2d 167.

FRIENDLY, CIRCUIT JUDGE.

While the United States Coast Guard vessel Tamaroa was being overhauled in a floating drydock located in Brooklyn's Gowanus Canal, a seaman returning from shore leave late at night, in the condition for which seamen are famed, turned some wheels on the drydock wall. He thus opened valves that controlled the flooding of the tanks on one side of the drydock. Soon the ship listed, slid off the blocks and fell against the wall. Parts of the drydock sank, and the ship partially did—fortunately without loss of life or personal injury. The drydock owner sought and was granted compensation by the District Court for the Eastern District of New York [in a bench trial]; the United States appeals.

* * *

Seaman Lane, whose prior record was unblemished, returned from shore leave a little after midnight on March 14. He had been drinking heavily; the quartermaster made mental note that he was "loose." For reasons not apparent to us or very likely to Lane,[4] he took it into his head, while progressing along the gangway wall, to turn each of three large wheels some twenty times; unhappily, as previously stated, these wheels controlled the water intake valves. After boarding ship at 12:11 A.M., Lane mumbled to an off-duty seaman that he had "turned some valves" and also muttered something about "valves" to another who was standing the engineering watch. Neither did anything; apparently Lane's condition was not such as to encourage proximity. At 12:20 A.M. a crew member discovered water coming into the drydock. By 12:30 A.M. the ship began to list, the alarm was sounded and the crew were ordered ashore. Ten

---

4. Lane disappeared after completing the sentence imposed by a court-martial and being discharged from the Coast Guard.

minutes later the vessel and dock were listing over 20 degrees; in another ten minutes the ship slid off the blocks and fell against the drydock wall.

The Government attacks imposition of liability on the ground that Lane's acts were not within the scope of his employment. It relies heavily on § 228(1) of the Restatement of Agency 2d which says that "conduct of a servant is within the scope of employment if, but only if: * * * (c) it is actuated, at least in part by a purpose to serve the master." Courts have gone to considerable lengths to find such a purpose, as witness a well-known opinion in which Judge Learned Hand concluded that a drunken boatswain who routed the plaintiff out of his bunk with a blow, saying "Get up, you big son of a bitch, and turn to," and then continued to fight, might have thought he was acting in the interest of the ship. Nelson v. American–West African Line, 86 F.2d 730 (2 Cir.1936). It would be going too far to find such a purpose here; while Lane's return to the Tamaroa was to serve his employer, no one has suggested how he could have thought turning the wheels to be, even if—which is by no means clear—he was unaware of the consequences.

In light of the highly artificial way in which the motive test has been applied, the district judge believed himself obliged to test the doctrine's continuing vitality by referring to the larger purposes *respondeat superior* is supposed to serve. He concluded that the old formulation failed this test. We do not find his analysis so compelling, however, as to constitute a sufficient basis in itself for discarding the old doctrine. It is not at all clear, as the court below suggested, that expansion of liability in the manner here suggested will lead to a more efficient allocation of resources. As the most astute exponent of this theory has emphasized, a more efficient allocation can only be expected if there is some reason to believe that imposing a particular cost on the enterprise will lead it to consider whether steps should be taken to prevent a recurrence of the accident. Calabresi, The Decision for Accidents: An Approach to Non–fault Allocation of Costs, 78 Harv.L.Rev. 713, 725–34 (1965). And the suggestion that imposition of liability here will lead to more intensive screening of employees rests on highly questionable premises.[5] The unsatisfactory quality of the allocation of resource rationale is especially striking on the facts of this case. It could well be that application of the traditional rule might induce drydock owners, prodded by their insurance companies, to install locks on their valves to avoid similar incidents in the future, while placing the burden on shipowners is much less likely to lead to accident prevention. It is true, of course, that in many cases the plaintiff will not be in a position to insure, and so expansion of liability will, at the very least, serve *respondeat superior's* loss spreading function. But the fact that the defendant is better able to afford damages is not alone sufficient to justify legal responsibility, and this overarching principle must be taken into account in deciding whether to expand the reach of *respondeat superior*.

---

5. We are not here speaking of cases in which the enterprise has negligently hired an employee whose undesirable propensities are known or should have been.

A policy analysis thus is not sufficient to justify this proposed expansion of vicarious liability. This is not surprising since *respondeat superior,* even within its traditional limits, rests not so much on policy grounds consistent with the governing principles of tort law as in a deeply rooted sentiment that a business enterprise cannot justly disclaim responsibility for accidents which may fairly be said to be characteristic of its activities. It is in this light that the inadequacy of the motive test becomes apparent. Whatever may have been the case in the past, a doctrine that would create such drastically different consequences for the actions of the drunken boatswain in *Nelson* and those of the drunken seaman here reflects a wholly unrealistic attitude toward the risks characteristically attendant upon the operation of a ship. We concur in the statement of Mr. Justice Rutledge in a case involving violence injuring a fellow-worker, in this instance in the context of workmen's compensation:

> Men do not discard their personal qualities when they go to work. Into the job they carry their intelligence, skill, habits of care and rectitude. Just as inevitably they take along also their tendencies to carelessness and camaraderie, as well as emotional make-up. In bringing men together, work brings these qualities together, causes frictions between them, creates occasions for lapses into carelessness, and for fun-making and emotional flare-up. * * * These expressions of human nature are incidents inseparable from working together. They involve risks of injury and these risks are inherent in the working environment.

* * *

Put another way, Lane's conduct was not so "unforeseeable" as to make it unfair to charge the Government with responsibility. We agree with a leading treatise that "what is reasonably foreseeable in this context [of *respondeat superior*] * * * is quite a different thing from the foreseeably unreasonable risk of harm that spells negligence * * *. The foresight that should impel the prudent man to take precautions is not the same measure as that by which he should perceive the harm likely to flow from his long-run activity in spite of all reasonable precautions on his own part. The proper test here bears far more resemblance to that which limits liability for workmen's compensation than to the test for negligence. The employer should be held to expect risks, to the public also, which arise 'out of and in the course of' his employment of labor." 2 Harper & James, The Law of Torts 1377–78 (1956). See also Calabresi, Some Thoughts on Risk Distribution and the Law of Torts, 70 Yale L.J. 499, 544 (1961). Here it was foreseeable that crew members crossing the drydock might do damage, negligently or even intentionally, such as pushing a Bushey employee or kicking property into the water. Moreover, the proclivity of seamen to find solace for solitude by copious resort to the bottle while ashore has been noted in opinions too numerous to warrant citation. Once all this is granted, it is immaterial that Lane's precise action was not to be foreseen. Consequently, we can no longer accept our past decisions that have refused to move beyond the *Nelson* rule, since they do not accord with modern understanding as to when it is fair for an enterprise to disclaim the actions of its employees.

One can readily think of cases that fall on the other side of the line. If Lane had set fire to the bar where he had been imbibing or had caused an accident on the street while returning to the drydock, the Government would not be liable; the activities of the "enterprise" do not reach into areas where the servant does not create risks different from those attendant on the activities of the community in general. We agree with the district judge that if the seaman "upon returning to the drydock, recognized the Bushey security guard as his wife's lover and shot him," vicarious liability would not follow; the incident would have related to the seaman's domestic life, not to his seafaring activity, and it would have been the most unlikely happenstance that the confrontation with the paramour occurred on a drydock rather than at the traditional spot. Here Lane had come within the closed-off area where his ship lay, to occupy a berth to which the Government insisted he have access, and while his act is not readily explicable, at least it was not shown to be due entirely to facets of his personal life. The risk that seamen going and coming from the Tamaroa might cause damage to the drydock is enough to make it fair that the enterprise bear the loss. It is not a fatal objection that the rule we lay down lacks sharp contours; in the end, as Judge Andrews said in a related context, "it is all a question [of expediency,] * * * of fair judgment, always keeping in mind the fact that we endeavor to make a rule in each case that will be practical and in keeping with the general understanding of mankind." Palsgraf v. Long Island R.R. Co., (dissenting opinion) (supra p. 175).

Since we hold the Government responsible for the damage resulting from Lane's turning the wheels, we find it unnecessary to consider Bushey's further arguments that liability would attach in any event because of later inaction of Lane and others on the Tamaroa * * *.

Affirmed.

NICHOLS v. LAND TRANSPORT CORP.

United States Court of Appeals, First Circuit, 2000.
223 F.3d 21.

LIPEZ, CIRCUIT JUDGE.

Robert Nichols brought this diversity action in the district court for the District of Maine to recover for personal injuries he suffered in a "road rage" attack by Oscar Gonzalez, a truck driver employed by Land Transport Corp. The [district court] granted Land Transport's motion for summary judgment, concluding that under Maine law Gonzalez was not acting within the scope of employment when he attacked Nichols.

We review a summary judgment de novo, viewing the record in the light most favorable to the nonmoving party to determine whether there exists a genuine issue of material fact. We agree with the magistrate judge and affirm the judgment.

On November 11, 1996, Nichols, driving his pickup truck, and Gonzalez, driving a tractor-trailer for Land Transport, were traveling westbound on Route 9 in eastern Maine. Driving recklessly behind Nichols, Gonzalez made multiple attempts to pass Nichols in no-passing zones, nearly causing a collision, and followed Nichols at an unsafe distance. Nichols responded twice with the predictable obscene gesture. When both drivers stopped at a red light in Brewer, Gonzalez exited his truck, confronted Nichols, and attacked him with a rubber-coated metal cable. In the ensuing struggle, Nichols briefly subdued Gonzalez, but then fell to the ground, and Gonzalez stabbed him in the thigh with a knife. Gonzalez was later convicted of aggravated assault.

Nichols seeks to hold Land Transport vicariously liable for Gonzalez's actions, alleging that Gonzalez was acting within the scope of employment. Maine courts apply the test of Restatement (Second) of Agency § 228 (1958) in determining whether conduct is within the scope of employment. See McLain v. Training & Dev. Corp., 572 A.2d 494, 497 (Me.1990). The Restatement test provides:

> Conduct of a servant is within the scope of employment if, but only if:
>
> (a) it is of the kind he is employed to perform;
>
> (b) it occurs substantially within the authorized time and space limits;
>
> (c) it is actuated, at least in part, by a purpose to serve the master, and
>
> (d) if force is intentionally used by the servant against another, the use of force is not unexpectable by the master.

Restatement (Second) of Agency § 228(1).

We confine our discussion to the third prong of the test because we conclude as a matter of law that Nichols has not satisfied that prong. There is no evidence in the record that Gonzalez was in any way motivated by a purpose to serve Land Transport when he fought and stabbed Nichols. Indeed, Nichols does not seriously contend otherwise. Instead, he argues that "an employer may be held liable for an assault by its employee when the assault arises out of an employment-related dispute and the assault occurs within work-related limits of time and place," regardless of whether the employee had a purpose to serve the employer.

Nichols's argument is plainly incompatible with the Restatement rule. This is obvious enough from the text of § 228. The Restatement commentary is even clearer, stating that a master is not liable

> if the servant has no intent to act on his master's behalf, although the events from which the tortious act follows arise while the servant is acting in the employment and the servant becomes angry because of them. The fact that the servant acts in an outrageous manner or

inflicts a punishment out of all proportion to the necessities of his master's business is evidence indicating that the servant has departed from the scope of employment in performing the act.

Restatement § 245 cmt. *f.*

There is, nevertheless, a split of authority on the issue of whether a purpose to serve the master is a requirement for respondeat superior liability. Nichols cites cases from a number of jurisdictions holding that an assault can be within the scope of employment if it arises out of an employment-related dispute, even if in committing the assault the servant lacked a purpose to serve the master. The cases from other jurisdictions that support Nichols's position represent a rejection, rather than an application, of Restatement § 228(1)(c).

For example, in a case heavily relied on by Nichols, Weinberg v. Johnson, 518 A.2d 985 (D.C.1986), the court purported to apply the Restatement in holding that it was a jury issue whether a laundromat employee acted in the scope of employment in shooting a customer who was leaving the laundromat after an argument with the employee concerning the customer's missing shirts. In reaching this conclusion, the court held that District of Columbia law had so evolved that the requirement of a purpose to serve the master "has become broad enough to embrace an intentional tort arising out of any dispute that was originally undertaken on the employer's behalf." Id. at 991. This outcome has been criticized. See Smith v. American Express Travel Related Servs. Co., 179 Ariz. 131, 876 P.2d 1166, 1171–72 (1994). It is unmistakably a departure from the Restatement rule.

Despite the departure in some jurisdictions noted by Nichols, many courts continue to hold that a purpose to serve the master is necessary under Restatement § 228(1) to bring a tort within the scope of employment. We have been given no reason to think that Maine would leave this company. * * * Under Maine law, a servant's tort is committed in the scope of employment only if it is actuated, at least in part, by a purpose to serve the master. It is not enough that the tort arises out of an employment-related dispute.

Although Kuehn v. White, 24 Wash.App. 274, 600 P.2d 679 (1979), is not a Maine case, it applies the Restatement test used in Maine to facts similar to the facts here and reached the same result. In response to reckless driving by a tractor-trailer driver, including unsafe passing attempts that almost caused a collision, the plaintiff motorist made the familiar obscene gesture (or at least the truck driver believed he had). Both vehicles pulled over to the side of the road, a confrontation ensued, and the truck driver struck the plaintiff repeatedly with a two-foot-long metal pipe. The truck driver was later convicted of assault. The Washington Court of Appeals affirmed the summary judgment for the trucking company, holding that where the evidence showed that the employee had "assaulted Kuehn because of his personal anger towards Kuehn and not because of any intent to serve the employer," as required by Restatement

§ 228, the scope of employment issue could be resolved in the employer's favor as a matter of law.

The same is true in this case. Because Gonzalez's attack on Nichols was not actuated by a purpose to serve Land Transport, it was not within the scope of Gonzalez's employment, and Land Transport may not be held vicariously liable. The magistrate judge did not err in entering summary judgment for Land Transport.

Affirmed.

PUSEY v. BATOR

Supreme Court of Ohio, 2002.
94 Ohio St.3d 275, 762 N.E.2d 968.

DOUGLAS, JUSTICE.

[Greif Brothers Corporation, a steel drum manufacturer, owned and operated a manufacturing plant in Youngstown, Ohio. In early 1987, Greif Brothers experienced several thefts from its parking lot. Lowell Wilson, the superintendent at Greif Brothers' Youngstown plant, decided to hire a security company to guard Greif Brothers' property. He engaged] Youngstown Security Patrol, Inc. ("YSP") to supply a uniformed security guard to "deter theft [and] vandalism" on Greif Brothers' property during specified hours. Wilson told YSP's owner and president, Carl Testa, that he wanted the security guard to periodically check the parking lot and the inside of the building. Other than those instructions, Wilson did not instruct Testa in the manner that YSP was to protect Greif Brothers' property.

The written security contract did not specify whether the guard was to be armed or unarmed, and Wilson and Testa both later testified that they never discussed the subject. At least some of the YSP security guards that were assigned to watch Greif Brothers' property carried firearms. Wilson was [well] aware of this * * *.

On June 30, 1991, Testa hired Eric Bator as a YSP security guard. Notes written on the bottom of Bator's application indicate that Bator was hired as an unarmed guard but that he would take the necessary training required by the state to become certified as an armed guard. Nevertheless, because he felt uneasy performing his security duties without a weapon, Bator took his gun, in a briefcase, to work with him. Bator testified that his supervisor, Bill Kissinger, knew that Bator carried a gun while working as a YSP guard and that Bator was not licensed to work as an armed guard. Kissinger testified that he had seen Bator's gun but denied knowing that Bator carried the gun while working as a YSP guard.

YSP employed several security guards, but only one guard per shift was assigned to guard Greif Brothers' property. Bator was the guard assigned to Greif Brothers' property from 11:00 p.m., August 11 to 7:00 a.m., August 12, 1991. At approximately 1:00 a.m., Bator looked out through a window in the guard office and saw two individuals, later identified as Derrell Pusey and Charles Thomas, walking through Greif Brothers' parking lot. Bator used the radio in the office to inform a YSP guard on duty at another location that two people were on Greif Brothers' property. [He then went outside, unarmed, to investigate. Because Thomas's and Pusey's responses seemed suspicious and potentially belligerent, Bator soon returned to the office to get his pistol. He then attempted to apprehend the two men. The situation deteriorated, and it ended in tragedy when Bator shot and killed Derrell Pusey.]

* * *

* * * [P]laintiff-appellant, Ethel Pusey, Derrell's mother, individually and as executor of Derrell's estate, filed a wrongful death and survivorship action against Bator, YSP, and Greif Brothers. YSP and Bator settled with Pusey soon after the jury trial began, leaving Greif Brothers as the only defendant.

After Pusey rested her case, Greif Brothers moved for a directed verdict * * *. The trial court granted Greif Brothers' motion. The court held that even if Derrell's death was the result of YSP's negligence, Greif Brothers was not liable because YSP was an independent contractor and, as a general rule, an employer is not liable for the negligent acts of its independent contractor. The court rejected Pusey's assertion that the nature of the work contracted for in this case qualified as an exception to the general rule.

Pusey appealed the trial court's decision to the Seventh District Court of Appeals. The court of appeals, in a split decision, affirmed the trial court's ruling and Pusey appealed to this court. The case is before this court upon our allowance of a discretionary appeal.

The issue for our determination in this case is whether the court of appeals erred in affirming the trial court's ruling directing a verdict in favor of Greif Brothers. A decision granting a directed verdict should be affirmed on appeal if, when the evidence is viewed most strongly in favor of the nonmoving party, reasonable minds could only find against the nonmoving party. In making its determination that Greif Brothers was not liable for the damages resulting from Derrell's death, the trial court first determined that YSP was an independent contractor and not an employee of Greif Brothers. This was an important factor in the court's ultimate decision because, whereas an employer is liable for the negligent acts of its employees committed within the scope of employment, an employer of an independent contractor generally is not liable for the negligent acts of the independent contractor. Because this finding was a pivotal factor in the trial court's decision, we review it first.

The chief test in determining whether one is an employee or an independent contractor is the right to control the manner or means of performing the work. If such right is in the employer, the relationship is that of employer and employee; but if the manner or means of performing the work is left to one responsible to the employer for the result alone, an independent contractor relationship is created.

We find that, even when viewed in the light most favorable to Pusey, the evidence clearly established YSP's status as an independent contractor. Greif Brothers specified the result to be accomplished, i.e., to deter vandals and thieves, but the details of how this task should be accomplished, with the exception noted above regarding periodic patrolling of the property, were left to YSP. Moreover, YSP, not Greif Brothers, hired the guards, supplied them with uniforms and equipment, paid them, and assigned them to their posts, and was responsible for training them and ensuring that they were state-certified as security guards. For the foregoing reasons, we agree with the trial court's conclusion, affirmed by the court of appeals, that YSP was an independent contractor.

As stated previously, an employer is generally not liable for the negligent acts of an independent contractor. There are, however, exceptions to this general rule, several of which stem from the nondelegable duty doctrine. Nondelegable duties arise in various situations that generally fall into two categories: (1) affirmative duties that are imposed on the employer by statute, contract, franchise, charter, or common law and (2) duties imposed on the employer that arise out of the work itself because its performance creates dangers to others, i.e., inherently dangerous work. Prosser & Keeton, The Law of Torts (5 Ed.1984) 511–512, Section 71; Albain v. Flower Hosp. (1990), 50 Ohio St.3d 251, 260–261, 553 N.E.2d 1038, 1047–1048. If the work to be performed fits into one of these two categories, the employer may delegate the *work* to an independent contractor, but he cannot delegate the *duty*. In other words, the employer is not insulated from liability if the independent contractor's negligence results in a breach of the duty.

Pusey claims that hiring armed guards to protect property creates a nondelegable duty because the work is inherently dangerous. Consequently, Pusey argues, even if YSP is an independent contractor, that status does not relieve Greif Brothers from liability for the damages arising from Derrell's death resulting from the alleged negligence of Bator.

Work is inherently dangerous when it creates a peculiar risk of harm to others unless special precautions are taken. Under those circumstances, the employer hiring the independent contractor has a duty to see that the work is done with reasonable care and cannot, by hiring an independent contractor, insulate himself or herself from liability for injuries resulting to others from the negligence of the independent contractor or its employees.

To fall within the inherently-dangerous-work exception, it is not necessary that the work be such that it cannot be done without a risk of harm to others, or even that it be such that it involves a high risk of such harm. It is sufficient that the work involves a risk, recognizable in advance, of physical harm to others, which is inherent in the work itself.

The exception does not apply, however, where the employer would reasonably have only a general anticipation of the possibility that the contractor may be negligent in some way and thereby cause harm to a third party. For example, one who hires a trucker to transport his goods should realize that if the truck is driven at an excessive speed, or with defective brakes, some harm to persons on the highway is likely to occur. An employer of an independent contractor may assume that a careful contractor will take routine precautions against all of the ordinary and customary dangers that may arise in the course of the contemplated work.

The inherently-dangerous-work exception does apply, however, when special risks are associated with the work such that a reasonable man would recognize the necessity of taking special precautions. The work must create a risk that is not a normal, routine matter of customary human activity, such as driving an automobile, but is rather a special danger to those in the vicinity arising out of the particular situation created, and calling for special precautions. 2 Restatement of the Law 2d, Torts, at 385 § 413 cmt. *b*; Prosser & Keeton at 513–514, Section 71.

Greif Brothers argues that hiring armed guards to protect property does not create a peculiar risk of harm to others and, therefore, does not fit within the inherently-dangerous-work exception. The common pleas court agreed with Greif Brothers and relied on the Twelfth District Court of Appeals' holding in Joseph v. Consol. Rail Corp. (Oct. 30, 1987), unreported, 1987 WL 19481, to support its decision.

In *Joseph,* the defendant, Conrail, hired an independent contractor to perform surveillance of an employee of Conrail to determine the validity of the employee's claim that he had injured his back. The investigators were consequently detected and confronted by the employee. In a subsequent action by the employee against Conrail for alleged damages resulting from the confrontation, the trial court granted summary judgment in favor of Conrail. [Affirming, the court of appeals rejected the plaintiff's contention that the inherently-dangerous-work exception was applicable and stated that that exception "is limited to dangerous work, and cannot be extended to proper work dangerously done."]

Although we agree with the holding in *Joseph,* we disagree with the trial court's determination that it is applicable to the facts of this case. One crucial difference between the work at issue in *Joseph,* i.e., surveillance, and the work at issue herein, i.e., an armed guard deterring thieves and vandals, is that an *armed* confrontation with a suspicious person may be *required* by the latter. Surveillance work, as emphasized by the *Joseph* court, is not inherently dangerous to the person being investigated because the purpose of the investigator is to remain undetected and unobtrusive. In contrast, *armed* YSP guards were instructed to "deter" thieves and vandals. Thus, the work contracted for contemplates a confrontation between an armed guard and persons entering the property. For the foregoing reasons, we do not agree with the trial court's determination that *Joseph* supports its conclusion that hiring armed guards to protect property is not inherently dangerous to those entering the property.

In affirming the trial court's decision, the court of appeals did not consider whether armed security satisfied the inherently-dangerous-work exception. * * * We find that work such as YSP was hired to perform does create a peculiar risk of harm to others. When armed guards are hired to deter vandals and thieves it is foreseeable that someone might be injured by the inappropriate use of the weapon if proper precautions are not taken. Thus, such an injury is one that might have been anticipated as a direct or probable consequence of the performance of the work contracted for, if reasonable care is not taken in its performance. Also, the risk created is not a normal, routine matter of customary human activity, such as driving an automobile, but is instead a special danger arising out of the particular situation created and calling for special precautions. We therefore hold that when an employer hires an independent contractor to provide armed security guards to protect property, the inherently-dangerous-work exception is triggered such that if someone is injured by the weapon as a result of a guard's negligence, the employer is vicariously liable even though the guard responsible is an employee of the independent contractor.

We do not mean to suggest by the foregoing that we have determined that Derrell's death resulted from YSP's negligence. That issue is to be determined by a finder of fact. If the fact finder so finds, however, then, pursuant to our holding herein, Greif Brothers is liable for the damages even though the negligence was that of an employee of an independent contractor.

For the foregoing reasons, we reverse the judgment of the court of appeals and remand the cause to the trial court for a fact-finder's determination whether Derrell's death was a result of YSP's negligence.

Judgment reversed and cause remanded.

COOK, JUSTICE, concurring in judgment only.

A majority of this court holds that the provision of "armed security guards to protect property" triggers, as a matter of law, the "inherently-dangerous-work exception" to the general rule that an employer is not vicariously liable for the negligence of its independent contractor.[3] Accordingly, the majority decides that Greif Brothers may be vicariously liable if the jury finds that Eric Bator acted negligently in shooting Derrell Pusey. Although I agree with the majority's decision to reverse the judgment and remand the cause, I would decline to hold that the work contracted by Greif Brothers to Youngstown Security Patrol ("YSP") was "inherently dangerous" to others as a matter of Ohio law. * * *

* * *

---

3. At least three courts have held that the provision of armed security personnel is *not,* in and of itself, an inherently dangerous activity. See Ross v. Texas One Partnership (Tex.App.1990), 796 S.W.2d 206, 214–215; Brien v. 18925 Collins Avenue Corp. (Fla.App.1970), 233 So.2d 847, 38 A.L.R.3d 1328; Schreiber v. Camm (D.N.J.1994), 848 F.Supp. 1170, 1177–1180.

If an independent contractor's work is "generically hazardous," such that the activity poses an inherent danger to others regardless of the skill with which the contractor performs the work, * * * a court may find that the work falls within the inherently-dangerous-work exception as a matter of law. * * * [The inherently-dangerous-work exception can also be applied to activities that are not "generically hazardous"—because they *can* be performed safely by taking proper precautions—when the employer has reason to know that his independent contractor is likely, *under particular circumstances,* to endanger others absent reasonable precautions. When the activity at issue is not "generically hazardous," the applicability of the exception depends on the fact-specific, particular circumstances under which any task is to be performed.]

I do not view the work YSP contracted to perform—providing security guards to protect Greif Brothers property—as falling within the "generically hazardous" branch of the inherently-dangerous-work exception. Whether the presence of security guards poses a peculiar risk to others depends on the particular circumstances of the job, such as the location of the guarded premises and the likelihood of the guards being armed. * * * [W]e should allow the trier of fact to decide whether the facts and circumstances surrounding this case bring YSP's work within the purview of the "peculiar risk"/"special danger" branch of the inherently-dangerous-work exception.

* * *

NOTES

1. As explained in the opinion of the court in *Pusey*, the concept of nondelegable duty may be applied in situations other than inherently dangerous work. An example is ColmenaresVivas v. Sun Alliance Insurance Co., Chapter III, section E, p. 104 supra.

2. There are other exceptions to the general rule of nonliability of one who employs an independent contractor. See, e.g., Jackson v. Power, 743 P.2d 1376 (Alaska 1987), subjecting a hospital to liability for the negligence of an independent contractor physician working in its emergency room because it had held him out to the public as its employee. (The court found support in both the agency and torts restatements. See Restatement (Second) of Agency § 267 (1958); Restatement (Second) of Torts § 429 (1965).)

CHAPTER IX

PROPORTIONATE LIABILITY

■ ■ ■

A. INTRODUCTION: AFFIRMATIVE DEFENSES IN NEGLIGENCE ACTIONS

The five elements of the plaintiff's prima facie case in a cause of action based on negligence are duty, breach, cause in fact, proximate cause, and damages. If these elements are established, there will be a recovery unless the defendant can establish an affirmative defense.

The term "affirmative defense" is not peculiar to tort law. In its general usage it means any matter that, if pleaded and proved by the defendant, will defeat or reduce the liability that plaintiff has otherwise established. Rule 8(c)(1) of the Federal Rules of Civil Procedure states that a defendant must "affirmatively [plead] any avoidance or affirmative defense" and sets out a non-exhaustive 19–item list that includes (from the torts realm) contributory negligence and assumption of risk. In this chapter we will look at those defenses, together with comparative negligence, failure to avoid consequences, and failure to mitigate damages.

The procedural rules that allocate the burden of pleading and proving these defenses vary somewhat from state to state. In most states, the defendant must plead and prove contributory or comparative negligence and assumption of risk.

B. REPLACING THE CONTRIBUTORY NEGLIGENCE DOCTRINE WITH COMPARATIVE FAULT[1]

Under the traditional common law doctrine of contributory negligence, defendants who were indisputably guilty of seriously negligent conduct often escaped liability. If such a defendant could prove a negligence case against the plaintiff—i.e., if the defendant could prove that the

---

1. Many of the issues treated in this and the following sections of this chapter are discussed in Robertson, Eschewing Ersatz Percentages: A Simplified Vocabulary of Comparative Fault, 45 St. Louis U.L. Rev. 831 (2001).

plaintiff, too, was guilty of negligent conduct that was a cause in fact and a proximate cause of the injurious event—the defendant would not be liable. This was true even though the defendant's negligence may have been far worse—more extreme or more blameworthy—than the plaintiff's. The theory of the contributory negligence rule was that any legally relevant negligence of the plaintiff, no matter how slight, would bar recovery completely.

The contributory negligence (total bar) doctrine was a peculiarity of Anglo–American law. In civil-law systems and in maritime law, plaintiffs and defendants have generally *shared* losses produced by their combined negligence. This loss-sharing approach is variously called "comparative negligence," "comparative fault," "comparative responsibility," "proportionate responsibility," and "proportionate liability." As we will see in the cases and notes below, the "comparative" or "proportionate" approach has swept the common-law contributory negligence doctrine aside in most of the United States.

England was ahead of the U.S. on this matter. The Law Reform (Contributory Negligence) Act, 1945, 8 & 9 George 6, c. 28, § 1, abolished the contributory negligence rule and replaced it with an agreeably simple principle:

> Where any person suffers damage as the result partly of his own fault and partly of the fault of any other person or persons, a claim in respect of that damage shall not be defeated by reason of the fault of the person suffering the damage, but the damages recoverable in respect thereof shall be reduced to such extent as the court thinks just and equitable having regard to the claimant's share in the responsibility of the damage * * *.

In modern England, negligence cases are tried to the bench, and the 1945 statute's simple "just and equitable" approach has worked well.But the United States remains committed to jury trial, and an approach giving judges fairly close control over the victim-fault penalty was felt to be needed. Rather than asking the jury to state what reduction in the plaintiff's total damages would be a "just and equitable" penalty for the plaintiff's own fault in the matter, almost all of the states require the jury to express its intended victim-negligence penalty in percentage terms. Thus, in a simple car-wreck case in which both drivers violated four-way stop signs and the plaintiff's total recoverable damages were $100,000, the jury is not instructed to return a verdict reducing the $100,000 by whatever is just and equitable. Instead, it is told to assume that the combined fault of the two drivers totaled 100% and to assign each driver a share of that fault, expressed in percentage terms. Typically, the trial judge in entering judgment then does the math and reduces the $100,000 to reflect the jury is percentage-fault findings. (By the way, don't bet on the jury's saying 50/50, not even in a simple case like the one posited. Sometimes juries say things like Driver A 43.75% and Driver B 56.25%,[2]

---

2. Petrolane Inc. v. Robles, 154 P.3d 1014, 1017 (Alaska 2007).

or even Driver A 68.94% and Driver B 31.06%.[3] Probably we don't even *want* to know what could be going on in the jury room to produce such parodies of precision.)

Not too long after the percentage-allocation tool came into the law for the relatively simple purpose of measuring the plaintiff-negligence penalty, courts and legislatures began using the tool for other purposes (as in *McIntyre* just below). Gradually, what looked at the beginning to be a very simple change in the law—to stop penalizing plaintiff negligence by killing the lawsuit and instead use a recovery-reduction penalty—has seemingly inexorably entailed many other changes. Many, perhaps most, aspects of negligence law and litigation have been (or are beginning to be) fundamentally affected in ways that were quite unforeseen when the shift from the contributory to the comparative negligence regime began.

McINTYRE v. BALENTINE
Supreme Court of Tennessee, 1992.
833 S.W.2d 52.

DROWOTA, JUSTICE.

* * *

In the early morning darkness of November 2, 1986, Plaintiff Harry Douglas McIntyre and Defendant Clifford Balentine were involved in a motor vehicle accident resulting in severe injuries to Plaintiff. The accident occurred in the vicinity of Smith's Truck Stop in Savannah, Tennessee. As Defendant Balentine was traveling south on Highway 69, Plaintiff entered the highway (also traveling south) from the truck stop parking lot. Shortly after Plaintiff entered the highway, his pickup truck was struck by Defendant's Peterbilt tractor. * * *

* * *

[McIntyre brought a negligence action against Balentine. In his answer, Balentine pleaded that McIntyre was contributorily negligent. After trial, the jury returned a verdict stating: "We, the jury, find the plaintiff and the defendant equally at fault in this accident; therefore, we rule in favor of the defendant." The trial judge entered judgment on the jury verdict for Balentine. McIntyre appealed, asserting that the trial judge erred by refusing to instruct the jury regarding the doctrine of comparative negligence. The Court of Appeals affirmed, stating:

> Under the law as it is presently constituted in the State of Tennessee, it is not permissible for the trier of fact to compare relative degrees of fault among the parties. In other words, comparative negligence is not the law of Tennessee. If comparative negligence is to be adopted in this state, then it must be adopted by either the Supreme Court of

---

3. Duncan v. Kansas City S. Ry. Co., 773 So.2d 670, 674 (La. 2000). See also Quady v. Sickl, 260 Wis. 348, 350, 51 N.W.2d 3 (1952) (drivers of four vehicles assigned 14.17%, 15.42%, 23.33%, 47.08%).

Tennessee or the General Assembly of Tennessee. It cannot be adopted by this Court or by the trial courts of this state, either directly or by subterfuge.]

I.

The common law contributory negligence doctrine has traditionally been traced to * * * Butterfield v. Forrester, 11 East 60, 103 Eng.Rep. 926 (1809). There, plaintiff, "riding as fast as his horse would go," was injured after running into an obstruction defendant had placed in the road. Stating as the rule that "[o]ne person being in fault will not dispense with another's using ordinary care," [the court] denied recovery on the basis that [the plaintiff] did not use ordinary care to avoid the obstruction.

The contributory negligence bar was soon brought to America as part of the common law, *see* Smith v. Smith, 19 Mass. 621 (1824),* and proceeded to spread throughout the states. This strict bar may have been a direct outgrowth of the common law system of issue pleading; issue pleading posed questions to be answered "yes" or "no," leaving common law courts, the theory goes, no choice but to award all or nothing. A number of other rationalizations have been advanced in the attempt to justify the harshness of the "all-or-nothing" bar. Among these: the plaintiff should be penalized for his misconduct; the plaintiff should be deterred from injuring himself; and the plaintiff's negligence supersedes the defendant's so as to render defendant's negligence no longer proximate.

In Tennessee, * * * we have [long followed] the general rule that a plaintiff's contributory negligence completely bars recovery. Equally entrenched in Tennessee jurisprudence are exceptions to the general all-or-nothing rule: contributory negligence does not absolutely bar recovery where defendant's conduct was intentional, where defendant's conduct was "grossly" negligent, where defendant had the "last clear chance" with which, through the exercise of ordinary care, to avoid plaintiff's injury, or where plaintiff's negligence may be classified as "remote."

In contrast, comparative fault has long been the federal rule in cases involving injured employees of interstate railroad carriers [see 45 U.S.C. § 53] and injured seamen [see 46 U.S.C. § 30104]. * * *

Between 1920 and 1969, a few states began utilizing the principles of comparative fault in all tort litigation.** Then, between 1969 and 1984, comparative fault replaced contributory negligence in 37 additional states. In 1991, South Carolina became the 45th state to adopt comparative fault, leaving Alabama, Maryland, North Carolina, Virginia, [the District of

---

* The facts of *Smith* were remarkably similar to those of *Butterfield*. *Smith* was "an action on the case for an injury done to the plaintiff's horse by a wood-pile, which the defendant had placed in the highway. * * * The horse was harnessed to a wagon loaded with [barrels of] cider." 10 Mass. at 662. [Ed.]

** Mississippi enacted the first comparative fault statute in 1920. The most influential early enactment was Wisconsin's (1931). [Ed.]

Columbia], and Tennessee as the only remaining common law contributory negligence jurisdictions.

Eleven states have judicially adopted comparative fault.[3] Thirty-four states have legislatively adopted comparative fault.

II.

Over 15 years ago, we stated, when asked to adopt a system of comparative fault:

> We do not deem it appropriate to consider making such a change unless and until a case reaches us wherein the pleadings and proof present an issue of contributory negligence accompanied by advocacy that the ends of justice will be served by adopting the rule of comparative negligence.

[Street v. Calvert, 541 S.W.2d 576, 586 (Tenn. 1976).] Such a case is now before us. After exhaustive deliberation that was facilitated by extensive briefing and argument by the parties, amicus curiae, and Tennessee's scholastic community, we conclude that it is time to abandon the outmoded and unjust common law doctrine of contributory negligence and adopt in its place a system of comparative fault. Justice simply will not permit our continued adherence to a rule that, in the face of a judicial determination that others bear primary responsibility, nevertheless completely denies injured litigants recompense for their damages.

We recognize that this action could be taken by our General Assembly. However, legislative inaction has never prevented judicial abolition of obsolete common law doctrines, especially those, such as contributory negligence, conceived in the judicial womb. Indeed, our abstinence would sanction "a mutual state of inaction in which the court awaits action by the legislature and the legislature awaits guidance from the court," thereby prejudicing the equitable resolution of legal conflicts.

Nor do we today abandon our commitment to *stare decisis*. While "[c]onfidence in our courts is to a great extent dependent on the uniformity and consistency engendered by allegiance to *stare decisis*, * * * mindless obedience to this precept can confound the truth and foster an attitude of contempt."

III.

Two basic forms of comparative fault are utilized by 45 of our sister jurisdictions, these variants being commonly referred to as either "pure" or "modified." In the "pure" form, a plaintiff's damages are reduced in proportion to the percentage negligence attributed to him; for example, a plaintiff responsible for 90 percent of the negligence that caused his injuries nevertheless may recover 10 percent of his damages. In the "modified" form, plaintiffs recover as in pure jurisdictions, but only if the

---

3. In the order of their adoption, these states are Florida [1973], California [1975], Alaska [1975], Michigan [1979], West Virginia [1979], New Mexico [1981], Illinois [1981], Iowa [1982], Missouri [1983], Kentucky [1984], and South Carolina [1991]. * * *.

plaintiff's negligence either (1) does not exceed ["51 percent" jurisdictions] or (2) is less than ["50 percent" jurisdictions] the defendant's negligence.

Although we conclude that the all-or-nothing rule of contributory negligence must be replaced, we nevertheless decline to abandon totally our fault-based tort system. We do not agree that a party should necessarily be able to recover in tort even though he may be 80, 90, or 95 percent at fault. We therefore reject the pure form of comparative fault.

We recognize that modified comparative fault systems have been criticized as merely shifting the arbitrary contributory negligence bar to a new ground. However, we feel the ["50 percent rule"] ameliorates the harshness of the common law rule while remaining compatible with a fault-based tort system. We therefore hold that so long as a plaintiff's negligence remains less than the defendant's negligence the plaintiff may recover; in such a case, plaintiff's damages are to be reduced in proportion to the percentage of the total negligence attributable to the plaintiff.

In all trials where the issue of comparative fault is before a jury, the trial court shall instruct the jury on the effect of the jury's finding as to the percentage of negligence as between the plaintiff or plaintiffs and the defendant or defendants. The attorneys for each party shall be allowed to argue how this instruction affects a plaintiff's ability to recover.

IV.

Turning to the case at bar, the jury found that "the plaintiff and defendant [were] equally at fault." Because the jury, without the benefit of proper instructions by the trial court, made a gratuitous apportionment of fault, we find that their "equal" apportionment is not sufficiently trustworthy to form the basis of a final determination between these parties. Therefore, the case is remanded for a new trial in accordance with the dictates of this opinion.

V.

We recognize that today's decision affects numerous legal principles surrounding tort litigation. For the most part, harmonizing these principles with comparative fault must await another day. However, we feel compelled to provide some guidance to the trial courts charged with implementing this new system.

First, and most obviously, the new rule makes the doctrines of remote contributory negligence and last clear chance obsolete. The circumstances formerly taken into account by those two doctrines will henceforth be addressed when assessing relative degrees of fault.

Second, in cases of multiple tortfeasors, plaintiff will be entitled to recover so long as plaintiff's fault is less than the combined fault of all tortfeasors.

Third, today's holding renders the doctrine of joint and several liability obsolete. Our adoption of comparative fault is due largely to considerations of fairness: the contributory negligence doctrine unjustly allowed the entire loss to be borne by a negligent plaintiff, notwithstanding that the plaintiff's fault was minor in comparison to defendant's. Having thus adopted a rule more closely linking liability and fault, it would be inconsistent to simultaneously retain a rule, joint and several liability, which may fortuitously impose a degree of liability that is out of all proportion to fault.

Further, because a particular defendant will henceforth be liable only for the percentage of a plaintiff's damages occasioned by that defendant's negligence, situations where a defendant has paid more than his "share" of a judgment will no longer arise, and therefore the Uniform Contribution Among Tort–Feasors Act, T.C.A. §§ 29–11–101 to 106 (1980), will no longer determine the apportionment of liability between codefendants.

Fourth, fairness and efficiency require that defendants called upon to answer allegations in negligence be permitted to allege, as an affirmative defense, that a nonparty caused or contributed to the injury or damage for which recovery is sought. In cases where such a defense is raised, the trial court shall instruct the jury to assign this nonparty the percentage of the total negligence for which he is responsible. However, in order for a plaintiff to recover a judgment against such additional person, the plaintiff must have made a timely amendment to his complaint and caused process to be served on such additional person. Thereafter, the additional party will be required to answer the amended complaint. The procedures shall be in accordance with the Tennessee Rules of Civil Procedure.

Fifth, until such time as the Tennessee Judicial Conference Committee on Civil Pattern Jury Instructions promulgates new standard jury instructions, we direct trial courts' attention to the suggested instructions and special verdict form set forth in the appendix to this opinion.

VI.

The principles set forth today apply to (1) all cases tried or retried after the date of this opinion, and (2) all cases on appeal in which the comparative fault issue has been raised at an appropriate stage in the litigation.

* * *

[For the foregoing reasons, the judgment of the Court of Appeals is reversed, and the case is remanded to the trial court for a new trial in accordance with the dictates of this opinion.]

Appendix

The following instructions may be used in cases where the negligence of the plaintiff is at issue. These instructions are intended for two-party litigation. Appropriate modifications would be necessary for more complex litigation.

Suggested Jury Instructions

[The following instructions should be preceded by instructions on negligence, proximate cause, damages, etc.]

1. If you find that defendant was not negligent or that defendant's negligence was not a proximate cause of plaintiff's injury, you will find for defendant.

2. If you find that defendant was negligent and that defendant's negligence was a proximate cause of plaintiff's injury, you must then determine whether plaintiff was also negligent and whether plaintiff's negligence was a proximate cause of his/her injury.

3. In this state, negligence on the part of a plaintiff has an impact on a plaintiff's right to recover damages. Accordingly, if you find that each party was negligent and that the negligence of each party was a proximate cause of plaintiff's damages, then you must determine the degree of such negligence, expressed as a percentage, attributable to each party.

4. If you find from all the evidence that the percentage of negligence attributable to plaintiff was equal to, or greater than, the percentage of negligence attributable to defendant, then you are instructed that plaintiff will not be entitled to recover any damages for his/her injuries. If, on the other hand, you determine from the evidence that the percentage of negligence attributable to plaintiff was less than the percentage of negligence attributable to defendant, then plaintiff will be entitled to recover that portion of his/her damages not caused by plaintiff's own negligence.

5. The court will provide you with a special verdict form that will assist you in your duties.* This is the form on which you will record, if appropriate, the percentage of negligence assigned to each party and plaintiff's total damages. The court will then take your findings and either (1) enter judgment for defendant if you have found that defendant was not negligent or that plaintiff's own negligence accounted for 50 percent or more of the total negligence proximately causing his/her injuries or (2) enter judgment against defendant in accordance with defendant's percentage of negligence.

* * *

Notes

1. ***Three types of comparative fault systems.*** The Restatement (Third) of Torts: Apportionment of Liability (2000) states that at the time of its compilation, five jurisdictions (four states and the District of Columbia) still had the contributory negligence doctrine, 13 states had the pure form, 21 the 51%-bar system, and 11 the 50%-bar system. (South Dakota has a slight-gross system.) Id. at § 7, Reporter's Note pp. 73–75.[1]

---

* We have not included the court's special verdict form, but we commend it to your attention as an exemplar for providing useful guidance to the jury. [Ed.]

1. State legislatures have been active in the proportionate liability field, so some shifts may have occurred since the Apportionment Restatement compilation.

2. *Special-purpose pockets of contributory negligence?* Indiana is a modified (51%) state, but it has retained the old contributory negligence defense on behalf of medical care providers (see Cavens v. Zaberdac, 849 N.E.2d 526 (Ind. 2006)) and governmental entities (see Penn Harris Madison School Corp. v. Howard, 861 N.E.2d 1190 (Ind. 2007)). There may be similar phenomena in other states.

3. *Judicial legislation; how McIntyre changed the law.* The contributory negligence doctrine was a judicial creation, but by the time courts became convinced it needed to be jettisoned, tort law in every state had become a complex and far-reaching system of intermingled common law and legislation, and the contributory negligence doctrine ran through those systems like a virus. In the late 1960s, an intermediate appellate court in Illinois tried to adopt a 50%-bar system of comparative negligence; the state's supreme court in *Maki v. Frelk*, 40 Ill.2d 193, 239 N.E.2d 445, 447–48 (1968) reversed, explaining (citations omitted):

> [S]uch a far-reaching change, if desirable, should be made by the legislature rather than by the court. The General Assembly is the department of government to which the constitution has entrusted the power of changing the laws. Where it is clear that the court has made a mistake, it will not decline to correct it, even though the rule may have been re-asserted and acquiesced in for a long number of years. But when a rule of law has once been settled, contravening no statute or constitutional principle, such rule ought to be followed unless it can be shown that serious detriment is thereby likely to arise prejudicial to public interests. The rule of Stare Decisis is founded upon sound principles in the administration of justice, and rules long recognized as the law should not be departed from merely because the court is of the opinion that it might decide otherwise were the question a new one.

> * * * The General Assembly has incorporated the * * * doctrine of contributory negligence as an integral part of statutes dealing with a number of particular subjects [such as injuries to firemen and policemen, counties' responsibility for highway defects, etc.], and the legislative branch is manifestly in a better position than is this court to consider the numerous problems involved.

From the *Maki* perspective, the *McIntyre* decision was a heroic feat of judicial legislation. Not only did the court replace the affirmative defense of contributory negligence with a new 50%-bar system, it made a surprising number of other changes in the law (in the process overtly expunging a chapter of the Tennessee statute books and probably implicitly eviscerating a significant number of other statutes). Note that many of the changes the court made were seemingly in no way connected with the facts of the case. We will take up these changes at appropriate points as we move through this chapter. Here's a list:

- Abolition of an age-old victim-fault penalty, the affirmative defense of contributory negligence.

- Abolition of old exceptions to the victim-fault penalty ("the doctrines of remote contributory negligence and last clear chance").

- Adoption of a new victim-fault penalty, the 50%-bar comparative negligence rule.

- Clarification that "in cases of multiple tortfeasors, plaintiff will be entitled to recover so long as plaintiff's fault is less than the combined fault of all tortfeasors."

- Provision that judges must instruct juries on (and that lawyers may argue to juries about) the effects of percentage-negligence findings.

- Abolition of joint and several liability and concomitant abolition of contribution among co-tortfeasors (expunging Tennessee's Uniform Contribution Among Tort–Feasors Act).

- Adoption of a new "affirmative defense" of nonparty percentage fault.

- Grant of permission to plaintiffs to join such nonparties as defendants.

- Creation of new pattern jury instructions.

- Creation of a new pattern jury verdict form.

If the Tennessee legislature had enacted the foregoing changes, they would have been generally accepted as legitimate law-making—even by those who strongly disagreed with their content—and thus brought some stability to the law. But when such far-reaching changes are made by a court—and when many of the changes were not at issue in the particular case and thus were not subjected to the vigorous testing inherent in adversarial litigation—they are unlikely to prove stable. (In everyday jurisprudential language, pronouncements not called forth by the facts and issues in the case are "dicta.") Eighteen years after *McIntyre*, the Tennessee Supreme Court in Banks v. Elks Club, 301 S.W.3d 214, 218 (Tenn. 2010), termed *McIntyre* "a sea-change in Tennessee's tort law" (when used to characterize a single judicial decision, "sea-change" is a disparaging term) and went on to chronicle the numerous ways in which the *McIntyre* regime fairly quickly proved unstable. The details of the *Banks* critique of *McIntyre* need not concern us, but we will take up an aspect of *Banks* in section G, infra p. 418.

4. ***Representative comparative fault statutes.*** In Apportionment Restatement terms, supra note 1, how should each of the following statutes be classified?

> *N.Y.Civ.Prac.Law § 1411*: In any action to recover damages for personal injury, injury to property, or wrongful death, the culpable conduct attributable to the claimant or to the decedent, including contributory negligence or assumption of risk, shall not bar recovery, but the amount of damages otherwise recoverable shall be diminished in the proportion which the culpable conduct attributable to the claimant or decedent bears to the culpable conduct which caused the damages.

> *Wis.Stat. § 895.045*: Contributory negligence does not bar recovery in an action by any person or the person's legal representative to recover damages for negligence resulting in death or injury to person or property, if that negligence was not greater than the negligence of the person against whom recovery is sought, but any damages allowed shall be diminished in the proportion to the amount of negligence attributed to the person recovering. The negligence of the plaintiff shall be measured

separately against the negligence of each person found to be causally negligent. * * *

Ark.Stat. § 16–64–122:

(a) In all actions for damages for personal injuries or wrongful death or injury to property in which recovery is predicated upon fault, liability shall be determined by comparing the fault chargeable to a claiming party with the fault chargeable to the party or parties from whom the claiming party seeks to recover damages.

(b)(1) If the fault chargeable to a party claiming damages is of less degree than the fault chargeable to the party or parties from whom the claiming party seeks to recover damages, then the claiming party is entitled to recover the amount of his damages after they have been diminished in proportion to the degree of his own fault.

(b)(2) If the fault chargeable to a party claiming damages is equal to or greater in degree than any fault chargeable to the party or parties from whom the claiming party seeks to recover damages, then the claiming party is not entitled to recover such damages.

(c) The word "fault" as used in this section includes any act, omission, conduct, risk assumed, breach of warranty, or breach of any legal duty which is a proximate cause of any damages sustained by any party.

(d) In cases where the issue of comparative fault is submitted to the jury by an interrogatory, counsel for the parties shall be permitted to argue to the jury the effect of an answer to any interrogatory.

5. ***Should the jury be told what the effects of its percentage-fault findings will be?*** *McIntyre* and section (d) of the Arkansas statute reflect a fairly recent trend[2] toward letting the jury know how its fault assessments will affect the parties. Can you see why the argument for such a provision is stronger in Arkansas and Tennessee than in New York or Wisconsin?

6. ***In modified systems, what is the cut-off point in multiple-defendant cases?*** Suppose the jury returns a verdict finding the plaintiff 40% at fault and each of two defendants 30% at fault. *McIntyre* says that in Tennessee, the plaintiff in that case is not barred from recovery. What is Wisconsin law on the point? Arkansas?

The Apportionment Restatement (Reporters' Note to § 7 cmt. *n*, p. 84) says the Wisconsin provision on this point is unique. Section 7 cmt. *n* implies that a court confronted with a statute that is ambiguous on the point should interpret it not to bar the plaintiff in the situation posed in this note.

WASSELL v. ADAMS

United States Court of Appeals, Seventh Circuit, 1989.
865 F.2d 849.

POSNER, CIRCUIT JUDGE.

The plaintiff, born Susan Marisconish, grew up on Macaroni Street in a small town in a poor coal-mining region of Pennsylvania—a town so

---

2. We *hope* it's a trend. The majority view at one time favored blindfolding the jury. For a recent case adhering to that view, see Brodsky v. Grinnell Haulers, Inc., 181 N.J. 102, 853 A.2d 940, 949–52 (2004).

small and obscure that it has no name. * * * After graduating from high school she worked briefly as a nurse's aide, then became engaged to Michael Wassell, also from Pennsylvania. Michael joined the Navy in 1985 and was sent to Great Lakes Naval Training Station, just north of Chicago, for basic training. He and Susan had decided to get married as soon as he completed basic training. The graduation was scheduled for a Friday. Susan, who by now was 21 years old, traveled to Chicago with Michael's parents for the graduation. The three checked into a double room at the Ron–Ric Motel, near the base, on the Thursday (September 22, 1985) before graduation. The Ron–Ric is a small and inexpensive motel that caters to the families of sailors at the Great Lakes Naval Training Station a few blocks to the east. The motel has 14 rooms and charges a maximum of $36 a night for a double room. The motel was owned by Wilbur and Florena Adams, the defendants in the case.

Four blocks to the west of the Ron–Ric Motel is a high-crime area: murder, prostitution, robbery, drugs—the works. The Adamses occasionally warned women guests not to walk alone in the neighborhood at night. They did not warn the Wassells or Susan.

Susan spent Friday night with Michael at another motel. On Saturday the Wassells checked out and left for Pennsylvania, and at the Wassells' suggestion Susan moved from the double room that she had shared with them to a single room in the Ron–Ric. Michael spent Saturday night with her but had to return to the base on Sunday for several days. She remained to look for an apartment where they could live after they were married (for he was scheduled to remain at the base after completing basic training). She spent most of Sunday in her room reading the newspaper and watching television. In the evening she went to look at an apartment.

Upon returning to her room at the motel, she locked the door, fastened the chain, and went to bed. She fell into a deep sleep, from which she was awakened by a knock on the door. She turned on a light and saw by the clock built into the television set that it was 1:00 a.m. She went to the door and looked through the peephole but saw no one. Next to the door was a pane of clear glass. She did not look through it. The door had two locks plus a chain. She unlocked the door and opened it all the way, thinking that Michael had come from the base * * *. It was not Michael at the door. It was a respectably dressed black man whom Susan had never seen before. He asked for "Cindy" (maybe "Sidney," she thought later). She told him there was no Cindy there. Then he asked for a glass of water. She went to the bathroom * * * to fetch the glass of water. When she came out of the bathroom, the man was sitting at the table in the room. [He then raped her.]

* * *

The rapist was never prosecuted; a suspect was caught but Susan was too upset to identify him. There had been a rape at the motel several years previously * * *. There had also been a robbery, and an incident in which an intruder kicked in the door to one of the rooms. These were the only serious crimes committed during the seven years that the Adamses owned the motel.

Susan married Michael, but the rape had induced post-trauma stress that has, according to her testimony and that of a psychologist testifying as her expert witness, blighted her life. She brought this suit against the Adamses on January 21, 1986. It is a diversity suit that charges the Adamses with negligence in failing to warn Susan or take other precautions to protect her against the assault. The substantive issues are governed by the law of Illinois. A jury composed of four women and three men found that the Adamses had indeed been negligent and that their negligence had been a proximate cause of the assault, and the jury assessed Susan's damages at $850,000, which was the figure her lawyer had requested in closing argument. But in addition the jury found that Susan had been negligent too—and indeed that her negligence had been 97 percent to blame for the attack and the Adamses' only 3 percent. So, following the approach to comparative negligence laid down in Alvis v. Ribar, 85 Ill.2d 1, 421 N.E.2d 886 (1981)—the decision in which the Supreme Court of Illinois abolished the common law rule that contributory negligence is a complete bar to a negligence suit—the jury awarded Susan only $25,500 in damages. This happens to be approximately the midpoint of the psychologist's estimate—$20,000 to $30,000—of the expense of the therapy that the psychologist believes Susan may need for her post-traumatic stress.

Susan's lawyer asked the district judge to grant judgment in her favor notwithstanding the verdict, on the ground either that she had been nonnegligent as a matter of law or that her negligence was immaterial because the Adamses had been not merely negligent but willful and wanton in their disregard for her safety. In the alternative, counsel asked the judge to grant a new trial on the ground that the jury's apportionment of negligence was contrary to the manifest weight of the evidence. * * * The judge denied the motion[s], and Susan appeals.

Had she filed her suit after November 25, 1986, she could not have recovered any damages, assuming the jury would have made the same apportionment of responsibility between her and the Adamses. Illinois' new comparative negligence statute bars recovery in negligence (or strict liability product) cases in which the plaintiff's "fault * * * is more than 50% of the proximate cause of the injury or damage for which recovery is sought." But as her suit was filed before that date, the new statute is inapplicable.

Susan Wassell's counsel argues that the jury's verdict "reflected a chastened, hardened, urban mentality—that lurking behind every door is evil and danger, even if the guest is from a small town unfamiliar with the area." He takes umbrage at the defendants' argument that Susan's "antennae" should have been alerted when she didn't see anyone through the peephole. He rejects the metaphor, remarking unexceptionably that human beings do not have antennae and that this case is not a Kafka story about a person who turned into an insect (i.e., is not *The Metamorphosis*). He points out that a person awakened from a deep sleep is not apt to be thinking clearly and that once Susan opened the door the fat was in the fire—if she had slammed the door in the rapist's face he might have kicked the door in, as had happened once before at this motel, although she didn't know that at the time.

* * * Susan's counsel insists that Susan was not negligent at all but that, if she was, she was at most 5 percent responsible for the catastrophe, which, he argues, could have been averted costlessly by a simple warning from the Adamses. To this, the Adamses' counsel replies absurdly that a warning would have been costly—it might have scared guests away! The loss of business from telling the truth is not a social loss; it is a social gain.

The common law refused to compare the plaintiff's and the defendant's negligence. The negligent plaintiff could recover nothing, unless the defendant's culpability was of a higher degree than simple negligence. Susan argues that the defendants were willful and wanton, which, she says, would make her negligence as irrelevant under a regime of comparative negligence as it would be in a jurisdiction in which contributory negligence was still a complete defense.

Both the premise (that the Adamses were willful and wanton) and the conclusion (that if so, her own negligence was irrelevant) are wrong. As we guessed in Davis v. United States, 716 F.2d 418, 429 (7th Cir. 1983), that it would, Illinois appears to be lining up with the states that allow the plaintiff's simple negligence to be compared with the defendant's "willful and wanton conduct." See State Farm Mut. Auto. Ins. Co. v. Mendenhall, 517 N.E.2d 341 (Ill.App. 1987). We say "appears to be" because * * * *Mendenhall* * * * is not a decision of the Illinois Supreme Court, and because a critical premise of the decision may be shaky. That is the proposition that "willful and wanton" under Illinois law denotes merely a heightened form of negligence, so that there is only a small difference between simple negligence and willful and wanton misconduct despite the ominous sound of the words "willful" and "wanton." As we noted in *Davis*, there are two lines of "willful and wanton" decisions in Illinois. One, which seemed to be in the ascendancy when we wrote *Davis*, * * * regards "willful and wanton" as merely a heightened form of "negligent." * * * But the cases since *Davis* appear to have swung round to the narrower concept, under which willful and wanton conduct denotes "conscious disregard for * * * the safety of others" or "knowledge that [the defendant's] conduct posed a high probability of serious physical harm to others." * * *

If the more recent formulations are authoritative, this would undermine the argument in *Davis* and *Mendenhall* for allowing a plaintiff's simple negligence to be compared with a defendant's willful and wanton misconduct. But it would not help Susan Wassell win her case. No rational jury could find that the Adamses *consciously* disregarded a *high* probability of *serious* physical harm. * * *

[So the] district judge was right to deny Susan's request for judgment notwithstanding the verdict. But was he right to deny her [motion] for a new trial? [In support of her new trial motion, Susan argues that the jury's finding that her negligence was so great as to outweigh the Adamses' by a factor or more than 30 was contrary to the manifest weight of the evidence.] * * *

The old common law rule barring the contributorily negligent plaintiff from recovering any damages came eventually to seem too harsh. That is why it has been changed in most jurisdictions, including Illinois. It was harsh, all right, at least if one focuses narrowly on the plight of individual plaintiffs, but it was also simple and therefore cheap to administer. The same cannot be said for comparative negligence, which far from being simple requires a formless, unguided inquiry, because there is no methodology for comparing the causal contributions of the plaintiff's and of the defendant's negligence to the plaintiff's injury. In this case, either the plaintiff or the defendants could have avoided that injury. It is hard to say more, but the statute requires more—yet without giving the finder of facts any guidance as to how to make the apportionment.

We have suggested in previous cases that one way to make sense of comparative negligence is to assume that the required comparison is between the respective costs to the plaintiff and to the defendant of avoiding the injury. If each could have avoided it at the same cost, they are each 50 percent responsible for it. According to this method of comparing negligence, the jury found that Susan could have avoided the attack at a cost of less than one thirty-second the cost to the Adamses. Is this possible?

It is careless to open a motel or hotel door in the middle of the night without trying to find out who is knocking. Still, people aren't at their most alert when they are awakened in the middle of the night, and it wasn't crazy for Susan to assume that Michael had returned without telling her, even though he had said he would be spending the night at the base. So it cannot be assumed that the cost—not to her (although her testimony suggests that she is not so naive or provincial as her lawyer tried to convince the jury she was), but to the reasonable person who found himself or herself in her position, for that is the benchmark in determining plaintiff's as well as defendant's negligence—was zero, or even that it was slight. As innkeepers (in the increasingly quaint legal term), the Adamses had a duty to exercise a high degree of care to protect their guests from assaults on the motel premises. And the cost to the Adamses of warning all their female guests of the dangers of the neighborhood would have been negligible. Surely a warning to Susan would not have cost the Adamses 32 times the cost to her of schooling herself to greater vigilance.

But this analysis is incomplete. It is unlikely that a warning would have averted the attack. Susan testified that she thought the man who had knocked on the door was her fiance. Thinking this, she would have opened the door no matter how dangerous she believed the neighborhood to be. The warning that was not given might have deterred her from walking alone in the neighborhood. But that was not the pertinent danger. Of course, if the Adamses had told her not to open her door in the middle of the night under any circumstances without carefully ascertaining who was trying to enter the room, this would have been a pertinent warning and might have had an effect. But it is absurd to think that hoteliers are required to give so obvious a warning, any more than they must warn guests not to stick their fingers into the electrical outlets. Everyone, or at least the average person, knows better than to open his or her door to a stranger in the middle of the night. The problem was not that Susan thought that she should open her bedroom door in the middle of the night to anyone who knocked, but that she wasn't thinking clearly. A warning would not have availed against a temporary, sleep-induced lapse.

Giving the jury every benefit of the doubt, as we are required to do * * *, we must assume that the jury was not so muddle-headed as to believe that the Adamses' negligence consisted in failing to give a futile warning. Rather, we must assume that the jury thought the Adamses' negligence consisted in failing to have a security guard, or telephones in each room, or alarms * * *. The only one of these omitted precautions for which there is a cost figure in the record was the security guard. A guard would have cost $50 a night. That is almost $20,000 a year. This is not an enormous number. * * * [But it] might be much greater than the monetary equivalent of the greater vigilance on the part of Susan that would have averted the attack.

The assumption that the jury was clear-thinking and instruction-abiding is artificial, of course. During its deliberations, the jury sent the judge a question about the duty to warn (the judge did not answer it). This is some indication that the jury thought that the Adamses' negligence consisted in failing to warn Susan. But it is equally plausible that the jury didn't think the Adamses were negligent at all toward Susan, but, persuaded that she had suffered terribly, wanted to give her a token recovery. Concern with sympathy verdicts appears to lie behind Illinois' new statute barring the plaintiff from recovering any damages if he is more than 50 percent negligent. * * * It may be more than coincidence that the jury awarded Susan just enough money to allow her to undertake the recommended course of psychological therapy. We are not supposed to speculate about the jury's reasoning process, and we have just seen that it would not necessarily strengthen Susan's case if we did. The issue for us is not whether this jury was rational and law-abiding but whether a rational jury could, consistently with the evidence, have returned the verdict that this jury did. If we were the trier of fact, persuaded that both parties were negligent and forced to guess about the relative costs to the plaintiff and to the defendants of averting the assault, we would assess the defendants' share at more than 3 percent. But we are not the trier of fact, and are authorized to upset the jury's apportionment only if persuaded that the trial judge abused his discretion in determining that the jury's verdict was not against the clear weight of the evidence. We are not so persuaded. It seems probably wrong to us, but we have suggested an interpretation of the evidence under which the verdict was consistent with the evidence and the law. And that is enough to require us to uphold the district judge's refusal to set aside the verdict.

AFFIRMED.

NOTES

1. ***Ameliorative doctrines and the multiple meanings of "willful and wanton."*** In *McIntyre* we saw the court abolish "the doctrines of remote contributory negligence and last clear chance" because these had been developed solely as exceptions to the harsh old contributory negligence rule and should therefore fall by the wayside once that rule is killed off. Such rules, intended solely to ameliorate some of the effects of contributory negligence, are sometimes called *ameliorative doctrines*. (See, e.g., § 3 of the Apportionment Restatement.) The question in *Wassell* was whether the Illinois "willful and wanton" doctrine was only an ameliorative doctrine or whether it had some independent justification.

As Judge Posner's opinion shows, the question was not easy. If the doctrine meant that a plaintiff could escape the contributory negligence doctrine by showing that the defendant's negligence conduct was significantly more culpable than plaintiff's, it was only an ameliorative doctrine that should disappear once a comparative fault regime is adopted. But if it meant that a plaintiff's negligence should not constitute a defense when the defendant's conduct was qualitatively different from negligence—because it included the element of *conscious* disregard of a highly unacceptable risk and thus seemed more like an intentional wrong than like negligence—then perhaps "mere" negligence on the victim's part should not affect the recovery (just as most courts seem to think it shouldn't in standard intentional tort cases). For other courts struggling with this difficulty, see Martel v. Montana Power Co., 231 Mont. 96, 752 P.2d 140 (1988) (jettisoning a "willful and wanton" doctrine); Danculovich v. Brown, 593 P.2d 187 (Wyo. 1979) (jettisoning the last clear chance doctrine but keeping a "willful and wanton" doctrine). Cf. Weaver v. Lentz, 348 S.C. 672, 561 S.E.2d 360 (App.2002) (holding that damages were properly reduced to reflect the plaintiff's decedent's negligence even though the defendant may have acted "recklessly").

2. ***What is being "compared?"*** Judge Posner's approach to the validity of the 97% assignment to Susan Wassell is intriguing, but it has not been influential; perhaps it was too tightly focused on only the "B" element in the Hand B<PL formula. It is doubtful whether the 97% assignment could have been upheld in a system following the approach of § 8 of the Apportionment Restatement:

Factors for assigning percentages of responsibility to each person whose legal responsibility has been established include

(a) the nature of the person's risk-creating conduct, including any awareness or indifference with respect to the risks created by the conduct and any intent with respect to the harm created by the conduct; and

(b) the strength of the causal connection between the person's risk-creating conduct and the harm.

The assignment of 97% to Susan Wassell would have been even less likely to withstand scrutiny in Louisiana, where the supreme court has decreed:

> In determining the percentages of fault, the trier of fact shall consider both the nature of the conduct of each party at fault and the extent of the causal relation between the conduct and the damages claimed. In assessing the nature of the conduct of the parties, various factors may influence the degree of fault assigned, including (1) whether the conduct resulted from inadvertence or involved an awareness of the danger, (2) how great a risk was created by the conduct, (3) the significance of what was sought by the conduct, (4) the capacities of the actor, whether superior or inferior, and (5) any extenuating circumstances which might require the actor to proceed in haste, without proper thought.

Watson v. State Farm Fire and Cas. Ins. Co., 469 So.2d 967, 974 (La. 1985). See also Eaton v. McLain, 891 S.W.2d 587, 592–93 (Tenn. 1994), where the court provides a multi-factor formulation very similar to that in *Watson*. Dobbs, The Law of Torts § 202, p. 508 (2000), cautions that formulations like those in *Watson* and *Eaton* are "merely familiar instances of the fundamental negligence analysis" and that "[i]nstructions that specify particular instances of the general principle may run risks of overemphasizing particular facets of the negligence issue."

In thinking about the way in which juries are supposed to arrive at percentage-fault assessments, it may help to realize that there is no need to directly compare one party's conduct with that of the other. Section 8 cmt. *a* of the Apportionment Restatement suggests that " 'assigning shares of responsibility' may be a less confusing phrase [than 'comparing conduct'] because it suggests that the factfinder, after considering the relevant factors, *assigns* shares of responsibility rather than *compares* incommensurate qualities." But the term "comparative" is deeply entrenched in the vocabulary of the proportionate liability regime.

3. ***In a pure comparative fault system, can the egregiousness of plaintiff's fault ever lead to total defeat?*** In the pure system in effect in Illinois when Wassell's case arose, her 97% fault assignment left her entitled to recover 3% of her total damages. In situations in which the plaintiff's blameworthiness is assessed at such a high level, some judges and other analysts have considered it appropriate to hold for defendant on the basis that plaintiff's fault was so extreme as to constitute the "sole proximate cause" of the accident. See, e.g., Soto v. New York City Transit Authority, 6 N.Y.3d 487, 813 N.Y.S.2d 701, 846 N.E.2d 1211, 1216 (2006) (Smith, J., dissenting); Hayden, Butterfield Rides Again: Plaintiff's Negligence as Superseding or Sole Proximate Case in Systems of Pure Comparative Responsibility, 33 Loy. L.A. L. Rev. 887, 945 (2000); cf. Minor v. Zidell Trust, 618 P.2d 392, 395 (Okla. 1980). Others argue strongly to the contrary. See, e.g., Judge Posner's opinion in Justice v. CSX Transp., Inc., 908 F.2d 119, 124 (7th Cir. 1990):

> [Arguing that the plaintiff's negligent conduct was the superseding or sole proximate cause of the accident is] a transparent effort to circumvent Indiana's comparative negligence statute, by relabeling contributory neg-

ligence as proximate cause and thereby using a victim's negligence to eliminate his cause of action rather than merely to reduce the size of the award to which he is entitled.

Dobbs, The Law of Torts § 196 (2000), tends to agree with Judge Posner but notes that the courts are divided on the question.

4. *Other devices for barring high-blame plaintiffs.* Suppose you negligently leave your car unlocked with the key in the ignition and an intoxicated person steals the car and injures himself in a wreck. In the contributory negligence era, he wouldn't have sued you—obviously, he would have been barred by his own fault. In a comparative fault system, especially a pure one, some new doctrine may be needed. (You may well win on the merits, but what you need is something that gets the complaint thrown out.) The New York judiciary has named its response to this kind of problem—i.e., an action by a plaintiff whose injury stems from the combination of defendant's negligent conduct and the plaintiff's illegal or highly immoral conduct—the "preclusion doctrine" and has used it to dismiss complaints by a bombmaker, a burglar, a car thief, a fleeing felon, and an unlicensed dentist.[1] There have been similar developments in other states. See generally Dobbs, The Law of Torts § 208 (2000); King, Outlaws and Outlier Doctrines: The Serious Misconduct Bar in Tort Law, 43 Wm. & Mary L. Rev. 1014 (2002).

5. *New no-duty rules for plaintiffs.* Suppose your preoccupation with a cellular phone conversation causes you to drive negligently and wreck your car, producing personal injuries that require hospitalization, and the negligence of an emergency-room physician makes your injuries worse. If your medical malpractice action had been brought during the contributory negligence era, the physician would not have been able to invoke your negligent driving against you; the last clear chance doctrine would readily have prevented it. Here the switch to comparative fault seems to necessitate the creation of new legal doctrine. The Apportionment Restatement § 7 cmt. *m* provides that "in a case involving negligent rendition of a service, including medical services, a factfinder does not consider any plaintiff's conduct that created the situation the service was employed to remedy." For a discerning application and discussion of this proposition, see the majority and dissenting opinions in Aden v. Fortsh, 169 N.J. 64, 776 A.2d 792 (2001) (action against insurance broker). Mercer v. Vanderbilt University, 134 S.W.3d 121, 128 (Tenn. 2004), says that "most jurisdictions have held that a patient's negligence that provides only the occasion for medical treatment may not be compared to that of a negligent physician" (citing cases from Georgia, Maine, Montana, Oklahoma, Texas, and West Virginia).

6. *Set off.* Under a contributory negligence regime, negligent parties are barred from recovery against one another, so set-off issues will not arise. Once a comparative fault rule has been instituted, though, set-off issues can become prevalent. In the first judicial adoption of comparative fault in the U.S., the court in Hoffman v. Jones, 280 So.2d 431 (Fla. 1973), opted for the pure system and assumed that it would regularly lead to situations in which traffic tortfeasors were enabled to recover from one another. The court decreed that in such situations—i.e., when the jury returns verdicts awarding damages to

---

1.   Guadamud v. Dentsply Int'l, Inc., 20 F.Supp.2d 433 (E.D.N.Y. 1998).

both the plaintiff and the defendant/counterclaimant—the court should "set off" the verdicts and enter one net judgment. This was not a good idea.* In Jess v. Herrmann, 26 Cal.3d 131, 161 Cal.Rptr. 87, 604 P.2d 208, 211–12 (1979), the court explained:

> The facts of the instant case illustrate the problem. [Jess sustained $100,000 in damages and was 40% at fault. Herrmann sustained $14,000 in damages and was 60% at fault.] If both Jess and Herrmann carry adequate automobile insurance, in the absence of a mandatory setoff rule, Jess would receive $60,000 from defendant Herrmann's insurer to partially compensate her for the serious injuries caused by Herrmann's negligence, and Herrmann would receive $5,600 from Jess' insurer to partially compensate her for the injuries suffered as a result of Jess' negligence. Under the setoff rule applied by the trial court, however—despite the fact that both Jess' and Herrmann's injuries, financial losses and insurance coverage remain in fact unchanged—Jess' recovery from Herrmann's insurer is reduced to $54,400 and Herrmann is denied any recovery whatsoever from Jess' insurer.

> As these facts demonstrate, a mandatory setoff rule in the typical setting of insured tortfeasors does not serve as an innocuous accounting mechanism or as a beneficial safeguard against an adversary's insolvency but rather operates radically to alter the parties' ultimate financial positions. Such a mandatory rule diminishes both injured parties' actual recovery and accords both insurance companies a corresponding fortuitous windfall at their insureds' expense. Indeed, in this context, application of a mandatory setoff rule produces the anomalous situation in which a liability insurer's responsibility under its policy depends as much on the extent of the injury suffered by its own insured as on the amount of damages sustained by the person its insured has negligently injured.

Apportionment Restatement § 9 provides:

> If two parties are liable to each other in the same suit, each party is entitled to a setoff of any recovery owed by the other party, except that, in cases in which one or both of the parties has liability insurance, setoff does not reduce the payment of a liability insurer unless an applicable rule of law or statute so provides.

C. PROPORTIONATE LIABILITY ISSUES IN MULTIPLE TORTFEASOR CASES

The kinds of changes *McIntyre* brought to Tennessee law have also occurred in a number of other states. Normally this has been an "incremental" process, extending over many years.[1] The chronological details

---

* The court soon corrected the mistake. See Stuyvesant Ins. Co. v. Bournazian, 342 So.2d 471 (Fla. 1977) (holding that set-off should not occur when it benefits liability insurers at the expense of the parties). See also Sitzes v. Anchor Motor Freight, Inc., 169 W.Va. 698, 289 S.E.2d 679 (1982) (agreeing with the *Stuyvesant* and *Jess* courts).

1. Staab v. Diocese of St. Cloud, 780 N.W.2d 392, 394 (Minn. App. 2010) (describing Minnesota law's movement toward restricting joint and several liability and allowing the assignment of percentage fault to nonparties). For other descriptions of similar "incremental"

vary from state to state, but the logical progression is as follows. (1) First, the jurisdiction begins using the percentage-fault tool to penalize plaintiff's fault. (2) Then it decides to use the percentage tool to measure the contribution shares of multiple defendants. (3) Then, on encountering cases in which "deep-pocket" defendants are jointly and severally liable despite having small percentage-fault assignments (and in which such defendants' contribution rights against high-percentage tortfeasors are worthless because these tortfeasors are impecunious and uninsured),[2] the legislature or judiciary is persuaded to abolish or limit joint and several liability. (4) Adjudicating percentage-fault assignments against nonparty tortfeasors comes to be allowed.

The foregoing four stages have often seemed to be a slippery slope, in this sense: Once the percentage-fault concept comes into the law to measure the victim-fault penalty, it tends to take over. Few if any jurisdictions have held the line after step one.[3] A significant number have drawn the line after step two.[4] A handful have drawn it after step three.[5] But at the time of the Apportionment Restatement compilation (2000), twelve states had gone all the way to full abolition of joint and several liability and provision for percentage-fault assignments against nonparty tortfeasors.[6] *McIntyre* is unusual in having gone all the way all at once.

change, see Richards v. Badger Mutual Ins. Co., 309 Wis.2d 541, 749 N.W.2d 581, 588–89 (2008); Piner, infra p. 412; Fabre v. Marin, 623 So.2d 1182, 1185 (Fla. 1993); Brochner, infra p. 377.

2. See, e.g., Kaeo v. Davis, 68 Haw. 447, 719 P.2d 387 (1986), in which the jury's negligence assessments of plaintiff 0%, City of Honolulu 1%, drunk driver 99% left the City with liability for plaintiff's full damages ($725,000) along with a worthless right to seek 99% contribution from the drunk driver. See also Walt Disney World Co. v. Wood, 515 So.2d 198 (Fla. 1987), where plaintiff was injured at an amusement park (Disney) when her fiancé crashed his bumper car into hers. The jury's negligence assessments of plaintiff 14%, fiance 85%, and Disney 1% left Disney owing 86% of plaintiff's damages.

3. For many years Mississippi held that line. See Standard Oil Co. v. Illinois Central R. Co., 421 F.2d 201 (5th Cir. 1969) (describing Mississippi law as using percentage-fault assignments to penalize negligent plaintiffs and a head-count system for measuring multiple tortfeasors' contribution shares (e.g., three defendants, 1/3 each)). Recent legislation has greatly altered Mississippi law. Massachusetts may still be using percentage-fault assignments to penalize negligent plaintiffs and a head-count system to measure contribution shares. See Zeller v. Cantu, 395 Mass. 76, 478 N.E.2d 930, 934 (1985). But the line is hard to hold; most would agree that the decision to use percentage-fault assignments to compare the fault of victims and tortfeasors "lead[s] ineluctably" to percentage-based allocation among multiple tortfeasors. Sitzes v. Anchor Motor Freight, Inc., 169 W.Va. 698, 289 S.E.2d 679, 688 (1982).

4. The Apportionment Restatement at p. 151 lists ten comparative-fault states as having retained full joint and several liability.

5. See id. at p. 154 (listing three states that have abolished joint and several liability but refused to allow percentage-fault assignments to nonparties).

6. Id. There have been a number of legislative changes since the Apportionment Restatement was published. This area of the law has grown steadily more complex. The trend of recent legislation has been toward restricting or abolishing joint and several liability, but there are myriad exceptions. See, e.g., Apportionment Restatement p. 151 (listing ten comparative-fault states that have retained joint and several liability); id. p. 153 (listing four states where innocent plaintiffs still benefit from joint and several liability); id. p. 157 (listing ten states where joint and several liability still applies against defendants whose fault exceeds a certain percentage); id. p. 159 (listing eight states where restrictions on joint and several liability differ depending on the type of damages at issue); Richards v. Badger Mutual Ins. Co. 309 Wis.2d 541, 749 N.W.2d 581 (2008) (holding that full joint and several liability is still applicable against defendants held liable on the basis of concerted action) (supra Chapter IV section C, pp. 127–38); Reilly v. Anderson, 727 N.W.2d 102 (Iowa 2006) (same); Bell v. Ren–Pharm, Inc., 269 Mich.App. 464, 713 N.W.2d 285,

1. JOINT–AND–SEVERAL LIABILITY AND NONPARTY TORTFEASORS

BROWN v. KEILL

Supreme Court of Kansas, 1978.
224 Kan. 195, 580 P.2d 867.

FROMME, JUSTICE.

This appeal is from a judgment for damage to plaintiff's automobile resulting from a two-car collision. The primary issues raised on appeal require a construction of the provisions of K.S.A. 60–258a, commonly referred to as the Kansas comparative negligence statute.

The plaintiff-appellant, Britt Brown, owned a Jaguar roadster. His son, Britt M. Brown, was the permissive driver of appellant's Jaguar at the time of the collision. * * * The defendant-appellee, Patricia L. Keill, was the driver of the other car involved in the collision. The collision occurred at a street intersection in Wichita. The reasonable cost of repair to the Jaguar amounted to $5,423.00. The circumstances surrounding the collision need not be detailed. Apparently the defendant-appellee settled her claim against the driver of the Jaguar out of court. The owner of the Jaguar then sued to recover his property loss. Defendant-appellee did not seek to have the son joined as an additional formal party to the action. She did not file a counterclaim or cross-claim.

* * *

At the close of a bench trial the court found: (1) The plaintiff-father, as bailor of the Jaguar, was guilty of no negligence; (2) the driver of the Jaguar was responsible for 90% of the causal negligence; (3) the defendant, Keill, was responsible for 10% of the causal negligence; (4) plaintiff sustained total damages in the amount of $5,423.00; and (5) pursuant to the comparative negligence statute of Kansas plaintiff was entitled to recover $542.30 or 10% of his total damage from the defendant, Keill. Judgment was entered for that amount and this appeal followed.

At the outset it should be noted that in the absence of evidence of a joint venture, agency or circumstances giving rise to vicarious liability the negligence of a bailee of a vehicle is not imputable to the bailor in an action by the bailor against a third party for damage to the bailed vehicle.* The plaintiff in this case accordingly was guilty of no contributory negligence.

---

287 (2006) (indicating that joint and several liability is still available in "medical malpractice action[s] in which plaintiffs have been determined to be without fault"); Barry v. Quality Steel Products, Inc., 280 Conn. 1, 905 A.2d 55, 62 & nn. 13, 14 (2006) (indicating that Connecticut law has separate regimes for negligence and products liability cases). In most jurisdictions, intentional tortfeasors are always jointly and severally liable. See Apportionment Restatement § 12.

    * Kansas law was typical in this respect. See infra section D, pp. 388–94. What this meant was that there was no substantive doctrine that could have supported imputing Brown, Jr.'s fault to Brown, Sr. If that result was to be attained, its justification had to be found in the comparative negligence statute. [Ed.]

[T]he two ultimate questions to be decided on appeal are: (1) Has the rule of joint and several liability of joint tortfeasors been retained in actions now governed by the Kansas comparative negligence statute, K.S.A. 60–258a; and (2) is the causal negligence or fault of all parties to a collision or occurrence giving rise to plaintiff's claim in a comparative negligence action to be considered even though one of said parties is not served with process or joined as a formal party to the action?

We will consider first the question as to joint and several liability.

* * *

[U]nder the Kansas law as it existed prior to statutory comparative negligence a plaintiff could choose his tortfeasor and a defendant had no right to bring in another joint tortfeasor to plaintiff's action. [I]f plaintiff sued and recovered a judgment against two tortfeasors plaintiff could proceed to collect the judgment from either judgment debtor. When one judgment debtor had satisfied the entire judgment he could then recover one-half of the amount paid from the other judgment debtor. The effect of these prior holdings was to make each defendant jointly and severally liable for all of plaintiff's damage regardless of whether others contributed to cause such injuries. The right of contribution between judgment debtors in such case was on a fifty-fifty basis. Plaintiff controlled his own lawsuit and could collect a judgment from any judgment debtor he chose. The inability of any judgment debtor to pay his half of the judgment would concern only the judgment debtor who satisfied the judgment and then sought contribution.

* * *

In 1974 the Kansas legislature passed [K.S.A. 60–258a § 1], which reads as follows:

An Act concerning tort liability; abolishing contributory negligence as a bar to recovery; and providing for the awarding of damages on the basis of comparative negligence.

Be it enacted by the Legislature of the State of Kansas:

(a) The contributory negligence of any party in a civil action shall not bar such party or his legal representative from recovering damages for negligence resulting in death, personal injury or property damage, if such party's negligence was less than the causal negligence of the party or parties against whom claim for recovery is made, but the award of damages to any party in such action shall be diminished in proportion to the amount of negligence attributed to such party. If any such party is claiming damages for a decedent's wrongful death, the negligence of the decedent, if any, shall be imputed to such party.

(b) Where the comparative negligence of the parties in any such action is an issue, the jury shall return special verdicts, or in the absence of a jury, the court shall make special findings, determining the percentage of negligence attributable to each of the parties, and determining the total amount of damages sustained by each of the claimants, and the entry of judgment shall be made by the court. No general verdict shall be returned by the jury.

(c) On motion of any party against whom a claim is asserted for negligence resulting in death, personal injury or property damage, any other person whose causal negligence is claimed to have contributed to such death, personal injury or property damage shall be joined as an additional party to the action.

(d) Where the comparative negligence of the parties in any action is an issue and recovery is allowed against more than one party, each such party shall be liable for that portion of the total dollar amount awarded as damages to any claimant in the proportion that the amount of his causal negligence bears to the amount of the causal negligence attributed to all parties against whom such recovery is allowed.

* * *

Both parties assert there are ambiguities in the comparative negligence statute, K.S.A. 60–258a, as passed by the Kansas legislature. We agree. Therefore, it becomes necessary to consider and apply rules of statutory construction. The fundamental rule of statutory construction, to which all others are subordinate, is that the purpose and intent of the legislature governs when that intent can be ascertained from the statute, even though words, phrases or clauses at some place in the statute must be omitted or inserted. In determining legislative intent, courts are not limited to a mere consideration of the language used, but look to the historical background of the enactment, the circumstances attending its passage, the purpose to be accomplished and the effect the statute may have under the various constructions suggested. In order to ascertain the legislative intent, courts are not permitted to consider only a certain isolated part or parts of an act but are required to consider and construe together all parts thereof in pari materia. When the interpretation of some one section of an act according to the exact and literal import of its words would contravene the manifest purpose of the legislature, the entire act should be construed according to its spirit and reason, disregarding so far as may be necessary the literal import of words or phrases which conflict with the manifest purpose of the legislature.

* * *

The appellant contends that the trial court erroneously ignored the principle of joint and several liability in entering judgment for only 10% of the total damages. He suggests that since K.S.A. 60–258a does not mention joint and several liability this court should construe the statute to retain joint and several liability, and adopt a rule of comparative contribution that would permit the joint judgment debtors to apportion damages on the basis of their relative fault. Under such a construction of the statute if plaintiff suffered damages in the amount of $5,423.00, as in this case, he could sue and recover said sum from either defendant regardless of such defendant's percentage of fault. In such case if the defendant against whom recovery was had was 10% at fault and the other defendant was 90% at fault, the plaintiff could collect the $5,423.00 from the defendant 10% at fault and such defendant would then have a right of contribution against the other joint tortfeasor for 90/100 × $5,423.00 or $4,880.70, based on proportion of fault.

The substance of defendant-appellee's argument in support of the present judgment is that the legislature by adopting subsection (a) as well as subsection (d) of the statute meant to equate both the amount to be recovered by plaintiff and the liability of a defendant with the individual's degree of fault in all cases where the plaintiff's negligence was less than the fault of all other parties to the collision or occurrence. If this were the intention of the legislature it would of necessity require this court to hold our prior rules as to joint and several liability had been abolished by the legislature in comparative negligence cases.

* * *

The perceived purpose in adopting K.S.A. 60–258a is fairly clear. The legislature intended to equate recovery and duty to pay to degree of fault. Of necessity, this involved a change of both the doctrine of contributory negligence and of joint and several liability. There is nothing inherently fair about a defendant who is 10% at fault paying 100% of the loss, and there is no social policy that should compel defendants to pay more than their fair share of the loss. Plaintiffs now take the parties as they find them. If one of the parties at fault happens to be a spouse or a governmental agency and if by reason of some competing social policy the plaintiff cannot receive payment for his injuries from the spouse or agency, there is no compelling social policy which requires the codefendant to pay more than his fair share of the loss. The same is true if one of the defendants is wealthy and the other is not. Previously, when the plaintiff had to be totally without negligence to recover and the defendants had to be merely negligent to incur an obligation to pay, an argument could be made which justified putting the burden of seeking contribution on the defendants. Such an argument is no longer compelling because of the purpose and intent behind the adoption of the comparative negligence statute.

It appears more reasonable for the legislature to have intended to relate duty to pay to the degree of fault. Any other interpretation of K.S.A. 60–258a(d) destroys the fundamental conceptual basis for the abandonment of the contributory negligence rule and makes meaningless the enactment of subsection (d). If it were not the intention of the legislature to abolish joint and several liability by adopting subsection (d) that subsection would have little or no purpose, because [subsections (a) and (b)] of the statute standing alone could have accomplished the legislative purpose urged by the appellant.

* * * Having considered the arguments in light of the statute, we hold [that] under the provisions of K.S.A. 60–258a the concept of joint and several liability between joint tortfeasors previously existing in this state no longer applies in comparative negligence actions. The individual liability of each defendant for payment of damages will be based on proportionate fault, and contribution among joint judgment debtors is no longer required in such cases.

We turn now to the second question raised in this appeal. Is the causal negligence or fault of all parties to a collision or occurrence giving rise to plaintiff's claim in a comparative negligence action to be considered even though one or more of said parties is not served with process or joined as a formal party to the action?

The appellant points out that, while subsection (c) of the statute permits "any party against whom a claim is asserted" to bring in another person on motion, there is nothing in the statute which specifically requires the plaintiff to bring his action or file a claim against any particular person or group of persons. Appellant further notes that under subsection (d) the causal negligence or fault of all parties "against whom such recovery is allowed" is to be proportioned. Nowhere in the act does it state that persons who are not parties to the action are to have any impact on the ultimate judgment to be entered. Therefore, appellant asserts it is incumbent upon a defendant to join such additional parties as he may deem necessary or advisable to determine their fault.

Appellee, on the other hand, points to subsection (d) of the statute and says the comparative negligence of all parties whose fault contributed to the collision or occurrence must be determined if "each such party shall be liable for that portion of the total dollar amount awarded as damages to any claimant in the proportion that the amount of his causal negligence bears to the amount of the causal negligence attributed to all parties against whom such recovery is allowed." In addition appellee contends that subsection (c) of the statute must be construed as permissive for it is impossible and fruitless in many cases for a defendant to attempt to join and bring into the action those who have settled out under a covenant not to sue and whose liability for damages no longer exists. Other instances are cited where no recovery by plaintiff may be obtained against a party who is or may be at fault, such as cases of interspousal immunity and where there is an absence of information as to the name or whereabouts of a party to the occurrence.

In examining K.S.A. 60–258a we note that subsection (a) is concerned with changing our prior rule which denied recovery to a claimant whose negligence contributed to cause the collision or occurrence. It provides that a party's negligence shall not be a bar if such negligence was less than the causal negligence of the party or parties against whom claim for recovery is made. It further provides the award of damages to such party shall be diminished in proportion to the amount of negligence attributed to such party. This section, as well as other sections of the statute, speaks in terms of parties in or to the action rather than plaintiffs and defendants. We note, however, this wording in the statute can be construed as a means of accommodating cases in which both claims and counterclaims are filed as a result of one collision or occurrence rather than to imply it relates to parties to the occurrence. The position taken by plaintiff in this action has support because of the use of the phrases "party or parties against whom claim for recovery is made" in subsection (a), and "all parties against whom such recovery is allowed" in subsection (d).

Before answering the ultimate question being considered, several preliminary questions bearing on multiple party cases should be examined. * * *

* * * May the plaintiff avoid proportionate liability by suing and making a claim against only one of several tortfeasors? Presumably subsection (c) permits a defendant to file a motion and join other tortfeasors. However, plaintiff may have settled with that tortfeasor and no liability exists when the action is filed. The statute is silent as to what position the added party occupies once that party is joined. It is doubtful if the plaintiff in such a case can be forced to make a claim against the added party. The legislative intent in including subsection (c) would appear to have been to * * * permit a defendant in a comparative negligence case to bring in other joint tortfeasors so their percentage of fault can be determined and their liability, if any, adjudged.

The next preliminary question that presents itself is will proportionate liability be defeated when a party joined under subsection (c) has a valid defense such as interspousal immunity, covenant not to sue and so forth? The added party in such case would not be a party "against whom such recovery is allowed" and if subsection (d) is taken literally such a party's percentage of fault should not be considered in determining the judgment to be rendered. It appears after considering the intent and purposes of the entire statute that such a party's fault should be considered in each case to determine the other defendant's percentage of fault and liability, if any. The proportionate liability of the other parties to the action under K.S.A. 60–258a(d) should not be increased merely because a party joined under subsection (c) has a valid defense to plaintiff's claim, other than lack of negligence.

Now we return to the ultimate question should the percentage of fault of one who is not or cannot be formally joined as a party under subsection (c) be considered under subsection (d) to arrive at the proportionate liability of the defendant or defendants?

After having answered the preliminary questions and having applied the rules of statutory construction previously set forth in this opinion, we conclude the intent and purpose of the legislature in adopting K.S.A. 60–258a was to impose individual liability for damages based on the proportionate fault of all parties to the occurrence which gave rise to the injuries and damages even though one or more parties cannot be joined formally as a litigant or be held legally responsible for his or her proportionate fault.

* * *

Judgment affirmed.

1. ***Respect for legislative language.*** On becoming convinced that the abolition of joint and several liability or the creation of a new affirmative defense of nonparty tortfeasor percentage fault is a wise move, a court is still obligated to examine relevant legislation to see if it impedes the desired change. In *McIntyre*, we saw the court essentially repealing the Tennessee Uniform Contribution Among Tort–Feasors Act. Did the *Brown* court do any violence to the Kansas statute? In thinking about this question, consider the following inquiries and data:

(a) What will be the role and purpose of subsection (c) of the statute in post-*Brown* litigation?

(b) How did the court define the phrase "all parties against whom such recovery is allowed" in subsection (d)?

(c) The legislature has not amended the statute to reflect any disagreement with the *Brown* court's interpretation of it.[1]

(d) Apparently unaware of Brown v. Keill, the court in Newville v. State, 267 Mont. 237, 883 P.2d 793, 802 (1994) cited subsection (d) of the Kansas statute for the proposition that "[a]lthough Kansas has abolished joint and several liability altogether, it does not allow apportionment of percentage of total damages to any person who is not a party [to the lawsuit]."

2. ***Pros and cons of abolishing joint and several liability.*** Both the *McIntyre* and *Brown* courts presented arguments for abolishing joint and several liability. Some of the counter-arguments were summarized in American Motorcycle Ass'n v. Superior Court, 20 Cal.3d 578, 146 Cal.Rptr. 182, 578 P.2d 899, 906–07 (1978), as follows:

[Here defendant AMA argues that Li v. Yellow Cab Co., 532 P.2d 1226 (Cal. 1975), in which this Court adopted the pure form of comparative negligence] undermined the fundamental rationale of the entire joint and several liability doctrine as applied to concurrent tortfeasors. In this regard AMA cites the following passage from Finnegan v. Royal Realty Co., 218 P.2d 17, 32 (Cal. 1950): "Even though persons are not acting in concert, if the results produced by their acts are indivisible, each person is held liable for the whole. * * * *The reason for imposing liability on each for the entire consequences is that there exists no basis for dividing damages and the law is loath to permit an innocent plaintiff to suffer as against a wrongdoing defendant.* * * *" (Emphasis added.) Focusing on the emphasized sentence, AMA argues that after *Li* (1) there is a basis for dividing damages, namely on a comparative negligence basis, and (2) a plaintiff is no longer necessarily "innocent," for *Li* permits a negligent plaintiff to recover damages. AMA maintains that in light of these two factors it is logically inconsistent to retain joint and several liability of

---

1. The statute was rewritten in 2010, but the changes appear purely cosmetic.

concurrent tortfeasors after *Li*. As we explain, for a number of reasons we cannot accept AMA's argument.

First, the simple feasibility of apportioning fault on a comparative negligence basis does not render an indivisible injury "divisible" for purposes of the joint and several liability rule. * * * [A] defendant has no equitable claim vis a vis an injured plaintiff to be relieved of liability for damage which he has proximately caused simply because some other tortfeasor's negligence may also have caused the same harm. * * * [T]he mere fact that it may be possible to assign some percentage figure to the relative culpability of one negligent defendant as compared to another does not in any way suggest that each defendant's negligence is not a proximate cause of the entire indivisible injury.

Second, abandonment of the joint and several liability rule is not warranted by AMA's claim that, after *Li*, a plaintiff is no longer "innocent." Initially, of course, it is by no means invariably true that after *Li* injured plaintiffs will be guilty of negligence. In many instances a plaintiff will be completely free of all responsibility for the accident, and yet, under the proposed abolition of joint and several liability, such a completely faultless plaintiff, rather than a wrongdoing defendant, would be forced to bear a portion of the loss if any one of the concurrent tortfeasors should prove financially unable to satisfy his proportioned share of the damages.

Moreover, even when a plaintiff is partially at fault for his own injury, a plaintiff's culpability is not equivalent to that of a defendant. [Often] a plaintiff's negligence relates only to a failure to use due care for his own protection, while a defendant's negligence relates to a lack of due care for the safety of others. Although we recognized in *Li* that a plaintiff's self-directed negligence would justify reducing his recovery in proportion to his degree of fault for the accident, the fact remains that insofar as the plaintiff's conduct creates only a risk of self-injury, such conduct, unlike that of a negligent defendant, is not tortious.

Finally, from a realistic standpoint, we think that AMA's suggested abandonment of the joint and several liability rule would work a serious and unwarranted deleterious effect on the practical ability of negligently injured persons to receive adequate compensation for their injuries. * * * [T]he joint and several liability rule * * * permits an injured person to obtain full recovery for his injuries even when one or more of the responsible parties do not have the financial resources to cover their liability. In such a case the rule recognizes that fairness dictates that the "wronged party should not be deprived of his right to redress," but that "[t]he wrongdoers should be left to work out between themselves any apportionment." (Summers v. Tice, 199 P.2d 1, 5 (Cal. 1948).) The *Li* decision does not detract in the slightest from this pragmatic policy determination.

3. ***Pros and cons of adjudicating the percentage fault of nonparty tortfeasors.*** *McIntyre* justified its creation of this new affirmative defense on "fairness and efficiency" grounds, and the tenor of *Brown* is to the same effect. Strong counter-arguments may have been overlooked or shortchanged.

It is easiest to see the pros and cons in the context of a pure comparative negligence system.

In a pure comparative fault system with full joint and several liability, assigning percentage fault to nonparties would generally benefit plaintiffs, because those assignments would siphon off some of the 100 fault points that might otherwise go to the plaintiff, and the rule of joint and several liability would mean that defendant would be charged with those points in addition to its own. But if the plaintiff believes that someone other than defendant is to blame, why shouldn't the plaintiff be required to sue that person or entity? (The jury will want to know this, too, which is why plaintiffs generally don't ask for nonparty percentage-fault adjudication.)

In a pure comparative fault system that has abolished joint and several liability, adjudicating percentage fault against nonparties is enormously beneficial to defendants. It siphons off some of the 100 fault points that would otherwise go to the defendant, and it charges the plaintiff with those points. (And the technique is also rhetorically powerful; it may enable the defendant to say, I did nothing wrong, and moreover this accident was someone else's fault.) Because of personal jurisdiction, statutes of limitations, immunities, and other issues, frequently it will not be feasible for plaintiff to amend the lawsuit to add as defendants the additional putative culprits nominated by the defendant. In that situation, plaintiff's counsel has a newly daunting task at trial: Not only must the defendant's conduct be inculpated and the plaintiff's exculpated; now the plaintiff must also try to exculpate the nonparty culprits nominated by the defendant. In *Newville*, supra note 1, the Montana Supreme Court cited these litigation realities as a significant reason for holding that a statute requiring the allocation of percentages of liability to nonparties "violates substantive due process" under the 14th Amendment to the U.S. Constitution. 883 P.2d at 802–803.

Some have argued that assigning percentage fault to nonparties brings greater clarity and accuracy to the fact-finding process. The argument seems unpersuasive. Certainly in the course of reconstructing an accident and deciding who is to blame, the jury needs to make decisions about the conduct of everyone involved, and in the process to come to a solid sense of who is more responsible than whom. But none of those determinations necessitates the expenditure of any of the precious 100 fault points on persons who will not be affected by being assigned such points.

4. *A frequent mistake: treating percentage-fault assignments as reflecting cause-in-fact shares.* Suppose that a bus tries to outrace a train (itself traveling at grossly excessive speed) to a grade crossing, loses, and the crash kills a bus passenger, whose estate brings a state-court action against Bus and Train.[2] The Train Company immediately files a bankruptcy petition in U.S. Bankruptcy Court. The bankruptcy court discharges the Train Company from any debt arising from the accident, and the state-court judge then dismisses the Train Company from the suit.[3] At the trial, the jury assigns 50% fault to Bus and 50% to Train. The law of the jurisdiction is unsettled on joint and several liability, enabling the Bus Company to argue vigorously: "How

---

2. See generally Baylor University v. Bradshaw, 52 S.W.2d 1094 (Tex.Civ.App. 1932).

3. See generally Brodsky v. Grinnell Haulers, Inc., 181 N.J. 102, 853 A.2d 940 (2004).

can we be liable for all of it when we caused only half of it?" It should be obvious that the court should answer as follows: "Nonsense. Your conduct was a cause in fact and a proximate cause of all of it. Do you deny that the man would still be alive today if you hadn't tried to outrace the train? The 50% assignment reflects your blameworthiness; it does not purport to estimate a causal share of an indivisible injury. The court assumes you agree that death is indivisible?"

Despite the confusion or obfuscation on which it rests, versions of the Bus Company's argument sometimes succeed.The mischaracterization at the heart of the Bus Company's argument is sometimes encountered in arguments for abolishing joint and several liability and for the new affirmative defense of nonparty percentage fault. See, e.g., Bartlett v. New Mexico Welding Supply, 98 N.M. 152, 646 P.2d 579 (1982).

5. Percentage-fault assignments to nonparties frequently bring practical complexity and confusion to multiple tortfeasor cases. See the next case.

VARELA v. AMERICAN PETROFINA COMPANY OF TEXAS, INC.

Supreme Court of Texas, 1983.
658 S.W.2d 561.

WALLACE, JUSTICE.

This is an appeal from a third-party negligence action brought by an employee covered by workers' compensation insurance. The trial court [required the jury to assess] the negligence of the employee, the employer, and the * * * defendant. Judgment was rendered for the amount of damages found by the jury reduced by the proportion of negligence of both the employee and the employer. The court of appeals affirmed. We reverse the judgments of the courts below and render judgment for the employee for the total amount of damages found by the jury reduced only by the proportion of negligence of the employee.

Robert O. Varela was employed by Hydrocarbon Construction Company (Hydrocarbon), who was performing a "turnaround" on a fluid catalytic cracking unit owned and operated by American Petrofina Company of Texas (Petrofina). During the course of performing the "turnaround" Varela was injured as a result of a fall due to an alleged premises defect. After settling his workers compensation claim with Hydrocarbon's workers compensation [insurer], Varela sued Petrofina for the damages resulting from his injuries. * * * [T]he jury apportioned the negligence of the parties as follows: Varela 15%, Hydrocarbon 42%, and Petrofina 43%. The jury further found damages for Varela in the sum of $606,800. The trial court rendered judgment for * * * 43% of the total damages. The court of appeals affirmed.

The sole question before us is whether an employer's negligence may be considered in a third-party negligence action brought by an employee arising out of an accidental injury covered by workers' compensation insurance. We hold that under applicable statutes, the employer's negligence may not be considered.

Article 8306, Sec. 3 states in pertinent part:

> The employees of [an employer covered by the workers' compensation system] shall have no right of action against their employer or against any agent, servant or employee of said employer for damages for personal injuries * * * but such employees * * * shall look for compensation solely to the [employer's workers' compensation insurer]. * * * If an action for damages on account of injury * * * is brought by such employee * * * against a person other than the [employer] * * * and if such action results in a judgment against such other person, or results in a settlement by such other person, the [employer], his agent, servant or employee, shall have no liability to reimburse or hold such other person harmless on such judgment or settlement * * *. No part of this Section is intended to lessen or alter the employee's existing rights or cause of action * * * against * * * any third party.

The above quoted statute abrogates the covered employee's right to recover common law damages from the employer for personal injury covered by the Workers' Compensation Act. However, the employee may seek recovery from a third party whose negligence contributed to the injury. In the event of recovery the negligent third party is barred from seeking contribution or indemnity from the employer, and the [employer's compensation insurer] is entitled to reimbursement for all compensation and medical expenses paid.

Article 2212a generally governs the liability of joint tortfeasors. Section 1 provides that a plaintiff shall recover if his negligence is not greater than the negligence of the defendant and " * * * any damages allowed shall be diminished in proportion to the amount of negligence attributed to the person or party recovering." Section 2(b) stipulates that " * * * contribution to the damages awarded to the claimant shall be in proportion to the percentage of negligence attributable to each defendant." Subsection 2(c) provides that "[e]ach defendant is jointly and severally liable for the entire amount of the judgment * * * except * * * a defendant whose negligence is less than that of the claimant * * *." Subsection 2(e) provides that in the event of a settlement with a defendant " * * * the settlement is a complete release of the portion of the judgment attributable to the percentage of negligence found on the part of the [settling] tortfeasor."

We hold that Article 8306, § 3 is an exception to Article 2212a, § 2(b). When read together those two Articles indicate the intent of the Legislature that where the * * * defendant's negligence is [equal to or] greater than that of the employee, the employee shall recover the total amount of damages as found by the jury diminished only in proportion to the amount of the negligence attributed to the employee.

Petrofina contends that upon settlement of the workers' compensation claim the employer became a settled tortfeasor and thus subsection 2(e) of Art. 2212a mandates that Petrofina be credited with a reduction of damages equal to that percentage of negligence attributable to Hydrocarbon. It simply stretches the concept of settlement too far to hold that by not rejecting coverage of workers' compensation insurance in writing within five days of commencing employment, an employee has settled any and all future claims against the employer. Further, a defendant's claim of contribution is derivative of the plaintiff's right to recover from the joint defendant against whom contribution is sought. The Workers' Compensation Act, Article 8306, § 3, precludes any right by Varela to a cause of action against Hydrocarbon for common law negligence. Since Varela had no cause of action against Hydrocarbon, Petrofina had no claim for contribution from Hydrocarbon. Since Petrofina had no claim for contribution, subsection 2(e) of Art. 2212a has no application to this case.

The judgments of the courts below are reversed and judgment is rendered for Varela in the amount of $515,780.00 plus interest from the date of judgment.

Notes

1. ***Should the employer's fault be assessed and used to diminish the employee's tort recovery?*** The central issue of *Varela*—whether the employee's tort recovery should be diminished to reflect the employer's percentage of fault—is a close one, and the law is unsettled. The U.S. Supreme Court has signaled its agreement with the *Varela* approach. See Edmonds v. Compagnie Generale Transatlantique, 443 U.S. 256, 99 S.Ct. 2753, 61 L.Ed.2d 521 (1979) (construing the Longshore and Harbor Workers' Compensation Act, 33 U.S.C. § 901 et seq.). According to the listing of states provided in the Apportionment Restatement (pp. 151–59), at the time of that compilation 24 states said no to the captioned question and 19 said yes. (By virtue of *Varela*, the Restatement had Texas in the no column. However, in 2003 Texas crossed over. See Tex. Civ. Prac. & Rem. Code §§ 33.003 and 33.004.)

2. In jurisdictions where the employer's percentage of fault does not diminish the employee's recovery against the "third party tortfeasor," is there any reason for making the employer a party defendant or submitting the issue of the employer's percentage of fault to the jury? Most courts have answered no. See, e.g., Teakell v. Perma Stone Company, 658 S.W.2d 563 (Tex.1983), a companion case to *Varela*. To the same effect see *Edmonds,* supra note 1.

3. ***Dealing with erroneous or unwanted percentage assignments: proportionate reallocation***. Fairly often in multi-party comparative fault cases, an appellate court will conclude that a fault percentage the trial court has assessed should not be given effect. For example, the appellate court may decide that a party who was assigned a fault percentage and cast in liability by the trial court was immune, owed no duty, was not guilty of negligence, or was not a proximate cause of the injuries. Or it may happen, as in *Varela,* that the appeals court disagrees with the trial judge as to the kinds of actors whose negligence should count. (During the present era, when comparative fault

systems are being enacted, developed, expanded, and tested in a variety of contexts, trial judges are likely to commit such mistakes.) The appeals court must then decide what to do with the now-unwanted percentage finding.

In *Varela* the trial court found fault as follows:

P (Varela): 15%

D (Petrofina): 43%

Employer (Hydrocarbon): 42%

No one doubted that the assessments against P and D should be factored into P's recovery. The question was what to do with the 42% assignment to Employer, who could not be made to pay anything because of the immunity conferred by the workers' compensation statute. As the case came to the supreme court, as a matter of logic there were four choices:

(a) Charge the 42% to P.

(b) Charge it to D.

(c) Ignore the unwanted finding—set it aside—and re-express the relative fault of P and D as 15/58 and 43/58. The Apportionment Restatement, § 7 cmt. *h*, calls this *proportionate reallocation*.

(d) Remand the case for a new trial so that the finder of fact can express the relative fault of P and D in percentage terms, without using any of the 100 fault points on Employer.

The trial court chose (a). The supreme court explained why that was wrong. The supreme court chose (b)—it awarded P 85% of his full damages—but without explaining why that was right.

Was it? As between (b) and (c), the pertinent question would seem to be, which more nearly reflects the jury's allocation of fault as between plaintiff and defendant. For decisions concluding that (c)—proportionate reallocation—is the better approach, see Munoz v. Union City, 148 Cal.App.4th 173, 55 Cal.Rptr.3d 393 (2007);[4] Davis v. Commercial Union Ins. Co., 892 F.2d 378 (5th Cir.1990);[5] Cartel Capital Corp. v. Fireco of New Jersey, 81 N.J. 548, 410 A.2d 674 (1980);[6] Haney Elec. Co. v. Hurst, 624 S.W.2d 602 (Tex.Civ.App. 1981).[7]

---

4. *Munoz* was an action alleging police misconduct resulting in a death. The jury assessed the victim with 5% fault, the police officer who fired the fatal shot with 50%, and the city with 45%. On appeal, it was determined that the 45% assessment against the city was erroneous. The court concluded that the victim's and policeman's assessments should be proportionately reallocated at 5/55 and 50/55. 55 Cal.Rptr.3d at 402–03.

5. *Davis* was functionally identical to *Varela*. The trier of fact assessed the injured worker with 60%, the defendant with 10%, and the worker's employer with 30%. Holding that under Louisiana law the assignment to the employer was improper, the appellate court held the defendant responsible for 10/70 of the worker's damages. 892 F.2d at 384–85.

6. *Cartel* was a products liability action in which the jury assessed the plaintiff with 41% fault and the two defendants (manufacturer and supplier of the defective product) with 30% and 29%. Holding that under New Jersey products liability law a consumer plaintiff's negligence should not be penalized, the court said that the two defendants' shares of the liability were 30/59 and 29/59. 410 A.2d at 685.

7. *Haney* was two consolidated cases, tried together, arising from a multi-vehicle tangle on a Dallas freeway. The jury assigned each of two plaintiff-drivers 30% fault and the defendant driver 40%. The court held that defendant owed each plaintiff 40/70 of that plaintiff's damages. 624 S.W.2d at 612–13.

Apportionment Restatement, § 7 cmt. *h*, recommends proportionate real-location to avoid a new trial except in three situations: when "eliminating the nonliable person from the factfinder's consideration might have substantially altered the jury's deliberations, such as when the nonliable person was assigned the vast majority of responsibility and the remaining persons only very small percentages,"[8] and when reallocation would put a party "on the other side of a discontinuity" in the jurisdiction's modified comparative fault rule[9] or joint-and-several-liability rules.[10]

2. INDEMNITY, CONTRIBUTION, AND PARTIAL SETTLEMENTS

BROCHNER v. WESTERN INSURANCE COMPANY

Supreme Court of Colorado, 1986.
724 P.2d 1293.

KIRSHBAUM, JUSTICE.

* * *

The Community Hospital Association (the hospital), which operates Boulder Community Hospital, granted staff privileges to Dr. Ruben Brochner in October 1964. Brochner performed numerous craniotomies at the hospital over the next few months. [A craniotomy is a type of brain surgery in which suspected abnormal or diseased brain tissue is removed.] In 1965, after reviews of those craniotomies indicated that tissue samples from many of the patients appeared normal, the hospital's executive committee orally required Brochner to obtain consultations before performing craniotomies if the relevant radiographic evidence did not clearly establish pathology. In 1966, the executive committee recommended to Brochner that he should obtain additional outside consultation on surgical pathological specimens.

In March 1968, the hospital's tissue committee received a report that fourteen of twenty-eight tissue samples taken from Brochner's neurosurgery patients were completely normal and that nine of the remaining fourteen samples indicated only low grade disease. An expert testified at trial that one normal tissue of 100 tissue samples was an acceptable ratio

---

8. See, e.g., Price v. Kitsap Transit Co., 125 Wash.2d 456, 886 P.2d 556 (1994). Plaintiff, a city bus passenger, was hurt when another passenger's 4–year–old reached into the driver's area and engaged the emergency stop switch. The trier of fact found that the plaintiff was blameless, the bus driver's fault was 10%, the 4–year–old's father's was 10%, and the 4–year–old's was 80%. Holding that the child was too young to be negligent, the court remanded the case for a new trial limited to the issue of "the proper apportionment of fault." Id. at 563.

9. E.g., in a jurisdiction with a modified (50%-bar) rule, suppose the jury finds that the fault assignments are P 40%, D–1 40%, and D–2 20%. The appellate court then determines that the assignment to D–2 was improper. Proportionate reallocation would put P at 40/80 = 50% = barred. The Restaters think this circumstance might call for a new trial.

10. E.g., in a jurisdiction that imposes joint and several liability on defendants whose fault is 50% or greater, the jury finds that the fault assignments are P 10%, D–1 40%, and D–2 50%. The appellate court then determines that the assignment to D–2 was improper. Proportionate reallocation would bring D–1 to 40/50 = 80% = jointly and severally liable. Here again, a new trial might be warranted.

and that two normal tissues out of twenty-eight samples would require investigation.

On November 9, 1968, Brochner performed a craniotomy on Esther Cortez which resulted in injury to Cortez. Cortez later filed a civil action against Brochner and the hospital. She alleged that Brochner negligently diagnosed her need for a craniotomy, that the hospital negligently continued Brochner's staff privileges when it knew or should have known that he was incompetent, and that the hospital negligently allowed Brochner to perform unnecessary surgery. The claim against Brochner was severed, and trial of the claims against the hospital commenced April 3, 1978. Prior to the conclusion of that trial, Cortez and the hospital agreed to a settlement of $150,000. Some time later, Cortez reached a settlement of her suit against Brochner, who was uninsured, for an undisclosed sum.

In 1979, the hospital and its subrogee, Western Insurance Company (Western), filed this indemnity action against Brochner, alleging that Brochner's negligence was the active and primary cause of Cortez's injuries while the hospital's negligence was passive and secondary. On September 15, 1982, the trial court entered judgment for Western and the hospital against Brochner as follows: (1) $150,000 as the sum paid by Western on behalf of the hospital to Cortez in settlement of her claim against the hospital; and (2) $10,000 to the hospital for expenses incurred in connection with the Cortez lawsuit not reimbursed by insurance. The trial court found that Brochner had breached a pre-existing duty to the hospital to abide by its rules and regulations, that Brochner's negligence was the primary cause of Cortez's injuries, that the hospital was independently negligent toward [Cortez], and that the hospital's negligence was only a secondary cause of [Cortez's] injuries. The trial court also awarded Western its attorney fees and costs incurred in defending the original lawsuit. The Court of Appeals affirmed the trial court's judgment.

* * *

[In 1977 the General Assembly adopted the Uniform Contribution Among Tortfeasors Act, §§ 13–50.5–101 to–106, 6 C.R.S. (1985 Supp.), which provided that joint tortfeasors owed] contribution among themselves based upon their relative degrees of fault. That principle is at odds with the essential characteristic of our present rule of indemnity that, without regard to apportionment of fault, a single tortfeasor may ultimately pay the expense of all injuries sustained by a third party as the result of negligent conduct by two or more tortfeasors. There can be no mistake concerning the intent of the General Assembly to establish the policy of responsibility related to proportionate fault in the context of personal injury litigation. * * * [Moreover, in 1986 the General Assembly] abolished the principle of joint and several liability. * * * This new provision extends the principle that liability for negligence should be based on proportionate fault.

In view of these legislative enactments, a tortfeasor no longer may unfairly be forced to pay all or a disproportionate share of damages suffered by an injured party as the result of negligent conduct by two or more joint tortfeasors. The principle of proportionate fault adopted by the General Assembly represents a rational and equitable approach to the problem of allocating ultimate responsibility between or among joint tortfeasors for the payment of damages to an injured party. Application of this principle will prove far more certain in varied factual contexts and will consequently promote more predictability than any continued effort to perpetuate ephemeral distinctions based on primary or secondary negligence concepts. For these reasons we conclude that the doctrine of indemnity insofar as it requires one of two joint tortfeasors to reimburse the other for the entire amount paid by the other as damages to a party injured as the result of the negligence of both joint tortfeasors, is no longer viable, and is hereby abolished.

* * *

The judgment of the Court of Appeals is reversed.

Notes

1. *What is left of tort indemnity in the comparative fault era?* In an omitted footnote the *Brochner* court stated: "The question of whether our common law doctrine of indemnity should be preserved or abolished in situations where the party seeking indemnity is vicariously liable or is without fault is not presented by the circumstances of this case." Many comparative fault jurisdictions have concluded that indemnity should be retained when a defendant is liable purely vicariously, when an innocent retailer is liable for a manufacturer's defective product, and when there is a contract for indemnity, but otherwise should be jettisoned in favor of comparative-fault allocation principles. This is the position taken in § 22 of the Apportionment Restatement.

2. *Contribution among tortfeasors.* Normally Cortez's suit against Brochner and the hospital would not have been severed. Brochner and the hospital would have cross-claimed against each other for contribution. At trial, each party would have been assigned a fault percentage by the trier of fact. Because the statute abolishing joint and several liability went into effect after the case arose, Cortez would have been able to collect her damages (reduced by any fault percentage assigned to her) from either Brochner or the hospital. Brochner and the hospital would have owed each other contribution measured by their respective shares of fault. For example, assume that the trier of fact found Cortez's full damages to be $100,000 and assigned fault percentages as follows: Cortez 0%, Brochner 75%, hospital 25%. The judgment would have provided that Brochner and the hospital were jointly and severally liable to Cortez for $100,000, and that Brochner and the hospital were entitled to contribution from each other such that ultimately Brochner should pay $75,000 and the hospital $25,000.

In the case as it actually developed, the hospital's separate action against Brochner sought contribution as a fall-back to the indemnity claim. The court denied the contribution claim, stating: "Because both Brochner and the hospital settled with Cortez * * *, neither is entitled to contribution from the other."

3. ***The abolition of joint and several liability greatly reduces the need for contribution.*** As we saw in *McIntyre*, supra p. 345, the abolition of joint and several liability means by definition that no defendant will be held liable for more than its percentage-fault-based share of the damages, so that defendants cast in judgment will have no need or justification for seeking contribution from one another. (However, in the partial settlement context, justifiable contribution claims may occasionally arise. See infra p. 387, note 3.)

4. ***Partial settlements.*** When the plaintiff enters into a settlement agreement with one or more of a group of multiple tortfeasors and continues to pursue others, complexities unavoidably arise. The principal ones relate to (a) whether and when settling and nonsettling tortfeasors have contribution rights against each other, and (b) whether and by what measure the plaintiff's judgment against nonsettling tortfeasors should be reduced to take into account the benefits of the settlement.

In the next case, the U.S. Supreme Court brought considerable clarity to the partial settlement area. The case arose under U.S. admiralty and maritime law, which is a pure comparative negligence system (plaintiffs are not barred, not even at 99%) with unrestricted joint and several liability.

McDERMOTT, INC. v. AmCLYDE

Supreme Court of the United States, 1994.
511 U.S. 202, 114 S.Ct. 1461, 128 L.Ed.2d 148.

JUSTICE STEVENS delivered the opinion of the Court.

A construction accident in the Gulf of Mexico gave rise to this admiralty case. In advance of trial, petitioner, the plaintiff, settled with three of the defendants for $1 million. Respondents, however, did not settle, and the case went to trial. A jury assessed petitioner's loss at $2.1 million and allocated 32% of the damages to respondent AmClyde and 38% to respondent River Don. The question presented is whether the liability of the nonsettling defendants should be calculated with reference to the jury's allocation of proportionate responsibility, or by giving the nonsettling defendants a credit for the dollar amount of the settlement. We hold that the proportionate approach is the correct one.

I.

Petitioner McDermott, Inc., purchased a specially designed, 5,000–ton crane from AmClyde. When petitioner first used the crane in an attempt to move an oil and gas production platform—the "Snapper deck"—from a barge to a structural steel base affixed to the floor of the Gulf of Mexico, a prong of the crane's main hook broke, causing massive damage to the deck and to the crane itself. The malfunction may have been caused by petitioner's negligent operation of the crane, by AmClyde's faulty design or construction, by a defect in the hook supplied by River Don Castings,

Ltd. (River Don), or by one or more of the three companies (the "sling defendants") that supplied the supporting steel slings.

Invoking the federal court's admiralty jurisdiction under 28 U.S.C. § 1333(1), petitioner brought suit against AmClyde and River Don and the three sling defendants. The complaint sought a recovery for both deck damages and crane damages. On the eve of trial, petitioner entered into a settlement with the sling defendants. In exchange for $1 million, petitioner agreed to dismiss with prejudice its claims against the sling defendants, to release them from all liability for either deck or crane damages, and to indemnify them against any contribution action. The trial judge later ruled that petitioner's claim for crane damages was barred by East River Steamship Corp. v. Transamerica Delaval Inc. 476 U.S. 858, 106 S.Ct. 2295 (1986).*

In its opening statement at trial, petitioner McDermott "accepted responsibility for any part the slings played in causing the damage." The jury found that the total damages to the deck amounted to $2.1 million and, in answer to special interrogatories, allocated responsibility among the respective parties: 32% to AmClyde, 38% to River Don, and 30% jointly to McDermott and the sling defendants. The Court denied a motion by respondents to reduce the judgment pro tanto by the $1 million settlement, and entered judgment against AmClyde for $672,000 (32% of $2.1 million) and against River Don for $798,000 (38% of $2.1 million).** Even though the sum of those judgments plus the settlement proceeds exceeded the total damages found by the jury, the District Court concluded that petitioner had not received a double recovery because the settlement had covered both crane damages and deck damages.

The Court of Appeals held that a contractual provision precluded any recovery against AmClyde and that the trial judge had improperly denied a pro tanto settlement credit. It reversed the judgment against AmClyde entirely and reduced the judgment against River Don to $470,000. It arrived at that figure by making two calculations. First, it determined that petitioner's "full damage award is $1.47 million ($2.1 million jury verdict less 30% attributed to McDermott/sling defendants)." Next, it deducted the "$1 million received in settlement to reach $470,000." * * *

II.

* * *

In [United States v. Reliable Transfer Co., 421 U.S. 397, 95 S.Ct. 1708 (1975)] we decided to abandon a rule that had been followed for over a century in assessing damages when both parties to a collision are at fault.

---

* In *East River* the Supreme Court held that under federal maritime law, pure economic loss, without personal injury or damage to property other than the product itself, is not recoverable under negligence or strict products liability. [Ed.]

** Technically the judgment should have held AmClyde and River Don jointly and severally liable for $1.47 million (70% of $2.1 million), with contribution rights against each other such that AmClyde would ultimately bear $672,000 and River Don $798,000. The trial court's technical glitch mattered not at all, because both defendants were fully solvent and insured. [Ed.]

We replaced the divided damages rule, which required an equal division of property damage whatever the relative degree of fault may have been, with a rule requiring that damages be assessed on the basis of proportionate fault when such an allocation can reasonably be made. Although the old rule avoided the difficulty of determining comparative degrees of negligence, we concluded that it was "unnecessarily crude and inequitable" and that "[p]otential problems of proof in some cases hardly require adherence to an archaic and unfair rule in all cases." Thus the interest in certainty and simplicity served by the old rule was outweighed by the interest in fairness promoted by the proportionate fault rule.

Our decision in *Reliable Transfer* was supported by a consensus among the world's maritime nations and the views of respected scholars and judges. No comparable consensus has developed with respect to the issue in the case before us today. It is generally agreed that when a plaintiff settles with one of several joint tortfeasors, the nonsettling defendants are entitled to a credit for that settlement. There is, however, a divergence among respected scholars and judges about how that credit should be determined. Indeed, the American Law Institute has identified three principal alternatives and, after noting that "[e]ach has its drawbacks and no one is satisfactory," decided not to take a position on the issue. Restatement (Second) of Torts § 886A, pp. 343–344 (1977). The ALI describes the three alternatives as follows:

> "(1) The money paid extinguishes any claim that the injured party has against the party released and the amount of his remaining claim against the other tortfeasor is reached by crediting the amount received; but the transaction does not affect a claim for contribution by another tortfeasor who has paid more than his equitable share of the obligation."

> "(2) The money paid extinguishes both any claims on the part of the injured party and any claim for contribution by another tortfeasor who has paid more than his equitable share of the obligation and seeks contribution." (As in Alternative (1), the amount of the injured party's claim against the other tortfeasors is calculated by subtracting the amount of the settlement from the plaintiff's damages.)

> "(3) The money paid extinguishes any claim that the injured party has against the released tortfeasor and also diminishes the claim that the injured party has against the other tortfeasors by the amount of the equitable share of the obligation of the released tortfeasor."

The first two alternatives involve the kind of "pro tanto" credit that respondents urge us to adopt. The difference between the two versions of the pro tanto approach is the recognition of a right of contribution against a settling defendant in the first but not the second. The third alternative, supported by petitioner, involves a credit for the settling defendants' "proportionate share" of responsibility for the total obligation. Under this approach, no suits for contribution from the settling defendants are permitted, nor are they necessary, because the nonsettling defendants pay no more than their share of the judgment.

The proportionate share approach[9] would make River Don responsible for precisely its share of the damages, $798,000 (38% of $2.1 million).[10] A simple application of the pro tanto approach would allocate River Don $1.1 million in damages ($2.1 million total damages minus the $1 million settlement). The Court of Appeals, however, made a different calculation. Because McDermott "accepted responsibility for any part the sling played in causing the damage," the Court of Appeals treated the 30% of liability apportioned to "McDermott/sling defendants" as if that 30% had been caused solely by McDermott's own negligence. The Court of Appeals, therefore, gave River Don a double credit, first reducing the total loss by the McDermott/sling defendants' proportionate share and then applying the full pro tanto reduction to that amount. This double credit resulted in an award of only $470,000 ($2.1 million minus 30% of $2.1 million minus $1 million).

III.

In choosing among the ALI's three alternatives, three considerations are paramount: consistency with the proportionate fault approach of *Reliable Transfer*, promotion of settlement, and judicial economy. ALI Option 1, pro tanto setoff with right of contribution against the settling defendant, is clearly inferior to the other two, because it discourages settlement and leads to unnecessary ancillary litigation. It discourages settlement, because settlement can only disadvantage the settling defendant. If a defendant makes a favorable settlement, in which it pays less than the amount a court later determines is its share of liability, the other defendant (or defendants) can sue the settling defendant for contribution. The settling defendant thereby loses the benefit of its favorable settlement. In addition, the claim for contribution burdens the courts with additional litigation. The plaintiff can mitigate the adverse effect on settlement by promising to indemnify the settling defendant against contribution, as McDermott did here. This indemnity, while removing the disincentive to settlement, adds yet another potential burden on the courts, an indemnity action between the settling defendant and plaintiff.

The choice between ALI Options 2 and 3, between the pro tanto rule without contribution against the settling tortfeasor and the proportionate share approach, is less clear. The proportionate share rule is more consis-

9. In this opinion, we use the phrase "proportionate share approach" to denote ALI Option 3. We have deliberately avoided use of the term "pro rata," which is often used to describe this approach because that term is also used to describe an equal allocation among all defendants without regard to their relative responsibility for the loss.

10. * * * AmClyde is immune from damages because its contract with McDermott provided that free replacement of defective parts "shall constitute fulfillment of all liabilities * * * whether based upon Contract, tort, strict liability or otherwise." 979 F.2d at 1075 (emphasis omitted). The best way of viewing this contractual provision is as a quasi-settlement in advance of any tort claims. Viewed as such, the proportionate credit in this case properly takes into account both the 30% of liability apportioned to the settling defendants (and McDermott) and the 32% allocated to AmClyde. This leaves River Don with $798,000 or 38% of the damages.

tent with *Reliable Transfer*, because a litigating defendant ordinarily pays only its proportionate share of the judgment. Under the pro tanto approach, however, a litigating defendant's liability will frequently differ from its equitable share, because a settlement with one defendant for less than its equitable share requires the nonsettling defendant to pay more than its share. Such deviations from the equitable apportionment of damages will be common, because settlements seldom reflect an entirely accurate prediction of the outcome of a trial. Moreover, the settlement figure is likely to be significantly less than the settling defendant's equitable share of the loss, because settlement reflects the uncertainty of trial and provides the plaintiff with a "war chest" with which to finance the litigation against the remaining defendants. Courts and legislatures have recognized this potential for unfairness and have required "good-faith hearings" as a remedy. When such hearings are required, the settling defendant is protected against contribution actions only if it shows that the settlement is a fair forecast of its equitable share of the judgment. Nevertheless, good-faith hearings cannot fully remove the potential for inequitable allocation of liability. First, to serve their protective function effectively, such hearings would have to be minitrials on the merits, but in practice they are often quite cursory. More fundamentally, even if the judge at a good-faith hearing were able to make a perfect forecast of the allocation of liability at trial, there might still be substantial unfairness when the plaintiff's success at trial is uncertain. In sum, the pro tanto approach, even when supplemented with good-faith hearings, is likely to lead to inequitable apportionments of liability, contrary to *Reliable Transfer*.

The effect of the two rules on settlements is more ambiguous. Sometimes the pro tanto approach will better promote settlement. This beneficial effect, however, is a consequence of the inequity discussed above. The rule encourages settlements by giving the defendant that settles first an opportunity to pay less than its fair share of the damages, thereby threatening the non-settling defendant with the prospect of paying more than its fair share of the loss. By disadvantaging the party that spurns settlement offers, the pro tanto rule puts pressure on all defendants to settle. While public policy wisely encourages settlements, such additional pressure to settle is unnecessary. The parties' desire to avoid litigation costs, to reduce uncertainty, and to maintain ongoing commercial relationships is sufficient to ensure nontrial dispositions in the vast majority of cases. Under the proportionate share approach, such factors should ensure a similarly high settlement rate. The additional incentive to settlement provided by the pro tanto rule comes at too high a price in unfairness. * * *

The effect of the two rules on judicial economy is also ambiguous. The pro tanto rule, if adopted without the requirement of a good-faith hearing, would be easier to administer, because the relative fault of the settling defendant would not have to be adjudicated either at a preliminary hearing or at trial. Nevertheless, because of the large potential for unfairness, no party or amicus in this suit advocates the pro tanto rule untamed by good-faith hearings. Once the pro tanto rule is coupled with a good-faith hearing, however, it is difficult to determine whether the pro tanto or proportionate share approach best promotes judicial economy. Under either approach, the relative fault of the parties will have to be determined. Under the pro tanto approach, the settling defendant's share of responsibility will have to be ascertained at a separate, pretrial hearing. Under the proportionate share approach, the allocation will take place at trial. The pro tanto approach will, therefore, only save judicial time if the good-faith hearing is quicker than the allocation of fault at trial. Given the cursory nature of most good-faith hearings, this may well be true. On the other hand, there is reason to believe that reserving the apportionment of liability for trial may save more time. First, the remaining defendant (or defendants) may settle before trial, thus making any determination of relative culpability unnecessary. In addition, the apportionment of damages required by the proportionate share rule may require little or no additional trial time. The parties will often need to describe the settling defendant's role in order to provide context for the dispute. Furthermore, a defendant will often argue the "empty chair" in the hope of convincing the jury that the settling party was exclusively responsible for the damage. The pro tanto rule thus has no clear advantage with respect to judicial economy.

In sum, although the arguments for the two approaches are closely matched, we are persuaded that the proportionate share approach is superior, especially in its consistency with *Reliable Transfer*.

IV.

Respondents advance [an additional argument] against the proportionate share approach: that it violates the "one satisfaction rule" * * *.

In the 19th and early 20th centuries, the "one satisfaction rule" barred a plaintiff from litigating against one joint tortfeasor, if he had settled with and released another. This version of the one satisfaction rule has been thoroughly repudiated. Respondents do not ask that the one satisfaction rule be applied with its original strictness, but rather in the milder form in which some courts still invoke it to reduce a plaintiff's recovery against a nonsettling defendant in order to ensure that the plaintiff does not secure more than necessary to compensate him for his loss. As a preliminary matter, it is far from clear that there was any danger of super-compensatory damages here. First, there is the question of the crane damages, which were not covered by the judgment against River Don. In addition, even limiting consideration to deck damages, the jury fixed plaintiff's losses at $2.1 million. Plaintiff received $1 million in settlement from the sling defendants. Under the proportionate share approach, plaintiff would receive an additional $798,000 from River Don. In total, plaintiff would recover only $1.798 million, over $300,000 less than its damages. The one satisfaction rule comes into play only if one assumes that the percent share of liability apportioned to McDermott and the sling defendants really represented McDermott's contributory fault, and that it would be overcompensatory for McDermott to receive more than the percentage of the total loss allocated to the defendants, here $1.47 million (70% of $2.1 million).

Even if the Court of Appeals were correct in finding that the proportionate share approach would overcompensate McDermott, we would not apply the one satisfaction rule. The law contains no rigid rule against overcompensation. Several doctrines, such as the collateral benefits rule, recognize that making tortfeasors pay for the damage they cause can be more important than preventing overcompensation. In this case, any excess recovery is entirely attributable to the fact that the sling defendants may have made an unwise settlement. It seems probable that in most cases in which there is a partial settlement, the plaintiff is more apt to accept less than the proportionate share that the jury might later assess against the settling defendant, because of the uncertainty of recovery at the time of settlement negotiations and because the first settlement normally improves the plaintiff's litigating posture against the nonsettlors. In such cases, the entire burden of applying a proportionate share rule would rest on the plaintiff, and the interest in avoiding overcompensation would be absent. More fundamentally, we must recognize that settlements frequently result in the plaintiff's getting more than he would have been entitled to at trial. Because settlement amounts are based on rough estimates of liability, anticipated savings in litigation costs, and a host of other factors, they will rarely match exactly the amounts a trier of fact would have set. It seems to us that a plaintiff's good fortune in striking a favorable bargain with one defendant gives other defendants no claim to pay less than their proportionate share of the total loss. In fact, one of the virtues of the proportionate share rule is that, unlike the pro tanto rule, it does not make a litigating defendant's liability dependent on the amount of a settlement negotiated by others without regard to its interests.

* * * In addition, * * * there is no tension between joint and several liability and a proportionate share approach to settlements. Joint and several liability applies when there has been a judgment against multiple defendants. It can result in one defendant's paying more than its apportioned share of liability when the plaintiff's recovery from other defendants is limited by factors beyond the plaintiff's control, such as a defendant's insolvency. When the limitations on the plaintiff's recovery arise from outside forces, joint and several liability makes the other defendants, rather than an innocent plaintiff, responsible for the shortfall. * * * [T]he proportionate share rule announced in this opinion applies when there has been a settlement. In such cases, the plaintiff's recovery against the settling defendant has been limited not by outside forces, but by its own agreement to settle. There is no reason to allocate any shortfall to the other defendants, who were not parties to the settlement. Just as the other defendants are not entitled to a reduction in liability when the plaintiff negotiates a generous settlement, so they are not required to

shoulder disproportionate liability when the plaintiff negotiates a meager one.

V.

The judgment of the Court of Appeals is reversed, and the case is remanded for further proceedings consistent with this opinion.

It is so ordered.

NOTES

1. Section 16 of the Apportionment Restatement adopts the rule in *AmClyde*.

2. ***Percentage-fault-based contribution and percentage-fault-based settlement credit are correlatives.*** In the *AmClyde* regime, a nonsettling tortfeasor cannot go against a settling tortfeasor for contribution; instead, the settling tortfeasor's percentage-fault-based share of the damages is deducted from plaintiff's recovery. A simple way to understand these cases is to consider the plaintiff's settlement with Tortfeasor *A* as having sold away the contribution right that Tortfeasor *B* would otherwise have had against *A*. Having sold away that right, plaintiff is obliged to restore it in the form of a credit against plaintiff's recovery from *B*. (For another expression of the same basic idea, see the penultimate paragraph of *Varela*, supra p. 375.)

3. ***Settling tortfeasors occasionally have contribution rights.*** Normally, a settling tortfeasor cannot seek contribution from a nonsettling tortfeasor. But there is a principled exception, as set out in Combo Maritime, Inc. v. United States United Bulk Terminal, 615 F.3d 599, 604 (5th Cir. 2010):

> If * * * the settling defendant discharges the plaintiff's entire claim as evidenced by a total release of all potential joint tortfeasors, then the settling defendant has met the requirements for a contribution claim. Because he is responsible for only his [percentage-fault-based] portion of the damages, and he has paid the entire amount, he has paid more than he owes. And, because he has obtained a release of all other potential joint tortfeasors, he has extinguished the plaintiff's claim. Therefore, he may bring a claim for contribution against the non-settling potential tortfeasors.

Note that, while *Combo* arose in a jurisdiction with full joint and several liability, the need for a contribution device in the situation treated in this note would be equally acute in a jurisdiction that has abolished joint and several liability. There, too, the tortfeasor who paid to settle the whole case would have "paid more than he owes."

4. The suggestion in note 2—that it helps to think of a plaintiff's settlement with Tortfeasor *A* as having sold away Tortfeasor *B*'s contribution right—is also worth keeping in mind in the context in which the tortfeasors are in an indemnity-justifying relationship with one another. When the plaintiff settles with Employee and continues to sue vicariously liable Employer, has the plaintiff sold away Employer's indemnity right against Employee,

thereby killing plaintiff's case against Employer? Some courts have said yes. See Apportionment Restatement § 16 cmt. *d.*

D. IMPUTED CONTRIBUTORY (COMPARATIVE) FAULT

Chapter VIII addressed the issue of when a *defendant* will be charged with the legal effects of someone else's fault under the doctrine of vicarious liability. This section addresses the issue of when the *plaintiff* will be charged with the legal effects of someone else's fault. The question is this: In a tort action in which *P* seeks damages from *D,* under what circumstances will *X*'s fault be attributed to *P*? The modern law answers this question affirmatively for only two types of cases: (a) cases in which the relationship between *P* and *X* is such that *P* would be vicariously liable for the damaging effects of *X*'s fault; and (b) cases in which *P*'s suit against *D* may be said to be somehow "derivative" of *X*'s potential rights against *D.*

The Apportionment Restatement treats the first group of cases in § 5, providing:

> The negligence of another person is imputed to a plaintiff whenever the negligence of the other person would have been imputed had the plaintiff been a defendant, except the negligence of another person is not imputed to a plaintiff solely because of the plaintiff's ownership of a motor vehicle or permission for its use by the other person.

CONTINENTAL AUTO LEASE CORPORATION v. CAMPBELL

Court of Appeals of New York, 1967.
19 N.Y.2d 350, 280 N.Y.S.2d 123, 227 N.E.2d 28.

KEATING, JUDGE.

Continental Auto Lease Corporation is engaged in the auto rental business. It sued Ralph B. Shepard for damage to its automobile as the result of an accident. Shepard died after the action was commenced and his administratrix, Doris B. Campbell, was substituted as defendant.

Continental leased the automobile to one Kamman for a four-day period for a fixed sum plus a charge for mileage. During the rental period, Kamman was involved in an accident with an automobile driven by Shepard. Upon the trial, the jury found both drivers negligent, but returned a verdict for Continental, as directed by the trial court. Judgment was entered accordingly, and affirmed, on appeal, by the Appellate Division, Fourth Department.

The question presented is whether the negligence of Kamman, the operator of Continental's automobile, is imputable to Continental so that [Continental] is barred by contributory negligence from recovery against Shepard.

At the outset, it should be noted that there is a distinction between imputed negligence and imputed contributory negligence. The effect of imputed negligence is to widen liability; the effect of imputed contributory negligence, to narrow it. Section 388 of the Vehicle and Traffic Law, Consol.Laws, c. 71 [provides in pertinent part:

> Every owner of a vehicle used or operated in this state shall be liable and responsible for death or injuries to person or property resulting from negligence in the use or operation of such vehicle, in the business of such owner or otherwise, by any person using or operating the same with the permission, express or implied, of such owner.]

[This provision] imputes to the owner of a motor vehicle the negligence of one who uses or operates it with his permission for the purpose of imposing on the owner liability to an injured third party. This enactment expresses the policy that one injured by the negligent operation of a motor vehicle should have recourse to a financially responsible defendant. The owner of the automobile is the obvious candidate, for he can most easily carry insurance to cover the risk.

This policy—broadened liability for the protection of the injured plaintiff—gives no support to the doctrine of imputed contributory negligence, which narrows the liability of a negligent defendant to a plaintiff innocent of actual negligence. Mills v. Gabriel, 284 N.Y. 755, 31 N.E.2d 512 [1940], is the leading case refusing to impute contributory negligence to an absentee owner. In that case an action was brought to recover damages for injury to plaintiff's automobile sustained in a collision between such automobile, driven with [plaintiff's] permission but in her absence, and an automobile owned and driven by defendant. It was conceded that both operators were negligent, and that the operator of plaintiff's automobile was using it for his own private purpose and not for the benefit or on the business of the plaintiff. On those facts, we held that former section 59 of the Vehicle and Traffic Law [which was identical to section 388] was no bar to plaintiff's common-law right of recovery.

In contrast, in Gochee v. Wagner, 257 N.Y. 344, 178 N.E. 553 [1931], we held, on a different fact pattern, that the owner of the vehicle was barred by imputed contributory negligence. There, the accident occurred while the car was driven by plaintiff's wife, with his permission, while plaintiff was sitting in the rear seat. His wife was found negligent in her operation of plaintiff's car. We held for defendant, reasoning that: "When the respondent entered the car, he regained dominion over it * * *. It was respondent's car, he was present and had the legal right to control its operation, and the negligent conduct of the driver was imputable to him. The mere fact that he chose to sit on the rear seat and refrained from directing its operation did not change his rights or limit his liability."

Gochee v. Wagner makes it clear that the touchstone of imputed contributory negligence is the existence of a relationship between the owner of the vehicle and the operator such that the operator of the vehicle is subject to the owner's control. Such control need not be actually exercised—it can be inferred, as in *Gochee,* when the owner is physically present in the car. Likewise, the requisite degree of control might be found in the master-servant or principal-agent relationship when the physical operation of the vehicle is for the benefit of the owner.

Defendant urges that Continental should be barred from recovery because it was benefiting financially under the terms of the lease for each mile that the car was driven, and that this "benefit" distinguishes the present case from the gratuitous bailment involved in Mills v. Gabriel. The mere fact that the bailment was commercial rather than gratuitous is not sufficient ground for denying to a plaintiff, guilty of no actual negligence, the right to recover his damages from a negligent defendant. If a car owner's relationship to the driver of his car is such that a degree of physical control over the driver can reasonably be deemed to exist, under Gochee v. Wagner the negligence of the driver can be imputed to the owner to bar the owner's recovery against a negligent third party. But Continental had no interest in where or when the vehicle was driven and no relationship to Kamman consistent with the inference that it had the right to control in any manner Kamman's conduct as a driver. Accordingly, Kamman's negligence should not be imputed to Continental to bar its recovery in this action.

The order of the Appellate Division should be affirmed, with costs.

NOTES

1. Vicarious liability statutes like New York's have been federally preempted (insofar as commercial lessors are concerned) by a provision in the fabulously-titled Safe, Accountable, Flexible, Efficient Transportation Act of 2005, 49 U.S.C. § 30106(a).

2. The *Continental* result is consistent with Apportionment Restatement § 5, quoted in the introductory note to this section. But is it sustainable under the controlling New York statute (quoted in the fourth paragraph of the opinion)? In thinking about this question, closely compare the New York statute's language with Iowa Code § 321.493, which provides in pertinent part that "in all cases where damage is done by any motor vehicle by reason of negligence of the driver, and driven with the consent of the owner, the owner of the motor vehicle shall be liable for such damage."

3. ***The effect of imputation.*** When the situation calls for charging someone else's fault to the plaintiff, the legal effect is the same as if the fault were plaintiff's own. Thus, in the contributory negligence era imputed contributory fault barred recovery. Today in comparative-fault jurisdictions it reduces recovery on a comparative fault basis and bars recovery only when the fault assigned to the plaintiff—which might consist of his own plus any that is properly imputed to him—takes the plaintiff over the particular jurisdiction's limit. (In this connection, see the next case.)

4. ***Imputation in derivative-claim situations.*** The Apportionment Restatement treats these cases in § 6, which provides:

(a) When a plaintiff asserts a claim that derives from the defendant's tort against a third person, negligence of the third person is imputed to the plaintiff with respect to that claim. The plaintiff's recovery is also reduced by the plaintiff's own negligence.

(b) The negligence of an estate's decedent affects the estate's recovery under a survival statute to the same extent that it would have affected the decedent's recovery had the decedent survived. * * *.

The comments go on to explain that the principal categories of derivative-claim situations are wrongful death and survival actions, claims for consortium, and what we have called "uninjured bystander" or Dillon v. Legg claims (see supra p. 243, note 1).[1]

WHITE v. LUNDER

Supreme Court of Wisconsin, 1975.
66 Wis.2d 563, 225 N.W.2d 442.

BEILFUSS, JUSTICE.

[Rosemary White was hurt in a boating mishap involving herself, her husband Lloyd, and defendant James Lunder. She sued Lunder for her personal injuries, and her husband sued for loss of consortium and medical expenses. Lunder did not file a counter or cross-claim against Lloyd White. The jury apportioned causal negligence among the parties thus: Rosemary White, 30%; Lloyd White, 33%; Lunder, 37%.

The Wisconsin comparative negligence statute provided:

Contributory negligence shall not bar recovery in an action by any person or his legal representative to recover damages for negligence resulting in death or in injury to person or property, if such negligence was not as great as the negligence of the person against whom recovery is sought, but any damages allowed shall be diminished in the proportion to the amount of negligence attributable to the person recovering.*

The trial judge determined that the statute called for charging Lloyd White with 63% of the causal negligence and accordingly denied recovery to him. He appealed.]

The issues are:

1.   Where wife sustains bodily injury by reason of causal negligence of herself, her husband, and a third party, is the negligence of the spouses combined for purposes of comparing negligence with that of

_____

1. The Reporters' Note to § 6 (p. 65) acknowledges that putting Dillon v. Legg cases on the derivative-claim list is an educated guess. There are few cases addressing the point, and they are divided.

* As the court notes four paragraphs below, a 1971 amendment to the statute did not apply to the 1970 accident in *White*. At pp. 352–53 supra we set forth the present version of the statute. [Ed.]

the third party and thereby determining whether husband recovers for medical expenses and for loss of consortium?

2. Where wife sustains bodily injury, are her husband's causes of action for medical expenses and for loss of consortium both derivative actions?

The issues are discussed together here because they are closely related and involve basically the same principles. * * *

* * *

[T]he question of whether a spouse's cause of action for loss of consortium arising in personal injury actions is derivative is not clearly settled and the cases are confusing.

We deem it appropriate to declare, for the purpose of applying our comparative negligence statute, that both the causes of action for medical expenses and loss of consortium shall be deemed derivative; and that the causal negligence of the injured spouse shall bar or limit the recovery of the claiming spouse pursuant to the terms of the comparative negligence statute.

* * *

To allow no recovery to the husband where, as here, the third party tortfeasor was more causally negligent than he, not only seems to be unjust but is not entirely consistent with our comparative negligence statute. It prohibits partial recovery only when the negligence of the claimant was equal to or greater than the person against whom the claim was made. ([It] was amended in 1971 to prohibit recovery only when causal negligence of the claimant is greater than the person against whom he seeks recovery. [The amendment was not applicable in this case, which arose in 1970.])

Likewise, it seems unjust for the husband to collect damages upon a formula that disregards either his causal negligence or that of his injured wife.

The comparative negligence statute does not by its terms specifically contemplate its effect in a situation like this where both spouses are causally negligent.

A workable construction, consistent with the statute, that will allow recovery in derivative actions where the causal negligence of the person against whom recovery is sought is greater than either the husband or wife can be accomplished by reducing the entire award for both medical expenses and loss of consortium by the percentage of negligence attributed to the injured spouse (here Rosemary White's 30 percent); and further reducing the entire award by the percentage of causal negligence attributable to the claiming spouse (here Lloyd White's 33 percent). By this method the person who was found to have been causally negligent in greatest degree cannot escape all liability but his liability is decreased by an amount proportionate to the two other tortfeasors.

By way of illustration, if the amount awarded for medical expenses and claimed by the husband was $5,000, the $5,000 would be reduced by 30 percent because it was a derivative claim and the injured spouse was 30 percent negligent. This reduction would be $1,500. The claimant husband's causal negligence also contributed 33 percent of the entire award. Therefore the entire award, namely, the $5,000 should be again reduced by 33 percent or $1,650. The total of these two deductions is $3,150; it is also 63 percent of the total causal negligence * * *. The husband's recovery in this hypothetical would be $1,850. Loss of consortium should be calculated upon the same basis.

If the causal negligence of the claiming spouse is greater than the person against whom the claim is made, he should be denied recovery because of the comparative negligence statute. Likewise, if the causal negligence of the injured spouse is greater than that of the person against whom recovery is sought, the claiming spouse should be denied recovery because his action is derivative.

Judgment reversed with directions to enter judgment consistent with this opinion on behalf of the plaintiff-appellant Lloyd White.

NOTES

1. ***A bias against using imputed negligence to bar recovery?*** In the "both ways" context, the court in *Campbell* arguably took some liberties with the language of the statute in order to avoid charging Continental with Kamman's negligence. In the derivative-claims context, cases from the contributory negligence era show courts similarly struggling to avoid imputation. See, e.g., Handeland v. Brown, 216 N.W.2d 574 (Iowa 1974) (refusing to impute minor child's negligence to father in father's action under a statute allowing parents to recover "for the expense and actual loss of services, companionship and society resulting from injury to or death of a minor child"). Plainly courts do not like the idea of barring a plaintiff entirely because of imputed fault. This disinclination probably explains the *White* court's creative reading of the Wisconsin comparative negligence statute. Did the court do any violence to the statutory language? Could the court's result have been achieved under a statute like the following (hypothetical) provision?

> Contributory negligence attributable to the plaintiff shall not bar recovery in an action by any person or his legal representative to recover damages for negligence resulting in death or in injury to person or property, if such contributory negligence attributable to the plaintiff was not as great as the negligence of the person against whom recovery is sought, but any damages allowed shall be diminished in proportion to the amount of contributory negligence attributable to the plaintiff.

2. ***No imputation "inter se."*** "The great weight of authority confines the doctrine of imputed negligence to claims against someone who is an outsider [to the relationship that gives rise to imputation]." Webber v. Sobba, 322 F.3d 1032, 1036 (8th Cir. 2003) (holding that a joint enterprise doctrine would support imputing a host driver's negligence to a passenger in the

passenger's suit against another negligent motorist but not in the passenger's action against the host driver).

E. ASSUMPTION OF THE RISK

In the pre-comparative fault era, the term "assumption of the risk" (or "assumed risk") indiscriminately covered a lot of territory. Most often, probably, the term referred to a victim-fault-related affirmative defense that was a close cousin to contributory negligence. But the term also had at least two other meanings. In the pre-comparative fault era, it was not important to sort these different meanings out, because all usages of the assumed-risk term announced the same result: plaintiff must lose.

Now that victim-fault-related affirmative defenses no longer guarantee defeat for plaintiffs, the various usages of the assumed-risk terminology need to be unpacked. To make a long story short, the close cousin to contributory negligence has come to be called *implied secondary* assumption of risk, and this (like indemnity between tortfeasors, supra section C.2 has largely been swallowed up by comparative fault principles. The other two main meanings have survived under the new names of *express* assumption of risk and *implied primary* assumption of risk.

1. EXPRESS ASSUMPTION OF RISK

HOJNOWSKI v. VAN SKATE PARK

Supreme Court of New Jersey, 2006.
187 N.J. 323, 901 A.2d 381.

JUSTICE ZAZZALI.

* * *

In January 2003, twelve-year old Andrew Hojnowski and his mother, Anastasia Hojnowski, visited a Vans Store in Moorestown, New Jersey. Defendant Vans operated the retail store that sold skateboards and related merchandise and maintained a recreational skateboard facility. To enter the skate park, Vans required Andrew's mother to sign an exculpatory release. [The release begins by stating:

> Please read this document. It affects Your legal rights against Vans, Inc. if you are injured. Do not sign this document unless you understand it. If You are a minor, Your parent or guardian is required to sign this legal document.

The document then provides, in relevant part:

2. Can You Make A Claim For Money If You Are Injured?

> If you are injured and want to make a claim, you must file a demand before the American Arbitration Association (the "AAA") * * *. You agree that any dispute between You and Vans will be decided by the AAA. Vans, Inc. will pay all costs of the arbitration for You * * *.

3. Vans Is Asking You To Give Up Legal Rights in Order to Enter This Park

Because using Vans' Park, or even entering the Park as a spectator may increase your risk of harm, Vans is asking you to give up certain valuable legal rights. Here are the rights you are giving up when you sign this document:

(a) You give up your right to sue Vans in a court of law.

(b) You give up your right to a trial by jury.

(c) You give up the right to claim money from Vans if you are injured unless Vans intentionally failed to prevent or correct a hazard caused by unsafe equipment or devices.

(d) You give up the right to claim money from Vans if you wait more than one year from the injury in order to make a claim.

(e) You give up the right to claim money from Vans, Inc. if you are injured by another person.

(f) You give up the right to recover damages to punish or make an example of Vans, Inc.

Andrew's mother answered "Yes" to the question: "Do You understand that You are giving up rights by signing this document if You are hurt?" The document also informed customers that "[b]y signing this document You agree that Vans, Inc. may rely on Your answers." Andrew's mother signed the release on Andrew's behalf in the space provided beneath this last provision.]

Plaintiffs claim that, during his use of Vans' facility in January 2003, Andrew suffered a fractured femur when an aggressive skateboarder, about whom his parents had complained to Vans, forced him off a skateboard ramp. Consequently, in August 2003, Andrew, acting through his parents as guardians *ad litem,* * * * filed suit against Vans. Their complaint alleges that Vans "negligently fail[ed] to supervise the activities at the skate park, negligently failed to control activities of aggressive skateboarders, negligently failed to warn Plaintiffs' parents that the activities of aggressive skateboarders would not be monitored, and negligently failed to provide a safe place to skateboard." * * * Vans responded by filing a demand for commercial arbitration with the American Arbitration Association. Plaintiffs then moved to enjoin the arbitration and to invalidate the pre-injury release signed by Andrew's mother, and Vans cross-moved for summary judgment. The trial court granted Vans' motion, dismissing plaintiffs' complaint without prejudice and ordering arbitration. The trial court, however, did not rule on the validity of the liability release, finding that the issue is "for the arbitrators to determine."

[The Appellate Division unanimously affirmed the trial court's grant of summary judgment upholding the validity of the arbitration provision, but held 2–1 that the liability waiver was invalid. Vans appealed the holding that the pre-injury release was invalid and the plaintiffs appealed the ruling that the arbitration clause was enforceable.]

II.

We first address whether New Jersey's public policy permits a parent to release a minor child's potential tort claims arising out of the minor's use of a commercial recreational facility. Plaintiffs argue that a parent may not waive a minor child's right to sue for negligence. * * * [P]laintiffs claim that the vast majority of states have held that a parent's attempt to waive a child's prospective cause of action is void as a matter of public policy. Plaintiffs assert that public policy disfavors pre-injury waivers of liability because they encourage tortious conduct by absolving a commercial enterprise of its ordinary duty to exercise due care. Plaintiffs also maintain that because a parent is not permitted to settle a child's post-injury tort claim without judicial approval, a parent should not be allowed to waive a child's potential claim before an injury occurs.

Defendant recognizes that the enforcement of parental liability waivers has been "treated in varied fashions by different states." However, defendant asserts that "[t]he more substantial and well-considered decisions favor enforcement of exculpatory agreements based on the fundamental right of parents to raise their children as they decide." Defendant further contends that it is "erroneous" to equate pre-tort releases of liability with post-tort releases because "[t]he conflict of interest and potential for harm to befall a minor are far different in the context of a release of an accrued tort claim where settlement funds are present and may be misappropriated." Finally, defendant claims that "[w]ithout enforceable [r]eleases many activities available to children may be forced to close due to liability concerns."

* * *

Exculpatory agreements have long been disfavored in the law because they encourage a lack of care. For that reason, courts closely scrutinize liability releases and invalidate them if they violate public policy. It is well settled that to contract in advance to release tort liability resulting from intentional or reckless conduct violates public policy. Further, courts have found that exculpatory agreements for negligence claims violate public policy in a variety of settings, such as in residential leases, or in connection with rendering professional services.

The relevant public policy implicated in this matter is the protection of the best interests of the child under the *parens patriae* doctrine. *Parens patriae* refers to "the state in its capacity as provider of protection to those unable to care for themselves." In keeping with that policy, the Legislature and the courts historically have afforded considerable protections to claims of minor children. The most significant of those protections concerns the compromise or release of a minor's post-injury claims. Under [the New Jersey Rules of Court,] *Rule* 4:44, after a minor has suffered a tortious injury, a minor's parent or guardian may not dispose of a minor's existing cause of action without statutory or judicial approval. That *Rule* applies regardless of whether suit has been filed on the minor's behalf, and its purpose is "to guard a minor against an improvident compromise [and] to secure the minor against dissipation of the proceeds."

Although the *Rule* governing post-injury settlements is not dispositive of our treatment of pre-injury releases, we find that the purposes underlying the post-injury settlement rule also apply in the present context. First, children deserve as much protection from the improvident compromise of their rights before an injury occurs as *Rule* 4:44 affords them after the injury. Moreover, at the time a parent decides to release the potential tort claims of his or her child, the parent may not fully understand the consequences of that action and may not have even read the waiver before signing. As the Utah Supreme Court has noted:

> These clauses are * * * routinely imposed in a unilateral manner without any genuine bargaining or opportunity to pay a fee for insurance. The party demanding adherence to an exculpatory clause simply evades the necessity of liability coverage and then shifts the full burden of risk of harm to the other party. Compromise of an existing claim, however, relates to negligence that has already taken place and is subject to measurable damages. Such releases involve actual negotiations concerning ascertained rights and liabilities. Thus, if anything, the policies relating to restrictions on a parent's right to compromise an existing claim apply with even greater force in the pre-injury, exculpatory clause scenario.

Further, in both the pre- and post-injury context, it is necessary to ensure that children retain the ability to seek compensation for an injury. When a parent signs a pre-injury release of liability and the child is later injured, the parent is left to provide for the child's injuries while the negligent party suffers no liability. If a parent is unable to finance the child's injuries, the child may be left with no resources to obtain much needed care or support.

Those concerns are even more acute in the context of commercial premises liability. * * * The operator of a commercial recreational enterprise can inspect the premises for unsafe conditions, train his or her employees with regard to the facility's proper operation, and regulate the types of activities permitted to occur. Such an operator also can obtain insurance and spread the costs of insurance among its customers. Children, on the other hand, are not in a position to discover hazardous conditions or insure against risks. Moreover, the expectation that a commercial facility will be reasonably safe to do that which is within the scope of the invitation, is especially important where the facility's patrons are minor children. If we were to permit waivers of liability, we would remove a significant incentive for operators of commercial enterprises that attract children to take reasonable precautions to protect their safety.

* * *

Although we recognize that jurisdictions are not uniform on the question of waiver, our research discloses that the only published decisions in which such agreements have been upheld are in connection with non-commercial ventures, such as volunteer-run or non-profit organizations. Without expressing an opinion on the validity of parental liability releases in such settings, it suffices to note that volunteer, community, and non-profit organizations involve different policy considerations than those associated with commercial enterprises. Such a distinction is buttressed by the fact that the Legislature has afforded civil immunity from negligence to certain volunteer athletic coaches, managers, officials, and sponsors of non-profit sports teams, while not providing similar immunities from negligence in the commercial realm.

Accordingly, in view of the protections that our State historically has afforded to a minor's claims and the need to discourage negligent activity on the part of commercial enterprises attracting children, we hold that a parent's execution of a pre-injury release of a minor's future tort claims arising out of the use of a commercial recreational facility is unenforceable.

* * *

We * * * reject defendant's argument that enforcing parental releases of liability is necessary to ensure the continued viability of businesses offering sports activities to minors. We do not view tort liability as an unreasonable economic restraint on the ability of business owners to operate commercial recreational facilities. Indeed, by invalidating pre-injury releases of liability executed by a parent on a minor's behalf, we are not altering the landscape of common-law tort liability principles by which commercial enterprises typically must abide. Rather, we are preserving the traditional duties owed by business owners to their invitees. Further, as noted, because such facilities derive economic benefit from their operation, they are better able to assume the costs associated with proper maintenance and the prevention of injury than are the children to whom they cater.

* * *

III.

The second issue that we must decide is whether a parent can bind a minor child to an agreement to arbitrate future disputes arising out of a commercial recreation contract. Plaintiffs contend that "[although] arbitration is an approved alternative to a jury trial, an unsophisticated parent, about to have [his or her] child enter a recreational facility, should not be permitted to bind [his or her] child to a waiver of a trial by jury." Defendant counters that * * * plaintiffs should be bound to arbitrate the present matter because public policy favors the arbitration of disputes. We agree and find that a parent's agreement to arbitrate a minor's potential tort claims is not contrary to public policy.

* * *

Federal policy has favored the enforcement of arbitration agreements for many years. In 1925, Congress enacted the Federal Arbitration Act (FAA), 9 U.S.C.A. §§ 1–16, to reverse then existing judicial hostility to arbitration agreements and "to place arbitration agreements upon the same footing as other contracts." To that end, § 2 of the FAA provides:

A written provision in any * * * contract evidencing a transaction involving commerce to settle by arbitration a controversy thereafter arising out of such a contract or transaction * * * shall be valid, irrevocable, and enforceable, save upon such grounds as exist at law or in equity for the revocation of any contract.

* * *

In light of the strong public policy favoring the settlement of disputes through arbitration, we conclude that allowing a parent to bind a minor child to arbitrate future tort claims is not contrary to our duty as *parens patriae* to protect the best interests of the child. As opposed to a pre-injury release of liability, a pre-injury agreement to arbitrate does not require a minor to forego any substantive rights. Rather, such an agreement specifies only the forum in which those rights are vindicated.

* * *

Although we recognize that certain cases from other jurisdictions have found a minor's claims to be non-arbitrable, those cases are distinguishable because they were decided solely on the basis of the individual contracts at issue in those appeals. They did not directly rule on the larger issue presented by this appeal—whether a parent can bind a minor child to arbitrate future disputes. Therefore, in the absence of any allegations relating to fraud, duress, or unconscionability in the signing of the contract or that the agreement to arbitrate was not written in clear and unambiguous terms, we conclude that a parent's agreement to arbitrate is valid and enforceable against any tort claims asserted on a minor's behalf.

IV.

We affirm the judgment of the Appellate Division and refer this matter to the arbitrator for further proceedings consistent with this opinion.

Justice LaVecchia, concurring in part and dissenting in part.

I am in full agreement with that portion of the majority's decision that affirms enforcement of the parties' agreement to subject their dispute to arbitration. I part company from my colleagues, however, in so far as they have chosen to invalidate the waiver of liability that the parties to this appeal executed as a condition of the minor Andrew's use of defendant's property to skateboard. Essentially, because a waiver of rights of the type entered into by these parties generally would be enforceable as against an adult, I see no reason why this Court should prevent a parent from ratifying such a waiver on behalf of a child, provided that a court or arbitrator determines that the release is reasonable.

* * * [A]lthough the majority notes that "[e]xculpatory agreements have long been disfavored in the law," that proposition has been invoked not to invalidate a waiver, as the Court does here, but rather to explain that such waivers should be narrowly construed. * * * The fact that exculpatory waivers receive narrow construction from courts does not render such waivers unenforceable. Previously, we have stated that "[w]here [exculpatory agreements] do not adversely affect the public

interest, exculpatory clauses in private agreements are generally sustained." The California Supreme Court's decision in Tunkl v. Regents of the University of California, 60 Cal.2d 92, 32 Cal.Rptr. 33, 383 P.2d 441, 445–46 (1963), provides arguably the most widely accepted test applied to exculpatory agreements. *Tunkl* set forth six factors, one of which is whether "[t]he party seeking exculpation is engaged in performing a service of great importance to the public, which is often a matter of practical necessity for some members of the public." In my view, recreational activities such as skateboarding do not implicate the "public interest."[1]* * *

* * *

I would have allowed the arbitrator to sort out the reasonableness and the reach of the waiver executed by the parties.

JUSTICE RIVERA-SOTO joins in this opinion.

NOTES

1. Section 2 of the Apportionment Restatement states: "In appropriate situations, the parties to a transaction should be able to agree which of them should bear the risk of injury, even when the injury is caused by a party's legally culpable conduct." Comments *a* and *d* impose conditions:

> A contract that limits liability must be expressed in clear, definite, and unambiguous language and cannot be inferred from general language. Generally, contracts absolving a party from intentional or reckless conduct are disfavored. When an individual plaintiff passively accepts a contract drafted by the defendant, the contract is construed strictly, favoring reasonable interpretations against the defendant. A contract is not unenforceable merely because it fails to use specific language naming the causes of action to which it applies. In a written consumer contract, the fact that language is in small print or otherwise is not conspicuous is a factor in determining whether the agreement is enforceable."

2. As the principal case indicates, some waivers of liability are unenforceable as a matter of public policy even as to adults. The leading case is *Tunkl* (cited in the dissent), which set forth a number of factors to be weighed. As summarized by § 2 cmt. *e* of the Apportionment Restatement, those factors are:

> [T]he nature of the parties and their relationship to each other, including whether one party is in a position of dependency; the nature of the

---

1. That conclusion is in accord with the majority of jurisdictions that have addressed the subject; they have concluded that recreational activities do not implicate the public interest. Courts have upheld liability waivers in the context of the following recreational activities: automobile racing, being a spectator at an automobile race, scuba diving, horseback riding, roller skating, skydiving, mountain biking, recreational sumo wrestling, weightlifting at a fitness center, motorcycle racing, go-cart racing, bicycling, and ski racing. Hanks v. Powder Ridge Rest. Corp., 276 Conn. 314, 885 A.2d 734, 752–53 (2005) (Norco, J., dissenting) (collecting cases). On the other hand, a minority of states have found that snow-tubing and skiing activities do implicate the public interest. I find those cases unpersuasive. To find that recreational activities implicate the "public interest," would strip that term of meaningful content.

conduct or service provided by the party seeking exculpation, including whether the conduct or service is laden with "public interest"; the extent of the exculpation; the economic setting of the transaction; whether the document is a standardized contract of adhesion; and whether the party seeking exculpation was willing to provide greater protection against tortious conduct for a reasonable, additional fee.

3. Clauses requiring disputes to be decided by arbitration have long been common in commercial contracts. Their use to govern tort claims by individuals against businesses is more recent, but it has spread rapidly. Not everyone would agree with the *Hojnowski* majority's assertion that an arbitration clause is merely a choice of forum. The drafter of the clause usually chooses the jurisdiction whose law will control; the opportunity to conduct discovery may be limited; there is no right of jury trial; and the arbitrator's interpretations of law usually are not appealable. See, e.g., Federal Arbitration Act, 9 U.S.C. §§ 1–16.

Occasionally courts refuse to enforce clauses requiring arbitration of personal injury claims on grounds of unconscionability, see, e.g., Broemmer v. Abortion Services of Phoenix, Ltd., 173 Ariz. 148, 840 P.2d 1013 (1992), but these decisions tend to be very fact-specific and the general trend is to enforce such clauses. See Thornburg, Contracting with Tortfeasors: Mandatory Arbitration Clauses and Personal Injury Claims, 67 Law & Contemp. Probs. 253 (2004).

2. IMPLIED ASSUMPTION OF RISK

BENNETT v. HIDDEN VALLEY GOLF AND SKI, INC.

United States Court of Appeals, Eighth Circuit, 2003.
318 F.3d 868.

MURPHY, CIRCUIT JUDGE.

* * *

In the early morning of February 7, 1998, [Breanne] Bennett went with two older male friends to Hidden Valley for a midnight ski session. At the time Bennett was 16 years old and a high school student. She had limited experience as a skier, all of which had been at Hidden Valley where she had skied once before and had snowboarded twice.

While Bennett was skiing down a slope marked for intermediate difficulty, she fell at a spot which the parties have variously referred to as a bump, a ridge, a jump, a ramp, or a mogul. She was thrown about five feet forward and hit the ground limp. * * * Both sides agree that the bump on the slope had not been intentionally created by Hidden Valley, but had formed as skiers and snow boarders cut across the slope and moved the snow. Bennett claims injuries as a result of the accident, including brain damage and a diminished future earning capacity.

[Bennett's action against Hidden Valley alleged that Hidden Valley was] negligent in the design, maintenance, and staffing of its skiing facilities; in the supervision of its customers "so as to prevent or cure

dangers created by such business invitees"; in providing its customers
with "unrestricted access to advanced and intermediate ski areas without
assessing [their] ski aptitude, ability, or experience"; in permitting obstructions, including trees and jumps, to "exist in the path of skiers at a
time when [it] should have known that such obstructions posed a hazard
or risk of injury"; in failing to "warn * * * of dangers and obstructions
which it knew or reasonably should have known were present at its
facilities and ski slopes"; and in failing "to guard against, barricade,
protect, or cushion known or reasonably knowable obstructions in the
path of skiers upon its ski slopes."

Hidden Valley denied negligence and raised assumption of risk as a
defense. It waived a defense of comparative fault, however, and agreed
that there was no issue as to whether Bennett had contractually released
Hidden Valley from liability because she was a minor at the time of the
accident.

The case proceeded to trial before a jury. Bennett * * * presented
witnesses who described the accident, as well as expert evidence, to prove
Hidden Valley's negligence and the extent of her injuries, including her
diminished future earning capacity. After she rested, Hidden Valley put on
evidence that it had exercised reasonable care and that the bump[s] * * *
on the slope were risks inherent in the sport of skiing, in support of its
assumption of risk defense. * * * At the close of all evidence, Bennett
moved for a judgment as a matter of law, claiming that Hidden Valley had
not established its affirmative defense of assumption of the risk. The
district court denied the motion. * * * [T]he jury returned a verdict in
favor of Hidden Valley.

[Bennett's most significant argument on appeal centers on the trial
judge's Instruction 7, which directed the jury to find for Hidden Valley] if
the conditions Bennett encountered "were a risk inherent in the sport of
skiing." Bennett further argues that the district court should have granted her motion for judgment as a matter of law because Hidden Valley did
not make out an assumption of risk defense. * * *

* * *

Instruction 7 was the verdict director for Hidden Valley's defense of
implied primary assumption of risk. Under Missouri law, this defense
"relates to the initial issue of whether the defendant had a duty to protect
the plaintiff from the risk of harm."[3] The defense applies where "the
parties have voluntarily entered a relationship in which the plaintiff
assumes well-known incidental risks." A plaintiff's consent to assume the

---

3. Missouri recognizes three forms of assumption of risk: express, implied primary, and
implied secondary. Only implied primary assumption of risk is at issue in this case. Express
assumption of risk "occurs when the plaintiff expressly agrees in advance that the defendant
owes him no duty," and both parties agree that Bennett made no such agreement. Implied
secondary assumption of risk "occurs when the defendant owes a duty of care to the plaintiff but
the plaintiff knowingly proceeds to encounter a known risk imposed by the defendant's breach of
duty." Hidden Valley did not claim that Bennett knowingly proceeded to encounter the particular
risks; it thus did not raise a defense of implied assumption of risk in the secondary sense.

risk is "implied from the act of electing to participate in the activity" and "[a]s to those risks, the defendant has no duty to protect the plaintiff."[4]

Instruction 7 stated, "Your verdict must be for the defendant if you believe that the conditions that plaintiff encountered on defendant's ski slope on the day of the occurrence were a risk inherent in the sport of skiing." Bennett contends that the instruction misstated Missouri law because it did not require the jury to find that she had knowledge of, and appreciated, the specific dangers causing her injury. Hidden Valley argues on the other hand that under Missouri law, a plaintiff assumes any risk inherent in a sport regardless of her actual knowledge of the risk.

In a diversity case such as this we must follow state law as announced by the highest court in the state. The Supreme Court of Missouri has explained that a participant in sport "accept[s] * * * those [hazards] that reasonably inhere in the sport so far as they are obvious and usually incident to the game." It has thus prevented a spectator injured by a foul ball at a baseball game from proceeding beyond the summary judgment stage, for

> [t]his risk [of being struck by a foul ball] is a necessary and inherent part of the game * * *. [It] is assumed by the spectators because it remains after due care has been exercised and is not the result of negligence on the part of the baseball club.

Anderson v. Kansas City Baseball Club, 231 S.W.2d 170, 173 (Mo.1950). Whether the plaintiff had subjective knowledge of the risk of being injured by a foul ball was immaterial. The risk assumed by a spectator was described in this way in [another Missouri Supreme Court case]:

> The patron * * * subjects himself to the dangers necessarily and usually incident to and inherent in the game. This does not mean that he "assumes the risk" of being injured by the proprietor's negligence but that by voluntarily entering into the sport as a spectator he knowingly accepts the reasonable risks and hazards inherent in and incident to the game.

Hudson v. Kansas City Baseball Club, Inc., 349 Mo. 1215, 164 S.W.2d 318, 323 (1942). These cases show that the Missouri Supreme Court has analyzed implied primary assumption of risk by focusing on whether the risk was incident to or inherent in the activity undertaken by the plaintiff, rather than on the plaintiff's subjective knowledge of the risk.

The lower courts in Missouri have generally taken the same approach. For example, injury to a professional hockey player was held not actionable because it was "part of the game of professional hockey." Similarly, a golf spectator injured by a rock hidden in the grass "assumed the risks ordinarily incident to watching such a match and to walking over the course." "Falling and colliding with other skaters is not an extraordinary

---

4. Because the doctrine of implied primary assumption of risk focuses on whether the defendant owed a duty to the plaintiff with respect to the risk in question, it is not strictly an affirmative defense. * * *

occurrence for those indulging in that form of exercise. One who skates assumes those risks * * *." "[P]ersons participating in sports may be held to have consented, by their participation, to those injuries which are reasonably foreseeable consequences of participating in the competition."

* * *

Bennett points to language in several Missouri cases to support her position that Hidden Valley had to show she knew that she might encounter conditions like those existing on the night she was injured. She cites Ross v. Clouser, a case in which a third basemen was injured by a sliding baserunner. 637 S.W.2d 11, 13 (Mo.1982) (en banc) (reversing a judgment notwithstanding the verdict which had been granted on the basis that the plaintiff had assumed the risk). Although the Missouri Supreme Court said in *Ross* that assumption of risk "bars recovery when plaintiff comprehended the actual danger and intelligently acquiesced in it," the court appeared to be speaking about implied secondary assumption of risk. * * *

* * *

We conclude that under Missouri law, a voluntary skier assumes the risks inherent in or incidental to skiing, regardless of her subjective knowledge of those risks. This principle can also be put in terms of duty: the proprietor of a ski area has no duty to protect a skier from those risks inherent in or incidental to skiing. Implied primary assumption of risk does not of course relieve a defendant of liability for negligence, because inherent risks "are not those created by a defendant's negligence but rather by the nature of the activity itself." By directing the jury to find for Hidden Valley if it determined that the conditions on the ski slope at the time Bennett was injured were inherent risks of skiing, Instruction 7 fairly and adequately submitted the issue to the jury. The district court therefore did not abuse its discretion by giving this charge.

* * *

[Affirmed.]

NOTES

1. *The inherent risks of sports and recreational activities.* Bennett is one of a number of recent cases standing for the proposition that the organizers of and participants in recreational and sports activities have no duty to guard against or warn of risks that are inherent in the activity. A number of other recent cases achieve roughly the same effect by holding that the duty owed by sports participants to one another is only to avoid intentional or reckless injury.

The inherent-risk formulation is probably a better expression of the governing principle in this area than the avoidance-of-intentional-or-reckless-injury expression. For one thing, it enables courts to treat actions against participants and sponsors under the same conceptual structure. For another, the inherent-risk formulation seems to be a more refined tool; in many sports, conduct that would be intentionally tortious or reckless in any other context is tolerated or even encouraged. See generally Phi Delta Theta Co. v. Moore, 10 S.W.3d 658 (Tex. 1999) (Enoch, J., dissenting from writ denial).

Recall that Overall v. Kadella, supra p. 47, expresses the same basic idea in treating the scope of the consent that a sports participant is deemed to confer on his fellow players.

2. ***Implied primary assumption of risk is not a very good name for this doctrine.*** The implied primary assumption of risk terminology is potentially confusing because its baggage includes a lot of victim-specific language about knowledge and consent, and also because it may imply that the rule is an affirmative defense. The *Bennett* court is probably right in saying that it isn't.

3. ***The core idea of the implied primary (inherent risk)doctrine.*** The inherent risk concept is reasonably coherent: the inherent risks of an activity are those that are permitted by the rules, customs, and mores of the activity. Another way to say this is that a risk is inherent in a sport if its elimination would chill vigorous participation in the sport or alter the fundamental nature of the activity. Sanchez v. Hillerich & Bradsby Co., 104 Cal.App.4th 703, 128 Cal.Rptr.2d 529 (2002), applied this test in concluding that the manufacturer of a hollow aluminum baseball bat with a pressurized air bladder was not entitled to summary judgment in an action by a pitcher who was struck by a line drive traveling at more than 100 m.p.h. Noting that the bat's inventor had himself complained to the company that it was too dangerous, the court decided that this particular risk was not inherent to college baseball.

4. ***The coverage of the implied primary (inherent risk) doctrine is less clear.*** The notion of "sports and recreational activities" has been given very broad extension, covering virtually every organized or organizable game imaginable, including the operation of personal watercraft (jet skis), paint-ball warfare, and amusement park rides. But there are a significant number of cases taking a narrower view. See, e.g., Van Guilder v. Collier, 248 Mich.App. 633, 650 N.W.2d 340, 342 (2001) (excluding the operation of off-road recreational vehicles from the category).

5. ***An occupational-injury offshoot.*** Dobbs, The Law of Torts § 285 p. 769 (2000), summarizes what is generally called *the firefighters' rule* as follows: "When firefighters or police officers are injured by perils that they have been employed to confront, they ordinarily have no claim against the person who created those perils." In Priebe v. Nelson, 39 Cal.4th 1112, 47 Cal.Rptr.3d 553, 140 P.3d 848, 852 (2006), the court discussed California's "veterinarian's rule, an offshoot of the 'fireman's rule,' which rules are also sometimes collectively referred to as 'occupational assumption of the risk.' " The court applied this rule to a kennel employee who was savagely bitten by a customer's 75–pound pit bull.

6. ***Implied secondary assumption of risk (contributory negligence's ugly old cousin).*** The affirmative defense of implied assumption of risk as an absolute bar to recovery was developed in the late nineteenth and

early twentieth centuries. The doctrine was complex and controversial. See, e.g., James, Assumption of Risk, 61 Yale L.J. 141 (1952); Keeton, Assumption of Risk and the Landowner, 20 Tex.L.Rev.562 (1942). It was developed first in the context of employees impliedly assuming the risks inherent in their jobs,[1] but was then expanded to non-employment situations. The doctrine was sometimes called "implied assumption of risk," sometimes "voluntary assumption of risk," and sometimes *volenti non fit injuria*. Today it is often called "implied secondary assumption of the risk." It applied whenever the plaintiff was subjectively aware of a risk that plaintiff then voluntarily undertook to encounter.

Courts spent a great deal of time and energy determining whether a plaintiff was actually aware of a risk and whether a plaintiff voluntarily undertook it. See, e.g., Meese v. Brigham Young University, 639 P.2d 720 (Utah 1981) (plaintiff lacked sufficient knowledge of risk); Marshall v. Ranne, 511 S.W.2d 255 (1974) (assumption was not voluntary).

After the advent of comparative negligence, many legislatures and courts abolished the affirmative defense of voluntary assumption of risk, concluding that a plaintiff's knowledge of the risk and voluntary conduct in encountering it are no longer a suitable basis for barring recovery but rather are appropriately factored into the question of whether, and by how much, the plaintiff's conduct was unreasonable. See, e.g., N.Y.Civ.Prac.Law. § 1411, supra p. 352; Ark.Stat. § 16–64–122(c), supra p. 353; Gilson v. Drees Brothers, 19 Wis.2d 252, 120 N.W.2d 63 (1963); Farley v. M M Cattle Co., 529 S.W.2d 751 (Tex. 1975); Murray v. Ramada Inns, Inc., 521 So.2d 1123 (La.1988). The abolitions are expressed in various ways; the thrust of Apportionment Restatement § 3 cmt. *c* is toward abolishing both the defense and the term.

The opinion in Perez v. McConkey, 872 S.W.2d 897, 903 (Tenn. 1994), is a thorough survey of the history and current jurisprudence of the assumed risk doctrine, concluding that only five states that have adopted comparative fault still retain the old total-bar assumed risk defense (listing Georgia, Nebraska, Mississippi, Rhode Island, and South Dakota).

F.   FAILURE TO AVOID CONSEQUENCES; FAILURE TO MITIGATE DAMAGES

HUTCHINS v. SCHWARTZ

Supreme Court of Alaska, 1986.
724 P.2d 1194.

COMPTON, JUSTICE.

Charles Hutchins and Donna Hutchins (Hutchins) appeal a jury verdict which awarded Hutchins $1,937.09 damages for injuries sustained

---

1. Tort actions by injured workers against their employers were bedeviled by what has been called the "unholy trinity" of a vigorous contributory negligence defense, the assumed risk defense, and the fellow servant rule. These defenses were so effective in cutting injured workers out of the protections of negligence law that—in a movement that began in Germany and England in the late 19th century—legislatures began enacting workers' compensation statutes. See Epstein, The Historical Origin and Economic Structure of Workers' Compensation Law, 16 Ga.L.Rev. 775 (1982). See also supra p. 148 note *.

in an automobile collision with Robert Schwartz (Schwartz). The jury determined that Hutchins was 40% comparatively negligent. On appeal Hutchins claims that the trial court erred 1) by admitting evidence of Hutchins' failure to wear a seat belt; [and] 2) by denying his motion for judgment notwithstanding the verdict (JNOV) and/or new trial * * *.

* * *

Hutchins was not wearing a seat belt at the time of the accident. He sustained cuts on his head, bruises on his chest, knee and wrist, and a broken big toe. * * *

Hutchins sued Schwartz for $275,000 compensatory damages. He filed a motion *in limine* to exclude evidence of his non-use of a seat belt. Judge Milton M. Souter denied the motion, ruling that evidence of Hutchins' failure to wear a seat belt could be used by Schwartz to argue for a reduction of damages.

At the end of the trial, Judge Souter granted Hutchins' motion for directed verdict on the seat belt issue. The jury was instructed to disregard all evidence relating to Hutchins' non-use of a seat belt.

The jury returned a verdict finding Schwartz 60% negligent and Hutchins 40% comparatively negligent. It awarded Hutchins $1,937.09 in damages.

Hutchins moved for JNOV and/or a new trial. The motion was denied.
* * *

Hutchins claims that the trial court erred by denying his motion *in limine* and allowing evidence on Hutchins' non-use of a seat belt. He contends that this error was not cured by the trial court's subsequent instruction telling the jury to disregard the seat belt evidence. Hutchins urges the court to follow the jurisdictions which reject evidence of non-use of seat belts.

* * *

We have not addressed whether failure to use a seat belt can be used in a personal injury action as evidence of comparative negligence.

* * *

The question is whether we should impose a duty upon a person to wear a seat belt when driving a car equipped with one.

Most jurisdictions, whether they have adopted comparative or contributory negligence, have rejected the proposition. In [Amend v. Bell, 89 Wash.2d 124, 570 P.2d 138 (1977)], the Washington Supreme Court stated the reasons upon which most courts rely when declining to impose a duty upon all persons riding in a car equipped with seat belts.

First, the defendant should not diminish the consequences of his negligence by the plaintiff's failure to anticipate defendant's negligence. Plaintiffs are not required to predict a defendant's negligence.

Second, seat belts are not required in all vehicles.

Third, a majority of motorists do not habitually use their seat belts.

Fourth, admission of evidence of non-use would lead to a "battle of experts" as to what injuries would have or have not been avoided if plaintiff had worn a seat belt.

Other courts have declined because the legislature has not mandated seat belt use. The decision as to whether people should wear seat belts is one of policy and best left to the legislature.

Other courts have declined because the duty to avoid a defendant's negligence and mitigate one's own damages does not arise until after the accident and injury have occurred. Hutchins argues that a defendant must take his plaintiff as he finds him under the "eggshell skull" theory.

The supreme courts of Florida and Wisconsin, however, have taken a contrary view.

In Bentzler v. Braun, 34 Wis.2d 362, 149 N.W.2d 626 (1967), the Wisconsin Supreme Court recognized that there was a demonstrable link between wearing seat belts and minimizing injuries. The failure to wear seat belts was not negligence per se but

> where seat belts are available and there is evidence before the jury indicating causal relationship between the injuries sustained and the failure to use seat belts, it is proper and necessary to instruct the jury in that regard. A jury in such case could conclude that an occupant of an automobile is negligent in failing to use seat belts.

In a subsequent case, [Foley v. City of West Allis, 113 Wis.2d 475, 335 N.W.2d 824 (1983)], the Wisconsin court stated that the seat belt defense

> is this court's recognition that in light of the realities of the frequency of automobile accidents and the extensive injuries they cause, the general availability of seat belts, and the public knowledge that riders and drivers should "buckle up for safety," those who fail to use available seat belts should be held responsible for the incremental harm caused by their failure to wear available seat belts.

The Wisconsin court suggested that the so called "seat belt defense" comports with the principles underlying comparative negligence. A plaintiff only recovers damages for injuries caused by defendant and not for those that plaintiff could have prevented by wearing a seat belt.

In Insurance Co. of North America v. Pasakarnis, 451 So.2d 447, 453 (Fla.1984), the Florida Supreme Court stated:

> As we have already expressly acknowledged, automobile collisions are foreseeable as are the so-called "second collisions" with the interior of the automobile. The seat belt has been a safety device required by the federal government for nearly twenty years. In a 1982 study by the United States Department of Transportation, it is reported that the evidence for the effectiveness of safety belts in reducing deaths and injury severity is substantial and unequivocal.

In light of the importance of the seat belt as a safety precaution and the minimal effort required to fasten an available seat belt, the court concluded that failure to wear one could be a pertinent factor for the jury to consider in determining damages.

We agree with the reasoning of the Florida and Wisconsin courts. These courts persuasively rebut the arguments of those holding the contrary.

Automobile accidents are foreseeable. The fact that many motorists do not wear seat belts may suggest that a failure to use a seat belt does not violate a standard of care. However, the fact that a majority of people act in a certain manner does not make that conduct reasonable especially when that conduct involves an unnecessary risk.

Most studies indicate that seat belt use is more advantageous than non-use since it prevents serious injuries.

As to a "battle of experts," juries are constantly evaluating expert testimony. This is not unique to the seat belt issue.

In *Pasakarnis,* the court responded to the argument that it should reject evidence of non-use absent specific legislation requiring the use of seat belts. The court stated that it has a duty to ensure that the law remains both fair and realistic as society and technology change. The court primarily modernized the law of torts as seen in its decisions of comparative negligence and loss of consortium. Additionally, the absence of a legislative mandate to wear seat belts means only that the failure to use one cannot constitute negligence per se.

Regarding a plaintiff's duty to mitigate damages before the injury occurs, the *Foley* court stated that when the plaintiff's pre-injury conduct does not cause the accident but aggravates the ensuing damages, then damage reduction is "the better view unless we are to place an entirely artificial emphasis upon the moment of impact, and the pure mechanics of causation."

We conclude that the failure to wear a seat belt is relevant evidence for the purpose of damage reduction. However, we do not choose to categorize such evidence as a "seat belt defense." Rather, the concept of comparative negligence contemplates the inclusion of all relevant factors in arriving at the appropriate damage award and non-use of a seat belt is a relevant factor for apportioning damages. We find it unnecessary to wait for legislative action on this subject.

Therefore, if under the facts and circumstances of the case a reasonably prudent person would have used a seat belt and if plaintiff suffered more severe injuries as a result of not wearing a seat belt, then the jury should be permitted to consider this factor in assessing damages.

In this case, we do not need to determine the extent to which seat belt evidence is relevant since the trial court directed a verdict against Schwartz on this issue.

We conclude that the trial court did not abuse its discretion by admitting evidence of Hutchins' failure to wear a seat belt. The court gave a subsequent jury instruction to disregard such evidence since it found that Schwartz presented insufficient evidence that the seat belt system actually worked and that Hutchins' injuries were caused by his failure to wear a seat belt. The subsequent instruction removed any possibility of jury confusion or prejudice.

* * *

Hutchins contends that the trial court erred in denying his motion for JNOV and/or new trial because there is no evidence showing that he was 40% comparatively negligent * * *.

* * *

After reviewing the evidence * * *, we conclude that reasonable minds could differ as to whether Hutchins' headlights were on or off. * * * Additionally, the jury could have concluded that Hutchins was traveling too fast for the road conditions. We conclude that there is an evidentiary basis for the jury's finding that Hutchins was 40% comparatively negligent.

* * *

[Affirmed.]

NOTES

1. ***Distinguishing among failure to avoid consequences, failure to mitigate damages, and contributory or comparative negligence.*** The law of negligence traditionally precluded recovery of any damages that the plaintiff could have avoided by taking prudent measures *after* the accident to prevent or reduce the severity of his injuries. This rule is known as the doctrine of mitigation of damages. In some jurisdictions this is not a full-fledged affirmative defense, because the defendant is not required to plead it. But in most respects the mitigation of damages rule functions as an affirmative defense; in practice the defendant must introduce evidence and persuade the trier of fact that reasonable care by the plaintiff after the accident would have avoided some of the damages.

The doctrine of mitigation of damages is sometimes also called the "doctrine of avoidable consequences." But in the recent cases and commentary, the "avoidable consequences" terminology is applied to the issue raised in *Hutchins*. A defendant who contends that the plaintiff should not be permitted to recover any damages that could have been avoided by wearing a seat belt is making an argument closely resembling the standard mitigation of damages argument, but the issue is different in this respect: the traditional mitigation of damages doctrine focuses on the victim's conduct after the accident, whereas the "avoidable consequences" argument in the seat belt and similar cases focuses on *pre-accident conduct*. Many recent judicial opinions have regarded that difference as an important one. Therefore, it seems best to highlight it by confining the term *mitigation of damages* to inquiries into the victim's post-accident conduct, and using the term *avoidable consequences* to refer to pre-accident conduct.

For clarity of analysis, avoidable consequences issues should also be distinguished from comparative (or contributory) negligence issues. Both terms focus on pre-accident conduct; but the difference—a clear and important one—is that conduct constituting comparative or contributory negligence was a cause in fact and a legal cause of the accident and hence of all of the victim's injuries, whereas conduct violative of the avoidable consequences doctrine will normally have been a cause in fact of only some of the injuries.

In summary, the preferred terminology in this area is as follows:

Comparative (or contributory) negligence: Pre-accident conduct by the victim that was a cause of the accident and hence of *all* of the injuries or damages.

Failure to avoid consequences: Pre-accident conduct by the victim that did not cause the accident but that was a cause of *some* (perhaps even all) of the injuries or damages.

Failure to mitigate damages: Post-accident conduct by the victim that was a cause of *some* of the injuries or damages.

2. *How should the penalty for failure to mitigate damages be measured?* Most states have handled the mitigation of damages issue via jury instructions. See, e.g., Michigan Standard Jury Instructions—Civil § 53.05 (2d ed. 1981):

A person has a duty to use ordinary care to minimize his damages after he has been injured. It is for you to decide whether plaintiff failed to use such ordinary care and, if so, whether any damage resulted from such failure. You must not compensate the plaintiff for any portion of his damages which resulted from his failure to use such care.

Note that this has the effect of precluding recovery for all of the damages that resulted from the plaintiff's failure to mitigate, even though those damages also resulted from the defendant's negligence in causing the accident. Many courts continue to follow this approach. See, e.g., Adams v. Chenault, 836 So.2d 1193 (La.App. 2003), involving a traffic accident in which the plaintiff was an innocent passenger. The court held that the plaintiff's negligent failure to mitigate her damages—by refraining from overindulgence in prescription painkillers—necessitated reducing her damages award from $110,000 to $55,000. The Apportionment Restatement (§ 3 cmt. *b*, illus. 4) calls for a different approach whereby a plaintiff's negligent failure to mitigate damages is penalized by a percentage-fault reduction rather than a total-bar rule.

3. *How should the penalty for failure to avoid consequences be measured?* Here again the Restatement (Third) calls for a percentage-reduction approach. Id., illus. 3. But some courts favor a total-bar approach (regarding the portion of the total damages that resulted from the plaintiff's culpable failure to avoid the consequences). See, e.g., Halvorson v. Voeller, 336 N.W.2d 118, 121 (N.D. 1983), setting forth the following jury instruction for cases involving injuries to motorcyclists:

> If you find (1) it was unreasonable for the plaintiff to not wear a helmet, and (2) the plaintiff would not have received some or all of his injuries had he worn a helmet, then (3) the amount of damages awarded the plaintiff for the injuries he sustained must be reduced in proportion to the amount of injury he would have avoided by the use of the helmet. The burden of proof on both (1) and (2) rests with the defendant.

The *Halvorson* court provided an example clarifying that it used the phrase "in proportion to the amount" to call for a cause-in-fact inquiry: What part of the plaintiff's total damages would the culpably-omitted helmet have prevented? Here is the example:

> Defendant's negligently-driven automobile collides with plaintiff's negligently-driven motorcycle, causing the plaintiff to sustain $100,000 in damages. The jury finds that the parties' accident-causing fault should be assessed 60% to defendant and 40% to plaintiff. The jury also finds that plaintiff should have been wearing a helmet and that, if he had been, he would have sustained only $40,000 in damages. The plaintiff should be awarded $24,000.

G. THE GRAVITATIONAL PULL OF PROPORTIONATE LIABILITY CONCEPTS: UNANTICIPATED CHANGES TO SUBSTANTIVE NEGLIGENCE LAW

"[T]he nearly universal adoption of comparative responsibility by American courts and legislatures has had a dramatic impact. * * * Comparative responsibility has a potential impact on almost all areas of tort law." Apportionment Restatement § 1 cmt. *a*. This is a huge phenomenon. Here we can take only a brief selective look at it.

PINER v. SUPERIOR COURT

Supreme Court of Arizona, 1998.
192 Ariz. 182, 962 P.2d 909.

FELDMAN, JUSTICE.

* * *

On his way to work on Friday, October 12, 1990, William Piner stopped his truck to let a pedestrian cross the street. While he was stopped, a car driven by Billy Jones hit Piner's truck from behind. Police were called to investigate the incident. Piner waited for the police to finish their investigation before calling his physician to complain of pain in his neck, upper back, left arm, and head. The doctor's staff told Piner that the doctor was unavailable but would call him back later that day. Piner then fixed the broken tail lights on his truck and went to work.

Later that day, Piner was driving to lunch when the car ahead of him stopped to let some pedestrians cross the street. Piner stopped and was again hit from the rear, this time by a vehicle driven by Cynthia Richardson. Feeling similar pain symptoms after this accident, Piner called his doctor's office and was again told that the doctor was occupied and would contact him later.

Piner was unable to see his physician until Monday. After examination, the doctor concluded that Piner suffered a number of injuries as a result of the collisions. Due to the nature of the injuries, however, neither she nor any other physician has been able to attribute any particular part of Piner's total injuries to one accident or the other.

Piner filed an action against Jones and Richardson * * * alleging indivisible injuries resulting from the successive impacts. Neither defendant has asserted that he or she could apportion the particular physical harm Piner suffered between the separate accidents. Apparently, all parties agree that both collisions contributed to Piner's total physical injuries.

Piner moved for partial summary judgment * * *. According to Piner, in a successive accident, indivisible injury case, defendants have the burden of proving apportionment; if neither defendant can demonstrate what portion of the total damage he or she caused, they should be held jointly and severally liable for the entire amount. [The trial judge denied Piner's motion, ruling that] A.R.S. § 12–2506 abolished the system of joint and several liability * * * "and that the plaintiff has to prove which accident caused which injuries, and if not, the plaintiff loses." [We granted Piner leave to file this interlocutory appeal.]

* * *

THE INDIVISIBLE INJURY RULE IN ARIZONA

A. *Evolution of the Rule of Joint and Several Liability: Causation and Apportionment of Damages*

Black-letter tort law tells us that as an essential element of the action, the plaintiff must provide evidence that the defendant's conduct caused plaintiff's damage. [Thus a] plaintiff's case failed if that plaintiff was unable to establish the damage attributable to a defendant's conduct. [But the] law eventually recognized an exception for multiple, culpable actors if the plaintiff, through no fault of his own, was unable to apportion [damages] * * *.

* * *

The evolution of Arizona law on the subject [began in 1924, when] Arizona recognized joint and several liability as a well-settled rule but one that applied only in cases involving tortious injury brought about by concerted action of two or more tortfeasors. See White v. Arizona Eastern R. Co., 26 Ariz. 590, 594, 229 P. 101, 102 (1924). [Subsequently, in Salt River Valley Water Users' Ass'n v. Cornum,. 49 Ariz. 1, 63 P.2d 639(1937), the court expanded the *White* principle, holding that] when the negligence of different tortfeasors "coincided in time, place, and character" [so as to produce a single indivisible result], joint and several liability could be applied even though the defendants' actions were not concerted.* When the plaintiff's case fell outside the exception, the plaintiff would have to apportion damage by causation or prove that one of the tortfeasors was the proximate cause of the entire injury. If the plaintiff was unable to do so, the case failed.

In 1966, [Holtz v. Holder, supra p. 143] recognized another circumstance in which a plaintiff could be excused from apportioning damages. The facts in *Holtz* [were] are similar to those in * * * the present case. Holtz, like Piner, suffered [injuries] from separate [traffic] accidents. [Holtz's injuries resulted from two collisions separated by five to ten minutes. Like Piner's, Holtz's injuries were theoretically divisible, but Holtz's doctor testified that it was "medically impossible to determine which impact caused which injuries," and that "the only way to tell would have been an examination of the plaintiff immediately after the first collision."] We held that the tortfeasors were jointly and severally liable for Holtz's entire damage. Such a result was "desirable as a matter of policy" even though it extended the exception recognized in * * * *Cornum* to include incidents of successive injury.

To reach this result, *Holtz* actually applied two different rules. First, when the injury was indivisible, even though caused by successive accidents, the plaintiff could assert a claim against all wrongdoers without having the burden of "proving the extent of damage or injury caused by each * * *." We described this as the "single indivisible injury rule." *Holtz* shifted the burden of apportionment to the defendants and gave them incentive to apportion cause by holding each liable for the entire amount of unapportioned damages. Successive tortfeasors are responsible for the entire amount of damages if "their acts occur closely in time and place" and the plaintiff receives successive injuries that "the trier of fact determines to be unapportionable between or among the several tortfeasors." * * *

Holtz's [second rule was that] damages were not to be apportioned on the basis of fault. Thus, all defendants were jointly and severally liable for the whole amount of damage. At common law, degrees of fault were never assigned to the parties * * *. This, [then], was the common law in Arizona—each tortious actor was jointly and severally liable for all of the damage caused by his conduct, even if one was much more at fault than another.

---

* For typical examples of such cases—in which the conduct of each of two independently acting tortfeasors was a but-for cause of an indisputably single and indivisible injury—see Austin Electric Ry. Co. v. Faust, 133 S.W. 449 (Tex.Civ.App. 1910) (holding a streetcar company and an ice company jointly and severally liable when a collision between a negligently operated street car and the ice company's negligently operated horse-drawn wagon caused the ice company's horses to bolt into a second collision with a nearby buggy in which the plaintiff was sitting at the time); Baylor University v. Bradshaw, 52 S.W.2d 1094 (Tex.Civ.App. 1932) (holding that a bus passenger hurt in a collision between the negligently operated bus and a negligently speeding train could recover in full from the bus company, which could then recover over in a third party action for contribution against the railroad). [Ed.]

B.   The Impact of UCATA

Defendants claim the Uniform Contribution Among Tortfeasors Act (UCATA) overruled *Holtz* and its progeny, thus requiring the factfinder to apportion damages between multiple actors and making each tortfeasor severally liable only for the portion of damages caused by his conduct. If the plaintiff is unable to provide enough evidence to form a basis for apportionment of damages, then, defendants argue, the claim must be dismissed. We disagree with this view because UCATA does not require limiting liability by apportioning damages but by apportioning fault.

The Arizona Legislature enacted its first version of UCATA in 1984. These provisions replaced [the common law rule of contributory negligence, whereby a plaintiff's negligent conduct barred his recovery entirely, with a statutory regime of comparative fault, under which a plaintiff's negligent conduct diminishes his recovery on a percentage-fault basis but no longer automatically bars all recovery. The 1984 UCATA also] abolished the rule forbidding contribution between joint tortfeasors. Under this new regime, the factfinder allocated a percentage of fault to each culpable actor. Even though the culpable defendants were still jointly and severally liable for all damages, the legislature established a right of contribution that allowed a defendant held liable for more than his share of fault to recover from the other tortfeasors in proportion to their several contributions of fault.** This change was intended to bring about a system in which each tortfeasor would eventually contribute only a portion of damage equal to the percentage of fault attributed to that tortfeasor by the factfinder. But Arizona's negligence law still produced harsh results when one defendant was insolvent, thus leaving the others unable to obtain contribution. See, e.g., Gehres [v. City of Phoenix, 156 Ariz. 484, 753 P.2d 174 (1987)] (defendants assigned five percent of fault held jointly and severally liable for one hundred percent of damages).

In response, the Arizona Legislature amended UCATA, abolishing joint liability and replacing it with a system that requires the courts to allocate responsibility among all parties who caused the injury, whether or not they are present in the action. A.R.S. § 12–2506(B). Under the present [statute], "the liability of each defendant is several only and not joint." § 12–2506(D). Taken in isolation, this wording tends to support defendants' argument, but several factors militate against such an interpretation. First, the legislative intent was to cure the *Gehres* "deep pocket" problem of a defendant only minimally at fault yet liable for the full amount of damages.

A second factor is that the old [pre-*Holtz*] rule [often] conditioned the plaintiff's recovery on the impossible: if unable to divide the indivisible, the plaintiff was denied relief and the culpable parties were relieved of all responsibility. The injustice inherent in this policy has been repeatedly

** In the pre-comparative fault era, contribution in cases like *Austin Electric* and *Bradshaw*, supra note *, was on a per capita (head count) basis. [Ed.]

recognized by our courts. We do not believe that when the legislature attempted to eliminate the injustice it perceived in the deep pocket problem, it also intended to reestablish an unfair regime under which an innocent victim is denied any relief because the damages caused by independent wrongdoers result in an indivisible, unapportionable injury.

Most important, the clear text of [§ 12–2506] does not require that a defendant's liability be limited by apportioning damages, but only by apportioning fault:

A.   In an action for personal injury, property damage or wrongful death, the liability of each defendant for damages is several only and is not joint * * *. *Each defendant is liable only for the amount of damages allocated to that defendant in direct proportion to that defendant's percentage of fault * * *. [T]he trier of fact shall multiply the total amount of damages recoverable by the plaintiff by the percentage of each defendant's fault,* and that amount is the maximum recoverable against the defendant * * *.

B.   In assessing percentages of fault the trier of fact shall consider the fault of all persons who contributed to the alleged injury * * *.

* * *

F.   (2) "Fault" means an actionable breach of legal duty, act or omission *proximately causing or contributing to injury or damages sustained by a person seeking recovery* * * *.

Thus, while [§ 12–2506] requires the plaintiff to prove that a defendant's conduct was a cause of injury, it does not instruct us to limit liability by apportioning damages. Instead, each tortfeasor whose conduct caused injury is severally liable only for a percentage of the * * * damages recoverable by the plaintiff, the percentage based on each actor's allocated share of fault.

We conclude, therefore, that [§ 12–2506] has left intact the rule of indivisible injury, relieving the plaintiff of apportioning damage according to causal contribution. When the tortious conduct of more than one defendant contributes to one indivisible injury, the entire amount of damage resulting from all contributing causes is the total amount "of damages recoverable by the plaintiff," as that term is used in § 12–2506(A). The second part of the *Holtz* rule, however, was abrogated by § 12–2506(A). Contrary to the common law and cases such as *Gehres*, the fault of all actors is compared and each defendant is severally liable for damages allocated "in direct proportion to that defendant's percentage of fault." § 12–2506(A). To determine each defendant's liability "the trier of fact shall multiply the * * * amount of damages recoverable by the plaintiff by the percentage of each defendant's fault, and that amount is the maximum recoverable against the defendant."

Thus in an indivisible injury case, the factfinder is to compute the total amount of damage sustained by the plaintiff and the percentage of fault of each tortfeasor. Multiplying the first figure by the second gives the maximum recoverable against each tortfeasor. This result conforms not only with the intent of the legislature and the text of the statute but also with common sense. When damages cannot be apportioned between multiple tortfeasors, there is no reason why those whose conduct produced successive but indivisible injuries should be treated differently from those whose independent conduct caused injury in a single accident. Like our predecessors in *Holtz*, we see no reason to employ a different rule if the injuries occur at once, five minutes apart or, as in the present case, several hours apart. The operative fact is simply that the conduct of each defendant was a cause and the result is indivisible damage.

* * *

CONCLUSION

In the present case, the trial judge erred in placing the burden of proof on apportionment on Piner. Assuming Piner proves that the conduct of both Jones and Richardson contributed to the final result, the burden of proof on apportionment is on them. If the judge concludes there is no evidence that would permit apportionment, then the case should be treated as one involving indivisible injuries. If the judge * * * concludes there is [evidence that might provide a basis for apportionment], the jurors should be instructed that if they are able to apportion damages, they should do so, allocating fault and damages for each accident separately. They should also be instructed that if they are unable to apportion damages, then they are to determine Piner's total damages resulting from both accidents. In such case, the indivisible injury rule will apply. * * * [But the jurors will also] be instructed to allocate fault in accordance with § 12–2506. The judge is then to multiply each tortfeasor's percentage of fault by the [total damages]. Each tortfeasor in an indivisible injury case is then severally liable for the product of that calculation.

* * *

The trial court's * * * order denying Piner's motion for partial summary judgment and * * * ruling regarding jury instruction content are vacated. The trial court may proceed in accordance with this opinion.

NOTES

1. ***Conceptual phases of a negligence action.*** In thinking about the intended and potential unintended effects of a jurisdiction's embrace of proportionate responsibility principles, it is useful to posit three separate conceptual phases of a negligence action. The plaintiff's prima facie case—plaintiff's satisfaction of the duty, breach, cause in fact, proximate cause, and damages requirements—is Phase One. The defendant's assertion and establishment of one or more affirmative defenses is Phase Two. The assessment, application, and effect of percentage-fault assignments is Phase Three. (These conceptual phases are not to be confused with the chronological stages of a negligence lawsuit as outlined in Chapter I. The conceptual phases do not

occur according to any chronology; they are a conceptual map of the whole case, and all of them are potentially in play throughout each chronological stage.)

In the pre-comparative fault era, none of the questions in Phases One and Two could properly have been addressed in percentage-fault terms; indeed, it would have been unthinkable to suggest this. In using the conceptual phases map in the present era, here is a very useful dogma: In the absence of a strong and clear legislative command, the adoption of comparative fault principles was not intended to affect anything in Phases One and Two.

2. From the viewpoint of the conceptual phases vocabulary, the defendants' argument in *Piner* was an effort to put Phase Three concepts to work on a Phase One issue. As we saw in Chapter IV, supra p. 143, the rule of Holtz v. Holder enabled the plaintiff to surmount a potentially grave difficulty with the factual causation component of the damages element in Phase One. The *Piner* defendants were arguing that the percentage-allocation-derived abolition of joint and several liability—a Phase Three artifact—should come over into Phase One and undo *Holtz*. The court resisted defendants' efforts, but the course of reasoning was not easy. The case might have been easier for the parties and the trial court—and the high court might have been spared the case—if plaintiff's counsel had looked at the conceptual phases map and realized the wisdom of rephrasing the *Holtz* argument to the trial judge. Rather than citing *Holtz* for the proposition that "if neither defendant can demonstrate what portion of the total damages he or she caused, they should be held jointly and severally liable for the entire amount," counsel should perhaps have changed the concluding clause to say "each should be deemed to have caused the entire amount."

BANKS v. ELKS CLUB PRIDE OF TENNESSEE 1102

Supreme Court of Tennessee, 2010.
301 S.W.3d 214.

WILLIAM C. KOCH, JR., J.

* * *

Alice J. Banks attended a social event at an Elks Lodge in Nashville on March 24, 2006. While she was there, the chair on which she was seated collapsed, causing serious injuries to Ms. Banks's back. Ms. Banks consulted with Dr. Robert H. Boyce, a physician affiliated with Premier Orthopaedics and Sports Medicine, P.C. ("Premier Orthopaedics"), who recommended lumbar surgery at the L3–L4 and L4–L5 levels. The procedure consisted of a decompression laminectomy and fusion. Ms. Banks agreed to have the procedure performed.

On May 16, 2006, Ms. Banks underwent surgery at Centennial Medical Center. While Dr. Boyce's operative report indicates that he performed a lumbar laminectomy and fusion at the L3–L4 and L4–L5 vertebrae as intended, he actually performed the surgery upon the L2–L3 and L3–L4 vertebrae. It was only after the surgery was completed that Dr. Boyce realized he mistakenly performed the surgery at the L2–L3, rather than the L4–L5 vertebrae. As a result, Ms. Banks was required to undergo a second surgery on May 17, 2006.

Following Ms. Banks's surgeries, she was transferred to Cumberland Manor Nursing Home ("Cumberland Manor") for further recuperation and rehabilitation. While a patient at Cumberland Manor, Ms. Banks developed a serious staphylococcus infection that required additional surgeries and extensive care and treatment.

* * *

[Banks sued the Elks Lodge and filed a separate lawsuit against Dr. Boyce and Premier Orthopaedics. Eventually the trial court entered an order consolidating the two cases. The defendants moved to amend their answers to assert the comparative fault of Cumberland Manor as an affirmative defense.* Banks opposed the defendants' motions, citing a long-standing common-law principle that imputes liability to an original tortfeasor for enhanced physical harm caused by the normal efforts of third persons to render aid that an injured personal reasonably requires.** In Banks's view, allowing defendants to assert a comparative fault defense based on Cumberland's negligence would violate that rule.] In their trial court briefs, the parties argued vigorously over whether what they referred to as the "original tortfeasor rule" or the "original tortfeasor doctrine"[3] survived this Court's decision in McIntyre v. Balentine, [supra p. 345]. * * *

[Accepting Banks's argument, the trial court denied the defendants' motions. The intermediate appellate court denied defendants' application for an interlocutory appeal, and the case made its way to the supreme court.]

* * *

The principles governing liability for successive injuries are settled. They recognize that there are circumstances in which an earlier tortfeasor may be held liable not only for the injury caused by its own negligent conduct but also for later injury caused by the negligent conduct of another tortfeasor. Liability in these circumstances arises when the subsequent negligent conduct is a foreseeable or natural consequence of the original tortfeasor's negligence.

Negligence in subsequent medical treatment of a tortiously caused injury is the most common invocation of this rule. * * * Tennessee's

---

* Remember that *McIntyre* authorizes this. See supra pp. 349, 351–352. [Ed.]

** See the discussion of "subsequent medical injuries" in Chapter V, supra p. 170. [Ed.]

3. The terms "original tortfeasor rule" and "original tortfeasor doctrine" are actually shorthand references to a concatenation of two common-law principles. The first principle is that "if one is injured by the negligence of another, and these injuries are aggravated by medical treatment (either prudent or negligent), the negligence of the wrongdoer causing the original injury is regarded as the proximate cause of the damage subsequently flowing from the medical treatment." The second principle is that the original tortfeasor is jointly and severally liable for the full extent of the injuries caused by the original tortfeasor and the successive tortfeasor.

courts have recognized and applied this principle for over one hundred years. * * *.

McIntyre v. Balentine involved a straightforward intersection crash * * *. It did not raise an issue of liability for successive injuries, and thus, this Court had no occasion to determine how the new comparative fault regime would mesh with the principle that, in proper circumstances, an earlier tortfeasor could be liable for the later negligent acts of another tortfeasor. To understand the effect of McIntyre v. Balentine on the original tortfeasor rule, the two principles in that rule—the original tortfeasor's liability for subsequent negligent acts of third parties and the original tortfeasor's joint and several liability with the subsequent negligent actors—must be unraveled and considered separately.

Today, we state unequivocally that our decision regarding joint and several liability in McIntyre v. Balentine did not alter Tennessee's common-law rules with regard to liability of tortfeasors for injuries caused by subsequent medical treatment for the injuries they cause. That rule is a rule that determines "when defendants are liable for the harm they caused." [Third Restatement of Torts § 35 cmt. *d*.] Thus, the rule in Tennessee is now, as it was before McIntyre v. Balentine was decided, that an actor whose tortious conduct causes physical harm to another is liable for any enhanced harm the other suffers due to the efforts of third persons to render aid reasonably required by the other's injury, as long as the enhanced harm arises from a risk that inheres in the effort to render aid.

However, at the same time, [we affirm the *McIntyre* principle that] the doctrine of joint and several liability no longer applies to circumstances in which separate, independent negligent acts of more than one tortfeasor combine to cause a single, indivisible injury. This [principle] is not inconsistent with our decision to retain the rule imposing liability on tortfeasors for subsequent negligent medical care for the injuries caused by the original tortfeasor. [As is explained in the Third Restatement of Torts § 35 cmt. *d*]:

> [M]odification of joint and several liability [does not] require or imply any change in the [subsequent medical injuries rule]. Modern adoption of pure several liability limits the liability of each defendant liable for the same harm to that defendant's comparative share of the harm. Several liability, however, does not provide rules about when defendants are liable for harm that they caused. When two or more defendants are liable for the enhanced harm suffered by a plaintiff, as may occur under [the subsequent medical injuries rule], and the governing law imposes several liability, each of the defendants is held liable for the amount of damages reflecting the enhanced harm discounted by the comparative share responsibility assigned by the factfinder to that defendant.

* * *

Most of the states that have adopted the principles of comparative fault or comparative responsibility have done so by statute rather than by judicial decision. The substance of these statutes differs because states have balanced the rights and interests of the parties in different ways. Accordingly, decisions from other state courts construing their own comparative fault statute provide only limited guidance to us. However, we note that a significant number of state courts that have addressed the same question we address in this case have, like this Court, concluded that comparative fault does not prevent the continuing imposition of liability on an original tortfeasor for subsequent negligent medical care for the injuries caused by the original tortfeasor [citing decisions from California, Florida, Idaho, Indiana, and New Mexico].

* * *

Ms. Banks and the Tennessee Association for Justice assert that public policy dictates retaining joint and several liability in circumstances where an injured person suffers enhanced physical harm due to the efforts of third persons to render aid to the injured person for injuries caused by the defendant's negligence. They assert that joint and severable liability is appropriate because * * * the original defendant is the proximate cause of the entire injury * * *. [This] argument overlooks the fact that in cases of this sort, the original tortfeasor's conduct is not the sole proximate cause of the plaintiff's indivisible injury. To the contrary, the independent tortious conduct of the original tortfeasor and one or more other parties are both proximate causes of the injury. The tortfeasors are not acting in concert, have not breached [a] common duty, and do not have a relationship triggering the application of vicarious liability. Therefore, this circumstance is governed by our * * * holding that joint and several liability is no longer applicable in circumstances "where the separate, independent negligent acts of more than one tortfeasor combine to cause a single, indivisible injury."

* * *

[The trial court erred by refusing to permit the Elks Lodge and Dr. Boyce to amend their answers to assert Cumberland Manor's comparative fault as an affirmative defense. We remand the case to the trial court for further proceedings consistent with this opinion.]

NOTES

1. ***The court's "conceptual phases" reasoning***. Here the court made two uses of the conceptual phases map (see note 1 following *Piner*, supra p. 417). (a) Defendants argued that the *McIntyre*-derived abolition of joint and several liability should travel from Phase Three to Phase One in order to wipe out a long-established proximate cause doctrine. The court used the Third Restatement's distinction between "rules about when defendants are liable" (Phase One) and rules about "the amount of damages" (Phase Three) as a way of rejecting that argument. (b) On the other hand, plaintiff argued that

the Phase One rule—"the original defendant is the proximate cause of the entire injury"—should travel to Phase Three to trump the abolition of joint and several liability. The court again said no, pointing to the independent integrity of the Phase Three principle.

2. The conceptual phases map seems to be a helpful way of thinking about a number of proportionate responsibilities puzzles. For another example, the question treated in note 3 following *Wassell*, supra p. 360—whether a superseding cause/sole proximate cause doctrine can be used to countermand a pure comparative fault rule—can usefully be phrased: Can the Phase One doctrine of superseding cause cross over into Phase Three and trump a pure comparative fault rule? This phrasing makes it clear that the answer should be no, which we (along with Judge Posner) think is the right answer.

H. PERCENTAGE–FAULT ASSIGNMENTS IN INTENTIONAL TORT CASES

Whether proportionate responsibility principles should apply in cases involving intentional tortfeasors entails two big questions. The first is whether an intentional tortfeasor can use the plaintiff's percentage of fault as an affirmative defense. Section 1 cmt. *c* of the Apportionment Restatement states:

> Although some courts have held that a plaintiff's negligence may serve as a comparative defense to an intentional tort, most have not. This Restatement takes no position on that issue.

Look at the New York, Wisconsin, Arkansas, and Kansas statutes on pp. 352–53, supra. Do any of them provide a clear answer?

The second big question is whether in a multiparty case involving both intentional and negligent tortfeasors, the intentional tortfeasor should be assigned a fault percentage. Here, quite a few courts and legislatures have answered yes. Section 12 of the Apportionment Restatement provides that intentional tortfeasors are always jointly and severally liable, even if joint and several liability has otherwise been abolished or modified. It provides that, in multiparty litigation, the fact finder assigns a percentage of responsibility to intentional tortfeasors for the purpose of applying a jurisdiction's rules about joint and several liability to other tortfeasors See id. §§ A19, B19, C19, D19, E19. But it also provides that, regardless of a jurisdiction's other rules about joint and several liability, "[a] person who is liable to another based on a failure to protect the other from the specific risk of an intentional tort is jointly and severally liable for the share of comparative responsibility assigned to the intentional tortfeasor in addition to the share of responsibility assigned to the person." Id. § 14.

CHAPTER X

STATUTES OF LIMITATIONS AND REPOSE

■ ■ ■

A. STATUTES OF LIMITATIONS

Statutes of limitations are not peculiar to tort law, of course; all causes of action are subject to them. This chapter treats only aspects of the subject that have special application to tort cases.

JOLLY v. ELI LILLY & CO.

Supreme Court of California, 1988.
44 Cal.3d 1103, 245 Cal.Rptr. 658, 751 P.2d 923.

PANELLI, JUSTICE.

* * *

Plaintiff Jolly was born in 1951. In 1972, she first learned that while she was *in utero* her mother had ingested the synthetic drug estrogen diethylstilbestrol (DES) for the prevention of miscarriage. Plaintiff was told in 1972 that DES daughters could suffer injuries. Therefore, she went to a DES clinic at the UCLA Medical Center for a check-up. She was diagnosed as having adenosis, a precancerous condition that required careful monitoring. In 1976, she had an abnormal pap smear and underwent a dilation and curettage, a surgical procedure to remove abnormal tissue. In 1978, plaintiff underwent a complete hysterectomy and a partial vaginectomy in order to remove malignancy. As of 1972, plaintiff was aware, or at least suspected, that her condition was a result of her mother's ingestion of DES during pregnancy.

Starting in 1972, plaintiff attempted to discover the manufacturer of the DES ingested by her mother. Efforts were increased in 1976 and 1978 when plaintiff's condition became acute. Unfortunately, the doctor who prescribed the drug had died, and plaintiff was unable to locate his records. Although the dispensing pharmacist did remember filling the DES prescription, he did not recall or have records pertaining to the specific brand used.

* * *

In March 1980, we decided Sindell v. Abbott Laboratories, 26 Cal.3d 588, 163 Cal.Rptr. 132, 607 P.2d 924, and held that if a plaintiff could not identify the precise drug manufacturer of the ingested DES, she could state a cause of action against the DES manufacturers of a substantial percentage of the market share of the drug.* Defendants would be liable, assuming the remaining material allegations in the complaint were proven, unless they could disprove their involvement. Almost one year after *Sindell,* plaintiff Jolly brought this action [against a number of DES manufacturers].

Defendants moved for summary judgment, asserting that the action [filed in 1981] was barred by Code of Civil Procedure section 340, subdivision (3), setting forth a one-year statute of limitations period for an action "for injury caused by the wrongful act or neglect of another." Although conceding the applicability of the one-year statutory period, plaintiff denied that the suit was time-barred. She asserted that the statute did not commence until she learned of the *Sindell* decision, because only then did she realize that she would be able to successfully bring her claim. [The trial court granted the defendants' motion. The Court of Appeal reversed and remanded, holding that the claim was not necessarily barred.]

* * *

[B]oth sides agree that the one-year limitations period of section 340, subdivision (3) applies to this case. Both sides also agree that the common law rule, that an action accrues on the date of injury applies only as modified by the "discovery rule." The discovery rule provides that the accrual date of a cause of action is delayed until the plaintiff is aware of her injury and its negligent cause.[4] A plaintiff is held to her actual knowledge as well as knowledge that could reasonably be discovered through investigation of sources open to her. The parties differ as to what constitutes sufficient knowledge to start the statute running.

The Court of Appeal applied Kensinger v. Abbott Laboratories, Inc., 171 Cal.App.3d 376, 217 Cal.Rptr. 313 (1985), a factually similar case, and found that it was a question of fact as to whether the statute of limitations began to run more than one year before plaintiff Jolly filed her complaint. The *Kensinger* court acknowledged the well established rule that ignorance of the legal significance of known facts or the identity of the defendant would not delay the running of the statute—only ignorance of one or more "critical facts" could have that effect.

---

* See Chapter IV, supra, pp. 131–34, 137–38.—Ed.

4. Defendants argue that the statute should commence when the plaintiff knows of her injury and its *factual* cause. Although that position has been adopted in some jurisdictions (see e.g., United States v. Kubrick (1979) 444 U.S. 111, 100 S.Ct. 352, 62 L.Ed.2d 259 [concerning the Federal Tort Claims Act]; Anthony v. Koppers Co., Inc. (1980) 284 Pa.Super. 81, 425 A.2d 428, 436, revd. on other grounds, (1981) 496 Pa. 119, 436 A.2d 181), it is not the rule in California. (See, e.g., Sanchez v. South Hoover Hospital (1976) 18 Cal.3d 93, 99, 132 Cal.Rptr. 657, 553 P.2d 1129; Gutierrez v. Mofid (1985) 39 Cal.3d 892, 896, 218 Cal.Rptr. 313, 705 P.2d 886.)

However, the key point in *Kensinger* was its determination that one "critical fact" was knowledge of some wrongful conduct. Specifically, the court held that a plaintiff may have "no knowledge of facts indicating wrongdoing by a particular defendant. In such a situation, litigation might be premature for lack of knowledge of any *factual basis* for imputing fault to a manufacturer rather than ignorance of supportive legal theories. Knowledge of the occurrence and origin of harm cannot necessarily be equated with knowledge of the factual basis for a legal remedy." Accordingly, the *Kensinger* court held that the statutory clock did not begin to tick until the plaintiff knew or reasonably should have known of the facts constituting wrongful conduct, as well as the fact of her injury and its relation to DES. The Court of Appeal, applying *Kensinger,* held that it could not be said that "as a matter of law" Jolly was or should have been aware of *facts* establishing wrongdoing, e.g., "either failure to test or failure to warn," until within one year of the date she filed suit.

The rule proposed in *Kensinger* goes too far.[6] Under the discovery rule, the statute of limitations begins to run when the plaintiff suspects or should suspect that her injury was caused by wrongdoing, that someone has done something wrong to her. A plaintiff need not be aware of the specific "facts" necessary to establish the claim; that is a process contemplated by pretrial discovery. Once the plaintiff has a suspicion of wrongdoing, and therefore an incentive to sue, she must decide whether to file suit or sit on her rights. So long as a suspicion exists, it is clear that the plaintiff must go find the facts; she cannot wait for the facts to find her.

* * *

The foregoing is fully consistent with the policy of deciding cases on the merits as well as the policies underlying the statute of limitations. [T]he fundamental purpose of the statute is to give defendants reasonable repose, that is, to protect parties from defending stale claims. A second policy underlying the statute is to require plaintiffs to diligently pursue their claims. Because a plaintiff is under a duty to reasonably investigate and because a *suspicion* of wrongdoing, coupled with a knowledge of the harm and its cause, will commence the limitations period, suits are not likely to be unreasonably delayed, and those failing to act with reasonable dispatch will be barred. At the same time, plaintiffs who file suit as soon as they have reason to believe that they are entitled to recourse will not be precluded.

While resolution of the statute of limitations issue is normally a question of fact, where the uncontradicted facts established through discovery are susceptible of only one legitimate inference, summary judgment is proper. In this case it is clear that application of the discovery rule supports the trial court's judgment. Plaintiff stated that as early as 1978

---

6. We recognize that some jurisdictions have adopted rules similar to that set out in *Kensinger.* (See, e.g., Anthony v. Abbott Laboratories (R.I.1985) 490 A.2d 43 (relied on in *Kensinger*); Dawson v. Eli Lilly & Co. (D.D.C.1982) 543 F.Supp. 1330; Lopez v. Swyer (1973) 62 N.J. 267, 300 A.2d 563.) However, as will be shown, the rule in California is otherwise.

she was interested in "obtaining more information" about DES because she wanted to "make a claim"; she felt that someone had done something wrong to her concerning DES, that it was a defective drug and that she should be compensated. She points to no evidence contradicting her candid statements. Thus, plaintiff is held to her admission; she suspected that defendants' conduct was wrongful during 1978—well over a year before she filed suit. This suspicion would not have been allayed by any investigation. To the contrary, a timely investigation would have disclosed numerous articles concerning DES and many DES suits filed throughout the country alleging wrongdoing.

* * *

In sum, the limitations period begins when the plaintiff suspects, or should suspect, that she has been wronged. Here, plaintiff suspected as much no later than 1978. Because she did not file suit until 1981, her suit, unless otherwise saved, is time-barred.

III. THE EFFECT OF *SINDELL*

Plaintiff's major argument, which was summarily rejected by the trial court and the Court of Appeal, is that our landmark decision in *Sindell*, constituted the "fact" that activated the statute. Plaintiff does not dispute the general rule that ignorance of the identity of the defendant does not affect the statute of limitations. However, she asserts that the rule does not apply to the facts of her case.

* * *

Sindell did not provide plaintiff with the critical "fact" that started the limitations period. Nor did it create a new tort with an independent starting date for purposes of the statute of limitations. Rather, *Sindell* demonstrated the legal significance of facts already known to plaintiff. The statute had started to run for plaintiff well before *Sindell* was decided.

At a less legalistic but more fundamental level, plaintiff argues, with some persuasive force, that prior to *Sindell* she could not have prevailed on her suit. She notes that during the time that defendants argue her action would have been timely, McCreery v. Eli Lilly & Co., 87 Cal.App.3d 77, 150 Cal.Rptr. 730 (1978) (overruled by *Sindell),* effectively barred her claim. In *McCreery,* the Court of Appeal held that a plaintiff who could not identify the precise manufacturer of the pills ingested by her mother did not allege a cause of action. Plaintiff undoubtedly fell into this group. The response to plaintiff's contention is that a change in the law, either by statute or by case law, does not revive claims otherwise barred by the statute of limitations.

* * *

[This] rule may work a harsh result. Nonetheless, it is justified in three ways. First, the rule encourages people to bring suit to change a rule of law with which they disagree, fostering growth and preventing legal stagnation. Second, the statute of limitations is not solely a punishment for slow plaintiffs. It serves the important function of repose by allowing defendants to be free from stale litigation, especially in cases where evidence might be hard to gather due to the passage of time. Third, to hold otherwise would allow virtually unlimited litigation every time precedent changed. For example, in Li v. Yellow Cab Co. (1975) 13 Cal.3d 804, 119 Cal.Rptr. 858, 532 P.2d 1226, this court held that contributory negligence was not a total bar to recovery. There were undoubtedly thousands of potential plaintiffs through the years who had been reasonably advised to the contrary by competent counsel and so failed to bring suit. Nevertheless, allowing them all to sue within a year after the *Li* decision would have been untenable. Courts simply are not equipped to handle cases dating back many years, eventually brought because the law has changed. This prohibition against revival of claims can obviously create a hardship on such unfortunate plaintiffs (and a windfall to fortunate defendants). However, the hardship is no greater than that incurred by plaintiffs who received an adverse final judgment based on the "old" law and are barred from relitigating their case by res judicata.

* * *

Moreover, in early 1978, plaintiff's legal situation was not as dismal as it initially appears. First, she was in no worse a position than Judith Sindell, who ultimately prevailed in changing the law. Second, there were other, more traditional theories available on which plaintiff could base her lawsuit, such as civil conspiracy or joint liability under Summers v. Tice [33 Cal. 2d 80, 199 P.2d 1 (1948)]. While it is true that these theories were not clearly meritorious (indeed they were ultimately rejected by us in *Sindell*), they did provide plaintiff with a nonfrivolous cause of action. Although in the latter part of 1978 *McCreery* appeared to foreclose such a suit, that case was an intermediate appellate court decision. In this regard, the last word on the subject had not been spoken, and other Courts of Appeal were free to disregard that case. Therefore, plaintiff was not entirely forestalled, even as a practical matter, from bringing a timely suit.

Finally, even without using any of the above theories, plaintiff could have filed a timely complaint under [Cal. Code of Civ. Pro. § 474], which allows suit to be filed against a Doe party. From the time such a complaint is filed, the plaintiff has three years to identify and serve the defendant. Hence, in the instant case, plaintiff could have brought a timely Doe action, effectively enlarging the statute of limitations period for three years. Had she done so, her complaint would have been pending when *Sindell* was decided.

In sum, plaintiff's argument that *Sindell* created or revived her cause of action must fail.

* * *

NOTES

1. The discovery rule, though widespread, is not universal. Some states apply it only in certain types of cases, such as product liability cases or medical malpractice cases involving foreign objects left in the patient's body. In its absence, the limitations period begins to run whenever the statute says it does, regardless of the plaintiff's knowledge at that time. The California statute, as interpreted by the courts, begins to run on the date of injury; the injury to DES daughters occurred before birth. The limitations period usually is "tolled", i.e., does not run, until the victim becomes an adult. If the age of majority in California at the time was 18, the statute would have run on Jolly in 1969, before she even learned that her mother had taken DES. That is the kind of injustice the discovery rule is designed to prevent.

2. With or without a discovery rule, there are many disagreements as to when the limitations period begins to run. Some statutes say it begins to run "when the tort occurs" and some say "when a cause of action accrues." Courts usually interpret both of these to mean "when injury occurs," on the ground that neither a tort nor a cause of action exists until there is both a tortious act and an injury. See, e.g., Lo v. Burke, 249 Va. 311, 455 S.E.2d 9 (1995) (limitations period began to run when plaintiff's cyst became cancerous, not when physician negligently interpreted CAT scan).

3. Under the discovery rule, the question is "discover what?" In the principal case the court says the discovery rule delays the running of the limitations period "until the plaintiff is aware of her injury and its negligent cause," but that this occurs when the plaintiff suspects negligence, even if she does not yet have proof. As the opinion acknowledges, some courts say discovery does not occur until plaintiffs knows or should know *facts* establishing wrongdoing (see footnote 6). On the other hand, some courts say discovery occurs when the plaintiff knows the factual cause, even if she does not yet suspect that it is a negligent cause (see footnote 4).

FELTMEIER v. FELTMEIER

Supreme Court of Illinois 2003.
207 Ill.2d 263, 798 N.E.2d 75, 278 Ill.Dec. 228.

JUSTICE RARICK.

[Plaintiff, Lynn Feltmeier, and defendant, Robert Feltmeier, were married in 1986 and divorced in 1997. In 1999, Lynn sued Robert for intentional infliction of emotional distress. She alleged that he engaged in a pattern of physical and mental abuse which began shortly after the marriage and did not cease even after its dissolution. Lynn alleged that Robert struck and kicked her, prevented her from leaving the house, threw things at her, abused her verbally, and, after the divorce, stalked her.

[Robert moved to dismiss on the ground that the complaint failed to state a cause of action and was barred by the statute of limitations and the terms of the divorce settlement. The trial court denied the motion to dismiss but certified all three issues for interlocutory appeal. The appellate court affirmed and Robert appealed. On the first issue, the supreme court held that the conduct alleged was sufficiently extreme, and the alleged distress sufficiently severe, to state a cause of action for intentional infliction.]

The second certified question we examine is whether Lynn's claim for intentional infliction of emotional distress based on conduct prior to August 25, 1997, is barred by the applicable statute of limitations. Robert contends that each separate act of abuse triggered a new statute of limitations so that "all claims by Lynn based upon incidents occurring prior to August 25, 1997," or more than two years before the date on which Lynn filed her complaint, would be time-barred. Lynn responds that Robert's actions constitute a "continuing tort" for purposes of the statute of limitations and that her complaint, filed within two years of the occurrence of the last such tortious act, is therefore timely. The appellate court majority agreed with Lynn.

Generally, a limitations period begins to run when facts exist that authorize one party to maintain an action against another. However, under the "continuing tort" or "continuing violation" rule, "where a tort involves a continuing or repeated injury, the limitations period does not begin to run until the date of the last injury or the date the tortious acts cease."

At this juncture, we believe it important to note what does *not* constitute a continuing tort. A continuing violation or tort is occasioned by continuing unlawful acts and conduct, not by continual ill effects from an initial violation. Thus, where there is a single overt act from which subsequent damages may flow, the statute begins to run on the date the defendant invaded the plaintiff's interest and inflicted injury, and this is so despite the continuing nature of the injury. For example, in [Bank of Ravenswood v. City of Chicago, 307 Ill.App.3d 161, 240 Ill.Dec. 385, 717 N.E.2d 478 (1999)] the appellate court rejected the plaintiffs' contention that the defendant city's construction of a subway tunnel under the plaintiff's property constituted a continuing trespass violation. The plaintiffs' cause of action arose at the time its interest was invaded, *i.e.*, during the period of the subway's construction, and the fact that the subway was present below ground would be a continual effect from the initial violation, but not a continual violation.

A continuing tort, therefore, does not involve tolling the statute of limitations because of delayed or continuing injuries, but instead involves viewing the defendant's conduct as a continuous whole for prescriptive purposes. Thus, in [City of Rock Falls v. Chicago Title & Trust Co., 13 Ill.App.3d at 364, 300 N.E.2d 331 (1973)], where the defendant city and its mayor had continuously engaged in various acts of tortious interference with the utilization of the plaintiff's property over a period of three years, the appellate court held that the violation of the plaintiff's rights was a continuing tort that did not cease until the date of the last injury or when the tortious acts ceased.

This court recently examined the issue of whether a continuing violation existed in Belleville Toyota, Inc. v. Toyota Motor Sales, U.S.A., Inc., 199 Ill.2d 325, 264 Ill.Dec. 283, 770 N.E.2d 177 (2002).* There it was held that the continuing violation rule did not apply where the defendants' misconduct in the allocation of vehicles to the plaintiff did not constitute "one, continuing, unbroken, decade-long violation" of the Motor Vehicle Franchise Act. Rather, each individual allocation, made two to four times per month, was a separate violation of the Franchise Act supporting a separate cause of action, because each allocation was the result of a discrete decision by the defendants "regarding the numerous adjustable parameters that drove the computerized allocation system."

In the instant case, Robert cites *Belleville Toyota* and maintains that "each of the alleged acts of abuse inflicted by Robert upon Lynn over a 12 year period are separate and distinct incidents which give rise to separate and distinct causes of action, rather than one single, continuous, unbroken, violation or wrong which continued over the entire period of 12 years." We must disagree. While it is true that the conduct set forth in Lynn's complaint could be considered separate acts constituting separate offenses of, *inter alia,* assault, defamation and battery, Lynn has alleged, and we have found, that Robert's conduct *as a whole* states a cause of action for intentional infliction of emotional distress.

* * *

As did the appellate court below, we find the case of Pavlik v. Kornhaber, 326 Ill.App.3d 731, 260 Ill.Dec. 331, 761 N.E.2d 175 (2001), to be instructive. In *Pavlik,* the court first found that plaintiff's complaint stated a cause of action for intentional infliction of emotional distress, where the defendant's persistent notes, sexually explicit comments, insistence on meetings to discuss his desire for sexual contact and lewd behavior in their employer-employee relationship were such that a reasonable person would perceive them to be sufficiently offensive and sinister to rise to the level of extreme and outrageous behavior. The court in *Pavlik* then found that the trial court had erred in dismissing the plaintiff's claim as untimely. While the defendant argued that his sexual advances took place outside the two-year statute of limitations for personal injury, the plaintiff had alleged an ongoing campaign of offensive and outrageous sexual pursuit that established a continuing series of tortious behavior, by the same actor, and of a similar nature, such that the limitations period did not commence until the last act occurred or the conduct abated.

We find the following passage, wherein the *Pavlik* court explains its reasons for applying the continuing tort rule to the plaintiff's action for intentional infliction of emotional distress, to be particularly cogent:

---

* *Belleville Toyota* involved a claim that the defendant had violated a statute that forbade auto manufacturers from adopting or implementing an arbitrary or capricious system of allocating cars to dealers and from engaging in arbitrary, bad faith, or unconscionable actions toward dealers.— Ed.

Illinois courts have said that in many contexts, including employment, repetition of the behavior may be a critical factor in raising offensive acts to actionably outrageous ones. It may be the pattern, course and accumulation of acts that make the conduct sufficiently extreme to be actionable, whereas one instance of such behavior might not be. It would be logically inconsistent to say that each act must be independently actionable while at the same time asserting that often it is the cumulative nature of the acts that give rise to the intentional infliction of emotional distress. Likewise, we cannot say that cumulative continuous acts may be required to constitute the tort but that prescription runs from the date of the first act. Because it is impossible to pinpoint the specific moment when enough conduct has occurred to become actionable, the termination of the conduct provides the most sensible place to begin the running of the prescriptive period.

* * *

We believe the appellate court herein properly applied this reasoning to the facts of this case where:

The alleged domestic violence and abuse endured by Lynn spanned the entire 11–year marriage. No one disputes that the allegations set forth the existence of ongoing abusive behavior. Lynn's psychologist, Dr. Michael E. Althoff, found that Lynn suffered from the "battered wife syndrome." He described the psychological process as one that unfolds over time. The process by which a spouse exerts coercive control is based upon "a systematic, repetitive infliction of psychological trauma" designed to "instill terror and helplessness." Dr. Althoff indicated that the posttraumatic stress disorder from which Lynn suffered was the result of the entire series of abusive acts, not just the result of one specific incident.

* * *

Therefore, based upon the foregoing reasons, we agree with the appellate court herein, the court in *Pavlik,* and with the growing number of jurisdictions that have found that the continuing tort rule should be extended to apply in cases of intentional infliction of emotional distress.

We note, however, that embracing the concept of a continuing tort in the area of intentional infliction of emotional distress "does not throw open the doors to permit filing these actions at any time." As with any continuing tort, the statute of limitations is only held in abeyance until the date of the last injury suffered or when the tortious acts cease. Thus, we find that the two-year statute of limitations for this action began to run in August 1999, because Lynn's complaint includes allegations of tortious behavior by Robert occurring as late as that month. Applying the continuing tort rule to the instant case, Lynn's complaint, filed August 25,

1999, was clearly timely and her claims based on conduct prior to August 25, 1997, are not barred by the applicable statute of limitations.

* * *

[The court held that language in the divorce settlement releasing all claims did not bar future claims and under the continuing tort theory Lynn's cause of action did not accrue until after the settlement was signed.]

NOTES

1. "The discovery rule, like the continuing tort rule, is an equitable exception to the statute of limitations." Feltmeier, 798 N.E.2d at 89.

2. Under the continuing tort rule, the key determination is whether there is one continuing wrong or several separate ones. Some torts are complete in a single incident—battery, for example. Others, like intentional infliction of emotional distress (or negligent failure to diagnose) may become actionable only after a series of events. In *Feltmeier*, the court distinguished the *Belleville Toyota* case on the ground that the tortious conduct complained of there involved "separate and distinct incidents," while Robert's conduct "as a whole" was the basis of the complaint in *Feltmeier*. In *Belleville Toyota*, the statutory tort was "adopting or implementing an arbitrary or capricious system of allocating cars to dealers," but the court focused on the individual allocation decisions to conclude that there was no continuing tort. In *Feltmeier*, some of Robert's alleged acts may have been batteries actionable in themselves, but the claim of intentional infliction also alleged other acts that may not have been tortious in themselves. Is that a sufficient basis for distinguishing the two cases?

Applying Illinois law, the Seventh Circuit determined that *Belleville Toyota*, not *Feltmeier*, controlled a case in which the defendant allegedly converted 269 forged checks over a six year period. The holding that each transaction gave rise to a discrete cause of action, even if it was part of a pattern of conduct, meant that those occurring more than three years before suit was brought were barred by the statute of limitations. See Rodrigue v. Olin Employees Credit Union, 406 F.3d 434 (7th Cir. 2005).

3. The continuing tort idea is frequently employed in medical malpractice cases to prevent the statute of limitations from beginning to run at least until the physician's negligence ceases, apparently on the theory that the defendant has a continuing duty to recognize the problem and try to remedy it. See, e.g., Farley v. Goode, 219 Va. 969, 252 S.E.2d 594 (1979). Some states hold that the statute does not begin to run until the course of treatment ends. See Borgia v. City of New York, 12 N.Y.2d 151, 237 N.Y.S.2d 319, 187 N.E.2d 777 (1962), aff'd, 15 N.Y.2d 665, 204 N.E.2d 207, 255 N.Y.S.2d 878. A similar rule sometimes delays the triggering of the statute in legal malpractice cases until the lawyer-client relationship terminates. See O'Neill v. Tichy, 19 Cal.App.4th 114, 25 Cal.Rptr.2d 162 (1993).

4. ***Tort claims in divorce actions.*** Some courts refuse to entertain claims for intentional infliction of emotional distress between divorced or

estranged spouses, on grounds that the events leading to marital breakdown inevitably produce emotional distress, or that vindictive claims are too likely, or that tort law should leave such matters to the divorce courts. See Pickering v. Pickering, 434 N.W.2d 758 (S.D. 1989); Hakkila v. Hakkila, 112 N.M. 172, 812 P.2d 1320 (App. 1991). In an omitted portion of the *Feltmeier* opinion, the court rejected these arguments. It said the requirements that the conduct be extreme and outrageous and that the distress be severe will confine tort actions to the most egregious cases of spousal abuse. It noted that in Illinois, as in most states, divorce courts are not are not allowed to consider marital misconduct in the distribution of property when dissolving a marriage, so abuse will go uncompensated unless tort law intervenes. "After examining case law from courts around the country, we find the majority have recognized that public policy considerations should not bar actions for intentional infliction of emotional distress between spouses or former spouses based on conduct occurring during the marriage. See Henriksen [v. Cameron, 622 A.2d 1135 (Me. 1993)] and cases cited therein."

B.　STATUTES OF REPOSE

BRADWAY v. AMERICAN NATIONAL RED CROSS

United States Court of Appeals, Eleventh Circuit, 1993.
992 F.2d 298.

TJOFLAT, CHIEF JUDGE.

* * *

I.

In April 1983, when she was twenty years old, Carol Bradway underwent reconstructive surgery for facial birth defects at the Emory University Hospital in Atlanta, Georgia. Mrs. Bradway received two units of whole blood by transfusion after surgery. The hospital obtained the blood from an American National Red Cross blood bank. The Red Cross had no direct contact with Mrs. Bradway.

In July 1988, Mrs. Bradway was admitted into a hospital after a diagnosis of pneumocystis. On July 19, 1988, Mrs. Bradway's doctor informed her that she had AIDS. On April 19, 1989, Mrs. Bradway and her husband David filed a complaint alleging that Mrs. Bradway contracted AIDS during her 1983 transfusion. The Bradways sought compensatory damages, contending that the Red Cross was negligent in screening blood donors and in testing blood samples for the presence of HIV. They specifically asserted that the Red Cross, by not asking potential blood donors whether they were homosexuals, negligently failed to identify individuals possessing a high risk of being infected with the AIDS virus.

* * *

The Red Cross moved the district court to dismiss the Bradways' action as barred by Georgia's statutes of limitation and ultimate repose for medical malpractice suits. See O.C.G.A. §§ 9–3–70–71 (1982 & Supp. 1992).[1] The Bradways contended that the action was one for "ordinary" negligence, not medical malpractice. The district court concluded that under Georgia law "an action against a blood bank for the negligent collection and supply of human blood is an action for medical malpractice," and dismissed the case as barred by O.C.G.A. § 9–3–71.

The Bradways appealed this dismissal, arguing that the district court erred in classifying the case as a medical malpractice action rather than an "ordinary" negligence suit.* Since this Court determined that the case turned on an unanswered question of Georgia law, we certified the following question to the Georgia Supreme Court:

> Is a suit alleging that a not-for-profit blood bank was negligent in collecting and supplying human blood—including screening volunteer blood donors and testing blood for the presence of human immunodeficiency virus (HIV)—an action for medical malpractice and thus subject to Georgia's statutes of limitation and repose for medical malpractice actions, O.C.G.A. § 9–3–71?

The Georgia Supreme Court answered our certified question in the affirmative [on the ground that the collection, processing, and distribution of blood "are medical services involving medical judgment."] Bradway v. American Nat'l Red Cross, 426 S.E.2d 849, 850 (Ga.1993).

II.

In certifying the question above to the Georgia Supreme Court, we reasoned that "resolution of this issue of Georgia law will determine whether the Bradways' suit was dismissed properly by the district court." 965 F.2d at 993. The Bradways contend, however, that it remains to be determined "when a cause of action accrues in a medical malpractice

---

1. O.C.G.A. § 9–3–70 states:

As used in this article, the term "action for medical malpractice" means any claim for damages resulting from the death of or injury to any person arising out of:

(1) Health, medical, dental, or surgical service, diagnosis, prescription, treatment, or care rendered by a person authorized by law to perform such service or by any person acting under the supervision and control of the lawfully authorized person; or

(2) Care or service rendered by any public or private hospital, nursing home, clinic, hospital authority, facility, or institution, or by any officer, agent, or employee thereof acting within the scope of his employment.

O.C.G.A. § 9–3–71 states, in pertinent part: (a) Except as otherwise provided in this article, an action for medical malpractice shall be brought within two years after the date on which an injury or death arising from a negligent or wrongful act or omission occurred.

(b) Notwithstanding subsection (a) of this Code section, in no event may an action for medical malpractice be brought more than five years after the date on which the negligent or wrongful act or omission occurred.

(c) Subsection (a) of this Code section is intended to create a two-year statute of limitations. Subsection (b) of this Code section is intended to create a five-year statute of ultimate repose and abrogation.

* As an "ordinary" negligence case, the suit would have been governed by O.C.G.A. § 9–3–33, which provides that "[a]ctions for injuries to the person shall be brought within two years after the cause of action accrues," and would have been subject to a discovery rule tolling the statute until Mrs. Bradway learned she had AIDS.—Ed.

action for injury from a hazardous substance such as the AIDS virus." They argue that the action did not accrue until the wrong was completed, i.e., when Mrs. Bradway became infected, and that "[i]t is a jury question as to when Carol Bradway became infected with the AIDS virus." We cannot agree.

The plain language of the [repose] statute indicates that the period begins on "the date on which the negligent or wrongful act or omission occurred." The relevant acts or omissions of the Red Cross—the "screening" of the blood, the release of the blood to the hospital—each occurred more than five years before this suit was filed.

Notwithstanding the language of the statute, the Bradways contend that the statute of repose runs from the time the wrong was completed. This legal theory, however, is not open to us. One week after responding to our certified question, the Georgia Supreme Court revisited the same statute of repose in Wright v. Robinson, 426 S.E.2d 870 (Ga.1993). The court reasoned:

> There is a distinct difference between statutes of limitations and statutes of repose. "A statute of limitations normally governs the time within which legal proceedings must be commenced after the cause of action accrues. A statute of repose, however, limits the time within which an action may be brought and is not related to the accrual of any cause of action. The injury need not have occurred, much less have been discovered."
>
> A statute of repose stands as an unyielding barrier to a plaintiff's right of action. The statute of repose is absolute; the bar of the statute of limitations is contingent. The statute of repose destroys the previously existing rights so that, on the expiration of the statutory period, the cause of action no longer exists.

The Georgia statute of repose for medical malpractice bars the Bradways' suit.[3] While we may regret the application of the statute of repose to the instant facts, we cannot honestly avoid it.

* * *

NOTES

1. *Delayed claims.* Statutes of repose are a response to the possibility that despite statutes of limitations, actionable claims may arise many years after the tortious act occurs. This can happen under any statute of limitations that does not begin to run until injury occurs, and the problem is exacerbated by the discovery rule, which makes it possible for late-discovered claims to be brought many years after the injury. This creates problems not only for defendants but also for their insurers, who want to have a time certain when they can close their books on potential claims. Long-delayed claims occur with

---

3. All statutes of repose prevent plaintiffs with otherwise legitimate claims from having those claims addressed by a court of law. In passing a statute of repose, a legislature decides that there must be a time when the resolution of even just claims must defer to the demands of expediency.

some regularity in medical malpractice and defective product cases, and it is these classes of potential defendants who have been most aggressive in persuading legislatures to protect them with statutes of repose. The statute in the principal case is typical.

2. ***Tolling the statute of limitations***. The discovery rule is the most important deviation from the strict deadlines imposed by statutes of limitations. But there are other exceptions, often judicially created, that prevent the limitations period from running while the plaintiff is mentally or legally incapacitated or while the plaintiff is unable to sue because of the defendant's fraud or coercion. Do statutes of repose cut off claims even under these exceptional circumstances? As in the principal case, the statutes usually recognize no exceptions for incapacity or fraud, and their intent plainly is to provide an absolute deadline. There is no reason to think courts will be any more sympathetic to plaintiffs whose inability to file within the repose period was caused by incapacity than to those whose inability was due to ignorance of their injury. Does fraud or coercion by the defendant provide a stronger case for an exception? Cf. M.E.H. v. L.H., 177 Ill.2d 207, 226 Ill.Dec. 232, 685 N.E.2d 335 (1997) (plaintiffs' claim of child abuse by father barred by 12–year–statute of repose; plaintiffs did not explicitly argue fraud or coercion, but they did claim that trauma had caused them to repress memory of alleged abuse for 40 years).

3. ***Constitutionality of statutes of repose.*** Some state constitutions contain provisions guaranteeing "open courts" or "a remedy for every injury." Statutes of repose are sometimes found to violate these provisions when they deny the plaintiff any opportunity to bring a claim. See, e.g., Kenyon v. Hammer, 142 Ariz. 69, 688 P.2d 961 (1984). But see Zapata v. Burns, 207 Conn. 496, 542 A.2d 700 (1988), upholding a statute of repose that cut off claims 16 years before the injury occurred.

Chapter XI

Immunities

■ ■ ■

Immunities protect certain types of defendants from all or some kinds of tort liability. They differ from the defenses addressed in Chapter IX in that they depend on the identity of the defendant, not on the nature of the plaintiff's conduct. Moreover, the subject of immunities goes beyond negligence liability; immunities often avail against intentional tort liability and strict liability as well as negligence. Claims of family or charitable immunity are usually treated as affirmative defenses, but governmental immunity may preclude subject matter jurisdiction.

At one time, federal and state governments were completely immune from suit and from liability for most forms of tortious conduct. The same was true of "charitable" corporations and institutions. Family members were sometimes immune from tort actions brought by fellow family members. Although the scope of all these immunities has been restricted in the years since World War II, enough remains to make immunity an issue in many tort cases.

Charitable immunity has been abolished in most states as a general common-law doctrine, but aspects of it have reappeared in legislation immunizing or limiting liability of specific charitable organizations. See, e.g., Tex. Civ. Prac. & Rem. Code § 87.003, immunizing sponsors of livestock shows and rodeos from liability for injuries to participants; Md.Cts. & Jud.Pro.Code § 5–632, capping liability of charity hospitals at the amount of their insurance coverage provided that is at least $100,000. The remnants of charitable immunity are too scattered and idiosyncratic to be further explored here.

A. GOVERNMENT IMMUNITY

1. STATE AND LOCAL GOVERNMENTS

HICKS v. STATE

Supreme Court of New Mexico, 1975.
88 N.M. 588, 544 P.2d 1153.

MONTOYA, JUSTICE.

This appeal arises from an order of the Santa Fe County District Court granting the motion of defendant State of New Mexico to dismiss on the ground that the action of plaintiff Ron E. Hicks was barred by the doctrine of sovereign immunity.

Suit was originally brought in the District Court of Santa Fe County on August 6, 1973, to recover damages for the wrongful death of plaintiff's wife and minor daughter due allegedly to the negligence of the State Highway Department. These deaths were the result of an accident near Fort Summer, New Mexico, on December 26, 1972, when a school bus collided with a cattle truck on a narrow bridge constructed and maintained by the State Highway Department. Subsequently, defendant filed a motion to dismiss. After a hearing, the motion was granted by order of the trial court * * *.

In a memorandum decision, the district court stated that the doctrine of sovereign immunity was a long-standing common law principle which could now be changed only by legislative action. We do not agree that a change in this age-old doctrine can only be made by the legislature.

* * *

* * * The doctrine of sovereign immunity has always been a judicial creation without statutory codification and, therefore, can also be put to rest by the judiciary. * * * Merely because a court-made rule has been in effect for many years does not render it invulnerable to judicial attack once it reaches a point of obsolescence.

* * *

The original justification for the doctrine of sovereign immunity was the archaic view that "the sovereign can do no wrong." It is hardly necessary for this court to spend time to refute this feudalistic contention. This and all other rationalizations which have been advanced to justify continued adherence to this doctrine are no longer valid in New Mexico. The argument has been presented that the elimination of sovereign immunity will result in an intolerable financial burden upon the State. We believe it is safe to say that adequate insurance can be secured to eliminate that possible burden in a satisfactory manner. In addition, it would appear that placing the financial burden upon the State, which is able to distribute its losses throughout the populace, is more just and equitable than forcing the individual who is injured to bear the entire burden alone. There are presently in New Mexico no conditions or circumstances which could rationally support the doctrine of sovereign immunity. We have long recognized that the doctrine is not applicable to municipalities when engaged in a proprietary function.

Several times in the recent past this court has cast aspersions upon sovereign immunity * * *. But unfortunately, in those cases, the issue was not squarely before us, as it is today. Thus, we take this opportunity to rid the State of this legal anachronism. Common law sovereign immunity may no longer be interposed as a defense by the State, or any of its political subdivisions, in tort actions. Sovereign immunity was born out of the judicial branch of government, and it is the same branch which may dispose of the doctrine. It can no longer be justified by existing circumstances and has long been devoid of any valid justification. In so doing, we join the growing number of States which have judicially abolished it.

We recognize that this is a far-reaching decision which, at first blush, does violence to the doctrine of "stare decisis." However, we do not feel that "stare decisis" should be used to perpetuate the harsh and unjust results which blind adherence to sovereign immunity rules mandated. We concede that there was ample authority which influenced our predecessors in adopting and upholding the doctrine of sovereign immunity. We also say that there is better reasoned authority to overturn it. We simply conclude that its continuance is causing a great degree of injustice.

In today's world, we cannot discount the extent of governmental intervention and actions which affect the conduct of human affairs. We agree with the reasoning of the Supreme Court of Pennsylvania in its discussion of the doctrine in Ayala v. Philadelphia Board of Public Education, 453 Pa. 584, 592, 305 A.2d 877, 881–82 (1973), when it stated:

> Today we conclude that no reasons whatsoever exist for continuing to adhere to the doctrine of governmental immunity. Whatever may have been the basis for the inception of the doctrine, it is clear that no public policy considerations presently justify its retention.

> Governmental immunity can no longer be justified on "an amorphous mass of cumbrous language about sovereignty * * *." As one court has stated:

> " * * * it is almost incredible that in this modern age of comparative sociological enlightenment, and in a republic, the medieval absolutism supposed to be implicit in the maxim, 'the King can do no wrong,' should exempt the various branches of the government from liability for their torts, and that the entire burden of damage resulting from the wrongful acts of the government should be imposed upon the single individual who suffers the injury, rather than distributed among the entire community constituting the government, where it could be borne without hardship upon any individual, and where it justly belongs." Likewise, we agree with the Supreme Court of Florida that in preserving the sovereign immunity theory, courts have over-

looked the fact that the Revolutionary War was fought to abolish that "divine right of kings" on which the theory is based.

Moreover, we are unwilling to perpetuate the notion that "it is better that an individual should sustain an injury than that the public should suffer an inconvenience." Russell v. Men of Devon, * * * [2 T.R. 667, 673, 100 Eng.Rep. 359, 362 (1788)]. This social philosophy of nonliability is "an anachronism in the law of today." As has been noted:

The social climate which fostered the growth of absolutism and the divine right of kings in England has long since been tempered with the warm winds of humanitarianism and individual freedom. The changes which have occurred in the last century with respect to the imposition of liability upon private corporate enterprises of any kind are well-known. Workmen's compensation laws have replaced the old theories which permitted the corporate organizations to escape liability under the fellow-servant rule or the doctrine of assumption of risk. Liability may now be predicated without fault merely on grounds that potential injuries to individuals must be calculated as a part of the cost of doing business, and must be paid for by the business enterprise. *There is widespread acceptance of a philosophy that those who enjoy the fruits of the enterprise must also accept its risks and attendant responsibilities.*

(Emphasis added) (footnote omitted).

* * *

Though the foregoing case decided by the Pennsylvania Supreme Court related to liability of a local school board, we believe that the principles and reasoning enunciated therein apply equally to a State agency.

We, therefore, conclude that the ancient doctrine of sovereign immunity has lost its underpinnings by the social and governmental changes which have occurred. This view was expressed with great clarity by Justice Cardozo in the following words:

A rule which in its origins was the creation of the courts themselves, and was supposed in the making to express the *mores* of the day, may be abrogated by the courts when the *mores* have so changed that perpetuation of the rule would do violence to the social conscience.

Cardozo, The Growth of the Law 136–37 (1924).

* * *

Accordingly all prior cases wherein governmental immunity from tort liability was recognized are expressly overruled and shall no longer be considered precedents in tort actions filed against governmental agencies.

Since this action involves a significant and major change in tort liability for governmental agencies, the question of its applicability to past, pending and future cases must be determined. * * * [I]t is our considered opinion that the rule of law announced herein shall have modified prospectivity. Consequently, the decision we announce herein applies to the case at bar, all similar pending actions and all cases which may arise in the future.

* * *

OPINION ON MOTION FOR REHEARING

McMANUS, JUSTICE.

[The issue on rehearing is limited to the issue of whether our] decision should apply: (1) only to cases arising in the future; (2) to cases arising in the future and to the case at bar; or (3) to cases arising in the future, to the case at bar and to all similar pending actions.

In the original *Hicks* decision we selected the third option. The briefs and arguments presented on rehearing developed this issue much more fully than had been done in the briefs and arguments on the appeal. We now conclude that the *Hicks* decision should apply only to cases arising in the future.

[The court quoted from an article by Justice Cardozo in 109 Pa.L.Rev. 13]:

It may appear unfair to deprive the present claimant of his day in court. However, we are of the opinion it would work an even greater injustice to deny defendant and other units of government a defense on which they have had a right to rely. We believe that it is more equitable if they are permitted to plan in advance by securing liability insurance or by creating funds necessary for self-insurance. In addition, provision must be made for routinely and promptly investigating personal injury and other tort claims at the time of their occurrence in order that defendants may marshal and preserve whatever evidence is available for the proper conduct of their defense.

We find this reasoning persuasive.

It is so ordered.

* * *

SOSA, JUSTICE, dissenting.

* * * I think this ruling is harsh and unjust. I would have made the ruling applicable to the case at bar and all those cases actually filed prior to our decision, which were undisposed. They were filed based on dicta that the doctrine's demise was near. I would not penalize those that took this court at its word.

The main reason for the abolishment of sovereign immunity was that it created an injustice in the law. I feel that the majority ruling making the ruling in the case effective beginning July 1, 1976, creates another injustice.

I respectfully dissent from the order on rehearing for the above stated reasons.

NOTES

1. ***Much immunity remains.*** The original opinion in *Hicks* displays an eagerness to be rid of sovereign immunity that was short-lived. As the opinions on rehearing indicate, the decision created a backlash and the court retreated slightly, making the decision prospective only. More significantly, the New Mexico legislature promptly restored that state's immunity, subject to broad exceptions. N.M.Stat. § 41–4–1 et seq. permits liability only for injuries arising out of specified activities, which include operation of motor vehicles, buildings, parks, machinery, airports, public utilities, hospitals, and highways, and intentional torts of law enforcement officers. Claims in these permitted categories are subject to a cap of $300,000 for medical expenses and $750,000 for all other claims. Despite the statutory exception for operation of streets and highways, claims like those in the principal case might still be barred because the legislature retained immunity for claims arising out of defective design of bridges. See N.M.Stat. § 41–4–11.

Most of the other states have at least partially abolished their sovereign immunity and that of their political subdivisions, either by judicial decision or by statute. Substantial amounts of immunity remain, however. State tort claims statutes often place dollar limits on the amount of recovery against a governmental entity, or limit recovery to the amount of the government's insurance policy. Often punitive damages are precluded. Some of the statutes authorize suits against governments only in specified classes of cases, such as motor vehicle accidents. Some prescribe different rules for cities and counties than for the state. Most contain an exception for discretionary functions similar to that of the Federal Tort Claims Act, which is excerpted below, but even where the language is the same, the federal cases do not control the interpretation of state statutes.

2. ***Cities.*** Municipal immunity was never as complete as that of the state and federal governments. The common law treated some municipal activities as "proprietary," rather than governmental, and held cities liable for torts arising from those activities. The proprietary-governmental distinction has often been criticized as inconsistent and arbitrary, but it survives in many states. For example, in states where the tort claims statute places a cap on damages, suits for torts arising from proprietary activities may not be subject to the cap on the ground that the liability in those cases derives from the common law, not the tort claims statute. It is impossible to know what activities will be treated as proprietary without a careful reading of the case law of the relevant jurisdiction. Some states have attempted to assimilate their case law into their tort claims act through long lists of municipal activities that are considered governmental or proprietary. See, e.g., Tex.Civ. Prac. & Rem.Code Sec. 101.0215 (containing a nonexclusive list of 36 types of activities considered governmental).

3. ***Constitutional immunity of states.*** Recent Supreme Court jurisprudence has added a federal constitutional dimension to the immunity of

state governments. The Court has held that states are immune from private suits in federal courts under either federal or state law, see Kimel v. Florida Bd. of Regents, 528 U.S. 62, 120 S.Ct. 631, 145 L.Ed.2d 522 (2000), and cannot be sued by private parties under federal law even in their own courts, see Alden v. Maine, 527 U.S. 706, 119 S.Ct. 2240, 144 L.Ed.2d 636 (1999). Congress has no power to authorize such suits except pursuant to § 5 of the 14th amendment, which gives Congress power to enforce civil rights, see Seminole Tribe of Fla. v. Florida, 517 U.S. 44, 116 S.Ct. 1114, 134 L.Ed.2d 252 (1996). This jurisprudence, which the Court has ascribed to the Tenth and Eleventh Amendments and pre-Constitutional notions of sovereignty, means that state governments cannot be subjected to liability under federal statutes other than civil rights laws unless they waive their immunity.

This has little effect on ordinary tort claims based on state law because those are not cognizable anyway unless the state has abrogated its sovereign immunity. It has significant consequences, however, for maritime law and for federal statutory tort schemes such as the Federal Employers Liability Act, 45 U.S.C. 51 et seq., and the Jones Act, 46 U.S.C. app. 688(a). Those often create liability where state tort law would not, but they are now unavailable in suits against state governments. The federal constitutional immunity does not apply to municipal governments, however; see Alden v. Maine, supra.

2. THE "PUBLIC DUTY" DOCTRINE

When governments are protected by sovereign immunity, it is unnecessary to decide what duties they owe to persons injured by their activities. Once immunity is abrogated, new duty issues emerge. In some areas, such as operation of motor vehicles, duties established in nongovernmental cases are easily adaptable to governmental defendants. But post-immunity claims often arise from activities that have no precise counterparts in the private sector, and as to which there are no established duty rules.

We saw this in Lacey v. United States, supra p. 205, where the question was whether the Coast Guard had a duty to rescue a pilot downed at sea, and in Galanti v. United States, supra p. 211, where the question was the FBI's duty to protect a third party put in danger by law enforcement activities. The courts resolved both of those cases by interpreting general duty principles to preclude liability. Sometimes, however, courts invoke a special duty rule to absolve governmental defendants from liability even when general duty principles would seem to make them potentially liable. In some states this rule, called the "public duty rule," is applied only to police protection, while in others it is applied widely to distinguish tort duties from broader governmental duties that the court believes are owed to the public at large but not to specific victims of governmental negligence.

RISS v. CITY OF NEW YORK

New York Court of Appeals, 1968.
22 N.Y.2d 579, 293 N.Y.S.2d 897, 240 N.E.2d 860.

BREITEL, JUDGE.

This appeal presents, in a very sympathetic framework, the issue of the liability of a municipality for failure to provide special protection to a member of the public who was repeatedly threatened with personal harm and eventually suffered dire personal injuries for lack of such protection. The facts are amply described in the dissenting opinion * * *. The issue arises upon the affirmance by a divided Appellate Division of a dismissal of the complaint, after both sides had rested but before submission to the jury.

[The dissenting opinion stated the facts as follows. Linda Riss, an attractive young woman, was for more than six months terrorized by a rejected suitor well known to the courts of this State, one Burton Pugach. This miscreant, masquerading as a respectable attorney, repeatedly threatened to have Linda killed or maimed if she did not yield to him: "If I can't have you, no one else will have you, and when I get through with you, no one else will want you." In fear for her life, she went to those charged by law with the duty of preserving and safeguarding the lives of the citizens and residents of this State. Linda's repeated and almost pathetic pleas for aid were received with little more than indifference. Whatever help she was given was not commensurate with the identifiable danger. On June 14, 1959 Linda became engaged to another man. At a party held to celebrate the event, she received a phone call warning her that it was her "last chance." Completely distraught, she called the police, begging for help, but was refused. The next day Pugach carried out his dire threats in the very manner he had foretold by having a hired thug throw lye in Linda's face. Linda was blinded in one eye, lost a good portion of her vision in the other, and her face was permanently scarred. After the assault the authorities concluded that there was some basis for Linda's fears, and for the next three and one-half years, she was given around-the-clock protection.]

It is necessary immediately to distinguish those liabilities attendant upon governmental activities which have displaced or supplemented traditionally private enterprises, such as are involved in the operation of rapid transit systems, hospitals, and places of public assembly. Once sovereign immunity was abolished by statute the extension of liability on ordinary principles of tort law logically followed. To be equally distinguished are certain activities of government which provide services and facilities for the use of the public, such as highways, public buildings and the like, in the performance of which the municipality or the State may be liable under ordinary principles of tort law. The ground for liability is the provision of the services or facilities for the direct use by members of the public.*

In contrast, this case involves the provision of a governmental service to protect the public generally from external hazards and particularly to control the activities of criminal wrongdoers. The amount of protection that may be provided is limited by the resources of the community and by a considered legislative-executive decision as to how those resources may be deployed. For the courts to proclaim a new and general duty of protection in the law of tort, even to those who may be the particular seekers of protection based on specific hazards, could and would inevitably determine how the limited police resources of the community should be allocated and without predictable limits. This is quite different from the predictable allocation of resources and liabilities when public hospitals, rapid transit systems, or even highways are provided.

Before such extension of responsibilities should be dictated by the indirect imposition of tort liabilities, there should be a legislative determination that that should be the scope of public responsibility.

It is notable that the removal of sovereign immunity for tort liability was accomplished after legislative enactment and not by any judicial arrogation of power.** * * *

When one considers the greatly increased amount of crime committed throughout the cities, but especially in certain portions of them, with a repetitive and predictable pattern, it is easy to see the consequences of fixing municipal liability upon a showing of probable need for and request for protection. To be sure these are grave problems at the present time, exciting high priority activity on the part of the national, State and local governments, to which the answers are neither simple, known, or presently within reasonable controls. To foist a presumed cure for these problems by judicial innovation of a new kind of liability in tort would be foolhardy indeed and an assumption of judicial wisdom and power not possessed by the courts.

* * *

For all of these reasons, there is no warrant in judicial tradition or in the proper allocation of the powers of government for the courts, in the absence of legislation, to carve out an area of tort liability for police protection to members of the public. Quite distinguishable, of course, is the situation where the police authorities undertake responsibilities to particular members of the public and expose them, without adequate protection, to the risks which then materialize into actual losses (Schuster v. City of New York, 5 N.Y.2d 75, 180 N.Y.S.2d 265, 154 N.E.2d 534 [1958]).

---

* Recall that Edwards v. Honeywell, supra p. 180, noted a split among the states as to the duties of public utilities.—Ed.

** New York state's immunity was abolished by statute in 1929. N.Y.Ct.Claims Act § 8. In Barnardine v. City of New York, 294 N.Y. 361, 62 N.E.2d 604 (1945), the New York Court of Appeals held that the statute implicitly waived the immunity of municipalities also.—Ed.

Accordingly, the order of the Appellate Division affirming the judgment of dismissal should be affirmed.

KEATING, JUDGE, dissenting.

* * *

No one questions the proposition that the first duty of government is to assure its citizens the opportunity to live in personal security. And no one who reads the record of Linda's ordeal can reach a conclusion other than that the City of New York, acting through its agents, completely and negligently failed to fulfill this obligation to Linda.

Linda has turned to the courts of this State for redress, asking that the city be held liable in damages for its negligent failure to protect her from harm. With compelling logic, she can point out that, if a stranger, who had absolutely no obligation to aid her, had offered her assistance, and thereafter Burton Pugach was able to injure her as a result of the negligence of the volunteer, the courts would certainly require him to pay damages. Why then should the city, whose duties are imposed by law and include the prevention of crime and, consequently, extend far beyond that of the Good Samaritan, not be responsible? If a private detective acts carelessly, no one would deny that a jury could find such conduct unacceptable. Why then is the city not required to live up to at least the same minimal standards of professional competence which would be demanded of a private detective?

* * *

The fear of financial disaster is a myth. The same argument was made a generation ago in opposition to proposals that the State waive its defense of "sovereign immunity". The prophecy proved false then, and it would now. The supposed astronomical financial burden does not and would not exist. No municipality has gone bankrupt because it has had to respond in damages when a policeman causes injury through carelessly driving a police car or in the thousands of other situations where, by judicial fiat or legislative enactment, the State and its subdivisions have been held liable for the tortious conduct of their employees. Thus, in the past four or five years, New York City has been presented with an average of some 10,000 claims each year. The figure would sound ominous except for the fact the city has been paying out less than $8,000,000 on tort claims each year and this amount includes all those sidewalk defect and snow and ice cases about which the courts fret so often. * * * Certainly this is a slight burden in a budget of more than six billion dollars (less than two tenths of 1%) and of no importance as compared to the injustice of permitting unredressed wrongs to continue to go unrepaired. * * *

* * *

* * * Bernardine v. City of New York, 294 N.Y. 361, 62 N.E.2d 604 [1945] * * * is cited generally for the proposition that the State's waiver of "sovereign immunity" is applicable to its subdivisions. What is of greater interest about the case is that it premised liability on pure common-law negligence. But although "sovereign immunity", by that name, supposedly died in Bernardine v. City of New York, it has been revived in a new form. It now goes by the name "public duty". The [public duty] rule is judge made and can be judicially modified. By statute, the judicially created doctrine of "sovereign immunity" was destroyed. It was an unrighteous doctrine, carrying as it did the connotation that the government is above the law. Likewise, the law should be purged of all new evasions, which seek to avoid the full implications of the repeal of sovereign immunity.

No doubt in the future we shall have to draw limitations just as we have done in the area of private litigation, and no doubt some of these limitations will be unique to municipal liability because the problems will not have any counterpart in private tort law. But if the lines are to be drawn, let them be delineated on candid considerations of policy and fairness and not on the fictions or relics of the doctrine of "sovereign immunity."

The Appellate Division did not adopt the "no duty" theory, but said there was no negligence here because the danger was not imminent. * * * This finding does not stand examination and to its credit the city does not argue that this record would not support a finding of negligence. The danger to Linda was indeed imminent, and this fact could easily have been confirmed had there been competent police work.

* * *

NOTES

1. ***The aftermath.*** Burton Pugach was convicted and served fourteen years in prison. Eight months after he was released, he and Linda Riss were married. After 23 years of marriage to Linda, Pugach was charged with threatening to kill another woman after she broke off her five-year extramarital affair with him. Linda testified as a character witness for Pugach. To a reporter, Pugach sang his version of a Frank Sinatra song: "The end is near. This is chapter three, the final chapter in a stupid life. But I did it my way. And boy, did I foul up." See A Tangle of Affairs of the Heart, N.Y.Times April 21, 1997, at B8. Pugach was ordered to undergo counseling and stay away from the woman he had threatened. See Wife Defends Man Ordered by Court to Avoid Mistress, Buffalo News, May 8, 1997 at A9.

2. The majority opinion draws a distinction between government activities that displace or supplement traditional private enterprises (e.g., hospitals, water companies) and those that have been the sole province of government (law enforcement, streets, traffic control). Even before the abolition of sovereign immunity, most states denominated the former as "proprietary" functions and denied them immunity, while preserving immunity for "governmental" functions. That distinction survives in many of the state tort claims statutes. See, e.g., Tex. Civ. Prac. & Rem. Code § 101.0215, which applies the state's tort claims act to a nonexclusive list of 36 "governmental" functions,

and excludes all other functions as "proprietary." (The effect is that suits arising from governmental activities are subject to caps on liability and other limitations of the act, but suits arising out of proprietary functions are not.)

3. In *Schuster,* cited near the end of the majority opinion, a police informant was killed. The police had publicized the informant's part in capturing a fugitive, and the informant told the police he had been threatened. His estate alleged that the police were negligent for exposing him to risk and for failing to supply him with a bodyguard. The court held that the allegation stated a cause of action.

4. ***Voluntarily assuming a duty.*** In Florence v. Goldberg, 44 N.Y.2d 189, 404 N.Y.S.2d 583, 375 N.E.2d 763 (1978), a first-grade student was hit by a taxicab at a busy intersection near his school. For the first two weeks of class, the police department had furnished a crossing guard at the intersection, and the victim's mother, having observed the presence of the guard, ceased accompanying her child to school. On the day the child was injured, the regular guard was ill and the police department failed to provide a substitute. The court held that "a municipality whose police department voluntarily assumes a duty to supervise school crossings—the assumption of that duty having been relied upon by parents of school children—may be held liable for its negligent omission to provide a guard. * * * The department's failure to perform this duty placed the infant plaintiff in greater danger than he would have been had the duty not been assumed * * *."

The court said "[d]eployment of these resources remains, as it must, a legislative-executive decision which must be made without the benefit of hindsight." But it seemed to suggest that the interference-with-resource-allocation problem could be solved by something short of a no-duty rule: "Had the city established that a shortage of personnel precluded assignment of a patrolman to cover the intersection * * * notification of this contingency to the school principal or other appropriate action would have been sufficient to relieve the police department and New York City from liability * * *." Is case-by-case adjudication a satisfactory answer to the resource allocation issue?

5. The "public duty rule" sometimes seems to reflect a belief that compensating all the injuries and property losses that could be attributed to police negligence would create too much liability. The dissent in *Riss* argues that this is simply untrue—that liability for these injuries would impose only a slight burden on the city. Another argument might be that even if the potential liabilities are large, the legislature in abolishing sovereign immunity decided that the amount of potential liability is not "too much." But in other areas of tort law, such as pure economic loss and emotional distress, courts have created no-duty rules for the apparent purpose of preventing "too much" liability. Is it possible that the legislature expected the courts to use similar techniques (such as the public duty rule) to prevent "too much" liability once sovereign immunity was abolished?

3. FEDERAL GOVERNMENT

a. Federal Tort Claims Act

(Act of Aug. 2, 1946. 28 U.S.C.A. §§ 1346(b), [2401(b)], 2402 & 2671 et seq.)

§ 1346.   United States as Defendant

* * *

(b) Subject to the provisions of [sections 2671–80], the district courts * * * shall have exclusive jurisdiction of civil actions on claims against the United States, for money damages, accruing on and after January 1, 1945, for injury or loss of property, or personal injury or death caused by the negligent or wrongful act or omission of any employee of the Government while acting within the scope of his office or employment, under circumstances where the United States, if a private person, would be liable to the claimant in accordance with the law of the place where the act or omission occurred.

§ 2401.   Time for commencing action against United States

* * *

(b) A tort claim against the United States shall be forever barred unless it is presented in writing to the appropriate Federal agency within two years after such claim accrues or unless action is begun within six months after the date of mailing, by certified or registered mail, of notice of final denial of the claim by the agency to which it was presented.

§ 2402.   Jury Trial in Actions Against United States

* * * [A]ny action against the United States under section 1346 shall be tried by the court without a jury * * *.

§ 2671.   Definitions

As used in this chapter and sections 1346(b) and 2401(b) of this title, the term—

"Federal agency" includes the executive departments, the judicial and legislative branches, the military departments, independent establishments of the United States, and corporations primarily acting as instrumentalities or agencies of the United States, but does not include any contractor with the United States.

"Employee of the government" includes officers or employees of any federal agency, members of the military or naval forces of the United States, members of the National Guard while engaged in training or duty under section 316, 502, 503, 504, or 505 of title 32, and persons acting on behalf of a federal agency in an official capacity, temporarily or permanently in the service of the United States, whether with or without compensation * * *.

"Acting within the scope of his office or employment", in the case of a member of the military or naval forces of the United States or a member of the National Guard as defined in section 101(3) of title 32, means acting in line of duty.

§ 2674.   Liability of United States

The United States shall be liable, respecting the provisions of this title relating to tort claims, in the same manner and to the same extent as a private individual under like circumstances, but shall not be liable for interest prior to judgment or for punitive damages.

If, however, in any case wherein death was caused, the law of the place where the act or omission complained of occurred provides, or has been construed to provide, for damages only punitive in nature, the United States shall be liable for actual or compensatory damages, measured by the pecuniary injuries resulting from such death to the persons respectively, for whose benefit the action was brought, in lieu thereof.

With respect to any claim under this chapter, the United States shall be entitled to assert any defense based upon judicial or legislative immunity which otherwise would have been available to the employee of the United States whose act or omission gave rise to the claim, as well as any other defenses to which the United States is entitled.

* * *

§ 2675.   Disposition by Federal Agency as Prerequisite; Evidence

(a) An action shall not be instituted upon a claim against the United States for money damages for injury or loss of property or personal injury or death caused by the negligent or wrongful act or omission of any employee of the Government while acting within the scope of his office or employment, unless the claimant shall have first presented the claim to the appropriate Federal agency and his claim shall have been finally denied by the agency in writing and sent by certified or registered mail. The failure of an agency to make final disposition of a claim within six months after it is filed shall, at the option of the claimant any time thereafter, be deemed a final denial of the claim for purposes of this section. The provisions of this subsection shall not apply to such claims as may be asserted under the Federal Rules of Civil Procedure by third party complaint, cross-claim, or counterclaim.

(b) Action under this section shall not be instituted for any sum in excess of the amount of the claim presented to the federal agency, except where the increased amount is based upon newly discovered evidence not reasonably discoverable at the time of presenting the claim to the federal agency, or upon allegation and proof of intervening facts, relating to the amount of the claim.

(c) Disposition of any claim by the Attorney General or other head of a federal agency shall not be competent evidence of liability or amount of damages.

§ 2680.   Exceptions

The provisions of this chapter and section 1346(b) of this title shall not apply to—

(a) Any claim based upon an act or omission of an employee of the Government, exercising due care, in the execution of a statute or regulation, whether or not such statute or regulation be valid, or based upon the exercise or performance or the failure to exercise or perform a discretionary function or duty on the part of a federal agency or an employee of the Government, whether or not the discretion involved be abused.

* * *

(h) Any claim arising out of assault, battery, false imprisonment, false arrest, malicious prosecution, abuse of process, libel, slander, misrepresentation, deceit, or interference with contract rights: Provided, That, with regard to acts or omissions of investigative or law enforcement officers of the United States Government, the provisions of this chapter and section 1346(b) of this title shall apply to any claim arising, on or after the date of the enactment of this proviso, out of assault, battery, false imprisonment, false arrest, abuse of process, or malicious prosecution. For the purpose of this subsection, "investigative or law enforcement officer" means any officer of the United States who is empowered by law to execute searches, to seize evidence, or to make arrests for violations of Federal law. * * *

(i) Any claim for damages caused by the fiscal operations of the Treasury or by the regulation of the monetary system.

(j) Any claim arising out of the combatant activities of the military or naval forces, or the Coast Guard, during time of war.

(k) Any claim arising in a foreign country.

* * *

MERANDO v. UNITED STATES

United States Court of Appeals, Third Circuit, 2008.
517 F.3d 160.

GREENBERG, CIRCUIT JUDGE.

[Merando's wife and daughter were killed instantly when a tree fell on a highway in the Delaware Water Gap National Recreation Area and crushed the car in which they were riding. More than ten years before the accident, the tree had been topped and delimbed. The tree died and the dead trunk was left leaning over the highway. Merando sued for wrongful death under the Federal Tort Claims Act. The district court dismissed on the ground that the discretionary function exception immunized the government from suit.]

* * *

A. The Discretionary Function Exception

The United States of America, as a sovereign, is immune from suit unless it consents to be sued. Nevertheless, under the FTCA, the United States has waived its sovereign immunity for:

> claims * * * for money damages * * * for injury or loss of property, or personal injury or death caused by the negligent or wrongful act or omission of any employee of the Government while acting within the scope of his office or employment, under circumstances where the United States, if a private person, would be liable to the claimant in accordance with the law of the place where the act or omission occurred.

The FTCA carves out a "discretionary function" exception, however, which provides that the Government cannot be sued for any claim based upon "the exercise or performance or the failure to exercise or perform a discretionary function or duty on the part of a federal agency or an employee of the Government, whether or not the discretion involved be abused." The plaintiff, here Mr. Merando, bears the burden of demonstrating that his claims fall within the scope of the FTCA's waiver of government immunity, but " '[t]he United States has the burden of proving the applicability of the discretionary function exception.' "

The discretionary function exception "marks the boundary between Congress' willingness to impose tort liability upon the United States and its desire to protect certain governmental activities from exposure to suit by private individuals." The exception's purpose is "to prevent judicial 'second-guessing' of legislative and administrative decisions grounded in social, economic, and political policy through the medium of an action in tort."

Courts make two-part inquiries to determine whether the discretionary function exception applies in any particular case. First, a court must determine whether the act giving rise to the alleged injury and thus the suit involves an "element of judgment or choice." "The requirement of judgment or choice is not satisfied if a 'federal statute, regulation, or policy specifically prescribes a course of action for an employee to follow,' because 'the employee has no rightful option but to adhere to the directive.' " The Supreme Court has stated:

> [I]f a regulation mandates particular conduct, and the employee obeys the direction, the Government will be protected because the action will be deemed in furtherance of the policies which led to the promulgation of the regulation. If the employee violates the mandatory regulation, there will be no shelter from liability because there is no room for choice and the action will be contrary to policy. On the other hand, if a regulation allows the employee discretion, the very existence of the regulation creates a strong presumption that a discretionary act authorized by the regulation involves consideration of the same policies which led to the promulgation of the regulations.

[United States v. Gaubert, 499 U.S. 315, 324 (1991).]

Second, even if the challenged conduct involves an element of judgment, the court must determine "whether that judgment is of the kind that the discretionary function exception was designed to shield."

> Because the purpose of the exception is to prevent judicial 'second-guessing' of legislative and administrative decisions grounded in social, economic, and political policy through the medium of an action in tort, when properly construed, the exception protects only governmental actions and decisions based on considerations of public policy.

The "focus of the inquiry is not on the agent's subjective intent in exercising the discretion conferred by the statute or regulation, but on the nature of the actions taken and on whether they are susceptible to policy analysis."

B. The Challenged Government Conduct

Before we can make the two-part *Gaubert* inquiry to determine whether the discretionary function exception immunizes the Government from a suit based on its conduct, we must identify the conduct at issue. [The court concluded that the only relevant conduct was the Park Service's alleged negligent failure to find and remove the hazardous tree.]

C. Whether the Discretionary Function Exception Immunizes the Government from a Lawsuit Based on its Conduct

Now that we have identified the Government's conduct at issue in this case, we determine whether the discretionary function exception immunizes it from a lawsuit based on that conduct. In this inquiry we first must decide whether a statute, regulation, or policy required the Park Service to locate and manage hazardous trees in any specific manner, or whether the Government's actions were discretionary because they involved an "element of judgment or choice." [*Gaubert*.]

* * *

Although the Park Service has not instituted a written hazardous tree management plan, its Roads and Trails crews follow an unwritten plan for identifying and removing hazardous trees in the Park. In areas of high visitor usage, i.e., where people are known to congregate and buildings are located, the Roads and Trails crews inspect trees on foot, looking at individual trees. In undeveloped, low usage areas, Roads and Trails crews perform "windshield inspections": while driving they survey the scene for dangerous conditions. If a tree or limb impedes traffic on the road, is leaning into the road, overhangs the road, or otherwise is made known to the crew as defective, the crew gets out and examines the tree more closely. There is no specific route or schedule for windshield inspections.

Once a Park Service crew identifies a hazardous tree, it will take steps to manage the problem the same or the next day, depending on the availability of proper equipment. Pursuant to the unwritten policy, Park

Service crews will not top trees and leave the trunk standing, because a topped tree quickly will die and become hazardous.

In considering whether the discretionary function exception protected the Government in this case, the District Court looked to three cases for guidance. Because we, too, find that these cases are particularly useful for our analysis, we will review them as well.

In [United States v. S.A. Empresa (Varig Airlines), 467 U.S. 797 (1984)], the Supreme Court held that the discretionary function exception immunized the Government from suit for its alleged negligence in certifying two separate planes for use in commercial aviation. The Government had devised a system of compliance review in which it would "spot-check" aircraft manufacturers' own inspections and tests to establish that an aircraft design conformed to safety regulations. The Court stated that the plaintiffs' "contention that the FAA was negligent in failing to inspect certain elements of aircraft design before certificating the [aircraft] necessarily challenges two aspects of the certification procedure: the FAA's decision to implement the 'spot-check' system of compliance review, and the application of that 'spot-check' system to the particular aircraft involved in these cases." The Court concluded that the discretionary function exception immunized the Government's decision to implement the "spot-check" system, and stated:

> the FAA has determined that a program of "spot-checking" * * * best accommodates the goal of air transportation safety and the reality of finite agency resources. Judicial intervention in such decisionmaking through private tort suits would require the courts to "second-guess" the political, social, and economic judgments of an agency exercising its regulatory function. It was precisely this sort of judicial intervention in policymaking that the discretionary function exception was designed to prevent.

The Court also determined that "the acts of FAA employees in executing the 'spot-check' program in accordance with agency directives are protected by the discretionary function exception as well," because the employees were specifically empowered to make policy judgments regarding the degree of confidence that might reasonably be placed in a given manufacturer, the need to maximize compliance with FAA regulations, and the efficient allocation of agency resources.

In Mitchell v. United States, [225 F.3d 361 (3d Cir. 2000)] we concluded that the discretionary function exception immunized the Government from a lawsuit brought by a plaintiff whose car collided with a concrete head-wall at the end of a drainage ditch in the Delaware Water Gap National Recreation Area. We found that the National Park Service's decision about how and when to reconstruct the road was a discretionary decision that required the Park Service to "balance its mission of preserving the parklands against the severity of design flaws and the different levels of deterioration of the road." We stated that "[t]he Service's choice to focus on a few highly dangerous portions of the road rather than to distribute its finite resources along the whole of Route 209 is a policy choice this court should not second-guess."

* * *

[In Autery v. United States, 992 F.2d 1523 (11th Cir. 1993)] a tree fell on a car as it drove through the Great Smoky Mountain National Park, killing one passenger and injuring another. At the time of the accident, the Government had an unwritten policy under which its personnel would conduct visual inspections of trees while driving along the road, and more closely inspect any tree that appeared hazardous. The issue before the court of appeals was "whether controlling statutes, regulations and administrative policies mandated that the Park Service inspect for hazardous trees in a specific manner. If not, then the Park officials' decision to employ a particular inspection procedure-and its execution of that plan-is protected by the discretionary function exception." The court found that there was no policy establishing a mandatory requirement so as to deprive Government personnel of discretion, and that "the inspection plan in effect at the time of the accident did not compel park employees to inspect certain trees on certain days or remove a particular number of trees per week." The court also noted that "there was no evidence presented in the district court that park personnel did not fully comply with the tree inspection procedure." The court then determined that the Government's discretionary conduct was susceptible to policy analysis:

> To decide on a method of inspecting potentially hazardous trees, and in carrying out the plan, the Park Service likely had to determine and weigh the risk of harm from trees in various locations, the need for other safety programs, the extent to which the natural state of the forest should be preserved, and the limited financial and human resources available.

Accordingly, the court held that the discretionary function exception deprived it and the district court of jurisdiction over a suit against the Government based on the decisions made by Government personnel in designing and implementing the unwritten tree inspection program in the park.

We conclude that the controlling statutes, regulations, and policies that led to the creation of the Park Service's unwritten plan did not mandate any particular methods of hazardous tree management. As the District Court noted, the Park Service "was responsible for choosing the methods by which it maintained the Park and protected its visitors. The [Park Service's] decisions concerning tree inspections, i.e. using windshield inspections for lower usage areas, involved the type of judgment or choice that the discretionary function exception protects." Like the Government's hazardous tree management plan in *Autery,* the unwritten inspection plan in this case "did not compel park employees to inspect certain trees on certain days or remove a particular number of trees per week." In these circumstances, both the Government's decision to implement "windshield inspections" for low usage areas of the Park and its selection of the method of execution of those inspections by Park Service personnel required the exercise of discretion.

Furthermore, both the Park Service's decision to implement the "windshield inspection" program and the execution of those inspections by Park personnel are susceptible to policy analysis, and thus they satisfy the second prong of the *Gaubert* inquiry for the Government to have immunity for its conduct. The Government had to consider how best to use its limited financial and human resources in a manner that balanced visitor safety with visitor enjoyment and conservation of the Park. * * *

* * *

In these circumstances, the District Court correctly concluded that the discretionary function exception immunized the Government from a lawsuit based on its decisions regarding the maintenance of the Park and the carrying out of that maintenance by the Roads and Trails crew. * * *

* * *

NOTES

1.   Note that the court asks only whether the Park Service's decisions were "susceptible to policy analysis"—not whether they actually were the product of a policy choice. That is as *Gaubert* instructs, and it has been criticized on the ground that it immunizes conduct on the basis of judicial speculation about possible policy motives when the more likely explanation for the act is simple negligence. See Dan B. Dobbs, The Law of Torts 700 (2000).

2.   In *Gaubert*, the Court gave two examples of decisions that would not be within the exception: a government employee's automobile driving decisions, and decisions based on mathematical calculations. The lower courts have not applied the exception quite as aggressively as that suggests, see, e.g., Deasy v. United States, 99 F.3d 354 (10th Cir. 1996) (permitting suit for negligently releasing dangerous vaccine), but they have tended to interpret the discretionary immunity broadly, sometimes treating routine governmental decisions as decisions of "policy" and sometimes treating any choice as immune even if it involves no social or economic matter. See Dobbs, supra note 1, at 702–03.

3.   An unstated assumption of the principal case is that the general rule of sovereign immunity is still in force. At the federal level that immunity is relaxed only to the extent that Congress has provided. Any suit that falls within one of the exceptions to the Tort Claims Act is therefore subject to the general rule of immunity.

4.   The Federal Tort Claims Act is the major, but not the only, abrogation of federal sovereign immunity in the tort area. For example, the claim in Ira S. Bushey & Sons, Inc. v. United States, supra p. 331, was permitted under admiralty and maritime statutes. Other statutes create immunity from claims that might otherwise be permitted under the FTCA. For example, 33 U.S.C. § 702c, immunizes the U.S. from liability for damage from floods.

5. The FTCA has three crucial procedural limitations. First, section 1346(b) gives the federal courts exclusive jurisdiction. Neither the government itself nor a federal employee charged with an employment-related tort can be sued in state court. Second, section 2402 precludes jury trial. Third, sections 2401(b) and 2675(a) require that the claim be presented to the governmental agency deemed responsible within two years after it arose. The claimant may file suit only if the agency denies the claim or fails to respond within six months.

6. ***Interpreting the FTCA.*** Until passage of the FTCA in 1946, torts committed by the government were dealt with through private claim bills, in which Congress authorized payment to specific claimants on a case-by-case basis. In the decade before passage, each session of Congress considered about 2,000 such bills and passed hundreds of them. This practice not only was a burden on Congress, it also undermined the notion that the government owed no obligation to pay for its torts. Passage of the FTCA in 1946 was the culmination of a 30–year struggle in Congress to turn the business of evaluating tort claims against the government over to the courts.

Almost from the beginning, the Supreme Court limited the effect of the Act. In 1950 it created an exception giving the government immunity to suits by military personnel for injuries that "arise out of or are in the course of activity incident to service." Feres v. United States, 340 U.S. 135, 71 S.Ct. 153, 95 L.Ed. 152 (1950). This was much broader than the exception written by Congress, which retained immunity only as to service members' claims arising out of "combatant activities * * * during time of war." A few years later, the Court gave an expansive interpretation to the discretionary function exception, holding that acts as mundane as stacking bags of ammonium nitrate fertilizer in the hold of a ship were discretionary and therefore immune. Dalehite v. United States, 346 U.S. 15, 73 S.Ct. 956, 97 L.Ed. 1427 (1953). The case arose out of the Texas City disaster of 1947, an explosion that leveled the city and killed more than 560 people. Until September 11, 2001, that was the worst nonnatural disaster in American history, in terms of lives lost. The parties had agreed to accept the result in the *Dalehite* case as controlling on the liability issue in 300 other cases arising from the explosion, and it has often been speculated that the cost of such massive liability influenced the outcome. Those early decisions have continued to set the tone for judicial interpretation of the FTCA, with the result that the federal government still enjoys a great deal of immunity.

The *Gaubert* case, which established the framework within which the court in *Merando* analyzed the discretionary function exception, was another case raising the spectre of massive liabilities. The claimant was an owner of a Texas savings and loan institution who had lost millions of dollars, allegedly as the result of the government's negligence after it took over his institution in the savings and loan crisis of the 1980s. Had Gaubert's claim succeeded, the government might have faced billions of dollars in claims from other savings and loan owners similarly situated.

Congress has shown no inclination to revise the FTCA since its original passage, and the Supreme Court sometimes cites that inaction as support for its interpretations. If the Court believes the FTCA exposes the government to too much liability, should it wait for Congress to make the correction, or try to avoid the kind of massive liabilities that might spur Congress to act? The decisions contain no explicit consideration of that choice.

b. Immunity for Government Contractors

1. ***Government contractor defense.*** Before the FTCA abrogated sovereign immunity, the Supreme Court held that private contractors could not be held liable for damages caused by the performance of work validly ordered by Congress. See Yearsley v. W.A. Ross Const. Co., 309 U.S. 18, 60 S.Ct. 413, 84 L.Ed. 554 (1940). Although it is apparent that permitting such suits would allow end runs around the government's immunity, the Court did not treat the matter as an extension of sovereign immunity. More recently, however, the Supreme Court has extrapolated from the FTCA's discretionary function exception to create a doctrine that immunizes government contractors for tort liability "for design defects in military equipment * * * when (1) the United States approved reasonably precise specifications; (2) the equipment conformed to those specifications, and (3) the supplier warned the United States about the dangers in the use of the equipment that were known to the supplier but not to the United States." Boyle v. United Technologies Corp., 487 U.S. 500, 108 S.Ct. 2510, 101 L.Ed.2d 442 (1988).

The Court described this doctrine as a federal common law rule justified by the federal interest in making sure the government gets the equipment it wants at prices that are not inflated by the contractor's risk of tort liability. Such liability would produce the same sort of second-guessing that the discretionary function exception aims to prevent when the decision in question is made by the government itself, the majority argued. Three dissenting justices argued that the decision ignored the basic tort law assumption that "the imposition of liability encourages actors to prevent any injury whose expected cost exceeds the cost of prevention." A state court applying the *Boyle* test said the decision gave defense contractors a result they had been unable to secure through 50 years of lobbying Congress. See Pietz v. Orthopedic Equipment Co., Inc., 562 So.2d 152, 156 (Ala. 1989).

The *Boyle* decision in terms applied only to military contractors, but some courts suggest that the defense applies to government procurement contracts generally, because its purpose is to protect the government's discretion in specifying what it wants its contractors to supply and that interest exists in civilian as well as military contexts. See, e.g., Bennett v. MIS Corp., 607 F.3d 1076 (6th Cir. 2010) (citing cases). See also Ackerson v. Bean Dredging LLC, 589 F.3d 196 (5th Cir. 2009) (relying largely on Yardsley in dismissing claims against civilian contractors whose work allegedly exacerbated harm from Hurricane Katrina). But see In re Hawaii Federal Asbestos Cases, 960 F.2d 806 (9th Cir. 1992), refusing to apply the doctrine to a nonmilitary contractor.

2. ***Expanding the contractor defense***. Congress expanded the contractor defense significantly with the SAFETY ("Support Anti–Terror-

ism by Fostering Effective Technologies") Act of 2002, 6 U.S.C. §§ 441–44 (2006). The statute applies to contractors who supply "qualified anti-terrorism technologies" to *any* government or private entity. A supplier qualifies by obtaining certification from the Department of Homeland Security that its product or service is intended for the purpose of combating terrorism. Certification creates a rebuttable presumption that the supplier is entitled to the government contractor defense in any tort action arising from an unlawful act "designed or intended to cause mass destruction, injury, or other loss to citizens or institutions of the United States." The presumption can be defeated by producing clear and convincing evidence that the supplier committed fraud in obtaining certification. The federal courts are given exclusive jurisdiction, and if a case survives the government contractor defense, punitive damages are not permitted, compensatory damages are limited, and the collateral source rule is abrogated.

Among those who have received certification are suppliers of bomb-sniffing dogs, the association that promulgates the National Fire Protection code, a company that provides alarm systems for commercial buildings, and the National Football League's guidelines for stadium security. See DHS Safety Act Approved Product List, http://www.safetyact.gov.

4. IMMUNITY OF GOVERNMENT OFFICIALS AND EMPLOYEES

In addition to the government's immunity, governmental officers sometimes have immunity from claims against them individually. All federal officers and employees enjoy virtually absolute immunity by virtue of the Federal Employees Liability Reform and Tort Compensation Act of 1988. Unless the tort involves violation of the Constitution or a federal statute, a federal employee sued personally is entitled to ask the attorney general to certify that the employee was acting within the scope of employment. If the attorney general so certifies, the United States becomes the defendant instead of the employee and the remedy against the government is exclusive. See 28 U.S.C. § 2679. Whether the government is liable for the employee's tort is determined pursuant to the Federal Tort Claims Act. See Williams v. United States, 71 F.3d 502 (5th Cir. 1995).

At the state level, judges, prosecutors, legislators and high-ranking executives usually have absolute immunity as long as they are acting within the powers of their offices. Other officials and employees usually have qualified immunity from personal liability for torts committed within the scope of their government employment, meaning that they are protected if they act in a good faith (though possibly unreasonable) belief that their actions are lawful. In most jurisdictions, the state or local government pays at least part of any judgment against an employee acting within the scope of employment.

B. FAMILY IMMUNITIES

PRICE v. PRICE

Supreme Court of Texas, 1987.
732 S.W.2d 316.

KILGARLIN, JUSTICE.

This case presents us with the opportunity to re-examine the validity of the doctrine of interspousal immunity. The case originated as a civil action of negligence for personal injuries brought by Kimberly Parmenter Price against her husband, Duane Price. Duane Price's motion for summary judgment was granted. The court of appeals affirmed that judgment. We reverse the judgment of the court of appeals and remand this cause to the trial court.

In July of 1983, Kimberly Parmenter * * * was injured when a motorcycle on which she was riding collided with a truck. The motorcycle was driven by Duane Price. Six months after the accident, Duane and Kimberly were married. After marriage, Kimberly brought this action seeking recovery from her husband, Duane, and from the driver of the truck, claiming that the negligence of these drivers had caused her injuries. The driver of the truck and his employer settled. The trial court, in granting summary judgment for Duane, relied on the doctrine that one spouse could not sue another for negligent conduct.

The doctrine of interspousal immunity is a part of the common law, having been judicially created. Its origins are shrouded in antiquity, but the basis of the doctrine is *"that a husband and wife are one person."*

A woman's disability during coverture was an essential ingredient in fostering the doctrine. As was stated in Thompson v. Thompson, 218 U.S. 611, 614–15, 31 S.Ct. 111, 54 L.Ed. 1180 (1910):

> At common law the husband and wife were regarded as one—the legal existence of the wife during coverture being merged in that of the husband; and, generally speaking, the wife was incapable of making contracts, of acquiring property or disposing of the same without her husband's consent. They could not enter into contracts with each other, *nor were they liable for torts committed by one against the other* (emphasis added).

An earlier thesis on American law expanded the concept of superiority of the husband over the wife even to the extent of restraining her liberty or disciplining her. While in this, the last quarter of the twentieth century, such views seem preposterous, recognition that those views were prevalent in the law makes easily understandable why suits by wives against husbands were not permitted.

However, the husband/wife unity argument as grounds for the doctrine was severely impeded by the adoption of what were known as Married Women Acts. These legislative acts occurred principally in the latter half of the nineteenth century and early twentieth century. These acts, while varying from state to state, generally gave wives the rights to own, acquire and dispose of property; to contract; and, to sue in respect to their property and contracts. Most importantly, many of the statutes specifically abolished the doctrine of the oneness of husband and wife. [One important consequence of these acts was permitting a wife to sue her husband for tortious damage to her separate property. Another was permitting binding contracts between husbands and wives. Thus, spousal immunity in modern times has been confined to personal injury suits.]

With the demise of the legal fiction of the merger of husband and wife into a single entity, the doctrine of interspousal immunity found support in considerations of marital harmony, as well as the potential for collusive lawsuits.

American jurisdictions, in upholding the doctrine, early on espoused the premise that a civil suit by one spouse against another would destroy the harmony of the home. One court, in a fire and brimstone opinion upholding the prohibition against suits between spouses, foresaw all manner of evil should the immunity doctrine be terminated. In Ritter v. Ritter, 31 Pa. 396 (1858), that court, while observing that a favorite maxim at common law was that marriage makes a man and woman one person at law, also said:

> Nothing could so complete that severance [of the marriage relationship] and degradation, as to throw open litigation to the parties. The maddest advocate for woman's rights, and for the abolition on earth of all divine institutions, could wish for no more decisive blow from the courts than this. The flames which litigation would kindle on the domestic hearth would consume in an instant the conjugal bond, and bring on a new era indeed—an era of universal discord, of unchastity, of bastardy, of dissoluteness, of violence, cruelty, and murders.

The second argument for barring interspousal suits, the possibility of collusive lawsuits, is entirely inconsistent with the subjugation of wife to husband and preservation of happy homes theses. Nevertheless, such inconsistency did not seem to trouble the courts. The possibility of collusion was alluded to in Abbott v. Abbott, 67 Me. 304 (1877), where it was suggested that a widow could raid her deceased husband's estate by claiming all sorts of wrongs by him during his lifetime. The fraud theory expanded into vogue with the advent of insurance to cover vehicular accidents. In Newton v. Weber, 119 Misc.Rep. 240, 196 N.Y.S. 113, 114 (1922), the court said of allowing a tort action by a wife against her husband, "[t]he maintenance of an action of this character, unless the sole purpose be a raid upon an insurance company, would not add to conjugal happiness and unison."

Without ascribing any reasons for doing so, Texas adopted the doctrine of interspousal immunity one hundred years ago in Nickerson and Matson v. Nickerson, 65 Tex. 281 (1886) * * *.

* * *

The doctrine remained firmly established as Texas law until Bounds v. Caudle, 560 S.W.2d 925 (Tex.1977). *Bounds* abrogated the rule as to intentional torts. In *Bounds,* this court concluded that suits for willful or intentional torts would not disrupt domestic tranquility since "the peace and harmony of a home" which had "been strained to the point where an intentional physical attack could take place" could not be further impaired by allowing a suit to recover damages.

Is there today any policy justification for retaining this feudal concept of the rights of parties to a marriage? Apparently, our colleagues on the Court of Criminal Appeals have decided "no" in respect to the marital discord argument. With their September 1, 1986 promulgation of Tex. R.Crim.Ev. 504, that court abolished the long-standing rule that one spouse could prevent the other from voluntarily giving testimony in a criminal prosecution. * * *

* * *

* * * It is difficult to fathom how denying a forum for the redress of any wrong could be said to encourage domestic tranquility. It is equally difficult to see how suits based in tort would destroy domestic tranquility while property and contract actions do not.

As to the potential for fraud and collusion, we are unable to distinguish interspousal suits from other actions for personal injury. In Whitworth v. Bynum, 699 S.W.2d 194, 197 (Tex.1985) [which held unconstitutional a statute limiting actions against automobile drivers by passengers who were close relatives of the driver], this court "refuse[d] to indulge in the assumption that close relatives will prevaricate so as to promote a spurious lawsuit." Our system of justice is capable of ascertaining the existence of fraud and collusion. * * *

* * *

The doctrine of interspousal immunity has previously been abrogated as to some causes of action in this jurisdiction. We now abolish that doctrine completely as to any cause of action. We do not limit our holding to suits involving vehicular accidents only, as has been done by some jurisdictions and as has been urged upon us in this case. To do so would be to negate meritorious claims such as was presented in Stafford v. Stafford, 726 S.W.2d 14 (Tex.1987). In that case a husband had transmitted a venereal disease to his wife, resulting in an infection that ultimately caused Mrs. Stafford the loss of her ovaries and fallopian tubes, ending for all time her ability to bear children. While we ruled for her, the issue of interspousal immunity had not been preserved for our review. To leave in place a bar to suits like that of Mrs. Stafford or other suits involving nonvehicular torts would amount to a repudiation of the constitutional guarantee of equal protection of the laws. This we will not do.

* * *

BROADBENT v. BROADBENT

Supreme Court of Arizona, 1995.
184 Ariz. 74, 907 P.2d 43.

CORCORAN, JUSTICE.

We must determine whether the doctrine of parental immunity bars Christopher Broadbent's action against his mother for negligence. We also discuss the viability of the line of Arizona cases creating and refining the parental immunity doctrine. * * *

Facts and Procedural History

I. Facts

Christopher and his mother, Laura J. Broadbent, went swimming at the family residence on April 13, 1984, their first day of swimming that year. Christopher was wearing "floaties," which are inflatable rings worn on the arms to assist a child in staying afloat. Laura understood that a child could still drown while wearing floaties and should be supervised. At the time of the accident, Christopher was two-and-a-half years old and did not know how to swim.

Laura and Christopher were by the side of the pool when the telephone rang. Laura left Christopher alone by the pool to answer the phone. Laura saw Christopher remove his floaties before she answered the phone. Laura talked on the phone 5 to 10 minutes and could not see Christopher from where she was talking. She also did not have on her contact lenses. Laura said that if she stretched the phone cord and her body, she could see the pool area, but when she did this, she could not see Christopher. She dropped the phone, ran toward the pool, and found Christopher floating in the deep end of the pool.

Laura administered cardio-pulmonary resuscitation and telephoned for the paramedics. Neither Laura nor the paramedics were able to revive Christopher. The paramedics took Christopher to the hospital where he was finally revived. As a result of this near drowning, Christopher suffered severe brain damage because of lack of oxygen. He has lost his motor skills and has no voluntary movement.

* * *

A complaint was filed on behalf of Christopher, as plaintiff, against his mother, alleging that she was negligent and caused his injuries. This action was brought to involve the Broadbents' umbrella insurance carrier in the issue of coverage. * * * The trial court granted Laura's motion for summary judgment and ruled that the parental immunity doctrine applied to the facts of this case.

* * *

Discussion

I. *History and Purpose of the Parental Immunity Doctrine*

A. *The Origins of Parental Immunity*

We begin by stating a few basic facts about the treatment of children under the law and family immunities. Under common law, a child has traditionally been considered a separate legal entity from his or her parent. Children have generally been allowed to sue their parents in property and contract actions.

The doctrine of parental immunity is an American phenomenon unknown in the English common law. Courts in Canada and Scotland have held that children may sue their parents in tort.

* * *

In Hewlett v. George, 68 Miss. 703, 711, 9 So. 885, 887 (1891), the Supreme Court of Mississippi held, without citation to legal authority, that a child could not sue her parent for being falsely imprisoned in an insane asylum because of parental immunity, a doctrine which that court created from whole cloth. As its rationale, the court stated:

> [S]o long as the parent is under obligation to care for, guide and control, and the child is under reciprocal obligation to aid and comfort and obey, no such action as this can be maintained. The peace of society, and of the families composing society, and a sound public policy, designed to subserve the repose of families and the best interests of society, forbid to the minor child a right to appear in court in the assertion of a claim to civil redress for personal injuries suffered at the hands of the parent.

Hewlett was followed by two cases that were also decided on parental immunity grounds, and these came to be known as the "great trilogy" of cases establishing the parental immunity doctrine. In McKelvey v. McKelvey, the Tennessee Supreme Court held that a minor child could not sue her father for "cruel and inhuman treatment" allegedly inflicted by her stepmother with the consent of her father. 111 Tenn. 388, 77 S.W. 664, 664–65 (1903). *McKelvey* cited *Hewlett* as the only authority for the doctrine of parental immunity and analogized the parent-child relationship to that of the husband-wife relationship, noting that the basis for the spousal immunity was, in part, the fact that husband and wife are a legal entity.

In Roller v. Roller, the Supreme Court of Washington cited *Hewlett* and held that a minor child could not sue her father for rape, even though he had been convicted of the criminal violation, because of the doctrine of parental immunity. *Roller,* 37 Wash. 242, 79 P. 788, 788–89 (1905). The *Roller* court argued that if the child recovered a money judgment from the parent and then died, the parent would then become heir to the property that had been taken from him. In addition, *Roller* argued that "the public has an interest in the financial welfare of other minor members of the family, and it would not be the policy of the law to allow the estate, which is to be looked to for the support of all the minor children, to be appropriated by any particular one."

This "great trilogy" was the inauspicious beginning of the doctrine of parental immunity, which was soon embraced by almost every state. * * * However, the courts soon began fashioning several exceptions to the doctrine, and in several states the doctrine has been abolished. * * * In several situations, parental immunity does not apply: if the parent is acting outside his parental role and within the scope of his employment; if the parent acts willfully, wantonly, or recklessly; if the child is emancipated; if the child or parent dies; if a third party is liable for the tort, then the immunity of the parent does not protect that third party; and if the tortfeasor is standing *in loco parentis,* such as a grandparent, foster parent, or teacher, then the immunity does not apply.

B.   *Parental Immunity in Arizona*

In 1967 the doctrine of parental immunity was first recognized in Arizona in Purcell v. Frazer, 7 Ariz.App. 5, 8–9, 435 P.2d 736, 739–40 (1967). In *Purcell,* the Arizona Court of Appeals held that the doctrine of parental immunity prohibited children from suing their parents for injuries resulting from a car accident allegedly caused by the parents' negligence. *Purcell,* however, was soon overruled in 1970 by Streenz v. Streenz, which held that an unemancipated minor could sue her parents for injuries resulting from a car accident. *Streenz,* 106 Ariz. 86, 88–89, 471 P.2d 282, 284–85 (1970). In *Streenz,* this court adopted the standard from the Wisconsin Supreme Court set forth in Goller v. White, 20 Wis.2d 402, 122 N.W.2d 193, 198 (1963). Under the *Goller* standard, parental immunity is abrogated except:

> (1) where the alleged negligent act involves an exercise of parental authority over the child; and

> (2) where the alleged negligent act involves an exercise of ordinary parental discretion with respect to the provision of food, clothing, housing, medical and dental services, and other care.

The cases following *Streenz* show the difficulty in applying this ambiguous standard.

In Sandoval v. Sandoval, a child sued his parents alleging that his father had negligently left the gate open, which allowed the 4–year–old child to ride his tricycle from the front yard into the street where he was run over by a car. 128 Ariz. 11, 11, 623 P.2d 800, 800 (1981). In *Sandoval,* this court devised a new test for applying the standard set forth in *Streenz:* the parent would not be immune if the parent had a duty to the world at large. If the parent's duty was "owed to the child alone and a part of the parental 'care and control' or 'other care' to be provided by the parents," then the parent was immune from liability. The court held that "the act of leaving a gate open should not subject the plaintiff's parents to suit." Further, the court noted that it did not limit the abrogation of the parental immunity doctrine to negligence in car accident cases and would, instead, "continue to consider, on a case by case basis, the actual cause of the injury and whether the act of the parent breached a duty owed to the world at large, as opposed to a duty owed to a child within the family sphere." The court reasoned that when a parent was driving a car, he had a duty to the world to drive carefully, whereas the duty to close the gate was a duty owed only to the child, and that the direct cause of the child's injuries in *Sandoval* was the car that struck him in the street, not the gate being open.

Applying *Sandoval*, the court in Schleier v. Alter held that the parents had a duty to the world at large and therefore were not immune from liability. *Schleier*, 159 Ariz. 397, 399–400, 767 P.2d 1187, 1189–90 (App.1989). In that case, the family dog, which had a history of attacking children, bit the Alters' 11–month–old child. The court of appeals characterized the duty that the parents owed as a general duty to the world to supervise their dog, which the court found to be the equivalent of a "dangerous instrumentality" to children.

The most recent Arizona case on parental immunity found the doctrine to be applicable. In Sandbak v. Sandbak, the Sandbaks' child wandered onto the next door neighbors' property where the neighbors' pit bull terrier severely mauled her. 166 Ariz. 21, 22, 800 P.2d 8, 9 (App. 1990). The parents knew that the next door neighbors owned pit bull terriers and that their daughter had a habit of wandering onto the neighbors' property. The court held that the child's claim of negligent supervision was barred, rejecting the child's argument that immunity only applied to parents' negligence with regard to legal obligations. The court rejected the Wisconsin Supreme Court's limiting interpretation of the *Goller* test in Thoreson v. Milwaukee & Suburban Transport Co., 56 Wis.2d 231, 201 N.W.2d 745, 753 (1972), which held that acts involving an "exercise of discretion with 'respect to the provision of food, clothing, housing, medical and dental services, and other care' " meant that parents were allowed "discretion in performing their legal duties." In *Thoreson*, the Wisconsin court concluded that the parent was not immune from liability for negligently supervising her child who wandered out of the house and into the street where he was injured.

Further, in *Sandbak,* the Arizona Court of Appeals rejected the argument that allowing the child to trespass on the neighbors' property was a violation of the parents' duty to the world at large, finding that violation of that duty, if it even existed, was not the proximate cause of the injury.

C. Analysis of the Policy Reasons Advanced in Support of Parental Immunity

Courts and commentators have postulated many policy reasons for the parental immunity doctrine. The primary justifications for this immunity are:

(1) Suing one's parents would disturb domestic tranquility;

(2) Suing one's parents would create a danger of fraud and collusion;

(3) Awarding damages to the child would deplete family resources;

(4) Awarding damages to the child could benefit the parent if the child predeceases the parent and the parent inherits the child's damages; and

(5) Suing one's parents would interfere with parental care, discipline, and control.

We believe that all of these justifications provide weak support for the parental immunity doctrine.

The injury to the child, more than the lawsuit, disrupts the family tranquility. In fact, if the child is not compensated for the tortious injury, then peace in the family is even less likely. In the seminal Arizona case on parental immunity, the court recognized that family tranquility would not be disturbed if the parents had liability insurance.

This fear of upsetting the family tranquility also seems unrealistic when we consider how such a lawsuit is initiated. The parent most often makes the decision to sue himself, and the parent is in effect prepared to say that he was negligent.

The danger of fraud and collusion is present in all lawsuits. We should not deny recovery to an entire class of litigants because some litigants might try to deceive the judicial system. The system can ferret out fraudulent and collusive behavior in suits brought by children against their parents just as the system detects such behavior in other contexts.

We note, too, that both of these arguments—disturbing domestic tranquility and danger of fraud and collusion—were also justifications for spousal immunity, which has been abrogated in Arizona. These same concerns could justify an immunity from suits brought by one sibling against another; however, this is an immunity that the courts have not felt the need to create. Furthermore, one of the justifications for spousal immunity was that husband and wife were considered a single legal entity, yet this legal fiction was not applied to the parent-child relationship. As noted earlier, children have always been able to maintain actions against their parents in contexts other than negligence actions, such as contract actions or for willful conduct by the parent. Therefore, the reliance on spousal immunity as a justification for parental immunity is not sound.

A damage award for the child will not deplete, or unfairly redistribute, the family's financial resources. These cases will generally not be brought if no insurance coverage is available, and therefore the worry that the family's resources will be depleted for the benefit of one child is illusory. The opposite is true. If a child has been seriously injured and needs expensive medical care, then a successful lawsuit against the parent and subsequent recovery from the insurance company could ease the financial burden on the family. It would not be a viable rule to say that liability only exists where insurance exists, but we recognize that lawsuits generally will be brought when there is potential insurance coverage.

The possibility that the parent might inherit money recovered by the child is remote. This becomes a concern only if the parent inherits as a beneficiary under intestate succession laws. This is a concern for the probate courts and the laws of intestate succession, not tort law. The remedy would be to prohibit inheritance by the parent—not to deny recovery to the injured child.

The Arizona courts have embraced the rationale that allowing a child to sue a parent would interfere with parental care, discipline, and control. See *Streenz,* 106 Ariz. at 89, 471 P.2d at 285. We have cited with approval the Wisconsin Supreme Court's statement that:

> [a] new and heavy burden would be added to the responsibility and privilege of parenthood, if within the wide scope of daily experiences common to the upbringing of children a parent could be subjected to a suit for damages for each failure to exercise care and judgment commensurate with the risk.

Sandoval, 128 Ariz. at 13, 623 P.2d at 802, quoting Lemmen v. Servais, 39 Wis.2d 75, 158 N.W.2d 341, 344 (1968).

The justification that allowing children to sue their parents would undercut parental authority and discretion has more appeal than the other rationales. However, if a child were seriously injured as a result of the exercise of parental authority, such as by a beating, then it would constitute an injury willfully inflicted, and parents are generally not immune for willful, wanton, or malicious conduct. Furthermore, such a willful beating would probably constitute child abuse and could be criminally prosecuted. See A.R.S. § 8–546 (Supp.1994).

We want to protect the right of parents to raise their children by their own methods and in accordance with their own attitudes and beliefs. The New York Court of Appeals aptly stated this concern:

> Considering the different economic, educational, cultural, ethnic and religious backgrounds which must prevail, there are so many combinations and permutations of parent-child relationships that may result that the search for a standard would necessarily be in vain. * * * For this reason parents have always had the right to determine how much independence, supervision and control a child should have, and to best judge the character and extent of development of their child.

Holodook v. Spencer, 36 N.Y.2d 35, 364 N.Y.S.2d 859, 867, 324 N.E.2d 338, 346 (1974) * * *. Though we recognize the importance of allowing parental discretion, we disagree that our searching for a standard would be "in vain." Parents do not possess unfettered discretion in raising their children.

II. The Abolishment of Parental Immunity and Adoption of the "Reasonable Parent" Standard for Parent–Child Suits

Although the above concerns make it difficult to draft a proper standard for the type of action a child may maintain against a parent, we will attempt to do so. We need to "fashion an objective standard that does not result in second-guessing parents in the management of their family affairs." First, we should make clear what the standard is *not*. We reject and hereby overrule *Sandoval,* which created the "duty to the world at large versus duty to the child alone" distinction. This distinction is not capable of uniform application and has no connection with the rationale for parental immunity. This is especially evident when we compare the facts of *Schleier* and *Sandbak.*

In *Schleier,* the negligent act was failure to restrain a dog, and the court found that this was a duty to the world; therefore, parental immunity did not apply. In *Sandbak,* the negligent act was failure to supervise a child who was bitten by a neighbor's dog, and the court found this was a duty to the child alone; therefore, parental immunity applied. The children in *Schleier* and *Sandbak* suffered similar injuries; neither case involved parental discipline, and neither case involved the "provision of food, clothing, housing, medical and dental services, and other care," unless "other care" is broadly defined. Both cases involved the negligent supervision of children. If we were to hold that parents are immune for negligent supervision of children, then the issue of liability would revolve around whether an activity could be described as "supervision" and whether lack of supervision was the cause of the injury. This would not involve a consideration of whether the activity infringed on the parents' discretionary decisions regarding care, custody, and control. Almost everything a parent does in relation to his child involves "care, custody, and control."

We add that parents always owe a parental duty to their minor child. The issue of liability should revolve around whether the parents have breached this duty and, if so, whether the breach of duty caused the injury.

In accord with the California Supreme Court, "we reject the implication of *Goller* [which this court approved in *Streenz*] that within certain aspects of the parent-child relationship, the parent has carte blanche to act negligently toward his child. * * * [A]lthough a parent has the prerogative and the duty to exercise authority over his minor child, this prerogative must be exercised within reasonable limits." *Gibson,* 479 P.2d at 652–53. We hereby reject the *Goller* test as set forth in *Streenz,* and we approve of the "reasonable parent test," in which a parent's conduct is judged by whether that parent's conduct comported with that of a reasonable and prudent parent in a similar situation.

A parent is not immune from liability for tortious conduct directed toward his child solely by reason of that relationship. And, a parent is not liable for an act or omission that injured his child if the parent acted as a reasonable and prudent parent in the situation would.

III.   Application to the Present Case

In this case, the trier of fact may find that the mother, Laura Broadbent, did not act as a reasonable and prudent parent would have in this situation. The finder of fact must determine whether leaving a two-and-a-half year old child unattended next to a swimming pool is reasonable or prudent. We fail to see why parents should not be held liable for negligence in failing to supervise their own children near the pool, when their liability would be clear had the children not been their own. We think that in most cases, if not all, the standard of care owed to a parent's own child is the same as that owed to any other child.

The paradox of parental immunity can be seen if we assume that a neighbor child from across the street was a guest and was injured at the same time and under the same circumstances as Christopher. Should the neighbor child be permitted to sue and recover damages from Laura but Christopher be denied the same opportunity?

A parent may avoid liability because there is no negligence, but not merely because of the status as parent. Children are certainly accident prone, and oftentimes those accidents are not due to the negligence of any party. The same rules of summary judgment apply to these cases as to others, and trial courts should feel free to dismiss frivolous cases on the ground that the parent has acted as a reasonable and prudent parent in a similar situation would.

Conclusion

We vacate the court of appeals' decision in this case, reverse the trial court's rulings on summary judgment, and remand to the trial court for proceedings consistent with this opinion. Laura Broadbent is not immune from liability in this case because of the doctrine of parental immunity, which we hereby abolish. We overrule *Sandoval* on the issue of parental immunity and no longer follow the *Goller* test as adopted in *Streenz*.

CHAPTER XII

MEDICAL MALPRACTICE

■ ■ ■

Medical malpractice is a species of negligence. As with any cause of action for negligence, the plaintiff must prove that the defendant failed to exercise reasonable care and that this substandard conduct was a factual and legal cause of the plaintiff's injuries. We present these medical negligence cases in a separate chapter because proving negligence and causation in a lawsuit against medical defendants presents special problems and issues.

A. PROFESSIONAL STANDARD OF CARE

MELVILLE v. SOUTHWARD

Supreme Court of Colorado, 1990.
791 P.2d 383.

CHIEF JUSTICE QUINN.

Plaintiff won a $56,000 judgment against a podiatrist for malpractice resulting in a permanent foot injury that interfered with plaintiff's ability to walk and balance herself. The court of appeals reversed and ordered judgment for the defendant on the ground that the plaintiff failed to present admissible evidence that the defendant was negligent.

Plaintiff consulted the defendant in 1980 about an ingrown toenail. Defendant removed the ingrown toenail but also suggested that the plaintiff should have a metatarsal osteotomy (cutting and shortening the metatarsal bone of a toe) to relieve discomfort. The podiatrist performed the surgery a month later in his office. He made a small incision in the top of the plaintiff's foot, used a drill to fracture the metatarsal bone and a dental burr to remove bone fragments, wrapped the foot in a bandage soaked in antibiotic, placed the foot in a half-shoe, and told the plaintiff to soak the foot in vinegar and water.

One week later plaintiff returned for a check-up. The defendant commented "I don't like the looks of this," rewrapped the foot and provided plaintiff with an antibiotic. After another week, the plaintiff complained that her foot was red, swollen, and painful. Defendant advised her to increase the amount of vinegar and soak the foot more frequently. Two days later, he told her the foot was healing and rewrapped it with clean bandages. The next day the plaintiff noticed fluid exuding from a sore near the incision and called her family physician, Dr. McGarry, who recognized that the surgical site was badly infected, admitted plaintiff to a hospital for X-rays and intravenous administration of antibiotics, and referred her to Dr. Barnard, an orthopedic surgeon.]

Plaintiff's counsel asked Doctor Barnard whether he had an opinion to a reasonable medical probability on whether the osteotomy was performed below the standard of care for such a surgical procedure. The defendant objected to this line of questioning on the basis that no foundation had been laid regarding Barnard's knowledge of the standard of care applicable to podiatry. The trial court overruled the objection and permitted Barnard to testify. Barnard testified that the osteotomy performed by the defendant was below the standard of care for two reasons: first, the surgery was unnecessary because none of the pre-surgical X-rays indicated a deformity in the metatarsal; and second, even assuming the surgery was necessary, the osteotomy was performed in an unsterile office environment and thereby subjected the bone to a high risk of infection. Barnard acknowledged in his testimony that he was unfamiliar with the standards applicable to podiatric foot surgery, was not familiar with podiatric literature, had never received any instruction on podiatry, and had never performed the surgical procedure involved in this case.

Doctor Barnard also testified, again over the defendant's objection, that the defendant's post-operative treatment of the plaintiff fell below the proper standard of care for treating an osteotomy. Barnard testified that there is a uniform physiological bone healing process for all types of bone surgeries and that proper post-operative treatment of foot surgery requires that the foot be elevated for 24 to 48 hours without weight-bearing as a means of reducing inflammation. Inflammation, according to Barnard, can cause infection. Barnard further testified that a review of the plaintiff's medical history and the defendant's notes, as well as an examination of the plaintiff's foot, revealed that the plaintiff had received inadequate post-operative treatment. Barnard based his opinion on the fact that the plaintiff's right foot had not been adequately immobilized and on the further fact that the soaking treatment provided only semi-antibiotic surface treatment of the wound and not the type of internal treatment necessary for the healing of a post-operative infection.

* * *

II.

In a medical malpractice case, * * * the plaintiff must establish that the defendant failed to conform to the standard of care ordinarily possessed and exercised by members of the same school of medicine practiced by the defendant. The standard of care in a medical malpractice action is measured by whether a reasonably careful physician of the same school of medicine as the defendant would have acted in the same manner as did the defendant in treating and caring for the plaintiff.

Unless the subject matter of a medical malpractice action lies within the ambit of common knowledge or experience of ordinary persons, the plaintiff must establish the controlling standard of care, as well as the defendant's failure to adhere to that standard, by expert opinion testimony. The reason for the requirement of expert opinion testimony in most medical malpractice cases is obvious: matters relating to medical diagnosis and treatment ordinarily involve a level of technical knowledge and skill beyond the realm of lay knowledge and experience. Without expert opinion testimony in such cases, the trier of fact would be left with no standard at all against which to evaluate the defendant's conduct.

* * *

The evidentiary standard for determining whether a member of one school of medicine may offer an opinion concerning the standard of care applicable to another school has been articulated by several appellate courts in various ways. One line of cases places emphasis on whether the expert witness is sufficiently knowledgeable of and familiar with the standard of care governing the defendant's specialty to offer an informed opinion on that issue. Another line of cases focuses primarily on whether the standard of diagnosis or treatment applicable to the expert witness' specialty is substantially identical to the standard for the defendant's practice.

There is merit in both of the above approaches. * * * In our view, therefore, the dispositive consideration in ruling on the admissibility of expert opinion testimony by a medical witness regarding whether the defendant, who practices in another school of medicine, has adhered to or deviated from the requisite standard of care in diagnosing or treating the plaintiff should be the following: (1) whether the testifying expert, although practicing a specialty different from that of the defendant, nonetheless is, by reason of knowledge, skill, experience, training, or education, so substantially familiar with the standard of care applicable to the defendant's specialty as to render the witness' opinion testimony as well—informed as would be the opinion of an expert witness practicing the same specialty as the defendant; or (2) whether the standard of care for the condition in question is substantially identical for both specialties.[1] If a

---

1. In 1988, the General Assembly enacted a statutory provision that purports to establish criteria for permitting an expert witness to testify in a medical malpractice action. The statutory provision in question, which was enacted as part of the Health Care Availability Act, applies to acts or omissions occurring on or after July 1, 1988. [It states that] "No person shall be qualified to testify as an expert witness concerning issues of negligence in any medical malpractice action or proceeding against a physician unless he not only is a licensed physician but can demonstrate by competent evidence that, as a result of training, education, knowledge, and experience in the evaluation, diagnosis, and treatment of the disease or injury which is the subject matter of the action or proceeding against the physician defendant, he was substantially familiar with applicable standards of care and practice as they relate to the act or omission which is the subject of the claim on the date of the incident. The court shall not permit an expert in one medical subspecialty to testify against a physician in another medical subspecialty unless, in addition to such a showing of substantial familiarity, there is a showing that the standards of care and practice in

proper foundation establishes either of these evidentiary predicates for admissibility, the witness should be permitted to offer an expert opinion on the standard of care applicable to the defendant's specialty and on whether the defendant breached that standard of care. * * *

III.

The practice of podiatry is defined by statute as "the diagnosis and the medical, surgical, mechanical, manipulative, and electrical treatment of disorders of the human toe and foot, including the ankle and tendons that insert into the foot." § 12–32–101(3), 5 C.R.S. (1985).[2] The practice of medicine, in contrast, includes the diagnosis, treatment, or prevention of "any human disease, ailment, pain, injury, deformity, or physical or mental condition, whether by the use of drugs, surgery, manipulation, electricity, or any physical, mechanical, or other means whatsoever." Section 12–36–106(1)(a), 5 C.R.S. (1985). Orthopedic surgery is a medical subspecialty that involves the utilization of medical, surgical, and physical methods in treating the extremities, spine, and associated structures, and, as such, includes not only foot surgery encompassed by the practice of podiatry but also other treatments and medical practices not within podiatric practices.

The fact that practicing podiatrists and orthopedic surgeons are authorized to perform surgical procedures on a patient's foot is not to say that the standard of care applicable to each discipline is necessarily the same. A patient seeking podiatric treatment is entitled to receive treatment in accordance with the principles and practices of podiatry, rather than some other school of medicine, and a podiatrist rendering treatment to a patient is entitled to be judged by the standard of reasonably careful podiatric practice exercised by members of that specialty, and not by some other school of medicine.

In this case Doctor Barnard, an orthopedic surgeon, testified that in his opinion the metatarsal osteotomy performed by the defendant did not conform to the standard of care applicable to such a surgical procedure and that the defendant did not adhere to the standard of care applicable to post—operative care and treatment of the plaintiff. We consider separately each aspect of the doctor's opinion testimony.

---

the two fields are similar. The limitations in this section shall not apply to expert witnesses testifying as to the degree or permanency of medical or physical impairment."

We express no opinion on the validity of this legislation or on what effect, if any, the statute would have on facts similar to those present here.

2. The statutory definition of podiatry in section 12–32–101(3) also states:

* * * except that "podiatry" does not include the amputation of the foot and the administration of an anesthetic other than a local anesthetic. Surgical procedures of the ankle below the level of the dermis may be performed only in a licensed or certified hospital by a podiatrist licensed in this state who is: (a) Certified by the American board of podiatric surgery; or

(b) Performing surgery under the direct supervision of a licensed podiatrist certified by the American board of podiatric surgery; or

(c) Performing surgery under the direct supervision of a person licensed to practice medicine and certified by the American board of orthopedic surgery.

A.

The trial court ruled that, because an orthopedic surgeon receives more training and education than a podiatrist, Doctor Barnard was qualified to render an opinion on the standard of care exercised by the defendant in performing the metatarsal osteotomy on the plaintiff's foot. The court of appeals disagreed with the trial court's ruling and held that Barnard's opinion testimony was nothing more than an expression of opinion that the general practice of podiatry did not meet the standard of care observed by an orthopedic surgeon in performing foot surgery. We agree with the court of appeals that the trial court erred in its evidentiary ruling.

The plaintiff failed to establish an evidentiary foundation that Doctor Barnard, by reason of his knowledge, skill, experience, training, or education, was so substantially familiar with the standard of care for podiatric surgery as to render his opinion testimony as well informed as that of a podiatrist. On the contrary, Barnard expressly acknowledged that he was not familiar either with podiatric foot care or with the standard of care applicable to a podiatrist. Under this state of the record, there was no evidentiary basis to accept Barnard, an orthopedic surgeon, as an expert witness on the standard of care applicable to the surgical procedure performed by the defendant and to permit the doctor to express the opinion that the defendant failed to exercise reasonable care in operating on the plaintiff. Nor did the plaintiff establish by way of an evidentiary predicate that the standard of care for a metatarsal osteotomy was substantially identical for both the practice of orthopedic surgery and podiatry. The court of appeals, therefore, correctly concluded that the opinion testimony of Doctor Barnard should not have been admitted on the issue of the defendant's alleged negligence in performing the metatarsal osteotomy in question.

B.

The plaintiff's malpractice claim was based not only on the defendant's alleged negligence in performing the metatarsal osteotomy but also in the defendant's post—operative care and treatment of the plaintiff. Again, a review of the record reveals that the plaintiff did not establish the necessary foundation for the admission of Doctor Barnard's expert opinion testimony on this aspect of the defendant's conduct.

The primary basis for the plaintiff's claim of negligent post-operative care and treatment was the presence of an infection that the defendant failed to adequately treat. The mere presence of an infection following surgery, however, does not establish a prima facie case of negligence. More importantly, although Doctor Barnard testified that there exists a uniform physiological bone healing process and that the diagnosis of an existing bone infection includes a consideration of such symptoms as localized swelling, redness, or drainage, and an analysis of X-rays in the case of suspected osteomyelitis, there was no foundation evidence in this case linking the particulars of Barnard's opinion testimony to the standard applicable to post-operative podiatric care and treatment. The plaintiff, for example, did not establish that Barnard, by reason of knowledge, skill, experience, training, or education, was familiar with the standard of care applicable to podiatric post-operative care and treatment of a metatarsal osteotomy. Nor did the plaintiff establish that the standard of care for treating such a condition is substantially identical for practitioners of orthopedic surgery and podiatric surgery.[3]

IV.

Although the trial court erred in permitting Doctor Barnard to offer opinion testimony on the defendant's failure to use reasonable care in the performance of the metatarsal osteotomy and in his post-operative care and treatment of the plaintiff, we believe the proper disposition of this case is not a dismissal of the plaintiff's complaint with prejudice, as ordered by the court of appeals, but a remand of the case for a new trial. In ordering the dismissal of the plaintiff's complaint, the court of appeals reasoned that when Doctor Barnard's opinion testimony was excluded from consideration, the other evidence offered by the plaintiff failed to establish a prima facie case of negligence. The plaintiff, however, never had reason to establish an adequate foundation for Barnard's opinion testimony because the trial court simply overruled the defendant's objection and thus admitted the opinion testimony without requiring any further foundation.

If the trial court had sustained the defendant's objections to Doctor Barnard's opinion testimony, as it should have done, the plaintiff might have been able to lay an adequate foundation for at least some of the doctor's opinion testimony. Although Barnard acknowledged that he was not familiar with the standard of care applicable to a podiatric metatarsal osteotomy, he might have been sufficiently familiar with the podiatric standard of care applicable to post—operative care and treatment or might have been of the view that the post—operative standard of care for a metatarsal osteotomy was identical for both orthopedic surgery and podiatry. Moreover, in the event the defendant's objection had been sustained, the plaintiff might have been able to present an adequate foundation through Doctor McGarry or some other expert witness for eliciting opinion testimony on the issue of the defendant's alleged post—operative negligence. In light of the particular circumstances of this case, we believe the appropriate disposition is to remand the case to the court of appeals with directions to return the case to the district court for a new trial. * * *

---

3. Later in the trial, after Doctor Barnard had completed his testimony, the defendant testified that podiatrists diagnose an infection in the same manner as orthopedic surgeons. The defendant also acknowledged that the X-rays relied on by Doctor Barnard for his diagnosis revealed the presence of a lytic area which, according to the defendant, could be symptomatic of osteomyelitis. This testimony of the defendant, however, occurred long after Doctor Barnard had offered his opinions on the defendant's surgical and post-surgical care and treatment of the plaintiff and cannot serve to remedy the foundational defect in Doctor Barnard's opinion testimony.

NOTES

1. In most negligence cases, the jury decides what reasonable care requires. In Chapter III we saw that industry custom, though relevant, is not controlling. The standard of the profession is controlling only in malpractice cases—not only in medical malpractice, but also in cases alleging malpractice by lawyers, accountants, engineers, and other professionals. Only rarely do courts allow recovery without proof of a violation of the professional standard. In one case, the Washington Supreme Court decided that glaucoma tests were so clearly desirable that it should be negligence as a matter of law not to give them to all ophthalmologic patients, even though the ophthalmology profession believed they were unnecessary for most patients under 40. See Helling v. Carey, 83 Wash.2d 514, 519 P.2d 981 (1974). The state legislature effectively reversed that decision, however. See Harris v. Robert C. Groth, M.D., Inc., 99 Wash.2d 438, 663 P.2d 113 (1983).

2. *Expert testimony.* The requirement that the standard of care of the profession must be established usually means that the malpractice plaintiff must find a physician who is willing to testify against a professional colleague. Courts often hold that experts offered are not qualified to testify about the matter at issue. In what is perhaps an extreme example, two physicians with many years of practice in a variety of private and public settings were held to be unqualified to testify about a nursing home's failure to guard against falls and failure to diagnose a hip fracture, on the ground that their experience was not "clinical practice" as specified by a statute. A nurse was disqualified because her experience was in hospitals, not nursing homes. The disqualifications left the plaintiff without expert testimony, resulting in dismissal of the case. See Perdieu v. Blackstone Family Practice Center, Inc., 264 Va. 408, 568 S.E.2d 703 (2002).

Sometimes the standard of care can be established through the defendant's own testimony. The defendant may agree as to what the standard is and deny only that he or she breached it. Or one defendant may establish the standard of care for a co-defendant to whom he or she seeks to shift responsibility. See, e.g., Clark v. Gibbons, 66 Cal.2d 399, 58 Cal.Rptr. 125, 426 P.2d 525 (1967) (defendant anesthesiologist's testimony established defendant surgeon's obligation to advise of duration of anesthesia needed).

Occasionally courts hold that the negligence is so obvious that the jury may infer lack of reasonable care without expert testimony. Sometimes they explain by saying: "The law is well established that expert testimony is not required where the common knowledge or experience of laymen is capable of inferring lack of care and also the required causal link." King v. Williams, 276 S.C. 478, 279 S.E.2d 618, 620 (1981) (defendant failed to order X-rays of plaintiff's injured foot despite pain and swelling that continued for nine months). Sometimes they explain by saying "res ipsa loquitur." See, e.g., Gold v. Ishak, 720 N.E.2d 1175 (Ind.App. 1999) (spark from surgical instrument used near an oxygen source caused fire); Funk v. Bonham, 204 Ind. 170, 183 N.E. 312 (1932) (sponge left inside patient's abdomen after surgery).

Practitioners of the healing arts come in many varieties. There are different "schools"—medical doctors, doctors of osteopathic medicine, chiropractors, etc. In most states the only practitioners authorized to use all methods of treatment are M.D.s and D.O.s. Practitioners of other schools are restricted; podiatrists, for example, are only authorized to treat conditions of the foot. Each of the schools has its own educational, internship, and residency requirements.It is therefore not surprising that courts insist that practitioners of one school not be judged by the standards of another. In the *Melville* case, the court did not clearly distinguish between testimony from practitioners of different schools and testimony from different specialists within the same school—internists, urologists, and pediatricians, for example, of all whom may all be found within the ranks of M.D.'s. Although the issue was whether a member of one school could testify against a member of another, the court applied a statute that speaks to testimony by experts from different medical subspecialties, not different schools of health care. But perhaps that makes sense; if the legislature intended to restrict choice of experts even among M.D.'s, it probably would be at least as insistent about restricting the choice across the presumably wider lines that separate different schools. When a patient chooses to be treated by a podiatrist or chiropractor, he or she is entitled to the standard of care of that profession, not the standards of medical doctors, and allowing testimony of an M.D. would be at least as objectionable as allowing testimony by one M.D. against another of a different specialty.

Some courts are less deferential to non-M.D. practitioners, limiting those professions' power to set their own standards. For example, in Rosenberg v. Cahill, 99 N.J. 318, 492 A.2d 371 (1985), the court held as a matter of law that a chiropractor must refer the patient to a medical doctor when the practitioner should realize that the problem is not amenable to treatment by his or her methods. Other courts adhere to the standards-of-the-profession approach, reasoning that the practitioner should not be required to make a determination—whether medical treatment is needed—that he or she may not be qualified to make. See, e.g., Kerkman v. Hintz, 142 Wis.2d 404, 418 N.W.2d 795 (1988) (requiring only that a chiropractor explain the limitations of his or her method of treatment).

Suppose the defendant is a holistic healer who treats a breast cancer with an herbal ointment, a midwife who attempts a breech delivery, or a person who treats a case of acute appendicitis by acupuncture. Would the court exclude a physician's testimony unless the physician claims knowledge of the standards of holistic healing, midwifery, or acupuncture?

3. ***Claims against HMOs and insurance companies.*** With recent changes in the delivery of health care, the cause of a medical injury may not be a physician or hospital, but a Managed Care Organization (MCO), a Health Maintenance Organization (HMO), or an insurance company. Often the contracts with these entities contain arbitration clauses, which largely exempt their actions from judicial scrutiny. When claims against them do reach the courts, they often fail. For example, in McKenzie v. Hawaii Permanente Medical Group Inc., 98 Hawai'i 296, 47 P.3d 1209 (2002), the court held that an MCO's refusal to permit its physicians to prescribe the safest drug was not actionable, asserting that cost-containment decisions were too complex to be evaluated in malpractice litigation. For extensive consideration of these is-

sues, see Symposium, The Legal Implications of Health Care Cost Containment, 36 Case Western L. Rev. 605 (1986).

B. INFORMED CONSENT

In some circumstances (for example, when immediate action is necessary to save a patient's life or prevent serious injury), a physician may proceed without obtaining the patient's consent (although generally not over the patient's objections). Normally, however, any medical procedure that would be an offensive (or harmful) touching if done by a stranger is actionable as battery if done by a physician without consent. See, e.g., Gragg v. Calandra, 297 Ill.App.3d 639, 231 Ill.Dec. 711, 696 N.E.2d 1282 (1998) (maintaining patient on life support despite contrary instructions in living will held to be actionable battery). Liability also may be based on battery in cases where the physician misrepresents material matters, because, as we saw in Chapter II, supra, consent obtained by misrepresentation is ineffective. But what of the far more common scenario, in which there was no misrepresentation but the plaintiff alleges she would not have consented if the physician had fully disclosed the risks? Such cases have generated their own special malpractice theory, grounded in negligence rather than battery.

HARRISON v. UNITED STATES

United States Court of Appeals, First Circuit, 2002.
284 F.3d 293.

TORRUELLA, CIRCUIT JUDGE.

[Dr. Louis Laz, an obstetrician and gynecologist, delivered Kenyeda Taft's second child, Melvin Harrison. Taft had informed Laz that her first child, because of its large size, suffered an injury to her shoulder during delivery, resulting in a permanent condition known as Erb's Palsy. She also informed Laz of other risk factors that increased the likelihood that her second baby would also be large, and therefore more likely to suffer similar complications during a vaginal birth: she was pregnant with her second child, and second children are usually larger than first; the fetus was male, and males are generally larger; Taft was an obese woman at the time of her pregnancy and had experienced excessive weight gain during the pregnancy. While Laz recognized these risk factors, he considered them to be normal birth risks and therefore did not discuss them with Taft. He testified that he did not discuss an elective C-section with Taft because records he obtained from the obstetrician who delivered Taft's first child indicated that that birth occurred "without any complications." Melvin weighed almost ten pounds at birth, and in the course of a difficult delivery the baby suffered an injury which resulted in Erb's Palsy, a condition that caused weakness in his arm and hand.

Taft filed suit on behalf of Melvin against Laz for medical malpractice. Since Laz was a federal employee at the time he treated Taft, the action was removed to the United States District Court for the District of Massachusetts, and the United States was substituted as the defendant under the Federal Tort Claims Act.* The plaintiff's suit alleged two grounds of negligence: (1) Laz's failure to meet the standard of care by not originally offering an elective C-section and by not performing a C-section during labor based on fetal heart monitorings; and (2) Laz's failure to obtain Taft's informed consent by not discussing the risks of vaginal birth and disclosing the alternative of a C-section. A bench trial began on December 18, 2000. At the close of the plaintiff's case, the district court granted the United States' motion for judgment as a matter of law on the question of Laz's compliance with the standard of care during labor.

At the conclusion of the bench trial, the district court determined that Laz did not fail to obtain the patient's informed consent and entered judgment for the defendant. The court found that, although the risks of vaginal birth for the baby were "something more than negligible," when these risks were balanced against the risks to the mother from a C-section, performing a cesarean section was not a reasonable medical judgment. Therefore, even though the court found that Ms. Taft would have opted for a C-section if informed of the possibility, the court concluded that "Dr. Laz was under no duty to afford [Taft] the opportunity to have a cesarean section." The plaintiff appealed the court's judgment only on the informed consent claim.]

* * *

III.

Under the Federal Tort Claims Act, 28 U.S.C. § 1346(b), state law is the source of substantive liability. To recover under a theory of informed consent in Massachusetts, a patient must prove that the physician has a duty to disclose certain information and that a breach of that duty caused the patient's injury. To establish a breach of the physician's duty of disclosure, the plaintiff must establish that: (1) a sufficiently close doctor-patient relationship exists; (2) the doctor knows or should know of the information to be disclosed; (3) the information is such that the doctor should reasonably recognize that it is material to the patient's decision; and (4) the doctor fails to disclose this information. In this case, only the materiality of the information to the patient is contested.

If a duty exists, a physician must disclose "sufficient information to enable the patient to make an informed judgment whether to give or withhold consent to a medical or surgical procedure." Harnish v. Children's Hosp. Med. Ctr., 387 Mass. 152, 439 N.E.2d 240, 242 (Mass.1982). Failure to do so constitutes medical malpractice.

There are two primary standards for determining the requisite scope of the physician's disclosure in informed consent cases: "customary practice" and "materiality." See Canterbury v. Spence, 464 F.2d 772, 786–87

---

* See Chapter XI section A–3.—Ed.

(D.C.Cir.1972). Many jurisdictions require a physician to disclose whatever information a reasonable physician in similar circumstances would customarily disclose. The Commonwealth of Massachusetts, however, has rejected the customary practice standard as providing insufficient protection for the patient's autonomy, which is the very purpose of disclosure.[4] Instead, Massachusetts has adopted the "materiality" standard, requiring the physician to disclose "information he should reasonably recognize is material to the [patient's] decision."

" 'Materiality may be said to be the significance a reasonable person, in what the physician knows or should know is his patient's position, would attach to the disclosed risk or risks in deciding whether to submit or not to submit to surgery or treatment.' " Material information "may include the nature of the patient's condition, the nature and probability of risks involved, the benefits to be reasonably expected, * * * the likely result of no treatment, and the available alternatives, including their risks and benefits."

Whether a risk of injury is material to a patient depends upon the severity of the potential injury as well as the probability of its occurrence. If the likelihood of an injury occurring is negligible, then the risk is not considered material, and the risk is insufficient to trigger the physician's duty to disclose.[5] See Feeley v. Baer, 424 Mass. 875, 679 N.E.2d 180, 182 (Mass.1997) (holding that physician had no duty to disclose risk of serious infection because plaintiffs failed to prove that there was "more than a negligible risk") * * *. Similarly, if the severity of the potential injury is "very minor," the risk is immaterial and need not be disclosed.

In the case at hand, the plaintiff, citing to *Feeley,* argues that any risk that is more than negligible automatically qualifies as a material factor that must be disclosed.* * *

* * *

The plaintiffs in *Feeley* [made the same argument]. On the particular facts, however, the *Feeley* court determined that the risk was *not* more

---

4. The Supreme Judicial Court of Massachusetts has, in prior cases, cited *Canterbury* with approval for its explanation rejecting the customary practice standard:

The decision to unveil the patient's condition and the chances as to remediation, as we shall see, is ofttimes a non-medical judgment and, if so, is a decision outside the ambit of the special [medical] standard. Where that is the situation, professional custom hardly furnishes the legal criterion for measuring the physician's responsibility to reasonably inform his patient of the options and the hazards as to treatment.

* * *

* * * Any definition of scope [of disclosure] in terms purely of a professional standard is at odds with the patient's prerogative to decide on projected therapy himself. That prerogative, we have said, is at the very foundation of the duty to disclose, and both the patient's right to know and the physician's correlative obligation to tell him are diluted to the extent that its compass is dictated by the medical profession.

464 F.2d 785–86.

5. We note, however, that there is no "magic number" for determining whether a probability of injury is sufficient to make the risk material. See *Canterbury,* 464 F.2d at 788 & n. 86 (citing cases, among which one percent chance of loss of hearing was material but 1.5 percent chance of loss of eye was not material).

than negligible. * * * The court was not, as plaintiff argues, declaring an affirmative duty to disclose any risk that is "more than negligible." Thus, the case law stands for the proposition that there is no duty to disclose negligible risks, not that all non-negligible risks are actionable if not revealed.

As a result, when the district court's analysis focused on whether the risks were "more than negligible" rather than on materiality, the district court applied the incorrect legal standard. Thus, we vacate the district court's judgment and remand the case to the district court judge to assess the materiality of the risks of vaginal birth to a reasonable person in Ms. Taft's position.[6]

Moreover, the court made a second legal error by balancing the risks to the child from a vaginal birth against the risks to the mother from a C-section and concluding that, because the C-section presented a greater risk and was therefore not medically recommended, the doctor had no duty to disclose the risks of either procedure. The materiality standard for disclosure does not incorporate a balancing test by which the court can weigh the risks of alternate treatments in deciding what information is material to the patient. An obstetrician in the delivery room is in the unique situation of having to take into account the best interests of two individuals, mother and child, in rendering medical care. As such, in recommending a course of treatment to his patients, the standard of care may require the doctor to consider the risks to the mother, the risks to the child, and the appropriate balance of these risks.

However, the standard of care that governs a conventional medical malpractice case differs from the materiality standard that governs informed consent cases. Under informed consent law, if a risk to the baby *or* a risk to the mother is material to the patient-mother's decision, the doctor has a duty to disclose that risk. Once these risks and other material information have been disclosed, it is the patient's prerogative to balance these risks and choose the form of treatment that best meets that patient's needs.

Thus, if, on remand, the district court finds that a risk existed either as to the mother's health *or* as to the child's health and that such information would have been material to a reasonable patient in Ms. Taft's position, then Dr. Laz had a duty to disclose that risk. Moreover, because there are only two methods of childbirth, if the district court finds the risk of vaginal birth to be material to the patient, then Dr. Laz also had a duty to present the alternative option of a C-section that might minimize such risk, regardless of his medical opinion on the proper course of treatment.[8]

* * *

---

6. Materiality, since it is a factual determination, is properly left for the district court to determine.

8. We emphasize that a duty to disclose, if it exists, does *not* necessarily indicate any duty to offer or to perform a C-section if the doctor does not consider one to be warranted in his medical

Notes

1. The informed consent doctrine gives the plaintiff a way to establish breach without showing that the physician violated the professional standard; it does not obviate the need to prove cause in fact. Suppose on remand the government's lawyer elicits testimony from Taft that she was aware that having a cesarean section was an option. The judge should then enter judgment for the government on the ground that the physician's failure to inform Taft of that option was not the cause in fact of the baby's injury. Note that the court says Laz was not required to offer to perform a C-section, only to inform her of the option.

2. Most courts do not allow the plaintiff to establish cause in fact merely by showing that he or she would have declined the treatment if properly informed, apparently because they distrust the plaintiff's testimony as to what he or she would have done. Instead, they require a showing that neither the patient nor a reasonable person in similar circumstances would have undergone the procedure. But see Arena v. Gingrich, 305 Or. 1, 748 P.2d 547 (1988) (holding that "What the patient in fact would have done after a full explanation is a question about that patient's behavior, not about some other 'reasonable' patient's * * *.")

3. The opinion in the principal case says the Massachusetts Supreme Judicial Court has "rejected" the customary practice standard with regard to disclosure. That may be an overstatement. *Harnish* and the other cases cited establish only that a patient may proceed on the informed consent theory even when the standards of the profession do not require disclosure. They do not suggest that the conventional theory is unavailable when the standards of the profession *do* require disclosure. There seems to be no logical reason why a plaintiff could not pursue both theories.

4. *The malpractice "crisis."* Many statutes have been passed in recent years to restrict liability for medical malpractice. Some of these create special tribunals to weed out claims before they get to court, e.g., Mass. Gen. L.Ann. 231 § 60B. Other statutes require dismissal of cases unless they are supported by detailed expert reports, e.g. Tex.Civ. Prac. & Rem. Code § 74.351; forbid the use of res ipsa loquitur in malpractice cases, e.g., N.H.Rev.Stat. § 507–C:2; or impose caps on damages, e.g., Cal.Civ.Code § 3333.2. Some forbid courts from using the informed consent theory, e.g., N.C.Gen.Stat. § 90–21.13, or restrict it to a list of specified risks developed by a panel, e.g., Tex. Civ.Prac. & Rem. Code § 74.102 et. seq.

The impetus for such legislation has been the perception that a proliferation of unfounded malpractice claims was driving up the cost of malpractice insurance, in some cases so much that physicians were forced out of practice. Whether this perception is grounded in fact is disputed. A study of claims in Texas during a period when there was alleged to be an insurance crisis showed that although premiums rose significantly, the cost of all settled and litigated malpractice claims rose very little. See Bernard Black, Charles Silver,

---

judgment. The duty to disclose is intended to be limited, so as not to unduly burden the practice of medicine.

David A. Hyman and William M. Sage, Stability, Not Crisis: Medical Malpractice Claims Outcomes in Texas, 1998–2002, 2 J. Empirical Legal Studies 207, 210 (2005).

The majority of medical mistakes do not result in malpractice claims. See, e.g., Paul C. Weiler et al, A Measure of Malpractice (1993) (reporting that 27,179 instances of negligent medical injuries produced only 3,682 claims). The Institute of Medicine, a branch of the National Academy of Science, estimated that medical errors cause between 44,000 and 98,000 deaths in hospitals each year—more than die from auto accidents or cancer. See Linda T. Kohn et al., To Err is Human: Building a Safer Health System (2000). The American Medical Association said those figures included patients who would have died anyway, and estimated that no more than 5,000 to 15,000 deaths a year are clearly caused by medical mistakes. See Rodney A. Hayward and Timothy P. Hofer, Estimating hospital deaths due to medical errors: Preventability is in the eye of the reviewer, J. of Am. Med. Ass'n, July 25, 2001.

Chapter XIII

Common Law Strict Liability

■ ■ ■

In the cases we have studied so far, the plaintiff has been required to prove that the defendant acted with "fault," that is, that the defendant either intentionally or negligently caused injury to the plaintiff.* Certain types of cases, however, are governed by doctrines under which the plaintiff need not prove negligence or intent. Courts usually refer to these doctrines as "strict liability." This chapter addresses two traditional strict liability contexts: trespassing animals and wild animals, and abnormally dangerous activities. A newer body of law, strict liability for product injuries, is addressed in Chapter XIV.

The term "strict liability" means that the plaintiff need not prove negligence or intent. It does not mean that a defendant who causes injury is automatically liable, without any means of escape. Making a defendant liable on the basis of factual causation alone would be "absolute liability" or "insurer's liability." Courts often emphasize that strict liability is not the equivalent of absolute liability. (Occasionally, however, "absolute liability" is used to *mean* strict liability.)

Strict liability means different things in different contexts. For example, the doctrine of strict liability for defective products is vastly different from strict liability for abnormally dangerous activities. The common thread is that both eschew the requirement that the plaintiff prove negligence or intent.

A. ANIMALS

The early common law rule was that the owner of animals was liable, without proof of fault, for damage caused by the animals' trespassing onto a neighbor's land. (Exceptions were made for livestock that wandered off the highway on their way to market and for wandering dogs and cats.)

The early English rule was not uniformly accepted in the United States. In several western states, where livestock needed to be left free to

---

* Some analysts put vicarious liability, supra Chapter VIII, in the strict liability category. See, e.g., Abraham, The Forms and Functions of Tort Law 166, 190 (3d ed. 2007).

graze, the English rule was rejected. The cattle-oriented states passed "fencing out" statutes that permitted courts to impose liability only if cattle broke through the complaining landowner's fence. Farm-oriented states passed statutes imposing liability unless ranchers fenced in their cattle. The current patchwork of laws on the subject of trespassing animals reflects conflict between ranching and farming interests in particular localities. These fencing statutes can also affect the respective rights of animal owners and highway users. A motorist whose vehicle collides with a cow in an open range area is in a different legal position from one who hits an animal that has escaped a statutorily required fence.

English and American courts also impose strict liability for injuries caused by wild animals. Under this rule a person who keeps a lion or tiger is liable without proof of negligence if the animal mauls or bites someone. This version of strict liability has been extended to domestic animals in the limited situation in which the owner has reason to know that the particular animal had vicious propensities. Otherwise, domestic animal owners are liable only if negligence or intent is shown. (This is the source of the common but somewhat misleading view that "every dog is entitled to one bite.") Negligence may be based upon the violation of a statute such as a leash law.

Although liability for injuries caused by wild animals is "strict," it is not "absolute." It extends only to the types of injuries that are foreseeable, given the nature of the animal. It also extends only to classes of persons to whom injury is reasonably foreseeable. The defendant may also be able to raise comparative negligence of the plaintiff as a defense.

B. ABNORMALLY DANGEROUS ACTIVITIES

RYLANDS v. FLETCHER

House of Lords, 1868.
L.R. 3 H.L. 330.

THE LORD CHANCELLOR (LORD CAIRNS).

My Lords, in this case the Plaintiff [Fletcher] is the occupier of a mine and [mine] works under a close of land. The Defendants [Rylands, et al.] are the owners of a mill in his neighbourhood, and they proposed to make a reservoir for the purpose of keeping and storing water to be used about their mill * * *. Underneath the close of land of the Defendants on which they proposed to construct their reservoir there were certain old and disused mining passages and works. There were five vertical shafts, and some horizontal shafts communicating with them. The vertical shafts had been filled up with soil and rubbish, and it does not appear that any person was aware of the existence either of the vertical shafts or of the horizontal works communicating with them. In the course of the working by the Plaintiff of his mine, he had gradually worked through the seams of coal underneath the close, and had come into contact with the old and disused works underneath the close of the Defendants.

In that state of things the reservoir of the Defendants was constructed. It was constructed by them through the agency and inspection of an engineer and contractor. Personally, the Defendants [do not] appear to have taken [any] part in the works, or to have been aware of any want of security connected with them. As regards the engineer and the contractor, we must take it from the case that they did not exercise, as far as they were concerned, that reasonable care and caution which they might have exercised, taking notice, as they appear to have taken notice, of the vertical shafts filled up in the manner which I have mentioned. [W]hen the reservoir was constructed, and filled, or partly filled, with water, the weight of the water bearing upon the disused and imperfectly filled-up vertical shafts [ ] broke through those shafts. The water passed down them and into the horizontal workings, and from the horizontal workings under the close of the Defendants it passed on into the workings under the close of the Plaintiff, and flooded his mine, causing considerable damage, for which this action was brought.

The Court of Exchequer * * * was of opinion that the Plaintiff had established no cause of action. The Court of Exchequer Chamber, before which an appeal from this judgment was argued, was of a contrary opinion, and the Judges there unanimously arrived at the conclusion that there was a cause of action, and that the Plaintiff was entitled to damages.

My Lords, the principles on which this case must be determined appear to me to be extremely simple. The Defendants, treating them as the owners or occupiers of the close on which the reservoir was constructed, might lawfully have used that close for any purpose for which it might in the ordinary course of the enjoyment of land be used; and if, in what I may term the natural use of that land, there had been any accumulation of water, either on the surface or underground, and if, by the operation of the laws of nature, that accumulation of water had passed off into the close occupied by the Plaintiff, the Plaintiff could not have complained that that result had taken place. If he had desired to guard himself against it, it would have lain upon him to have done so, by leaving, or by interposing, some barrier between his close and the close of the Defendants in order to have prevented that operation of the laws of nature.

* * *

On the other hand if the Defendants, not stopping at the natural use of their close, had desired to use it for any purpose which I may term a non-natural use, for the purpose of introducing into the close that which in its natural condition was not in or upon it, for the purpose of introducing water either above or below ground in quantities and in a manner not the result of any work or operation on or under the land—and if in consequence of their doing so, or in consequence of any imperfection in the mode of their doing so, the water came to escape and to pass off into the close of the Plaintiff, then it appears to me that that which the Defendants were doing they were doing at their own peril; and, if in the course of their doing it, the evil arose to which I have referred, the evil, namely, of the escape of the water and its passing away to the close of the Plaintiff and injuring the Plaintiff, then for the consequence of that, in my opinion, the Defendants would be liable. * * *

My Lord, these simple principles, if they are well founded, as it appears to me they are, really dispose of this case.

The same result is arrived at on the principles, referred to by Lord Blackburn in his judgment, in the Court of Exchequer Chamber, where he states the opinion of that Court as to the law in these words:

> We think that the true rule of law is, that the person who, for his own purposes, brings on his land and collects and keeps there anything likely to do mischief if it escapes, must keep it in at his peril; and if he does not do so, is *prima facie* answerable for all the damage which is the natural consequence of its escape. He can excuse himself by showing that the escape was owing to the Plaintiff's default; or, perhaps, that the escape was the consequence of *vis major,* or the act of God; but as nothing of this sort exists here, it is unnecessary to inquire what excuse would be sufficient. The general rule, as above stated, seems on principle just. The person whose grass or corn is eaten down by the escaping cattle of his neighbour, or whose mine is flooded by the water from his neighbour's reservoir, or whose cellar is invaded by the filth of his neighbour's privy, or whose habitation is made unhealthy by the fumes and noisome vapours of his neighbour's alkali works, is damnified without any fault of his own; and it seems but reasonable and just that the neighbour who has brought something on his own property (which was not naturally there), harmless to others so long as it is confined to his own property, but which he knows will be mischievous if it gets on his neighbour's, should be obliged to make good the damage which ensues if he does not succeed in confining it to his own property. But for his act in bringing it there no mischief could have accrued, and it seems but just that he should at his peril keep it there, so that no mischief may accrue, or answer for the natural and anticipated consequence. And upon authority this we think is established to be the law, whether the things so brought be beasts, or water, or filth, or stenches.

My Lords, in that opinion, I must say I entirely concur. Therefore, I have to move your Lordships that the judgment of the Court of Exchequer Chamber be affirmed, and that the present appeal be dismissed with costs.

Judgment of the Court of Exchequer Chamber affirmed.

NOTES

1. ***The basis of liability in* Rylands *is not clear*. The case was decided at a time when English courts were starting to apply negligence rather than strict liability to certain types of cases. (See supra pp. 66–68.) For example, in 1856 the Court of Exchequer had decided Blyth v. Birmingham Waterworks Co., 11 Ex. 781, 156 Eng.Rep. 1047 (1856). The defendant's pipes

burst in "[o]ne of the severest frosts on record." A plug had been installed to relieve pressure, but it failed because it was encrusted with snow and ice. The escaping water damaged the plaintiff's house. The court held that the defendant was not negligent and, therefore, was not liable. Baron Bramwell, who later dissented in Fletcher v. Rylands in the Court of Exchequer by voting in favor of liability, stated in *Blyth* that "the plaintiff was under quite as much obligation to remove the ice and snow which had accumulated as the defendants."

At the time of *Rylands,* trespass to land cases were governed by strict liability. But Fletcher did not sue for trespass, perhaps because Rylands acted through an agent rather than directly.

Lord Blackburn's opinion in the Exchequer Chamber seemed to portray a background system of liability that generally applied strict liability, with certain exceptions where negligence was required. He argued that the common thread of the cases in which negligence was required was that, in all of them, the plaintiff could be viewed as having assumed the risk, such as by venturing out on the public highway. On that view, the *Rylands* plaintiff had an uncomplicated strict liability case. (Lord Blackburn did not cite *Blyth,* but he might have distinguished it on the ground that it involved a defendant acting in accordance with a municipal charter.)

Lord Cairns' opinion in the House of Lords had a different flavor. Unlike Lord Blackburn, Lord Cairns did not distinguish the growing number of cases requiring proof of negligence. He believed that strict liability governed any case in which a person brings something onto his land that later escapes to injure someone else's land.

Note that Lord Cairns distinguished the defendant's reservoir from water (or some other substance) that occurs naturally on the defendant's land. We saw a similar distinction in Chapter VI in connection with the duties of owners and occupiers of land. There is no overt reliance in Lord Cairns' opinion on the unusual or abnormal nature of a reservoir in a coal-mining region of England. Instead, his point seems to have been that owners and occupiers of land were strictly liable for artificial (non-natural) conditions on their land that caused injury to their neighbour's land.

2. ***American strict liability for "abnormally dangerous" activities***. Notwithstanding the ambiguity of the original basis of liability in *Rylands,* the case was later interpreted by American courts and scholars to embody a special island of strict liability in a sea of negligence. Ultimately, courts and scholars came to interpret *Rylands* as embodying strict liability for abnormally dangerous (that is, abnormal *and* dangerous) activities. These courts and scholars pointed to the fact that a reservoir was unusual or abnormal in a coal-mining region. They then relied on this fact to interpret Lord Cairns' reference to "non-natural" uses as meaning "abnormal" or "unusual" uses.

This interpretation is both broader and narrower than *Rylands* might have been interpreted. It is broader because it applies to situations other than injury to land. It is narrower because it does not apply to all non-natural uses of land; it applies only to abnormally dangerous activities.

A famous American case adopting strict liability for abnormally dangerous activities is Exner v. Sherman Power Construction Co., 54 F.2d 510 (2d Cir.1931). The defendant stored dynamite for use on a construction project. The dynamite exploded, and the concussion injured the plaintiff and his real property. The court held that blasting cases are governed by strict liability. The opinion, written by Augustus Hand, did not make absolutely clear why this was so. At times Judge Hand relied on the fact that trespasses to land had historically been governed by strict liability. But at other times he suggested that the distinction between trespassory and non-trespassory causes of action was not controlling. (*Exner* itself did not involve an action for trespass in the traditional sense; the plaintiff and his land were injured by the concussion, not by any debris.) Thus, as with *Rylands,* the basis of liability in *Exner* is somewhat obscure. Nevertheless, *Exner* too came to be interpreted as an example of strict liability for abnormally dangerous activities, irrespective of whether the case involved an injury to land.

Not all American courts have adopted the "doctrine of Rylands v. Fletcher." For example, in Turner v. Big Lake Oil Co., 128 Tex. 155, 96 S.W.2d 221 (1936), the defendant used artificial ponds to collect salt water residue from its oil well operations. When the salt water escaped and polluted a neighbor's ponds, the neighbor sued. The Court rejected strict liability under the "doctrine of Rylands v. Fletcher." It instead required the plaintiff to prove negligence. The Court reasoned that a reservoir might have been an abnormal use of land in a coal-mining region of England, but artificial ponds are normal and essential in semi-arid portions of Texas. Moreover, salt water ponds are normal and essential in oil-producing portions of Texas. Under this reasoning, the Court could have approved the concept of strict tort liability for abnormally dangerous activities and then declined to apply it to the facts of *Turner.* The Court's language, however, clearly rejected the doctrine of strict liability itself.

A significant group of courts, backed by the Restatements of Torts, have relied on *Rylands* and applied strict liability to abnormally dangerous activities. The next case is an example.

SIEGLER v. KUHLMAN

Supreme Court of Washington, 1972.
81 Wash.2d 448, 502 P.2d 1181.

HALE, ASSOCIATE JUSTICE.

Seventeen–year–old Carol J. House died in the flames of a gasoline explosion when her car encountered a pool of thousands of gallons of spilled gasoline. She was driving home from her after-school job in the early evening of November 22, 1967, along Capitol Lake Drive in Olympia; it was dark but dry; her car's headlamps were burning. There was a slight impact with some object, a muffled explosion, and then searing flames from gasoline pouring out of an overturned trailer tank engulfed her car. The result of the explosion is clear, but the real causes of what happened will remain something of an eternal mystery.

Aaron L. Kuhlman had * * * been driving for Pacific Intermountain Express for about 4 months, usually the night shift out of the Texaco bulk plant in Tumwater. * * * Before leaving the Texaco plant, he inspected the trailer, checking the lights, hitch, air hoses and tires. Finding nothing wrong, he then set out, driving the fully loaded truck tank and trailer tank * * *. Running downgrade on [a freeway] offramp, he felt a jerk, looked into his left-hand mirror and then his right-hand mirror to see that the trailer lights were not in place. The trailer was still moving but leaning over hard, he observed, onto its right side. The trailer then came loose. Realizing that the tank trailer had disengaged from his tank truck, he stopped the truck without skidding its tires. He got out and ran back to see that the tank trailer had crashed through a chain-link highway fence and had come to rest upside down on Capitol Lake Drive below. He heard a sound, he said, "like somebody kicking an empty fifty-gallon drum and that is when the fire started." The fire spread, he thought, about 100 feet down the road.

* * * When the trailer landed upside down on Capitol Lake Drive, its lights were out, and it was unilluminated when Carol House's car in one way or another ignited the spilled gasoline.

Carol House was burned to death in the flames. There was no evidence of impact on the vehicle she had driven, Kuhlman said, except that the left front headlight was broken.

Why the tank trailer disengaged and catapulted off the freeway down through a chain-link fence to land upside down on Capitol Lake Drive below remains a mystery. * * *

* * *

* * * From a judgment entered upon a verdict for defendants, plaintiff appealed to the Court of Appeals which affirmed. We granted review and reverse.

In the Court of Appeals, the principal claim of error was directed to the trial court's refusal to give an instruction on res ipsa loquitur, and we think that claim of error well taken. * * *

But there exists here an even more impelling basis for liability in this case * * * and that is the proposition of strict liability arising as a matter of law from all of the circumstances of the event.

Strict liability is not a novel concept; it is at least as old as [Rylands v. Fletcher, supra p. 486]. In that famous case, where water impounded in a reservoir on defendant's property escaped and damaged neighbouring coal mines, the landowner who had impounded the water was held liable without proof of fault or negligence. Acknowledging a distinction between the natural and non-natural use of land, and holding the maintenance of a reservoir to be a non-natural use, the Court of Exchequer Chamber imposed a rule of strict liability on the landowner. The ratio decidendi included adoption of what is now called *strict liability,* and * * * announced, we think, principles which should be applied in the instant case:

[T]he person who for his own purposes brings on his lands and collects and keeps there anything likely to do mischief if it escapes, must keep it in at his peril, and, if he does not do so, is prima facie answerable for all the damage which is the natural consequence of its escape.

[Not all] of the Justices in [*Rylands*] [drew] a distinction between the natural and non-natural use of land, but such a distinction would, we think, be irrelevant to the transportation of gasoline. The basic principles supporting the [*Rylands*] doctrine, we think, control the transportation of gasoline as freight along the public highways the same as it does the impounding of waters and for largely the same reasons.

In many respects, hauling gasoline as freight is no more unusual, but more dangerous, than collecting water. When gasoline is carried as cargo—as distinguished from fuel for the carrier vehicle—it takes on uniquely hazardous characteristics, as does water impounded in large quantities. Dangerous in itself, gasoline develops even greater potential for harm when carried as freight—extraordinary dangers deriving from sheer quantity, bulk and weight, which enormously multiply its hazardous properties. And the very hazards inhering from the size of the load, its bulk or quantity and its movement along the highways presents another reason for application of the [*Rylands*] rule not present in the impounding of large quantities of water—the likely destruction of cogent evidence from which negligence or want of it may be proved or disproved. It is quite probable that the most important ingredients of proof will be lost in a gasoline explosion and fire. Gasoline is always dangerous whether kept in large or small quantities because of its volatility, inflammability and explosiveness. But when several thousand gallons of it are allowed to spill across a public highway—that is, if, while in transit as freight, it is not kept impounded—the hazards to third persons are so great as to be almost beyond calculation. As a consequence of its escape from impoundment and subsequent explosion and ignition, the evidence in a very high percentage of instances will be destroyed, and the reasons for and causes contributing to its escape will quite likely be lost in the searing flames and explosions.

* * *

Recently this court, while declining to apply strict liability in a particular case, did acknowledge the suitability of the rule in a proper case. In Pacific Northwest Bell Tel. Co. v. Port of Seattle, 80 Wash.2d 59, 491 P.2d 1037 (1971), we observed that strict liability had its beginning in [*Rylands*], but said that it ought not be applied in a situation where a bursting water main, installed and maintained by the defendant Port of Seattle, damaged plaintiff telephone company's underground wires. There the court divided—not on the basic justice of a rule of strict liability in some cases—but in its application in a particular case to what on its face was a situation of comparatively minor hazards. Both majority and dissenting justices held, however, that the strict liability principles of [*Rylands*], should be given effect in some cases; but the court divided on the question of whether underground water mains there constituted such a case.

The rule of strict liability, when applied to an abnormally dangerous activity, as stated in the Restatement (Second) of Torts § 519 (Tent. Draft No. 10, 1964), was adopted as the rule of decision in this state in Pacific Northwest Bell Tel. Co. v. Port of Seattle, supra, as follows:

(1) One who carries on an abnormally dangerous activity is subject to liability for harm to the person, land or chattels of another resulting from the activity, although he has exercised the utmost care to prevent such harm.

(2) Such strict liability is limited to the kind of harm, the risk of which makes the activity abnormally dangerous.

As to what constitutes an abnormal activity, § 520 states:

In determining whether an activity is abnormally dangerous, the following factors are to be considered:

(a) Whether the activity involves a high degree of risk of some harm to the person, land or chattels of others;

(b) Whether the gravity of the harm which may result from it is likely to be great;

(c) Whether the risk cannot be eliminated by the exercise of reasonable care;

(d) Whether the activity is not a matter of common usage;

(e) Whether the activity is inappropriate to the place where it is carried on; and

(f) The value of the activity to the community.

* * *

Transporting gasoline as freight by truck along the public highways and streets is obviously an activity involving a high degree of risk; it is a risk of great harm and injury; it creates dangers that cannot be eliminated by the exercise of reasonable care. That gasoline cannot be practicably transported except upon the public highways does not decrease the abnormally high risk arising from its transportation. Nor will the exercise of due and reasonable care assure protection to the public from the disastrous consequences of concealed or latent mechanical or metallurgical defects in the carrier's equipment, from the negligence of third parties, from latent defects in the highways and streets, and from all of the other hazards not generally disclosed or guarded against by reasonable care, prudence and foresight. Hauling gasoline in great quantities as freight, we think, is an activity that calls for the application of principles of strict liability.

The case is therefore reversed and remanded to the trial court for trial to the jury on the sole issue of damages.

ROSELLINI, ASSOCIATE JUSTICE, concurring:

I agree with the majority that the transporting of highly volatile and flammable substances upon the public highways in commercial quantities and for commercial purposes is an activity which carries with it such a great risk of harm to defenseless users of the highway, if it is not kept contained, that the common-law principles of strict liability should apply. In my opinion, a good reason to apply these principles, which is not mentioned in the majority opinion, is that the commercial transporter can spread the loss among his customers—who benefit from this extrahazardous use of the highways. Also, if the defect which caused the substance to escape was one of manufacture, the owner is in the best position to hold the manufacturer to account.

I think the opinion should make clear, however, that the owner of the vehicle will be held strictly liable only for damages caused when the flammable or explosive substance is allowed to escape without the apparent intervention of any outside force beyond the control of the manufacturer, the owner, or the operator of the vehicle hauling it. I do not think the majority means to suggest that if another vehicle, negligently driven, collided with the truck in question, the truck owner would be held liable for the damage. But where, as here, there was no outside force which caused the trailer to become detached from the truck, the rule of strict liability should apply.

* * *

NOTES

1. What the court quoted was a tentative version of Restatement (Second) of Torts §§ 519 and 520. The ALI ultimately adopted a version that was virtually identical to the version quoted in *Siegler*. In the Third Restatement, the corresponding provision is simpler. An activity is abnormally dangerous and therefore subject to strict liability if it "creates a foreseeable and highly significant risk of physical harm even when reasonable care is exercised" and it is "not one of common usage." Third Restatement § 20.

2. Most American jurisdictions now apply some form of strict tort liability to abnormally dangerous activities. As the court's discussion of *Pacific Northwest Bell* suggests, the recurrent litigation point is whether a specific activity is "abnormally dangerous."

3. Note that § 519(b) of the Second Restatement limited liability to "the kind of harm, the possibility of which makes the activity abnormally dangerous." The Third Restatement's general scope-of-liability provision, § 29, which similarly provides that "[a]n actor's liability is limited to those harms that result from the risks that made the actor's conduct tortious," applies to strict liability cases. See Third Restatement § 29 cmts. *j* & *l*.

4. Justice Rosellini states that strict liability would not obtain if the explosion had been caused by a negligent motorist's colliding with the tanker truck. Do you think the majority agreed?

In Klein v. Pyrodyne Corp., 117 Wash.2d 1, 810 P.2d 917 (1991), the court held that a pyrotechnic company conducting a public fireworks display was subject to strict liability under Second Restatement §§ 519 and 520. The defendant, citing Justice Rosellini's concurring opinion in *Siegler* and dicta in a subsequent Washington Supreme Court case, argued that the manufacturer's improper construction of the shell that caused the accident was an intervening or outside force that cut off its liability. The court noted that § 522 of the Second Restatement took an opposite position: even the "unexpectable" negligent or reckless conduct of a third person did not affect liability. The *Klien* court adopted a middle ground, holding that because improper manufacture was not unforeseeable, the defendant remained liable, but rejecting the Restatement's view that an unforeseeable intervening force would not affect liability. The Third Restatement appears to abandon the position of the Second that would extend liability to unforeseeable events. See Third Restatement § 29 & cmts. *j* & *l*.

CHAPTER **XIV**

PRODUCTS LIABILITY

■ ■ ■

A. INTRODUCTION

"Products liability" refers to civil liability for injuries caused by defective products. It generally covers several different theories of liability, including negligence, breach of warranty, strict tort liability, and misrepresentation. These theories are not mutually exclusive, but can be combined in the same lawsuit. The Restatement (Third) of Torts: Products Liability, adopted by the American Law Institute in 1998, suggests that courts should combine these traditional theories into a single theory of liability for selling a "defective product." Restatement (Third) of Torts: Products Liability § 1 cmt. *a*, § 2 cmt. *n* (1998). Nevertheless, most courts still speak the language of the traditional categories.

Negligence, misrepresentation, and breach of warranty were developed primarily outside of the context of product injuries. We have already studied negligence. Warranty law was developed primarily in the context of commercial dealings. Its roots are in contract law, and most of its aspects are addressed in the contracts course. The law of misrepresentation was also developed primarily in the context of commercial dealings. Its roots are in tort law. It is addressed in courses on commercial torts.

Unlike the other three theories, so-called strict tort liability was developed as a special theory to deal with injuries caused by defective products. After a brief discussion of the other three theories in the context of product cases, this chapter focuses on strict tort liability. A more detailed examination of the other three theories in the context of product injuries may be made in an upper level course on products liability.

Negligence

Today, courts apply negligence principles to products cases much as they apply negligence principles to any other case involving personal injury. The plaintiff must prove that the defendant failed to use reasonable care in manufacturing, designing, or marketing the product and that this failure was a cause-in-fact and a proximate cause of the plaintiff's injuries. The question of reasonable care turns in large part on whether the defendant created a foreseeable, unreasonable risk of injury, judged from the perspective of the defendant's expertise concerning the product. The defendant can escape or reduce its liability by proving that the plaintiff was also negligent.

The full applicability of negligence law to product injury cases was a relatively recent development. See the introductory note to section B, Chapter VI, supra p. 196. At the turn of the twentieth century, courts did not apply normal negligence principles to product cases. Instead, they applied a limited duty rule that protected manufacturers from liability for their negligence except to the immediate purchaser, that is, except to persons who were in privity of contract with the manufacturer. Because manufacturers seldom sell directly to the public, and because a plaintiff usually cannot prove a retailer was negligent, the privity rule virtually eliminated recovery for injuries caused by negligently manufactured products.

The origin of the privity rule was Winterbottom v. Wright, 10 M. & W. 109, 152 Eng.Rep. 402 (1842). The court there held that a person who negligently repaired a stagecoach could not be held liable to a coach driver who was injured in an accident caused by the negligence. The court based its decision on the fact that the driver did not have a contract with the repairer. In the last half of the nineteenth century, courts began to recognize an exception to the privity rule for "imminently" or "inherently" dangerous products. A leading case was Thomas v. Winchester, 6 N.Y. 397, 57 Am.Dec. 455 (1852). The defendant's negligence caused a poison (belladonna) to be placed in a bottle labeled as extract of dandelion. The defendant sold the bottle to a druggist, who in turn sold it to a customer. The court held that the customer could recover from the defendant, notwithstanding the absence of privity, because poison is inherently dangerous.

Then, in 1916, in a famous opinion by Judge Cardozo, the New York Court of Appeals decided MacPherson v. Buick Motor Co., 217 N.Y. 382, 111 N.E. 1050 (1916). Buick sold a car with a defective wheel to a retailer, who in turn sold it to the plaintiff. The court held that the "inherently dangerous" exception to the privity requirement applies to products that are "dangerous if defective," not just to products, like poisons, that "in their normal operation are implements of destruction."

Although *MacPherson* purported to address an exception to the privity requirement, it came to stand for the proposition that privity is never required in a negligence case involving a defective product. Courts in virtually all states have followed *MacPherson*. This does not mean, however, that liability extends to anyone injured by a negligently manufactured product; liability extends only to plaintiffs injured by a "reasonably foreseeable use" of the product. Products Restatement § 2 cmt. *m*.

Even after abolition of the privity rule, some courts applied a "no duty" rule that protected a product seller from liability for negligence if the product danger was "open and obvious." Most courts have now abandoned the special rule, holding that the obviousness of the danger is only a factor in evaluating the defendant's conduct. See, e.g., Micallef v. Miehle Co., 39 N.Y.2d 376, 384 N.Y.S.2d 115, 348 N.E.2d 571 (1976). Some courts, however, continue to apply a categorical "no duty" rule. See, e.g., Pressley v. Sears–Roebuck and Co., 738 F.2d 1222 (11th Cir.1984) (applying Georgia law). The rule is similar to the "no duty" rule for open and obvious dangers for owners and occupiers of land.

MacPherson and *Micallef* eliminated special *doctrinal* obstacles to recovery for negligence in products cases, but practical problems remained. In most early product cases, the plaintiff's theory of negligence was that an employee in the manufacturer's factory engaged in a specific act of negligence, such as not tightening a nut on a bolt. Such conduct occurred before the plaintiff bought the product and outside the view of persons other than the defendant's employees. Discovery practices did not offer plaintiffs the same access to manufacturers' records that plaintiffs have today. Under those circumstances, plaintiffs had a difficult time producing direct proof of acts of negligence. Courts commonly granted directed verdicts for defendants, refusing to let juries infer negligence from the mere existence of a defect. In time some courts applied *res ipsa loquitur* to help plaintiffs overcome the problem of direct proof. See, e.g., Escola v. Coca Cola Bottling Co. of Fresno, 24 Cal.2d 453, 150 P.2d 436 (1944). Other courts and scholars began to suggest applying other theories of recovery that did not require proof of negligence, specifically breach of warranty and strict tort liability.

Warranty

Warranties have a dual significance for products liability law. First, although strict tort liability has shed most of its warranty heritage, warranty law spawned strict tort liability and influenced its early development. Second, warranty law still provides an effective remedy for injured consumers. Plaintiffs can join claims of strict tort liability and breach of warranty, and an action for breach of warranty can provide a victim with certain remedies that are not available under strict tort liability, such as recovery of pure economic damages and a variety of remedies available under some states' consumer protection and deceptive trade practices statutes.

Because warranty law developed primarily to regulate commercial dealings, it covers a variety of issues that are not relevant to products liability litigation. The basic source of warranty law is Article 2 of the Uniform Commercial Code, which was adopted in most states in the 1960s and early 1970s. Some warranties are also governed by the federal Magnuson–Moss Act (15 U.S.C. §§ 2301–12) or by state consumer protection or deceptive trade practice legislation. Most states also have common law warranties for certain transactions that are not covered by the various statutes.

Before the U.C.C., most states had developed a fairly extensive body of warranty law either as a body of common law or as an interpretation of their version of the old Uniform Sales Act. A landmark case in applying warranty law to a product injury was Henningsen v. Bloomfield Motors, Inc., 32 N.J. 358, 161 A.2d 69 (1960). Mr. Henningsen purchased a Plymouth from Bloomfield Motors and gave it to his wife as a gift. Ten days after delivery of the car, Mrs. Henningsen was injured in an accident caused by the steering's failing suddenly and without warning. She sued Bloomfield Motors and Chrysler for breach of express and implied warranties and for negligence. The court held that Mrs. Henningsen could recover for breach of implied warranty even though she was not in privity of contract with either defendant and even though the sales contract, in fine print, contained a disclaimer of the warranty. *Henningsen* is important historically because it influenced the codification of warranty law in Article 2 of the U.C.C.

Warranties respecting the sale of goods are now governed principally by Article 2 of the U.C.C. Section 2–313 governs express warranties, section 2–314 governs implied warranties of merchantability, and section 2–315 governs implied warranties of fitness for a particular purpose.

Section 2–318 governs the privity requirement. The drafters gave states three options. Under alternative A, purchasers, family members, and household guests can recover for breach of warranty. Under alternative B, any foreseeable plaintiff who suffers personal injury or property damage can recover. Under alternative C, any foreseeable plaintiff can recover, regardless of the type of injury.

Sellers of goods can do much to avoid liability for breach of warranty by disclaiming warranties (section 2–316) and by limiting the buyers' remedies (section 2–719). The ability of sellers to disclaim warranties and limit remedies is not absolute, however, and much warranty litigation involves questions about the validity of specific disclaimer and remedy limitations. Nevertheless, disclaimers and remedy limitations have turned out to be significant obstacles to recovery. So too has the requirement of section 2–607 that an injured buyer give timely notice of injury to the seller.

The details of the law governing the Article 2 warranties can be complex. They are addressed in the first-year contracts course and in upper-level courses on products liability.

Misrepresentation

Most states apply the misrepresentation principles set forth in § 9 of the Restatement (Third) of Torts: Products Liability, which summarizes the more detailed § 402B of the Restatement (Second) of Torts. Section 9 provides:

> One engaged in the business of selling or otherwise distributing products who, in connection with the sale of a product, makes a fraudulent, negligent, or innocent misrepresentation of material fact concerning the product is subject to liability for harm to persons or property caused by the misrepresentation.

Section 9 is an outgrowth of the law of intentional misrepresentation (fraud) and negligent misrepresentation, both of which were developed primarily in non-product cases. The law of fraud and negligent misrepresentation is important in products cases for two reasons. First, by relying directly on fraud and negligent misrepresentation, a plaintiff can recover for pure economic loss. (In many states, negligence, strict tort liability, and innocent misrepresentation under § 9 do not allow a plaintiff to recover for pure economic loss.) Second, other than the issues addressed by § 9—such as the defendant's state of mind—many of the general rules governing fraud and negligent misrepresentation are applicable to innocent misrepresentation under § 9.

B. EMERGENCE OF STRICT TORT LIABILITY

GREENMAN v. YUBA POWER PRODUCTS, INC.

Supreme Court of California, 1963.
59 Cal.2d 57, 27 Cal.Rptr. 697, 377 P.2d 897.

TRAYNOR, JUSTICE.

Plaintiff brought this action for damages against the retailer and the manufacturer of a Shopsmith, a combination power tool that could be used as a saw, drill, and wood lathe. He saw a Shopsmith demonstrated by the retailer and studied a brochure prepared by the manufacturer. He decided he wanted a Shopsmith for his home workshop, and his wife bought and gave him one for Christmas in 1955. In 1957 he bought the necessary attachments to use the Shopsmith as a lathe for turning a large piece of wood he wished to make into a chalice. After he had worked on the piece of wood several times without difficulty, it suddenly flew out of the machine and struck him on the forehead, inflicting serious injuries. About ten and a half months later, he gave the retailer and the manufacturer written notice of claimed breaches of warranties and filed a complaint against them alleging such breaches and negligence.

After a trial before a jury, the court ruled that there was no evidence that the retailer was negligent or had breached any express warranty and that the manufacturer was not liable for the breach of any implied warranty. Accordingly, it submitted to the jury only the cause of action alleging breach of implied warranties against the retailer and the causes of action alleging negligence and breach of express warranties against the manufacturer. The jury returned a verdict for the retailer against plaintiff and for plaintiff against the manufacturer in the amount of $65,000. The trial court denied the manufacturer's motion for a new trial and entered judgment on the verdict. The manufacturer and plaintiff appeal. Plaintiff seeks a reversal of the part of the judgment in favor of the retailer, however, only in the event that the part of the judgment against the manufacturer is reversed.

Plaintiff introduced substantial evidence that his injuries were caused by defective design and construction of the Shopsmith. His expert witnesses testified that inadequate set screws were used to hold parts of the machine together so that normal vibration caused the tailstock of the lathe to move away from the piece of wood being turned permitting it to fly out of the lathe. They also testified that there were other more positive ways of fastening the parts of the machine together, the use of which would have prevented the accident. The jury could therefore reasonably have concluded that the manufacturer negligently constructed the Shopsmith. The jury could also reasonably have concluded that statements in the manufacturer's brochure were untrue, that they constituted express warranties, and that plaintiff's injuries were caused by their breach.

The manufacturer contends, however, that plaintiff did not give it notice of breach of warranty within a reasonable time and that therefore his cause of action for breach of warranty is barred by section 1769 of the Civil Code. Since it cannot be determined whether the verdict against it was based on the negligence or warranty cause of action or both, the manufacturer concludes that the error in presenting the warranty cause of action to the jury was prejudicial.

Section 1769 of the Civil Code provides: "In the absence of express or implied agreement of the parties, acceptance of the goods by the buyer shall not discharge the seller from liability in damages or other legal remedy for breach of any promise or warranty in the contract to sell or the sale. But, if, after acceptance of the goods, the buyer fails to give notice to the seller of the breach of any promise or warranty within a reasonable time after the buyer knows, or ought to know of such breach, the seller shall not be liable therefore."

Like other provisions of the uniform sales act (Civ.Code, §§ 1721–1800), section 1769 deals with the rights of the parties to a contract of sale or a sale. It does not provide that notice must be given of the breach of a warranty that arises independently of a contract of sale between the parties. Such warranties are not imposed by the sales act, but are the product of common-law decisions that have recognized them in a variety of situations. It is true that in many of these situations the court has invoked the sales act definitions of warranties (Civ.Code, §§ 1732, 1735) in defining the defendant's liability, but it has done so, not because the statutes so required, but because they provided appropriate standards for the court to adopt under the circumstances presented.

The notice requirement of section 1769, however, is not an appropriate one for the court to adopt in actions by injured consumers against manufacturers with whom they have not dealt. "As between the immediate parties to the sale [the notice requirement] is a sound commercial rule, designed to protect the seller against unduly delayed claims for damages. As applied to personal injuries, and notice to a remote seller, it becomes a booby-trap for the unwary. The injured consumer is seldom 'steeped in the business practice which justifies the rule,' [James, Product Liability, 34 Texas L.Rev. 44, 192, 197] and at least until he has had legal advice it will not occur to him to give notice to one with whom he has had no dealings."

(Prosser, Strict Liability to the Consumer, 69 Yale L.J. 1099, 1130, footnotes omitted.) * * * We conclude, therefore, that even if plaintiff did not give timely notice of breach of warranty to the manufacturer, his cause of action based on the representations contained in the brochure was not barred.

Moreover, to impose strict liability on the manufacturer under the circumstances of this case, it was not necessary for plaintiff to establish an express warranty as defined in section 1732 of the Civil Code. A manufacturer is strictly liable in tort when an article he places on the market, knowing that it is to be used without inspection for defects, proves to have a defect that causes injury to a human being. Recognized first in the case of unwholesome food products, such liability has now been extended to a variety of other products that create as great or greater hazards if defective.

Although in these cases strict liability has usually been based on the theory of an express or implied warranty running from the manufacturer to the plaintiff, the abandonment of the requirement of a contract between them, the recognition that the liability is not assumed by agreement but imposed by law, and the refusal to permit the manufacturer to define the scope of its own responsibility for defective products make clear that the liability is not one governed by the law of contract warranties but by the law of strict liability in tort. Accordingly, rules defining and governing warranties that were developed to meet the needs of commercial transactions cannot properly be invoked to govern the manufacturer's liability to those injured by their defective products unless those rules also serve the purposes for which such liability is imposed.

We need not recanvass the reasons for imposing strict liability on the manufacturer. They have been fully articulated in the cases cited above. The purpose of such liability is to insure that the costs of injuries resulting from defective products are borne by the manufacturers that put such products on the market rather than by the injured persons who are powerless to protect themselves. Sales warranties serve this purpose fitfully at best. In the present case, for example, plaintiff was able to plead and prove an express warranty only because he read and relied on the representations of the Shopsmith's ruggedness contained in the manufacturer's brochure. Implicit in the machine's presence on the market, however, was a representation that it would safely do the jobs for which it was built. Under these circumstances, it should not be controlling whether plaintiff selected the machine because of the statements in the brochure, or because of the machine's own appearance of excellence that belied the defect lurking beneath the surface, or because he merely assumed that it would safely do the jobs it was built to do. It should not be controlling whether the details of the sales from manufacturer to retailer and from retailer to plaintiff's wife were such that one or more of the implied warranties of the sales act arose. "The remedies of injured consumers ought not to be made to depend upon the intricacies of the law of sales." (Ketterer v. Armour & Co., D.C., 200 F. 322, 323 [S.D.N.Y. 1912].) To establish the manufacturer's liability it was sufficient that plaintiff proved that he was injured while using the Shopsmith in a way it was intended to be used as a result of a defect in design and manufacture of which plaintiff was not aware that made the Shopsmith unsafe for its intended use.

* * *

The judgment is affirmed.

NOTES

1. ***The Restatements.*** The Restatement of Torts (Second) § 402A (1965) adopted the rule embodied in *Greenman*. It provided:

§ 402A. Special Liability of Seller of Product for Physical Harm to User or Consumer

(1) One who sells any product in a defective condition unreasonably dangerous to the user or consumer or to his property is subject to liability for physical harm thereby caused to the ultimate user or consumer, or to his property, if

(a) the seller is engaged in the business of selling such a product, and

(b) it is expected to and does reach the user or consumer without substantial change in the condition in which it is sold.

(2) The rule stated in Subsection (1) applies although

(a) the seller has exercised all possible care in the preparation and sale of his product, and

(b) the user or consumer has not bought the product from or entered into any contractual relation with the seller.

Section 402A was replaced in 1998 with the Restatement (Third) of Torts: Products Liability. The new Restatement reflects an extensive body of case law that followed the basic rule in section 402A. Section 1 contains the basic rule of liability. It provides:

One engaged in the business of selling or otherwise distributing products who sells or distributes a defective product is subject to liability for harm to persons or property caused by the defect.

2. ***Do the policy justifications that have been proposed for strict tort liability support it?*** Courts and scholars have advanced a variety of policy justifications for strict tort liability. Five of them are set forth below. As you study strict liability, consider whether these policies are valid and whether the courts are effectively implementing them. Consider also whether these policies provide an adequate justification for applying strict liability to product injuries, even though proof of negligence is generally required for all other types of injuries. See generally Powers, A Modest Proposal to Abandon Strict Products Liability, 1991 Ill.L.Rev. 639.

a. Compensation (or loss spreading). Losses inevitably result from the use of products. These losses can have a disastrous effect on the individual who experiences them. It is humane and fair to shift these losses to all consumers of the product. This can be accomplished by imposing liability on manufacturers, forcing them to raise prices enough to pay for the losses or insure against them.

b. Cost internalization. Forcing manufacturers to raise prices in order to pay for harm caused by their products will lead to a more efficient allocation of resources. The prices of products will then more nearly include all of their true costs, including accident costs. Being aware of the true costs of products, consumers will make more intelligent decisions about which products to purchase.

c. Deterrence. Tort liability increases costs to manufacturers, but competition induces manufacturers to minimize these costs. Imposing liability provides manufacturers with an incentive to market safer products. In theory, strict liability may create more deterrence than negligence-based liability, since negligence imposes liability only if the defendant fails to take measures that a plaintiff can prove a reasonable person would have taken. Strict liability induces manufacturers to do more if the cost of the added safety measures is less than the potential cost of liability.

Nevertheless, courts also want to encourage useful products. Although compensation and deterrence are most commonly cited as the bases for strict tort liability, they are clearly not the only considerations because they almost always point in the direction of imposing liability. No court has imposed the liability of an insurer on manufacturers by requiring them to pay for all harm caused by their products. This is because of the fear that such absolute liability would place unreasonable burdens on manufacturers and discourage them from producing useful products. The policy of avoiding over-deterrence by balancing the needs of defendants against the needs of plaintiffs is clearly at work, although it is seldom articulated.

d. Proof problems. Quite often the manufacturer of a defective product is negligent. Modern industrial and technological complexities, however, frequently make it very difficult for the plaintiff to establish this. This is particularly so because any negligent conduct usually occurred before the plaintiff purchased the product and at a place controlled by the defendant. Imposing strict liability relieves the plaintiff of the burden of proving specific acts of negligence.

e. Protection of consumer expectations. Consumers should be protected from unknown dangers in products. This is particularly true when advertising and marketing techniques induce consumers to rely on manufacturers to provide them with safe, high-quality products.

C. DEFECT

LINEGAR v. ARMOUR OF AMERICA, INC.

United States Court of Appeals, Eighth Circuit, 1990.
909 F.2d 1150.

BOWMAN, CIRCUIT JUDGE.

This action was brought as a products liability case and heard under the District Court's diversity jurisdiction. Armour of America, Inc. (Armour) appeals a judgment based on a jury verdict in favor of the widow and children of Jimmy Linegar, a Missouri State Highway Patrol trooper who was killed in the line of duty. The jury found that the bullet-resistant vest manufactured by Armour and worn by Linegar at the time of the murder was defectively designed, and it awarded his family $1.5 million in damages. We reverse.

On April 15, 1985, as part of a routine traffic check, Linegar stopped a van with Nevada license plates near Branson, Missouri. The van's driver produced an Oregon operator's license bearing the name Matthew Mark Samuels. Linegar ascertained from the Patrol dispatcher that the name was an alias for David Tate, for whom there was an outstanding warrant on a weapons charge. Linegar did not believe the driver matched the description the dispatcher gave him for Tate, so he decided to investigate further.

A fellow trooper, Allen Hines, who was working the spot check with Linegar, then approached the passenger's side of the van while Linegar approached the driver's side. After a moment of questioning, Linegar asked the driver to step out of the van. The driver, who was in fact David Tate, brandished an automatic weapon and fired at the troopers first from inside and then from outside the van. By the time Tate stopped firing, Hines had been wounded by three shots and Linegar, whose body had been penetrated by six bullets, lay dead or dying. None of the shots that hit the contour-style, concealable protective vest Linegar was wearing—there were five such shots—penetrated the vest or caused injury. The wounds Linegar suffered all were caused by shots that struck parts of his body not protected by the vest.

The Missouri State Highway Patrol issued the vest to Linegar when he joined the Patrol in 1981. The vest was one of a lot of various sizes of the same style vest the Patrol purchased in 1979 directly from Armour. The contour style was one of several different styles then on the market. It provided more protection to the sides of the body than the style featuring rectangular panels in front and back, but not as much protection as a wrap-around style. The front and back panels of the contour vest, held together with Velcro closures under the arms, did not meet at the sides of the wearer's body, leaving an area along the sides of the body under the arms exposed when the vest was worn. This feature of the vest was obvious to the Patrol when it selected this vest as standard issue for its troopers and could only have been obvious to any trooper who chose to wear it. The bullet that proved fatal to Linegar entered between his seventh and eighth ribs, approximately three-and-one-fourth inches down from his armpit, and pierced his heart.

The theory upon which Linegar's widow and children sought and won recovery from Armour was strict liability in tort based on a design defect in the vest.* * * [W]e hold that, as a matter of law, the evidence was insufficient to present a submissible products liability case * * *.

* * *

The parties agree that Missouri substantive law controls in this diversity case. Under Missouri products liability law, plaintiff potentially had available to her three theories of recovery: negligence, strict liability, and breach of warranty. In 1969, the Missouri Supreme Court adopted section 402A of the Restatement (Second) of Torts, which imposes strict liability in tort upon sellers and manufacturers for selling "any product in a defective condition unreasonably dangerous to the user or consumer" that results in injury to the user or consumer. The strict liability theory is further divided into liability for defective design of a product and liability for failure to warn of an inherent danger in the product. Although here the first amended complaint stated claims against Armour on all of Missouri's products liability theories, plaintiff later elected to dismiss all claims except Count I, strict liability for defective design, and the case was submitted to the jury only on that theory.

* * *

Under the Missouri law of strict liability in tort for defective design, before a plaintiff can recover from the seller or manufacturer he must show that "the design renders the product unreasonably dangerous." Nesselrode v. Executive Beechcraft, Inc., 707 S.W.2d 371, 377 (Mo.1986) (en banc). Ordinarily, that will be a jury question, and "the concept of unreasonable danger, which is determinative of whether a product is defective in a design case, is presented to the jury as an ultimate issue without further definition," as it was here. In this case, however, there was simply no evidence that the vest's design made it unreasonably dangerous, and the District Court should have declared that, as a matter of law, the vest was not defective, and directed a verdict or granted judgment for Armour notwithstanding the verdict.

The Missouri cases leave the meaning of the phrase "unreasonably dangerous" largely a matter of common sense, the court's or the jury's. The Missouri Supreme Court has stated, however, that a product is defectively designed if it "creates an unreasonable risk of danger to the consumer or user when put to normal use." Nesselrode, 707 S.W.2d at 375. Among the factors to be considered are "the conditions and circumstances that will foreseeably attend the use of the product." The conditions under which a bullet-resistant vest will be called upon to perform its intended function most assuredly will be dangerous, indeed life-threatening, and Armour surely knew that. It defies logic, however, to suggest that Armour reasonably should have anticipated that anyone would wear its vest for protection of areas of the body that the vest obviously did not cover.

Courts applying Missouri law also have applied what has become known as the "consumer expectation" test for unreasonable dangerousness: "The article sold must be dangerous to an extent beyond that which would be contemplated by the ordinary consumer who purchases it, with the ordinary knowledge common to the community as to its characteristics." Restatement (Second) of Torts § 402A cmt. *i* (1965); accord id. cmt. *g.*

The consumer expectation test focuses attention on the vest's wearer rather than on its manufacturer. The inherent limitations in the amount of coverage offered by Armour's contour vest were obvious to this Court, observing a demonstration from the bench during oral argument, as they would be to anyone with ordinary knowledge, most especially the vest's wearer. A person wearing the vest would no more expect to be shielded from a shot taken under the arm than he would expect the vest to deflect bullets aimed at his head or neck or lower abdomen or any other area not covered by the vest.

Plaintiff insists that the user's expectations should not be considered by us, since doing so would effectively afford Armour the benefit of the "open and obvious" defense, inappropriate, they say, in a defective design strict products liability action. We disagree. Although not conclusive, "[t]he obviousness of a defect or danger is material to the issue whether a product is 'unreasonably dangerous.' " McGowne v. Challenge–Cook Bros., 672 F.2d 652, 663 (8th Cir.1982) (applying Missouri law * * *). * * *

We have no difficulty in concluding as a matter of law that the product at issue here was neither defective nor unreasonably dangerous. Trooper Linegar's protective vest performed precisely as expected and stopped all of the bullets that hit it. No part of the vest nor any malfunction of the vest caused Linegar's injuries. The vest was designed to prevent the penetration of bullets where there was coverage, and it did so; the amount of coverage was the buyer's choice. The Missouri Highway Patrol could have chosen to buy, and Armour could have sold the Patrol, a vest with more coverage; no one contests that. But it is not the place of courts or juries to set specifications as to the parts of the body a bullet-resistant garment must cover. A manufacturer is not obliged to market only one version of a product, that being the very safest design possible. If that were so, automobile manufacturers could not offer consumers sports cars, convertibles, jeeps, or compact cars. All boaters would have to buy full life vests instead of choosing a ski belt or even a flotation cushion. Personal safety devices, in particular, require personal choices, and it is beyond the province of courts and juries to act as legislators and preordain those choices.

In this case, there obviously were trade-offs to be made. A contour vest like the one here in question permits the wearer more flexibility and mobility and allows better heat dissipation and sweat evaporation, and thus is more likely to be worn than a more confining vest. It is less expensive than styles of vests providing more complete coverage. If manufacturers like Armour are threatened with economically devastating litigation if they market any vest style except that offering maximum coverage, they may decide, since one can always argue that more coverage is possible, to get out of the business altogether. Or they may continue to market the vest style that, according to the latest lawsuit, affords the "best" coverage. Officers who find the "safest" style confining or uncomfortable will either wear it at risk to their mobility or opt not to wear it at all. See Transcript Vol. II at 333 (testimony of Missouri Highway Patrol Trooper Don Phillips that he continued to wear the Armour contour-style vest with his summer uniform, even though the Patrol had issued him a wrap-around vest). Law enforcement agencies trying to work within the confines of a budget may be forced to purchase fewer vests or none at all. How "safe" are those possibilities? "The core concern in strict tort liability law is safety." *Nesselrode*, 707 S.W.2d at 375. We are firmly convinced that to allow this verdict to stand would run counter to the law's purpose of promoting the development of safe and useful products, and would have an especially pernicious effect on the development and marketing of equipment designed to make the always-dangerous work of law enforcement officers a little safer.

The death of Jimmy Linegar by the hand of a depraved killer was a tragic event. We keenly feel the loss that this young trooper's family has suffered, and our sympathies go out to them. But we cannot allow recovery from a blameless defendant on the basis of sympathy for the plaintiffs. * * *

The judgment of the District Court is reversed. The District Court shall enter a final judgment in favor of Armour.

PHILLIPS v. KIMWOOD MACHINE COMPANY

Supreme Court of Oregon, 1974.
269 Or. 485, 525 P.2d 1033.

HOLMAN, JUSTICE.

Plaintiff was injured while feeding fiberboard into a sanding machine during his employment with Pope and Talbot, a wood products manufacturer. The sanding machine had been purchased by Pope and Talbot from defendant. Plaintiff brought this action on a products liability theory, contending the sanding machine was unreasonably dangerous by virtue of defective design. At the completion of the testimony, defendant's motion for a directed verdict was granted and plaintiff appealed.

As is required in such a situation, the evidence is recounted in a manner most favorable to the plaintiff. The machine in question was a six-headed sander. Each sanding head was a rapidly moving belt which revolved in the direction opposite to that which the pieces of fiberboard moved through the machine. Three of the heads sanded the top of the fiberboard sheet and three sanded the bottom. The top half of the machine could be raised or lowered depending upon the thickness of the fiberboard to be sanded. The bottom half of the machine had powered rollers which moved the fiberboard through the machine as the fiberboard was being sanded. The top half of the machine had pinch rolls, not powered, which, when pressed down on the fiberboard by use of springs, kept the sanding heads from forcefully rejecting it from the machine.

On the day of the accident plaintiff was engaged in feeding the sheets of fiberboard into the sander. * * * During the sanding of * * * thick sheets, a thin sheet of fiberboard, which had become mixed with the lot, was inserted into the machine. The pressure exerted by the pinch rolls in the top half of the machine was insufficient to counteract the pressure which the sanding belts were exerting upon the thin sheet of fiberboard and, as a result, the machine regurgitated the piece of fiberboard back at plaintiff, hitting him [in] the abdomen and causing him the injuries for which he now seeks compensation.

Plaintiff asserts in his complaint that the machine was defective in its design * * * because there were no safety devices to protect the person feeding the machine from the regurgitation of sheets of fiberboard.

While we do not here attempt to recount all of the testimony presented by plaintiff concerning the defective design of the machine, there was evidence from which the jury could find that at a relatively small expense there could have been built into, or subsequently installed on, the machine a line of metal teeth which would point in the direction that the fiberboard progresses through the machine and which would press lightly against the sheet but which, in case of attempted regurgitation, would be jammed into it, thus stopping its backward motion. The evidence also showed that after the accident such teeth were installed upon the machine for that purpose by Pope and Talbot, whereupon subsequent regurgitations of thin fiberboard sheets were prevented while the efficiency of the machine was maintained. There was also evidence that defendant makes smaller sanders which usually are manually fed and on which there is such a safety device.

It was shown that the machine in question was built for use with an automatic feeder and that the one installed at Pope and Talbot is the only six-headed sander manufactured by defendant which is manually fed. There also was testimony that at the time of the purchase by Pope and Talbot, defendant had automatic feeders for sale but that Pope and Talbot did not purchase or show any interest in such a feeder. Pope and Talbot furnished a feeding device of their own manufacture for the machine which was partially automatic and partially manual but which, the jury could find, at times placed an employee in the way of regurgitated sheets.

* * *

In defense of its judgment based upon a directed verdict, defendant contends there was no proof of a defect in the product, and therefore strict liability should not apply. This court and other courts continue to flounder while attempting to determine how one decides whether a product is "in a defective condition unreasonably dangerous to the user." It has been recognized that unreasonably dangerous defects in products come from two principal sources: (1) mismanufacture and (2) faulty design. Mismanufacture is relatively simple to identify because the item in question is capable of being compared with similar articles made by the same manufacturer. However, whether the mismanufactured article is dangerously defective because of the flaw is sometimes difficult to ascertain because not every such flaw which causes injury makes the article dangerously defective.

The problem with strict liability [for] products has been one of limitation. No one wants absolute liability where all the article has to do is to cause injury. To impose liability there has to be something about the article which makes it dangerously defective without regard to whether the manufacturer was or was not at fault for such condition. A test for unreasonable danger is therefore vital. A dangerously defective article would be one which a reasonable person would not put into the stream of commerce if he had knowledge of its harmful character. The test, therefore, is whether the seller would be negligent if he sold the article knowing of the risk involved. Strict liability [imposes] what amounts to constructive knowledge of the condition of the product.

On the surface such a test would seem to be different than the test of 2 Restatement (Second) of Torts § 402A cmt. *i*, of "dangerous to an extent beyond that which would be contemplated by the ordinary consumer who purchases it." This court has used this test in the past. These are not necessarily different standards, however. As stated in Welch v. Outboard Marine Corp., [481 F.2d 252 (5th Cir.1973),] where the court affirmed an instruction containing both standards:

> We see no necessary inconsistency between a seller-oriented standard and a user-oriented standard when, as here, each turns on foreseeable risks. They are two sides of the same standard. A product is defective and unreasonably dangerous when a reasonable seller would not sell the product if he knew of the risk involved or if the risks are greater than a reasonable buyer would expect.

To elucidate this point further, we feel that the two standards are the same because a seller acting reasonably would be selling the same product which a reasonable consumer believes he is purchasing. That is to say, a manufacturer who would be negligent in marketing a given product, considering its risks, would necessarily be marketing a product which fell below the reasonable expectations of consumers who purchase it. The foreseeable uses to which a product could be put would be the same in the minds of both the seller and the buyer unless one of the parties was not acting reasonably. The advantage of describing a dangerous defect in the manner [we now use] is that it preserves the use of familiar terms and thought processes with which courts, lawyers, and jurors customarily deal.

While apparently judging the seller's conduct, the test set out above would actually be a characterization of the product by a jury. If the manufacturer was not acting reasonably in selling the product, knowing of the risks involved, then the product would be dangerously defective when sold and the manufacturer would be subject to liability.

In the case of a product which is claimed to be dangerously defective because of misdesign, the process is not so easy as in the case of mismanufacture. All the products made to that design are the same. The question of whether the design is unreasonably dangerous can be determined only by taking into consideration the surrounding circumstances and knowledge at the time the article was sold, and determining therefrom whether a reasonably prudent manufacturer would have so designed and sold the article in question had he known of the risk involved which injured plaintiff. The issue has been raised in some courts concerning whether, in this context, there is any distinction between strict liability and negligence. The evidence which proves the one will almost always, if not always, prove the other. We discussed this matter recently in the case of Roach v. Kononen, 525 P.2d 125 (Or.1974), and pointed out that there is a difference between strict liability for misdesign and negligence. We said:

> However, be all this as it may, it is generally recognized that the basic difference between negligence on the one hand and strict liability for a design defect on the other is that in strict liability we are talking about the condition (dangerousness) of an article which is designed in a particular way, while in negligence we are talking about the reasonableness of the manufacturer's actions in designing and selling the article as he did. The article can have a degree of dangerousness which the law of strict liability will not tolerate even though the actions of the designer were entirely reasonable in view of what he knew at the time he planned and sold the manufactured article. As Professor Wade points out, a way of determining whether the condition of the article is of the requisite degree of dangerousness to be defective (unreasonably dangerous; greater degree of danger than a consumer has a right to expect; not duly safe) is to assume that the manufacturer knew of the product's propensity to injure as it did, and then to ask whether, with such knowledge, something should have been done about the danger before it was sold. In other words, a greater burden is placed on the manufacturer than is the case in negligence because the law assumes he has knowledge of the article's dangerous propensity which he may not reasonably be expected to have, had he been charged with negligence.

525 P.2d at 129.

To some it may seem that absolute liability has been imposed upon the manufacturer since it might be argued that no manufacturer could reasonably put into the stream of commerce an article which he realized might result in injury to a user. This is not the case, however. The manner of injury may be so fortuitous and the chances of injury occurring so remote that it is reasonable to sell the product despite the danger. In design cases the utility of the article may be so great, and the change of design necessary to alleviate the danger in question may so impair such utility, that it is reasonable to market the product as it is, even though the possibility of injury exists and was realized at the time of the sale. Again, the cost of the change necessary to alleviate the danger in design may be so great that the article would be priced out of the market and no one would buy it even though it was of high utility. Such an article is not dangerously defective despite its having inflicted injury.

In this case defendant contends it was Pope and Talbot's choice to purchase and use the sander without an automatic feeder, even though it was manufactured to be used with one, and, therefore, it was Pope and Talbot's business choice which resulted in plaintiff's injury and not any misdesign by defendant. However, it is recognized that a failure to warn may make a product unreasonably dangerous. Comment *j*, Section 402A, Restatement (Second) of Torts, has the following to say:

> In order to prevent the product from being unreasonably dangerous, the seller may be required to give directions or warning, on the container, as to its use. The seller may reasonably assume that those with common allergies, as for example to eggs or strawberries, will be aware of them, and he is not required to warn against them. Where, however, the product contains an ingredient to which a substantial number of the population are allergic, and the ingredient is one whose danger is not generally known, or if known is one which the consumer would reasonably not expect to find in the product, the seller is required to give warning against it, if he had knowledge, or by the application of reasonable, developed human skill and foresight should have knowledge, of the presence of the ingredient and the danger. Likewise in the case of poisonous drugs, or those unduly dangerous for other reasons, warning as to use may be required.

It is our opinion that the evidence was sufficient for the jury to find that a reasonably prudent manufacturer, knowing that the machine would be fed manually and having the constructive knowledge of its propensity to regurgitate thin sheets when it was set for thick ones, which the courts via strict liability have imposed upon it, would have warned plaintiff's employer either to feed it automatically or to use some safety device, and that, in the absence of such a warning, the machine was dangerously defective. It is therefore unnecessary for us to decide the questions that would arise had adequate warnings been given.

In Anderson v. Klix Chemical, 256 Or. 199, 472 P.2d 806 (1970), we came to the conclusion that there was no difference between negligence and strict liability for a product that was unreasonably dangerous because of failure to warn of certain characteristics. We have now come to the conclusion that we were in error. The reason we believe we were in error parallels the rationale that was expressed in the previously quoted material from Roach v. Kononen, supra, where we discussed the difference between strict liability for misdesign and negligence. In a strict liability case we are talking about the condition (dangerousness) of an article which is sold without any warning, while in negligence we are talking about the reasonableness of the manufacturer's actions in selling the article without a warning. The article can have a degree of dangerousness because of a lack of warning which the law of strict liability will not tolerate even though the actions of the seller were entirely reasonable in selling the article without a warning considering what he knew or should have known at the time he sold it. A way to determine the dangerousness of the article, as distinguished from the seller's culpability, is to assume the seller knew of the product's propensity to injure as it did, and then to ask whether, with such knowledge, he would have been negligent in selling it without a warning.

* * *

The case is reversed and remanded for a new trial.

NOTES

1. ***Three categories of defective products.*** As the opinion in *Phillips* suggests, courts have identified three categories of product defect. A "manufacturing defect" or "flaw" involves a product that does not conform to the manufacturer's specifications or intentions, such as a bottled soft drink with a piece of glass in it. A "design defect" involves a product that is like every other product in the line, but the entire line has a feature that is unreasonably dangerous. A "warning defect" involves a product that is made unreasonably dangerous because of the warning or instructions for use, or lack thereof, such as a drug that does not have a warning that it has adverse side effects for fetuses. See Restatement (Third) of Torts: Products Liability § 2 (1998).

2. Most early products liability cases involved flaws. In these cases, the consumer expectation test (used in comments *g* and *i* of section 402A and in *Gray*) was intuitively easy to apply. In design defect cases and in more complex cases generally, however, it is often difficult to determine what ordinary consumers expect, even assuming they have any specific expectations about the details of the product. As cases became more complex, more courts began using the risk-utility test that was used in *Phillips*. The Restatement (Third) of Torts: Products Liability § 2 (1998) adopts the risk-utility test for design defects and warnings. Consumer expectations about a product may affect risk and utility, but consumer expectations do not constitute an independent test. Id. cmt. *g*. The new Restatement provides that a product has a manufacturing defect when it "departs from its intended design, even though all possible care was exercised in the preparation and marketing of the product."

Some courts use a different test for different types of defect, and some courts use a test that combines risk-utility and consumer expectations. The leading case applying a combined test is Barker v. Lull Engineering Co., 20 Cal.3d 413, 143 Cal.Rptr. 225, 573 P.2d 443 (1978). The court held that the jury should be instructed that a product is defective if it either fails to meet ordinary consumer expectations or has risks that outweigh utility.

3. In applying the risk-utility test, courts consider a variety of factors, including product cost and product performance. The analysis properly focuses on the particular product feature, not on the product as a whole. For example, in *Phillips* the appropriate focus was on the risks and benefits of not having teeth on the sander, not on the overall risks and benefits of the sander.

4. The plaintiff must prove that the defect existed when the product left the defendant's control. This burden is not difficult to meet in most cases involving design defects and warnings. In cases involving flaws, however, defendants commonly claim that the product became flawed after it left the defendant's control.

A common situation is a product sold in a sealed container. As the court said in McKisson v. Sales Affiliates, Inc., 416 S.W.2d 787 (Tex.1967), "[w]hen it is shown that the product involved comes in a sealed container, it is inferrable that the product reached the consumer without substantial changes in the conditions in which it was sold." If other evidence proves that the sealed container was invaded or that the product became flawed after it left the defendant's control, however, the inference breaks down. See, e.g., Klein v. Continental–Emsco, 445 F.2d 629 (5th Cir.1971); Carroll v. Ford Motor Co., 462 S.W.2d 57 (Tex.Civ.App.–Houston [14th Dist.] 1970, no writ).

A product's failure caused merely by normal wear is not sufficient to establish that it was defective when it was sold. The plaintiff need not, however, prove that the product failed immediately upon delivery. If the product is designed or manufactured to have a propensity to deteriorate more quickly than normal, it might be defective when it is delivered, even though the danger is not manifested until later. In such cases, the defect is the propensity to deteriorate too quickly, which was present when the product was delivered.

5. The court in *Phillips* discussed the possibility of applying a hindsight test to evaluate either an alleged design defect or a failure to warn. Such an approach would evaluate the product with current ("time-of-trial") knowledge rather than the state of knowledge when the product was sold. The inquiry would nevertheless focus on the risks and benefits that the product actually had at the time it was sold. It is important to observe that the *Phillips* court nowhere indicated that the case before it actually presented a situation in which the relevant risks of the product were unknown at the time of sale and discovered later. For cases involving alleged design defects or failure to warn, most courts today take into account only risks that were *reasonably* foreseeable when the product was sold. See Restatement (Third) of Torts: Products Liability § 2 cmt. *m* (1998). Even courts that use a hindsight test for design defects nevertheless use a foresight test to cases involving a failure to warn. The risk-utility test from a foresight perspective is very close, if not identical, to negligence.

POTTER v. CHICAGO PNEUMATIC TOOL CO.

Connecticut Supreme Court, 1997.
241 Conn. 199, 694 A.2d 1319.

KATZ, J.

[Shipyard workers sued tool manufacturers, claiming they were injured as a result of using defectively designed pneumatic hand tools manufactured by defendants. The trial court entered judgment on a jury verdict for plaintiffs and denied defendants' post-trial motions.]

Section 402A [of the Restatement (Second) of Torts] imposes liability only for those defective products that are "unreasonably dangerous" to "the ordinary consumer who purchases it, with the ordinary knowledge common to the community as to its characteristics." [§ 402A cmt. *i.*] Under this formulation, known as the "consumer expectation" test, a manufacturer is strictly liable for any condition not contemplated by the ultimate consumer that will be unreasonably dangerous to the consumer.

* * *

In Barker v. Lull Engineering Co. [(1978)] the California Supreme Court established two alternative tests for determining design defect liability: (1) the consumer expectation analysis, and (2) a balancing test that inquires whether a product's risks outweigh its benefits. Under the latter "risk-utility" test, the manufacturer bears the burden of proving that the product's utility is not outweighed by its risks in light of various factors. * * *

Other jurisdictions apply only a risk-utility test in determining whether a manufacturer is liable for a design defect. * * *

* * *

* * * In Garthwait v. Burgio [(1965)] this court * * * became one of the first jurisdictions to adopt the rule provided in § 402A. * * *

This court has long held that in order to prevail in a design defect claim, "[t]he plaintiff must prove the product is unreasonably dangerous." We have derived our definition of "unreasonably dangerous" from cmt. *(i)* to § 402A, which provides that "the article sold must be dangerous to an extent beyond that which would be contemplated by the ordinary consumer who purchases it, with the ordinary knowledge common to the community as to its characteristics." * * *

The defendants propose that it is time for this court to abandon the consumer expectation standard and adopt the requirement that the plaintiff must prove the existence of a reasonable alternative design in order to prevail on a design defect claim. We decline to accept this invitation.

* * *

In support of their position, the defendants point to the second tentative draft of the Restatement (Third) of Torts: Products Liability (1995), which provides that, as part of a prima facie case, the plaintiff must establish the availability of a reasonable alternative design. Specifically, § 2(b) of the Draft Restatement [Third] provides: "[A] product is defective in design when the foreseeable risks of harm posed by the product could have been reduced or avoided by the adoption of a reasonable alternative design by the seller or other distributor, or a predecessor in the commercial chain of distribution, and the omission of the alternative design renders the product not reasonably safe." The reporters to the Draft Restatement Third state that "[v]ery substantial authority supports the proposition that [the] plaintiff must establish a reasonable alternative design in order for a product to be adjudged defective in design."

* * * [O]ur independent review of the prevailing common law reveals that the majority of jurisdictions *do not* impose upon plaintiffs an absolute requirement to provide a feasible alternative design.[11]

In our view, the feasible alternative design requirement imposes an undue burden on plaintiffs that might preclude otherwise valid claims from jury consideration. Such a rule would require plaintiffs to retain an expert witness even in cases that infer a design defect from circumstantial evidence. Connecticut courts, however, have consistently stated that a jury may, under appropriate circumstances, infer a defect from the evidence without the necessity of expert testimony.

Moreover, in some instances, a product may be in a defective condition unreasonably dangerous to the user even though no feasible alternative design is available. In such instances, the manufacturer may be strictly liable for a design defect notwithstanding the fact that there are no safer alternative designs in existence. Accordingly, we decline to adopt the requirement that a plaintiff must prove a feasible alternative design as a sine qua non to establishing a prima facie case of design defect.

Although today we continue to adhere to our long-standing rule that a product's defectiveness is determined by the expectations of an ordinary consumer, we nevertheless recognize that there may be instances involving complex product designs in which an ordinary consumer may not be able to form expectations of safety. In such cases, a consumer's expectations may be viewed in light of various factors that balance the utility of the product's design with the magnitude of its risks. * * *

In our view, the relevant factors a jury *may* consider include, but are not limited to, the usefulness of the product, the likelihood and severity of the danger posed by the design, the feasibility of an alternative design, the financial cost of an improved design, the ability to reduce the product's danger without impairing its usefulness or making it too expensive, and the feasibility of spreading the loss by increasing the product's price. The availability of a feasible alternative design is a factor the plaintiff may, rather than must, prove in order to establish that a product's risks outweigh its utility.

* * * [O]ur adoption of a risk-utility balancing component to our consumer expectation test does not signal a retreat from strict tort liability. In weighing a product's risks against its utility, the focus of the jury should be on the product itself, and not on the conduct of the manufacturer.

* * * [W]e emphasize that we do not require a plaintiff to present evidence relating to the product's risks and utility in every case. * * *

---

11. Our research reveals that * * * six jurisdictions affirmatively state that a plaintiff need not show a feasible alternative design to establish a manufacturer's liability for a design defect; sixteen jurisdictions hold that a feasible alternative design is merely one of several factors the jury may consider in determining whether a product design is defective; three jurisdictions require the defendant, not the plaintiff, to prove the product was not defective; and eight jurisdictions require that the plaintiff prove a feasible alternative design to establish a prima facie case of design defect.

[T]he ordinary consumer expectation test is appropriate when the everyday experience of the particular product's users permits the inference that the product did not meet minimum safety expectations.

* * *

* * * It is the function of the trial court to determine whether an instruction based on the ordinary consumer expectation test or the modified consumer expectation test, or both, is appropriate in light of the evidence presented. * * *

[Because of various errors committed by the trial judge, the case is remanded for a new trial.]

D. PLAINTIFF-CONDUCT DEFENSES

DALY v. GENERAL MOTORS CORP.

Supreme Court of California, 1978.
20 Cal.3d 725, 144 Cal.Rptr. 380, 575 P.2d 1162.

RICHARDSON, JUSTICE.

The most important of several problems which we consider is whether the principles of comparative negligence expressed by us in Li v. Yellow Cab Co. (1975) 13 Cal.3d 804, 119 Cal.Rptr. 858, 532 P.2d 1226, apply to actions founded on strict products liability. We will conclude that they do. * * *

* * * In the early hours of October 31, 1970, decedent Kirk Daly, a 36–year–old attorney, was driving his Opel southbound on the Harbor Freeway in Los Angeles. The vehicle, while travelling at a speed of 50–70 miles per hour, collided with and damaged 50 feet of metal divider fence. After the initial impact between the left side of the vehicle and the fence the Opel spun counterclockwise, the driver's door was thrown open, and Daly was forcibly ejected from the car and sustained fatal head injuries. It was * * * undisputed that had the deceased remained in the Opel his injuries, in all probability, would have been relatively minor.

* * * The sole theory of plaintiffs' complaint was strict liability for damages allegedly caused by a defective product, namely, an improperly designed door latch claimed to have been activated by the impact. It was further asserted that, but for the faulty latch, decedent would have been restrained in the vehicle and, although perhaps injured, would not have been killed. Thus, the case involves a so-called "second collision" in which the "defect" did not contribute to the original impact, but only to the "enhancement" of injury.

* * *

Over plaintiffs' objections, defendants were permitted to introduce evidence indicating that: (1) the Opel was equipped with a seat belt-shoulder harness system, and a door lock, either of which if used, it was contended, would have prevented Daly's ejection from the vehicle; (2) Daly used neither the harness system nor the lock; (3) the 1970 Opel owner's manual contained warnings that seat belts should be worn and doors locked when the car was in motion for "accident security"; and (4) Daly was intoxicated at the time of collision, which evidence the jury was advised was admitted for the limited purpose of determining whether decedent had used the vehicle's safety equipment. After relatively brief deliberations the jury returned a verdict favoring all defendants, and plaintiffs appeal from the ensuing adverse judgment.

* * *

In response to plaintiffs' assertion that the "intoxication-nonuse" evidence was improperly admitted, defendants contend that the deceased's own conduct contributed to his death. Because plaintiffs' case rests upon strict products liability based on improper design of the door latch and because defendants assert a failure in decedent's conduct, namely, his alleged intoxication and nonuse of safety equipment, without which the accident and ensuing death would not have occurred, there is thereby posed the overriding issue in the case, should comparative principles apply in strict products liability actions?

* * *

[In Li v. Yellow Cab Co. we adopted] a "pure" form of comparative negligence which, when present, reduced but did not prevent plaintiff's recovery. We held that the defense of assumption of risk, insofar as it is no more than a variant of contributory negligence, was merged into the assessment of liability in proportion to fault. Within the broad guidelines therein announced, we left to trial courts discretion in the particular implementation of the new doctrine.

* * *

Those counseling against the recognition of comparative fault principles in strict products liability cases vigorously stress, perhaps equally, not only the conceptual, but also the semantic difficulties incident to such a course. The task of merging the two concepts is said to be impossible, that "apples and oranges" cannot be compared, that "oil and water" do not mix, and that strict liability, which is not founded on negligence or fault, is inhospitable to comparative principles. The syllogism runs, contributory negligence was only a defense to negligence, comparative negligence only affects contributory negligence, therefore comparative negligence cannot be a defense to strict liability. While fully recognizing the theoretical and semantic distinctions between the twin principles of strict products liability and traditional negligence, we think they can be blended or accommodated.

The inherent difficulty in the "apples and oranges" argument is its insistence on fixed and precise definitional treatment of legal concepts. In the evolving areas of both products liability and tort defenses, however, there has developed much conceptual overlapping and interweaving in order to attain substantial justice. The concept of strict liability itself, as we have noted, arose from dissatisfaction with the wooden formalisms of traditional tort and contract principles in order to protect the consumer of manufactured goods. Similarly, increasing social awareness of its harsh "all or nothing" consequences led us in *Li* to moderate the impact of traditional contributory negligence in order to accomplish a fairer and more balanced result. We acknowledged an intermixing of defenses of contributory negligence and assumption of risk and formally effected a type of merger. * * *

Furthermore, the "apples and oranges" argument may be conceptually suspect. It has been suggested that the term "contributory negligence," one of the vital building blocks upon which much of the argument is based, may indeed itself be a misnomer since it lacks the first element of the classical negligence formula, namely, a duty of care owing to another. A highly respected torts authority, Dean William Prosser, has noted this fact by observing, "It is perhaps unfortunate that contributory negligence is called negligence at all. 'Contributory fault' would be a more descriptive term. Negligence as it is commonly understood is conduct which creates an undue risk of harm to others. Contributory negligence is conduct which involves an undue risk of harm to the actor himself. Negligence requires a duty, an obligation of conduct to another person. Contributory negligence involves no duty, unless we are to be so ingenious as to say that the plaintiff is under an obligation to protect the defendant against liability for the consequences of his own negligence." (Prosser, Law of Torts, § 65, p. 418 [4th ed. 1971].)

We think, accordingly, the conclusion may fairly be drawn that the terms "comparative negligence," "contributory negligence" and "assumption of risk" do not, standing alone, lend themselves to the exact measurements of a micrometer-caliper, or to such precise definition as to divert us from otherwise strong and consistent countervailing policy considerations. Fixed semantic consistency at this point is less important than the attainment of a just and equitable result. The interweaving of concept and terminology in this area suggests a judicial posture that is flexible rather than doctrinaire.

We pause at this point to observe that where, as here, a consumer or user sues the manufacturer or designer alone, technically neither fault nor conduct is really compared functionally. The conduct of one party in combination with the product of another, or perhaps the placing of a defective article in the stream of projected and anticipated use, may produce the ultimate injury. In such a case, as in the situation before us, we think the term "equitable apportionment or allocation of loss" may be more descriptive than "comparative fault."

Given all of the foregoing, we are, in the wake of *Li,* disinclined to resolve the important issue before us by the simple expedient of matching linguistic labels which have evolved either for convenience or by custom. Rather, we consider it more useful to examine the foundational reasons underlying the creation of strict products liability in California to ascertain whether the purposes of the doctrine would be defeated or diluted by adoption of comparative principles. We imposed strict liability against the manufacturer and in favor of the user or consumer in order to relieve injured consumers "from *problems of proof* inherent in pursuing negligence * * * and warranty * * * remedies * * *." As we have noted, we sought to place the burden of loss on manufacturers rather than " * * * injured persons *who are powerless to protect themselves* * * *."

The foregoing goals, we think, will not be frustrated by the adoption of comparative principles. Plaintiffs will continue to be relieved of proving that the manufacturer or distributor was negligent in the production, design, or dissemination of the article in question. Defendant's liability for injuries caused by a defective product remains strict. The principle of protecting the defenseless is likewise preserved, for plaintiff's recovery will be reduced *only* to the extent that his own lack of reasonable care contributed to his injury. The cost of compensating the victim of a defective product, albeit proportionately reduced, remains on defendant manufacturer, and will, through him, be "spread among society." However, we do not permit plaintiff's own conduct relative to the product to escape unexamined, and as to that share of plaintiff's damages which flows from his own fault we discern no reason of policy why it should, following *Li,* be borne by others. Such a result would directly contravene the principle announced in *Li,* that loss should be assessed equitably in proportion to fault.

* * *

A second objection to the application of comparative principles in strict products liability cases is that a manufacturer's incentive to produce safe products will thereby be reduced or removed. While we fully recognize this concern we think, for several reasons, that the problem is more shadow than substance. First, of course, the manufacturer cannot avoid its continuing liability for a defective product even when the plaintiff's own conduct has contributed to his injury. The manufacturer's liability, and therefore its incentive to avoid and correct product defects, remains; its exposure will be lessened only to the extent that the trier finds that the victim's conduct contributed to his injury. Second, as a practical matter a manufacturer, in a particular case, cannot assume that the user of a defective product upon whom an injury is visited will be blameworthy. Doubtless, many users are free of fault, and a defect is at least as likely as not to be exposed by an entirely innocent plaintiff who will obtain full recovery. In such cases the manufacturer's incentive toward safety both in design and production is wholly unaffected. Finally, we must observe that under the present law, which recognizes assumption of risk as a complete defense to products liability, the curious and cynical message is that it profits the manufacturer to make his product so defective that in the event of injury he can argue that the user had to be aware of its patent defects. To that extent the incentives are inverted. We conclude, accordingly, that no substantial or significant impairment of the safety incentives of defendants will occur by the adoption of comparative principles.

In passing, we note one important and felicitous result if we apply comparative principles to strict products liability. This arises from the fact that under present law when plaintiff sues in negligence his own contributory negligence, however denominated, may diminish but cannot wholly defeat his recovery. When he sues in strict products liability, however, his "assumption of risk" *completely bars* his recovery. Under *Li,* as we have noted, "assumption of risk" is merged into comparative principles. The consequence is that after *Li* in a negligence action, plaintiff's conduct which amounts to "negligent" assumption of risk no longer defeats plaintiff's recovery. Identical conduct, however, in a strict liability case acts as a complete bar under rules heretofore applicable. Thus, strict products liability, which was developed to free injured consumers from the constraints imposed by traditional negligence and warranty theories, places a consumer plaintiff in a worse position than would be the case were his claim founded on simple negligence. This, in turn, rewards adroit pleading and selection of theories. The application of comparative principles to strict liability obviates this bizarre anomaly by treating alike the defenses to both negligence and strict products liability actions. In each instance the defense, if established, will reduce but not bar plaintiff's claim.

A third objection to the merger of strict liability and comparative fault focuses on the claim that, as a practical matter, triers of fact, particularly jurors, cannot assess, measure, or compare plaintiff's negligence with defendant's strict liability. We are unpersuaded by the argument and are convinced that jurors are able to undertake a fair apportionment of liability.

* * *

We note that the majority of our sister states which have addressed the problem, either by statute or judicial decree, have extended comparative principles to strict products liability.

* * *

Moreover, we are further encouraged in our decision herein by noting that the apparent majority of scholarly commentators has urged adoption of the rule which we announce herein.

* * *

Having examined the principal objections and finding them not insurmountable, and persuaded by logic, justice, and fundamental fairness, we conclude that a system of comparative fault should be and it is hereby extended to actions founded on strict products liability. In such cases the separate defense of "assumption of risk," to the extent that it is a form of contributory negligence, is abolished. While, as we have suggested, on the particular facts before us, the term "equitable apportionment of loss" is more accurately descriptive of the process, nonetheless, the term "comparative fault" has gained such wide acceptance by courts and in the literature that we adopt its use herein.

[The court then held that its decision would not be applied retroactively, not even to the case before it. Under the law existing at the time of trial, evidence of the plaintiff's intoxication and failure to use a seat belt should have been excluded.]

The judgment is reversed.

JEFFERSON, JUSTICE, concurring and dissenting.

* * *

The majority * * * does not consider it significant that it is unable to determine what labels should be given to the new comparative principles—whether the new doctrine should be known as comparative fault, equitable apportionment of loss, or equitable allocation of loss. This inability to give the new doctrine an appropriate label is some indication of the shaky ground upon which the majority has decided to tread.

The majority rejects what I consider to be a sound criticism of its holding—that it is illogical and illusory to compare elements or factors that are not reasonably subject to comparison. The majority states that it is convinced that jurors will be able to compare the noncomparables—plaintiff's negligence with defendant's strict liability for a defective product—and still reach a fair apportionment of liability.

I consider the majority conclusion a case of wishful thinking and an application of an impractical, ivory-tower approach. * * *

* * *

What the majority envisions as a fair apportionment of liability to be undertaken by the jury will constitute nothing more than an *unfair reduction* in the plaintiff's total damages suffered, resulting from a jury process that necessarily is predicated on speculation, conjecture and guesswork. Because the legal concept of negligence is so utterly different from the legal concept of a product defective by reason of manufacture or design, a plaintiff's negligence is [not] capable of being rationally compared with a defendant's defective product * * *.

* * *

The guessing game that will be imposed on juries by the application of comparative negligence principles to defective product liability cases will be further enhanced in those cases in which several defendants are joined in an action—some being sued on a negligence theory and others on the defective product theory and where there are several plaintiffs whose conduct may range from no negligence at all to varying degrees of negligence. The jury will be required to determine percentages of fault with respect to all the parties (and perhaps some nonparties) by seeking to compare and evaluate the *conduct* of certain parties with the *product* of other parties to produce 100 percent of fault as the necessary starting point in order to calculate a reduction in the damages suffered by each plaintiff found to be negligent. I cannot agree with the majority that such a process is reasonably workable or that it will produce an equitable result to injured plaintiffs. If a just or fair result is reached by a jury under the majority's holding, it will be strictly accidental and accomplished by pure happenstance.

* * *

MOSK, JUSTICE, dissenting.

* * *

This will be remembered as the dark day when this court, which heroically took the lead in originating the doctrine of products liability and steadfastly resisted efforts to inject concepts of negligence into the newly designed tort, inexplicably turned 180 degrees and beat a hasty retreat almost back to square one. The pure concept of products liability so pridefully fashioned and nurtured by this court for the past decade and a half is reduced to a shambles.

The majority inject a foreign object—the tort of negligence—into the tort of products liability by the simple expedient of calling negligence something else: on some pages their opinion speaks of "comparative fault," on others reference is to "comparative principles," and elsewhere the term "equitable apportionment" is employed, although this is clearly not a proceeding in equity. * * *

* * *

The defective product is comparable to a time bomb ready to explode; it maims its victims indiscriminately, the righteous and the evil, the careful and the careless. Thus when a faulty design or otherwise defective product is involved, the litigation should not be diverted to consideration of the negligence of the plaintiff. The liability issues are simple: was the product or its design faulty, did the defendant inject the defective product into the stream of commerce, and did the defect cause the injury? The conduct of the ultimate consumer-victim who used the product in the contemplated or foreseeable manner is wholly irrelevant to those issues.

* * *

The majority deny their opinion diminishes the therapeutic effect of products liability upon producers of defective products. It seems self-evident that procedures which evaluate the injured consumer's conduct in each instance, and thus eliminate or reduce the award against the producer or distributor of a defective product, are not designed as an effective incentive to maximum responsibility to consumers. The converse is more accurate: the motivation to avoid polluting the stream of commerce with defective products increases in direct relation to the size of potential damage awards.

In sum, I am convinced that since the negligence of the defendant is irrelevant in products liability cases, the negligence—call it contributory or comparative—of the plaintiff is also irrelevant. * * *

* * *

NOTES

1. As the opinion in *Daly* indicates, most states that have comparative negligence schemes apply some type of comparative scheme to strict tort liability.

2. Justice Mosk's opinion in *Daly* reflects a common objection to applying comparative negligence principles to strict tort liability. Why is it that Justice Mosk thinks an analysis of the plaintiff's negligence is intrinsically incompatible with the theory of strict tort liability?

3. Once a court adopts a comparative scheme for strict tort liability, it must decide what the contours of that scheme will be. For example, will it be a pure comparative scheme—in which a plaintiff assigned more than 50% "fault" can still recover—or a modified comparative scheme—in which such a plaintiff is completely barred from recovery?

4. Restatement (Second) of Torts § 402A cmt. *n* provided that negligence that was merely a failure to discover or guard against the possibility of a product defect was not a defense against strict tort liability. The idea seems to be that a consumer should not be denied recovery altogether merely because he or she failed to inspect the product for defects. After the advent of comparative responsibility, comment *n* created difficulties. In a case involving claims of negligence and strict tort liability, possibly against different types of defendants, a jury might have to consider the plaintiff's negligent failure to discover or guard against the possibilities of a defect with respect to recovery against some defendants, but not others. Moreover, the advent of comparative responsibility lowered the stakes with respect to plaintiff negligence by reducing the plaintiff's recovery, rather than barring it altogether. Consequently, most courts now count all forms of plaintiff negligence, including a plaintiff's negligently failing to discover or guard against a product defect. See Restatement (Third) of Torts: Products Liability § 17 & cmt. *b* (1998).

CHAPTER XV

NUISANCE

■ ■ ■

A private nuisance is a substantial and unreasonable interference with quiet use and enjoyment of real property. A public nuisance is an unwarranted interference with public safety, health, convenience, or morals. This chapter deals primarily with private nuisance.

The law of private nuisance is relatively amorphous, having little theory or structure. Courts sit almost as though they were zoning commissions charged with the task of resolving disputes over competing uses of land. Their decisions are usually fact specific. They sometimes incorporate bits of doctrine from other torts, such as negligence, and they sometimes develop "rules" for resolving disputes. But these rules tend to be fluid, and adjudication tends to be ad hoc.

A plaintiff who proves a private nuisance has available several remedies. If the nuisance is temporary, the plaintiff can recover lost rental value and consequential damages, such as lost profit, damage to the real property, damage to crops and livestock, and personal injury. If the nuisance is continuous or permanent, the plaintiff can recover lost market value of the land and consequential damages. In some cases, a plaintiff can get an injunction.

AMPHITHEATERS, INC. v. PORTLAND MEADOWS
Supreme Court of Oregon, 1948.
184 Or. 336, 198 P.2d 847.

BRAND, JUSTICE.

[Plaintiff owned an outdoor drive-in movie theater. Defendant owned a horse race track on adjacent property. The race track was equipped with lights for night racing. The plaintiff sued for damages on the basis of trespass to land and nuisance, claiming that the lights from the race track interfered with the movie screen. The trial court directed a verdict for the defendant on both theories. The portion of the Supreme Court's opinion dealing with trespass to land is reproduced in Chapter II, section F, supra p. 33. In that portion of the opinion, the Court held that the trial court did not err by directing a verdict in favor of the defendant on the trespass theory.]

In installing outdoor moving picture theaters, it is necessary to protect the premises from outside light interference. For that purpose the plaintiff constructed wing fences for a considerable distance on each side of the screen and along the westerly line of Union Avenue for the purpose of shutting off the light from the cars traveling on that arterial highway. It was also necessary to construct a shadow box extending on both sides and above the screen for the purpose of excluding the light from the moon and stars. The testimony indicates that the construction of the shadow box was necessary if a good picture was to be presented on the screen. The extreme delicacy of plaintiff's operation and the susceptibility of outdoor moving pictures to light in any form was conclusively established by the evidence.

* * *

As its second assignment, the plaintiff asserts that the trial court erred in failing to submit the case to the jury on the theory of nuisance.

This is a case of first impression. It differs in essential particulars from any case which has received consideration by this court. The nuisance cases appearing in our reports fall into four easily recognizable classes: (1) Cases involving harm to human comfort, safety or health by reason of the maintenance by a defendant upon his land of noxious or dangerous instrumentalities causing damage to the plaintiff in respect to legally protected interests of the plaintiff in his land. (2) Cases involving illegal or immoral practices, most of them being public as distinct from private nuisances. They relate to bawdy houses, gambling, abortions, lotteries, illegal possession of liquor, and acts outraging public decency. (3) Cases involving obstructions to streets, public ways, common rights, access to property and the like. (4) Cases involving damage to the land itself, as by flooding. The cases, with the exception of those falling in the first class, bear no resemblance to the one at bar, and require no further comment.

* * *

The cases listed in the first class are the only ones which bear any faint resemblance to the case at bar. Examination of those cases will disclose that no Oregon decision has ever held that the casting of light in any quantity or form upon the land of another gives rise to a cause of action upon any legal theory. If the cases involving smoke, noxious odors, flies and disease germs are claimed to be analogous to the case at bar, it must be answered that in every case the activity or thing which has been held to be a nuisance has been something which was, 1, inherently harmful, and 2, an unreasonable and substantial interference with the ordinary use or enjoyment of property. No one can contend that light is inherently harmful to persons in the ordinary enjoyment of property.

Since there is no Oregon precedent to support plaintiff's contention we must go back to fundamental principles. Plaintiff relies upon the general definition of a nuisance * * *. A private nuisance is defined as "anything done to the hurt, annoyance, or detriment of the lands or hereditaments of another, and not amounting to a trespass." Definitions in such general terms are of no practical assistance to the court. * * *

The statement of Addison, Torts, 8th Ed. 66 [(1906)], that "[t]he due regulation and subordination of conflicting rights constitute the chief part of the science of law" is peculiarly applicable in the field of private nuisance, for the rights of neither party in the use and enjoyment of their respective properties are absolute. "What is a reasonable use and whether a particular use is a nuisance cannot be determined by any fixed general rules, but depend upon the facts of each particular case, such as location, character of the neighborhood, nature of the use, extent and frequency of the injury, the effect upon the enjoyment of life, health, and property, and the like."

Notwithstanding the fact that the existence vel non of a nuisance is generally a question of fact, there have arisen several rules of law which guide and sometimes control decision. It is established law that an intentional interference with the use and enjoyment of land is not actionable unless that interference be both substantial and unreasonable.

Again it is held that whether a particular annoyance or inconvenience is sufficient to constitute a nuisance depends upon its effect upon an ordinarily reasonable man, that is, a normal person of ordinary habits and sensibilities. * * * This doctrine has been applied in many cases involving smoke, dust, noxious odors, vibration and the like, in which the injury was not to the land itself but to the personal comfort of dwellers on the land.

* * *

[T]he plaintiff's only basis of complaint is the fact that it is attempting to show upon the screen moving pictures, and * * * the operation is such a delicate one that it has been necessary for the plaintiff to build high fences to prevent the light of automobiles upon the public highway from invading the property and to build a shadow box over the screen to protect it from the ordinary light of moon and stars, and * * * it now claims damage because the lights from the defendant's property, which it has not excluded by high fences, shine with the approximate intensity of full moonlight upon the screen and interfere thereby with the showing of the pictures. We think that this is a clear case coming within the doctrine of the English and American cases * * * that a man cannot increase the liabilities of his neighbor by applying his own property to special and delicate uses, whether for business or pleasure.

* * *

By way of summary, we have found no case in which it has been held that light alone constitutes a nuisance merely because it damaged one who was abnormally sensitive or whose use of his land was of a peculiarly delicate and sensitive character.

It is not our intention to decide the case upon authority alone, divorced from reason or public policy. The photographic evidence discloses that the properties of the respective parties are not in a residential district, and in fact are outside the city limits of Portland, and lie adjacent to a considerable amount of unimproved land. Neither party can claim any greater social utility than the other. Both were in process of construction at the same time, and the case should not be decided upon the basis of the priority of occupation. The case differs fundamentally from other cases, all typical cases of nuisance, in that light is not a noxious, but is, in general, a highly beneficial element. The development of parks and playgrounds equipped for the enjoyment of the working public, whose recreation is necessarily taken after working hours, and frequently after dark, is a significant phenomenon in thousands of urban communities. The court takes judicial knowledge that many lighted parks and fields are located adjacent to residential property and must to some extent interfere with the full enjoyment of darkness (if desired), by the residents.

We do not say that the shedding of light upon another's property may never under any conditions become a nuisance, but we do say that extreme caution must be employed in applying any such legal theory. The conditions of modern city life impose upon the city dweller and his property many burdens more severe than that of light reflected upon him or it.

In this case, the court directed a verdict for the defendant. We recognize the general rule to be that the existence or nonexistence of a private nuisance is ordinarily a question of fact for the jury, but the rule is subject to exceptions. * * *

* * * We limit our decision to the specific facts of this case and hold as a matter of law that the loss sustained by the plaintiff by the spilled light which has been reflected onto the highly sensitized moving picture screen from the defendant's property 832 feet distant, and which light in intensity is approximately that of a full moon, is *damnum absque injuria.*

The trial court did not err in directing a verdict. The judgment is affirmed.

NOTES

1. *Public vs. private nuisance.* The court in *Amphitheaters* referred to "four easily recognizable classes" of nuisance. Categories (2) ("[c]ases involving illegal or immoral practices") and (3) ("[c]ases involving obstructions to streets * * * and the like") are examples of public nuisance. Public nuisance is a different tort from private nuisance. Generally speaking, it involves an unwarranted interference with public safety, convenience, health, or morals. Usually, only a public entity such as the state can sue for public nuisance. An exception exists when a private individual suffers special harm, not merely the kind of harm suffered generally by the public. Private nuisance, on the other hand, involves an interference with a private person's interest in quiet use and enjoyment of land.

2. ***Private nuisance factors.*** Courts have referred to a variety of factors in determining whether a specific interference constitutes a nuisance. One important factor is the propriety of the defendant's activity to the time and place. Church bells ringing for ten minutes at eleven o'clock in the morning are not a nuisance, but they probably are in a residential neighborhood at three o'clock in the morning. Similarly, a court might distinguish between factory smoke in an industrial area and in a residential neighborhood.

It is not conclusive which competing use was first. A plaintiff can sometimes "move to a nuisance" and recover, if the defendant's activity is inappropriate to the area as it has evolved. However, the timing of the competing uses can be significant. (Note that the parties in *Amphitheaters* "were in process of construction at the same time.")

3. Courts often say that the defendant's state of mind is not a crucial element of nuisance. In fact, however, most nuisances are intentional, at least in the sense that the defendant continued the activity, knowing with a substantial certainty that the interference was taking place.

4. When considering the law of nuisance, it is useful to compare its features to those of trespass to land.

BOOMER v. ATLANTIC CEMENT CO.

Court of Appeals of New York, 1970.
26 N.Y.2d 219, 309 N.Y.S.2d 312, 257 N.E.2d 870.

BERGAN, JUDGE.

Defendant operates a large cement plant near Albany. These are actions for injunction and damages by [eight] neighboring land owners alleging injury to property from dirt, smoke and vibration emanating from the plant. A nuisance has been found after trial, temporary damages have been allowed; but an injunction has been denied. [The plaintiffs appealed, urging that the injunction should have been granted.]

The public concern with air pollution arising from many sources in industry and in transportation is currently accorded ever wider recognition accompanied by a growing sense of responsibility in State and Federal Governments to control it. Cement plants are obvious sources of air pollution in the neighborhoods where they operate.

But there is now before the court private litigation in which individual property owners have sought specific relief from a single plant operation. The threshold question raised by the division of view on this appeal is whether the court should resolve the litigation between the parties now before it as equitably as seems possible; or whether, seeking promotion of the general public welfare, it should channel private litigation into broad public objectives.

A court performs its essential function when it decides the rights of parties before it. Its decision of private controversies may sometimes greatly affect public issues. Large questions of law are often resolved by the manner in which private litigation is decided. But this is normally an incident to the court's main function to settle controversy. It is a rare exercise of judicial power to use a decision in private litigation as a purposeful mechanism to achieve direct public objectives greatly beyond the rights and interests before the court.

Effective control of air pollution is a problem presently far from solution even with the full public and financial powers of government. In large measure adequate technical procedures are yet to be developed and some that appear possible may be economically impracticable.

It seems apparent that the amelioration of air pollution will depend on technical research in great depth; on a carefully balanced consideration of the economic impact of close regulation; and of the actual effect on public health. It is likely to require massive public expenditure and to demand more than any local community can accomplish and to depend on regional and interstate controls.

A court should not try to do this on its own as a byproduct of private litigation and it seems manifest that the judicial establishment is neither equipped in the limited nature of any judgment it can pronounce nor prepared to lay down and implement an effective policy for the elimination of air pollution. This is an area beyond the circumference of one private lawsuit. It is a direct responsibility for government and should not thus be undertaken as an incident to solving a dispute between property owners and a single cement plant—one of many—in the Hudson River Valley.

The cement making operations of defendant have been found by the court of Special Term to have damaged the nearby properties of plaintiffs in these two actions. That court, as it has been noted, accordingly found defendant maintained a nuisance and this has been affirmed at the Appellate Division. The total damage to plaintiffs' properties is, however, relatively small in comparison with the value of defendant's operation and with the consequences of the injunction which plaintiffs seek.

The ground for the denial of injunction, notwithstanding the finding both that there is a nuisance and that plaintiffs have been damaged substantially, is the large disparity in economic consequences of the nuisance and of the injunction. This theory cannot, however, be sustained without overruling a doctrine which has been consistently reaffirmed in several leading cases in this court and which has never been disavowed here, namely that where a nuisance has been found and where there has been any substantial damage shown by the party complaining an injunction will be granted.

* * *

Although the court at Special Term and the Appellate Division held that injunction should be denied, it was found that plaintiffs had been damaged in various specific amounts up to the time of the trial and damages to the respective plaintiffs were awarded for those amounts. The effect of this was, injunction having been denied, plaintiffs could maintain successive actions at law for damages thereafter as further damage was incurred.

The court at Special Term also found the amount of permanent damage attributable to each plaintiff, for the guidance of the parties in the event both sides stipulated to the payment and acceptance of such permanent damage as a settlement of all the controversies among the parties. The total of permanent damages to all plaintiffs thus found was $185,000. This basis of adjustment has not resulted in any stipulation by the parties.

This result at Special Term and at the Appellate Division is a departure from a rule that has become settled; but to follow the rule literally in these cases would be to close down the plant at once. This court is fully agreed to avoid that immediately drastic remedy; the difference in view is how best to avoid it.*

One alternative is to grant the injunction but postpone its effect to a specified future date to give opportunity for technical advances to permit defendant to eliminate the nuisance; another is to grant the injunction conditioned on the payment of permanent damages to plaintiffs which would compensate them for the total economic loss to their property present and future caused by defendant's operations. For reasons which will be developed the court chooses the latter alternative.

* * *

[T]o grant the injunction unless defendant pays plaintiffs such permanent damages as may be fixed by the court seems to do justice between the contending parties. All of the attributions of economic loss to the properties on which plaintiffs' complaints are based will have been redressed.

The nuisance complained of by these plaintiffs may have other public or private consequences, but these particular parties are the only ones who have sought remedies and the judgment proposed will fully redress them. The limitation of relief granted is a limitation only within the four corners of these actions and does not foreclose public health or other public agencies from seeking proper relief in a proper court.

It seems reasonable to think that the risk of being required to pay permanent damages to injured property owners by cement plant owners would itself be a reasonable effective spur to research for improved techniques to minimize nuisance.

* * *

The judgment, by allowance of permanent damages imposing a servitude on land, which is the basis of the actions, would preclude future recovery by plaintiffs or their grantees.

This should be placed beyond debate by a provision of the judgment that the payment by defendant and the acceptance by plaintiffs of perma-

---

* Respondent's investment in the plant is in excess of $45,000,000. There are over 300 people employed there.

nent damages found by the court shall be in compensation for a servitude on the land.

Although the Trial Term has found permanent damages as a possible basis of settlement of the litigation, on remission the court should be entirely free to re-examine this subject. It may again find the permanent damage already found; or make new findings.

The orders should be reversed, without costs, and the cases remitted to Supreme Court, Albany County to grant an injunction which shall be vacated upon payment by defendant of such amounts of permanent damage to the respective plaintiffs as shall for this purpose be determined by the court.

JASEN, JUDGE, dissenting.

* * *

It has long been the rule in this State, as the majority acknowledges, that a nuisance which results in substantial continuing damage to neighbors must be enjoined. To now change the rule to permit the cement company to continue polluting the air indefinitely upon the payment of permanent damages is, in my opinion, compounding the magnitude of a very serious problem in our State and Nation today.

* * *

I see grave dangers in overruling our long-established rule of granting an injunction where a nuisance results in substantial continuing damage. In permitting the injunction to become inoperative upon the payment of permanent damages, the majority is, in effect, licensing a continuing wrong. It is the same as saying to the cement company, you may continue to do harm to your neighbors so long as you pay a fee for it. Furthermore, once such permanent damages are assessed and paid, the incentive to alleviate the wrong would be eliminated, thereby continuing air pollution of an area without abatement.

It is true that some courts have sanctioned the remedy here proposed by the majority in a number of cases, but none of the authorities relied upon by the majority are analogous to the situation before us. In those cases, the courts, in denying an injunction and awarding money damages, grounded their decision on a showing that the use to which the property was intended to be put was primarily for the public benefit. Here, on the other hand, it is clearly established that the cement company is creating a continuing air pollution nuisance primarily for its own private interest with no public benefit.

This kind of inverse condemnation may not be invoked by a private person or corporation for private gain or advantage. Inverse condemnation should only be permitted when the public is primarily served in the taking or impairment of property. The promotion of the interests of the polluting cement company has, in my opinion, no public use or benefit.

* * *

I would enjoin the defendant cement company from continuing the discharge of dust particles upon its neighbors' properties unless, within 18 months, the cement company abated this nuisance.

It is not my intention to cause the removal of the cement plant from the Albany area, but to recognize the urgency of the problem stemming from this stationary source of air pollution, and to allow the company a specified period of time to develop a means to alleviate this nuisance.

I am aware that the trial court found that the most modern dust control devices available have been installed in defendant's plant, but, I submit, this does not mean that better and more effective dust control devices could not be developed within the time allowed to abate the pollution.

* * *

NOTES

1. At the conclusion of the trial, the plaintiffs had achieved an aggregate award of damages to the time of trial of $44,835, an implicit recognition that they could return to court and sue for similar damages in the future, and a determination that their permanent damages came to $185,000. They obviously preferred not to stipulate that payment of the latter sum would forever resolve their controversy with Atlantic Cement. Instead, they appealed, contending that they were entitled to an injunction in addition to the $44,835 damages award. From the plaintiffs' perspective, did appealing turn out to be a good idea?

2. In real property law, "condemnation" (sometimes also called "eminent domain" and occasionally called "expropriation") refers to a governmental entity's or public utility's legally authorized taking of private property for public use on payment of just compensation. The dissenter's term "inverse condemnation" was a way of characterizing the majority's decision as having authorized Atlantic Cement to force the plaintiffs to sell it their clean-air rights.

3. Note that the court had no difficulty concluding that the cement factory constituted a nuisance, notwithstanding its social value. The only difficult issue was whether to issue an injunction.

On the question of whether a nuisance exists, courts often say that the interference must be unreasonable, but "unreasonable" apparently means something different in nuisance than in negligence. *Prosser and Keeton* states that "if it appears to be fairer and more feasible, technologically and economically, to internalize [the harm] as a cost of carrying on the defendant's industrial or business enterprise, the interference will be regarded as unreasonable." Prosser and Keeton on Torts, § 88, p. 627 (5th ed. 1984). Similarly, § 826 of the Restatement (Second) of Torts states:

An intentional invasion of another's interest in the use and enjoyment of land is unreasonable if

(a) the gravity of the harm outweighs the utility of the actor's conduct, or

(b) the harm caused by the conduct is serious and the financial burden of compensating for this and similar harm to others would not make the continuation of the conduct not feasible.

Comment *f* to section 826 states that "[i]t may sometimes be reasonable to operate an important activity if payment is made for the harm it is causing, but unreasonable to continue it without paying."

4.   Historically, English courts of law could not grant injunctions; by and large they could only award money damages. The chancellor, who was an officer of the king, could grant various forms of "equitable" relief, including injunctions, if the "legal" remedy was inadequate. Over time, formal courts of equity were established with a complex set of substantive and procedural rules of their own. A party seeking relief from a court of equity was required to show more than the violation of a legal right. He was also required to show, among other things, that he would suffer irreparable harm that could not be remedied by money damages and that equitable relief would not disserve the public interest.

During the last hundred years, American jurisdictions have "merged" courts of law and courts of equity. Today in most states, only one courthouse exists with one set of judges. Nevertheless, a plaintiff must still make a special showing to obtain equitable relief.

5.   Refusing an injunction for "equitable" reasons is not unique to the law of nuisance. In Crescent Mining Co. v. Silver King Mining Co., 17 Utah 444, 54 P. 244 (1898), the defendant laid a pipe across plaintiff's "barren, valueless land." Even though the defendant's conduct was clearly a trespass to land, the court refused to enjoin it. The court balanced the harm to the plaintiff, which was minimal, with the harm an injunction would cause the defendant, which was great.

INDEX

References are to Pages

RETALIATION
Self-defense distinguished, 54

SCOPE OF LIABILITY
See Legal Cause, this index

SELF-DEFENSE
Deadly force, 54
Reasonable force, 54
Retaliation compared, 54
Retreat, 54

SEXUALLY TRANSMITTED DISEASES
Battery claim, 50

SHOCK
Negligent infliction of emotional distress, 233

SPRING GUNS
Generally, 61

STANDARD OF CARE
Generally, 55 et seq.
Capacity of defendant, 81
Children, 85
Duty questions, distinguishing, 158
Foreseeability, 73
Foresight and hindsight standards, 73
Handicapped person, 81
Industry custom, 77
Intoxicated defendant, 81
Learned Hand formula, 74
Medical malpractice
Generally, 471
Expert testimony, 477
Objective standard of negligence, 81
Ordinary care, 76
Premises liability, see Owners' and Occupiers'
Duties, this index
Prima facie elements of negligence generally, 69
Professional malpractice
Generally, 471
Expert testimony, 477
Reasonable care standard
Generally, 70, 72
Owners' and occupiers' duties, 265, 272, 273
Recreational use statutes, 278
Res ipsa loquitur, 104 et seq.
Superior abilities of defendant, 81
Violation of statute, 89 et seq.
Willful or wanton conduct
Generally, 273
Recreational use statutes, 273

STATUTES OF LIMITATION AND RE-POSE
See Defenses, this index

STRANGERS
See Privity of Contract, this index

STRICT LIABILITY
Generally, 485 et seq.
See also Products Liability, this index
Abnormally dangerous activities, 486
Absolute liability distinguished, 485

STRICT LIABILITY—Cont'd
Animals, damage caused by, 485
Common law, 485 et seq.
Dangerous activities, 486
Immunities, this index
Insurer's liability distinguished, 485
Policy considerations, 503
Products liability claims, 496

SUMMARY JUDGMENT
Generally, 2

SUPERSEDING CAUSE
Generally, 179

SURVIVAL ACTIONS
Generally, 307 et seq.

THIRD PARTIES
See Privity of Contract, this index

TORT REFORM MOVEMENT
Generally, 306
Caps on damages, 319
Medical malpractice, 483
No-fault insurance, 320
Punitive Damages, 321
Statutes of repose, 433

TRANSFERRED INTENT
Battery, 18
Definition, 18

TRESPASS ON THE CASE
Writs, common law, 67

TRESPASS TO CHATTELS
Generally, 41
Consent as defense, 45
Conversion compared, 44
Defense of property, 55
Defenses, 45 et seq.
Intent, 44
Necessity, 61
Physical harm, 42
Self-defense, 51

TRESPASS TO LAND
Generally, 33 et seq.
Air pollution, 36
Airplane overflights, 35, 36
Animals, damage caused by, 485
Consent as defense, 45
Damages, 36
Defense of property, 55
Defenses, 45 et seq.
Direct vs. indirect entry, 40
Intent, 35
Light as interference, 33
Necessity, 61
Nuisance compared, 35, 529
Reasonableness of defendant's conduct, 36
Self-defense, 51
Title disputes, 36
Writs, common law, 40, 67

TROVER
Generally, 41

†